NIJINSKY
AND
ROMOLA

NIJINSKY
AND
ROMOLA

Biography
by

Tamara Nijinsky

BACHMAN & TURNER

LONDON

UNITED ARTS

PUBLISHERS LTD

NIJINSKY AND ROMOLA

First published in 1991 by Bachman & Turner, a division of
United Arts Publishers Ltd, 11 Uxbridge Street, London W8 7TQ.

British Library Cataloguing in Publication Data

Nijinsky, Tamara
NIJINSKY AND ROMOLA
1. Ballet
2. Title
792.82092

ISBN 0 85974 138 9

Typeset by Phoenix Photosetting, Chatham, Kent.
Printed by Ipswich Book Company Limited, Ipswich, Suffolk.

To my grandson, Mark Gerard.
The future is his, but I want
him to feel pride in the past

Tamara Nijinsky
Phoenix, Arizona

ACKNOWLEDGEMENTS

I wish to extend my deepest thanks to all my relatives, loyal friends, colleagues and even strangers, who with a phrase or more, often unknown to themselves, helped me accomplish my challenging task. There is one person in particular to whom I am indebted that this book became a reality, a person with implicit faith in me who spurred me on with unshakeable, honest criticism, Romola and Waslaw's granddaughter, my daughter Kinga Szakáts Gaspers.

Thanks are also due to my collaborator and editor, Marta Thyer-Turner, and the two of us wish to acknowledge the co-operation of various individuals and institutions, our two lists being amalgamated as below:

A & C Black (Publishers) Ltd for extracts from *Ballet Annual*
British Broadcasting Corporation
Richard Buckle
Dr Mihály Cenner, author of *Márkus Emilia* c 1961
Harold Clark
Denise Collett-Simpson, Librarian, Royal Academy of Dance, London
Dance and Dancers, London
Dance Magazine, New York
Father Joseph Daries
Ian Ferguson
F L Grant for permission to publish his mother's letter
George Hoare, archivist at the Stoll Music Archives, Theatre Royal, London
Alice Gannon Jacques
Dr E F Kunz, Melbourne, Australia, author of *Blood and Gold – Hungarians in Australia*
Nesta MacDonald
Kyra Nijinska Markevitch
Robert Mead
National Film Archives, London
Dr Peter Ostwald, Professor of Psychiatry, University of California, author of *Schumann, Music and Madness*

Psychic News, London
Irina Nijinska Raetz
Françoise Reiss, author of *Nijinsky ou la Grace*
Patricia Gannon Scully
Tom Shapcott, Director, Literary Arts Board, North Sydney, Australia, author of *White Stag of Exile*
Sydney Opera House Trust, Australia
Takarazuka Theatre, Japan

and to various publishers for permission to quote from works they have published, all of which are included in the Bibliography.

CONTENTS

LIST OF ILLUSTRATIONS

FOREWORD TO NIJINSKY AND ROMOLA

After Romola's death in Paris, I happened to overhear snatches of a conversation about her. '. . . over-ambitious, selfish, shrewd, a calculating woman who exploited and shamelessly manipulated her husband for her own purposes . . . she lived in luxury . . . it was a bed of roses for the widow of Waslaw Nijinsky!'

I listened with growing anger and dismay, They were, after all, talking about my mother. Alongside my indignation, I felt a growing urge to write about her and, in doing so, to create a detailed account of the woman who faithfully supported her husband for thirty-one years after incurable mental illness ended his brilliant career.

There were many complex sides to Romola's nature. Relentlessly, if not ruthlessly, she pursued the course she set upon – not to sever the life-line that connected Waslaw with the outside world. To many, she was an enigma. Capable of great passion and devout friendship, yet she was unable to give outward signs of love to her daughters, Kyra and myself.

It would hardly be possible to present any proper picture of my mother's life without writing about my father, too, stressing the remarkable relationship between them.

I have read my mother's books about my father and they tell me much about the writer as well as the subject. Letters, press interviews, books about Nijinsky, the 'God of Dance', and other sources provide material to extend my own experience and the memories I share.

To Emilia, my maternal grandmother, with whom I lived for many years, I owe special thanks. Day after day, she fed my childish curiosity with stories of my mother's life as a young girl, sometimes as a child and at other times as the beautiful debutante who thrilled to the sight of Waslaw Nijinsky on the stage of the Budapest Opera House.

Tamara Nijinsky
Phoenix, Arizona

PUBLISHERS' NOTE

The original manuscript for this book was provided by the author, Tamara Nijinsky, who relied on her memory and sundry letters, many translated from Hungarian, French, German and Russian, as well as information in newspapers, magazines and books. Her collaborator, Marta Thyer-Turner, has, as much as possible, verified this material and supplemented it through additional research wherever she had the authority to do so. Tamara spells her father's name *Waslaw* as that is how he himself signed his name.

As far as possible, the list of Acknowledgements reflects all the help and support given, but mention should be made of all those officials in various organisations, embassies, ministries and professional bodies, who have willingly devoted time and effort to answering enquiries. The magic of the name 'Nijinsky' still inspires respect and attention!

THÉOPHILE GAUTIER

LE SPECTRE DE LA ROSE

Soulève ta paupière close
Qu'effleure un songe virginal ;
Je suis le spectre d'une rose
Que tu portais hier au bal.
Tu me pris encore emperlée
Des pleurs d'argent de l'arrosoir,
Et parmi la fête étoilée
Tu me promenas tout le soir.

O toi qui de ma mort fus cause,
Sans que tu puisses le chasser,
Toute la nuit mon spectre rose
A ton chevet viendra danser.
Mais ne crains rien, je ne réclame
Ni messe ni *De profundis* ;
Ce léger parfum est mon âme,
Et j'arrive du paradis.

Mon destin fut digne d'envie :
Pour avoir un trépas si beau,
Plus d'un aurait donné sa vie,
Car j'ai ta gorge pour tombeau,

Et sur l'albâtre où je repose
Un poëte avec un baiser
Écrivit : Ci-git une rose
Que tous les rois vont jalouser.

1837.

Leányom

Pulszky Romoald
/Romola/ Flavia

Ludovika Polyxena

Consuelo /Marie de

la consolation/

született 1891 évben

február 19 én hajnal-

ban ¾ 4 kor.

Isten kegyém áldd meg őt.

CHAPTER 1

ROMOLA'S FAMILY
AND HER CHILDHOOD

'My daughter
Pulszky Romoalda
(Romola) Flavia
Ludowika Polyxena
Consuelo Marie de la Consolation
was born in the year 1891
on the 19th February at dawn 3.45 am
God, my Father, bless her.'

From the prayerbook of Emilia Márkus

The above inscription in Hungarian is to be found in the prayerbook that had belonged to my grandmother Emilia Márkus. This prayerbook, bound in rich leather and with Emilia's name inscribed in gold-leaf lettering, was given to her by her husband, Károly Pulszky.

What a strange mixture of Roman, Greek and French names, but they aptly reflect the complexity of the extraordinary human being, who was later to become the wife of Waslaw Nijinsky.

It was not inappropriate that Romola should have made her debut in this world in the family's private suite on the first floor of the *Tudományos Akadémia* (Academy of Science) in Budapest. Situated on the left bank of the Danube, the *Akadémia* was connected to the National Museum of Fine Arts, located on the second floor.

According to Emilia, her younger daughter *'... was in such a hurry to arrive that she was born two months prematurely. I used to worry a great deal about her. She was always so pale and her steel-blue eyes used to gaze at me with such frightened expression ... I remember, too that during my pregnancy I often admired an oil painting of Saint Catherine of Siena. Romola resembled her.'*

On her father's side, Romola could trace her ancestors to 14th-century Wallonia, in what today is Belgium. The family's original

1

name was De la Poule. When the persecution of the Huguenots began in the 16th-century in the reign of Charles V of Spain, the De la Poules fled from Wallonia to escape torture and possible burning at the stake. Their flight led them eastward, eventually ending in Poland, where they settled.

In Poland, the De la Poules changed the family name to de Pulszky. For 200 years they served their new homeland faithfully and with distinction in various capacities. For their services they were rewarded by the King, who granted them a baronetcy, together with a considerable estate. In time, they became quite wealthy. In the 17th-century, one branch of the family crossed the south eastern border of Poland into Hungary. There, where they acquired extensive vineyards and an opal mine, they were soon involved in politics, several of them becoming eminent statesmen. They also worked for the cause of their own Lutheran Church and for other Protestant churches, generally distinguishing themselves in all they undertook.

The Empress Maria-Theresa of Habsburg (Hungary was then part of the Austro-Hungarian Empire) bestowed noble titles of *Lubocz* and *Cserfalva* on the Pulszky family, together with the immense landed estates that appertained to those titles.

During the decades that followed, they married within the nobility and aristocracy. Among those illustrious names to whom they became related as a result was Count Moric Benyovszky, the noted Polish adventurer. Ferenc Pulszky's father, Károly, was married twice. His first wife was Judith Várady-Szakmáry; her brother, Donát, was the son-in-law of Benyovszky. While fighting in Poland, Moric was captured by the Russians. Together with a handful of comrades he managed to escape and fled to France. His venturesome spirit brought him to the Island of Madagascar which he acquired for France. As a reward he was proclaimed Viceroy of the island. Whoever gave rise to this legendary title, King of Madagascar, I do not know, but many years later, Romola's sister Tessa, when seized by delusions of grandeur, would sign her name with a flourish: *Madame Tessa de Pulszky-Schmedes, Princess of Madagascar!* There are countless family chronicles concerning extramarital affairs involving the ladies of the Pulszky family. Krisztina, in the 17th-century, was said to have returned the 'warm feelings' of the great Hungarian national hero, Imre Thököly. Some of the beautiful jewellery he gave her was willed to her descendants. A

2

pair of pearl earrings in particular were to play a dramatic part in my own life. I wonder if the errant lady's husband was aware of her affairs or chose to turn a blind eye to her peccadillos to further his own career. When the chilling winds of revolution swept through Europe in the 19th-century, the young Habsburg Emperor Franz Josef, realising that his throne was insecure, found himself forced to take drastic measures to quench the rebellious Hungarian people, still dreaming of their past freedom. They had now been aroused from their slumber, their Magyar pride inflamed. At the heart of the freedom movement was my great-grandfather, Ferenc Pulszky. The son of Károly in his second marriage to Apollonia Fejérdváry, he was a tall man with a high forehead and, in keeping with the fashion of the day, his features were graced by a moustache and a small goatee. Ferenc was a brilliant scholar, a fluent linguist and a lawyer by profession. He was also a politician, an archeologist with excavations in Greece and Egypt to his credit, a connoisseur of the fine arts as well as a distinguished author and publicist. His most salient characteristics were his integrity and his unflinching devotion to a democratic philosophy.

His first wife, Therese (Teréz as she was subsequently called in Hungary) was Austrian. Her father was the director of the famous Walter Bank in Vienna. Their house, the *Palais Rasumovsky,* was the centre of the intellectual, artistic and political life in the capital and they were famed for their hospitality; everybody of importance came to their receptions, members of the Imperial family, Prince Metternich, Franz Liszt, among other luminaries. It was rumoured that Teréz had fallen deeply in love with the latter. The composer features frequently in the personal history of the Pulszky family. Emilia recalled how she had sat on his lap when she was a mere slip of a girl. Aunt Janka, the wife of Emilia's eldest brother, Jozsef Márkus, who for a short period was Mayor of Budapest, was one of Franz Liszt's prize pupils, and Polyxena, Romola's aunt, took care of Liszt; in Romola's own words 'kept his household in order, when in his old age he was appointed President of the Academy of Music in Budapest.'

Teréz, endowed not only with considerable wealth, but with remarkable intelligence and pleasing appearance, had many suitors but showed no hurry to relinquish her spinsterhood, much to her parents' disappointment. They envisaged her married to a member of the Austrian aristocracy. Instead, to their intense chagrin, she lost her heart to a 'wild, barbaric Hungarian', Ferenc Pulszky. His redeeming features in the eyes of his prospective in-laws were that he came from an aristocratic background and that his family owned vast estates in northern Hungary. And thus, although they were not sanguine about the union, they were forced to give their blessing.

Teréz quickly adapted herself to the Hungarian way of life, learned to speak the language fluently, and devoted herself wholeheartedly to raising a family and seeing to the welfare of the peasants on their domains.

Lajós Kossuth, the renowned Hungarian patriot and statesman, was at this time agitating for political and economic independence from Austria, and Ferenc Pulszky became his staunch aide. Together they travelled to America in the early 1850's to seek help for Hungary. Both appeared before a joint session of Congress in Washington DC to plead their cause. I recall how proud Romola was to have in her possession a silk coat which her grandmother, Teréz, had worn on that historic occasion.

One of the interesting outcomes of the American visit was a book published in English entitled *White, Red, Black – Sketches of Society in the United States during the Visit of Their Guest*. It was printed in London in 1853 (Trübner & Co.). In addition to being a book about their travel, it dealt with the conditions of the Red Indians, the Whites and the Blacks in the States, together with an outspoken denunciation by Ferenc Pulszky of what he called the barbaric practice of slavery. He and Teréz had several books to their credit, among them, *A Memoir of A Hungarian Lady*, also printed in London (Henry Colburn 1850). As recently as 1986 it was published in Hungarian in Budapest. A friend of mine sent me a copy and I dipped into it eagerly. Romola must have inherited from my great-grandmother her sophistication and intelligence but the warmth and compassion that flow out of the pages, she sadly lacked. However, they had one distinction in common, both were strong women who fought for their causes. Ferenc wrote a massive bibliography, *Eletem és Korom* (My Life and Times), which was published in four volumes in Budapest and later republished in Germany circa 1880.

After the failure of the Hungarian Revolution of 1848, Lajós Kossuth and his faithful comrades-in-arms had to flee the country and go into exile. Ferenc and Teréz took refuge in England, where they had been offered asylum through the intervention of Lord

Palmerston. Ferenc worked for a time as a political journalist for *The London Times*. According to certain reference sources both Karl Marx and Friedrich Engels, who lived in England at that time, followed Ferenc's political activities with keen interest, although it is not clear from their letters whether they had any personal contact with Ferenc.

Károly, Romola's father, was born in Highgate, London on the 10th November, 1853. His godfather was Giuseppi Garibaldi.

From London, the Pulszkys moved first to Florence and then Turin. Pulszky gave staunch support to the Italian freedom fighter Garibaldi in his struggle for the unification and freedom of Italy. In 1866, his beloved wife Teréz and three of their six children returned to Hungary to administer some of the numerous properties still in their possession. Tragedy struck because, while there, a cholera epidemic broke out and claimed their lives. Pulszky, devastated by the news, naturally wished to return to his country for the funeral and on the advice of close friends sought an audience with the Emperor Franz-Josef (Ferencz-József). The Emperor not only received him but granted him the title of Count and restored to him his lands that had been confiscated in 1849 after the failure of the revolution, on the condition that he would retire from politics and raise his remaining three children as loyal patriots to the Empire.

Ferenc withdrew to his Estate, raised his children as stipulated by the Emperor, and in due course became the Director of the National Fine Arts Museum and head of several other cultural institutions. At the ripe old age of 72, he married Rozsa Gestner.

Ferenc Pulszky's favourite son was without a doubt Károly. He was highly educated and could boast degrees from the Universities of London, Turin and Leipzig. He spoke eleven languages. Ferenc was keen for his son to dedicate himself to the history of the Arts and the latter duly complied with his father's wishes. He became an art historian and his knowledge was so profound, he was regarded as the greatest Renaissance expert at that time in Hungary. At first appointed Curator of the Museum of Folk Art, his reputation soon gained him the directorship of the National Galley. Károly was dashingly handsome, and with his background and social position he could have chosen his bride from the highest aristocracy, but the twists and turns of fate led him to Emilia Márkus. An actress!

'The Blonde Wonder' was the *soubriquet* bestowed upon her by her adoring public because of the extraordinary splendour of her hair that glistened like gold thread in sunlight and cascaded down her shoulders covering her like a cloak, stretching almost to the ground. She had a sylph-like figure and the bearing of a queen. Her luminous forget-me-not blue eyes were usually gentle and warm, but they could also flash steely-grey when she was angry. Added to these admirable characteristics was her rich, velvety voice, never forgotten by the thousands of theatre-goers who heard her on the stage. No one could remain impartial to Emilia Márkus; people either went into raptures and worshipped her or, because of extreme jealousy, despised her.

Emilia was to be regarded by most Hungarian critics as the greatest actress of all times, unsurpassed even by Sarah Bernhardt, Réjaneor Duse. Her repertoire ranged from the naïve, romantic ingénue through the liberated women of social dramas, to the remarkable heroines of Shakespeare and the classic Greek tragedies.

She was born on September 10th, 1860, in Szombathely in Hungary (although some reference works give the date September 8, 1862). She claimed she was born in a mill which at the time of her birth was on fire, and that she had a mark on her hip to prove it. Oddly enough, she was never afraid of fire and on one occasion at least she was instrumental in saving people from death by fire. During a theatre performance, the kerosene lamp on stage overturned and a tablecloth burst into flames. The audience jumped up in panic, but Emilia reacted coolly and promptly. Without flinching she grasped hold of the four corners of the tablecloth and thus extinguished the fire. In her calm, melodious voice she bade the audience resume their seats so the performance could continue. For this she received an appreciative ovation.

Emilia was the youngest of eight children born to József Márkus and Anna Horvát. József was a prosperous mill owner. Anna's background must have been equally solid. Her elder brother Boldizsar was the Minister of the Interior. I must, however, confess my ignorance regarding my grandmother's early ancestors. When I was a child, she would regale me with stories of how she was a descendant of Marcus Aurelius, that her family were Roman in origin. I am quite certain all this was a figment of her ever-creative imagination, wishful thinking stemming from her classical drama studies. Most likely, it is closer to the truth that the Márkus family were of German descent from the proximity of the western border with Hungary.

Father József died quite young and it was left to Anna to rear their brood. She moved to Budapest to ensure a better chance of education for her children. They grew up to embark on widely different careers. István, for example, studied law; Miklós became a poet and Emilia used to love to tell how she as a child would hide under the billowing tablecloth in the kitchen and thrill to listen to him recite his poetry, and she frequently imitated his recitations; József studied for the priesthood but left the seminary after a few years because he found the food so abominable. Instead he procured work in the city and rose to become Mayor of Budapest. One brother studied architecture but died at the age of twenty. Emilia's sister Irma, tranquil by nature, found her greatest happiness when engrossed in her studies. Both girls had been sent to the Convent of the English Ladies of Loretto to further their education.

When Emilia was fourteen years old, she caused an upheaval by announcing that she wished to study to be an actress. Anna was distressed; Emilia had a weak constitution and was described as a pale and nervous girl, too frail for such a demanding occupation. She obdurately refused to listen to her mother's pleading against her taking such a step and found an ally in her uncle, who was then the Minister of Justice, and also loyal support from her brothers. Anna was forced to capitulate and accede to her strong-willed daughter's wish. Consequently, Emilia was enrolled in the Royal Academy of Drama in the year 1874. The Director was so delighted with her ability and progress that in 1877 he gave her the role of Juliet, which she played with outstanding success at the National Theatre. This was the beginning of a meteoric career that was to span sixty-odd years on the Hungarian stage. Emilia even played Juliet at the age of fifty!

The high opinion of Emilia's talents was by no means confined purely to her own countrymen. No less a person than the director of the *Comédie Française* saw her performance on stage and invited her to study French and perform at the *Comédie*. This invitation was said to be the first of its kind presented to a foreigner since the establishment of the *Comédie* by Molière in 1660. As regards her ability to play contemporary drama, Henrik Ibsen, while visiting her in her dressing-room on one occasion during a performance of *A Doll's House* kissed her hand and proclaimed 'You are my best and greatest Nora.' Edmond Rostand considered her the equal of both Bernhardt and Duse as Roxane in *Cyrano de Bergerac*.

Emilia fell passionately in love with a young man of whom her family did not approve. They called upon her to put an end to the romance and Emilia, though heartbroken, apparently did not offer any strong resistance to their wishes. It was shortly afterwards, that Károly Pulszky met one of Emilia's brothers and through the latter was introduced to her. Károly developed an immediate, intense attachment for the young actress but she did not reciprocate his interest. The family unanimously approved of Károly and pressed Emilia to accept his proposal. Although she tenaciously fought against it for some time, she finally capitulated and in 1882 she and Károly were married.

The much publicised wedding ceremony took place on June 7th, 1882, in the *Egyetem Templom* or University Catholic Church, after which the young couple, families and friends, as well as scores of distinguished guests, gathered at the National Museum for the reception. Afterwards, Károly and his young bride set forth on their honeymoon to Italy. It was Emilia's first trip abroad. They visited Venice, Ravenna, Assisi and other cities notable in the world of the Arts. It was a rather unusual honeymoon, to say the least, because *Charlie had also invited his younger brother Garri along on the trip. Garri was quite infatuated with Emilia and followed her around like a shadow. From early morning until late at night, the trio wandered from museums, to churches, to *palazzi,* in order to satisfy Charlie's passion to study, to discover and to estimate *objets d'art* and Renaissance treasures in particular. Hardly Emilia's idea of a honeymoon!

Upon their return to Budapest they moved into the Palace of the Academy of Science. Charlie's classic taste and expertise were instrumental in surrounding Emilia with items of indescribable elegance. Intricately woven Gobelin tapestries adorned the walls, vying in beauty with some of the paintings of the Renaissance masters acquired by Charlie on his many visits to the auction rooms in the capitals of Europe. Greek vases and carved furniture from India crowded the many niches in the apartment. The library was lined with innumerable leatherbound volumes, mostly first editions, selected not merely for display but for their content. Charlie was an avid reader of the classics and to further Emilia's knowledge of English, for instance, he would read to her almost daily from George Eliot's novel, *Romola.* He so admired this book, he was

---

* Because of his English birthright Károly was popularly called Charlie.

later to translate it into Hungarian and had it published under a *nom de plume.* Little wonder it inspired Emilia to ask that they should call their second daughter Romola. One may speculate if the name of their first-born, Tessa, was also derived from that novel, because Tito's baby-faced wife was so called, or whether she was simply named after her maternal grandmother Teréz Walter.

From this opulent period in Emilia's life there was one item of furniture that gave me a special thrill when I as a little girl first came to live with her in the Villa she shared with her second husband, Oskar. It was an enormous Renaissance Bishop's chair and I can still vividly recall how I would gently trace its elaborate reliefs and inlays with my fingertips.

János Temple painted a life-size portrait of Emilia in the costume she wore as Desdemona. It occupied a conspicuous place in the apartment. Guests invited to the glittering soirées and dinner parties were often at a loss for words afterwards to describe in sufficiently glowing terms the dazzling good looks and *belle tournure* of their hostess, the *savoir faire* and charm of their host, the lavish splendour of the salon and the sparkling flow of conversation. With each gathering there could always be found a sprinkling of well-known names from the intelligentsia, the theatre, the arts, and politics, that grew grander as the months sped by – Gustav Mahler, and Bernard Berenson on his first ever visit to Budapest, to name but two.

In the euphoria of their first years of marriage Charlie took Emilia all over the continent and introduced her to renowned personalities. She was delighted to meet Franz Liszt at a private musical soirée and used to refer to his brilliant piano recitals to the end of her days. She had not found Richard Wagner sympathetic, however, dismissing him as a 'cold, unpleasant little man', who never looked up and thus forced everyone to bend down to his level. Contrarily, she was obsessed by his operas and would not dream of missing a single performance of his work at the Opera whenever her heavy schedule at the National Theatre so permitted. When she was pregnant with Romola, she attended several performances of *The Flying Dutchman,* every time more and more enraptured by the music.

On May 5th, 1883 she gave birth to a daughter, who was to be christened Tessa Paula Gizella Beatrix. Emilia recorded the event in her leather prayerbook given to her by Károly '...*in the night between 12-1 o'clock. God my Father bless her.*'

The Pulszky family were strict Lutherans; Emilia's family, Catholics. When Károly married Emilia he had to sign an affidavit according to the ruling of that time to the effect that if children resulted from their union, daughters would have to take their mother's religion; sons their father's. Hence, both Tessa and Romola were brought up in the Catholic faith.

Károly did everything in his power to ensure Emilia's success, not only in Society but also in her career. Thus, when Tessa was born, it was he who personally chose a nanny for her, so that Emilia would be free to accept the many parts proffered to her. Miss Palmer, who was later to care for Romola as well and become both girls' governess, was a British import. She was only a few years older than Emilia. Tall and bony, she wore her reddish-blonde hair plainly and primly combed back in a neat chignon. 'Pretty' was not an adjective that could readily have applied to her but her appearance and manner denoted a vibrant worldly personality. She had been a friend of Charlie's during his London years, and had then evidently been extremely fond of him, perhaps nourishing the hope of one day becoming his wife. Ironically, she was instead to assume the role of 'substitute mother' to his children. She had met Emilia on the occasion Charlie had returned to London to introduce his bride and like most people who came in contact with Emilia, Miss Palmer had been deeply impressed by her. Surely, one must suspect, however, that she had been torn with doubt when Charlie later wrote and made his proposition. Would she be able to live under the same roof as his wife? But whatever flames of passion had burned within her must long since have died. Financially, she sorely needed work at the time and, as she was to confess to Emilia, she longed to escape her humdrum life in London.

I have wanted briefly to sketch the milieu in which Tessa and Romola spent their first formative years. Already as a youngster Tessa showed an aptitude for music and singing. Both girls were taken on trips on the continent and in 1894 they met Eleonora Duse in Venice, a meeting which Romola could hardly have remembered, as she was then only three years old. It was inevitable that the Pulszky daughters were to be strongly influenced by their environment. Throughout their lives, neither could quench her taste for luxury and a high life style. Both had absorbed a craving for the finest fashion, and money was to run through their fingers like grains of sand.

Surprisingly, when it came to her profession, Emilia never lost her sense of perspective, spoiled and pampered by Károly though she was, and elevated to the heavens by her audiences. She fully acknowledged her beauty, ability and talent yet an inherent common sense and a worrying nature always left her aware that the very people who held the reins in the theatre could one day quite callously forsake her art and genius for those of a less gifted actress desperate by fair means or foul to take over Emilia's mantle.

In complete control of herself on stage, she often acted like an irresponsible *enfant terrible* off-stage. Throughout her life she was cursed by extreme jealousy, a feminine weakness that according to the gossips took bizarre forms, like locking her husband up in her dressing-room during rehearsals and keeping the key in her pocket. She would take no chances that his roving eyes should stray in the direction of a younger colleague or understudy. Rather illogical, considering she was tolerant of Charlie's mistresses, both at home and abroad. Mistresses on whom he squandered vast sums. She was kept *á jour* of these indiscretions by the numerous obliging, wagging tongues of so-called 'friends'. Perhaps she philosophically considered what was 'out of sight' was 'out of mind'. Too, in those days it was accepted as perfectly natural that a husband might be a philanderer. For her part, Emilia flirted shamelessly with every man in sight, from the fireman stationed on guard in the wings during a performance, to the postman or every male guest clustering around her at a party. Yet her game, so I have been told – the conquest of as many adulating admirers as possible – was in truth so innocent, nobody took those performances seriously. On the contrary, they enjoyed participating in her charades. Never in the years I lived with my grandmother did I hear a breath of scandal connected with her private being.

At the risk of jumping decades ahead in my story, I must relate the following touching and revealing vignette. The day before she fell into a coma at the age of eighty-nine, Emilia received the last sacrament. She turned to my husband and myself, who were keeping vigil at her bedside, and with a coquettish gleam in her eyes said, 'This young Franciscan priest, is he not handsome in his habit? And did you notice his deep brown eyes?'. It has been said that only three men had captured her heart absolutely: the young man she had not been allowed to marry because of her family's opposition; A.K., a well-known newspaper publisher and writer, with whom she had a prolonged, intense liaison; and Oskar, her second hus-

11

band. Everyone had scoffed at this marriage, prophesying its early termination. Instead, it lasted for forty-two years until Oskar's death.

Those first few years of marriage Emilia set forth on her kaleidoscopic parade of characters created by such great dramatists as Shakespeare, Schiller, Dumas, Sardou, Bataille, Calderon de la Barca, Echegaray, Goethe, Ibsen, Emeric Madách – the list seems endless. Thanks to Charlie, she had acquired a cultural background, a broad understanding of world history and a profound appreciation of the fine arts, that helped her comprehend in depth both the classics and the more contemporary roles.

Emilia not only turned men's heads but occasionally women's. A rather weird story proving the latter circulated at the time Romola and Waslaw were staying in Budapest during World War 1. An elderly dresser, an unsightly and deformed woman, had managed to inveigle Emilia to take her on. Emilia, generous and warm-hearted to a fault, particularly when someone less fortunate sought her help, had even seen to it she was employed by the theatre and mainly used to perform menial tasks for Emilia. After a while it dawned on Emilia that the wretched woman had fallen in love with her. Although repelled by the mere thought, Emilia tried at first to ward off the unwelcome advances by simply ignoring them and dismissing the absurd situation as a harmless albeit distasteful 'comedy of errors'. Until one day it became grim reality when the frenzied woman attempted to kill Emilia in her bath. Emilia, wishing to obliterate the whole painful episode from her mind, refused to press charges. Neither would she allow the police to interfere. Instead, the pitiful woman was summarily dismissed from the theatre, and out of her own pocket Emilia sent her two months' wages, knowing the woman would otherwise be destitute.

Many years later, Romola was to record a completely different version of the incident in her notes for the new book she was hoping to write.

'As a child I used to have very vivid dreams. Many of them were prophetic or telepathic dreams – they foretold events which later actually happened. Some were dreams of warning, others foreboding happy events. At the time I was a rather nervous and sensitive child...psychic phenomena were unknown and my mother hastily took me to one of the foremost neurologists of

my native country, Professor Dr Ranschburg. At once I was
given bromide and was forbidden to read before going to bed at
night, or to go too often to the theatre. "The child is full of
imagination, highly strung...". A lot of fresh air, long walks in
the country, skating and swimming were ordered. But in spite
of everything I...continued to dream.'

In an interview which appeared in *Psychic News,* London, on November 28th 1964, Romola related the following dream to Anne Dooley. Briefly, her story was that she had dreamed that her mother, while dressing, was combing her long, golden hair when suddenly her dressing gown was pierced by a bullet, the shot fired by a small stout woman. Trembling with fear, Romola had rushed into the bedroom shared by her mother and stepfather and related the dream. Comforted by Emilia, she had been tucked into the latter's bed. At about eight o'clock the next morning Emilia had gone to her dressing-room to prepare for a rehearsal at the theatre. Suddenly a scream had rung out and when Romola and her stepfather rushed into the room, they found Emilia slumped over the dressing-room table (in the interview, lying on the floor) wounded by a bullet. A small stout woman had stood there with a pistol in her hand, a theatre dresser who had been dismissed because of her alcoholic habits and who erroneously had thought that Emilia was responsible for her dismissal. Somehow, she had managed to steal into the apartment where she had hidden, biding her opportunity. Luckily Emilia was not dangerously hurt, but later the dresser shot herself. I do not wish to pass judgment as to which story about the unbalanced woman is true, and neither Emilia nor Romola can give the answer.

To all outward appearances the Pulszky couple were united in a harmonious, happy marriage. Although Emilia harboured only lukewarm feelings toward her husband she was scrupulously honest in her assessment of her indebtedness to him. If there was a cloud on the horizon, it was in the form of Polyxena, Emilia's sister-in-law, who had grown to hate 'that actress', partly out of class snobbishness, partly out of envy. She was incensed by the fact that Károly had chosen a woman she sneeringly referred to as the *bourgeoisie.* She availed herself of every opportunity to malign Emilia, dropping devious hints in an effort to blacken her character and artistic ability.

Most members of Károly's family harboured quite different feelings towards his wife. His father Ferenc, for example, loved her dearly and was exceedingly proud of her, eager to show her off to his many influential friends. Sadly, he was to die in 1897, at a time when Emilia most desperately needed loyal support.

While his 'Blonde Wonder' experienced triumph upon triumph in her theatrical career, Károly was fired with an ambition to make his gallery the finest in Hungary, if not in the whole of Europe. His stamina never flagged as he tore from city to city – Cologne, Paris, London, Rome, Brussels, Milan, Venice – to procure the choicest pieces of art for his country. He did not miss an auction or art sale to bid for paintings he deemed as 'musts' to enhance the Gallery. He was delighted when in 1894 Parliament accepted his plan for the enlargement of the Museum of Fine Arts to coincide with the Millennium celebration to take place in 1896, and he was entrusted with a fair budget to be used for the procurement of additions to the existing collection. The Millennium was to celebrate the establishment by St Stephen of Hungary as a Kingdom in 896 AD after the settlement of the Magyar tribes on the shores of the Danube. Added to his role as director of the Fine Arts Museum, Károly was Guard of the Hungarian Crown and in this capacity he took the liberty to advise the Government that the Magyars' sacred emblem, the Crown of St Stephen, originally given to the Hungarian people by Pope Sylvester, should be restored for the Millennium. He was elected to Parliament in 1884 and held this seat for eight years.

Károly became overzealous in his feverish quest for specific works of art and, in an attempt to outwit other art dealers on the Continent, he used a rather infamous Countesss, whose lover he was rumoured to be, to bid for a painting on his behalf at the Gallery Scarpa auction in Milan. The painting, *Portrait of a Man*. Károly was later to swear he had purchased it in the full knowledge it was a work by Sebastiano del Piombo and that he had paid a very reasonable price for it, but his adversaries were to claim he had passed it off as a painting by Raphael. In actual truth, art experts had for years been unable to agree as to which of those two famous names to attribute it.

Political intrigue now intruded. For years Károly and his brother Agost, who had been Secretary of State and was currently a candidate for the post of Minister of Justice, had had strong enemies among the Opposition led by a clever lawyer, Géza Polonyi. Polonyi was after their scalps but because of their wealth and the influence of the Pulszky family, he had not dared confront them openly. At once he saw his golden opportunity and accused Károly of fraud, of embezzlement of Government funds!

Many years later, in her manuscript about her mother, Romola wrote: '...*my father went regularly to Italy and other European countries on behalf of the government to purchase paintings and sundry works of art. He was usually accompanied by a financial secretary, selected by the Ministry, who handled the administrative and financial affairs, but it so happened that in 1895, Károly went alone to Italy. Upon his return from Florence he had brought with him a painting which he attested unequivocally was an original and which he had purchased with government money for a very reasonable sum. Polonyi grasped this as a godsend to accuse Károly of passing off a fake on the government. The allegation gave rise to an official investigation. European art experts were called in. They agreed that the painting was an original Italian painting from the Renaissance but could not agree that it was a Raphael. Károly was incarcerated during the lengthy investigation. He was deeply wounded that his integrity had been doubted and that the powers-that-be could think that he would steal from them....*' In vain he had tried to explain that what he had bought for such a modest sum was a genuine bargain because, as he steadfastly claimed, it was an original Piombo.

The smear campaign against Károly Pulszky had commenced. He was put on trial, the target of slander. The whole of Budapest buzzed about the case, the newspapers wrote about little else. The legal battle was to be an arduous one – of accusations and counter accusations. Károly was derided by his enemies in Parliament. Jeers amidst raucous laughter echoed in the vast Assembly Hall whenever Polonyi thundered the name 'Piombo'.

While this tragic drama was moving slowly towards its climax, Romola, then barely five years old, searched daily through the corridors of the Academy of Science for her Charlie-Papa, not finding him at his desk in the library. How could Emilia and Tessa, the latter now old enough to have an inkling of what was happening, explain to a tiny girl the reason for her father's absence? Romola idolised her father. He was the pivot around whom her world turned. He was her story-teller, who on those wonderful rare occasions when he was at home, would read to her tales of magical places. He loved to read to both girls from works written by their grandparents, Ferenc and Teréz Pulszky – *Memoirs of a Hungarian Lady* and *Tales and Traditions of Hungary*.

Emilia resiliently held her blonde head high throughout the whole of the turbulent months that were to come. She bravely shook off the unkind, often snide remarks of her colleagues at the theatre, pride forbidding her to show how offended and wounded she was. Even Tessa had to suffer the cruel jibes of many of her playmates.

Relatives and 'well-meaning' meddlers were unanimous in their opinion she should seek a divorce. Malicious scandalmongers insisted that was precisely what Emilia intended to do. The rumours were wholly groundless, however. She had too much self-esteem and courage for that. Besides, Károly was the father of her two daughters, who loved both their parents, but she was faced with the appalling dilemma of where to find cash to pay the very high penalties imposed upon Károly. She had to make the agonising decision to move out of their luxurious apartment at the Academy of Science and sell most of her valuable jewellery and furs, even some of the priceless art treasures. By now she had to shoulder the unenviable task of being the breadwinner of the family.

In early 1896 Károly was suspended from office. He was released by the authorities from a brief spell in prison, albeit reluctantly, while the trial dragged on and on. His defence aimed to prove that he had been authorised by the Minister for Cultural Affairs to handle vast sums of money but had been given no competent assistance. That here was an art expert who had been forced to travel to the capitals of Europe to seek bargains for the Gallery at a pace that would have killed a lesser man. At the same time he had had to shoulder the mantle of cashkeeper, bookkeeper and despatcher. The strain had been too great and he had started to drink excessively. His condition had deteriorated to such a degree that he had suffered a nervous breakdown. Medical experts who were called in agreed that he must have acted with 'diminished responsibility' and he was later to be acquitted on those grounds, in addition to the lack of substantiating evidence that he had misappropriated funds.

Meanwhile, Polyxena discreetly arranged the transfer of her brother into a sanatorium where he was to spend one-and-a-half years. It was a satisfactory arrangement for all concerned. No stigma was attached to such a confinement. There, visitors could come and go at their leisure, the patients' rooms were comfortably furnished, and all meals were served in spacious dining-rooms.

To have Charlie at the sanatorium indefinitely was no solution, however. Emilia wanted to reach some agreement to have him at home. The girls needed him. She had the will-power and strength of character to cope with it but Polyxena and Agost took matters in their own hands. They has unanimously agreed that once Charlie was cleared, he would have to leave the country. Their objective was to erase, as speedily as possible, the dishonour that has befallen the Pulszky name. Charlie had to leave Hungary never to return, since he showed no inclination to do them the favour of ending his life like a gentleman – by committing suicide.

Not heeding Emilia, Charlie bowed submissively to his sister's demands and decided that the best course of action would be to return to London, his birthplace, where he had studied and still had some friends. He filled his many empty hours at the sanatorium preparing for his new venture. His spirits rose as replies to his letters to England hinted that he might be able to teach at a university there or even secure a position in the British Museum.

What ensued I have pieced together from fragmentary monologues my grandmother used to indulge in when I was a teenager and committed to ritually brushing her long tresses before she retired for the night. Tessa, too, would sometimes lift the curtain on that traumatic phase in their lives when Charlie-Papa vanished forever. Even Romola, young as she was, never could obliterate from her mind the anguish it caused her. In aftermath, I feel it must have been a form of therapy for Emilia to unveil to someone her actions at the time, to unburden herself and to free herself of any feeling of guilt she may have harboured over her harsh attitude toward her husband when he most desperately needed her support.

Usually, Emilia brought Tessa and Romola along to visit their father but on a certain Sunday morning Charlie had sent a message that he must see her alone. He had serious matters to discuss that would be unsuitable to thrash out in front of their daughters. Emilia had felt edgy and apprehensive about what he might have to impart. Upon entering his room, she had found him deeply engrossed in reading a letter. At the sound of her voice he jumped up. No doubt in that fleeting moment he had hungrily taken in her majestic figure, the heavy golden hair pinned up on her beautifully shaped head like a regal crown.

17

To Emilia, ritual meetings had reached a point where they had become increasingly an unpleasant duty, to be endured and dispersed with as quickly and painlessly as possible. She was even to admit years later that sometimes, studying him closely, she had been assailed by doubts concerning his innocence. No one knew better than she how weak-willed a man he was, but she was usually able to chase such gloomy suspicions away by clinging to the certainty of his inherent honest nature. Now, however, she was tired, drained, from the previous evening's performance and wanted the business to be over and done with so that she could go home.

He tried to embrace her but she suddenly felt a wave of repugnance flood over her and, brushing him aside, rather sharply demanded to hear what he had to tell her. He was pained by her impatience and aloofness and ruefully reminded her that he was due to leave for England within a few days.

Twitching nervously, he pleaded with Emilia to show some compassion and then, unexpectedly and dramatically, he produced a revolver from a brown suitcase on the floor. Noticing the startled expression on her face, he relented and, tossing the revolver to one side, assured her she need not worry. He would do nothing foolish. In the same breath he raised the vital issue of her visit. He beseeched her to join him in England with their children.

Emilia had been taken aback. Then she regained her composure and scoffed at the suggestion. If she too vanished it would be an open admission of guilt. No, he would have to go alone and then later, when the whole affair had quietened down – people's memories were so short – he should return to Budapest. Nothing he could say would change her attitude, she was adamant. Realising he had lost, he begged her for one last favour, that she book a table for dinner in the private dining-room of the Vadászkürt so that on the evening of his departure he could be with his family. To that she readily agreed.

Let us visualise the following scene. Emilia sank down in the horse-drawn carriage that was taking her home. She heaved a sigh of relief and relaxed as it moved along at a slow, rhythmical pace. Lost in her own reveries she saw, yet did not see, the familiar landmarks that they passed, the lane where the tall chestnut trees stood guard, the Chain Bridge with its four 'tongueless' lions, the St Stephen's Basilica, where Romola had been baptised.

It was not until the silhouette of the National Theatre loomed up in the foreground that she smiled. How thrilled she was with her latest role. It was at that precise moment, after ruthless self-interrogation, she was forced to admit to herself that there lay the true reason why she so flatly refused to accompany Charlie on his trip. The stage, the roles she played, the characters she portrayed, that was her life. To stand in front of the footlights, listen to the sweet music of the applause and cheering. To feel that exuberant sense of achievement. Perhaps, searching into the depths of her soul, she admitted she was unremittingly selfish in the pursuit of her career. Besides, she did not genuinely love Charlie, never had. She had to confess the truth even though it produced a justifiable tingle of shame. After all, she was beholden to him for so much. He had opened many doors for her, deepened her knowledge of the humanities and philosophies, introduced her to some of the most interesting people of her era, to wonderful foreign places they had explored together. He was the father of Tessa and Romola. Charlie had many good attributes but was irresolute. She was unable to withhold the tears as she cast her mind back to the young man she had been so ardently in love with and whom she had been forced to relinquish in obedience to her family.

The years were never to diminish his memory. She was always to speak of him with deep emotion. Now, when she approached the new residence where she and the girls lived, she felt as grey as the clouds that covered the sun like an impenetrable dull cloth. She was trapped. Did she perhaps recoil from the remembrance of those horrifying nights in the last few years when Charlie would come drunk and stumbling into their bedroom...

But Emilia kept her promise to her husband. A table was reserved at the Hotel Vadászkürt in a narrow patrician street in Budapest where Charlie was to spend his last evening with the family.

When Emilia had been compelled to leave their home at the Academy of Science, she had moved to a modest apartment at the Hotel Royal. Although the surroundings did not boast the same grandeur, each of the girls had her own room furnished in her own individual style, already exhibiting their different personalities. And how contrasting they were. Tessa, blonde, blue-eyed, robustly built, in her early teens physically resembled her mother and, in some ways, temperamentally too. Bohemian by nature, carefree, ready for anything that was a lark, maybe just a shade too flirtatious in her manner; a hint of laughter suspiciously ready to bubble over at the slightest provocation.

Romola, on the other hand, was frail in body. Emilia would lament that a breeze could blow her away. But the girl compensated for it by her self-possessiveness and perseverance and she was so clever, a true Pulszky. Emilia could never refrain from feeling that her younger child respected her but did not genuinely love her, and it was a heavy cross Emilia was to bear all her life because, despite all the grief and hurt Romola was to inflict upon her, it was she who would be closest to Emilia's heart.

Tessa's room was utterly feminine – a cascade of clothing strewn haphazardly over chairs and the bed. A large mirror adorned the dressing-table in front of which she would sit for hours on end preening herself and trying on her sizeable wardrobe of frilly bonnets. Books by her favourite authors were piled unceremoniously on the floor by her armchair, where she would curl up in the evenings absorbed in the company of Goethe's poems, the stories of Maupassant, and falling in love with the swashbuckling heroes she encountered in the works of Alexandre Dumas Père.

By contrast, a sombre, fastidious air pervaded Romola's room. Deep, red silk wallpaper with a design of Imperial gold laurel wreaths covered the walls. The bed was a copy of Madame Recamier's chaise longue. The thick silk bedspread matched the colour and design of the wallpaper. Books were neatly stacked on the bedside table and a glance at the titles revealed an early interest in serious subjects. Among the more predominant writers were Anatole France and Zola. Years later I inherited my mother's furnishings which had been transported to the Villa Emilia had built; wallpaper and all.

Romola's devotion to her father was unimpaired by separation. On the evening of the farewell dinner she subconsciously became plagued with fear it might be the last time she would see him. A shrewd child, she had taken in the many preparations, the packing of her father's large trunk that had accompanied the move to the new home. She sensed that the atmosphere was laden with upheaval of some kind. She had missed him so much during those endless months the adults had said he was 'away' on business. And now she had just begun to look forward to the visits to the Sanatorium where he was 'recuperating after an illness', only to learn he would be whisked away from her. She noticed how agitated both her mother and Miss Palmer were. Extremely clothes conscious even at that tender age, she was years later able to recall the dress she had worn on that joyless occasion. She had wanted to make a good impression on Papa. It was of navy blue wool, with long sleeves and high neck. A wide écru collar had lent a touch of grown-up elegance to the outfit. Her auburn hair had been combed straight back and two rows of braids tightly crowned her head. Ill-at-ease with her mother, she had plied Miss Palmer with questions. Miss Palmer, doing her utmost to skirt the issue as delicately as possible, reminded Romola of the many years her father travelled all over Europe to collect fine arts and that he now was faced with the prospect of doing so again. I must record what transpired that fateful day on trust; it had indelibly registered in her mind. According to her story their conversation at this point had been interrupted by Emilia, nervously pulling her long lilac gloves over her fingers. She was a breathtaking sight – dressed in a lilac silk robe. The upper part of the gown was made of muslin of the same subtle lilac shading. An antique silver brooch held the straps together around her neck. On her bosom the material lay in layers of folds and her wasp waist was held in by an armour-like girdle underneath. From the waist down, the silk cascaded to the floor in elegant pleats. A deep pink silk flower was pinned to the cleavage of her gown. A huge hat hid most of the mass of golden hair, the wide brim artfully concealing the black shadows under her eyes, tell-tale marks of lack of sleep.

Coquettish Tessa kept them all waiting while she decided what hat to wear but the trio had finally made their way to the rendezvous with Charlie-Papa. Like rewinding an old film Romola described in detail what the child, far too mature for her age, experienced. They had entered the hotel's private dining-room where Charlie impatiently awaited them. It was an intimate room, old-fashioned rose and gold wallpaper adorning the walls. A thick deep-red carpet absorbed the sound of footsteps. The table was set with the purest white damask, bone china and glittering silverware and lead crystal glasses, the latter sparkling like diamonds from the reflection of the chandelier.

Charlie was dressed in utilitarian travelling gear clashing with the festive chic of his 'girls'. The conversation at the dinner table was subdued, the aim to avoid mention of Charlie's impending departure. They all enacted their allotted roles: Charlie, outwardly the urbane man of the world, most certainly fighting his private battle to suppress his heartache at leaving his family, to hide from them his loss of self-esteem; Emilia, drained after an arduous rehearsal as Marguerite in *La Dame aux Camélias* had reached a peak of ennui and tried to disguise it and instead enliven the conversation for the sake of her little Molly (her pet name for Romola), whose unhappy pallid face was a mirror of her grief at losing her father. His promises to send her postcards from exotic foreign countries to enable her to follow him on his travels uncannily enough failed to convince her that he would ever return.

Tessa, on the threshhold of womanhood, was acutely aware that a significant change was about to transpire in their lives and although she did not share the same devout attachment to her father as did Romola, she was a very tender-hearted girl and intuitively realised what a psychological ordeal he must be going through. She did her utmost to please him by relating her progress in her musical studies; how much she enjoyed playing the piano. She felt a strong allegiance to both her parents and was determined to keep up the charade with cheerful patter.

Romola's rather shrill voice suddenly sounded through the room. The superficial, well-guarded flow of conversation came to an abrupt halt as everybody stared at her. She pushed her dinner plate to one side and refused to eat a single morsel of the white chicken breast that had been served. Her hysterical behaviour gave rise to a sharp exchange of words between Emilia and Charlie. Charlie, in a last bid to assert himself as the paternal head of the family, rebuked his daughter in no uncertain terms and ordered her to eat what was placed before her or else she would be punished. Romola looked at him with pained questioning eyes. She could not believe that the father she so adored would speak to her in such a tone on their last evening together. Even so, she steadfastly refused to touch the piece of hated chicken challenging her from the plate. No matter how Charlie bullied, she was adamant. They glared at each other – two Pulszkys – both just as stubborn.

In the Sixties, when I was invited one day to lunch at Sausolito together with my mother and her cousin Paul, he told me that Romola could never touch the white meat of fowl, but she thoroughly enjoyed the 'Bishop's nose' and he confessed that to his embarrassment Romola would order three to four pieces of this delicacy in the most exclusive eating-places in Europe. Incidentally, it was on this particular occasion Romola talked about the sad dinner party prior to Charlie-Papa's departure.

Later that night Charlie returned to the apartment with his family to collect his luggage, after which Emilia, Romola, Tessa and Miss Palmer accompanied him to the railway station. They waved good-bye to him as he stood on the rear platform of the train, his figure growing smaller and smaller as the train receded into the fog, bound for Vienna.

The little group had lingered immobile on the platform for a while, listening to the rattling of the wheels until nothing more could be heard. Darkness engulfed them. Romola stood there, a pathetic little body, her back stiff as a ramrod, her lips tight. It was not until they returned to the sanctuary of the apartment that the floodgates opened and her slender frame was racked with sobs. With a frenzied gesture she shrugged off Emilia's attempts to comfort her or even to touch her. It was left to Miss Palmer to quieten the distraught child and to lead her up to the bedroom. Tessa, noticing their mother's look of total fatigue, feared she was on the verge of collapse and solicitously guided her to her room and forced her to lie down on the chaise longe. Gently she covered her with a cashmere shawl and then sank down on the floor beside her, feeling at last the strain of the past hours. She could not refrain from asking herself, 'Dear God, why did you let this happen?'

Romola could not come to terms with the physical loss of her father and daily expressed her longing to join him. She induced Miss Palmer to take her to Aunt Poly, in whom she felt she had an ally. Polyxena patiently explained to her that if she really wanted her father to be proud of her then her first duty was to grow up and to carry on her studies in the manner he would have wished.

The bond of friendship between aunt and niece grew stronger and stronger much to the dismay of Emilia but she was powerless to intervene. It chagrined her to see her younger daughter being weaned away from her by a woman she loathed, yet however much she brooded over the fact, she found no tenable answer.

Days, weeks, months went by, crossed off the calendar one by one. Emilia made valiant efforts to maintain the same standard of living as they had enjoyed in earlier days, now that she was the master of their household as well, an unenviable role to play considering how pampered she had been. She had sparse news from Charlie. He had arrived safely in London but had not found the warm welcome he had been led to expect. His hopes of obtaining a professorship at one of the universities, a promise vaguely made by friends, had dwindled with each passing day. In late 1898 he eked out a meagre living acting as an agent in the antiques trade. Both Poly and Agost had bombarded him with letters designed to push him further and further away from the the European continent. Separated from Emilia, who had been his moral pillar of strength, he finally succumbed to their wishes and boarded a boat to Australia.

One spring evening in 1899, just as Emilia and her daughters were finishing dinner, they were disturbed by a heavy thud from above, followed by the shattering of glass. They rushed up to Emilia's bedroom whence the noise had come and, upon flinging the door open, found the large portrait of Charlie lying face down on the floor. Emilia was visibly shaken. Superstitious, like most of her colleagues in the theatre, she saw it as a bad omen – an omen of death. Romola had burst into a tantrum and begged that in future the portrait be hung in her room.

On the 6th of June a young girl, sent to collect firewood near the coast of Myrtletown, Australia, stumbled across the body of a man in the bush. Charlie Pulszky had ended his life with a single bullet to the heart only a few months after he had reached the 'promised land'. He was identified by a leather wallet engraved 'Baba'. It contained a photograph of Emilia and their two little daughters. There were also receipts for three registered letters posted on April 10th. None of these was addressed to Hungary. One had been sent to London, one to Sydney and one to Kalgoorlie.

Charlie had gone to Brisbane but had been unable to cope in an atmosphere totally alien to him. The pioneering life there had been too primitive; his only world had been that of arts and literature. And the poignant or rather bitter truth was that he had lost virtually everything to live for – his honour, his beloved family, his country, his position and political career. His crushed spirit could take no more...

The devastating news of her father's death was to linger in Romola's memory for many years. She had been in her room when she had heard a commotion in the corridor and her mother had entered, supported on the arm of Emilia's uncle, Boldizsár Horvát, and a distraught Aunt Poly in tow.

In her diary in which she recorded the events of that fateful morning, Romola wrote '...*I do not remember clearly, but I can see her (Emilia) in front of me, in a red plaid dress, nervously sobbing, her golden hair hanging in a tangled mass over her face, her body shaking, her eyes red from crying... I was eight years old when Father died. It was a terrible loss to me. I would have given anything to be able to be with him. I loved him so very much. He was the one closest to me, the only one who understood me. I keep his memory in my heart...*'

The impact of the cruel blow subsided in due course to a dull, aching pain but Romola, young as she was at the time, made a solemn vow that was to guide her throughout her entire life – a vow to Charlie-Papa that she would strive to become the knowledgeable woman of whom he would have been proud. One can truthfully say that she kept that promise. In her late sixties, for example, she studied Japanese, her seventh language. She wished to learn Japanese in order to fulfil an engagement to give a lecture tour in Japan. By then she was already an authority on ballet, had written a number of books, edited her husband's diary, lectured all over the world.

It was not until many weeks after his death that Romola and Tessa were each to receive a letter written by their father a day or two before he committed suicide.

'Brisbane, 4th June 1899

My sweet little Romola,

Mama wrote in her last letter that this year you have once more studied seriously and with perseverance, and that you will pass your examinations successfully. I am very proud that my little girl so completely lives up to my expectations and I believe that from here on you will carry on being clever and diligent but trust me when I say that having perseverance is even more important in attaining your goal and becoming a genuine source of joy to your relatives. When you one day begin your schooling, do not forget that what you learn there is only a portion of that which you must learn. If you have time at home you must study languages – English, German, French – which they do not teach at school or, if they do, not as well as would be preferred. The wise and good little girl that you are, I know you

25

will strive to make your mother happy by always being obedient to her, and if she leaves your education to a governess, then observe obedience to her as well. Just as you used to do when I was at home. I hope that you are able to comfort your mother through your kindness, if there is anything troubling her, and to take care of her when she is weak and unwell. Continue to do this from now on, since both you and Tessa are in a position to do everything for the best. The two of you are the only ones who can cause her both happiness and sadness, but I know that both of you will try to make her life pleasant and calm. Never envy Tessa her mother's love for her since you will never on this earth have better friends than they. I am very far away from you, my poor little one, so much so I do not know if I will ever see you again. But do not forget that I love you dearly and that I am very proud of the fact that you are always kind and good.

God bless you.

Many kisses

Charlie'

and to Tessa, he wrote in the same vein.

'Brisbane, Australia
1899, 4th June

My Dear Tessa,

By the time you receive this letter, your exams will have been over a long time but I hope that you were successful with them. However, if the results were not as good as you would have liked, don't let that discourage you. Sometimes, this is due to making a poor start in a subject that does not interest you and it is extremely difficult to catch up later. It will not be long before you begin training for a career. Have you given thought to what you want to do? At one time you expressed a desire to study music, so I should not be surprised if you decide to apply for entrance to the Academy of Music.

He admonished her not to neglect the study of the theory of music should she desire to become a singer, that she should learn composition and counterpoint even though these might seem boring subjects, as otherwise she would never attain the heights of a true artist. She must under no circumstances brush the study of foreign languages to one side. He implored her to continue reading serious literature, otherwise she might find herself estranged in the company of cultured people. At the end, he beseeched her never to alienate herself from her family but keep them closest in her heart.

'...and now that you are a young lady, I know you understand how much assistance you can give your mother in every way, including Romola's upbringing...gain Romola's complete confidence so that she can turn to you with her problems knowing you will willingly help her...From here, I shall probably soon go on, so for that reason do not write until I give you my new address. God bless you, my sweetest daughter, many kisses.

Your loving father.

Charlie.'

Curiously enough, Charlie's last, long letter to Emilia was postdated three days after his untimely death. Reading through it, one is left in no doubt but that he was devoted to his wife and their two young daughters. His love for them is clearly defined as are his anguish and self-reproach over the past, which could not be turned back. *'The more I reflect on the past, the more I understand that the basic cause of our many sufferings was brought about by my weakness...if I could have been more forceful with myself and with you, all that has happened would not have ensued...I can never restore the lost balance...don't ever allow your self-confidence to diminish by misunderstanding the memories and accusing yourself.'*
As in his letters to Romola and Tessa he goes on in much the same vein to advise Emilia on the course to take with regard to her own life, both professionally and privately, as well as to her relationship with their beloved daughters. *'Don't take offense for my writing these things...But I am prompted by my love for you and my anxiety for your future and tranquillity. It's all that is still worthy in me.'*
Although he did not express it bluntly in so many words, surely at the time of writing he must already have been contemplating his

own demise. *'Now I could possibly do something to your advantage by being able to perish, as I cannot actively better your position. But this is the secret of the future...Many kisses to all three of you; do love each other as I love you all wherever my destiny will take me...Only the knowledge of your unity can give me peace– by now the only thing I am yearning for.* God bless you, dear Emma, think of me without bitterness.*

Charlie'

Romola's father, my grandfather, Károly Pulszky, was post-humously exonerated by the Courts when a further investigation proved beyond doubt that through a party-political ruse he had been used as the scapegoat to bring discredit to the Pulszky family.

The famous Piombo painting is to this very day a precious treasure of the Hungarian National Art Gallery in Budapest.

In the Toowong Cemetery in Brisbane, Australia, there is a simple inscription over a grave:

> In Memory of Charles Pulszky
> Born in London 10th Nov. 1853
> Died in Myrtletown 6th June 1899

On February 19th, 1900, Romola celebrated her ninth birthday. It was barely eight months after the tragic death of Charlie-Papa and she was still bewildered, still dwelt upon the memory of him, often overcome by her loss, withdrawn into her shell with fits of moodiness. How is it possible to explain the bond that had grown up between them; she was, after all, only five when he first vanished out of her life. After that she had only experienced the sporadic visits to the sanatorium.

Emilia was acutely conscious of the fact it was her younger daughter's first birthday after her father's death and hence she endeavoured to make the occasion as festive as possible in an attempt to divert Romola's thoughts. The relationship between mother and daughter was still strained. Emilia was not a fool; however deeply she probed for the reason, she realised that her love for her little Molly was not reciprocated. Romola was always to harbour an ambivalent attitude towards her mother. She was torn between admiration for the career woman at the same time that she was jealous of her; yet she was inexplicably contemptuous of Emilia the mother. It was not until later in life she was to become more dependant on Emilia, sought her shoulder to cry on when she was in dire trouble, and yearned for the love she had once spurned.

A major upheaval had come about in the wake of Charlie's death and it was with mixed emotions Emilia pondered over how her headstrong young daughter would react to Emilia Hegedüs, the young woman she had employed as a chaperone and governess for Romola.

Emilia Hegedüs came from a genteel but poor family. She was a grade teacher at the time she was introduced to Emilia through mutual friends, but found the prospect of a position in the household of the Great Márkus so tempting she had been unable to refuse.

A few months after Charlie's death Emilia had called Miss Palmer to her and tactfully terminated her agreement with the thinly veiled excuse that Romola had to improve her knowledge of her native tongue, whilst implying, too, that as a widow her financial position did not permit the extravagance of a governess. Miss Palmer had taken it in her stride and left without acrimony. Both women had been aware it was a charade, that the underlying reasons were otherwise. Emilia wished to sever all her ties with the past; Miss Palmer had belonged to Charlie's past. Maternal jealousy had also reared its ugly head. Romola had shown far too much affection for her governess.

Miss Hegedüs was a new face, devoid of shadows from yesteryears. Her duties were fairly straightforward; to come for a few hours daily to coach Romola in her grade school studies and to prepare her for her exams; to accompany her on promenades, to the skating rink, and to visits to relatives.

Decades later Romola was to describe her ninth birthday to me. Like other events of a specific nature, it had lingered like a cameo of childhood. Friends and relatives had all been invited. Emilia had presented her with a beautiful doll with a delicately chiselled porcelain face. The birthday table had been decorated in true Central European mode of the *siècle*– with the finest blue and white bone china, and an enormous bouquet of wild flowers as the centrepiece. A separate table was laden with a tantalising array of presents. Cups of piping hot chocolate, topped with mounds of whipped cream and generously dusted with cocoa, were on the marble buffet, alongside trays of *mazsolás kuglof,* a Hungarian speciality. A *dobos torta* ('drum cake'), a delicious layercake with a filling of Dutch chocolate and sweet butter, and covered with burnt sugar, was ceremoniously brought in by the maid, the cake's nine lit candles reflecting a merry dance. It was a tradition in the Pulszky family to have this cake on all festive occasions.

Aunt Poly gave Romola a diary bound in leather, with a gold trim, and fastened with a tiny gold lock. A diary, Aunt Poly told her, in which to confide her secret thoughts when she did not have the chance to visit her aunt. The gift Romola treasured most, however, and which became her mascot, was a pendant hung on a thin gold chain. The pendant was a miniature of the Little Infant Jesus of Prague. The original statue can be found in a church in Prague. It represents Jesus as a small child but dressed in the robes of a king. It has a crown on its head and in one hand the Apple of the Kingdom and in the other, the Sceptre. The statue is dressed in an ornate garment made of a satiny material. The colour of the robe is changed in accordance with the Feast Days. On ordinary days, for example, the garment is green, on special Feast Days it is red and white, and at Christmas, golden. A replica of the statue can be seen in almost every Catholic Church.

By nature an introvert, Romola was very much a loner in those formative years. Her arrogant aloofness did not endear her to her classmates. She rather despised girls of her own age whom she scornfully dismissed as being solely occupied with silly nonsense. A contributing factor to her unpopularity in school was her fluent mastery of languages. In addition to Hungarian, she spoke French, English and German at the age of nine. She possessed a remarkable knowledge of literature.

Emilia had had difficulty in memorising her parts ever since she first stood on a stage; surprising, as she otherwise had a prodigious memory. Throughout her career she was to require someone to signal her cue when she was studying a new role. A duty passed on from one member of the family to another. It is doubtful that Charlie ever had time to give this support, but Tessa, Romola, Emilia's second husband Oskar, and later on I myself were among those who faithfully and patiently shouldered this task. Hence, it was in this *milieu* that Romola so early became a close friend of the famous characters in plays and novels. As a small child she was able to recite eloquently from *Maria Stuart,* one of Schiller's plays.

Judging from some of the notes she left behind, scribbled by hand with countless alterations, my mother was planning to write her own memoirs, which would include vignettes about famous people who had crossed her path. The episode on Rudolph Valentino, which appears later in this book, I am almost certain was to have been one of them.

Going back to her childhood, I feel it imperative to quote from one 'essay' she had entitled *The Franz Léhar Story*. I find it difficult to believe that it was more than a figment of her fertile imagination. The facts are hazy and ill-defined, to say the least, but her self-portrait is quite revealing. If true, arrogance was her second nature. Her precociousness and self-assurance were enviable.

Having lauded Emilia, the actress, effusively and emphasising the family's high social standing, she goes on:

'She (Emilia) had immense influence with the government, city officials, among artists and industrialists. Her charitable character was widely known, and no one turned to her in vain. My mother was widowed at this time and she thoroughly spoiled me. Taught by excellent teachers, I had an English and French governess to look after me and a legion of servants to attend to my wishes. Life was wonderful; after school hours I used to ride with my governess in an equipage to the park. In the winter I skated on the frozen lake of the city. The evenings were spent at opera performances, or those of the Royal National Theatre. At the age of seven I knew the whole English, French, German literature by heart and could recite any part of Shakespeare, Molière or Ibsen's plays. Music held no secrets from me. The operas of Mozart, Rossini, Wagner, I knew from beginning to end. At my mother's house I frequently met the visiting foreign and native artists: Duse, Sarah Bernhardt, Ibsen, Puccini and others and in time I became quite an expert in the arts...But in spite of all that, being a child I loved to play. One of my favourite pastimes was to open the front door and talk to the visitors and tradesmen who happened to come...One spring Sunday afternoon in the year 1906 my mother was at rehearsal. The servants were having their siesta in the domestic quarters when the bell rang. I raced excitedly down...A plump, fair, middle-class man stood rigidly before the front door, almost at attention. He seemed rather shy, in ill-fitting clothes. He

clasped under one arm a huge flat, dark "album". ...He spoke
Hungarian with a slight Swabish accent.'

The visitor was anxious to talk to Emilia about a matter of vital importance. Romola had asked him to state his errand and he had smiled and replied: 'My dear child. You would hardly understand.' At this Romola had thrown her head back in anger and haughtily replied: 'In this house my wish is law...I would advise you to submit your request to me.'

With infinite care and tenderness he had handed over to her the mysterious black album. 'Please, please, take very good care of it. I have worked for months and months on this score. It is my life's hope, it is my first opera. I am certain I am a good musician and if I only had the chance to have it submitted to the Director of the Royal Opera House – if he would only glance at it – I might have a chance. For weeks I have been in his antechamber at the Opera House and was not admitted.'

In her own words Romola had hastened to assure him that she knew Csepke Bácsi, the porter who had turned him away. It was his duty to keep outsiders from disturbing the Director. She, however, would see to it that her mother personally took the score to him. When questioned by Romola what his background was, the young man had said that his family were Swabish; they were poor and he was one of four children. He had had to make a living at an early age and although he joined the Army, his one interest was music. Currently he was the conductor of the Wilhelm Regiment Number Five. His opera was called *Kukoschkie*. When he returned to Emilia's apartment two weeks later, *'I received him and asked him with the air of a perfect hostess to sit down. My mother with her ravishing beauty and charm swept the young man off his feet but with her wonderful tact put him at ease and made him talk.'*

The tale is filled with loopholes, the most glaring one that Lehár's opera *'Kukuska'* was performed already in 1896; he was not Swabish; there were no rehearsals at the National Theatre on Sundays, and so on. I have no surviving evidence that there is a shred of truth in the story; certainly, my grandmother never related to me that she had been instrumental in 'discovering' Lehár. But then, the young composer to whom Romola referred, was possibly somebody wholly different and in later years her memory dimmed. Whatever physical likeness I have inherited from my mother, and there are those who say I bear an uncanny resemblance to her, I cannot lay claim to possessing her imperious, self-assured characteristics. They were both her strength and her weakness. Did she know when she crossed the borderline between fact and fiction?

Emilia soared to the very peak of her career during her first year of widowhood. She was given a tumultuous standing ovation upon her reappearance on the National stage while she was still in mourning. She was signally cognizant of the warmth that exuded from the audience and she threw herself into a schedule of work unheard of previously in the theatre. In one single season, for instance, she played between twenty to thirty new leading roles.

Of 'the Blonde Wonder' it was said that if she were to recite the telephone book, she could still captivate her listeners, hold them spellbound by her presentation. Her femininity and charismatic personality radiated an aura of sensual excitement that brought not only flamboyant admirers at her feet – aristocrats, wealthy businessmen and landowners – but also the critics. The latter likened her to a chameleon, because of her uncanny transformation into whatever character she was portraying, from the *amoureuse,* the sinful female, to the virgin, the innocent victim of man's lust. A *demimonde* one night, Ophelia in *Hamlet* the next.

Mari Jászai, the great tragedienne, who had preceded Emilia as the star on the Hungarian stage, was a towering figure of a woman, whose voice was charged with deepest pathos even in everyday life. She was living proof of the fact that if a person desires to reach a certain goal, it can be achieved. She had been illiterate until the age of twelve when she had assiduously conquered the art of reading and writing. As a teenager she had taken part in the 1848 Hungarian Revolution as a *markotányosnö* – worked in the field side by side with the soldiers, providing food and drinking water. She was the embodiment of tragedy on the stage but was not as colourful as Emilia. Although she must have envied Emilia's youth and beauty, she was honest enough to express sincere admiration for her talent – a compliment, indeed, coming from such a mature trouper.

Indirectly, it was through Mari that the adolescent, sensitive Romola was to be dealt yet another harsh blow. A year before Charlie's departure from Hungary, the actress had introduced Emilia to Oszkár Andor, a prosperous young businessman, who had also served in the Army. He came from a *petite bourgeoise* Jewish family in Nagykanizsa, the western part of Hungary. Endowed with extremely good looks, dark-haired, with a black moustache and an abundance of charm, he was in addition well-educated, suave, a brilliant, clever man who could handle any situation with ease.

From the moment of their very first meeting Emilia had been unable to dismiss her new young admirer from her mind. His whole demeanour was totally different from the many who haunted the corridor to her dressing-room. But she was then burdened with Charlie's hapless situation and concerned for her daughters whom she at all cost wanted to shield from the continuing vicissitudes. Too, she was engulfed in financial problems. She had therefore reluctantly brushed to one side any further thoughts about him. Widowhood changed all that. Although she genuinely mourned her husband at first, her wounds quickly healed, and not long thereafter Oskar re-entered her life. He was infatuated with her and began attending every performance, night after night, waiting for her patiently after each rehearsal, showering her with exotic bouquets of flowers and costly gifts. Gallant gestures such as these were not uncommon from the numerous devoted men in Emilia's entourage, but the observant onlooker could easily discern that Oskar meant far more to her than all the others. On that score she showed no discretion.

When the malevolent gossipers circulated the juicy titbit that the Great Márkus had a new lover, the Pulszky family were up in arms, incensed with fury. There is no evidence that Emilia flaunted her relationship with Oskar publicly but certainly they were constant companions for three years. In 1903 the bomb exploded – Emilia legalised her union with Oskar in a simple civil ceremony. To please Emilia, Oskar changed his surname to Párdány. On stage she used the name P Márkus Emilia (P for Pulszky) and she wished to keep the initial 'P'. Thirty years later I was present at the church ceremony which hallowed Emilia and Oskar's marriage. He had already been converted to the Catholic faith in 1903.

Her mother's marriage proved too much for Romola. She was twelve and still grieved for the loss of the father she had worshipped. Her fiercely loyal temperament saw Emilia's action as a betrayal to Charlie-Papa. She suffered a severe emotional shock and was unable to reconcile herself to the fact that another man had taken his place in her mother's affections. In furious protest she managed to win Miss Hegedüs over to accompany her to Aunt Poly as often as feasible. There she found solace in the sanctuary of a kindred spirit. Seeing her aunt's violent reaction to the turn of events, she felt justified in her own feelings and her antipathy towards Oskar turned into sheer hatred. Aunt Poly, on hearing the announcement of Emilia's new matrimonial union, had given orders to her family and intimate friends to sever all ties with that 'shameful' woman who had had the audacity to renounce the noble name of Pulszky and thus drag her children into the gutter. She declared that someday the ill-matched pair would bring disgrace upon all of them.

One can truly say that Oskar had literally walked into a hornet's nest soon after he had wooed and wed Emilia. The young bridegroom – he was only thirty-two, his bride eleven years his senior – found the atmosphere in the household laden with undercurrents of animosity emanating not only from Romola but also curiously enough – to a lesser degree from Tessa. Two stepdaughters, each with her own reason for wishing to make life a misery for the poor man. Emilia insisted that they call him Oti-Papa. To her the nickname seemed obvious, after all they had called their own father Charlie-Papa. To Romola, in particular, it was adding insult to injury.

Tessa, by then twenty years old, was a dreamer who neither understood nor gave the slightest consideration to the stark realities of life. She dearly loved her mother and sister, willing to give them staunch support in any way she knew how. Already introduced to society, the belle of the ball, her hours were crammed with visits to friends, to the theatre and to concerts. She was an accomplished pianist. Most days, however, her favourite pastime was flirting with the innumerable young beaux who swarmed around her. Her mother's marriage to Oskar had filled her with mixed feelings; she had no qualms whatsoever about the fact that her mother had 'dared' to renounce the distinguished name of Pulszky for a mere 'nobody'. Instead she experienced a twinge of annoyance that this very attractive young man displayed no interest in her. It puzzled and exasperated her. A Hungarian saying goes 'Look at the mother and marry the daughter'. That the process had now been reversed sparked off sufficiently strong negative sentiments in Tessa to create fertile ground for Romola to turn her vacillating sister against Oskar.

Not long after Emilia and Oskar's wedding, the family moved to another apartment, still in the vicinity of the National Theatre, taking with them the residue of the Pulszky furniture and fine art. Oskar was to be jolted out of the reverie of a honeymoon period by a problem as grave as the ill will of two stepdaughters. He was faced with the daunting task of trying to unravel Emilia's tangled financial standing. Almost from the day she set foot on the stage, Emilia had received a star's salary, far more than her colleagues, but she was totally inept at handling money, which flowed through her fingers and purse like so much silver dust. Frugality, economy of means, were unknown factors to her. She had been pampered by Charlie, who himself had treated the golden horn of plenty as a permanent fixture in their lives. After his death she was in such desperate straights she once had to seek special dispensation to be allowed to play in any theatre in the provinces during her summer holidays. The members of the Hungarian National Theatre were on yearly contracts with fringe benefits and they were likewise paid for their holidays, but an ironclad rule was that the members did not perform on any other stage than the National Theatre's. Not infrequently, Emilia had paid visits to the Ministers for Culture and Finance to plead her case and it was said that the Emperor Franz-Josef often reached into his purse to help his favourite Hungarian actress.

To be fair to Emilia, she was also a giver and would never let anyone go from her door empty-handed. She was likewise determined that her daughters should enjoy the same lifestyle to which she had been accustomed, and except for a brief period following Károly's departure, Romola was brought up in the lap of plenty. To her, only the best was good enough and this maxim was to dominate her behaviour all her life. In later years, when Romola was faced with the problem of providing for her own family, she found it a well-nigh Herculean struggle because of her high demands for both herself and them.

Whatever tensions existed between Romola and her mother, they shared one common denominator, the theatre. Romola seldom missed a première at the National Theatre. She would sit in her mother's dressing-room and watch with rapt attention as her mother skilfully applied her make-up and changed before her very eyes into the character she was to portray that evening.

On those special occasions that Emilia invited friends to an intimate dinner on her nights off from the theatre, or whenever she threw a large dinner party, she always made a habit of allowing her daughters to be present. She could see no harm in training them from the start to mingle with adults, nor was she a strict mother who insisted that her children should abide by set rules and regulations. Romola, who mixed very little with other youngsters of her own age, would listen attentively to the conversation around her and carefully file away in the back of her mind matters that she could not clearly comprehend. These she would take up later with her Aunt Poly. Poly, who was then forty-two, had a daughter Beatrix, some years older than Romola. Beatrix was a rather dull, sullen girl and obviously it gave Polyxena greater stimulation to chat with her niece. Perhaps, too, she experienced a sense of triumph, a mild form of revenge against Emilia, that the latter's daughter should find her a more intimate companion.

Because Emilia had such a soft place in her heart for her younger child, she indulged her every whim. If Romola indicated she had a slight headache, Emilia would keep her at home, and in the cosiness of her own room Romola could curl up in bed and immerse herself in some of the noteworthy history books or literary works she had been longing to read. Lunch and dinner would solicitously be brought up to her. She was free to withdraw to the blissful solitude of her own private world.

Although she had numerous acquaintances, Romola became attached to only one classmate, Lisbeth, the daughter of the Executive President of the International Insurance Company of Hungary. They were like twin sisters and their separate upbringing had many similarities. Lisbeth's father, who was English, had been a dear friend of Charlie's and when the latter died, he had paid out the life insurance to Romola and Tessa's guardian, a questionable action as it was not considered legal to pay out insurance to the beneficiaries of a person who had committed suicide. That Charlie had taken the precautionary measure of appointing a guardian was most likely due to the fact that he had comprehended only too well his Emilia's foible as far as money was concerned and had wanted to safeguard his daughters' future.

Lisbeth's father was transferred to a post in Paris and the loss of her only true friend made Romola very sadhearted. She vowed that she would join her. She felt the environment of the home more and more pleasureless with what she called 'the intruder' in their midst. And so she started to draw up her campaign. She was a Francophile, had yearned to see Paris, and she decided the time had come to grasp the opportunity. Had not her Aunt Poly preached to her that in order to achieve something in life one had to think it through thoroughly and lay plans, step by step. Which was exactly what she did. Behind Emilia's back Romola bombarded Lisbeth with lengthy letters, pleading with her to convince her parents to enrol Romola in the Lycée Fénélon, the school that Lisbeth attended.

The waiting list was normally long because it was the custom that girls from aristocratic and wealthy families were enrolled at the school from birth. Romola's dogged determination bore fruit and thanks to the influence of Lisbeth's father, she was accepted. Emilia had at first been stunned when she learned of the oblique way in which Romola had behaved, wholly without her knowledge. But she cast her mind back to when she herself defied her family in order to achieve her goal at the age of fourteen and was forced to give in gracefully. One consolation was that she knew Romola would be in good hands.

'...the Lycée Fénélon is in St Mande in the woods of Vincennes, the surroundings are very pleasing. We arrive by carriage in the morning and return by the same manner. We are thirty girls, all English or French with the exception of myself. As there are no Hungarian or German students, all conversation is carried on in French. I am well treated and, thank God, I like it here very much....'

This is an extract, typical of the numerous letters she wrote. After three years of study at the Lycée, Romola graduated with highest honours.

Lisbeth's parents were genuinely sorry when Romola's sojourn in Paris came to an end. She had wielded a stabilising influence on their own daughter, who was rather scatter-brained and averse to taking her studies seriously.

The summer and Christmas holidays had always brought Romola home to Budapest and even though she may have lost her girlish heart to Paris, she was quite happy to be reunited with Tessa at the end of the three years. They hardly went of bed the first nights after her return but carried on a breathless chatter about their experiences. Romola had her older sister entranced with her description of life in the French capital, stories about her studies, explaining with solemn enthusiasm what she had learned about Napoleon's life and philosophy. She had brought back a whole trunkful of treasures; books and memorabilia relating to the Little Corporal and his son, nicknamed *L'Aiglon*. Like a magician with his tricks, she had pulled out a hat, an identical copy of one that Napoleon had worn in his youth. A pair of black boots came next, to be followed by a cloak she had tossed nonchalantly over her shoulders. Thus garbed she had stood in front of her amazed sister and recited in faultless French a speech attributed to have been made by the Little Corporal before a major battle.

But after the initial enthusiasm had abated, Romola found it hard to acclimatise herself to the unspectacular life in Budapest compared to the pulsating, exciting, *allégresse* of her beloved Paris. She regretted every hour away from it. She became quickly bored to distraction, surprising, considering the glamour that did surround her in the shadow of her mother's social engagements.

She absolutely loathed accompanying Emilia on the latter's summer tours in the provinces. The towns were dreary, the shabby hotels often primitive, and Romola would shudder on recalling one particular nasty occasion when she and Emilia had to spend a whole night sitting bolt upright in their bed, which as an emergency measure they had pulled into the middle of the room, with an open umbrella clutched in their hands, to protect themselves from their uninvited nocturnal guests – bedbugs, of which there was an abundance in Hungary in those days.

However, the tours did have a brighter side as well. They brought home to Romola the realisation how accomplished an actress her mother was, and how very much loved. She spoke proudly of those occasions when, after a performance, enthusiastic crowds, waiting outside the stage door, jostling and nearly crushing one another to catch a glimpse of their star, would remove the harness from the horses, and themselves pull Emilia's carriage to her hotel.

Tessa, too, had chosen to pursue her studies abroad; her destination had not been Paris but Dresden, and later on, various parts of Italy. Despite her outwardly giddy and capricious manner it was said by at least one member of the family that her knowledge was deeper and more thorough than Romola's. Her virtuosity at the piano was acclaimed and she was a frequent visitor to the home of her and Romola's cousin Lily. Lily was to become an almost legendary character in the family...her mother Janka had been one of Franz Liszt's most talented pupils and when she decided to marry József, Emilia's brother, Franz Liszt is reputed to have said that he was very upset at the thought of losing such a gifted pupil. He had tried to talk her out of marrying and had sternly advised her to dedicate her life to music. Love, however, had conquered, and of her two children, Lily Márkus had inherited Janka's musical talent.

It was Lily who played the piano for Waslaw on a number of occasions during the First World War at the time he was composing the choreography for *Tyl Eulenspiegel*. Retracing yesteryears, I can still visualise my aunt, who, to me, resembled a tiny gnome. She could only have been in her sixties when I first met her, yet to my youthful eyes she looked ancient. I can even now see her face before me, two paprika red dots on her cheeks, glaring grotesquely from a heavily-powdered chalk-like face. It always made me think of a clown's make-up. She had a slight hump on her back, and her thin straggly wisps of white hair were poorly dyed. When I used to visit her, she would embrace me and welcome me with great warmth and love, only to switch seconds later to the stentorian voice of an instructor, impressing upon me the importance of music. Each time she would guide me into her private apartment, every nook and corner of which was crammed with music sheets, faded yellow newspaper clippings, write-ups of her past glory. A wilted laurel wreath hung among the countless photographs showing her at her many concerts. She had a maid but even so, her apartment looked as though it never had been subjected to the touch of a dustcloth or a broom. In this artistic ambiance Lily's husband Lala was to be found, himself an artist. I remember how we used to giggle when the telephone rang and one of us announced: 'It is Lylly-Lala calling...'

Tessa had blossomed into a dazzling beauty who turned men's heads. Her escapades were not well received by the Pulszky clan, least of all Polyxena. Emilia herself was unhappy and alarmed and found it hard to accept her daughter's unrestrained behaviour. Apparently, she turned to Oskar for advice, recognising the fact that drastic measures had to be taken to stave off a disaster. Oskar suggested they get in touch with a mutual friend of theirs who was the director of the Burgtheater in Vienna, and, who had once said, catching a glimpse of the blonde Tessa, '...*if she is as talented as she is beautiful we will have a second Emilia Márkus...*'

When the matter was broached as delicately as possible to Tessa, she was delighted and accepted the suggestion with alacrity. She spoke German fluently and had dear friends in Vienna. Emilia personally supervised the packing of trunks and hatboxes filled to overflowing with exquisite attire befitting a young lady in her quest to conquer the magical city of music and waltzes. From Emilia's ragbag of memories a picture of Tessa's introduction to Vienna unfolded itself; how she installed her daughter in one of the better class *pensions* to which she had been recommended. A maid, in a stiff starched uniform, had ushered them into the parlour. The tall, round stove, covered with decorative porcelain tiles, added a cosy warmth to the room; its gleaming brass oven doors wide open to display friendly glowing embers from the coal inside. The waxed parquet floor was polished to perfection and Tessa had whirled round, admiring her own reflection.

On the train journey back to Budapest Emilia had been beset by qualms at leaving her daughter alone in the foreign city, without a chaperon, and questioned whether, after all, she had done the right thing. True, Tessa would be surrounded by numerous friends, including Romola's godfather who was in charge of the Imperial Family Archives, but was this sufficient to tighten the reins of a wild young filly? For a short while Tessa behaved in an exemplary manner and diligently attended rehearsals at the Burgtheater, where she was given minor roles to play. Her drama coach promised her a glittering career if, and this was the crux, she would work very, very hard. But it proved impossible for her to seriously embark on such a path. Her fondness for the male species prevented her from applying herself zealously to anything else and before long she had thrown herself wholeheartedly into the gay life that beckoned to her. It was then she encountered Erik Schmedes. Due to her influential relative at the Opera she had soon become part of the coterie there and she was introduced to Erik, their leading Wagnerian tenor.

Erik Schmedes was born in Gentofte, near Copenhagen, Denmark on the 27th of August, 1866. Rumour would have it that he was related to the Danish royal family. He had studied with Rothmuhle in Berlin, Ress in Vienna and Padilla in Paris and had made a brilliant début as a baritone in Wiesbaden in 1891 and as a lyric tenor at Nürnberg in 1894, continuing his career in Dresden until 1897. From there he went to Vienna where he remained through the great Mahler years until 1924. He excelled in Wagnerian roles and was accredited with being a fine actor as well. In 1899 he sang Siegfried in *Parsifal* at Bayreuth. Tessa fell madly in love with him. There was a snag, however. Erik was married to an unsophisticated woman he had met in his early youth, a woman who did not share his artistic and cultural interests. They had one daughter, Dagmar.

Nothing deterred Tessa from obtaining what she wanted. Not long after their meeting, she moved out of the select *pension* where Emilia so conscientiously had placed her, and joined Erik, who was by then separated from his wife. The shocking, scandalous news spread swiftly to Budapest and Polyxena took matters into her own hands. In a state of emotional agitation and fury over the fact that once more the name of Pulszky was in jeopardy of being dishonoured, Polyxena went to Vienna and personally brought her sinful niece back to Emilia, who greeted her wayward daughter with as much compassion and forgiveness as she could muster. She felt extremely defeated and thwarted.

Tessa made one traumatic scene after the other, threatening to escape, no matter what the consequences. Emilia did not know how much longer she could endure her daughter's hysterical outbursts when salvation arrived in the form of the suitor himself. Schmedes formally requested Tessa's hand in marriage as soon as his divorce was finalised. In 1908 he and Tessa were quietly wed in Vienna, with Emilia, Oskar and Romola as the only witnesses.

CHAPTER 2

ROMOLA AND WASLAW
The Turning Point

Immediately after Tessa's wedding, Emilia and Oskar returned to Budapest and Romola to Paris. There she entered the Sorbonne in order to perfect her French and to broaden her knowledge of the Fine Arts. She was fortunate to have the use of a cosy *pied-à-terre* in the proximity, belonging to a British friend. She settled down happily; the lectures at the university absorbed much of her time as did visits to the Louvre, where she spent hours studying at close hand the masterpieces that had been discussed in class. Surely her consummate passion for the Arts had seeped into her subconscious mind as a small child under the influence of Charlie-Papa.

Occasionally, she would drop in to the Church of St Germain l'Auxerrois located not far from the Louvre and the Châtelet Theatre, the latter, unbeknown to her at the time, destined to play an important role in her life. She would spend some brief moments in meditation at the Church and then stroll through the surrounding street, her passionate love affair with the city growing stronger with each passing month.

Her rather serious nature, however, did not preclude her from cultivating an intimate clique of carefully selected friends with whom she enjoyed afternoon teas at the more fashionable haunts; concerts and theatre evenings were regularly on the agenda.

Although not as vain as Tessa, Romola was meticulous about her appearance as in everything else and the influence of Parisian *haute couture* was to dominate her thirst for material things that were the most luxurious, the most exquisite – a palate which again had its origin in her childhood, inflamed by both her parents. She would feel exasperated and frustrated in turn because she was not always to have the finance with which to quench her thirst. Yet she learned the art of stretching her budget shrewdly and always looked chic. She graduated from her Parisian 'finishing-school' with honours, a cultivated, well-spoken, graceful young woman.

Correspondence home had been scant and it was to Aunt Poly she mostly addressed her laconic letters, not as yet having acquired the gift for writing that later was to become her livelihood.

She felt a strong affinity to England where her dear Papa had been born, and she crossed the Channel as often as she could to stay as a guest with some of her father's old friends. In fact, according to Richard Buckle, Romola also had another English governess, a Miss Johnson, with whom she spent a year in England, staying mostly at Eastbourne but on at least one occasion at Southsea, in August 1909, when the Tsar of Russia reviewed the British Fleet. Going through bundles of letters, yellowed with age, I came across one from her, substantiating the fact that she indeed was in England that year.

Graylingwell, Chichester
England

13th July 1909

Dear sweet Aunt Poly,

I want to apologise for not thanking you until now for your kindness in giving me letters of introduction to friends in London. I had a very, very good time there. Jozsef Földváry was invited to dinners at the same time I was...

At this moment, I am here in the countryside, hopefully staying a few days onward. I hear that Beatrix is going to Switzerland; please tell that naughty girl that she should write to me.

I hope that your stay in Budapest in the heat of summer is not too uncomfortable...

Once again, many, many thanks – kezeit csókolja

Romola

Then a year later

Paris, France
1st July, 1910

Sweet Aunt Poly,

It was with great sadness I gathered from Mother's last letter that you have been ill. I sincerely hope it is now all behind you and that this finds you in the best of health.

It was when Kelemen Feri came to visit, he mentioned that you, dear Aunt Poly, were indisposed, but added that you are much better, and that you went to see the Aviation Show.

I am staying here a bit longer and if there is anything you wish me to bring back to you or Beatrix on my return to Budapest, I would be more than happy...

Romola

July, 1911, found Emilia and Oskar in Karlsbad. Romola had accompanied them and it was there her path crossed once more with a young man to whom she had been introduced a year-and-a-half earlier at one of Aunt Poly's soirées. His name was Bandi Hatvany and for a short interlude he was to become her fiancé.

As opposed to her sister, Romola shunned the company of admirers and showed no inclination to embark on any romantic attachments. Her very aloofness attracted scores of beaux but she sought intellectual companionship and disdained the sentimental nonsense a dancing partner would murmur in her ear.

Polyxena, who had taken upon herself the role of head of the Pulszky family, nurtured the very special bond that had sprung up between her and her niece and felt it was her responsibility to arrange a suitable match for Romola. She launched a campaign to introduce her protégée to the most eligible bachelors in Budapest, choosing them with infinite care, weighing up social background and financial status. For once, Emilia did not raise any objections. Although she and her sister-in-law were still at daggers drawn, she, too, wanted a perfect husband for her Molly, and thus meekly swallowed the bitter pill that Romola listened more to her aunt than to her mother. Emilia grudgingly had to admit that Polyxena was a far more powerful and influential woman in aristocratic circles than she herself was. She did voice her opinion, though, that love must play the dominant part to guarantee a happy marriage, reflecting ruefully on her own union with Charlie.

Baron Hatvany Bandi (Andras) came from a wealthy, industrial family, who had purchased their title together with an extensive country estate. The Hatvanys also possessed a splendid palace in Buda.

According to eyewitness reports, it had been fairly obvious that the young baron had immediately fallen in love with Romola when he first laid eyes on her. She, on the other hand, had been extremely reserved and unimpressed by his fawning. But after that chance encounter in Karlsbad they began to meet more frequently. Bandi would be her faithful escort to the Opera, to concerts, to the fashionable patisseries, such as the famous Kugler, later renamed Gerbeaud. There would always be a chaperone in attendance.

There is no evidence to suggest that Romola at any time harboured strong feelings of affection for her ardent admirer but she gradually became flattered by his intense courting. He was intelligent, well-bred, and showered her daily with dozens of long-stemmed roses and the costliest boxes of bon-bons.

Their love affair, if one can call it that, became a most controversial story within the family, changing with each person who told it. Allegedly, it was Bandi's mother who prodded her son into wooing Romola. A ruthless social climber, she wished to be united with the old aristocracy and to reach this goal she schemed to find the right partners for her daughter and two sons.

No matter what was true or untrue, the whole affair nearly ended in disaster already in the first act. Bandi was plagued with a persistent bronchitis and had gone to the Magas Tátra, a fashionable cure resort, to convalesce. The Baroness invited Romola to join him for a few days. She accepted with alacrity, looking forward to a stay at one of the elegant hotels there. Hastily tossing some clothes into a bag, she kissed Emilia goodbye and set forth with Emilia Hegedüs, her chaperone, to catch a train which would take them up into the towering mountains of Tátra*, surrounding the northern part of Hungary. What exactly transpired that fateful weekend, only the two young persons concerned could have divulged. Emilia confided the story to me as she knew it when I was in my late teens.

Barely two days after Romola had departed in such high spirits she had unexpectedly stormed into Emilia's room and flung herself into her arms, sobbing hysterically. Stroking her daughter's hair in an effort to comfort her and to calm her down, Emilia gleaned fragments of what had happened interrupted only by fresh outbursts from Romola. It seemed that in the afternoon of her arrival, Romola and Bandi had gone for a brisk walk together in the nearby woods. Bandi had been overjoyed to see her and proudly proclaimed he was fit and well. They had engaged in a snowball fight

* The Tátra mountains are today part of Czechoslovakia.

and Bandi had gallantly allowed her to win. Hand in hand they made their way back to the hotel. Miss Hegedüs had excused herself, saying she had a few letters to write, and without thinking, Romola found herself in Bandi's room – alone with him. The atmosphere had been so warm and inviting, the glow from the fire in the hearth had beckoned her to stay. While Bandi ordered hot chocolate to be brought up to the room, Romola had discarded her thick, woolly sweater and scarf and had gone over to the window to admire the setting sun.

Suddenly she had felt Bandi's arms entwined around her waist and he had begun to kiss her bared neck. Apparently, he had lost control of himself and had taken her in a passionate embrace. The physical contact had shocked Romola; no man had touched her before. She had struggled wildly to disengage herself and rushed in panic to her own room. Between sobs and convulsions shaking her slim frame, Romola poured out her tragic little tale to her mother of how she had rushed down to the lobby to enquire when the next train left for Budapest and then ordered her chaperone to arrange their departure. She had refused to see Bandi, who had frantically tried to reach her. Emilia, cradling her Molly, had then and there realised how overprotective she had been, not explaining to her daughter the plain facts of life. Poor, distraught Romola had actually confessed she feared she might have a baby – so naïve and innocent was my mother when she was eighteen, she believed a kiss could make a girl pregnant.

Emilia had endeavoured to soothe her and to reason with her, to explain it was only natural for a man to show his affections in such a manner but Romola remained adamant. She would not see Bandi again and despite daily messages from him, accompanied by the most seductive roses money could buy, it was to take time before she swallowed her pride and admitted she had behaved in a foolish manner.

It was finally the Baroness Hatvany who took matters into her own hands and paid a visit to Romola. The maid announced her arrival and she swept into the salon, dressed in an enormous, bulky black fur coat trimmed with a wide, white fur collar. Her hands were concealed in a huge fur muff, her head covered with a turban-style white fur hat with a long white feather perched in the middle and swaying gently to and fro as she spoke. Romola had been fascinated by her attire which she surmised had come straight from Paris.

Bandi's mother, ignorant of the incident up in the mountain but aware that something had gone acutely wrong and that her son, temporarily at least, was *persona non grata,* had donned her most ingratiating manner together with the latest fashion and invited Romola to join her in a sleigh ride and to a cup of chocolate in her favourite patisserie. She excused her unannounced visit by saying how worried she had been at not seeing Romola for some time and hoped that she was in good health. Romola must have experienced a sense of triumph that Bandi's mother was doing her utmost to make up for her son's shameful behaviour and therefore graciously accepted the invitation. How could she know that the ensuing mundane chat between them would spark off a chain of events that were dramatically to alter her entire life.

The Baroness had regaled Romola with the latest news about fashions she had seen in Paris and then plunged into a glowing account of a fantastic performance she had recently witnessed, a Russian ballet troupe directed by a certain Sergei Diaghilev. She was at a loss to find superlatives colourful enough to describe the dancing which had been electrifying. She promised Romola that if the group came to Budapest she would invite her to the first night. She also extended an invitation to Romola to join her and her family at the forthcoming Széchěnyi Ball.

The Social Season in those days was centred around grandiose festivities under the auspices of such patrons as the Ministry of Justice, the Military, the doctors, the lawyers, to name but a few, each of them trying to outdo the others in magnificence and ostentation. Budapest set the pace with the Széchěnyi Ball. It took place at the Vigadó, also used as the Concert Hall, a neo-classic building majestically stretched out on the left bank of the Danube, across from the Royal Palace.

In childhood I would listen enraptured to Emilia's portrayal of these events of a bygone era. Her eyes would sparkle and her cheeks acquire a rosy glow as she, in her inimitable style, described the pageantry of some of the balls. Her recollections unfolded to me a glamorous world, far more exciting than any fairy tale, and it was in particular the Széchěnyi Ball that captured my imagination because it was the first my mother attended as a young woman.

Preparations for the occasion had commenced weeks, possibly even months, earlier. Mothers and daughters would pore over the latest fashion magazines from Paris and then order the finest

4. Emilia Márkus with her
   daughter Romola de
   Pulszky, circa 1901

5. Károly Pulszky in
   Hungarian Gala garment,
   1881

6. Romola de Pulszky in her
   Napoléonic costume bought
   in Paris in 1907

7. Romola in her early teens

8. Tessa de Pulszky, Romola's sister

9. Emilia Márkus and Oskar Párdány (Emilia's second husband) with Tamara Nijinsky, Emilia's younger granddaughter

10. Waslaw Nijinsky as Harlequin in *Carnaval* in Paris, 1910 (believed to have been given to Romola Nijinsky by Mrs Margaret Power)

Chantilly lace, moiré, heavy satin, silks, often richly embroidered with beads and pearls in intricate designs. Tirelessly, the ladies in the family would shop around, debating every minute detail, ruffle and bow, for hours on end with the dressmaker. And the colour of their long gloves and shoes had to be a perfect match. The men's only duty was to dig deep into their pockets to pay the bills that poured in like water from a tap.

On the eve of the Ball, Bandi arrived early to collect Romola and her party. Emilia noted with approval how handsome her future son-in-law looked in his tails, stiff starched shirt, white tie and white *glacé* gloves. Ferencz and István, two swains in Romola's social entourage, were there already as the guests of Emilia and Oskar. Carriages had been called for about eight o'clock.

Emilia and her daughter must have caused many heads to turn when they entered the vast marble hall where the Baroness Hatvany was waiting. Emilia was then barely fifty-two, still radiantly beautiful according to the critics; her golden hair piled high on her head, her jewellery adorning a neck and bosom still as smooth as a young girl's. Only a few evenings previously her sensuous voice had enthralled a vast audience in her unforgettable performance as Lady Milford in Schiller's *Ármány és Szerelem. Emilia, the actress, was perhaps by then blasé about the stir she created whenever she appeared at social functions, but Emilia, the mother, felt her heart swell with pride that Romola, too, was the focus of attention that evening. She was dressed in a pale pink chiffon gown, tiny delicate handmade silk rosebuds scattered in the folds of her long skirt. A single strand of pearls adorned her slender neck. She loved pearls. Her dark auburn hair was coiffed in Greek manner high up on the top of her head. One shell-pink thornless rose graced her bosom, a corsage sent to her earlier by Bandi.

The Ball was officially opened with the majestic Hungarian dance, the *Palotás*, stately and slow-moving, to be followed by the rhythmic, ever popular Strauss waltzes, among them the *Császár-Keringö,* composed especially for the Emperor Ferencz-Jószef. What a magnificent kaleidoscope the dance floor with its whirling couples must have presented to the beholder. Each branch of the Military wore the dress uniform, *Attila:* cherry red for the Artillery, deep green for the Army, and the Cavalry (the smart Huszárs) wore light blue. Over the uniform

* Kabale und Liebe

the young men wore a short jacket-like mantle made from velour, trimmed with ermine and attached to the shoulder with a gold braid and button. A more sombre touch was provided by the black and white formal attire of the non-militia. The ladies in their exquisite ballroom gowns fluttered on the arms of their partners like myriads of butterflies.

It was in the middle of a waltz that Bandi proposed to Romola, begging to be forgiven for his previous behaviour. She had anticipated it, yet when the moment did arrive, she had become flustered, avoided his eyes, and engaged in a flirtatious banter to avoid capitulating then and there. As she later confessed to her mother, she was still in a turmoil, uncertain of what she wanted from the future.

She was spared an immediate reply by the arrival of waiters carrying huge silver trays laden with *hors d'oeuvres* that included *paté de foie gras* and Hungarian Balatoni *fogas* (fish) in aspic, decorated with Russian caviar. The young couple hastened to rejoin their families at the table where the guests were already toasting each other with the golden wine of Hungary, poured into tall crystal goblets. By the time dessert was served, the hauntingly wild music from the gypsy band had taken over the entertainment.

At the stroke of midnight the *csárdás* commenced, the characteristic Hungarian dance. Later, the orchestra took over again to play the popular melodies of the day, the one-step, the polka and, of course, the waltz. In the early hours of the morning, confetti was thrown down from the balcony like multi-coloured snowflakes, and streamers intertwined the dancers with each other. It was the signal to break up and an unforgettable evening had come to an end for Romola, who had still not given her answer to Bandi.

Throughout December 1911 and the beginning of 1912 Romola threw herself with abandon into a carefree life, continuing the rounds of jollities and balls which overflowed during the festive season in the capital. Rather surprising, as she had previously preferred 'splendid isolation', prone to wrinkle her nose at what she termed frivolous or superficial pastimes. Perhaps she reflected on what her life would be once she was married; restricted, if she were forced to don a matronly guise.

On New Year's Eve she attended a party on the estate of one of Emilia's friends. At midnight, all the guests gathered together in the vast kitchen for the traditional 'pouring the lead', an entertaining and harmless form of fortunetelling, commonly observed in those days in Hungary. The equipment was simple, just pieces of lead and big spoons. Each person heated the lead in a spoon over the flame burning in the huge grate and then, with a swift movement, plunged it into a receptacle filled with cold water. As soon as the boiling lead came into contact with the water, it would assume all sorts of different weird shapes. Peals of laughter reverberated round the walls as the guests vied in guessing what each piece resembled. Flights into fantasy as to what the solidified lead symbolised for the future were limitless. When it came to Romola's turn, she eagerly rescued her 'masterpiece' from the water. At first it had not been clear what it resembled, then slowly, before her eyes, it materialised into the shape of a ship and on the bow, a delicate dancing figure. Like her Little Jesus of Prague, the piece of lead became a precious mascot.

In February, Tessa came for a few days from Vienna to celebrate Romola's birthday and to assist in the move to Emilia's new villa on the outskirts of Budapest. Partly through Charlie's influence in their early years of marriage, partly through her portrayal on stage of heroines of that particular period, Emilia had come to visualise herself as a Renaissance princess and dreamed of a Renaissance palace. Sadly, with the meagre financial resources at her disposal coupled with the assistance of architects lacking in talent or imagination, the Villa, when completed, was but a poor imitation of what she had aspired to create. But, still, it was to be her pride and joy for the remainder of her life.

Built in a neo-classic style, it boasted two floors and a tower. Six steps guarded by two stone lions led to the portico covered with red, octagonal-shaped tiles. A most unusual feature was the five entrances. Three arched glass doors in front and one entrance on either side. Two round terracotta bas-reliefs adorned the two side doors. The one to the right was in daily use, the one to the left only if many guests were expected. The vast marble Atrium was square-shaped with four green marble columns supporting the ceiling; the height was equal to three floors. Wall-size mirrors, facing each other, created an illusion of an immense hall. The ceiling was impressive with its five round frescos painted by Károly Lotz; they represented allegorical figures. From the Atrium one stepped into the Gobelin Salon, so named because of the two enormous sixteenth century Flemish tapestries adorning the walls.

To the left was the Red Salon that derived its name from the red silk upholstery that covered the ebony black furniture. The room faced north and part of the floor was laid with marble. Shelves on one wall contained Charlie's leatherbound first editions from which Emilia had been unable to part, together with a sizeable collection of contemporary books. Nothing, however, could change the frozen atmosphere that prevailed in this room. I was always to harbour an intense dislike for the Red Salon. It had an indefinable aura that made one ill at ease.

A wide staircase with ebony railing led from the Atrium to the upper floor where the bedrooms were located. The stairs were covered with a thick vieux-rose coloured carpet. On the landing was János Temple's famous life-size painting of Emilia as Desdemona. Another relic from her past. In a niche stood the bust of Emilia made by Alajos Stróbl in 1899.

May I be forgiven for having gone into such detail about the Villa but, after all, it was to be a refuge for my mother and father during two periods of their lives, and it was the home where I was later brought up with so much love from Emilia and Oskar.

Adhering strictly to tradition, Bandi Hatvany paid a formal visit to Emilia to ask for her daughter's hand in marriage. A wedding date was not set, but Emilia decided to plan a magnificent reception for some time in March in honour of the official engagement. Within the space of a few days, however, certain disturbing events took place to jolt her out of her complacency with regard to Romola's future.

Shortly after news of the engagement had spread, Romola was invited to the Hotel Hungaria for afternoon tea by Gina, distantly related to the Pulszky family. Her mother and Ferenc Pulszky's mother were sisters. Her son, Paul Bohus – a cousin to Romola – was to play a prominent part in Romola's life. Gina was looked upon by the family as a rather vulgar woman in addition to being a notorious intriguer. The purpose of her chat with Romola had simply been to embroider further on the malicious rumour that to Bandi it was a union of convenience to enable his mother to tie her own family more strongly to the true Hungarian aristocracy. Thus, she felt it her solemn duty to warn Romola. She also hinted broadly at lurid stories circulating about Bandi, although she refused to be more forthcoming. Romola had recoiled from her veiled innuendoes and, having spoken to Emilia about what had transpired, promptly tossed the unpleasant accusations out of her mind. Emilia kept her own counsel, but experienced serious qualms and wished she could get to the truth behind the gossip before it was too late.

From her own account, Emilia shortly thereafter experienced an unwelcome and, to her, rather distressing visit from Bandi's mother. The latter announced herself one day under the pretext that she wished to discuss their children's future. Emilia had developed an antipathy bordering almost to contempt toward the other woman that she found hard to stifle and the afternoon in question she suffered from fatigue after a strenuous rehearsal at the theatre. However, she greeted her visitor politely and escorted her into the Red Salon. What a contrast the two must have made. Emilia's theatrical eye for costume had taken in every detail of the Baroness's appearance; a tailored suit made of the finest mohair in a taupe shade, the 'hobble skirt', so popular among wealthy women, sweeping Emilia's carpet as she walked. A high close-fitting collar shielded her neck and a cravat completed the outfit. Emilia, by contrast, was casually dressed in her long, warm burgundy coloured robe, which she loved to don when at home. A beautiful shawl in a rich shade of honey was draped around her shoulders.

For Romola's sake she forced herself to show Bandi's mother every courtesy but after a brief exchange of polite nothingness, she lost her patience and bluntly wished to know the reason for the visit.

The Baroness had the grace to blush but had then come to the point. It concerned Romola's trousseau. She had heard it was *magnifique* and expressed a desire to see it. Emilia held back a sharp retort and instead conducted the prying woman up to Romola's bedroom. Quite shamelessly, Baroness Hatvany opened the Biedermeier armoir and scrutinised the exquisite French silks and the lace lingerie from Brussels. She had the effrontery to chide Emilia about her daughter's rather extravagant taste and intimated she should be more frugal in future. Emilia had taken it as a slur against her, fully aware that her financial problems were an everyday topic of conversation in the city, and had brought the visit to a close.

Another strange happening was to follow. Bandi had invited Romola to have lunch with him and his mother at the Restaurant Gundel, an elegant family establishment noted for its cuisine. It was located on the edge of Varosliget, the vast, lush public park. It had been a balmy day with a hint of Spring in the air. Bandi and Romola had decided to take a stroll together before joining the Baroness. The horse-drawn carriage had kept a slow pace behind them, the clop-clop of the horse's hooves echoing on the cobblestones. Bandi had noticed a little flower vendor standing on the street corner with a basket of the first arrivals of the season, shy violets and pure white snowdrops. Just as he handed Romola a bouquet of velvet-petalled violets, the air had been rent with the raucous voice of the newspaper-boy screaming out the latest sensational headlines. The suicide of a young aristocrat jilted by a young sugar baron. To Romola it conveyed nothing but Bandi's whole manner changed. He rushed over to buy a paper and to her astonishment she saw how his lips trembled as he scanned through the front page, beads of perspiration forming on his forehead.

Almost brusquely, he bundled her into the carriage and in silence they had continued to the restaurant. He offered no explanation to her bewildered query and having escorted her to the table where his mother was waiting, he bid a hasty farewell. The following morning a bouquet of tea roses was delivered to Romola with a note begging forgiveness for his abrupt departure but still without any explanation as to why. Naturally puzzled, she yet again turned to Emilia. Sophisticated though she was, Romola had no knowledge of the many complex physical aspects of sex. She had not yet experienced the true meaning of love between a man and a woman. Her fiancé had not aroused her to any emotional feelings. She still shrank from physical contact with him. How was she then to know of the existence of love and passion between men; between women? Certainly, Emilia had not prepared Romola for the years ahead when she was to come face to face with tortuous human frailties into which she herself was to be plunged.

Whatever reservations assailed Emilia regarding the suitability of her daughter's husband-to-be, and by now she could surely not be blind to his dual nature, in the capricious month of March she commenced the preliminary arrangements for Romola's engagement dinner. Why? What motivated her? She had emphatically declared to Polyxena that her Molly must marry for love. She abhorred the Baroness. Was it the god of Mammon who won the struggle of her conscience? Security above all for her daughter? She never made it clear.

Oskar gave Emilia his unfailing support because, although a marvellous hostess, she had little knowledge of the more practical aspects of housekeeping. The couple whiled away long evenings poring over the guest list. There were three families to consider,

Márkus, Pulszky and Hatvany; the acting profession must not be neglected; members of the diplomatic corps; writers and artists, including the famous sculptor Alajos Stróbl. Apparently, Romola had taken little notice of the hubbub of activity around her. Was she beginning to awaken to the hypocrisy of tying herself down for life to a man, whose erratic behaviour the past few months she had been unable to fathom. Something must have stirred in the depths of her subconscious so that a jarring note crept into the relationship between her and her fiancé which at its best was luke-warm on her part. She did not voluntarily bring up the subject of a fixed date for the wedding. Dutifully, she visited her future mother-in-law now and again, and quite dispassionately shrugged off the latter's lectures over her extravagant habits and what she referred to as her 'royal' trousseau. She had developed a distinct coolness to the older woman.

Romola did thaw, however, when the Baroness, in keeping with the earlier promise, invited her in early March 1912 to the opening Gala Night of the *Ballets Russes* at the Municipal Opera House, the pride of the citizens of Budapest. The remarkable performance made an enormous impression upon Romola. The scenery alone overwhelmed her as each ballet with its exuberant colours and artistic presentation unfolded itself to the captivated audience. The brilliance of the dancers was such it was impossible to feast one's eyes on any particular individual. At the end of the evening she was left breathless, enchanted by what she had seen take place on stage. Yet she was told that the company's most magnetic star had not performed that evening due to a slight indisposition.

Sensing Romola's keen disappointment, the Baroness generously invited her to the following night's performance, when Bandi had promised to accompany them. More and more frequently of late he had absented himself from the many social functions with one lame excuse after the other. Nor did he put in an appearance that second evening until the first intermission but by then Romola hardly noticed him. She had donned her favourite long black, velvet evening dress and waited with almost feverish anticipation for the Baroness to collect her. At the Opera she sank down in her seat in the front row beside her hostess. The orchestra was tuning up. The lights dimmed and the curtain slowly rose for the first ballet, *Cleopatra,* performed as brilliantly as on the previous evening. Then the scene changed for Schumann's *Carnaval.* That was the moment, too, that Romola's life changed. And only Romola's own words can do justice to the impact that first 'introduction' to Waslaw Nijinsky made on her.

*'Suddenly a slim, lithe, cat-like Harlequin took the stage. Although his face was hidden by a painted mask, the expression and beauty of his body made us all realise that we were in the presence of a genius...Intoxicated, entranced, gasping for breath, we followed this superhuman being, the very spirit of Harlequin incarnate; mischievous, lovable. The power, the featherweight lightness, the steel-like strength, the suppleness of his movements, the incredible gift of rising and remaining in the air and descending in twice as slow a time as it took to rise – contrary to all laws of gravitation – the execution of the most difficult pirouettes and *tours en l'air* with an amazing nonchalance and apparently no effort whatever, proved that this extraordinary phenomenon was the very soul of the dance- ...*This magnificent vision was Nijinsky.* My one desire, from that moment on, was to know more about the extraordinary manifestation of art embodied in this entire company, and the individuals who had succeeded in creating it...'

At the end of the evening's performance, the audience, intoxicated by what they had witnessed, went wild; the sophisticated people of Budapest unashamedly gave vent to their innermost feelings, shouting *bravo* until their voices grew hoarse; clapped until their hands became numb; pelted flowers, programmes, anything within reach onto the stage, leaving the *Ballets Russes* in no doubt they had conquered yet another capital of Europe.

To Romola, her fiancé Bandi, simpering at her side and proffering his apologies for his belated appearance, ceased to exist from that evening onward. How ironic a twist of fate, that the Baroness, encapsulated by her egocentric desire to climb the social ladder, was the indirect cause of the loss of her aim.

Emilia had invited Romola to join her and a party of friends at a late supper at the Hotel Dunapalota after the performance. Romola, still in a daze after what she had experienced, had mechanically replied to questions thrown at her about her impression of the Russian ballet and then sat there silently, toying with her food, obli-

* From 'NIJINSKY' by Romola Nijinsky.

56

vious to the din of conversation around her. The only time she lit up was when she noticed some of the members of the *Ballets Russes* enter the dining room. She eagerly scanned their faces, searching for *Harlequin*. And suddenly, there he stood in the doorway. She later described her impression – that of a stocky, colourless young man, rather ill at ease in a tuxedo hanging limply on his lithe body. He had not resembled the god-like figure who only hours previously had electrified his audience. One of his contemporaries described Nijinsky, the man, as having 'a pale face, high cheekbones, small and slightly Mongol eyes, thin hair nondescript in colour; taciturn, glum and slightly bewildered.' His transformation into the characters he portrayed in his dance was therefore all the more astonishing. Not only was he a virtuoso in the skill of applying make-up and in changing his physical appearance, but the inner spirit of the character seemed to penetrate his soul.

Quite certainly, for the first time since the death of the father she had worshipped, she experienced an inward glow of happiness and a *raison d'être*. She became determined to join the company, and set about carrying out her plan. It presented no problem to Romola to make the acquaintance of the *Ballets Russes* because the Villa's doors were always open to distinguished guests who wished to pay their respects to the country's incomparable actress. Emilia was only too pleased to entertain the Russian troupe. A true artist herself, she appreciated and respected genuine artistic perfection in others. A sumptuous banquet was held and Romola mingled with the dancers and other members of the entourage but neither Diaghilev nor Nijinsky put in an appearance. On a later occasion she met Adolf Bolm, their principal character dancer, and the warm friendship that developed between them was to prove extremely beneficial. He was the son of the concert master of the Imperial Orchestra and was a likeable, popular person with the Ballet. Discreetly, Romola caught him in her web; invited him home, showed him the sights of Budapest and, with feminine wiles, learned as much as possible about the others in the company.

When the day finally arrived that the *Ballets Russes* departed to continue their conquest of the Western world, Romola's mind was made up. She decided to abandon all thoughts of the pursuit of a theatrical career, which involved giving up her lessons with the famous French actress Réjane and with Le Bargy to concentrate instead on dance. Even before meeting Waslaw, she had taken ballet lessons from Guerra at the Budapest Opera. What drove her on at that early stage to dramatically cut herself free from her carefree living? Although perhaps already in her innermost heart overwhelmed by the genius of Nijinsky, it is also certain that she harboured a burning ambition to prove to her father's memory that she, Romola de Pulszky, was *somebody* in her own right. And she was unable to rid herself of a deep-rooted jealousy of her own mother. She could not aspire to equal Emilia in *her* profession, therefore it would be wiser to embark on another. Emilia was loved by so many as the full-blooded woman that she was; Romola, cool and by her own volition, withdrawn, must sometimes have felt left out; admired, but from a distance.

During the Ballet's stay in the capital she had callously ignored Bandi, who surely must have suffered attacks of misgiving that something had gone wrong between him and his betrothed. She had scrupulously avoided him for days. The engagement dinner was approaching, yet Romola, racking her brain as to how to achieve her golden vision, had completely forgotten it until a letter from Tessa, wanting to know the exact date of the 'blissful' event, jolted her out of her reveries.

One must assume that she suffered a twinge of conscience as she took the coward's way out of her dilemma – by bolting temporarily from the scene. One morning, after Emilia had gone to a rehearsal and Oskar to the Ministry, she gathered a few personal belongings and departed on a train to Vienna and her sister, leaving behind a scribbled note to Emilia with the white lie that Tessa had urgently required her presence as she was despondent after a violent attack of influenza but that she, Romola, would come back home in a few days.

Simultaneously, she wrote to Bandi, unequivocally breaking off their alliance while begging his forgiveness. Enclosed with the letter was the exquisite gold bracelet set with rubies that he had given her.

Emilia was furious over what she had termed her headstrong daughter's disgraceful action. In fairness to Emilia, she had not so much minded the severance of relationships with the Hatvanys – she had long harboured suspicions Bandi would make an unsuitable husband – but she seethed with frustration over the fact she exercised no authority whatsoever over her daughters. Now Romola was following her sister's footsteps, taking no heed of Emilia's advice.

When she felt certain the storm had subsided, Romola returned from Vienna and broke the news to Emilia she could not see herself perpetuate a career in the theatrical profession and that she intended instead to secure for herself a niche in the world of ballet. Toward that aim she had decided to return to Paris to obtain proper training there. Emilia was devastated by the thought of her Molly taking such a precarious step – after all, she was past the age considered the minimum for a dancer to start – but tried to accept her daughter's resolve with outward dignity and calm.

In need of sympathy and advice, Romola had once more paid Polyxena a visit. The latter had prudently stressed two vital factors overlooked by Romola; she would require a substantial sum of money for her venture and a chaperone must accompany her.

Pampered as she had been by both Emilia and Oskar, Romola had prior to that scorned to consider a subject as sordid as finance. She turned to her step-father for help and felt frustrated and humiliated when he declined. He claimed that construction of the Villa, Emilia's own extravagant lifestyle and last but not least, the money hitherto lavished on Romola, had exhausted all available resources, at least temporarily. A violent quarrel ensued with Romola blaming *that outsider* for everything.

Realising tantrums would get her nowhere, she sat down and calmly took stock of the situation. It would present no problem to stay in Paris or Vienna, as she had a sufficient number of friends in either city who would be willing to help her with accommodation but she required money for travel expenses, to buy clothes, to pay for her tuition at a ballet school, and to support Anna, the young chaperone she had agreed to take on. Once more, it was Aunt Poly who came to her rescue, reminding her she had a small inheritance to come from Charlie-Papa's estate.

She immediately contacted Simon Krausz, a successful Jewish banker, who had also been a friend of the family for many years. He had at first been reluctant to release Romola's share without discussing the matter with Emilia, not wishing to be a partner to any deception, but Romola, with her persuasive and engaging manner, weakened his professional ethics and he agreed to grant her a temporary loan on her legacy.

And so the day came to pass that Romola left her sheltered youth behind her. With her chaperone Anna in tow lugging a heavy suitcase crammed with paraphernalia, she boarded the train to

Paris, leaving a tear-drenched Emilia standing on the platform.

It had not taken Romola long to install herself comfortably in the city that was virtually her second home. She admitted much later she had partaken in the daily ballet lessons with mixed emotions. Intelligent as she was, she was quite aware of the fact she had embarked upon a new career too late in life to make a genuine success of it. But she carried on with dogged determination. In her spare time she would rush over to the Bibliothèque Nationale, where she would engross herself in every printed word she could find about ballet, its origin, its history, until her eyes smarted. She would revisit the Louvre but now only to study the works of art connected with dance.

When the *Ballets Russes* returned to Paris to present their new programmes, Romola took advantage of the opportunity to rekindle her acquaintance with Bolm. And again, she sat enraptured evening after evening, watching the troupe's latest creations in which they surpassed themselves.

She haunted the hotel where the dancers were staying in the hope of catching a glimpse of Nijinsky, and early one afternoon as she was having tea with a friend, her prayers were answered. She had looked up to find him standing opposite her, with what she interpreted to be a flicker of recognition. He had, however, swiftly turned on his heels and vanished through one of the doors into a corridor. Acting upon impulse, like a stage-struck teenager, she hastily mumbled an excuse to her friend and rushed after him. Following the echo of his footsteps through the labyrinth of swinging doors and endless corridors, she had finally reached the tradesmen's entrance. Stepping out into a narrow alley, she could see no trace of him, only his companion and bodyguard, Vassily.

Rather shamefacedly, Romola had found her way back, forced to admit her prey had escaped. Her friend comforted her, remarking he had in all likelihood been late for an appointment. Romola failed to notice the significant smile on the other woman's lips. It was common knowledge to a select circle that Nijinsky, to break away from Diaghilev and assert himself as a man, would from time to time seek the company of Parisian prostitutes.

> '...I liked Paris tarts when I was with Diaghilev.
> He thought I went out for walks, but I was chasing tarts...I was
> very young and so did silly things...I did not like what I was

doing, but my habits became more complex and I took to look-
ing for them every day...'

Waslaw Nijinsky, Villa Guardamunt, 1919

Romola did not return to Budapest until the Christmas holidays, when the posters outside the Opera again proudly proclaimed the season's highlight, a return engagement of the *Ballets Russes.*

Emilia was delighted to have her prodigal daughter once more ensconced in the Villa and catered to her every whim. As on the previous occasion, she opened her doors and gave numerous parties for the Russian guests. Bolm was always present but to Romola's bitter disappointment, not even Emilia's fame could draw either Nijinsky or Diaghilev to her home. It was through Bolm that Romola got to know Enrico Cecchetti better. He was the troupe's teacher, Italian by birth, but for some thirty odd years he had been the *Maestro* to the most famous names at the Imperial School of Dancing in St Petersburg. Romola did everything in her power to win him over on her side; to help her achieve her goal to become a member of the *Ballets Russes.*

Whenever Waslaw Nijinsky was practising, Romola would hide herself in the wings, making herself as inconspicuous as possible. It was an unwritten law that Nijinsky should work undisturbed and at all times he was closely guarded by the master brain behind the Ballet, Sergei Pavlovitch Diaghilev himself, or by Vassily, the servant. Although by now, they had been introduced *en passant,* her idol would totally ignore her if their paths crossed in the corridors, a fact which hurt Romola intensely. Evening after evening, performance after performance, Romola would sit in the stalls, her eyes glued on the God of Dance. Nothing else mattered around her. The monotony of the hitherto grey humdrum hours of the day were wiped out by the presence of the lively Russians, by their vibrant, intoxicating lifestyle, their colourful costumes.

Romola derived pleasure from watching Waslaw and his sister Bronia dance together. She relished listening to the juicy titbits about the various members of the company. In particular about Mathilda Kchessinskaya, who was the Tsar's mistress and the toast of Russia. The stories surrounding her became legendary. Thus the days flew by with Romola breathing the intense atmosphere of the divine dancers. Cecchetti gave her every possible encouragement to join the company but advised her to seek an audience with Diaghilev. Only the *Maestro,* with his sensitive intuition of human nature, recognised her infatuation for Waslaw Nijinsky. The others in the company thought she was interested in Bolm. But Cecchetti, a shrewd and very wise man, was to give her a warning she never heeded. Seeing her devour her idol with her eyes one day at rehearsal, he gently admonished her, 'Beware, Nijinsky is like a sun that pours forth light but never warmth.'

When the company left for Vienna, so did Romola. There she made the fullest use of her family connections to gain access to the Opera House – her godfather was close to the Emperor Franz-Josef and head of the Imperial Family's archives, her brother-in-law, Erik Schmedes, was the leading Wagnerian tenor. Oddly enough, however, it was a Hungarian critic, Ludwig Kárpáth, who was instrumental in introducing Romola to Diaghilev. With everything against her, namely her age, her lack of experience as a ballet dancer, she still had the audacity to ask Diaghilev if she could join his company. With wit and ingenuity, she managed to convince the Impresario that she was suitable. The interview over, she flew on the wings of truimph to the *Maestro,* who told her that she would be studying under him and that she consequently would have to make preparations to join the Ballet in London in February, 1913.

Perhaps at this stage it would be fitting to introduce my father, Waslaw Nijinsky, to the uninitiated reader, who has never read my mother's biography nor in fact, any of the countless books written about him and his artistic career. As I mentioned in my Introduction, it would not be either prudent nor possible for me to go into detail about his amazing career which had reached its zenith when he met my mother. The experts have already covered that ground and done so skilfully and thoroughly. Bronislava Nijinska, his sister, graphically recorded his childhood and adolescence in her own memoirs and largely thanks to her wealth of knowledge I am able to describe briefly my father's early years.

What was the exact date of my father's birth? No one seems to know. On my own birth certificate it is down as 1st January 1890. The inscription on his tomb gives his date of birth as 28th November 1889. Bronislava declared in her early memoirs that the correct date was the night between February 27th-28th, 1889 (N.S. March 12th). To this day his birthdate is a continuing source of controversy. Some half a dozen dates have been given, with as many different substantiating bits of evidence, all too complicated to go into here. An interesting and in-depth article was written some years ago on the subject by Ian Ferguson and published in *The Dancing Times*. Perhaps it would suffice to say that Waslaw Nijinsky was born in Kiev between 1888 – 1890. However, I do have in my possession a copy of an official document stamped in Warsaw on June 3rd, 1921, stating that Nizyinski Waclaw was born on December 28th, 1889. (According to the Gregorian calendar, the 10th of January, 1890.) Parents: Thomas and Eleonora. Religion: Catholic. Possibly, this document was brought over by Bronislava when she departed from Russia for Paris in 1921. There remains the distinction between December 29th and February 28th (the date on the Russian calendar at that time, which did not change until 1923). In an often told anecdote, Waslaw's mother is said to have wished her son to appear to be nine months older to avoid military service (which was calculated to commence in September) and thus hope to gain for him another year's studies.

Waslaw's mother, Eleonora Nicolaevna Bereda, a sweet, gentle woman, devoutly religious, was the daughter of a Polish cabinet maker. He and his wife died within weeks of one another, leaving five orphaned children. Eleonora was then only seven years old. Together with a sister Stephanie Marie she became a member of the Theatrical Ballet School of the Wielki Theatre in Warsaw. After an unfortunate engagement to a young Russian artillery captain, Eleonora rejoined the ballet company and she met Thomas Lavrentiyevich Nijinsky when both were working with the Setov Enterprise in the Odessa Opera Theatre. Thomas was a strikingly handsome man, a skilled classical dancer and ballet master. Unlike her, he was temperamental to the extreme, prone to violent outbreaks of rage. His father had been a freedom fighter during the Polish Insurrection of 1863. Oddly enough, although both Thomas and Eleonora chose the world of dance as theirs, neither could boast professional dancers among their ancestors.

After their marriage, the young couple toured Russia with their own troupe, giving performances in every town and village they visited. They lived a true gypsy existence. In the space of six years they had three children; Stanislav (Stassik), their first-born, was tragically injured from a fall out of the window when he was barely three. In an unguarded moment he had climbed onto a broad window sill, attracted by the sound of a band marching down the street, and had fallen three stories to the cobblestones below. It was later generally assumed that his mental illness, which took violent forms as he grew up, was a direct result of the accident; Waslaw Fomitch (Watsa), the second son, came a year later to be followed by a daughter, Bronislava (Bronia).

According to his sister, Waslaw was a precocious child, far from introverted, mischievous and playful, mixing especially well with circus people and gypsies. Thus, to all appearances, his early childhood was both uncomplicated and filled with interesting happenings. He was a sound and healthy child, who loved to go fishing and on climbing jaunts in the country. The almost nomadic travels of the family were a continuous source of great adventure. But then the clouds began to gather on his horizon. One incident that left an indelible mark on him and was to remain with him as a vivid recollection, even during those twilight years when he wrote his diary, occurred when he had reached his sixth birthday. His father callously threw him into the Neva one day in an impatient endeavour to teach his son to swim. Waslaw, terrified, was on the point of drowning. When grown-up he claimed it was only the inborn strength of his legs that saved him as he leapt high out of the water and managed to grasp a rope for support.

Then the traumatic separation of his parents cast a dark shadow over his existence. His father Thomas abandoned his family for a mistress, a young Jewish dancer, Rumiantseva, whom he had met while on tour in Finland. With her he started a new family, a daughter named Marina, and left Eleonora to feed herself and the three children. Waslaw recalled how he had seen his beautiful mother weeping: 'Why do you cry?' he had asked. In a barely audible voice she had replied, 'Your father has left us.' She adamantly refused to give Thomas a divorce. To add to her worries Stanislav's illness took on violent forms and when he became a teenager it was deemed necessary to commit him to an asylum. Waslaw's whole attitude changed; he no longer joined his sister in music and song and his conduct and attention to lessons, aside from dance, plummeted to a low ebb. He was averse to visiting Stassik; felt physically ill at the thought, and it was only on rare occasions he could bring himself to visit his brother at the sanatorium. Stassik died years later of a liver complaint in the psychiatric hospital.

Sadly, though he inherited the gentle nature of his mother, Waslaw was also to suffer the uncontrollable rages so similar to his father's. But from Thomas, too, he inherited the incredible jumps for which he was to become famous. Unquestionably, Waslaw was a child prodigy, for he had danced solo in public already at the age of five in a children's Christmas show. The audience, fascinated by his high leaps, had applauded so long he had to dance an encore of the *Bopak*. He learned quickly to master a number of musical instruments, a remarkable achievement as he had never been taught any of them. Later, at the Imperial Ballet, he required only to listen to a musical score once and could then go home and play it faultlessly on the piano. He memorised whole operas such as *Eugene Onegin, Faust* and *Tannhäuser*.

The family, now reduced to four, moved to a flat in St Petersburg. A sea of troubles engulfed the abandoned family from the start. Stassik and Bronia had as yet not recovered from typhoid fever and had to spend lonely hours isolated from their new, exciting environment. Waslaw had to communicate his impressions of the neighbourhood, most often through a transom as he was strictly forbidden to enter the room in which they lay. He had by that time enrolled in a preparatory school.

Thomas's sporadic returns to the home and the distress these caused their mother dampened the children's spirits. Despite all this, however, Bronia in her *Early Memoirs* has painted a delightfully nostalgic and colourful picture of those early years, in which Watsa is lovingly depicted as a 'very lively and adventurous boy'. Eleonora was a conscientious mother who wanted to give her children a genteel upbringing. She took care to introduce them to the Stieglitz Museum not far from where they lived and as often as possible to the grand palaces and the Hermitage to admire the Imperial treasures.

Although their father still contributed his share of rubles to the household and Eleonora had part-time work as a ballet teacher, frugality had to be practised, and some years later, after the definitive break between Eleonora and Thomas, the monetary situation became distressful. According to his sister, the severance of all ties was indirectly brought on by Waslaw, who, while visiting his father, engaged in a quarrel uncontrolled on either side, when the latter insisted his son should meet Rumiantseva. In protest at this slur against his mother, Waslaw had stormed out without a backward glance. Neither Waslaw nor Bronia was ever to see Thomas again.

When Stassik developed his first indications of psychological disturbance Eleonora lavished all her love on the younger son, nurturing lofty ambitions for his future. But it was to prove impossible for her to protect him from the jibes of children in his class at school, envious perhaps of his talent. They would taunt him – for his poverty, his Polish accent, his Mongolian features. They nicknamed him 'the little Jap' and succeeded in making his hours in class a misery. Bronia recalls in her book how heartbroken he was over being teased that he was perhaps a girl, he danced so well. Maybe it was then that slowly but inevitably the foundation was laid for his inferiority complex; he began to imagine he was hounded for his genius and he developed a strong fear of punishment. With hindsight it must be concluded he was too sheltered by his mother at that stage to cope with the outside world, even though he did not take bullying from fellow classmates meekly – he would defend himself and get into fights.

His closeness to his mother made him keenly aware of her anguish at being left alone with three mouths to feed. Acutely sensitive, he was upset over the degradation she suffered in her struggle to bring them up as a family of substance and it was this which one day would spur him on to make money for the family even though his moral integrity was to be the high price he would pay. At the age of nine he was taken by his mother to the Imperial School of Ballet in St Petersburg. She prayed he would be accepted as a pupil. The State would then provide for him and his education and a career would be assured for him as a dancer; he would be well taken care of. Bronia was soon after to follow in his footsteps. In submitting his application, Waslaw derived a certain advantage through his parents' acquaintance with Enrico Cecchetti; they had both worked with him, and Eleonora went to him to seek his support. He passed his entrance examination with flying colours; he was one of five chosen from 150. Waslaw was quickly to be promoted to the class of Nicolas Legat, whose sharp eyes for talent had observed his fantastic leaps, and recognised the making of a brilliant dancer in his physique, perfect for the ballet.

For two years young Waslaw would daily walk home from the Imperial School, a walk that took him nearly half an hour. He developed an intense dislike for French lessons and Divinity classes. Music was his favourite pastime – Rimsky Korsakov and Wagner were his most loved composers – but he also became an avid reader and devoured works by Dostoevsky (he found it hard to understand

The Idiot, claiming he was too young to fully comprehend it), Gogol and the poems of Pushkin. In general subjects, unrelated to the arts, he was considered 'dull' and did not do very well, except for mathematics.

He wrote about his childhood:

> *'We did not have bread. My mother did not know what to give us to live. My mother joined the Ciniselli Circus in order to make a little money. She was ashamed of such work because she was a well-known actress in Russia. I realised it all even though I was a child. I wept in my heart. My mother also wept...'.*

Later, however, life apparently brightened for a brief space of time. With Bronia, too, at the Imperial School, Eleonora decided to run a boarding house. Waslaw recalled in his writings that they soon thereafter had enough bread to eat. His mother enjoyed entertaining friends and Waslaw would sit and listen rapturously to the grown-ups' conversation. He understood them and was therefore drawn to them. Children of his own age did not understand him.

After two years of probation Waslaw was enrolled as a Resident Student of the Imperial School. It was then he was awarded the much prized Didelot Scholarship. When a pupil was admitted, the parents relinquished all rights; the pupil was virtually adopted by the Tsar. Waslaw now lived in comfortable quarters at the School yet he was still an 'outsider' to his fellow classmates. He made his first appearance in the Mariinsky Theatre; he danced in numerous opera performances with older students as well as in ballet performances. His sister told of how proud he was to receive a total of three rubles and fifty kopeks for seven performances. A freak accident in 1901 very nearly ended Waslaw's budding career. He participated in a high-jump prank in the large dance hall in the school, slipped and fell to the floor with such force he was rendered unconscious. He was rushed to hospital where he did not regain consciousness until the fifth day. It was not until many weeks later he could resume where he had left off and such was his skill at dancing, he was promoted at the end of term with the other pupils. His high-spirited nature involved him in numerous boyish pranks and one brought about his expulsion from the school. Trying to prove his skill with a bow and arrow and egged on by other pupils while they were being driven by carriage for a matinée performance at the Mariinsky Theatre he missed the target and instead hit a government official. He was summarily dismissed and told *never to return* to the School but Inspector Vladimir Pisnyatchevsky and his teachers, realising the talent that would be lost, interceded on his behalf. Bronislava has movingly described the degradation he suffered when stripped of his splendid uniform and losing his status as residential pupil. It filled Waslaw with shame in addition to which the transition from the luxury of his room at the School to the comparatively shabby home jolted him rudely to his real situation. He vowed henceforth to study diligently and become famous.

Eleonora, devoutly religious and a strict disciplinarian, had little idea, it seemed, of what went on inside a boy's head during puberty. Thus, although she smothered him with love and affection, reciprocated by Waslaw, he was unable to confide to her his growing interest in the opposite sex. The Imperial School of Ballet could be likened to a combination of convent and barracks. Girls and boys were taught separately and, when brought together in class, they were strictly chaperoned. It was to be Bronislava who became his 'mother confessor' and to whom he poured out his secrets, how he would creep along the corridors to the girls' dressing-rooms and, safely hidden in the shadows, would steal glimpses of them changing their tutus for street clothes. It was she who perceived how he suffered from the torment of the others in his class. It was she who many years later recalled that he did not acquire one single friend during his eight long years at the school. She recollected, however, his first sweetheart, a gentle little girl, who lived on the floor below them and who gave Waslaw her photograph when the Nijinsky family left for a stay in Dudergoth; how his mother had recoiled with horror on finding the photograph in Waslaw's pocket and demanded he tear it up.

Snubbed and ridiculed by his classmates he may have been, but his teachers did not fail to encourage the incipient genius they had in their care. It was perhaps the most remarkable era in the history of Russian ballet that Waslaw was to experience and he was to dance with the most brilliant stars of that generation of which he was to prove to be the brightest.

When not wrapped up in his world of dance and music he loved to while away leisure hours strolling through the galleries of paintings, admiring most of all the Italian masters of the Renaissance, as he was to reveal in later years. What a wealth of culture surrounded him. And it was the era in ballet that burst into full bloom; the Italian ballet was to dazzle St Petersburg with names like Enrico Cecchetti, Carlotta Brianza and Pierina Legnani, to name but a few. Diaghilev, Bakst, Benois entered the scene, the creators of *Mir Istkustva*, the magazine 'The World of Art'. Alexandre Benois was an artist with an eminent theatrical family background. Tamara Karsavina, Michael Fokine, Kchessinskaya, Anna Pavlova, Chaliapine; Waslaw breathed the air they breathed, studied them, admired them, and was in due course to become a partner to a number of them.

Waslaw was promoted to the class of Mikhail Obukhov, who acknowledged his superb skill with the highest grade he had ever given to a pupil. Thomas was so proud of his son, he sent a hundred rubles. Obukhov decided to show him off in a student performance, the first public appearance of Waslaw Nijinsky. To be chosen for a *pas de deux* while only a young student was an honour seldom bestowed by the school. His sister Bronia, who herself danced at the Mariinsky that memorable night, recorded for posterity every movement, every step young Waslaw made. She was thrilled by the brilliance of his performance, by the spontaneous applause of the audience, a sound that was to be music to his ears hundreds of times throughout his brief meteoric career.

In late autumn 1905 he had a narrow escape. Strikes and disruptions had been rife and the masses rebelled, unable to bear their poverty any longer. On his way home he saw the Cossacks on horseback mow down the frenzied mob, and was himself dealt a blow by one of them but fortunately was not severely hurt. Others were not so lucky.

According to Bronia, Waslaw had several ardent admirers among the young girl students and on one occasion a *billet doux* intended for a partner, Tonya Tchumakova, was apprehended and in accordance with the strict rules of the School, he was forbidden to dance with her again. He matured, shunned his contemporaries to seek the company of those older than he. No longer did he idle away hours with boyish pranks but studied hard and gave dance lessons to better the family's income.

Eight years after he had become accepted as a pupil graduation tests faced him. To quote from Bronia 'though Nijinsky in dancing, art and music had the highest possible grade, A 12, his overall average grade was 11, and so he was second in the graduation class'. He was admitted to the Imperial Theatre (the Mariinsky). Matilda Kchessinskaya had noticed him and had expressed a wish for him to become her partner. Thus, incredibly, he never had to perform in the *corps* but became a soloist at the start. He danced solo before Tsar Nicholas II and received a gold watch bearing the Imperial cypher.

Imbued with a new sense of security he and his mother and Bronia took a cottage near Krasnoe Selo to enjoy the summer season, but he still had to commute to St Petersburg thrice weekly for rehearsals. Anatole Bourman came to visit Waslaw to the annoyance of both women, who distrusted him and instinctively feared he might have a damaging influence on Waslaw. He was in the same class as Waslaw and also became a member of the Diaghilev Ballet.

Eleonora rented a larger apartment not far from The Hermitage. To make more money Waslaw gave lessons in social dancing to rich aristocrats and some claim it was in this circle he was introduced to Prince Pavel Dmitrievitch Lvov in one of St Petersburg's most famous restaurants, an introduction purposely engineered as the Prince had seen Waslaw perform and had become captivated by him.

This meeting led young Waslaw onto a path hitherto alien to him. Persuaded by the Prince to believe that a beautiful cousin of Lvov's was interested in him, Waslaw was swept into the maelstrom of the debauched society of the wealthy aristocrats. He became the handsome prince's lover, although his sister Bronislava categorically stated that her brother was by nature not homosexually inclined; on the contrary he much preferred the company of women. But Lvov not only opened Waslaw's eyes to luxurious living, to smart clothes, to the finest cuisine, the taste for drinking, he also became a benefactor to the dancer's family, helping them financially. It was he who insisted Waslaw take lessons from Cecchetti. Lvov paid for these lessons with the understanding Waslaw could pay him back once he was famous. Too, according to Bronia, it was he who provided Waslaw with a much-longed for piano.

Bronislava has written very warmly about Prince Lvov. He was a tall man, dark-haired, with distinctive aristocratic features; his manners were impeccable and he exuded geniality and warmth to all he met, irrespective of social standing. In her book is a fascinating description of a visit to Prince Lvov's home on the Bolshaya Morskaya Ulitza to celebrate her birthday. Eleonora, Bronia and Waslaw were the only guests. She had been overwhelmed by the antique treasures that filled every room of this magnificent mansion. The dinner alone had been like something out of a fairy-tale; footmen serving, resplendent in black tailcoats and white gloves; gold plates heaped with caviar and other palatable delicacies. She had been struck by awe that her brother, Waslaw, was a frequent guest in these sumptuous surroundings. It became manifestly clear that the younger man felt a strong attachment to Lvov. The latter, however, evidently did not develop the same strong feeling for his charge, disappointed, perhaps bored, at finding him not to be his type. Consequently, he was not averse to introducing his protégé to, among others, a Polish Count, Tishkievitch. Then came the fateful meeting, a meeting that was to have unforeseen consequences; how is it possible for anyone to surmise what Waslaw Nijinsky's life would have been like if he had not been presented to Sergei Pavlovitch Diaghilev, 'Chinchilla', as he was then nicknamed. Prince Lvov was instrumental in bringing the two together, presumably at a party.

Waslaw was to write:

'...invited by telephone to Diaghilev. I had come to the Hotel Europa where he was staying. I hated him for his voice which was too sure of itself but I went in search of fortune. I found fortune there because I immediately loved him. I trembled like an aspen leaf. I hated him but I pretended that I agreed with all his views. I realised that I had to live and therefore it did not matter to me what sacrifice I had to offer. I worked a great deal at dancing and therefore always felt tired. But I pretended that I was cheerful and not tired in order that Diaghilev should not be bored...Diaghilev liked boys...'

A partnership was formed, one that was to bring audiences all over Europe to their feet. Diaghilev realised his dream to take the Russian Ballet to the Western World. He brought Waslaw with him to Paris. According to Bronia, it was during that period Prince Lvov had visited her at her home to bid farewell to her and Eleonora. The latter later said Diaghilev had requested Lvov to sever his bonds with Waslaw as he would only stand in the way of his success. Lvov told Eleonora he had agreed and, in fact, backed the Russian Season in Paris financially.

Waslaw was years later to elucidate further on his impressions of his 'benefactor'; that the trouble within Diaghilev's Russian Ballet began when the Impresario visualised himself as its soul. He quarrelled with Fokine, Bakst, Benois, Stravinsky and with many others as soon as they tried to stand on their own two feet; belittled them or dismissed them altogether. One of his weaknesses was that he had a very possessive nature and wanted to own his protégés body and soul. In Nijinsky's own words:

> 'Diaghilev thinks he is the God of Art. I want people to understand Sergei Pavlovitch as I worked for him for five years without any rest. I know all his sly tricks and habits. I know him better than he does himself. I was nineteen years old when I met Diaghilev, I sincerely admired him, and when he told me that love for a woman was a terrible thing I believed him. I understood later that he lied to me, that his outlook on life was wrong and I felt deeply hurt. Diaghilev cheated me. I no longer trusted him and I began to work independently pretending that I was still his pupil. I started to hate him but when I wanted to leave him, he struck me with his stick. After this, for a long time we were together but I lived sadly and sorrowed alone. I was afraid of life. He did not like me, when I did not give him all my earnings, all my savings...'.

The invasion of Europe commenced. Enrico Cecchetti was in Paris at the Châtelét Theatre and it was there, too, that Diaghilev's ballet troupe gave its first performance. 19th May 1909 – an historic date in the annals of ballet when the *Saison Russe* presented their *répétition générale* to an illustrious audience, the great critics embracing all the art forms; editors, dignitaries representing government, foreign embassies, famous dancers; the roll call of celebrities was endless. It was then that in *Le Pavillon d'Armide* Waslaw stunned the spectators with his brilliantly executed part as Armida's Favourite Slave. His leap, unparalleled in ballet history, evoked thunderous applause. By now Waslaw was a self-assured performer. He was immaculate in everything he did. Pedantic with his wardrobe. His make-up could only be compared to that of Chaliapine's. No one was to be allowed into his dressing-room prior to a performance. He was wholly dedicated to his art, never experienced stage fright and was in perfect control of every gesture.

Léon Bakst, the Russian painter, a genius in his own right, who revolutionised the art of stage decor for the Diaghilev Ballet, was responsible for the costumes. Michel Fokine choreographed Waslaw's dances. The critics went mad with excitement over the new star, over the Russian Ballet in every respect. *Le Dieu de la Danse* became famous overnight. Success followed success. His leaps – single leaps front stage to back – soaring to impossible heights, were the talk of Paris, leaps higher than any dancer, including Auguste Vestris, had attempted before him. Jean Cocteau, Auguste Rodin, Marcel Proust and a host of others vied to make his acquaintance. It was the Golden Age of Culture.

Diaghilev took his protégé to Karlsbad together with Bakst to allow the former to enjoy a well-earned rest. Afterwards they all continued to Vienna where Waslaw met the poet Gabriele D'Annumzio and Isadora Duncan. Waslaw was far from impressed by her style of dance. It is reputed that it was on that occasion, Isadora Duncan suggested they have a child together. Waslaw had coolly turned the offer down.

A triumphant return to Russia heralded the third season at the Mariinsky Theatre. By then, Diaghilev and Waslaw were inseparable. They shared the same views on art in all its forms and worked together in perfect harmony. Waslaw's repugnance for the physical aspects of their life together was only revealed much later in his Diary.

When the Russian Ballet returned to Paris on their second visit, tickets had been sold out weeks in advance. Parisians were the first to see *Schéhérazade* in which Ida Rubinstein danced the title role and Waslaw the Slave. The ballet was a triumph not only for Bakst but also for Waslaw. He was fêted like a hero, every door was open to him, *le beau monde* competed to have him on their guest list; expensive gifts were lavished upon him. Bronislava was now with the *Ballets Russes* as well and Eleonora had accompanied her to Paris to see both her children dance.

For many months Nijinsky continued to dance at the Mariinsky Theatre in St Petersburg until the last week in January, 1911, when a tempest broke out over his use of costume as Albrecht in *Giselle*. Numerous colourful versions of the incident have been cited, depending on observers' viewpoints at the time and later deductions. What appears certain is that Nijinsky wore the same costume designed for the role (in the first act) by Alexandre Benois, when the company were in Paris. Allegedly, it was in sharp contrast to that of the traditional Russian Renaissance style ballet, the customary trunks worn over the tights having been omitted, thus revealing too much of the dancer's anatomy. The Dowager Empress was in the audience as were many members of the aristocracy. Adverse criticism, possibly fanned by some mischief-maker, who either wished to seek revenge on Diaghilev or who was jealous of Waslaw Nijinsky, was to take on scandalous proportions in an atmosphere already rife with intrigue.

Waslaw was asked to apologise for his near-naked appearance on stage or else he would be expelled. He intransigently refused to apologise and suffered the consequence of immediate dismissal. The management of the Imperial Theatre, awakening to the stark fact that they were losing their finest dancer, retracted and attempted to woo Waslaw back. But to no avail. Diaghilev must have rubbed his hands with delight at the thought that Waslaw was now his – and nobody else's – property and proceeded to lay plans for tours of his ballet company. He had cleverly manipulated it so that Waslaw should refuse the highest offer of salary ever put before a Russian dancer and thus, in the Spring of 1911, Waslaw departed with him for extensive tours of Europe little dreaming at the time that he would never return to Mother Russia. He would have found it an almost impossible choice had he but known because he was devoted to his country and his people. He was to refer to this repeatedly in his notes, 1918-1919:

'I am a Pole through my mother and my father but I am a Russian. I was brought up there. I love Russia...The Russian people are like a child. Must be loved and well-governed. I love the Russian land. I shall build a dam in Russia...Russia is the mother of all states...Russia is not a policy. Russia is love. Russia is not the Bolsheviks. Russia is my mother.'

And so his *Odyssey* commenced but his wanderings were not to bring him back to his homeland. Together with the *Ballets Russes* he toured every major city of Europe. As his fame grew, royalty demanded to see the great Nijinsky perform. Sarah Bernhardt, when she saw Waslaw in *Petrouchka,* proclaimed she had seen the finest actor in the world. Ellen Terry enthused over him when he appeared on the London stage. A slightly sour dissenting note came from Marcel Proust in Paris, who proclaimed he did not like Nijinsky off-stage.

When Waslaw danced *Le Spectre de la Rose* in London – beautifully inspired by Théophile Gautier's poem and considered to be an exquisite classic among Fokine's compositions – his famous last leap, a *tour de force,* rendered Marinelli, the London impresario, speechless, then recovering, he insisted on inspecting Waslaw's shoes to see whether they had rubber soles.

It was in England Waslaw was to make the acquaintance of a woman who became his first real friend – Lady Ripon. She took him protectively under her wing and her deep, genuine fondness for him was clearly expressed in the ensuing years. She introduced him to Lady Ottoline Morrell, hostess and confidante of the Bloomsbury set.

Like other members of the troupe he was thrilled by the exotic atmosphere of Monte Carlo, its richly-coloured and fragrant flora, the blueness of the Mediterranean. Both climatically and scenically this southern strip of coastline, in those days so unspoilt, must have been paradise in his eyes. Tenderhearted and solicitous towards his mother, with whom he so wished to share his good fortune, he arranged for her to come to visit him in Monte Carlo on one occasion.

An odd incident occurred when the company was in Berlin. It was during a rehearsal there that Waslaw received the news that his father Thomas had died, quite unexpectedly, of pneumonia, in Kharkov. Adolph Bolm had proffered his condolences, and had been deeply shocked by Waslaw's reaction. The latter had thanked him, while a faint smile hovered on his lips. The natural assumption was that he was heartless, without feeling. But years later Romola was to point out that he had a reverse reaction to sorrow and joy; tears for joy, a smile for tragedy. A psychological quirk to his nature.

After a whirlwind tour of most of the famous stages of Europe, the company opened the season in Vienna at the Hofoper in mid-February 1912. Towards the end of the company's stay Waslaw became ill but insisted that he continue on to Budapest. And it was there that the whole pattern of his life would slowly but inevitably start to change. Is our life predetermined, no matter what path we take? Would the great Nijinsky's star have shone brighter and longer on the firmament, had he not encountered a young woman, who labelled him her hero and who, with dogged determination, pursued him to reach her own goal? There is no prophet to give the answer.

It was in that same year, on the 29th of May, that *L'Après-midi d'un Faune* had its sensational première, music by Debussy, and the ballet choreographed by Nijinsky; his first. The stark, sensual realism of Waslaw's performance as the Faun had the sophisticated Parisian audience rivetted to their seats in shocked silence. The movements of the Faun in the final seconds that he embraced the veil left behind by one of the nymphs were so explicit as to leave no one present in doubt but that they had observed a sexual act. Pandemonium had broken out and for weeks the ballet was on everyone's lips with both critics and audiences divided – in condemnation or in praise. One of the greatest names to praise Nijinsky's performance was Auguste Rodin who wrote in an article published in *Le Matin* that 'Nijinsky had never been so remarkable as in his latest role...nothing could be more soul-stirring than his movement when he throws himself down and passionately kisses the discarded veil...He is a dancer of genius...'.

The Aga Khan, upon being introduced to Waslaw, immediately invited him to India, an invitation he regretfully was unable to accept. Painters and sculptors queued to immortalise him. Rodin asked him to pose for him at Meudon, and a cordial friendship was struck up between the young dancer and the much older sculptor, of such intensity as to ignite a feeling of jealousy in Sergei Pavlovitch. It is said that he prevented further sittings, having unexpectedly arrived at the studio to find the two blissfully asleep following an apparently wholly innocent drinking bout after a lengthy session in extremely hot weather. Although deprived of the presence of his famous model Rodin must have carried on and completed the statue contrary to what Romola wrote in her book: 'The statue of Nijinsky was unfortunately never finished... The incident was never mentioned, but he (Diaghilev) energetically hindered any further sittings, and because of this he undoubtedly robbed the world of a masterpiece.'

However, as often happens with regard to famous pieces of art, controversy broke out in later years concerning the true identity of the sculpture which today is housed in the Rodin Museum in Paris. I have shown Dr Albert Elsen, Professor of Art History at Stanford University, the photograph of Rodin's 'incomplete' statue and he claims: 'It *is* Nijinsky; it is an étude; it is completed.' Serge Lifar, on the other hand, is said to have disclaimed the statue as being that of Waslaw Nijinsky on the grounds that it instead bore a stronger resemblance to a role that Nijinsky never danced and that hence the model had been another artiste. This information is to be found in a biography about Rodin (*Rodin,* Martigny, 1974).

Waslaw, who hitherto had possessed a very limited wardrobe and had not owned more than a few simple practice costumes, now went on a lavish spending spree and commissioned one of the most fashionable shirtmakers of the day to make him dozens of dance shirts in the finest silks after his own special design. He indulged in hundreds of pairs of dance-shoes. He developed a passion for jewellery, sapphires in particular, and Jean Cocteau presented him with a gold pencil ornamented with a sapphire cabochon.

He became very friendly with Debussy who had been delighted with the sensation created by *The Faun.* Richard Strauss and his wife Paula saw him in Paris. Although he spoke not a word of English and his French was relatively meagre, he struck up a deep and genuine friendship with Lady Ottoline Morrell. Having learnt more and more about him from the books I have read by people who knew him well, and from snatches of conversation with my mother in latter years, I believe he was wholly unimpressed by titles; he was wrapped up in his art for which he lived and breathed; he only felt rapport with people on the same wavelength. His speech was marked by brevity and succinctness; his eyes would furtively seek means of escape from people fawning upon him; only when he danced did the incredible metamorphosis take place; he became bewitched, a godling from another planet. Money in itself meant little or nothing to him and all the sordid details pertaining to contracts and financial matters, he trusted Sergei Pavlovitch to attend to. Creatively, it has been said he was to reach pinnacles above Diaghilev. Nor was the latter going to be able to keep him in the bondage of intimate relationship much longer. Waslaw Nijinsky worshipped womanhood in an old-worldly manner. He adored his mother and his closest friend was his sister Bronia. On the 15th of July 1912 she married a fellow dancer, Alexander Vladimirovitch Kotchetovsky, in the Russian Orthodox Chapel of the Russian Embassy in London. Waslaw was the best man and Eleonora

Bereda the witness; Diaghilev, replacing the father, gave the bride away. It was a sad turning-point for Waslaw. He lost more than a beloved sister, he lost the one person with whom he was united in a a passionate love of ballet. Her marriage unwittingly was to create a barrier between them.

He was too reserved, too inhibited, to take up a flirtation with a member of the company, although he deeply admired Tamara Karsavina. In December 1912 a young woman, Miriam Ramberg (later to take the name of Marie Rambert), a dancer of Polish-Russian origin, joined the *Ballets Russes*. Possibly, she replaced his sister, because with Miriam he was able to discuss his art and found a sympathetic ear. She fell in love with him; his feelings were purely platonic. Diaghilev, on the other hand, always fearing a rival, male or female, saw to it that the trusted Vassily kept a watching eye on Waslaw. It was Romola, who when she met Miriam Ramberg, nestled her way in to her confidence as a means of getting to know more about her idol, Waslaw, his likes and dislikes, his habits, his movements in society. Miriam felt flattered that the young Hungarian aristocrat sought her company and never dreamed that behind it lay an ulterior motive.

The theatre programmes from those brief yet fruitful years embraced London, Paris, Monte Carlo, Berlin, Cologne, Frankfurt... and, of course, Budapest; the curtain went down to deafening applause for *Les Sylphide, Cléopátre, Carnaval, Schéhérazade, Prince Igor, Le Spectre de la Rose, Le Pavillon d'Armide, Giselle, Le Lac des Cygnes, Daphnis et Chloë, Le Dieu Bleu* not to forget *Jeux, Le Sacre du Printemps* and *l'Après-midi d'un Faune*.

Jeux, with music by Debussy and settings by Bakst, did not awaken the enthusiasm amongst critics and audiences that Waslaw had hoped. Possibly he tried too soon to create a ballet free from the traditional paraphernalia. He was later to write '...*The Faun* and *Jeux* were ballets composed by me under the impression of my life with Diaghilev. *The Faun* is myself and *Jeux* the kind of life Diaghilev dreamed of. Diaghilev wanted to have two boys. He told me many times of this aim of his, but I showed him I was angry. Diaghilev wanted to love two boys at the same time and wanted these boys to love him...'.

Romola was present at the Champs-Elysées Théâtre on the 29th of May, 1913, when Waslaw's *Sacre du Printemps* was first performed. It was actually on the anniversary of the première of

78

L'Après midi d'un Faune. The music was by Stravinsky. Everybody had been tense, pulses rising rapidly, but no one had been prepared for the furore that ensued. The fracas that broke out was of such intensity that the police had to be called in to quell the riot because the otherwise dignified audience behaved like street gamins. According to Romola 'Beautifully dressed women were slapping their escorts; one spat in the face of a demonstrator. The Princesse Edmond de Polignac left her box, declaring: "I am sixty years old but this is the first time that anybody has made a fool out of me." Pierre Monteux was desperately striving to continue the music, Gabriel Astruc ordered the lights turned on.' Astruc was then the manager of the Théâtre des Champs-Elysées. In Richard Buckle's version of the incident, he attributes the biting retort to Comtesse René de Pourtalès. Romola went on to say that the din was such one could not hear the orchestra. Waslaw could be seen in the wings, overwrought by emotion. Her heart had gone out to him. To him it was his finest creation to date but once more, people had been unprepared for its new approach and startling innovations. He was accused of too much dangerous experimentation.

Waslaw was reported to have said:

'(Nikolai) Roerich, the great painter and scholar of archaic Russia, inspired me to create this new ballet. I started to search for the primitive architectural clear lines and the creation of a new form of expression. The heavy steps and unusual strides were difficult for the classically trained dancers to execute. Stravinsky finished the musical score by the end of November 1912. When he played it to us at the first rehearsal, we found that part of it could not go on the already existing choreography. We had a rather violent discussion.'

Accompanied by her faithful Anna, Romola travelled hundreds and hundreds of miles across the European continent with a single-minded purpose, to be near Waslaw Nijinsky. She even tried to get reservations on the same train but was only rarely successful. On one occasion fate was kind to her and she claimed she actually found herself in the compartment next to that of *Le Petit* on the midday express going from Gare du Nord to Calais. To Romola the journey literally became a trip to paradise because they stood side by side in the corridor and he saluted her with a few words in broken French.

She, on the other hand, had erupted in a flow of nervous speech, bubbling about England, their mutual destination, so carried away by emotion she did not realise until much later the conversation had been utterly one-sided. But he had smiled at her with his slanted eyes. And hungrily she had taken in every detail of his appearance, every item of clothing he wore with such panache. The cross-channel trip had been very rough. All the passengers suffered from *mal-de-mer*. Poor Anna had thrown herself prostrate onto a berth, unable to move, vowing she would never want to set foot on a ship again. In her book Romola related how she herself had been overcome by nausea from the stuffy confined atmosphere of the cabin and had decided to brave the onslaught of the turbulent sea up on deck, having been advised that fresh air would be the best cure. At first she thought the deck was deserted but then to her immeasurable joy she spotted a lone figure leaning against the railing and to all appearances in high spirits. Again, he greeted her and in pantomime they carried on an animated 'conversation'. No medicine could have cured her faster from her sea-sickness than to be in the presence of her idol.

Diaghilev was waiting impatiently at Victoria while Nijinsky doffed his cap to say goodbye to her. Romola stayed at the Hotel Stafford in St James's but as often as possible she would wine and dine in the company of her friends at the Savoy Grill, the favourite eating place of Sergei Pavlovitch and Waslaw. To be fair to her, she did not shirk her lessons; in fact maestro Cecchetti warned her not to overwork.

The season in London was a fantastic success. Romola thrilled to every curtain call *Le Petit* received. How could any of the characters involved in those glorious moments dream that the performances they witnessed would be the last that Londoners would see of Nijinsky with the Diaghilev Company? In what could be likened to carnival spirit, bouquets and programmes were hurled onto the stage. The cultural élite took the greatest dancer of them all to their bosom. He was their pampered darling. The rumble of any adverse comments on the *Ballets Russes* performances was drowned in the praise lavished by most of the critics. Stories about Waslaw – what he said, his wit, his perception, his latest daring and bold interpretation of a role, his liaison with Sergei Pavlovitch, their quarrels, the latter's tears of genuine pain when the favourite disagreed with him – all this and much, much more made delicious titbits to mull over in the exclusive clubs of London. The God of Dance was then not more than twenty-four years old.

Although during this period Romola was at no time part of the côterie to which Waslaw belonged, subsequent events surely must prove that he for a long time had been aware of the willowy shadow that followed him all over. Every detail of her face and figure must have registered itself in his brain, even if only subconsciously.

Then came the rumour that the Ballet was soon to go on a South American tour. Romola's heart would have skipped a beat as she posed to herself the vital question of how she could induce the *Maestro* to engage her as a member of the troupe. She refused to accept that at this stage her 'quarry' would escape. Had she not sacrificed her secure, comfortable niche in society to be near him – Waslaw Nijinsky? With indefatigable determination she set about plotting how to accompany them. Once that barrier was overcome, she also had to gain permission from her family. As luck would have it, a number of the dancers did not wish to make the long journey. The *Maestro* had to look around for replacements and again Romola's friendship with him paid off. He convinced Diaghilev she should come along. To win Emilia over proved rather more difficult. When she learned of her headstrong daughter's plans, she hastily packed a suitcase and with Oskar in tow took the boat train to London. To Romola's intense relief, Baron Dmitri de Gunsbourg, patron of the Ballet and its treasurer, assured Emilia that he would keep a protective eye on her Molly. Emilia had long before been introduced to him through mutual friends and she trusted him implicitly. Later events were to show that Gunsbourg was a steadfast ally of Romola's. Drobetsky, too, a charming Austro-Polish man, married to the dancer Sophia Pflanz, promised to look after her. And thus a victorious young woman reserved a first-class cabin for herself while Anna was given the second-class ticket to which she, Romola, was entitled as a junior member of the troupe. Romola had carefully seen to it that her stateroom would be in the proximity of Waslaw's.

The company dispersed to enjoy a brief two weeks' holiday before setting off. Romola visited her old governess who lived in Sussex. There, in the peaceful surroundings of the English countryside she must have day-dreamed about the forthcoming journey together with the man who intrigued her more than any other living mortal; she had carefully diagnosed her feelings and firmly resolved to become part of his life. Many years later Richard Buckle claimed she had confessed to him she had not been in love with Waslaw when she married him. Perhaps the truth is, that like any adolescent today who idolises her favourite pop star, she worshipped her God of Dance. According to Buckle she learned to love Waslaw later because he was such a good man. Surely her tireless crusade on his behalf after he retreated from the outside world bears witness to how much she cherished him; he was the pivot of her existence.

Waslaw had gone to Baden-Baden in the company of Diaghilev. They had been joined there by Alexandre Benois and had settled down to a working session on a forthcoming ballet. As a distraction Waslaw had been taken on a tour of notable palaces and churches in the region. And now yet another 'last time' was enacted unbeknown to the two principals involved because Sergei Pavlovitch and Waslaw were never again to be alone together.

On August 15th, 1913, the S.S. *Avon* sailed from Southampton. As the shore line disappeared from view, Romola was overcome by misgivings as to the wisdom of her action because she had suddenly been unnerved by a sharp feeling of loneliness. It was her first real sea voyage; the luxurious ocean liner's size overwhelmed her; she could not speak a word of Russian and the other members of the troupe were already divided into little cliques to which she did not belong. But she sought solace and strength in the thought that she was to be near *him* for weeks to come. Imagine her anguish when she discovered that the sole object of this mad adventure was not on board. Nor was Diaghilev. The appalling thought struck her that they might have decided to take a faster ship, following the example of Karsavina who was leaving by an Italian liner in the company of her husband. In near hysteria Romola rushed down to Anna, who was by then busily unpacking and making the cabin more home-like for her mistress. She poured out her distress and bewilderment over this blow to her well-laid plans. But then, taking herself in hand, she went up to study the passenger list and once more her heart leapt with joy and relief. Waslaw and Diaghilev were to board the ship at Cherbourg. As it turned out, the latter did not come. The official reason for his absence on this important tour was that the Impresario had vital business matters to attend to in Europe and it was not until much later that Waslaw confided the real reason to Romola. Diaghilev had a horror of water and had blankly refused to undertake the ocean voyage. Each time that he and Waslaw had crossed the Channel Sergei Pavlovitch had broken out in paroxysms of fear. Years previously in St Petersburg a gypsy had foretold that he would die on water.*

So again, fate played into Romola's hands. Her chief adversary was out of the way. Together with many of the other passengers she rushed up on deck to catch a glimpse of Waslaw as he boarded the ship. He looked carefree and debonair in his fashionable Parisian attire. With the ever faithful Vassily at his side he vanished in the direction of his stateroom.

According to Romola's own account twenty-one days lay ahead of her to make her conquest. She shook off all reserve and with abandon threw herself into the social life on board, spending much of her time in the company of Dmitri Gunsbourg and Adolf Bolm. Their little group also included Ekaterina Oblokova (Gunsbourg's mistress) and Josefina Kovalevska. Slowly but surely everyone slipped into the leisurely rhythmic routine of shipboard life. Although she rather disliked walking, Romola spent hours on the promenade deck, strolling past the deck-chair in which Nijinsky would recline, engrossed in reading his favourite Russian books or jotting down notes. She confessed it exasperated her to the point of tears that he never once appeared to take notice of her in that way which had so delighted her on previous rare occasions.

Shipboard activities were enlivened by visits ashore whenever the *Avon* docked at various ports. Lisbon was the last port of call in Europe. But Romola's plans to be in the same party as Nijinsky on going ashore were foiled. Likewise, when the ship anchored on the roads off Madeira, Romola was shattered at not being given the opportunity to join her idol's party, which included Rhené-Baton, the famous Parisian conductor, who had conducted the last five performances of the *Ballets Russes* at Drury Lane. It was he, according to Romola, who so admired Nijinsky that he had shouted *'Quel enfant adorable, quel simplicité, c'est moi qui serai votre nana pendant le voyage'* when they had met on board the first morning of the trip. And, true to his word, he had shown loving devotion to his 'child' throughout the journey as only a doting nurse could.

The excursion on Madeira very nearly ended in disaster for Romola and her little group, comprised of Bolm, Gunsbourg,

* Authors's note: Oddly enough, Diaghilev died surrounded by water – in Venice in 1929, although water was not the cause of his death.

Oblokova, Pflanz, Kovalevska and a few others. The merrymakers decided to have lunch at the hotel on top of the hill reached by the funicular. There they had a panoramic view of the picturesque island. Chatting and drinking, they became oblivious of time and the gathering dusk. It was only when they heard the piercing signal from the ship far below that they realised they were in grave danger of missing the boat. Little comfort was gained from the islanders' bland assurance that another ship was due to pass by in three weeks' time. Romola felt thwarted; her blood ran cold at the thought of not seeing Nijinsky again until Buenos Aires. They all made a hazardous run from the sleighs to the landing pier, only to see the last launch vanish in the distance. Frantically, they started screaming at the top of their lungs; each one had his or her personal reasons for wanting to be with the ship when it sailed. Finally, they managed to attract the attention of a local boatman and after some haggling over payment, they were speedily rowed toward the *Avon*. By then their absence had been noticed by Gunsbourg, and a motor-launch was on its way to pick them up. Romola must have heaved a sigh of relief upon entering her stateroom and one can almost certainly assume that she would have rushed over to her picture of *The Infant Jesus of Prague* and humbly thanked him. It was to Him she always turned when in need.

To the soothing accompaniment of the billowing waves against the ship's sides, the hours of the days slipped by; during the afternoons most of the company were resting in their cabins or sunken deep in armchairs in one of the comfortable saloons, engrossed in their favourite literature. Not so, Waslaw Nijinsky. It had become a source of growing agitation to Romola that she rarely saw him on deck but she soon uncovered his secret. Near the main dining-room was a piano and it was here that he and Rhené-Baton were working on the Bach ballet; the latter at the piano and *Le Petit* leaning against it, his eyes closed, his fingers moving as he composed. Romola sat huddled at the bottom of the stairs, listening and watching, only to be brusquely told to leave by one of the stewards. Doggedly, she returned the following day to be asked by Baton to depart. Surprisingly, however, Nijinsky had gestured that she might remain. One can only conclude that he was quite aware, indeed, of the young Hungarian girl, who so relentlessly pursued him. In fact, Romola's insistence that they first 'met' through an introduction arranged by Chavez differs from her sister-in-law Bronia's reminiscences in which she wrote that already in a letter posted from Madeira, Waslaw had mentioned being together with a beautiful young woman who was also alone on board.

Quite early another morning she discovered purely by chance a small crowd of passengers gathered in one corner of the upper deck. They were admiring Waslaw, who was practising. Williams, an Englishman and the dancer's masseur, was present. Romola made his acquaintance and feigned interest in his profession and his hobbies. Never before having shown the slightest inclination to be a fan of either sports or athletics, even less the various techniques of massage, she proceeded to draw Williams out on his pet subjects and his family and in this circumspect way, she also learned more about the body of Nijinsky, every perfectly controlled muscle. Williams had apparently abandoned a previous position to travel with the dancer and to give him an hour's massage daily.

Romola was not at a loss for admirers and although she was completely uninterested in them, she would use her *beaux* shamelessly in order to attract the attention of Nijinsky; parading up and down the deck arm in arm with one or the other, flirtatious and gay in her demeanour yet inwardly despondent when he seemingly did not notice her.

How exasperated she must have been as she tore off leaf after leaf in her calendar and saw with growing consternation that the voyage was rapidly drawing to a close. To ease her tension she participated in the usual shipboard rounds of dances and masquerades; the ceremonial baptism by Father Neptune as they crossed the Equator, the occasion being celebrated with a generous flow of champagne. Then, finally one evening, the miracle happened. According to her story she was strolling with a small party on deck when one of them, Chavez, an Argentinian-French couturier with whom she had struck up a friendship, taunted her that she apparently was afraid of the great Nijinsky. Would she not like to be introduced to him? She had been taken off her guard and possibly felt humiliated over the fact she had indeed been introduced to him on previous occasions but that he had ostensibly dismissed her from his thoughts. Chavez had laughingly pulled a defiant Romola in the direction of Waslaw, who was leaning against the railing cooling himself with a small black fan ornamented with a rose painted in gold.

No setting could have been more romantic. It was moonlight. The *Avon* was gliding through the calm waters. Not a breeze was stirring and the only sound to break the tropical stillness aside from the hum of conversation here and there on the decks was the gentle throbbing of the ship's engines.

Let Romola describe in her own words that moment when she came face to face with her *Dieu de la Dance.*

'I was trembling as Chavez said, *"Monsieur Nijinsky, permettez moi de vous presenter Mademoiselle de Pulszky."* He did not move; his eyes just closed with an imperceptible *nuance* and he slightly inclined his head. Kovalevska at once began to explain to him who I was and all about my love of dancing. Nijinsky listened without saying a word...I felt a chaos of emotion, saw nothing and nobody anymore except the dark graceful silhouette of Nijinsky and his fascinating eyes. I suddenly heard myself speaking. *"Je veux vous remercier que vous avez élevé la danse à la hauteur des autres arts."* Kovalevska translated. Suddenly he (Nijinsky) looked at the small ring I wore. I followed his gaze, and, pulling it off my finger, I passed it to him, explaining: "My father brought it from Egypt; it is a talisman supposed to bring luck. My mother gave it to me as I left with the Russian Ballet." It was a green-gold serpent whose head was crushed by a scarab... Nijinsky held it for one moment and then put it on my finger, saying in Polish, "It will bring you happiness, surely." We all four of us began to walk around the deck... For a long time we watched (the motion of the sea) in silence. Then I began to talk in French, choosing the easiest words about dance, music and Wagner, whose work I idolised... I don't know if he understood a word of what I said, but he seemed to listen attentively. I had to talk to hide my nervousness, my confusion. Then Chavez called us.'

What puzzles me, however, is the fact Romola throughout her record of those early years together with Waslaw emphasised time and again their lack of communication due to his inability to speak French. It was obligatory for all pupils at the Imperial Theatre School to study French and although foreign languages may not have been a subject in which he excelled, he did receive 9 points for French on his reportcard during his school year 1906-07. (The reportcard is in the Nijinska Archives).

I would like to think that Waslaw himself instigated the introduction. After all, Chavez frankly claimed that he was on extremely friendly terms with Nijinsky and it is evident that Romola had excited the latter's interest in her. Decades later, after the success of her first biography on Waslaw, Romola made it known she was going to write a more outspoken book dealing with her own family, her childhood etc., and about Waslaw and herself. I found a folder with the 'outlines' of certain chapters, some handwritten like the 'Léhar' story, others typed in English. Fifteen pages, largely comprised of an analysis of Diaghilev, his ballet company and its stars, flows from third person singular into first person, i.e. Waslaw talking.

'Maestro Cecchetti requested Diaghilev to take along his private pupil who travelled the last six months with our company. She was a Hungarian society girl, the daughter of an eminent family and Hungary's greatest dramatic actress. When Diaghilev asked me in Vienna, past Winter, if he should take her along, I told him not to, I disapproved of any dilettante to join us. But Diaghilev felt it was good publicity. I saw her many times, going to my training with the Maestro. I saw her at the theatre backstage watching with religious awe our dancing, Pavlova's and my practising. I noticed she loved our art. I met her again on the boat, the *Avon,* on which we sailed for the Argentine. On the boat one evening when we went to the steerage to watch the Ball of the Italian peasants, Kovalevska translated to me that Mademoiselle de Pulszky had the little pillow my mother gave me and which I forgot in the Monte Carlo hotel. That thinking I would be happy to get it back, she brought it along for me. I understood that her affection was not only for my art, but also for me. Then and there I decided to marry her.'

Was that perhaps the true story? Romola has confessed in *Nijinsky* how she would walk around the Place de la Casino in Monte Carlo, her eyes fixed on Waslaw for hours at a stretch as he supped on the terrace of the Hôtel de Paris with Sergei Pavlovitch or Chaliapine. She must also have haunted the corridors of the Hôtel Riviera Palace, where he was staying. What could have been easier for a love-sick girl than to stealthily enter his room, perhaps while it was being cleaned by a chamber-maid.

She went back to her cabin and knelt before the picture of the Infant Jesus of Prague. One wish had now been fulfilled. She had formally been introduced to Nijinsky. But she became conscience-stricken over the fact she had been totally wrapped up in self-interest, that she had prayed to her Saviour with only one purpose in mind, to have Nijinsky all to herself. And so she changed her tactics and for long hours into the morning beseeched Him to forgive Nijinsky his sins, to give him happiness and protect him from the evils of this world. Nonetheless, uppermost in her mind was the nagging fear that Diaghilev's hold on his favourite would be a hindrance to the realisation of her own hopes.

The following day her optimistic and light-hearted mood changed rapidly to melancholy as Nijinsky with distant politeness acknowledged her greeting when they came face to face on deck. Gone was the radiant glow of the previous evening. Her spirits must have slumped to a low ebb, throwing her into a gamut of mixed emotions. The voyage was rapidly drawing to a close and she was no nearer her objective.

Did she perhaps seek strength from the slim leather-bound volume of poetry she always brought with her?

'How do I love thee; Let me count the ways. I love thee to the depth and breadth and height
My soul can reach...'.

Emilia, never having forgotten her initiation by Charlie into the world of English literature had wielded much influence over her daughters' choice of reading material when they were growing up and among Romola's most loved were *Sonnets from the Portuguese* by Elizabeth Barrett Browning.

And then, according to Romola, an unbelievable event transpired. On Saturday, the 30th of August, to be precise. The *Avon* was steaming along the coast of Brazil on course for Rio de Janeiro. Romola had gone to the bar to have a drink and a chat with a few of her friends, when Dmitri Gunsbourg intervened, insisting he must talk to her privately on a matter of utmost urgency. Unnaturally for him, he appeared to be in a state of acute agitation. Romola became alarmed, fearing she had committed some unpardonable mistake when practising her dance routine.

She followed Gunsbourg to a secluded corner on deck. Striking a formal pose he uttered one sentence 'Romola Carlovna, as Nijinsky cannot speak to you himself, he has requested me to ask for your hand in marriage.'

Again, in her own words, she stared at him in disbelief and then, losing all control of herself, fulminated against him, accusing him of playing a ghastly joke on her. Sobbing, she turned on her heels and rushed down to her cabin where she locked herself in, succumbing to a state of near hysteria, shame welling up in her as she realised that her infatuation for Nijinsky had been too transparent, that the entire troupe had been ridiculing her behind her back all the time. She made up her mind to remain in the cabin until the ship docked in Buenos Aires and that she would then return home by the fastest possible boat.

Frantic knocking on her door went unheeded and not even Anna was permitted entry. Are we to believe Romola's version of events, Dmitri Gunsbourg must have felt frustrated in his attempts to act as go-between. Finally he had slipped a note through Romola's cabin door to the effect that Nijinsky was impatiently awaiting a reply. It had the desired effect. Romola pulled herself together, allowed her faithful Anna in and with her nimble assistance refreshed her tear-drenched, tousled appearance. Attired in one of her most attractive evening-gowns she swept into the saloon but her suitor was nowhere to be seen. She went up on deck, most probably to catch a breath of fresh air and to calm down, when from behind the shadows Nijinsky approached her. His proposal was short and to the point – spoken in the few words of French he had mastered: *'Mademoiselle, voulez-vous, vous et moi?'* Her reply had been as simple, *'Oui, oui, oui.'* With those few words the destiny of two young people was sealed. The news of their forthcoming union would reverberate throughout the artistic world and cause incredulity, scepticism, anger, or sorrow depending on the nature of the association of the people concerned with either of the two. In later years there would be those whose voices rose in dissent over Romola's version of the event, those who claimed Waslaw Nijinsky had been ruthlessly snared into the proposal, skilfully manipulated by Romola, possibly in conjunction with her mainstays – of whom Gunsbourg was the foremost – who perhaps for one reason or another would wish that the dancer's liaison with Diaghilev be severed. The dead cannot rise to defend themselves, they are long since silenced. All that remain are Romola's own words and Waslaw's. She never wavered on the issue of the proposal. In his Notes, written in Guardamunt in 1918, my father plainly declared his feelings for his wife time and again on the rambling pages. '*I do not wish my wife ill. I love her more than anyone...*'. And that was at a stage where his conscious mind was beginning to blur and he was speaking from the inner recesses of his soul without fear of retaliation because he was then beyond such actions.

Surely, it seems plausible that he, of whom it had been proven longed for the company of women, felt it was a golden opportunity to discard the shackles that bound him to a man for whom he was later to divulge he harboured a secret revulsion.

On board, however, Romola woke up the next morning barely able to fathom that her dream had come true. Josefina Kovalevska was the first to rush in and congratulate her. Many of her colleagues were still too stunned by the tidings to do likewise. Mim Ramberg had broken down and cried bitterly. For a long time she had secretly harboured a passion for Nijinsky. It was he who had advised her while on board to break off with the *Ballets Russes* and go her own way. And despite the fact that their delicate bond of friendship also broke, she did follow his sage advice; as Marie Rambert she founded the famous British ballet company, Ballet Rambert.

Many eyebrows had been raised. In the uproar that ensued unsubtle questions had surfaced. What would *Chinchilla,* the great Impresario, say? What would his reaction be? Was Romola so artless, she had no inkling about the true relationship between her fiancé and Diaghilev? The unattached ballerinas in the troupe must have become livid with jealousy. A number of them had tried to attract Nijinsky's attention but when he had failed to respond, they had assumed he was one hundred percent homosexual and wholly devoted to Diaghilev. Adolf Bolm was perhaps the only one genuinely concerned about Romola's future happiness. There was a special affinity between them and he felt responsible for her as a friend of her family. He did his utmost to warn her, to impress on her what a very complex individual Nijinsky was, however charming and kindly he could appear; he pointed out the language barrier – as yet they were unable to communicate with each other except in a few halting words of French and by mime. Was she fully aware that Nijinsky's friendship with Diaghilev was far stronger than a purely professional one? Almost brutally, he tried to convince her that her fiancé emotionally was without normal human feelings, a condition Bolm had witnessed on innumerable occasions. His warning fell on deaf ears. Romola took no heed of what he was trying to convey. She floated on air. Perhaps she saw herself as the victor in a duel, a duel in which she had used all her cunning.

No stage set could have been more suitable than the beautiful, exotic city of Rio de Janeiro in which to celebrate an engagement. Let us assume that like any carefree young couple Romola and her betrothed enjoyed a few fleeting moments of sheer happiness there. Together with Kovalevska as their interpreter they set forth on a tour of exploration but first they headed for one of the jewellery shops along a wide boulevard where two wedding bands were selected, to be called for that evening when the inscriptions would be ready. They then proceeded up the Sylvestre Mountain where they had lunch in tropical splendour.

'We were very gay during our lunch. It was the first time I ever sat with Nijinsky at a table. We decided to drive through the dense forests, with their towering, orchid-laden trees, amidst flowers, millions and millions, quaint unwholesome-looking but sensual blooms, in all kinds of shades – violent reds, greens, blues, we were lost, plunged into this ocean of foliage. The air was tepid and caressing, and suddenly, by certain turns of the narrow road, a stream of icy-cold current hit us for a second. It was all like a dream, this drive, all the time sitting between Kovalevska and Nijinsky.'

On the way back to the steamer the rings were collected. The engraving was plain: *Vaslav – Romola 1/9/1913*.

The two were surrounded by the entire troupe upon their return on board. They risked being crushed as everybody crowded around them, questions on their lips demanding answers. Utterly exhausted by the events of the day, Romola decided to retire and Nijinsky escorted her to her cabin. She quivered with apprehension – would Nijinsky follow her in? Theoretically, she had by now learned the facts of life but in practice she was still as innocent as when Baron Hatvany had tried to seduce her on that fatal week-end many months ago. In Hungary it was the custom that an engagement signalled the right to an intimate relationship prior to the actual marriage ceremony. But Nijinsky merely smiled, kissed her hand, before turning on his heels and departing. Could one not reasonably surmise that Bolm's warning words had momentarily flickered through her mind. Later she was to learn of the deep, almost sacred respect Nijinsky felt for womanhood.

The ensuing day, practical formalities had to be attended to, the most vital one a cable to Emilia Márkus from Nijinsky, asking for her daughter's hand in marriage. The request, translated into fluent French by Dmitri Gunsbourg, was an important hurdle to overcome as it was required by the laws of Hungary. There had been some discussion of a wedding ceremony being performed on board ship but Romola had set her heart on a proper church wedding. Both she and Waslaw were Roman Catholics. That same evening Baron Gunsbourg hosted a gala dinner in honour of the engaged couple. In true Russian style the champagne flowed freely and congratulations were once more showered on the two.

The *Avon* continued the last lap of its voyage up the Rio la Plata where the anchor was dropped in the port of Buenos Aires on Saturday, the 6th of September 1913. The company dispersed to find their way to their various hotels. Momentarily, the practicalities at hand had to be dispensed with. Nijinsky and Romola were both to stay at The Majestic; he in a suite and she in a room on another floor.

On Sunday, Romola joined with some others on a tour of the city and its environs. As rehearsals were to commence on Monday, Nijinsky had gone straight to the *Teatro Colón,* the city's splendid Opera House. Already on Monday morning Romola was to be rudely roused from her starry-eyed reveries when she was called to the theatre by Nijinsky to practise some steps. An entirely new side to her future husband unfolded before her. In her book she was to write of the psychological stress she suffered. She had been aghast to find herself confronted by a total stranger. He treated her as impersonally as if he had never laid eyes on her until then. She fully expected him to shout abuse at her. Instead he handled her with patience and courtesy when she stumbled and showed her the correct step. It was then and there she learned what a hard taskmaster he was; driven by the sole aim to ensure perfection regardless of whom he was coaching. In the same manner, she was never permitted to enter his dressingroom prior to a performance after they were married.

While the ballet troupe were busily engaged in rehearsals and practising, it befell Dmitri Gunsbourg to finalise the arrangements for the wedding. Complications arose; the respective embassies had to be involved as Nijinsky was a Russian subject, Romola, Hungarian by birth. Too, she was under age. Oblokova had taken it upon herself to help Romola with her *trousseau* and to buy wedding gifts. Somehow or other, Gunsbourg pulled the right strings and the immediate problems evaporated. He saw to it that the young couple went to Confession as otherwise the Church would refuse to marry them. The priest could not have had much joy out of Nijinsky's confession. The latter spoke Russian and Polish, a smattering of French, the priest only Spanish. Romola abhorred confessions; she always stoutly declared she had no sins to regret. On this occasion the priest wanted her to promise that she would prevent Nijinsky from dancing in *Schéhérazade,* a ballet deemed as wholly immoral by the Church.

Only a handful of the colleagues closest to them attended the civil ceremony which was held at the City Hall on Wednesday, 10th of September. Romola was dressed in blue with a bunch of soft roses pinned to her waist, giving her a splash of colour.

'A squat Spaniard came out with a huge ribbon in the Argentine colours across his chest. He looked terribly formal, and stood before us. On the desk full of flowers stood a crucifix on a dark green blotter, which was covered with a huge parchment document on which a lady was floating, holding a band on which our names and the date were printed in huge red letters. It was the smartest certificate of marriage, in full accordance with Argentinian taste. Then this kind old gentleman asked questions in Spanish. Baton pulled out a notebook and gave dates and names in French, which were immediately translated to the Mayor by the official interpreter. The two ministers confirmed it in Spanish. Then Waslaw was questioned and asked in Russian. I talked in Hungarian and French. Finally the Mayor made a speech in Spanish, to which we listened very attentively. We were made to sign the document which made us man and wife.'

After the ceremony a wedding breakfast was held at the Majestic Hotel, at which the entire company was present. Toasts were proposed, glib-tongued speeches made, only a few of them were genuinely sincere. From her own account, one gathers she was sublimely unaware of the stilted atmosphere. Only through reading the comments made much later by impartial witnesses, does one get an inkling of the strong undercurrent of doom that prevailed. Most of those assembled had gnawing misgivings about the marriage. The day that was to have been the happiest in Romola's life could perhaps more honestly be described as an ordeal, brought on by more *mondain* matters. Already exhausted she had to face a superstitious Anna, who adamantly refused to allow her to get married in church in a pale blue dress that she, Romola, had thought would be suitable. Anna had ranted on about the colour being unlucky. To preserve the peace Romola had capitulated and found herself frantically rushing around the exclusive boutiques with Oblokova and Madame Baton in tow. After a frenzied search they found a full-length cream-coloured gown of thick silk. White satin shoes and a white turban with a veil completed the bridal outfit. The turban replaced the traditional orange blossoms unknown to all the florists they visited.

By the time she returned to the hotel, she found Gunsbourg almost in tears. By then his nerves must have been strained, taking into account all his efforts to ensure that this rather odd marriage could take place. To crown it all, the bride would now be late. Romola made a quick change worthy of her actress mother. It was fast approaching seven o'clock; the wedding guests – members of the *Ballets Russes,* many dignitaries, and notables from Argentinian society – were impatiently waiting in the Iglesia St Miguel.

Utterly dazed, Romola arrived and was led down the aisle to the altar on the arm of Dmitri Gunsbourg to the wedding march from *Lohengrin.* The gown weighed heavily on her fragile shoulders and the turban fitted too snugly. In a blur she observed the face of her husband-to-be, his look of anxiety that she was late.

'Was it true or only a dream? Could it be really possible that in a few moments, before God and men, I was to be given in marriage to the *Spectre de la Rose.*'

The perfume from the exquisite flowers that decorated the sanctuary was almost overpowering. She glanced furtively at the man standing by her side; he was impeccably attired in a formal suit, his anxious expression had by then given way to one of solemnity. The two young persons were joined together by a bond of such mag-

94

nitude it was never to desert the bride, although the path that should only have been strewn with roses was later to be paved with thistles. The sensational marriage made the headlines internationally. A beautiful Hungarian aristocrat was at last united in holy matrimony to her Russian-Polish God of Dance, the great Nijinsky.

In the carriage which took the newlyweds back to the hotel, Waslaw gently placed a superb yellow-pink pearl ring over the wedding band on Romola's finger. There was no conversation between them. Instead of retiring from the world to their suite, they faced a bizarre wedding night. Waslaw had hurried to his rooms to change, Romola to hers. It was the dress rehearsal of *Schéhérazade*. Romola was to dance Almée; Nijinsky, of course, the Golden Slave. Did the memory of what she had half-promised the priest at Confession flicker through her mind that evening? One wonders.

At the *Teatro Colón* the corps de ballet rushed up to Romola, eager to see her beautiful ring. Romola had made herself ready, waiting for her cue. Just as she was about to go on stage, she became paralysed with fear at the thought of dancing with her husband. Something must have snapped within her because she was totally unaware of how she made her entrance and then to her acute embarrassment she fell headlong on the stage. She was forced to remain in her prone position while the others continued as though nothing had happened. Romola believed that this unfortunate incident had gone unobserved by the audience.

After the last curtain call Romola retreated to her dressingroom, changed, and hurried back to the hotel. The feeling of having made a fool of herself in front of her husband must have left her unstrung. And she faced yet another bewildering ordeal that day. To be alone at last with Nijinsky, her husband. She was about to spend her first night with him, the ecstatic moment she had visualised for so long. How often had she not knelt down in prayer in front of her Little Jesus of Prague? And now that ecstatic moment was imminent. But was she prepared for it? What was marriage and the physical act of love all about? The strict and sheltered upbringing of her childhood at the turn of the century had not clearly defined the answers to her.

Anna had seen to it that Romola's room was ready to receive a guest for supper. A round table had been romantically set for two and a meal had been ordered. Romola slipped into a Poiret gown in shades of palest turquoise while Anna helped put her silky auburn hair like a crown on her head and secured it with a fine silvery bead. As soon as Nijinsky arrived, Anna had discreetly excused herself.

'We ate in silence...I was getting more and more nervous, being left alone with Nijinsky. But he only smiled and served me attentively. We were both so embarrassed that we could not even express ourselves in pantomime. And when, after supper, Nijinsky kissed my hand and left me, I was so relieved that I almost cried from thankfulness.'

Romola went to the theatre the following morning to practise as usual. She studiously tried to ignore the knowing smirks that greeted her by some members of the ballet. She could not help reflecting rather ruefully what they would have said, had they been aware of the fact that her bridegroom had not stayed the night.

As the days progressed, Romola regained some of her assurance and it was Bolm who with tact and friendliness helped her overcome her stage fright. But she was again and again to experience the metamorphosis that came over Nijinsky when he was at the theatre. Everything around him ceased to exist except the part he was portraying. It made no difference to their working relationship that he and Romola were now man and wife. He continued simply to ignore her or treat her coolly like a stranger. On these occasions an immense void separated them. A genius, wholly wrapped up in his world of dance, he was unapproachable.

Yet every morning he sent Romola a wonderful bouquet of white roses. And she would join him for lunch and dinner, most often in the company of Dmitri as translator. Slowly they both grew to know each other better. Nijinsky's detached manner would give way to laughter and mischievousness on their outings. Together they would explore the Zoological Gardens and enjoy studying the motley mixture of animals and vibrantly-coloured birds. On those excursions he opened Romola's eyes to the beauty of the world around them and he would be relaxed and smiling like an eager young boy.

It was not long before Romola had moved down to Waslaw's magnificent suite on the floor below hers – five rooms comprising a dining-room, two small drawing-rooms and two bedrooms. Nearly every evening after a performance upon their return to the hotel he would sit down and write a letter to his mother Eleonora Bereda. And then, at last:

'My fear of Nijinsky began to vanish. The charm of his personality, the tenderness of his whole being, radiated so much goodness, such beauty, that the evening he chose to remain I felt I was making an offering on the altar of happiness.'

CHAPTER 3

MARRIED LIFE: ON A NEW PATH

How did those who had been closely linked to Romola and Waslaw accept the news of their marriage?

Sergei Pavlovitch Diaghilev received a cable from Waslaw, the contents of which were unbelievably artless: he announced his marriage to Romola and in the same sentence proclaimed his undying friendship to Diaghilev and his devotion to the *Ballets Russes*. It showed all too clearly Waslaw's childlike outlook on life, how far removed he was from understanding the basic human emotions of his fellow men.

It has been said that Diaghilev erupted into paroxysms of rage and jealousy at having lost his lover to a girl, whom ironically, he himself had engaged against his better judgment. He was powerless to intervene, the act was *fait accompli;* the headlines in the international press screamed out the sensational news of the marriage of the century, each with its own interpretation of the union.

Diaghilev's pride was wounded beyond repair, although rumour would have it that he had already earlier that year become disenchanted with Nijinsky as a lover. But he must have feared losing his star performer and choreographer. Sadly, he was to take his revenge after the South American tour was over. Under the pretext that Nijinsky had breached his contract, missing a performance in Montevideo, (categorically denied by Romola), a cable was sent to Waslaw while visiting his in-laws in Budapest terminating his services with the *Ballets Russes*. Hell hath no fury like a *man* scorned. Albeit, unwittingly, was not perhaps Diaghilev to a certain extent instrumental in bringing about the spiritual death of one of the greatest dancers of all times?

Eleonora Bereda, Waslaw's mother, how did she react? I have only his sister Bronislava's description of her state of mind. Bronia had first been made aware of the event when the headlines had leapt out at her from the front page of a newspaper she was reading during breakfast. She was spontaneously overjoyed for his sake and fervently hoped it would heal the rift that had sprung up between them after her own marriage. Eleonora Bereda, on the other hand, had been deeply distressed. Her son, otherwise so thoughtful and loving, had not sought her consent and blessing. It was not until a few days later that she was to receive a cable signed by 'Vatsa and Romuska' confirming the marriage. Bronia claimed that Romola, under duress, was to admit that she had been a party to preventing Waslaw from giving advance notice to his family and, indeed, Sergei Pavlovitch; it stemmed from the fear they would prevent it. Waslaw's mother was of the old school – tradition and parental respect meant everything – and thus she was inconsolable, unable to fathom that her beloved Waslaw had not confided in her. From Bronia's recollections it appears that Eleonora Bereda recalled that a young woman had persistently turned up next to her during performances in London and Paris. She had been extremely agitated by her presence. Now she pieced two and two together and realised it must have been Romola. Again, wounded pride and jealousy raised their ugly heads. She found it impossible to accept the news gracefully and became gripped by forebodings that the marriage would end unhappily. But one must understand her hostility. Waslaw had been close to her. He had been her joy and strength when her husband Thomas deserted her; when Stassik had to be committed to a psychiatric hospital.

She was destined to meet her daughter-in-law under the most tragic of circumstances, when in 1921 she fled from Russia to Vienna in the company of Bronislava and her two children, Irina, who was then seven, and Leo, who was two. By then Waslaw was in the Steinhof Sanatorium, withdrawn into his private realm. When his mother rushed forward in eager anticipation to embrace him, he merely stared at her blankly, without a glimpse of recognition. Only after Bronia persevered with a discussion on dance, her own ballet in particular, did his eyes light up.

In Budapest, Emilia had been better prepared for the announcement of the wedding. After all, it was she who had to cable her agreement to the ceremony. Despite that, she, too, had become apprehensive and asked herself had she done the right thing.

Oti-Papa was to tell of that fateful day, when Emilia had to face the first interviewer from the press. Journalists had besieged her with requests for interviews, clamoured for details she was unable to produce. The first audience she granted was to a young man eager to get as sensational a scoop as possible for one of Hungary's leading magazines. Regally dressed in an ankle length pure silk gown over which she had casually thrown a thick velvet robe, the actress answered the barrage of questions hurled at her. When he finally departed, Emilia collapsed, unable to carry on the charade any longer, trouper though she was. She clung to Oskar for solace, dissolved in tears. She had been flooded with misgivings that Nijinsky was not the right husband for her Molly; a genius of ballet, unquestionably, but would he bring her daughter security and happiness? When she had met him, she had recognised in him the pure artist, who, if need be, would ruthlessly sacrifice everything else in the pursuit of his career. And, naturally, the titillating stories circulating about him and Diaghilev had not gone unheeded in Hungary. Like Eleonora, Emilia had a foreboding of disaster.

Oblivious to the fire and fury that their marriage had created, the newly-weds were unreservedly preoccupied with each other. According to Romola, her husband 'became himself at last. His genius had always bloomed irresistibly, but now Nijinsky himself grew up and became a man...' She carried on with pride to say Waslaw danced 'more wonderfully than ever'. Like any young couple in love, they wished to probe each other's minds and hearts; there was no abatement in their discussions on matters of the most intimate kind. Yet one must remember the language barrier was still a hurdle to overcome. However glibly they may have conversed in French about trifling matters, Baron Gunsbourg had to continue his role of interpreter regarding serious issues. Nijinsky talked frankly about his relationship with Diaghilev and euphemistically assured Romola that the latter's friendship would not waver. With his innate honesty he told her about his brother Stassik; that he was incurably insane. Romola asked him to give her his forthright opinion regarding her own future as a dancer; his candid reply resulted in her decision to give it up. She had been too old when she started on her new career. And, after all, had not this burning ambition to become a ballet dancer merely been a means to an end, a pretext, a ruse to capture her idol?

Even on such a delicate matter as to the question of when they should have a child, it was necessary to turn to Gunsbourg to translate. Romola was wrapped up in her love for Nijinsky; she had no desire to become burdened with motherhood. Waslaw, on the other hand, had replied: 'For five years we shall live for art and our love, but the supreme happiness and the fulfilment of life and marriage is to have a child, and, after that time, when we will be in our permanent home, we shall have one.'

Things did not always go as Romola planned, however, because already in Montevideo she felt faint and overcome with nausea. The tour was to end in Rio de Janeiro and there her symptoms escalated. As she herself has related, the whole of Brazil reeked with the odious smell of coffee, which made her extremely ill. The doctor who was consulted confirmed her worst fears, she was pregnant. But Waslaw was delighted. Jubilantly, he had cried out in Russian 'Thank you, God, for giving us a son.' Never for a moment did he doubt that Romola would give birth to a boy, a great dancer, and he then and there nicknamed the unborn child 'Le Petit Nègre'.

The sea voyage back to Europe was harrowing for Romola in her condition. To while away the time she began to touch upon their future; bared to him her dreams of the life of luxury she intended to resume, spoiled as she was. She bubbled about the wardrobe she would equip herself with in Paris; the Callot dresses, Reboux hats, and, of course, exquisite jewellery. She was dumbfounded to note that Waslaw showed marked disapproval of such frivolous thoughts although he promised he would do his utmost to accede to her demands; it showed, however, a new twist to his nature because, when he had become Prince Lvov's intimate friend, he had displayed an insatiable appetite for life's luxuries.

They disembarked at Cadiz and from there continued to Paris where the couple were entertained royally, fêted and showered with the most sumptuous wedding gifts. Romola revelled in it. This was how she had imagined her new path would be. Nijinsky had hoped to meet Diaghilev, but the Impresario was absent.

In Vienna, Tessa and her husband Erik prepared to meet the newlyweds prior to their onward journey to Budapest. Tessa had been thrilled and jubilant over the marriage and eagerly looked forward to meeting her famous brother-in-law. Romola, bursting with pride, had carefully planned their route from Paris – a brief stop in Vienna between trains, then on to her home and Emilia. From there they intended to go to St Petersburg, where Waslaw would be reunited with his family and introduce his bride.

The Schmedes were waiting on the platform when the Paris Express rolled in, eager for a glimpse of the couple among the crowd of disembarking passengers. After introductions had been dealt with, the foursome sat down together in the bleak and dreary station restaurant. It would have been amusing and somewhat bewildering to eavesdrop on their conversation; Erik in German, Romola and Tessa in Hungarian and Waslaw in Russian and mime, all interspersed with a smattering of French.

The homecoming to Romola's birthplace, Budapest, did not culminate in the family affair they had envisaged. Instead, they were appalled to find the entire press gathered, camera bulbs flashing, as they got off the train, and jostling crowds of well-wishers surging forward to greet them.

Emilia had anticipated the visit of her precious Molly and her newly acquired son-in-law with mixed emotions. She had been unable to shake off her less than lukewarm acceptance of the world-famous dancer as a suitable match for her favourite daughter; the winds of notoriety around his person had been chilling, and she brooded over what the future would hold in store for them. She tried her best to alleviate her fears, to analyse them clinically in the bright light of day. Many years later when I, her granddaughter, stood on the threshold of marriage to a brilliant young actor, she was to react in the same manner. She explained to me then her belief that a man could be a great writer, musician or painter without losing his identity but it did not apply to an actor or dancer. She carefully spelled out her theory to me; exhibitionism in the form of applying make-up in front of a mirror in a dressing-room, donning costumes to suit a particular role, often as not exotic, and then go on the stage to portray a personality alien to one's own, was inherent in a woman's nature but not normal to a man.

Oskar, relatives and friends tried everything in their power to allay her qualms. Nijinsky was a renowned celebrity at the peak of his career, earning vast sums of money. Romola would travel with him, their headquarters would most likely be in Paris. She would become the toast of society, fraternising with royalty and heads of state. I am almost certain Emilia listened patiently to their contentions and then in the peaceful privacy of her bedroom she would whisper to the Madonna from Zsolna (a green-gold bas-relief she treasured), *'Édes jó Szüs Anyám ovd meg gyermekemet'.

Once she had held Romola in her arms and seen how radiantly happy she looked, Emilia succeeded in shaking off her gloom and despondency. She hastened to organise receptions and intimate

* My dear, sweet Virgin Mother, protect my child.

dinners in honour of the young couple but it befell Aunt Poly to provide the gala dinner to introduce Waslaw to the aristocracy of Budapest. The menu from that memorable evening was still in Emilia's possession when I lived in the Villa. Food and wine in those opulent pre-war years were an important 'ingredient' in setting the scene for glittering social events and Polyxena must have outshone herself, famous hostess that she was.

The feast commenced with a toast in champagne to the bridal couple. Clear bouillon flavoured with brandy had been the first course, followed by freshly caught fish from Lake Balaton, washed down with the famous white wine from the hills of Badacsony. Spicy *Töltött káposzta* and *Erdélyi rakott káposzta* were also on the menu, both prepared with pork, ham and sour cream. The main course was succulent duckling accompanied by the choicest vegetables of the season. Chestnut purée garnished with lashings of thick whipped cream was the dessert. Waslaw's reputation for having a sweet tooth must have preceded him.

The guest list had been a distinguished one. Among those present was a young student, Paul Bohus, Romola's distant cousin. He was born on March 17, 1897; six years younger than Romola, he was slightly-built with undistinguished features.

Paul was studying at a Jesuit school near Vienna and had by chance come to Budapest for a short break. The invitation was to alter his whole life. There must have been brief encounters with Romola in his childhood but now grown to manhood, the moment he laid eyes on her as she entered the salon, he had met his Destiny as the future was to prove. To the day she died, and it was he who was at her bedside then, his devotion, loyalty and friendship never wavered. He was to weave in and out of her life like a strong thread to which she was to cling for support time and again. A firm bond developed between him and Waslaw as well, to be severed only when Waslaw's recognition of the world around him went into a total eclipse.

Mother and daughter had little time alone together what with Emilia's commitments to the theatre and the social engagements into which Romola was drawn. Romola suffered increasingly from misgivings about her pregnancy. In no way did she feel ready for motherhood and she confided as much to Emilia. Romola was to

---

* Stuffed cabbage and Transylvanian layered cabbage.

claim that the latter seized upon her indecision, quite selfishly despairing over the fact that she would become a grandmother while still so youthful. She harboured fears that the image to her adoring public would be damaged. Decades later, Emilia gave her version; how she had been *against* abortion because of her own tragic experience. At the age of forty-four she was expecting a child by Oskar and suffered a miscarriage. She was told it would have been a son. Nevertheless, Romola was adamant and the house physician was consulted. His decision was that Romola was too frail to endure childbirth without risk to her health. All the necessary steps were taken but at the very last moment Romola became fainthearted at the thought of what was about to transpire and changed her mind. She was rewarded by her husband's joy at the announcement. *'Thank God, what He has given nobody has the right to destroy.'*

Their stay in Budapest was rapidly nearing an end. Waslaw kept pressing for them to proceed to St Petersburg as quickly as possible; he longed to see his mother and Bronia again. Meanwhile, he cabled Diaghilev to ask when rehearsals were to commence on two new ballets he had worked on while in South America. He wanted a reply before going to Russia. And the fatal reply did arrive – two days before their departure. It was curt, brutally to the point. Waslaw had been summarily dismissed, his services to the *Ballets Russes* were no longer required. The pretext given was that he had broken his contract by not appearing in a performance while in South America. Diaghilev had truly wreaked his vengeance on Waslaw. There had never been a contract. The tangled legal web that was to emerge and continue for many years to come was far too complicated for me to attempt to unravel here. Suffice to say, Romola has told how Waslaw had stared at the cable in utter disbelief. She had broken down and sobbed unrestrainedly. The full realisation of what it could mean to her beloved husband had suddenly dawned on her and the horrifying thought must have assailed her that perhaps it was she who inadvertently had brought about her husband's downfall – destroyed the very being for whom she had dreamed of doing so much good. Magnanimously, Waslaw had tried to shake off his own misery to console her. He still suffered the misapprehension it was all a mistake. Incongruous though it may seem, although he had breathed little else than the air of ballet, he had apparently been unaware of the jealousies and self-interested politics that governed the inner circle of the *Ballets Russes*. And even though he had confessed to Romola immediately after their marriage about his intimate relationship with Sergei Pavlovitch, he still assumed this friendship would not be broken. He hastened to write a long letter to Igor Stravinsky, asking him to intervene, above all to find out why Diaghilev had behaved in so cruel a fashion, and entreating Igor to plead with Sergei to write to him.

Hurt and defiant at the same time, he advised the French newspapers that he was no longer in the employ of Diaghilev.

The rug of security literally pulled from under him, he stood there alone, responsible for a wife and their unborn child. Diaghilev owed him vast sums of money for the South American tour; Romola's family demanded to know how he would support her; the world press hounded him, looking for sensational revelations in the break with Diaghilev; impresarios and agents from all four corners of the globe waved tempting offers in front of him, from music hall engagements to opera performances, all of which he refused because he feared being unfaithful to his art. To him there was only one future for his creativity – with the *Ballets Russes*. His mind was bursting with ideas for new ballets – to further his skills in that direction.

'I loved the Ballets Russes. I gave my whole heart to it. I worked like an ox. I lived like a martyr...was busy with dancing, and composed new ballets by myself. He did not want me to do by myself things which went against his grain...I often quarrelled with him...Diaghilev liked showing that Nijinsky was his pupil in everything...'.

Within the cloistered atmosphere of the Diaghilev ballet he had not been encumbered with the responsibility of finance, administration, nor any of the donkey work entailed in the running of a ballet company.

The birth of their first child was imminent, and Waslaw had to bow to the stark practicalities of life – to accept some form of work otherwise there would be insufficient funds to pay the bills. Temporarily, their trip to Russia was shelved. Instead he pulled himself together and commenced planning for the future. The story of what transpired has been variously interpreted depending on the writer. Romola claimed they left Budapest for Vienna to escape the intolerable friction that had arisen due to Emilia and Oskar's intervention in their affairs. According to Bronia, she received a letter from Waslaw with the news that he was negotiating a contract with the Opera in Paris. While she and her husband were in Prague a cable arrived from her brother, asking if she would consider leaving the *Ballets Russes* together with her husband Sasha Kotchetovsky. Intensely loyal to Waslaw, Bronia readily acquiesced and forthwith broke her contract with Diaghilev. A further cable from Waslaw of January 27th, 1914, offered them a two-year contract. She and Sasha hastened to Paris where they were reunited with Waslaw and introduced to his wife. Bronia described her as pretty and was pleased to note marriage appeared to agree with him and that it was already bearing fruit.

To Bronia's astonishment the Paris contract had not been finalised, instead Waslaw poured out his news that a contract had been signed with Alfred Butt of the Palace Theatre in London. At first, she had been taken aback as she was only too well aware of Waslaw's reservations about performing on the stage of a variety theatre. Had he accepted the eight-weeks' engagement as a *force majeure* under the prevailing circumstances or was he gulled into believing it really would enhance his reputation?

Against all odds the *Saison Nijinsky* was rushed through its preliminary stages with numerous stumbling blocks on its thorny path. Waslaw wanted top artists to assist him but many doors were closed in front of him out of fear of reprisal from Diaghilev. The impresario's threat to 'thrust Nijinsky into the depths from the heights he had placed him' were stealthily creeping to the fore. With tears often lurking in his otherwise inscrutable eyes, Waslaw persevered; worked like a demon in Paris. Bronia departed to Russia and returned with a reasonably competent group of dancers. Others were signed on when the company arrived in London.

Faithful friends, headed by Lady Ripon and Lady Morrell, did all in their power to make Waslaw and Romola feel welcome. They were delighted he had entered into a matrimonial haven. Emilia and Oti-Papa journeyed all the way from Budapest to be present at the opening night of *Saison Nijinsky*. Everything augured well yet nearly everything went catastrophically wrong. Diaghilev lashed out in a tantrum, slapping an injunction against Bronia for breach of contract, which prohibited her from performing the first night. Mercifully, he lost the case. According to Bronia, Pavlova sent a snide cable to Waslaw, with best wishes to 'a music hall artist'. This in retaliation for a remark innocently made by Waslaw long ago, but one for which the great diva never forgave him. Butt agitated Waslaw by demanding that he should include typically Russian ballets in the repertoire. The sensitive genius and purist must have felt himself trapped like an animal by what was virtually sabotage to his artistic talent. How he must have quailed at performing on the same programme as cabaret singers and clowns. It had nearly broken Romola's heart to witness her husband's anguish every time he stood poised to leap onto the stage.

With nerves taut to breaking point, it was a wonder that the dancers performed as successfully as they did. The critics praised them but by all accounts not as enthusiastically as in the past. Perhaps with so many odds against him, the sparkle had deserted the God of Dance. Bronia was to claim that at the end of their second week Waslaw broke into a fury painful to behold when from his dressing-room he heard the wrong introductory music played for *Spectre de la Rose*. He had defiantly flung his costume on the floor and refused to carry on. She had been forced to wheedle him to get ready. That performance on the 14th of March was to be his last with the *Saison Nijinsky*. The following morning Romola was horrified to find he was running a high temperature. A doctor was hastily summoned and diagnosed influensa; he also stated that Waslaw's condition had been worsened by a dose of aspirins given him by Romola. Apparently, Waslaw had an athlete's heart and the wellmeant cure could have proved fatal. He was to confess:

> '*I collapsed from overwork and had a fever. I was at death's door. My wife wept. She loved me. She suffered when she saw I worked so much. She realised that all that was for money.*'

As Nijinsky was unable to perform, the *Saison Nijinsky* contract was terminated. Waslaw had been under the misapprehension that his contract gave him the right to three days' sick leave during the engagement. When it came to the crux and reading the black, printed text word for word, the message was clear; if he was absent three consecutive days, he had breached the terms of the contract with instant effect. Bitterly, Bronia placed the blame on Romola's shoulders. Was it not she and she alone who could read English fluently and who had prided herself on being Waslaw's business advisor?

Whoever was to blame, the *Saison Nijinsky* had been a fiasco. All costs for scenery, costumes, music and salaries had to be funded by Waslaw personally. Because of their trust in him, he paid the dancers a full year's salary each, all thirty-odd. Fortunately, he still had some savings in a Paris bank, revenue received when dancing before royalty and such wealthy patrons of the arts as the Aga Khan and others. But now the nest egg had dwindled considerably. Bronia and Romola are at variance in their stories of how long the Nijinskys stayed in London. Romola wrote that she and Waslaw remained there two whole months; Bronia, that they departed fairly soon after the legal tangles and payments had been dealt with; that they had returned to Vienna and that Sasha and she had seen them off at the station.

Sifting through my mother's papers, I came across a few letters which prove that during that period, despite Romola's condemnation of her step-father, Oskar was acting on Waslaw's behalf in attempts to negotiate other contracts. On June 17th, 1914, Wollheim Ltd, International Theatrical Offices at number 17 Charing Cross Road, London, wrote to '*Sehr geehrter Herr Párdány*' that they were expecting an American director the following Tuesday and that they would immediately talk to him about a possible engagement. They went on to say that according to London newspapers Nijinsky would be appearing at the Drury Lane Theatre. Was there any truth in this? Rumours must already then have been circulating about the reunion of Waslaw with the *Ballets Russes* in their forthcoming appearance in London. Oskar received a further letter on the 19th of June from Wollheim Ltd offering his son-in-law an engagement at the Châtelét in Paris in early December. The theatrical agent had spoken to Monsieur Fontanes, director of the theatre, with regard to 'a grand festival to include ballet performances, and which in decor and originality will surpass everything seen so far. Mr. Nijinsky's participation would obviously be limited to the ballet.'

The agent was anxious to know what terms Waslaw would accept. The performances would be limited to one a day except for Thursdays when there would also be a matinée. He finished off by emphasising that his agency was convinced the part would guarantee Mr. Nijinsky great success.

On the same date a letter was despatched to Oskar from H.B. Marinelli Ltd in Paris regarding the draft contract (dated May 30th) between Jacques Rouche, Director of the *Académie Nationale de Musique et de Danse, Théâtre Nationale de l'Opéra,* and Monsieur Nijinsky. Having learnt a costly lesson through his ignorance in undertaking the complexities of the previous contract with Butt, Waslaw had cautiously requested Oskar to act on his behalf and carefully consider the fourteen articles laid down by Rouche. Oskar was advised that 'Unfortunately, it would appear to be somewhat difficult to find a clause which would exclude unforeseen events from the contract.' Certain other issues which had been raised were discussed and Marinelli Ltd went on to say that Monsieur Rouche wished to bring the matter to a speedy close; either Monsieur Nijinsky signed the existing contract or else confirmed that he no longer was interested in the engagement, which, incidentally, would have covered a period of three years with rehearsals to commence in January 1915. Nijinsky would be paid monthly the 4th part of the fixed sum of ninety thousand francs per season. In the same letter, Marinelli Ltd wondered if Nijinsky would accept an engagement at the Wintergarten in Berlin; the directors there were extremely interested.

How defenseless we mortals are to a large extent in planning our lives. Waslaw was once more on the threshold of a brilliant career, of a 'comeback', without being shackled to Diaghilev or subject to his almost paranoic desire to ruin his former protégé. Paris had again beckoned Nijinsky back. But Fate was to intervene, not only for him but millions of other hapless people when on the 28th of June shots rang out in Sarajevo murdering the Archduke Franz Ferdinand and his consort, the Duchess of Hohenberg; an event that was to unleash the tension fermenting for a long time between Germany, France and Russia.

After Romola and Waslaw returned to Vienna, Waslaw received an invitation in May to dance for the King and Queen of Spain. It was a command performance at a wedding reception to be held in the American Embassy. He could not refuse and besides, the fee was exceedingly high. Oskar accompanied him to Madrid. The *accueil* there was as genuine as it had been in the past and their Majesties went out of their way to make Nijinsky feel appreciated. Daily, he wrote to his *femmka* – brief notes in Russian. Romola treasured every one as she was acutely aware of his aversion to letterwriting. This was his way of letting her know she was never out of his thoughts. Before, it had only been his mother to whom he had written so faithfully.

However much the expectant father must have wished to return to his wife as quickly as possible, the artist Nijinsky could not refrain from stopping over in Paris on his journey home, primarily to be present at the première of *Joseph and Potiphar (La Légende de Joseph)* with music by Richard Strauss, and performed by the *Ballets Russes*. Strauss had earlier expressed deep disappointment upon hearing that Waslaw Nijinsky would not be dancing in his ballet. Waslaw made his entrance as unobtrusively as possible, taking his seat in an orchestra stall, but the eagle-eyed press and many in the audience recognised their former idol. He later told Romola how he had gone to Misia Sert's box in the intermission. Madame Sert was a rich, influential and very close friend of Diaghilev's. Jean Cocteau, among others, had been her guest. According to Waslaw, a frozen silence had greeted him as he entered. Then, laughingly, Cocteau had turned to him and remarked: 'This year, your creation is a child. The *Spectre de la Rose* chooses the part of a father. How utterly disgusting is birth.' Waslaw had felt deeply wounded but as he stood up he replied with quiet dignity: 'The entrance of the *Spectre de la Rose's* child will be quite as beautiful as his own, which you always admired.' Having said which, he had bowed and made his exit.

On the 19th of June 1914, a daughter was born to Romola and Waslaw in the Loew Sanatorium, Mariannengasse 20, Wien. Not *Le Petit Nègre* that Waslaw had prayed for. Tessa, who had been in the corridor with him when the nurse came and announced that it was a girl, claimed he had momentarily lost control of himself and given vent to his dashed hope by throwing his gloves on the floor. But he was never to utter a word of regret to Romola, and Kyra Vaslavovna Nijinskaya was adored by both parents. From her birth, she strongly resembled Waslaw and she was to inherit his wonderful artistic talents. Kyra is the Russian word for 'Queen'.

During her stay at the Loew Sanatorium Romola received a number of visits from her sister Tessa. Tessa's own marriage was childless and she urged Romola to come and stay with her and Erik during her post-natal convalescence. Erik, it seemed, had pressed her to make the request. He had a daughter, Dagmar, from his former marriage, whom he sorely missed. It was at this stage that Romola's sharp eyes noticed something was acutely awry with her sister, normally so gay and carefree. Under pressure, Tessa divulged the secret that was to mar her marital life until its tragic disbandment in divorce years later. Erik Schmedes, the gifted Wagnerian tenor with the golden voice, was on an alcoholic's downward path. Scene after scene had erupted at home; she was fearful not only for his brilliant career but for his health.

Emilia swept into the hospital from Budapest to have a look at her first grandchild, bitterly upset that Romola had not wished to have her present at the birth. Acrimonious words had been exchanged between the two women, both endowed with a rebellious nature and strong will, and in the ensuing abusive verbal battle both Waslaw and Oti-Papa had been drawn into the fray, much against their own volition. The older couple had taken their leave in a huff. Sadly, conflicts between mother and daughter were to become an endless series of melodramas, not to end until the death of Emilia. It is so difficult to put into words, the love-hate relationship that existed between them. Perhaps they were too much alike in temperament. Living under the same roof as my grandmother, I was to observe at close hand how she worshipped her headstrong Molly. When I reached maturity and read my mother's book, it grieved me to learn how she had so misjudged Emilia and how scathing and unwarranted her criticism had been.

Barely two weeks after Kyra's birth, Waslaw had to desert his family and go back to London. Lady Ripon had refused to give up her efforts to reconcile Waslaw and Diaghilev and to bring the former back to the fold of the Russian Ballet Company. The rumour, that had started as a whisper, grew to actual fact. Using all her skill and diplomacy under the mantle of the Production Committee of the Russian Ballet Performances at Drury Lane, she manoeuvred to get an agreement to the effect that unless Nijinsky was allowed to dance with the company the remainder of the season would be called off. Waslaw was elated. He had been accused of seeing his friendship with Diaghilev *en couleur de rose.* Now he would be able to prove everyone wrong; he and Sergei Pavlovitch would be reunited, co-partners once more on the ballet scene. His dream was shortlived. Upon his arrival at the Drury Lane theatre, he was shattered to find that the company with one or two exceptions turned their backs on him, froze him out. It was as if their former star did not exist. And Diaghilev refused to see him. One single excruciating and humiliating rehearsal produced the effect Sergei wanted.

Broken in spirit, unable to face more of what was clearly an unalterable situation between him and his former colleagues, Waslaw reached the painful decision to withdraw from it all. In the solitude of his room at the Savoy, he swiftly penned a brief note to Lady Ripon, thanking her for her wonderful support but explaining openly the impossibility of remaining under the prevailing circumstances and that he was immediately returning to Vienna. He must have written yet another letter, this time to Sasha, his brother-in-law, because Bronia was to speak of how Waslaw had written to them weeks before, requesting that both or at least Sasha should join him for the Diaghilev Season in London. Sasha had arrived by boat from St Petersburg and rushed to the hotel only to be handed a letter left by Waslaw, regretting that he had been forced to leave unexpectedly, having had a cable from Romola that she urgently needed him. Would Sasha kindly go to the theatre and proffer his apologies. The impairment to his pride and his artistic being must have been too great for him even to consider telling them the truth. The message delivered, Sasha had gone to Waslaw's dressing-room. Floral tributes filled the room from the many fans, who did not know then that they would never see the star dance on a London stage again.

In the meantime, Romola had stayed on at the Sanatorium, coming to terms with her new role as a mother. On the 28th of June, in the tranquillity of her bedroom, her reveries had been broken by the unintermittent tolling of church bells. Their peals reverberated ominously in the stillness of the beautiful summer's day. Their message was clear; a catastrophe had occurred. It was to be the young assistant doctor who, on his usual round, brought Romola the tidings about the murders in Sarajevo. Her godfather, Lájos Thallóczy, was able to fill in all the details when next he visited Romola. Close to the Imperial Family, he had access to confidential information. But Romola admitted in her book that she had paid scant attention to what he said. A tragic incident, but then life held many such tragedies. She was not a politically-minded person and would never have dreamt of interpreting it as a foreshadow of the horror that was to befall a large portion of mankind.

Soon after Waslaw's homecoming, the young couple resumed plans for their postponed trip to St Petersburg. Yet again would the chain of events that was to lead to its ultimate cataclysmic climax have been prevented, had Waslaw heeded Lady Ripon's urgent entreaty that he come back to London with his family? She must have sensed that war was inevitable. Can one therefore assume she feared that Nijinsky would be cut off from the outside world were he to remain in the eastern part of Europe? He, however, misjudged her actions, believing she was attempting to bring him back to the fold of Diaghilev's ballet.

Romola was still frail and her physician warned her that any lengthy voyage at that stage would prove far too strenuous. Using that as an excuse, Waslaw turned down Lady Ripon's invitation. Instead, he and Romola made the unfortunate decision to stop over in Budapest for a week before continuing to St Petersburg, albeit fraught with reservations on how they would get along with Romola's mother. The steps they took were to have grievous consequences for Waslaw. He was never to see his homeland again.

The young Nijinsky family arrived in Budapest a sultry, hot day in late July 1914. They settled down for a few days' rest before embarking on the last stage of their trip.

It must have been in the early evening of the 29th of July that Waslaw had gone with Romola's parents to a touring circus. He returned in an exhilarated, boyish mood, moved in true Russian fashion by the sight and smell of the Big Top, so nostalgic to him from his boyhood. Emilia and Oskar, on the other hand, were intoxicated by the news they had just heard, that Austria-Hungary had declared war on Serbia. They had foregone to explain the screaming headlines to Waslaw, forgetting he could not understand them. Like a forest fire the flames were to engulf country after country. Within the spate of a few days Russia had mobilised her troops; Germany was to follow; by August, 1st war commenced between Russia and Germany and by August 3rd, France and England had been drawn into the grim encounter.

Waslaw's sensitive nature had always condemned wars as a solution to any dispute, and seeing all the soldiers marching by, he is reputed to have said, 'All these young men marching to their death, and for what? *I love the world, there must be no wars.*'

Romola feverishly hastened to make reservations to get them on the Nord Express only to be told the Eastern frontier was hermetically closed. In desperation she turned to the Russian Embassy for assistance but they themselves were in turmoil, unable to cope with a situation that had come like a bolt from the blue. It was too late.

Doggedly, Romola persisted in trying to find a way of escape. She contacted her uncle, Garibaldi de Pulszky, president of a private railway company, to seek his aid in smuggling them over to Italy. At the last minute, this plot failed.

Emilia took a firm grip on the reins of the swelling household and prepared an apartment for her daughter and son-in-law in the 'Tower', which was the family nickname for the top floor of the Villa. It consisted of three rooms, bathroom and kitchenette. One of the rooms had been newly decorated and the windows were hung with crisp, white Swiss batiste curtains. It was to serve as a nursery and it was there that Kyra was to spend the first year and more of her life. From the spacious, rectangular terrace there was a splendid view of the mountains of Buda.

But despite the idyllic surroundings and Emilia's determination to make her charges' involuntary stay as comfortable as possible, she was unable to protect them from the psychological stress that was to be inflicted upon them. One chilly morning Emilia was warned of the arrival of a visitor by the furious barking of her German Shepherd dog. When she opened the door she was confronted by a man in civilian dress, who nervously blurted out his message. Monsieur and Madame Nijinsky were to report to the Prefecture of Police immediately. Emilia demanded to know the reason and was bluntly told she was harbouring an 'enemy' Russian under her roof. Strict orders had been issued that all aliens in the country were to be placed in internment camps.

Worse still, when Romola and Waslaw confronted the head of the Bureau they were informed they would be placed under arrest as enemies of Hungary. Prisoners of war! To Romola it seemed the ultimate straw. She was Hungarian, her mother was the greatest actress of Hungary, her uncle was the Minister of the Foreign Office, Waslaw had never been in the Army; as a dancer with the Imperial Ballet he had been exempt from military duty; and was he not Nijinsky, the world renowned dancer? To no avail. According to Emilia's story, it was she who went to the Ministry and after a long, drawn-out duel of wits, achieved the meagre concession that the three members of the Nijinsky family be under 'house arrest' which implied that they would be able to move freely in the city of Budapest but that it befell Emilia to shoulder the responsibility of seeing to it that they did not leave the country. Three red passes were issued with their names in bold print and they would have to report to the police once a week.

Romola raged and rebelled at the disgraceful attitude adopted by her own countrymen, cried in despair over the humiliation they suffered. Nor would her feeling of guilt leave her for since Waslaw had married her a series of misfortunes had befallen him. Now to add to it all, he was being persecuted in her homeland, deprived of his freedom. How could he support a wife and child without any source of income, confined to an intensely electrified atmosphere dominated by a mother-in-law who, for all her good traits, would never accept 'no' for an answer. He found it hard to practise because of lack of space in the Villa. In fact, his *Diary* provides some clues to his own interpretation of that dreadful time. He must have succumbed to lonely bouts of melancholia and he was to write that he was bored.

> *'I lived in my wife's mother's house and ate a lot...I was bored...I took care of my notation system. I wanted to forget myself and so started writing down my ballet 'The Faun' on the basis of my notation system. This was a long occupation. I took about two months to write it down, the ballet took ten minutes to perform. I realised my mistake and threw away the work. Again I felt bored. I grieved, I wept because I was bored...I lived from day to day. I did dancing exercises. I started to develop my muscles. My muscles became firm but my dancing was bad.'*

He had no friends and the few people he did come in contact with found communication almost impossible because of the language barrier. His greatest concern, however, was for his own family in Russia, totally cut off from them as he was.

As the days and weeks dragged on, more and more tendentious stories circulated in Budapest and stirred up indignation over the fact that a Russian was in their midst. Forgotten was the adulation for the dancer, now the bigoted minds saw this gentle and compassionate man as their sworn enemy. Headlines appeared taunting Romola, demanding she divorce her husband to prove her patriotism. Emilia and Oskar, much as they wished to remain loyally by their side, began to teeter under the strain, incapable of coming to terms with the effect it was having on their own lives. Emilia's colleagues at the theatre gave vent to their callous sentiments and Emilia feared the consequences the whole affair might have on her career and, indeed, on Oskar's, who at the time was with the Press Department of the Prime Minister. Another grave problem was purely materialistic – the financial burden of three additional mouths to feed. She, who loved to lavish money on culinary delights, now found her purse strained beyond its capacity.

Although he must have bled inwardly from the wounds inflicted upon him by malice and hatred, outwardly it was Waslaw who retained his calm and dignity. There was no rancour in either his speech or behaviour. Yet how he must have suffered. He claimed later that he was referred to as that 'Russian barbarian'. Romola wrote: 'One very patriotic young poet, who used to rave about Vaslav, spat on the ground before us as we passed in the street.' But dire though their predicament was, there was also a bright side. Confined to the intimacy of a small space, perhaps it was in that little apartment 'at the top' that they were to experience their happiest hours together. Thrust daily in each other's company, they learned to explore each other as never before. And they were by then able to converse quite fluently in a mixture of French and Russian. Waslaw's French had improved considerably since their wedding day and Romola had made it one of her goals to conquer the Russian language. After rummaging through a number of secondhand bookshops, she had found and purchased a pocket-size French/Russian dictionary and she was to carry it around with her as faithfully as she did her precious Jesus of Prague.

From Romola's own account she and Waslaw ventilated all the topics they had been longing to discuss from the moment they first met. He had been extremely outspoken about his love/hatred relationship with Diaghilev, a part of his past he would never forget, nor, more important, regret, no matter how hard the outside world might condemn it. 'I will never regret what I have done, for I believe that all experience in life, if made with the aim of truth, is uplifting. No, I do not regret my relationship with Sergei Pavlovitch, even if ethics condemn it.' He had gone so far as to claim that it was she who had made him realise how wrong the physical side of that bond had been; that he had awakened to the longing for a woman when he saw her on board the *Avon*. To her, he was a loving and caring husband, a passionate and tender lover, a companion with whom she had wandered hand in hand in nature and who had opened her eyes to the beauty of the surroundings she had formerly taken for granted. During the tedious winter months they read the treasures of Russian literature. He unravelled for her the depths of meaning in the works of Tolstoi, Chekhov and many others. Dostoievsky's

La Maison des Morts left the most lasting impression on her. To her, a similar fate appeared to have befallen Waslaw.

He worshipped Kyra and was everything a child could wish for in a father. When he felt Romola needed to stay in bed longer in the morning, it was he who saw to it the child was bathed and dressed. He spent days redecorating her room in an explosion of colours. With a few strokes of the paintbrush, he transformed the otherwise clinical room into a fairyland. With his skilled hands he carved toys for her, using his wealth of imagination as choreographer and dancer to create flamboyant characters out of mere strips of dull wood.

One day, Kyra's wet nurse had to be told to leave. The hostility towards the 'alien' family had finally infected her and she had refused to give Kyra her milk, declaring she would not feed a Russian while her own people were starving. From that day onward Waslaw shouldered the 'maternal' responsibilites to perfection, acquiring his knowledge from an illustrated book on the care of infants; how to bottle-feed his daughter, change her diapers, no task was to demeaning for him. The day was to arrive, when she took her first faltering steps, the classic example of joy in parenthood.

In her book Romola was to denounce Emilia and Oskar bitterly and harshly without a word of gratitude for what they had tried to do to assuage a situation governed by deep psychological stress. She was almost hysterical in her condemnation of them, that they boasted to Waslaw of the number of Russians taken prisoner, the battles his countrymen lost, how Emilia would fly into a rage and unjustly accuse Waslaw of committing the most trifling misconduct. Who am I to pass judgment on the truth or fallaciousness of her statements after all these years, but I refuse to believe Emilia would ever knowingly have wished to hurt her Molly. But neither would it be justifiable to canonize my grandmother. She was only human and the pressures brought upon her from the world outside the Villa must have been nigh on insufferable. Again, in his *Diary*, Waslaw was to confess: *'My wife's mother, Emma, was a nervous woman. She liked me for my success with the public. She liked my dancing... We were both nervous. I did not like her and therefore found fault with every trifle.'*

To escape the claustrophobic confinement in the home and make the days more bearable, Romola would take Waslaw out as much as possible, often to the National Museum where they relaxed and strolled side by side through the cool, arched corridors. Waslaw was particularly intrigued by a painting by Károly Lotz – *The Huszárs' Camp*. It must have roused memories of his lost childhood, of the rebellion of 1905, when the whip of the Russian Cossack had accidentally struck his face, narrowly missing his eyes. With pride Romola had explained that the six large canvases, representing mythological figures on the ceiling of the atrium in the Villa, had been painted by the same artist. Another painting that had caught Waslaw's attention was a huge portrait of a man in profile with quite a long nose, a reddish moustache, and a goatee. It was Ferenc Pulszky, Romola's grandfather. A friend of the family, Wolfgang Bohm, had painted the portrait in London during Ferenc's exile. Romola bore a striking resemblance to her grandfather.

Many years later when we were reconciled in the States, and when she was in one of her rare talkative moods, Romola would linger over the many excursions she and Waslaw made by carriage to the Fisherman's Bastion up the curving Hunyadi János Road. I could see it all vividly in front of me because the route was so familiar to me; the breathtaking panorama of the city of Buda, its ridge of hills, old towers, silhouetting the sky, the dwarflike crooked houses, some of them still standing from the time of the Turkish occupation, never ceased to hold a fascination for Waslaw with his keen artistic eye, not only for the beauty nature offered but also the superb 'stage' settings laid out before him. The sprawling flat Pest with the dividing line of the immortalised Danube provided yet another view. The Romans some two thousand years previously had discovered the admirable strategic possibilities of the area and they had also found the hot springs and built the town of Aquincum (Pannonia), the region where Emilia's forebears were said to have their roots. The very same factors which had so attracted the Romans were to bring the Huns, Goths, Slavs, and lastly, the conquering Magyar tribe, who stubbornly established their foothold in the fertile valley of the Danube and the Tisza. Buda had been the stronghold of the kings of Hungary when they had to struggle against the barbaric Turks. The thick stone walls and the Royal Palace along the Fortress Hill had protected its inhabitants from the Sultan's savage attacks in the sixteenth century. In later years, many political refugees had found safety in the vaulted underground labyrinths, which were built in such an intricate way that a person in need of hiding could stay there for months and wander from one side of the district to the other without the risk of detection.

Whenever they paid a visit to the Gothic Coronation Church, Romola made a habit of afterwards taking Waslaw to the charming old-world Ruszwurm Patisserie. It had a delightful interior filled with polished, heavy oak furniture, each piece an exquisite example of handwork made with loving care by artisans long, long ago. The small round tables were always covered with white damask table-cloths. And in the summertime each table would be adorned with a vase, usually filled with arrangements of blue cornflowers, scarlet poppies and golden sheafs of wheat. As the seasons changed, so would the bright floral bouquets. Under glass, tempting rows of the choicest sweets, laid out on Rosenthal china, would patiently wait to be selected by the beholder. It must have been the highlight of an outing for Waslaw for there he could indulge in his weakness for sugary confections. I can visualise him, his face lit up in anticipation, as he ordered giant slices of *Dobos torta* and a cup of steaming hot chocolate topped with a mountain of whipped cream.

But those brief idyllic interludes were few. The grisly war pursued its relentless course. And after an exceptionally unpalatable crisis involving Emilia and Waslaw, Romola decided the time had come to take drastic action to get away from her mother's household, even so far as to be sent to a prisoner-of-war camp. She escorted Waslaw to her Aunt Poly and left him there for the day while she went by train to Vienna, only four hours distance from Budapest. She wished to consult her godfather, His Excellency Dr Lájos Thall-óczy at the War Office. She took a desperate risk as she was for-bidden to leave the city, let alone the country. Somehow she managed to make the journey there and back undetected but her mission had not been very successful. When she had poured out her tale of woe concerning Emilia's attitude to Waslaw, he had diplo-matically tried to make her understand Emilia's position. He made no secret of the fact he had been madly in love with Emilia in his youth; that he still admired and respected her but that he sympa-thised with Romola in her current predicament. Emilia was not the most tolerant of women. Above all, she was an artist through and through. He attempted to analyse her behaviour toward Waslaw. Was perhaps an undercurrent of jealousy combined with frustration at the root of it? She, who had reached the heights in her own country, had never achieved the accolade of international stardom. Yet now she was housing a son-in-law under her roof – an alien –

who had established his fame throughout the world. When he had finished his little sermon, he advised Romola to return to Budapest immediately, otherwise she was in serious danger of being caught. She was strengthened by his parting words; he broadly hinted that international strings were being pulled at the highest level to get the great Nijinsky out of Hungary and cautioned her to exercise patience while waiting for further developments.

And so Romola slipped back once more to the daily routine. She longed to attend Opera performances but resisted the temptation because she feared it would disturb Waslaw to see the stage of his earlier triumphs. To take him to the theatre was unthinkable as he did not speak Hungarian. With one exception; he expressed a wish to see Emilia as Juliet in *Romeo and Juliet.* Although Emilia had by then passed the half century mark, she gave a brilliant performance, lauded by the critics.

There was one outsider who understood and felt deep sympathy for Nijinsky the artist. It was Romola's cousin Lily, the brilliant pianist. She took it upon herself to play for him to help fill the artistic void in his life. Once in a while she would insist that he play piano duets with her on the two black Bösendorfer grand pianos facing each other. For some time Waslaw had been giving much thought to a medieval theme for a ballet but it had as yet not crystallized. Then, late one evening, Lily played Strauss's tone-poem *Tyl Eulenspiegel's Lustige Streiche.* For Waslaw, that evening was the birth of a wonderful ballet. All else faded into insignificance, the genius had awakened from his slumber, the creativity that had slowly withered and been in danger of disintegrating in captivity, sprang back to life. In the strange environment in which he found himself, Nijinsky was to begin the creation of his most colourful and extraordinary ballet based on the thirteenth century Flemish *Robin Hood.* His jubilation at having found the key that would unlock the door to new horizons inspired him to dance some of the wild gypsy dances of Russia. His audience, Romola and Lily, watched spellbound, as he gave himself, body and soul, to the haunting and almost savage movements of the dances.

It was also during this period that he spent hours devising his complicated system of notation for the recording of dance steps. This pastime was to have dire consequences. One day, both Romola and Waslaw were summarily called to the Chief of Police and interrogated at great length. It transpired that an informer had told the police that Waslaw was working in code on secret, military plans. Only after several days of uncomfortable cross-examination by experts in music and mathematics was Waslaw able to convince the authorities of his complete innocence. He was, in fact, warmly congratulated instead for what he had accomplished. Who actually instigated the totally false and obnoxious accusation was to remain a mystery. Romola accused Emilia and Oskar. I refuse to believe it to this day. My own theory is that some people plagued by jealousy, the seeds of which had been sown years previously, were spreading vilifying rumours about Emilia and Oskar, the worst of which was that Oskar at Emilia's behest had informed the police about Waslaw's notation; that Emilia, fiercely patriotic, had been fed up with having an enemy in her house, fed up with the jeers of the public and her colleagues, and hence dearly wished to see the young couple out of the country. It seems impossible, with hindsight, to give any credence to such an act having been committed by either Emilia or Oskar. It would most certainly have jeopardised Oskar's position in the Government and Emilia's public image more than it would have harmed Waslaw Nijinsky. But in the extreme tension that prevailed, even Romola regarded her mother and step-father with implausible suspicion.

When the commotion around them was at its peak, the Nijinskys' morale was boosted by an unexpected letter from Lady Ripon, smuggled in by a mutual friend. She wrote of her undying fondness for Waslaw and that she was ceaselessly trying to find a way to help him.

Late in the autumn of 1915, a cryptic report reached Waslaw through a Hungarian impresario to the effect that the latter had met Diaghilev while on a visit to Switzerland and heard that Sergei Pavlovitch was planning a North American tour and that it was essential for Waslaw to be included in the Company. Waslaw was understandably dubious regarding the authenticity of such news and brushed it aside.

A mysterious communiqué which neither Waslaw nor Romola could decipher arrived from her godfather in Vienna simultaneously with an order from the Ministry of the Interior that they should both appear before the Minister. It was a matter of grave urgency. When they arrived in his office, accompanied by Emilia, they were told they were to be transferred to Karlsbad and that the necessary documents for their departure would be ready in a matter of days. They were also advised to keep the information strictly confidential and that under no circumstances were they to divulge it to anybody else.

They were puzzled and suspicious. Surely, they were not offered freedom, merely transfer from one captivity to another? The Minister proffered his apologies for the shameful way that the great Nijinsky had been treated; that it had gone against the grain of all true Hungarian patriots but that they had to honour the agreement which, by international law, stated that any alien in time of war must be placed in a camp. Romola persisted in wanting to know what it was all about. One short sentence in reply paved their way to liberation. An official medical report from the professor at the Loew Sanatorium in Vienna certified that due to complications she had suffered during childbirth it was essential that Romola undergo minor surgery at the Sanatorium in the immediate future.

Later, Romola and Waslaw were to find out that this seemingly convenient solution for obtaining their release out of Hungary had been prompted by separate schemes, including one arranged by Count Thallóczy and some high-ranking members of the Austro-Hungarian Cabinet.

Overjoyed by the news that Vienna was to be their destination, they hurriedly started preparing for their journey, and a few days later they bade farewell to Emilia and Budapest at the *Nyugati Pály-audvar* (the railway station to the west of the city).

CHAPTER 4

TYL EULENSPIEGEL:
NEW YORK AND THE AMERICAN TOUR

Tatakaboy. I had always been intrigued and puzzled by the origin of this affectionate name which both Kyra and I had been taught to use for our father. Apparently, it had quite simply come about on the journey from Budapest to Vienna in early January 1916. Kyra had shown increasing signs of boredom as the train sped faster and faster away from the Nijinsky family's 'prison'. She had clearly demonstrated her emotions by giving vent to howls which escalated alarmingly in volume.

Waslaw, far more tolerant and patient a parent than Romola, had balanced his screaming daughter on his knees. Cooing with joy and satisfaction at having gained her beloved father's attention, she had repeated again and again 'ta-ta...ta-ta-ka.... How it came to pass that the word 'boy' was tacked on remained a mystery, however, but from that day onward Kyra addressed him as *Tatakaboy* and, not unnaturally, I was to follow suit.

FREEDOM must have been the one word that echoed and re-echoed in Romola's ears that eventful day. Although technically they were still prisoners-of-war, they had at least escaped the bondage imposed upon them in Hungary.

Romola had received precise instructions to report to the head of police immediately upon their arrival. Foreseeing that she and Waslaw would have to seek temporary accommodation in the city, and quite possibly shrewdly calculating what prestige the presence of her brother-in-law would bring to bear, she had asked Erik Schmedes to join them at the police headquarters and there to collect Kyra, so that she and Waslaw could move about unhampered until they found suitable lodgings.

Erik Schmedes was still the *Kammersänger* of the *Hofoper,* still *Wien's* most adored Lohengrin and Tristan. No matter that he was slightly bald, his features prematurely lined, his weakness for *Sligovica* insatiable, he wielded a charismatic influence and gave invaluable support to the young couple. Consequently, their first battle was easily won during the interview with the police chief. Short of being given the keys to the city, they were free to do as they pleased.

The proprietor of the Hôtel Bristol was delighted when his former resident approached him regarding a room. Waslaw's embarrassed and almost abject apology over the fact that he momentarily was out of funds was grandly brushed to one side and instead he was offered a suite for an indefinite period of time.

The Spanish Embassy proved to be equally helpful. There, Romola and Waslaw were told that King Alfonso, a steadfast admirer and supporter, had intervened on Waslaw's behalf and expressed a solemn desire to give as much assistance as possible. When Waslaw once more felt impelled to raise the delicate matter of money, the first secretary had dismissed this as a mere bagatelle, declaring Waslaw would be guaranteed funds against his letter of credit on Paris.

Both Waslaw and Romola were overwhelmed and deeply moved to learn of the massive support that had come from all quarters in securing their release from Hungary. The list of names was impressive: Emperor Franz Josef, Queen Alexandra, the Marchioness of Ripon, the Dowager Empress Maria Feodorovna, even as eminent a figure as His Holiness the Pope.

For just a few split seconds of Eternity, fate seemed to be on their side. They received a pass to all performances and rehearsals at the *Hofoper* and Waslaw was offered the use of the stage of the *Theater an der Wien* in lieu of the *Hofoper*. Wartime restrictions forbade him from practising there. Once more the availability of a proper stage came like a godsend; he was able to plunge with frenzy into the completion of his new choreographic work, *Mephisto Valse,* to music by Franz Liszt. It required forty-five dancers. How he must have revelled in the euphoria of creativity once more. For months he had been a man starved, disengaged from ballet, smothered by hostility, deprived of a chance to give outlet to the fire of genius burning within him.

He found a sincere ally in Erik Schmedes with whom he went over the possibility of utilising Wagnerian operas as themes for new ballets, dreaming of performing them in Bayreuth once peace returned.

It was through the hospitality of Tessa and Erik in their spacious apartment in the Allé Gasse that Waslaw met Oskar Kokoschka, the famous Viennese painter, who was only too amenable to immortalise Nijinsky by making a drawing of him. And there, too, in the Schmedes' salon, Waslaw again encountered Richard Strauss. On that notable evening the two found they were soul mates. Strauss had been most favourably impressed with Waslaw's idea of adapting *Tyl Eulenspiegel* for a ballet and readily gave his consent to it being produced. So enthusiastic was he about the project he even offered to make any changes Waslaw might desire and Romola had to intervene in her rôle of interpreter to assure Strauss that her husband found the music perfect and that he did not wish a single note to be altered. It was she who could lay claim to being the inspiration behind the project, she who had tirelessly read and reread the story to him, kindled his first glow of enthusiasm for choreographing *Tyl*.

Tyl Eulenspiegel's Lustige Streiche had already become one of the most significant of contemporary musical compositions. Strauss, who had been considered a *Wunderkind* at the age of six, was a perfect match for Waslaw's choreographic calibre.

How blissfully happy Romola and Waslaw must have been during those irrepressible, carefree weeks. They crammed their days and nights with events of the most varied sort, intoxicated by the atmosphere that still prevailed in the Emperor's *Wien,* in spite of the continuous and terrible war. Two autumns had passed and 'the boys did not return with the fall of rusty leaves'. Vienna had as yet not been contaminated. It was a city wrapped in music and merriment that poured out from the celebrated cafés, from the palatial salons of the aristocrats, along the lanes of the Prater lined with chestnut trees.

Whenever Romola was in a nostalgic mood, she would recall little episodes reflected in the mirrors of her mind; they would not be of any particular importance, yet they meant so much to me – they brought *Tatakaboy* to life. Like a mischievous boy he had loved to visit the Prater time and again, and always insisted on going on the *Riesenrad.* When telling the incidents, Romola would involuntarily shudder, then go on to say how she had steeled herself for those joy rides and bravely accompanied her Waslaw.

Evenings they would while away with friends, when not at the Opera or concerts. Hand in hand they would browse through the many museums during the day when Waslaw was not practising. They experienced the pleasure of being invited by Arnold Schönberg, the American (Austrian-born) composer to his villa in

Hitzing. Schönberg and Waslaw pursued a lengthy discourse on music and drama, spiced by rather heated differences of opinion.

Now and then they were invited to dine at the Hotel Sacher. One must presume that Madame Anna herself, dressed in strictest black, would rush forward to greet her guests warmly. After all, it had been a favourite haunt of Diaghilev and his entourage. This splendid hotel had a distinguished history; the playground of the Hapsburg dynasties, the meeting place of the notables and the diplomatic corps. I have often wondered what secrets its walls would reveal could they but speak.

Perhaps in after years the most poignant of Romola's memories were the hours she and Waslaw spent alone together in the *Theater an der Wien*. There she had sat in the stalls and watched Nijinsky dance; she had been just as captivated then as the evening in Budapest when she first set eyes on her *Harlequin*. When he performed the parts of the forty-five dancers of the *Mephisto Valse* in his practice costume:

'I forgot that it was one person dancing and not a whole troupe. And he danced, with infinite lightness and brilliancy, the part of the maiden. Never, never, have I seen among all the great *prima ballerinas* anybody so tender, so maidenly, so light, so harmonious, so perfect in their attitudes, and so matchlessly equal on their toes.'

Afterwards, he would sink down beside her and in the venerable atmosphere of the theatre they would sit back and relax whilst exchanging fragmentary bits of their knowledge of dance.

Romola was eager to impart to Waslaw all she had absorbed about ballet those intensive weeks she had spent in Paris. She told him how he was now practising on the very stage where Fanny Elssler had reached the peak of her career as a ballerina in the nineteenth century. Fanny had risen to fame from a humble origin. Her father, Johann Florian Elssler, had been copiest to Haydn; her mother, Theresa Prinster, a gifted embroideress. Similarly to Waslaw, Fanny had been fêted by the crowned heads of Europe. Her only rival had been Taglione, the daughter of upper-class parents; the mother, Swedish, the father the famous Phillip Taglione, descendant from a long line of Italian ballet dancers. But Fanny had temporarily overshadowed her rival because of her personal beauty and charm.

In the gathering dusk, the tranquillity of the theatre would embrace them and they felt as though the spirits of a bygone age were there, present with them. Romola unfolded the history of the place and how, in the nineteenth century, an immensely wealthy Hungarian magnate, Count Pálffy, had become the director of the theatre.

And then, out of the blue, came the telephone call that was to dislodge them from their recently acquired cocoon of security. At the time they hailed the message with joy – the fantastic news from the American Embassy that the Nijinsky family was free to leave for the United States of America. To sum it up briefly – the *Ballets Russes* were in New York, having completed their first season; Diaghilev, too, and they were set to go on a tour. Otto Kahn of the Metropolitan Opera had insisted that for the second season Nijinsky be included. The Americans had felt cheated out of a box-office name. It had been left to Sergei Pavlovitch to swallow the bitter pill of wounded pride, pull strings to get his former favourite back. At first, the terms stipulated for the release of Waslaw had been harsh; under no circumstances would he be allowed to go to Russia and Romola and Kyra were to remain in Austria virtually as hostages until he returned. The latter condition Waslaw was wholly unwilling to comply with. Either his family went with him or none of them would go. His resoluteness triumphed and almost within hours the little family of three were once more on a train, now bound for Switzerland. Throughout the night a sleepless Romola had observed train after train roll past with grimy, unkempt, silent soldiers staring out of the windows – on their way to more fighting and to death.

Obstacles were yet to pursue the trio. At the frontier they were forced to get off the train and to stay at a hostelry until their papers were cleared, their baggage scrupulously checked. The villagers were friendly but Romola had the distinct impression that they were constantly under surveillance. The military police were taking no chances. After a week that was yet again to test their nerves and their patience, they boarded a train that took them over the border to Switzerland.

Certainly, one can say they experienced life's seesaw – up, down, up, down. In Berne, their short stay had been extremely congenial. Banquets were given in their honour. And to Romola the sight of bountiful food proved almost too much:

'...we ordered a big lunch (that was on their arrival). Cream, butter, chocolate, sugar, all in profusion, we did not dare to touch. It first seemed unreal – then we fell on it. Vaslav stopped us very wisely; even so, Kyra and myself were upset for days by these unusual delicacies....'

From Berne they continued to Lausanne where they met the representative of the New York Metropolitan Opera House. Mr Russell rendered a full account of the situation leading up to the Nijinskys' sudden release. Diaghilev, overzealous to make as much money as possible, had signed a contract to bring to the Metropolitan the original troupe, incorporating its leading stars. He had harboured no illusions that this would be possible; Michel Fokine was in Russia, Tamara Karsavina was pregnant with her first child, and Waslaw was incarcerated in Hungary. Optimistically, he had brushed aside all such matters, assured that the name of Diaghilev and the *Ballets Russes* would be sufficient to carry on. However, when pressure had been brought upon him to produce the great Nijinsky, he had acted quickly.

It was also at this stage that Waslaw learned he had won the lawsuit against the Russian Ballet concerning the vast sum of money owed to him – an empty victory as the chances of collecting the half-million gold francs were very slim.

Igor Stravinsky and his family lived at Morges not far from Lausanne and Romola and Waslaw had taken time off to visit him. His villa had been transformed into a home that breathed the soul of Russia. According to Romola they deeply appreciated the warm hospitality accorded them although at one point Stravinsky and Waslaw had had a sharp exchange of words when in an animated discourse on music Stravinsky had lashed out against the German composers. A human frailty observed all too often – to involve politics with art. Waslaw could not understand why a war between nations should provide an excuse to denigrate the great names of the past such as Bach, Beethoven, Brahms... Stravinsky was also up in arms against Diaghilev because the Impresario had promised him an official invitation would be forthcoming for him to conduct his own ballets in America: a promise promptly forgotten after it was made. Stravinsky was furious and wanted Waslaw to refuse to perform in the States without him, a commitment Waslaw found impossible to undertake although a mild request was sent off to Diaghilev, who ignored it.

Waslaw was himself to write critically of Stravinsky:

'I know what life is. Igor Stravinsky does not know what life is because he does not like me. Igor thinks that I am hostile to his aims. He seeks riches and fame... Stravinsky is a good composer of music but he does not write about life... Stravinsky is my friend who loves me in his heart because he feels, but he considers me his enemy because I am in his way... Stravinsky saw me off at the railway station. I shook hands with him very coldly. I did not like him and therefore wanted him to feel it, but he did not feel me because he kissed me. I don't know whether his kiss was a Judas one or a friendly one, but I had a nasty feeling. I went to America. I remained in America for eighteen months...'.

A whirlwind round of activities in Paris preceded Romola and Waslaw's departure. A veritable mountain of paperwork had to be gone through – passports, visas etc. to be acquired before they arrived there from Berne on March 24th. The French were extremely courteous and helpful and the Comtesse de Greffuhle placed herself at their disposal for a spending spree in the finest boutiques. A nurse for Kyra and a maid were employed to accompany them to the States. The money to finance their sudden reinstatement to luxurious living must have come from Waslaw's Paris account. Romola never made any mention of this 'minor' detail in her book but she did stress that they were elegantly dressed and that their baggage comprised of sixteen trunks. To have accumulated that much wearing apparel in the spate of twenty-four hours is a clear indication of Romola's stamina when it came to untying the purse strings.

They boarded a French liner at Bordeaux, accompanied by Henry Russell. In her book, Romola dismissed the two weeks at sea in a few short paragraphs. The crossing had been rough but on the whole uneventful. Much of the time Waslaw had been preoccupied in the company of Louis Moret, a renowned etcher, serving during wartime as ship's doctor. The two had discoursed at great length on the subject of Waslaw's system of notation.

On April 4th, 1916, they had their first glimpse of the Statue of

Liberty and the breathtaking skyline of New York City. How their hearts must have beat faster, their pulses quickened in anticipation of what lay ahead. The United States of America; sweet land of liberty; of golden opportunities; of fame and success.

Immigration officers swarmed on board and close on their heels, hordes of journalists and cameramen. Questions were fired at Waslaw at a gruelling pace to the discomfiture of his interpreter, Russell. Camera bulbs flashed. On the whole, they were a friendly, gum-chewing lot and Waslaw warmed to them. Smitten by their amiable scuffling around him as each journalist hoped to make a scoop for his particular newspaper, and overcome with *joie de vivre* on beholding the panoramic view spread out before him, he executed a few of his phenomenal leaps on deck to the delight of the newspaper men.

The ensuing first act of the Nijinsky American drama has been described time and again. On the pier a large group of people had been waiting impatiently; representatives from the Metropolitan Opera House, some of the members of the *Ballets Russes,* including Leonide Massine, Diaghilev's current favourite. But the foreground had been dominated by one figure, that of the Impresario himself, arrogant as ever, dressed in an impeccably tailored overcoat with velvet lapels, a monocle in his eye. In Romola's own words, she

'walked down first and he (Diaghilev) bowed very low and, kissing my hand, offered me a beautiful bouquet of American Beauties. Vaslav, carrying Kyra, followed me closely. Sergei Pavlovitch kissed him on both cheeks, according to the Russian custom, and Vaslav, with a quick gesture placed Kyra in his arms. He looked embarrassed, and handed the child to the next person standing near to him. Drobetsky was smiling like the full moon. Massine was introduced, then Sergei Pavlovitch walked away with Vaslav, and I prayed that this might prove a real pact of friendship.'

Romola was to be rudely awakened from her wishful thinking only a short time later. Meanwhile, however, Romola and Waslaw were conducted to their hotel whilst Diaghilev and Massine returned to the Ritz where they were staying. No sooner had the Nijinskys unpacked before trouble started. Prodded by Romola,

Waslaw demanded that the debt owed to him by Diaghilev should be paid in full before he danced one step at the Met. The settlement of financial transactions of this kind is usually rather sordid, especially if one party adamantly refuses to pay. Romola took it upon herself to place the matter in the hands of an eminent lawyer, a Mr Untermeyer, whose niece, Madeleine, she had become friendly with in Karlsbad when a young girl. A nephew in the law firm, Laurence Steinhardt, was to prove to be an invaluable support to Romola for years to come. A compromise was reached within a few days and Waslaw was to receive a weekly payment from Diaghilev under the terms of a special contract drawn up by the Metropolitan Opera. Possibly it was from that period on that Waslaw was to rely more and more on Romola to handle their finances.

But let us revert to the morning after their arrival. NIJINSKY THE DANCER ARRIVES – NIJINSKY WILL DANCE – NIJINSKY IN TWO BALLETS – those and similar headlines appeared in the *New York Times* and other newspapers.

For Waslaw, a hectic and nerve-racking period lay ahead. The *Ballets Russes* had performed in the States for nearly three months, commencing with a two-week engagement at the rather insignificant Century Theatre in New York. This theatre had been placed at their disposal because the official opera season at the Metropolitan was still on. The troupe had then gone on tour to seventeen cities and their new season had already begun at the Metropolitan on the 3rd of April. Their success had been moderate, the critics lukewarm in their praise. The glittering stars had been noted by their absence. Hence the cries for the appearance of the magnetic and charismatic Nijinsky were intensified.

The strain upon a man as sensitive as Waslaw must have been almost unbearable from the start. At no time did Diaghilev attend the rehearsals nor did he even go the the première. It is true that he had given implicit instructions that Nijinsky be allowed as many rehearsals as he required and that he be treated with courtesy by the other members of the company, and have their full backing. But did he? According to reliable sources Bolm was one of the few who showed loyalty and friendship. Waslaw had been quick to sense the air of antagonism that impregnated the atmosphere during rehearsals. He became tormented yet again by his fear of people and entered into a withdrawal process. As a result his behaviour was misinterpreted. Poisonous tongues were quick to spit out venom without any knowledge of actual facts; that he was creating a fuss about money, that he was out of form, had gained too much weight; that he was morose and had started scratching his fingers. Was perhaps that debut in America the beginning of the end? Even Romola, however much she loved her husband, could not fathom the depths of his soul, understand how much he probably missed the support of the man who it might be said had been his Svengali and with whom he had shared a passionate love for the art of dance.

Romola had been the victor in the bitter 'tug-of-war' for Waslaw Nijinsky. And inadvertently she must have been the one on whose shoulders lay the blame for the quenching of any hopes of reconciliation, when she immediately in New York took up the fight for money owed by entering into litigation against Diaghilev. Waslaw had been deeply hurt when she so relentlessly pursued the claim against his former mentor. To him, to express himself in his art, to be able to dance, was all important. To Romola, money meant security for her two 'children'. She had been indoctrinated by Emilia in the belief that a great artist should live in grand style and be surrounded by luxury; alas, she became blinded to the fact that her goal harmed rather than abetted her husband.

Tossing all worries to one side, she blossomed; she was in her element once more. The name Nijinsky was an *Open Sesame* to High Society where she felt she rightfully belonged. She was young, good-looking, she charmed all she met, had everybody at her feet with her wit and personality. She relished being in the company of celebrities. Was that not the environment in which she had been brought up?

Wednesday, the 12th of April arrived. The Metropolitan Opera House proudly advertised DIAGHILEFF'S BALLETS RUSSES, with the price of tickets ranging from $1.00 to $5.00. Four ballets were on the matinée programme, of which Nijinsky danced in two, *Le Spectre de la Rose* and *Petroushka*. The entire Social Register must have been in attendance that afternoon. When Waslaw appeared on stage as *Le Spectre*, the audience stood up as one man and rose petals, like a flurry of snowflakes, soon covered the stage and the performer. The critics were unanimous that Nijinsky was the greatest of all male dancers and the music editor of the *Globe* concluded he was 'not of this earth'.

After his second appearance, one critic wrote that it was apparent that the presence of the famous male dancer had a bracing effect on his colleagues as there was a brilliance and vitality about the presentations in which he took part that had been lacking before. With Nijinsky in the title role of any of the subsequent performances of the *Ballets Russes,* his name had sufficient appeal to draw the largest audiences than had attended any of the previous performances outside the subscription series.

Carl Van Vechten, who recalled Waslaw's European triumphs, wrote that Nijinsky 'had surpassed himself', that his movements 'contained the unbroken quality of music, the balance of great painting, the meaning of fine literature and the emotion inherent in all these arts.' He went on to say that 'the dancer makes of himself what he will, he can look tall or short, magnificent or ugly, fascinating or repulsive.'

Superlatives rained on him. Sifting through the old newspaper cuttings, I feel impelled to include a few more, selected at random. One commentator on Nijinsky's New York première went so far as to say that 'it took only ten minutes yesterday afternoon for Vaslav Nijinsky to demonstrate to the Metropolitan Opera House audience that he is the greatest dancer among men that this country has ever seen...'.

'His art was never in question after his first step. He combined grace with elegance and imagination in every gesture, pose or attitude... His part in *Spectre de la Rose* was intelligent, poetic and enhancing.' – *New York American.*

'Nijinsky has the face of a child, the frank smile of a boy, and he seems to have stolen the missing arms of Venus of Milo. For combining delicacy with strength, bodily grace with manly beauty, he recalls no equal. And aside from the wonderful pair of waving arms, this dancer has two legs built on lines of classic form and strong as iron.' –*New York Evening Sun.*

'...He dances with a bodily rhythm no man has ever shown Americans, and with every movement of head, limbs and torso, as well as his facial expressiveness, has a meaning that is well nigh perfect.' – *New York World.*

'...his movements have the grace of a woman, and he lands from his prodigious leaps as lightly as a bit of thistle down. He is a great artist, probably the greatest whom the present generation has seen here.' – *New York Herald.*

Romola was to say that Waslaw had difficulty in coping with the idolatry that greeted him. He was acutely discomposed by the mass hysteria he encountered, often surrounded in the wings by admirers who tried to touch him, feel his legs, his muscles. There were harrowing incidents like when a crowd rushed on to the stage to look for some 'gimmick' that enabled him to 'fly across the stage and stay in the air, suspended...'. At a charity function a group of women even besieged his dressing-room and took his underwear.

But she also recalled the brighter side. How rewarded he felt when he and Romola pored over the reviews each morning. How he loved exploring 'the New World' with her. On those rare occasions that they would be free for an evening, they would stroll along Broadway, dazzled by the myriad twinkling illustrated signs advertising the latest hits on the Great White Way. Waslaw became an ardent 'movie' fan. He foresaw a wonderful future for the motion picture industry as a new art form. It is amazing that no film mogul thought to perpetuate Nijinsky's fabulous leaps for posterity. According to Robert Mead, a rumour was spread years ago that a short strip of film showing Nijinsky dancing is owned by a wealthy American, who keeps it in a vault and only brings it out on occasion for privileged guests. Sadly, this astonishing memorabilia has never been traced nor its existence confirmed.

Waslaw and Romola attended a performance of the much acclaimed Ziegfield Follies and they also savoured their introduction to the 'new fangled' music called Jazz. Romola said that Waslaw would listen attentively just once to a Ragtime rhythm and then he would execute a brilliant rendition of it by tapping it out with his feet and hands. Sometimes, late at night, like a couple of teenagers, they would sneak in to a soda fountain, climb up on the high stools and satiate their palates with various flavours of ice cream. Excursions such as these were blessings bestowed upon them in their few private moments.

More and more, their 'official' engagement calendar was to spill over the pages. Invitations arrived by the score for Waslaw to open exhibitions, attend charity functions and bazaars. Hostesses vied with one another to entertain the couple and the guest list would embrace all the notables of the day. Caruso became a friend. Mrs William Vanderbilt asked Waslaw to dance at a Special Benefit performance in aid of the homeless in Venice after a catastrophic flood. For the occasion Waslaw was dressed in a black and gold Carpacciso Gondolier costume. Richard Strauss, who was visiting New York, gave a luncheon in honour of Waslaw and the guest list included

Fritz Kreisler and his wife and also Isadora Duncan. Romola cited in her book a memorable conversation between Isadora Duncan and Waslaw.

'You remember, Nijinsky, years ago in Venice I proposed to you that we should have a child together. What a dancer we could have created! The idea did not seem to appeal to you then; I see you are changed now; you are less intolerant towards us women.' A frozen, embarrassed silence followed her words. Vaslav smilingly replied to her challenge; 'I did not change. I love everybody, as Christ did.'

Among the many acquaintances, friends and admirers in New York at the time, was also Baron de Meyer, one of the fashionable photographers of the day. He had met Waslaw in Paris already in 1911 and had then taken some exquisite photographs of him. Meyer's wife Olga was allegedly the illegitimate daughter of one of the royal families in Europe. So that he would be able to move more freely in the circle of the Royal Court, Adolf Meyer had been given a baronetcy when he married his Olga. Using his wife's social connections, his own aplomb and a camera, he had thus begun to take pictures of the famous in the world of the arts, and the clique of the very rich.

In his final performance of the season, the 29th of April 1916 to be exact, Waslaw Nijinsky danced in *Le Spectre* at the matinée and in *La Princesse Enchantée* and *Schéhérazade* in the evening. Both performances had drawn a vast audience whose enthusiasm had been clearly expressed. A brief announcement appeared in the press to the effect that Messrs Nijinsky and Bolm as well as Mme Revalles would remain in the States until the following season but that Sergei Pavlovitch Diaghilev and his company would leave for Spain on May the 6th on the Italian liner *Dante Alighieri*. The company was to dance at the Teatro Real in Madrid at the request of the King of Spain.

The formal announcement concealed the deep rift that divided Diaghilev and Nijinsky. According to Romola, Diaghilev's 'hatred was ferocious and his pursuit of Vaslav relentless'. Apparently, he circulated the most untrue rumours about Waslaw and the bitter wrangle over money and lawsuits never seemed to end.

Quite naturally, the savagery of Diaghilev's attacks on his former star and the disturbing effect it had on Nijinsky did not go unnoticed. Otto Kahn had his heart set on arranging a coast-to-coast tour of the Russian Ballet in the autumn but he did not wish Diaghilev's presence to mar it. A contract was consequently drawn up with the Metropolitan Opera House calling for an engagement lasting forty weeks; the first three weeks to be in New York. There was one precondition – that Diaghilev was not to return to the United States but that Waslaw Nijinsky was to be the artistic director, and also supervise the tour, an arrangement that in Kahn's mind would avoid further friction between the two men. In other words, the company was to be subcontracted to the Met by Diaghilev and the sole responsibility placed on Nijinsky's shoulders. To both Diaghilev and the many who had witnessed Nijinsky's failure in London years previously, the whole idea seemed to be a preposterous one, doomed to failure from the start. Both Waslaw and Romola were totally inexperienced and were taking a foolhardy risk. But Romola was optimistic and took upon herself to become Waslaw's business manager. She was wise enough to realise, however, that, ignorant as she was in legal matters, she would require a sound legal adviser and she again turned to Laurence Steinhardt.

Casting to the four winds all thoughts of the gruelling work that lay ahead, Romola and Waslaw decided to enjoy to the full the American summer. To escape the heat of New York, weekends were often spent in millionaires' homes on Long Island. '…Vaslav loved especially the bathroom attached to each bedroom, with their towels and bathmats in the same vivid colours as the salts and scents. *Très Ballets Russes.*' Waslaw was an excellent swimmer and leapt like a dolphin in the water. Such was his prowess and skill that crowds used to gather round the pool to watch him.

On June 19th, they celebrated Kyra's second birthday in a traditional Hungarian way. The élite had all been invited and in generous American fashion had poured gifts on the great Nijinsky's daughter. Romola recalled how cuddly, woolly, stuffed toys larger than the child herself had crowded every available corner of the room. A huge chocolate *gâteau,* topped with three candles, had been ordered from one of New York's leading confectioners, two for the age she had reached and one for the forthcoming year.

During the summer, an epidemic of infantile paralysis broke out and to escape the congested city where the risk for Kyra was much higher, Romola and Waslaw drove to Bar Harbor in Waslaw's new

136

Peerless. He was inordinately proud of his hastily-acquired ability as a car-driver but, not surprisingly, Romola was to remain dubious after the rather hair-raising trip, taking into consideration the many hazards encountered during the six day journey before they reached their destination! '...he knew nothing about the engine...drove on the wrong side...almost ran into a tramcar, but at the last moment pirouetted aside – trouble with the carburetter... never quite sure which gear to take a hill, so he tried them all in turn, and then, when the car refused to pull, he just let it slide backwards, to Kyra's immense joy.'

From Romola's rendition of their short stay at Bar Harbor, they had a very relaxing time. She described the place as one of the most beautiful she had ever visited. Waslaw loved to take Kyra, her nurse and the favourite painted duck to the seaside. Or he would practise on the lawn of a neo-Greek marble temple that stood in magnificent solitude on the top of a hill, surrounded by pine trees. Kyra would chortle with delight at every high jump he made. 'Tatakaboy, how he leaped and flyed.' For many years Kyra claimed she could actually remember from that tender age how she would attend rehearsals with Romola in New York. She vividly recalled him dancing in *Sylphides* and the dark velvet clothing he wore with white sleeves. 'He flew in the moonlight,' she used to say.

Concerts were held once weekly in the temple which was converted into a theatre, and the list of performing artists was impressive; all the great names who had not been able to get back to Europe because of the war – Harold Bauer, Josef Hofmann, Fritz Kreisler, Efrem Zimbalist... A young harpist, Carlos Salzedo, also visited Waslaw and Romola during their stay and Robert Edmond Jones, whom Waslaw had been introduced to in New York, arrived with his ideas for costumes and scenery for *Tyl Eulenspiegel.* Jones was an American scenic painter who had worked with Max Reinhardt in Berlin. Laurence Steinhardt also came. He wished to go through the final arrangements for the forthcoming tour and the clauses in the contract. Romola had become alarmed over the almost diabolic workload which had been assigned to Waslaw. The itinerary alone for the comprehensive tour of some fifty-odd cities was daunting, added to which he had his own two new ballets to rehearse as well as the usual repertory.

And so the idyllic sojourn had to come to an end, the quiet life of their holiday haven to be replaced by unmitigated chaos. There is no doubt that some of the blame had to be placed on Nijinsky's shoulders. Insecure and unsure of himself, he had rebuffed the most competent men he could have had from Diaghilev's entourage and instead surrounded himself with the wrong managerial staff. Too, when the company arrived in New York on board the *Lafayette,* he did not greet them but confronted his troupe only on the first day of rehearsal. Thus, he built up an invisible yet impenetrable wall between himself and the staff and dancers. He would devote hours practising alone or in the company of Romola and Kyra, his appreciative audience of two, the only observers he would permit to be with him.

On October 16th, the new season was to open at the Metropolitan Opera House. Waslaw 'blindfolded' himself to the basic truth – he had taken upon himself too much. He became a victim of misadventure after misadventure. Only days after their arrival, the company went on a two day strike, when a dispute blew up. Waslaw was the artistic director, which entailed that not only did he have to work on the choreography, the costumes and the scenery for his cherished *Tyl,* he had to go over all the technical problems, lighting, the orchestra, acquaint the dancers with their new roles. In addition, he was scheduled to appear on stage himself in a number of performances. He became more and more edgy, quite unable to deal diplomatically with the likewise temperamental people around him.

Tyl Eulenspiegel, in which Waslaw himself was to dance the part of *Tyl,* was an extravaganza with some twenty main characters and extensive supporting cast. The costumes by Robert Jones were spectacular in their vivid colours but Waslaw had been dissatisfied with the sets and had broken out into an almost uncontrollable rage. On top of that, an incident occurred which was near-fatal to the opening of the season. Waslaw had jumped on stage to correct a dancer's steps, when he slipped and fainted. Fortunately, as it transpired, he had merely sprained his ankle but was still advised to take a complete rest for several weeks. His spirits must have sunk to an even lower ebb. Everything conspired against him! His *Mephisto Valse* had to be cancelled, the première of *Tyl Eulenspiegel* postponed until a later date.

'I have composed a ballet on the music of Richard Strauss. I composed this ballet in New York... They insisted I should produce it in three weeks. I wept and said that I could not produce

that ballet in three weeks because this was beyond my strength. Then Otto Kahn...said he could not give me more time than that...I agreed...because there was nothing else I could do. I knew that if I did not agree, I would not have enough money to live on... I worked like an ox. I never let up. I slept little...My wife saw all that work and was sorry for me...I commissioned an artist...to make the sets. The artist seemed to understand me, but...he was worried all the time. I was not worried. I enjoy myself... He drew for me what I was telling him. His costume drawings were better. Their colours were full of life... I was sure of success. I worked like an ox. The ox was driven too hard, for he twisted his ankle. The ox was sent to Dr Abbé. He was a good doctor... The American public loved me because it had confidence in me. It saw that my foot hurt. I danced badly, but the public enjoyed it. "Tyl" was a success but it was produced too soon... I made this a comic ballet because I felt the war. Everyone was sick of the war and therefore people wanted to be cheered up... I showed "Tyl" in all its beauty. "Tyl's" life was simple. I showed that it was the German people...'.

Waslaw Nijinsky, Villa Guardamunt

Waslaw was confined to his bed, from where he held conferences regarding the ongoing preparations for *Tyl*. Romola complained he was an irritable, difficult patient. And the presence of two of the dancers at his bedside was to have a significant bearing on his life later on. At first their soothing influence on her husband had been accepted by Romola but future events were to prove the detrimental and tragic consequences their grip on him wielded. They were Dmitri Kostrovsky, a newcomer to the company, and Nicolas Zverev. Almost imperceptively they began to preach about Tolstoy and his philosophy to Waslaw. Wearied by his continual battle against the other members of the troupe, whom he felt were antagonistic toward him, he became an easy prey.*

---

* They urged him to adopt Count Tolstoy's doctrine. In the guise of a moral philosopher and not as the novelist, Tolstoy had evolved a new Christianity. He held that God and His Kingdom were 'within' each individual; that Mankind must learn to love one another; man must free himself of lust and greed; abstain from partaking of meat of slaughtered animals; renounce worldly possessions and live solely by manual work.

Anna Pavlova was dancing in New York at the same time as the *Ballets Russes* and Romola tells the rather amusing story of how she sent an enormous basket of flowers to Waslaw when she heard of his mishap. 'One morning she asked me personally to the telephone. "Please tell me the truth; Vaslav Fomitch has broken his leg, hasn't he?" "No, fortunately, though we thought so at first." "Oh, really not?" And her voice dropped, as though she was disappointed. I did not say anything about it to Vaslav.'

Needless to say, she had hoped that her rival in drawing the public to the box office would be incarcerated for as long as her own programme at the Globe Theatre was running. In fact, attendance at the Met did drop noticeably for those performances when Nijinsky's name did not appear on the billboards.

His foot healed remarkably fast. When Dr Abbé showed Romola the X-rays he explained that Vaslav's foot anatomically was not constructed like that of other human beings, but was a mixture of the construction of man and bird... 'it is atavism – fifth generation of dancers. The result not only of his training and constant practising, but of those of the ancestors. This is the secret of his amazing elevation; no wonder he can fly; he is a human bird.'

With his foot bandaged, Waslaw limped back to rehearsals. His feverish mind was bursting with all the ideas that had been amassing there since he had first dreamed of creating a ballet on the theme of *Tyl*. He strove for perfection so as to make the audience gasp, and inside his head he kept churning over and over *pour faire rire*. The audience *must* be made to laugh with *Tyl* at his antics.

Carlos Salzedo was to write: 'I believe myself to be one of the few outsiders who has had the privilege of attending partial and ensemble rehearsals of *Tyl*. Nijinsky's choreography is admirably attuned to the fanciful rhythms of each episode of the score, without being enslaved by them. He has evolved tremendously since his staging of *L'Après-midi d'un Faune*. Nijinsky is music personified. As I was playing the music, it seemed to filter through his relaxed, motionless body, as if in a trance.'

The ballet centres around the mischievous *Tyl,* the Flemish folk hero, who plays his merry pranks against the rich and the professional people of Brunswick to mirror society's injustice and bias. Twenty characters, representing all walks of life; the lords and ladies, the wealthy merchants, the clergy, the police, the professors, the burghers, the beggars and urchins. With a pixieish sense of humour, he pokes fun at the rich and the snobbish, and turns them into fools, all except the poor whom he entices to join him in dance, a dance of Revolution and Equality. The pageantry of a medieval market place is brilliantly brought to life, a tapestry of vivid and subdued colours. Drolly, *Tyl* ties the townspeople together in a wide roll of the finest cloth only to snip their bond asunder with a pair of tailor's scissors. In the tumult that follows, the poor scramble to help themselves to everything available from the rich merchants' stalls. *Tyl* is surrounded by soldiers and brought to justice. His penalty, death by hanging. Laughing and dancing he goes to the scaffold, with a smile on his lips, believing it all to be a joke. The people mourn their protector and feel responsible for his death. Then, suddenly, amongst a group of weeping women, his 'spirit' springs forth. *Voilà, Tyl* is once more his gay self and the masses proceed with their merrymaking, cheered by their *Tyl.*

This incredible ballet lasted just eighteen minutes. The applause was deafening and Waslaw had the satisfaction of taking fifteen curtain calls with the members of his troupe. The première took place on Monday, the 23rd of October, and *Tyl Eulenspiegel* was heralded as Waslaw Nijinsky's finest choreography. Ironically, it was also to be the last new ballet by Nijinsky. The American public loved his interpretation of a 'comic' ballet and again the critics heaped praise upon him. It was a moment of triumph for Waslaw because *Tyl* was the first piece of work he had created without any influence or aid from Diaghilev. Waslaw had proven to himself and to the world he could do it alone. It was the only ballet performed by his company that the Impresario never saw.

As mentioned earlier, Waslaw's tireless work on *Tyl Eulenspiegel,* the endless press conferences in connection with the forthcoming tour, the never-ending crises to be overcome behind scenes, placed upon Romola's shoulders the responsibility of meeting, if only briefly, the incalculable number of people who daily besieged the hotel, crying for interviews with Nijinsky.

She was not emcumbered by wifely chores in a home and stepped blithely into her role of taking charge of her husband's affairs with absolute confidence. And he, in turn, leaned on his *Romushka* more and more to handle Government officials, artists and musicians, and last but not least the gentlemen of the press who wanted the latest gossip about the star for the society columns.

There were days when she had to attend as many as ten social functions and receive some thirty people privately. Although she was at the pinnacle of her youth and possessed a heroic stamina, at the end of a fortnight even she wilted under the terrific strain.

She was compelled to ask her French secretary to be more restrictive in her selection and to spurn lesser known names. But then she relented, and in an article she wrote in Zürich in 1966, she explained the reason why. A sensitive chord had been struck when she remembered how she as a young well-born Hungarian girl never got a chance to approach the august and aloof dancers of the *Ballets Russes,* when her whole being and heart ached to speak just once to the great Nijinsky himself...

In that same article she goes on to say how one day a young visitor was announced. He had tried in vain for several days to see Waslaw but had been turned away; he had even attempted to waylay him as he left the hotel or went into the dining-room but to no avail. It was the note she subsequently read that intrigued her. The writer had to see Waslaw Nijinsky, it was a matter of life and death. The note was signed Rodolfo Guglielmi. She felt she had to know what it was that he wanted of them.

When he entered the drawing-room, she saw in front of her a tall, slender, extremely good-looking young Italian. He had limpid brown eyes and jet black silky hair, brushed very close and smooth. He could only be in his early twenties. He moved gracefully, quietly, like a cat. His manners were good and he seemed quite self-possessed, although at a glance Romola deducted he came from humble origin. At first he appeared somewhat embarrassed, at a loss just how to begin.

Romola asked him to be seated and offered him a cigarette, which he declined. He stumbled through a few conversational phrases and then launched into his story. '*Signora,* I am forever indebted to you for granting me this interview. I had lost all hope of ever getting to see Signor Nijinsky, I don't know how to thank you. Believe me, I would never have dared to disturb you were it not for me such a vital matter. It is a very long story, I don't know how to tell you how it happened, so that you will understand and forgive me.'

He poured out his heart to her, all about his family back home in Castellaneta, his birthplace in southern Italy. His mother was French, his father, an army captain, who had died when he was thirteen. How he was sent to a Military Academy but did not like it there and how his burning ambition had been to come to the United States, the 'land of milk and honey'. How he had quickly become disillusioned. Romola was unable to stop his flow of words in broken English. He pressed on about how he had had to take all sorts of menial jobs to eke out an existence: garbage collecting, shoe polishing, washing dishes in restaurants. The streets of the great city of New York had not been paved with gold. He confessed how girls and mature women pursued him, he was unable to understand his success with them. Nor did he know how to escape them. He had found a friend from Sicily who had already been in the States for a number of years and who used to be in 'Tin Pan Alley' and knew from there some of the powerful and important people in the world of show business; Ziegfield, who ran the Century Theatre; the great Adolph Zukor, Hungarian Czar of the new fangled craze, the movies; Sam Goldwyn, who used to make gloves in Philadelphia; the Schuberts and many others.

Through this friend, Rodolfo was given work as an extra in a film and was paid the handsome sum of five dollars a day. He had found the work easy, but sometimes they had had to wait for hours, even days, before being used on the set. He had, however, carefully studied the actors from the sidelines – newcomers to stardom who earned thousands of dollars. It was a strange world, quite different from that of the backstage of the opera at home where he had once in a while worked unloading scenery and doing odd jobs. He had been fascinated by it all, the studio where houses and streets sprang up overnight and even mountains were built before one's very eyes; the intense heat from the strong lights under which they worked. Watching those stars perform in front of a camera, he had vowed he could do the same if only given a chance. He had tried to attract the attention of the director, the cameramen, anybody, but had merely been pushed out of the way until the script girl had noticed him. Eileen, that was her name, had been the director's girl friend for a long time. Her word weighed heavily with the cast and little by little she pushed Rodolfo into the front line; he got 'bit' parts and his love scenes impressed the director. But by then he was deeply involved with Eileen and she became wildly jealous. He had been in a quandary as he did not love her and was surrounded by other attractive and enamoured women. His dilemma was that he wanted to get away and he had learned that the studios were moving to Los Angeles. He was promised a contract provided his application was accepted. But he had to fill out a long form about his origin, his education, previous experience, and above all, his artistic background. He had lied when he put down that he had acted on the stage in Sicily, certain that they would never be able to check its validity. He had also been required to elucidate on any special talents and had written that he was a professional dancer.

At this point in his narrative he threw himself on his knees in front of Romola and beseeched her to forgive him...he had committed the unpardonable sin of writing that he was a pupil of the famous Maestro Nijinsky. Would she ask her husband to back him up should he be approached by the studio? He gazed at her pleadingly, his eyes filled with tears.

Romola felt pity for the young man, who so bewitched her with his story. She assured him that Nijinsky was not only a great artist but a most kind and understanding man. She would discuss the matter with him. 'And so it was that my kind Vaslav actually showed him a few steps and movements and Rudi became his only pupil...'.

His full name was Rodolfo Alfonzo Raffaelo Pierre Filibert Guglielmi Di Valentino D'Antonguolia. To his adoring fans he was to be known as Rudolph Valentino. He rapidly rose to fame when he was cast as Julió in *Four Horsemen of the Apocalypse*. It became one of the great box office successes of cinema history.

In the last paragraph of her article Romola told of how she was to meet him some years later at the home of a friend in New York. He was then at the height of his fame but already a doomed man. It was June and they had stood on the terrace of their host's apartment overlooking Central Park.

'...the whole of New York lay before us, the thousands of lights in this unique city glittered below, while millions of stars twinkled above in the sky. We could hear very faintly the ceaseless murmur of the city's traffic, and Valentino said, "*Carissima* Romola, I have known many women, lovable, enchanting, wonderful women, but I have never met one who was as kind, as loyal or more understanding than you..." This was the last time I saw Valentino because shortly afterwards he died and the whole world mourned him. He is still not forgotten and remains the symbol of a great lover. He is now beyond all suffering, hardship, success and admiration."

Valentino died in New York in 1926. His illness was at first not diagnosed as serious but he died of peritonitis.

On October 30th, 1916 the transcontinental tour commenced and it was to last until February 24th the following year. The management of the Metropolitan spared no expense in advertising the tour and the following statement was issued:

THE COMPANY

For this tour, the full strength of the Diaghileff organisation has been mobilized, and more than two score performers will make the trip.

At the head of the company stands the incomparable Nijinsky, whose belated appearance in New York last season sufficed to establish beyond dispute his preeminence as a dancer. In one performance he earned such plaudits from the metropolitan critics as they bestow only on superlative genius...

Last season M. Nijinsky secured his parole from Austria only in time to appear at the second New York engagement of the Ballet. He has never appeared in this country outside of New York. This year the spectacle of his incomparable technique will be accessible to the art-lovers of fifty cities. During the interim, the great dancer has practised continuously, as well as having completed the choreography of several new ballets of his own conception.

While Waslaw was engrossed in his work –setting up an itinerary that was to cover fifty-three cities in all was a programme that would have broken the resilience of a weaker man – Romola had to concentrate on planning a suitable wardrobe to conform with the changes in climate and the varied functions that she would be facing. Little Kyra was to remain in New York at the home of friends together with her nanny. It had been mutually agreed that the strain of so much travel would be far too trying for a small child. Nonetheless, Waslaw was deeply concerned about his little daughter, full of remorse at having to leave her in the hands of comparative strangers for so long. In 1919 he was to write about the impending trip to the States:

*'...I went to Morges to see Stravinsky and asked him, in the
absolute certainty that he would not refuse, whether he and his
wife would agree to take in my child and keep her for a bit. I
knew he had many children and I realised therefore that he
could keep my Kyra if I went to North America. I did not want
to take my child with me. I wanted to leave her in the care of
another loving mother. Feeling happy about it, I asked Stravinsky whether he could take my Kyra and keep her for a
while...'.*

Stravinsky had refused on the grounds that he and his wife would
not want to be burdened with the responsibility for another man's
child. Suppose she caught an infection and died?

*'His wife burst into tears and Stravinsky said he was sorry...
She is a woman and therefore feels what it means to have a child
in a train and ship. She was sorry for me. I know that she did not
agree with her husband because he spoke very quickly and deci-
sively and made his wife realise he did not want it. I told him I
would pay all Kyra's expenses. He did not agree...he advised
me to leave Kyra with one of the governesses...I could not leave
my child in a stranger's hands...I want to say that children must
always be with their mothers.'*

Romola, however, did not share his feelings. Almost callously it
seemed, she brushed aside Waslaw's anxiety. To her, the forthcoming months beckoned as the commencement of a glorious
adventure. She must have felt the spirit of the pioneers surging
through her veins; broadening her horizon by meeting new and
exciting people, acquainting herself with another culture, absorbing
the changes of seasons and scenery in a country as big as Europe.
And she was part of the *Ballets Russes;* her Watza leading a tour
unparalleled in the history of Diaghilev's Company.

And thus the magnificent folly got under way. Scenery, lighting,
baggage, costumes were stacked in a separate train carrying the
technical staff. They were to make up the advance guard and ensure
that the stage was set for each performance. A twelve car railroad
train carried the dancers and the musicians, in all over 120 individuals. A frenzied period of living in a gypsy ambience was to be
theirs for many weeks. Two books in my possession give chrono-

146

logical descriptions of the fantastic venture; one, Richard Buckle's *Nijinsky*, in which the emphasis is on the ballets performed, their reception by the critics, etcetera; the other is Romola's book which quite naturally dwells on the more personal highlights of the trip. I shall attempt to summarise as briefly as possible her impressions, revealing the lighter, more human aspects of the tour, but perhaps most significantly, some of the events portrayed give an indication, unbeknown to her then, of the tragedy that lay ahead. And it was during those weeks, too, that for the first time since she had laid eyes on her God of Dance, Romola, at one stage, felt impelled to leave him because of the baffling change that was taking place.

An itinerary covering the tour from the day it started on October 30th at the Opera House, Providence, Rhode Island, to February 24th, 1917, at the Harmanus Bleeker Hall, Albany, New York, circulated on tour sheets of 'Masque Studio' paper records each engagement. It is not in Romola's handwriting but in certain places she added some cryptic comments of her own in Hungarian. Against the date December 7th Romola had written in her tiny script *Kigyo,* meaning snake. To whom or what was she referring? December 11th, *free masons,* and *valtoztatjak a szerepeket,* meaning 'they have changed the roles'. December 13th, 14th, *Bevá-sárlás, indianok,* 'shopping', 'Indians'. Further down the page she made a note, *vészekédes, kirándulás* – 'quarrelling, picnic'.

From the very start of the tour she tried to keep up as normal a daily routine as possible and to find suitable hotels where Waslaw would be assured of a pause from the almost unbearable pressure imposed upon him. Quite ruthlessly he set a rigorous pace, not only for himself but for the company as a whole to keep in trim. He suffered discomfort in the narrow bed provided in American sleepers. 'He needed space, in sleeping as much as dancing'.

But it was not 'all work and no play' as they frequently renewed old acquaintances and made fresh contacts. In Boston, Waslaw was overjoyed to have a few quiet moments in the company of John Singer Sargent. He had met the painter in London when the artist had made the famous head of Nijinsky in the turban from *Le Pavillon d'Armide*. This charcoal drawing was to have a very chequered history.

In Boston, too, Waslaw and Romola spent a relaxing evening together with George Copeland, the pianist, who played Debussy for them. On a more jarring note, Waslaw had become deeply upset by rumours being spread that he was a deserter from the Russian Army and by a report in one of the newspapers to that effect.

It was not only in the actual performance of his dance that Waslaw was meticulous. He would go to the theatre about two hours before curtain time, even if he was not due to appear in the first ballet. His dresser would describe to Romola what ensued within the hallowed walls of the dressing-room. From the moment he stepped inside, Waslaw would completely disengage himself from the outside world. During those hours he would sit immobile on a chair, or, if a couch was available, lie down, eyes shut. It was then that his metamorphosis began; mentally he was slowly transforming himself into the character he was to dance.

His dresser would make himself as inconspicuous as possible, settling down in some dark corner, while keeping a wary eye on the door to prevent any intrusion that might break the spell. Then the supreme moment arrived when Waslaw would seat himself in front of the mirror and commence the ritual of applying his make-up. It was a skill in which he excelled and in which he was utterly self-taught. All the years he had spent studying paintings in museums, storing in the back of his mind the minutest details of the portraits, came to his aid as did his keen observation of people; their characteristics and mannerisms peculiar to them. Deftly, he would first apply a brownish base, then subtle shades of colour, and lastly the powder. Within minutes the desired mask was finished; The Golden Slave, the *Spectre de la Rose*...depending on which role he was dancing.

There is an amusing anecdote concerning him and Emilia which dates back to when he and Romola were staying at the Villa during the First World War. Whatever their differences on many matters, Emilia was sufficiently impressed by his professional skill in the art of make-up to implore him on one occasion to assist her with her own make-up. It was for a part she was to play at variance to her usual heroines. An ageing woman who managed a brothel! Emilia was forced to admire his superb technique. But vanity was one of her 'deadly' sins and she was shattered to study herself in the looking-glass and confront a face much older and rather vulgar. When she complained over this, Waslaw had calmly and patiently explained to her that 'you have to look convincing as the character you are portraying, and your role is that of an ageing burnt-out *Madame.*'

I still have in my possession a small, worn, metal make-up box comprising two compartments and an upper tray, given to me by my grandmother Emilia, which had belonged to my father. It was the one he had accidentally left behind those many years ago in Budapest.

Towards the end of November the company reached Washington, D.C. There, Waslaw performed in the presence of President Wilson and almost the entire *Corps Diplomatique*. It gave him the opportunity to express his thanks in person to the United States for the part the country had played in obtaining his release. The President must have made a lasting impression upon him because he was later to make countless references to Wilson in the most praiseworthy terms in his *Diary*.

> *'Wilson is a man of peace who did not want war...I want Wilson to realise his aims because his aims are nearer to truth...Wilson is a big man. The size of his head is small but it contains a lot...'*

In Atlanta, Georgia, Waslaw suffered a rather disturbing interruption to his tour. An official summons greeted him from the Russian military authorities that he would have to report to them in St. Petersburg within ten days. However willing he might have been to return to his homeland – one must remember his deep anxiety for his family there – a number of factors barred his going. Firstly, as a member of the Imperial Ballet he had been exempted from military service for all time; secondly, there was no physical way of transporting himself to Russia within the stipulated time; thirdly, he was tied to a firm contract with the Metropolitan Opera, and lastly but not least, he was theoretically still a prisoner-of-war to Austria and the only condition for his release had been that he remain in a neutral country for the duration of the war. Romola stayed on with the troupe while Waslaw left for Washington under escort to sort out the matter with the Russian Embassy there. It was agreed that he catch up with the company in New Orleans.

The train journeys would have been unbearably tedious and boring were it not for the friendships that were formed. Romola and Waslaw were mostly together with Mr and Mrs Herndon (he represented the Metropolitan on the tour) and with the concert master Fradkin and his wife. Both couples were outward-going and agreeable and Waslaw was at ease with them. The rest of the company for-

149

med their own little cliques, played dominoes and cards together. And all were avid readers. Waslaw had taken upon himself to purchase a fairly extensive library and Kostrovsky had been placed in charge as the chief librarian. Also during the tour Romola took lessons in Russian from an old member of the staff, a Mrs Spessivsteva, who had been a ballet dancer in Moscow in her younger days.

New Orleans, the 'Crescent City', captivated them with its mixture of old-world charm; the narrow streets with ornate houses, whose architecture had been influenced by the French and the Spanish, with intricate wrought-iron work enhancing the beauty of the façades and the patios. Semi-tropical in climate, the city boasted an abundance of exotic trees and plants. The French Opera House, designed by Gallier, was lovely and in exquisite taste. Romola and Waslaw experienced a gourmet lunch at the famous French restaurant, Antoine's, and enjoyed the delectable *omelette surprise,* served by the restaurateur himself.

Surprisingly, Romola wanted to go with some of their friends to a brothel, described to her as one of the 'high spots' to visit. Waslaw had at first refused to accompany her 'but I insisted; I had never been to such a place and was curious to go...He warned me I would be very much disgusted. I told him he could not know, as he had never been to any.' Either she feigned ignorance of his Parisian experiences or honestly did not know about them at the time she wrote her biography.

Touring the southern states raised a rather delicate problem. *Schéhérazade* had to be scrapped from the repertoire because the cast were not permitted to make up as blacks. Years later it was revealed in a New York Herald Tribune tribute on Waslaw's death that, even in the North, an audience had been shocked by the harem scene. Perhaps the ballet on the whole was too bold for Americans at that time.

To ease the tension which was inescapable on such a long journey and within the confines of the limited space that a train could afford, practical jokes were played. For instance, Waslaw and the concert master decided to swap roles. When they arrived at Tulsa, Oklahoma, Waslaw pretended to be Fradkin and *vice versa.* The gathering of newsmen had been not a little taken back when they were introduced to a rather rotund 'Nijinsky'. Nor could the strenuous schedule prevent some disagreeable incidents from springing to life among the staff. Petty misunderstandings, intrigues, all the human frailties raised their ugly heads in spite of everything. Waslaw tried his utmost to pacify everybody. Minor strikes erupted for one reason or another, weariness and *tristesse* started to infiltrate into the very souls of all on board and nerves were sorely frayed at the edges. And on the whole the critics were cooler in their appraisal of the performances. It was mostly when Waslaw performed solo that hardcore critics' commentaries were laudatory.

Romola was beginning to find the constant nearness of Dmitri Kostrovsky and Nicolas Zverev more and more irksome. They would invade the Nijinsky compartment and engage Waslaw in prolonged discussions in Russian and her instinctive distrust of them grew with each passing hour.

Salt Lake City introduced Romola to Mormonism. The Mormons, or Latter-Day Saints, are a religious society founded by Joseph Smith and associates at Fayette, Seneca County, New York, in 1830. Meeting one of the elder statesmen, Romola also made the acquaintance of his four wives and learned about their peaceful solution to co-habitation. Surprisingly, she was not shocked but wrote that she found their way of life a sensible one.

Christmas Eve everyone in the company entered into the spirit of the season in true European fashion. A splendid banquet was laid out on long tables in one of the carriages, the orchestra played favourite melodies and an informal dance commenced. Later, Romola and Waslaw invited them all to their private compartment where a gaily decorated Christmas tree created a welcome atmosphere. With Romola's assistance, Waslaw had earlier been shopping for presents and the gifts were handed out amidst merriment.

On the 25th of December they arrived in Los Angeles; the snow and winter landscape left behind, the warm sun and orange groves greeted them. The stay was to be one of the longest on the tour and consequently Romola and Waslaw shared an apartment with Fred Fradkin and his wife. The opportunity arose to make a number of fascinating excursions, among which perhaps the one to excite their curiosity most was their visit to the film studios in Hollywood. Waslaw strongly felt that motion pictures were part of the heritage of future generations and was keen to see a film being made on actual location. It so happened that Charlie Chaplin, balletomane that he was, had been among the audience every evening during the company's performances and naturally Waslaw and Romola were invited by him personally to his studio.

Lillian Gish had accompanied Chaplin one evening to see Nijinsky dance in *Le Spectre de la Rose*. She confessed in later years that ever since that evening she had dreamed of dancing in the same ballet herself. In 1984 her dream was to be fulfilled, when the Metropolitan Opera staged a belated gala in honour of its centenary of the performing arts. The wealthy audience paid $1,000 each for their seats to watch most of the star performers of today do their bit. Among the entertainment was also a 'stroll down memory lane'. The taped voice of Lillian Gish filled the vast theatre and told of her dream as a young girl, when she had seen the great Nijinsky. The curtain went up to reveal Gish, now eighty-seven years old, seated in a wing back chair, and Patrick Dupond vaulting through the window attired in a bepetalled costume similar to Nijinsky's. As Joan Ross Acocella related in *Dance Magazine*: 'The dance that followed was remote from any *Spectre* I have seen, not to mention the fact that it was purely solo. Gish...remained in her chair. This was not the most suitable frame for Dupond's remarkable talents, but no one begrudged Lillian Gish the fulfilment of her dream.'

I have read that Chaplin, a genius in his own right, had acknowledged Nijinsky as one of the greatest he had encountered, but that it had disturbed him to note that Nijinsky had been unable to smile at Chaplin's antics in front of the camera. Chaplin said of him that he was a serious, sad man, more like a monk. How perceptive the little man in the bowler hat and big shoes had been. It was not long after, that the breaking point came when Romola could no longer endure the strain of seeing the accelerating inexplicable transformation in her husband.

From Los Angeles the tour continued to San Francisco and there Waslaw went on his first ever airplane ride, all for the price of $2.50. Romola beseeched Waslaw not to be foolhardy. To her eyes the flying machine looked like an abandoned sewing-machine. No one had been able to restrain him and before Romola knew it, he was in the contraption that circled over the heads of the terrified onlookers. Romola could only stand there and pray that he would come down safely. When he did, he exclaimed it had been a glorious, exhilarating adventure and that from above the world looked beautiful.

On New Year's Eve a disturbing incident took place. Barocchi, an Italian, a member of the managerial staff of the company, told their fortunes. He was said to be an excellent clairvoyant. When it

11. The Russian Ballet on board the S/S *Avon* heading for the
    South American tour 1913

12. Romola and Waslaw
    Nijinsky after their wedding
    in Buenos Aires on
    September 10th, 1913

13. Waslaw Nijinsky, New
York, 1916

14. Romola Nijinsky, New
York, 1916

15. Waslaw Nijinsky as *Le Spectre de la Rose*, a photograph dedicated to André de Badet in 1917

The Last Photograph of Nijinsky, Taken in Buenos Aires.

16. Photograph of Nijinsky from his last performance as The Golden Slave in *Schéhérazade* in Buenos Aires, 1917

17. In Emilia Márkus's Villa, 1917   Seated: Tessa de Pulszky Schmedes, Katharina Schratt, Emilia Márkus and Frau Schratt's companion   Standing: Ferencz Árpád Odry, Oskar Párdány, Georg Reimers, Hedvig Leurey, Francis Herczog, Károly Marffy

18. Romola Nijinsky with daughters Kyra and Tamara, Budapest, late 1921

came to Romola's turn to have her palm read, he promised good health and a long life but added: 'Within five years you will be separated from Vaslav Fomitch. I see a divorce, but not exactly...'. Then he looked at Waslaw's palm and as though he had received a blow, staggered back and covered Waslaw's hands with his own. 'I don't know, I can't say...sorry, it is strange...'. Waslaw had asked him pointblank if he was going to die. Barocchi had hesitated and stammered 'No, no, certainly not, but...but this is worse...worse.'

During their stay in San Francisco Romola tried to analyse what was happening between her and her Watza. Something was terribly amiss. She could see his whole attitude changing, not only toward his art but toward her. There was by now not a member of the company who could avoid noticing the poisonous influence of the two Tolstoyans, Kostrovsky and Zverev, on Waslaw. They clung to him like leeches, rarely letting him out of their sight. They hammered into his brain the preachings of Tolstoy and Christ. They exercised such power over him that they induced him to become a vegetarian much to Romola's alarm. He required nourishing food for his arduous work; a sufficiency of meat in his diet to strengthen his muscles. She did not know which way to turn. Throughout the month of January the tour went on; city after city slipped by, unnoticed by Romola, who found herself in a nightmare. She seldom saw her husband; when not performing he was locked in conversation with Kostrovsky and his confederate.

> 'I am Tolstoy because I love him. I know men will say that I,
> too, am a Bolshevik because I love Tolstoy.
> I shall say that Tolstoy is not a Bolshevik...
> My digestion works better because I do not eat meat.
> Meat is a terrible thing. My lust disappeared after I stopped
> eating meat...
> I eat vegetables and all kinds of vegetarian food.
> I am a vegetarian...I am a man and not an animal...'

> *Waslaw Nijinsky*

In her book, Romola wrote of the trauma she went through at the time and how finally, at her wits' end, she reached the following desperate decision.

'At the time of our arrival in Chicago I declared that on account of this interference with our life I would return to New York and stay with Kyra, and if he really decided to live the life of Tolstoi I would return alone to Europe. He could keep Kyra if he wanted, as I could never adjust myself to that life. Waslav took me to the station, and he looked so sad and so humble that I could not help telling him that whenever he needed me he had only to call and I would always come.'

And so Romola packed her suitcase and departed for New York. There she resumed her social life where it had been broken off for the tour. She enjoyed being reunited with her little daughter, whom she thought resembled Waslaw more and more. The tour lasted for another six long weeks and she loyally kept in touch with Waslaw by telephone almost daily. It was during one of their conversations Waslaw told Romola that Diaghilev had contacted him and asked him to join the company in Spain and afterwards to proceed on a second tour of South America.

On February 14th, 1917, Diaghilev's *Ballets Russes* gave their last performance in the States in the Harmanus Bleeker Hall in Albany, New York. A surge of relief swept over Romola at the railway station when Waslaw arrived in New York City; he was smiling, dressed in one of his elegant suits. Her debonair husband had come back, gone was the monklike vegetarian. He, in turn, was overcome with joy at being together with his family and showered Romola with the luxuries he knew would make her eyes light up; jewellery and furs. Together they went up to Laurence Steinhardt's office to discuss Diaghilev's proposals and also to make their wills, the latter a precautionary measure as they were to set sail for Europe on troubled seas where submarine warfare was raging. Romola was deeply moved to learn that Waslaw left everything he had earned in the States to her.

As they both stood on the upper deck of the steamer bound for Spain, they were overcome by emotion, waving goodbye to the many friends on the pier below, watching the impressive skyline of New York fade away in the mist. Romola admitted to bursting into hysterical sobbing and even Waslaw's eyes welled with tears. It was farewell to a safe refuge, liberty, and success.

'I love America. I have earned money in America. I want America's happiness. Democracy is a perfect party where everybody has the same rights.'

From *The Diary*

CHAPTER 5

LE SPECTRE'S FAREWELL PERFORMANCE

Whatever the strain on their physical and mental constitution during those months in the United States, Romola and Waslaw had been spared living under the dark clouds of war that by then ravaged most of Europe. In Budapest, Emilia and Oskar were struggling to pursue the course of their lives as normally as possible despite the morass enveloping them. Overshadowing it all was Emilia's anxiety over the fate of her younger daughter as she had not been the recipient of any news from her since their hurried departure for America.

Although now approaching her sixties, my remarkable grandmother still enraptured her audiences. Albeit the number of suitable roles was diminishing, her fluency in adapting herself to new characters became more and more mature and polished. Early in 1917 she played the leading role in yet another Ibsen drama, *Rosmersholm*. But the ostentatious life was not like before; parties and receptions dwindled, mainly, of course, due to the war. The Golden Era was on the way out, Budapest was never to be the same again.

With a good deal of manipulation, and balancing the budget with the skill of a professional juggler, Oskar was more or less able to hold his extravagant wife in check, curbing her never-ending flow of bills. Their carriage was replaced by a motorcar, one of the few to be seen in the streets of Budapest. It was a blessing to Emilia as the Villa was seventeen miles from the National Theatre, a distance she as a rule had to cover twice daily.

One indulgence Emilia stubbornly refused to sacrifice was her popular afternoon teas. When I was a teenager, she used to love to bring out her photograph albums and we would browse through them together. My grandmother would point to the faces of those people she had felt a close kinship with and tell me something about them.

Among her distinguished guests to tea one day in 1917 was Katharina Schratt, die *Gnädige Frau,* who in her prime had been the reigning star at the Burgtheater in Vienna; one of the theatre's foremost actresses, she possessed a magnetic personality and a marvellous voice. For more than thirty years she had been a close *confidante* of Emperor Franz Josef. They were reputed to have met at a command performance at the Court in Vienna in honour of the Tsar and Tsarina of Russia; the Emperor was fifty-six at the time, Katharina Schratt, thirty-three. It was said that the eccentric Empress Elisabeth herself had approved of her husband's friendship with the actress. Allegedly, their relationship was purely platonic. To dispel any rumours to the contrary it was even whispered that documents unearthed in archives in Bavaria claimed her to be a daughter of the Emperor. However unfounded the various rumours were, they kept tongues wagging for years to come. The more intimate circles within the Court even called the Emperor *Herr Schratt* behind his back. It was an open secret that he wrote passionate and most unmajestic letters to her until the end of his life. It was said that she was present with the Empress and Emperor Franz Josef when the tragic news was brought to them that the only son and heir to the Austrian throne, Rudolf of Hapsburg, was found dead in his hunting lodge at Mayerling on the 30th of January, 1889, together with the beautiful seventeen-year old Baroness Marie Vetsera. The most extraordinary rumours circulated around the event, even with political undertones suggesting that Rudolf had been murdered. To silence the many nasty allegations involving other people, it was officially announced that Rudolf, in a fit of passion and frustration at the thought of losing his lover, first shot her and then turned the pistol on himself. A tight bond of secrecy hermetically sealed access to any documents pertaining to the case. Katharina was again to be of strength and comfort to the Emperor when his Empress Elisabeth was assassinated in Geneva on the 10th September 1898. Before the period of mourning was over, several members of the royal household conspired to oust die *Gnädige Frau* from her influential position but failed. Katharina, incidentally, had been married to a Hungarian nobleman and by him had a son, Toni.

Emperor Franz Josef died on November 21st, 1916, and at the time of Katharina's visit to Emilia, she had as yet not recovered from the loss of her devoted royal friend. She was still unofficially in mourning and had expressed a wish to visit Emilia, not at a large reception, but in the intimacy of the salon at teatime. The guest list at that auspicious tea party included Tessa, Katharina's faithful companion Madame E., George Riemers, (actor at the Burgtheater in Vienna), Ferenc Herczeg, Emilia's next-door neighbour, a handful of the most fashionable contemporary writers of the day, and two of Emilia's colleagues from the National Theatre.

Emilia's social life was to become further restricted by the fact that she had opened her doors to the wounded soldiers of Hungary, who kept pouring back from the front, crushed, not only physically, but also in spirit. A zealous patriot, Emilia did everything in her power to help them back to health and to rekindle hope in their eyes. She tried to bolster them by reciting poetry, telling them stories in her sensuous, melodious voice; to coax them to laugh and forget their pains. For her indefatigable, patriotic participation, she was later to receive the highest Red Cross decoration awarded for war efforts in Hungary.

Her worries about Romola grew with every passing day. The strong affiliation she harboured for her surmounted all the squabbles and discord between them. And she contacted everybody she could think of who might possibly be able to bring her news of her Molly so far away across the ocean. Oskar unswervingly stood by her and eventually his endeavours were crowned with success. He was called to the Chief of Police who handed him a bulky, brown envelope. Close scrutiny revealed it had been posted two months earlier in Spain; that it had been opened by the censors. Romola was still under suspicion as the wife of an enemy Russian.

Emilia had been so overcome with relief that she had read the contents to the accompaniment of sobs and laughter. I can still picture her reclining on her favourite Recamier chaise-lounge, dressed in one of her richly embroidered Renaissance-style velvet robes she loved to slip into on evenings at home after the theatre. She had Oskar as her sole audience. Romola had written in detail about the North American tour, about their stay in Spain and that she and Waslaw were due to go back to South America with the *Ballets Russes*. Several clippings from the *New York Times* and other newspapers, singing the praises of her son-in-law, were enclosed with the letter. Sleep had come easily that night after many fretful weeks of worry and uncertainty.

Having completed a tour of Italy in April, 1917, Diaghilev and the *Ballets Russes* were in Paris when Waslaw and Romola arrived in Spain. They had endured an exhausting voyage from New York on a Spanish ship, which according to Romola lacked all customary comfort and was so rat-infested that she had slept on deck throughout the trip, defying the bitterly cold wind and storm. Waslaw had bravely stayed below deck together with little Kyra.

Feeling desperately in need of a holiday, they made the decision to stay in Madrid while waiting for Diaghilev to arrive. Waslaw knew the city well from his previous performance there. To Romola, it was yet another galvanic exploration of a new city. They were provided with generous hospitality by the many who wished to renew their acquaintance with Waslaw, among them the Duc and Duquesa de Durcal, who were related to the King. Once more, Romola was given the opportunity to shine as the wife of the great Nijinsky. She and Waslaw passed a few pleasant weeks being entertained, visiting the theatres, the numerous museums, the sidewalk cafés where they were enchanted by the dancing of the gypsies. Waslaw could spend hours in the Prado Museum; his eyes never tired of feasting themselves on the paintings by Goya. They paid a visit to Toledo, where the famous painter had lived and worked. As always, when they could enjoy the luxury of being alone together, they would devote many hours to reading. Romola wrote how they used to sit in the gardens of the Prado where she would translate for him the poems of Oscar Wilde, the works of the Swedish writer Selma Lagerlöf, and the philosophical poetry of Rabindranath Tagore. While they would thus be engrossed, Kyra was close at hand, enjoying her own little world of make-believe among the flowers.

Waslaw had been given free rein to practise at the Royal Theatre and there he spent much of his time when not working hard at his system of notation, which he was eager to discuss with Diaghilev. The abdiction of the Tsar passed him by as an incident of little or no importance, assured within himself that whatever change took place in his homeland would be a peaceful one, that Art would always be appreciated in Russia and that there still would be a place for the likes of Diaghilev and himself.

From Romola's account, their own life at that time was one of harmony until the day a jarring note interrupted their quietude. A trivial incident in itself; Romola had cried in despair when one morning she found some of her lovely new clothes had been badly damaged by mice. Waslaw had launched into a sermon about the unimportance of worldly goods.... 'So, after all, Tolstoi was still preying on his mind.' A warning sign!

Waslaw awaited the reunion with Sergei Pavlovitch with relish and when in early June the Impresario arrived from Paris with his Ballet, he embraced Waslaw with warmth and affection as though there had never been a schism between them. Waslaw was above reproaches and behaved like a young boy, overjoyed that all traces of acrimony were gone. Hours at an end they sat and talked. Airily, Diaghilev dismissed the matter of the South American contract and launched into a discussion of immediate plans for performances in Spain – the Theatre Royal in Madrid, then on to Barcelona. Massine had created some new ballets. Sergei Pavlovitch wanted Waslaw's opinion about them. They went over the situation in Russia; Waslaw ventilated his hopes of setting up a school and festival theatre there but Diaghilev was adamant about not wishing to return. Europe was now his base.

Unbelievably, Diaghilev instilled in Waslaw yet again his sincerity and his belief in their future together. Even Romola was smitten by his 'hypnotic power'. He did his utmost to ingratiate himself with her, invited them to dinners to meet members of his charmed circle, to which also Stravinsky had been attracted. Romola wrote:

'He brought Picasso, who was very little known at that time, to us one day. He was reticent and very Spanish looking, and when he began to explain anything, he became full of excitement, and used to draw on the table-cloth, the menu cards, and on the top of Sergei Pavlovitch's walking stick.'

With naïve assurance, Waslaw at one stage exclaimed to her, *'Tu vois, femmka, je t'ai toujours dit qu'il sera notre ami.'* Pathetic faith and trust in the light of what was to come.

One of Romola's unforgettable moments was when they all went to the theatre to hear Pastora Imperio, the idol of Spain, sing. Romola wrote how she had made little impression on her at first, '...a rather faded, stout southern woman...' but that when she commenced her performance, 'With a few gestures she offered the history and soul of Spain.'

With the Madrid Season in full swing, Waslaw behaved like a man in a dream come true. Forgotten was the crucifixion he had earlier been subjected to; he was once more dancing with the *Ballets Russes;* Diaghilev had proved him right in his guileless assertions that the former would always be a loyal, protective friend; he was surrounded by his loving family, Romola and daughter Kyra; he danced before King Alfonso and the Queen. What more could he possibly wish? He felt no rancour nor jealousy of Massine, who was Diaghilev's current protégé. Instead, he heaped praises over him; wholly unselfish in his all-absorbing devotion to Dance, he was happy to encourage advancement within that field. He confessed much later:

> *'Diaghilev loves Massine and not me... Massine pretends he likes me. I do not pretend. I noticed this because when I was in Madrid and saw his ballet which Diaghilev had composed, I went to congratulate him, and when I was in his dressingroom I kissed him. Massine thought I was kissing him with a Judas kiss because Diaghilev had convinced him that my actions were evil... I was another Massine in Diaghilev's service for a period of five years.'*

The dream bubble was soon to burst. The stage was being set to seal Waslaw's doom as predicted in the States the previous year. The two Tolstoyans returned from their holiday and descended once more on Waslaw, their gullible victim.

> *'Tolstoy's dream is life and therefore he must be read... I am Tolstoy's tree. I am Tolstoy's roots. Tolstoy is mine. I am his. Tolstoy lived at the same time I did. I loved him but I did not understand him. Tolstoy is great and I was afraid of the great'.*

> *Waslaw Nijinsky*

The breach between husband and wife widened once more. It went so far that Waslaw one day confronted Romola and stated categorically that celibacy should be practised, not to be broken unless they planned to have another child. Romola was to confide how she practically drove him into the arms of the beautiful Duchess of Durcal, who confessed to being madly in love with him. How she must have been racked with torment – to sacrifice her husband to another woman rather than to risk him being in the clutches of his fanatic 'teachers'.

'At lunch, on the terrace (the Escorial) Vaslav seemed to have regained his mischievous ways. He said to me, "Please, *femmka,* do not leave me so much alone with her (the Duchess)!" He was too discreet to give her away, but too honest not to put me on my guard.'

Yet she goes on to say:

'Our intimate life was ideally happy. Sometimes the strangest feeling would come over me, and I felt that the women of mythology may have felt as I did when a God came to love them. There was the exhilaration and inexpressible feeling that Vaslav was more than a human being. The ecstacy that he could create in love as an art had a purifying quality, and yet there was something intangible in his being that one could never reach.'

So there were blissful episodes but cruel, disheartening ones as well. She became more and more suspicious that Diaghilev's intentions were not well-meaning, that in an underhanded manner he was attempting to wean Waslaw from the marital bed back to the fold of the *Ballets Russes* without being shackled to a family. One day she came across Diaghilev talking in a conspiratorial manner to Zverev. Her antagonism toward the Impresario flared up afresh. And her hatred and distrust of the two men she regarded as her rivals came to a climax one evening when she 'declared open war' on them. On the verge of a breakdown, she demanded that the two leave the apartment and, if they did not comply, threatened to leave Waslaw. She found the whole situation intolerable, sordid and humiliating. Waslaw had stood paralysed by her attack on his friends, because to him that was what they were. She claims she walked out on him that night and that he had found her the following day in the Prado. He had beseeched her to return. 'It shall be as you wish,' in other words Kostrovsky and Zverev were not to set foot in their home again.

Whatever the irritations, the piteous squabbles about his person, Waslaw did not let them interfere with his work. He allowed nothing to distract him from participating in rehearsals and offering advice and coaching whenever he deemed so necessary. He was totally unbiased, all he strove for was to seek perfection in the one art form that was his *raison d'être*.

The company continued to Barcelona to give a number of per-

162

formances there. In their tow was also the Duchess of Durcal, which pleased Romola, illuminating how she regarded her as the weapon to use against the Tolstoyans. During an outing to Montserrat, the party, which included Kostrovsky and his shadow, sat down to partake of a luncheon at a tavern. The two had earlier whisked Waslaw off to a visit to a monastery on the summit of the mountain.

'Kostrovsky, having ordered a vegetarian lunch, reproved Vaslav for ordering meat, but Vaslav said, "I approve of the idea of vegetarianism, but I cannot, unfortunately, carry it out; as long as I dance, I need solid nourishment." Kostrovsky said, "Then give up dancing."'

The evenings were spent in the company of the Duchess who, according to Romola, was by then hopelessly in love with Waslaw and wished to become his mistress.

'Jealousy never entered into my head, and I was even rather pleased when Vaslav returned later than usual one night, but this escapade had quite a different effect upon him than I had expected. He was mournful and told me frankly: *"Femmka,* I am sorry for what I did. It was unfair to her, as I am not in love, and the added experience, that you perhaps wanted me to have, is unworthy of us."'

Shortly after that, the storm that had been gathering under the surface between Diaghilev and Waslaw broke out in full fury. It concerned the latter's contract. Apparently, Waslaw had second thoughts about embarking on the South American tour. Although she never said so directly, I feel certain that Romola was behind this decision. She wanted him to be free of the wretched Tolstoyans' strangling hold. She must have convinced him it would not be the creative tour he had envisaged. And he must have shrunk back from yet again leaving their daughter behind. He realised it would be impossible to include Kyra – after all, it was wartime. Far too hazardous a journey to endanger her life.

But Diaghilev was having a hard struggle to keep the *Ballets Russes* above ground. He, too, had to grapple with the grotesque conditions imposed on mankind by the war. If Waslaw, his trump card, deserted him at this stage, it posed a potential threat to the existence of the Ballet. And so he used his cunning by binding Nijinsky to a cable the latter had despatched from America, in which he agreed in principle to dance not only in Spain but also in South America. Evidence once more of Waslaw's *naïveté* as he had not for one moment thought such a cable could be construed to be a legal document. Naturally, Romola's version was biased against Diaghilev but it would stand to reason that neither she nor Waslaw stood a chance to emerge as winners in the legal jungle that involved professional contracts of any kind.

A pitiful story was to unfold itself. Convinced that he was under no obligation to stay, Waslaw departed with his family one afternoon for the station with the intention of boarding the express train out of Barcelona. This dramatic leave-taking of the Ballet had been preceded by a violent argument with Sergei Pavlovitch. No sooner had they boarded the Madrid Express when they were summarily seized and to their disbelief and shock taken under escort to the Police Station and notified that they were under arrest. Waslaw was even threatened with imprisonment if he did not perform that evening. Pale, but determined, he had replied he would rather face gaol than dance. He was not under any contract and besides, he was far too upset to dance. Romola took charge and telephoned the Duc de Durcal, who forthwith secured their release. By then the train had departed. Defeated, they made their way back to their hotel room only to find the hysterical director of the Teatro Liceo waiting for them. He was in a state of collapse and burst into a tirade of how he would face financial ruin if Waslaw did not perform. Waslaw could not help but feel sympathy for his plight and agreed to fulfil his part of the engagement.

The following morning he was to learn from Señor Cambo, the Spanish lawyer in all likelihood provided by the Duke, that he had lost his battle to opt out of the South American tour. He was to rue the day he had not listened to the exhortation of Laurence Steinhardt in New York; that he had allowed Kostrovsky to draft the ill-fated cable. He was at the mercy of Diaghilev and no plea to him would unbend his will. Diaghilev was the victor. According to Spanish law, the cable was as good as a contract and could not be violated. The friendship which had hung on a fragile thread ever since Waslaw's marriage, terminated there in Spain, never to be resumed. Diaghilev saw Waslaw Nijinsky dance for the very last time on the 30th of June, 1917, at the Teatro Liceo in Barcelona.

164

'Diaghilev and Massine and sixteen dancers departed for Italy, and we left with the troupe in the middle of July for South America. This time the troupe was in the hands of Grigoriev. Vaslav seemed worn out by the excitement of the last few days, especially by the blow that had clearly unmasked Diaghileff's attitude; now he knew that an understanding was for ever impossible.

On the journey, Michel said how sorry he was that Sergei Pavlovitch and Vaslav could not agree. "I wanted to, I did everything, I am heartbroken about it," replied Vaslav.'

Kyra was sent off to a well-established children's school in Lausanne; Romola and Waslaw lingered a few days in Madrid. For the second (and last) time, Romola and Waslaw prepared for their departure to South America. The vessel this time was the *Reina Victoria Eugenia*. The date July 4th, 1917. Maestro Cecchetti, their faithful friend, was also on the trip. He was distressed over the intolerant, vindictive and overt act taken by Diaghilev and heartily disapproved of the way he had handled the situation. Concerned and caring, he tried to ferret out from Romola if she was still happy with her God of Dance. After all, was it not he who many months ago had warned her that her life with him would not be an easy one. But Romola assured him with pride that their marriage was still one of conjugal bliss. Cecchetti confessed to her his own disillusionment with the Russian Ballet, that he was tired, this would be his last trip.

Contrary to the first voyage when she devoted many letters to shipboard activities and the pursuit of her Harlequin, she wrote sparsely about the second trip. Briefly, she introduced a young Chilean, Georges de Cuevas, 'a typical gigolo, extremely well bred and dressed'. He had attached himself to the Nijinskys from the moment the ship sailed. He was an expert dancer of the tango and Waslaw was evidently so impressed by him, he took lessons from Cuevas. Romola summed him up as an adventurer on the look-out for an heiress. Oddly enough, he was later to inherit a Spanish title from an uncle and as Marquis de Cuevas he did indeed marry an American heiress in the Rockefeller family.*

An alarming occurence took place during the voyage. Kostrovsky suffered an epileptic fit and his wife sought Waslaw's help. He

* Later, he founded several ballet companies.

became acutely worried about his friend and resolved to seek medical consultation once they reached their destination.

I have not been able to find any notes from Romola dating from this period and have therefore had to rely solely upon her story and that of others. There appears to be a number of discrepancies in her version; their first stop was Rio, other sources state it was Montevideo. In the intervening years before writing her book Romola had been catapulted into a series of events of ferocious magnitude. Might she not perhaps be excused for confusing dates and places. At the best of times she had been a poor diarist, never keeping consistent chronicles of her movements.

Kostrovsky was taken to a specialist in Montevideo. I would like here to quote Richard Buckle and his interpretation of that episode. It is a chilling thought that Waslaw Nijinsky's life might have taken an entirely different course had Kostrovsky's illness been diagnosed much earlier.

'As she spoke a little Spanish, Romola interpreted the diagnosis, which was that the unfortunate man was incurably and dangerously insane. He was to be sent back to Russia. It is curious to conjecture how differently things might have turned out if this diagnosis had been made in Madrid. Romola would have had no reason to fear the Tolstoyan menace and might have encouraged Nijinsky to go to South America. Nijinsky would therefore never have had the difference with Diaghilev which led to their final break. He might have continued with the Russian Ballet for many years and made a number of new ballets. He might have revived 'Sacre du printemps', with the result that it might have survived intact to this day. Continued work with the Ballet might have averted his illness or postponed it'.*

In Montevideo, Romola and Waslaw were lavishly entertained by the French Minister Jules Lefaivre and the British Minister Mitchell Innes.

Their first objective when they set foot in Rio was to pay a nostalgic visit to the Hotel Sylvestre for a luncheon. It was there they celebrated their engagement four years previously. They were greeted

* From *Nijinsky* by Richard Buckle

with open arms by their Brazilian friends; the glittering, charmed circle of the Corps Diplomatique rivalling with each other to include them on their guest lists. Among their hosts were the American Ambassador Edwin Morgan, and Tscherbatchkoi, the Russian Ambassador, who took them to his summer residence in the hills behind Rio.

The famous poet and dramatist, Paul Claudel, whose lyric style was to become one of the richest in the French language, was then the French Ambassador. He was in Brazil for a period of three years. The early part of his diplomatic career had been spent in China, in the beginning as consul in various cities and then posted in Peking as first secretary, where he seriously took up the study of Chinese philosophy and way of life. It was he who indoctrinated Waslaw in the wonders of Oriental art. Romola described how he went out of his way to make their stay congenial, taking them for long drives through the magnificent, tropical countryside outside the city limits. At one luncheon he gave, he introduced them to Darius Milhaud, then a comparatively young man but already a talented composer and known for his chamber music. He became one of the group known as *Les Six.* Inspired by the atmosphere of Brazil, he wrote *Saudades de Brazil,* an effective dance suite for orchestra. It was at the time that Romola and Waslaw were in Rio that Milhaud and Claudel were composing two ballets, *L'homme et son désir* and *La Création du Monde.* They asked Waslaw if he would like to do the choreography for them and he readily agreed. It is to be deplored that the idea never came to a head.

They became friendly with the composer Estrade Guerra and his wife Niniha, a pianist. The two couples frequently dined together and it was in the cool shade of some secluded garden corner, they would sit and exchange pleasantries.

According to Guerra, Waslaw never said anything insulting about the Impresario, although he inwardly must have felt strong animosity toward Sergei Pavlovitch. On the contrary, he would appear to have avoided such a delicate topic and instead would launch into a discussion about his daughter Kyra, of whom he was fiercely proud. He always carried a snapshot of her on his person and his face would light up radiantly whenever he spoke about her.

Françoise Reiss in *Nijinsky ou la Grace* goes on to cite a conversation between Guerra and Waslaw; how it had flowed smoothly in French. Quite naturally, the subject of ballet had been raised and

Waslaw voiced the opinion that his sister Bronislava and Karsavina were the foremost of all contemporary dancers. By that time he must clearly have come face to face with the cruel realisation that the odds were against him carrying on in the *Ballets Russes* because he told Guerra that he wished to withdraw from Russian ballet '*pour suivre sa voie propre et, de toute façon, cette tournée Sud Américaine devait être la dernière.*'

When later he was to learn of Nijinsky's insanity, Guerra was overcome with disbelief. So many persons were 'wise after the event', proclaiming they had noticed the warning signals already years before. Not so Guerra. He had found Waslaw a highly intelligent, lucid and unpretentious man, who recognised his own genius without vanity. Of course, he was highly strung; he surrounded himself at times with an air of mysticism, but then, was he not a great artist and a Slav? Guerra spoke warmly of Romola, how harmonious the two young people appeared to be in each other's company; how lovely her features were; delicate and with blue eyes.

The chain of events during this last tour becomes more and more confusing as one reads one version after the other. Romola claimed they went by boat to São Paulo; others, that they took the train. In fact, according to Richard Buckle, much of the décor for some of the ballets was destroyed by fire, due to a spark from the engine igniting that particular carriage. Important to me is to record Romola's personal impressions of people and places, to untangle the web that would be beyond my capacity and has little bearing on my story.

In São Paulo 'Calmette, the head of the Research Institute…brother of Calmette of *Figaro*, who had caused so much fracas at the first performance of *Faune*, showed us round his extremely interesting place, where serums against snake bites and insects are prepared.'

The pattern of social acclamation and activity was repeated in Buenos Aires. There, the priest who had married them, gave a luncheon in their honour. 'Vaslav surprised me with a beautiful bag of heavy gold, and a vanity case set in sapphires.' Purely by chance, they encountered Pavlova in the grill-room of the hotel one day. She was also dancing in Buenos Aires at the time. Romola's only comment on that encounter was that Pavlova spoke sweetly to Waslaw in Russian. Romola had regarded her curiously, unable to forget her telephone call at the time of Waslaw's accident in New

York. They were effusively greeted by some old acquaintances, among them Señor Quintana, son of the ex-President, and also Georges de Cuevas, their tango-dancing friend.

However unclouded their private life, behind the scene at the theatres, Waslaw's world must have been sheer hell. Endless rifts flared up spurred on by Sergei Grigoriev, the company's *régisseur* and a loyal supporter of Diaghilev. Sensitive soul that he was, Nijinsky was again sucked into the vortex. London, Buenos Aires, New York…it followed the same nightmarish pattern all over again. Most of the members adopted a very cool attitude toward their star, some behaving vindictively toward the man who had done them no harm, who merely wanted to dance, dance, dance… Silly, inexplicable accidents happened once they were back at the Teatro Colón. Waslaw began to feel persecuted; dreading to perform on stage. Once, he stepped on a rusty nail during a performance. How could a rusty nail have been left on the boards that were supposed to be scrupulously examined? Another time, had he not instinctively leapt out of reach, he would have been hit by an iron weight falling down. During a performance of *Petroushka* the puppets' booth was not secured properly and it collapsed with Waslaw on top of it. Inwardly, he must have been torn asunder yet Romola swore that he never outwardly betrayed it nor did he condemn anyone. She, on the other hand, openly blamed the incidents on his enemies. In fact she was so convinced that they were deliberate, she arranged for detectives to watch over Waslaw at the theatre. Because of a clause in his contract to the effect that were he unable to fulfil his engagements, he would incur a penalty of 20,000 dollars, she felt certain that there was a plot to bring this about.

Romola tells a rather garbled story of how she had been contacted by a relative she merely identifies as Don de B, who welcomed her and Waslaw to South America and who wanted to meet them. He was described as a brilliant lawyer who wasted his talents on seamier hobbies and hence had been sent off in disgrace to the Argentine. Every family appears to have its black sheep.

'His passion was to expose people's private lives. He knew the law so well that he could always get away with his attacks, on leading politicians, officers of the general staff, and society women, in a paper he edited himself. Even his own family was not exempt from his attacks. However, he got into trouble when he exposed a high Hungarian general, and was then exiled to the Argentine...'.

Romola was invited to his home:

'...and there he showed me his beautifully arranged dossiers of all the important people of the Argentine; every peccadillo, every love-affair, was recorded. "But what is the idea? Why do you waste your time in this way?" He replied, "You do not understand. To become a great politician, one has to know all the weaknesses of the leaders of society...".'

He had the audacity to supply the press in Buenos Aires with a faked interview with Waslaw which was backed by a photograph wheedled out of Romola under false pretences. She learned that rumours were being spread about liaisons that she and Waslaw were supposed to have had with others. Don de B must have been the pen behind it all. He forced money out of Romola with the improbable story that he had to prevent a newspaper slander on Waslaw by a member of the company. Nearly everyone came under attack from his virulent and poisonous tongue. His accusations were almost obscene; his relentless and sordid evil-doing must have caused additional pain and suffering, especially to the oversensitive Waslaw. I have never been able to find out Don de B's true identity.

On the 26th of September, 1917, the last performance by Waslaw Nijinsky with the Diaghilev *Ballets Russes* took place at the Teatro Colón, Buenos Aires. He appeared in *Le Spectre de la Rose* and *Petroushka*. The tour had been an outstanding success, the appreciative audiences never suspecting the dramas that had taken place behind the scene. From the last curtain call onward, Romola and Waslaw had one wish only, to leave as soon as possible and to be reunited with their beloved daughter Kyra; to breathe freely again the neutral air of Switzerland, to leave behind the venomous atmosphere they had endured within the company. They started to make plans for their homeward journey but not before Waslaw had taken part in a Gala Matinée in Montevideo, for wounded soldiers, victims of the terrible war. On the 22nd of September, 1917, he wrote a letter from the Plaza Hotel, Buenos Aires, to André de Badet requesting his assistance. He expressed a wish to dance in aid of the English and French Red Cross. He was writing at the same time to Lefaivre and Mitchell Innes in the hope that they would organise the fête. He would be in Montevideo between the 27th and 30th and would be agreeable to dancing two to three dances, accompanied by piano. He asked Badet to assist him by reciting some verse, 'avec notre concours nous fairons une après-midi artistique.'* Waslaw begged Badet to be in charge of the proceedings and to give a reply by return. Badet was a diplomat whom Waslaw had become friendly with at one of the many social functions. Years later, Badet was to write, 'Il avait compte inclure dans ce spectacle MINSTRELS de Debussy car, ainsi qu'il m'en parle dans une autre lettre il m'avait demandé de jouer une scene de PELLÉAS et MÉLISANDE avec Madame Violette Supervielle de Lasala.'** The latter scene could not be performed because Waslaw was unable to assemble the costume he required as the major portion of his luggage was already on its way to Europe. In addition to Minstrels, the programme consisted of a recital by Artur Rubinstein, who happened to be touring the country at the time, and a few opera arias were sung by a tenor, whose name Badet could not remember. A young local pianist, Domingo Dente, accompanied Waslaw.

It was an historic occasion in the world of Dance because as Badet quite rightly commented, who would have thought, in the midst of the ovations that saluted the man who was universally known as Le Dieu de la Danse, that Nijinsky was performing publicly for the very last time – a divine flame to be extinguished forever?

Mercifully, neither Romola nor Waslaw himself could have dreamed of it at that moment.

* 'With our mutual interest, we will make it an artistic afternoon.'

** 'He had counted on including Minstrels by Debussy in this spectacle, at the same time that he told me in another letter that he had asked me to play a scene from Pelléas et Mélisande with Madame Violette Supervielle de Lasala.'

CHAPTER 6

'FEMMKA COURAGE...
car il y a un Dieu'

The Villa Guardamunt, located in St Moritz Dorf, Switzerland, became Romola and Waslaw's first real home. They leased it complete with inventories from Herrn Chr. Gartmann for the sum of Frs 4,500, half to be paid on the 31st December, half on the 1st of August, 1918. Waslaw signed the contract in his bold handwriting on the 11th of December, 1917.

When Romola had stood on the deck of the ship carrying her and her husband away from Buenos Aires, she must have given much thought to what lay ahead. There is no doubt in my mind but that she was fully aware that all ties with Sergei Pavlovitch and the *Ballets Russes* were severed. After all, was it not she who felt certain that the Impresario was conducting a vendetta against her husband? Had not the strange series of inexplicable accidents proved that? Her genuine loathing for Diaghilev blinded her to any form of sound reasoning. As Richard Buckle was to point out in his biography of Nijinsky, it would hardly have seemed likely that 'the goose that laid the golden eggs (for the *Ballets Russes*) should be killed, or even cast on one side.'

Waslaw was incapable of harbouring long-standing grudges against any other creative artist. He acknowledged that Massine had taken his place and he was merely eager to have the opportunity to carry on creating new ballets of his own, preferably in Russia, there to establish a ballet school under his directorship. He dreamed, too, of a *pied-à-terre* in Paris, the city that had mesmerized him from his very first glimpse of it. But it was still wartime and when would the carnage on the battlefields of Europe come to an end?

The homeward journey had been uneventful by all accounts. The only unpleasant moment had been the boarding of the ship by English officers from a cruiser not long after their departure. Romola had panicked and rushed down to her stateroom and destroyed her precious 'icon', the Infant Jesus of Prague, because the text on the back of the picture was in German.

172

'...I tore it in two and threw it into the sea. As the picture floated on the waves, I could see the small head of the miraculous Jesus turned upwards, looking at me. I uttered a scream. I wanted to get it back, but it was already sinking slowly, and I had the uncanny presentiment that my happiness was sinking with it...'.

Waslaw spent most of his time busily correcting his revision of the system of notation. Immediately upon their arrival at the European shores, they took the Sud Express from Spain to Paris and then on to Lausanne. They were both eager to curtail the agonising separation from their little daughter. Romola's description of Waslaw's reunion with Kyra is very moving.

'She was sitting in her bed and seemed almost as big as the teddy-bear Vaslav had given her before leaving Spain. She looked more like Vaslav than ever. He clasped her in his arms and danced around the room. Kyra screamed with joy. It was remarkable how the child changed the moment Vaslav entered the room. It seemed almost as though they had been one person split apart, and constantly wishing to be reunited. Sometimes I almost felt as if I was intruding on them. They were both essentially and fundamentally Russian...'.

Kyra was left behind at the school when they returned to St Moritz to hunt for a place to live early in December, 1917. They both fell in love with Villa Guardamunt, St Moritz Dorf, such a contrast to their rootless touring from continent to continent, hotel to hotel. The village lay nestled in the Engadine Valley, miles above sea level. A tiny lake sparkled like a diamond at the foot of the hills. The winding mountain roads lined with tall pine trees, like sentinels, led to the Roseg Alps and Piz Margna Mountain. Snow covered the roofs of the châlets like white ermine bonnets, reflecting the sun's glittering light. The atmosphere of St Moritz Dorf was one of tranquillity, a rural place where the Swiss themselves lived and worked, leaving St Moritz Bad for the tourists.

It had given Romola a great thrill to fill the house with their personal belongings and to cram the entrance with all the paraphernalia pertaining to winter sports – skis, heavy boots, a child's gaily-painted sled. Almost certainly Romola's favourite photographs of

Waslaw were given strategic positions in the various rooms.

Then came the day when Waslaw adventurously set off on his own to collect Kyra. He was totally unused to the practicalities of everyday life and could not speak a word of German. He had never before booked a room in a hotel nor purchased a railway ticket. Romola was the first to admit that such mundane matters were foreign to him, and consequently she had been fairly nervous at letting him go off on his own. However, he returned with Kyra without a mishap and the family settled down to their new life.

'The balcony on the ground floor was cleared. There, every morning, for two hours, Vaslav did his exercises, with Kyra looking on and patiently watching *Tatakaboy* dance, and when he leaped, she used to cheer and clap her hands, then often Vaslav, forgetting his iron discipline, caught her in his arms and waltzed round, singing, *"Votre amabilité, maia Kotyik, maia Funtyiki".*'

Kyra recalls to this day how our father often used his pet name for her, *Funtyiki,* meaning little pound. She also likes to remember how he would take her steel-sled racing on his back. 'It was very dangerous.' This glimpse of childhood must stem from the brief years in St Moritz.

In addition to Kyra's nurse, the household was increased with the arrival of two comely girls, Louise and Maria, in their capacity as maid and cook. Romola wrote that the servants worshipped Waslaw. He was always willing to give them a hand, to carry their parcels from the village, to help feed the fire with the weighty coal.

One gets the impression they had a blissfully happy time. She described how, that first winter, they became involved in the life of the villagers, sitting long evenings in front of blazing log fires, discussing the latest reports about the war, ruminating about life in general, often in the company of the mayor and the local doctor. Dr Bernhard's home was the meeting place of many prominent foreigners and important persons in the Swiss community. Often, Romola and Waslaw would go to Hanselmann's before lunch for an *apéritif* or a glass of *Glühwein* and to taste the superb *Käse-stängel* made by the famous *confiseur* himself. Hanselmann, an Austrian, was a colourful personality and seemingly became a true friend.

In February, 1918, Romola celebrated her twenty-eighth

birthday; auburn-haired, vivacious and lovely-looking, exquisitely groomed in the finest Parisian fashion, she must have felt on top of the world. For the first time she was mistress of her very own home and she had already acquired a select circle of friends; she rhapsodised about her intimate dinner parties at which she served Hungarian specialities, praised as high-lights in the neighbourhood. She took part in the winter sports with alacrity although Waslaw at first abstained. This did not prevent him, however, from offering his advice on technique and balance, particularly on the art of ice-skating. But he did develop one passion: at the reins of a horse-drawn sleigh he let loose his craze for speed, just as he had with his automobile. The sleighs for hire were open and roomy, often painted in brilliant colours, and would seat four persons comfortably. The horses were as ornately decorated as the sleigh, the bells of their harness tinkling merrily as they trotted along the well-worn routes through the mountain passes. It was Waslaw who loved to prod them into a terrifying gallop, much to Kyra's glee and Romola's distress.

February melted swiftly away but before the arrival of Spring, Tessa and Erik came over from Vienna. It had been Waslaw's idea to cable the invitation; he was eager to reciprocate their generous hospitality of previous years, and besides, he liked Erik. They were kindred spirits in the realm of music and art.

Romola has only mentioned their stay in a brief sentence. It was to be later, when Tessa apparently came on her own, that we have a record of Waslaw's impressions of her presence in their home. That was when his brilliant mind was crumbling, when he jolted down his disjointed thoughts in his little black copy books.

A luxuriant wealth of Alpine flowers burst into bloom and heralded the coming of Spring, '...the pink alpen-roses, the sweet-smelling purple violets, and the cornflower blue gentians. The snow retreated to the summits of the peaks, which were now so familiar to us and had each its own meaning for Vaslav. We used to run up to the Alp Giop and throw ourselves down among the flowers...'. It was Waslaw who had opened up Romola's eyes to the intoxicating splendour of flora and fauna on their sightseeing strolls that first tour to South America. He encouraged her to regard the world around her with the same perceptive vision that was his; to appreciate the richness of colours, the harmony of lines, be they on canvas or in *Belle Dame Nature*. With regard to his skill in creating the right characters for the different dance roles, Romola remarked, 'Vaslav was able, on seeing the lines and materials of a costume, to reconstruct the proper gestures of a period. He literally put bodies into the empty costumes of any historical period.'

In the early summer of 1918 Waslaw was more preoccupied than ever before, teaching Romola once more. His mind overflowed with ideas for new ballets, among which was a version of Debussy's *Chanson de Bilitis*. It was his wish that Romola dance the role of Bilitis. He also spent much time creating a choreographic poem he claimed was to mirror his own life. This particular ballet was based on the circle, just as was his system of notation.

'You know, *femmka,* the circle is the complete, the perfect movement. Everything is based on it – life, art, and most certainly our art. It is the perfect line.'

Romola commented on his dancing at this stage:

'He seemed lighter than ever; the number of his pirouettes and *entre-chats* was infinite, and, watching him make his *battements* and *pliés,* it sometimes seemed to me he was lighter than the snow-flakes themselves. But his strength was of steel, and he bounded like a rubber ball.'

This brief summer and early autumn, unbeknown to its central characters, was building up to a horrendous, tragic climax. Romola had been seized by malaise off and on since Kyra's birth and had to go into hospital in Berne for a minor operation. Once it was over she cabled Waslaw to come and for two solid weeks he stayed dutifully by her bedside. His one escape from the confines of the hospital was to watch a performance by the dancers Clothilde and Alexander Sakharoff. He had not been impressed. When the leaves had turned to copper and the air was nippy, giving a forewarning of an early winter, they returned home. And life to all appearances proceeded at a normal pace. Waslaw was eager to help with the heavier household duties. An item of news that affected him deeply, though, was the sudden and wholly unexpected mental illness of the husband of Kyra's Swiss nanny. He had been sent to an asylum in a straitjacket. Waslaw had become very silent and morose upon hearing the details, Not long after that a letter arrived from Bronia saying that Stanislav had died. Romola must have been nonplussed how to break the news as she knew better than anyone how much Waslaw loved his brother. He had died in the asylum from a liver complaint aggravated by pneumonia. She was astounded to find that Waslaw reacted to his brother's death exactly as he had done to his father's. 'He looked at me smiling, but with a strange and deep quietness.' It had unnerved her.

Romola was besieged at this time by offers from impresarios from far and wide who wished to lure Waslaw back to the stage but she refused them all. Why? Was it because Waslaw genuinely could not bring himself to dance until peace had come, or did Romola feel the offers were not grand enough? Who can really tell, so long afterwards. Would subsequent events have been avoided, or at least forestalled?

The 11th of November, Romola rushed home to Guardamunt after a shopping expedition to convey to Waslaw joyous news – Armistice had been declared, the dreadful war was over. His only comment: 'Peace, peace. There can be no peace under those terms. War will go on, but in a hidden, different way.' She had shrugged off his gloomy prophecy. To her, only one thing mattered, that they embark on a brilliant new future together. The horrid fighting had stopped, the distant rumble of cannon fire from across the mountains had been silenced. Instead, virginal snow once more draped the slopes of the Alps and the countryside around them in a snug blanket.

Through mutual acquaintances visiting St Moritz Romola had disturbing news from Emilia. Hungary was on the threshold of a revolution that was rapidly spreading from Russia. Russian agitators were seeping in through the open front. She gathered that some Hungarians had been quick to adapt to the new idealogy and that 'Lenin boys' were common sights on the streets of Budapest, dressed in black leather overcoats. These 'boys' were infiltrating into the existing Social Democratic party and were involved in an inveiglement to nationalise mines and factories and to take over many of the estates of the nobility. So far, the 'coup' had been bloodless, but for how long? Romola decided that she would invite Emilia and Oskar to come over for a visit once the holidays were over.

Waslaw was busy with a new ballet of his own creation, its theme was sex, its central character a once beautiful cocotte who, although physically a wreck as a result of her profligacy, spiritually still dealt in all the aspects of love. He called the ballet *Les Papillons de Nuit*.

'I want to show both the beauty and the destructive quality of love.' Throughout that winter, too, he kept his mind occupied with a series of inventions – a windscreen wiper and an eversharp pen. He developed a fixation about the importance of a pen, discoursed later at great length in his copybooks. He spent many hours on his drawings, an amazing technique of producing portraits out of circles. He read as much as ever, concentrating chiefly on Maeterlinck's *La Mort* and Nietzsche's *Ecce Homo*.

Romola devoted herself to preparations for the forthcoming Yuletide celebrations, determined to make them memorable for her family; to celebrate the peace that had returned to Mankind and the anticipation of glorious years ahead in their new home. She wrote to Tessa in Vienna to ask for the traditional recipes she remembered from her childhood. In after years I found she had committed to memory almost every hour of that nearly flawlessly happy Christmas, the only one the young Nijinsky family were destined to have together.

Every once in a while Waslaw would slip into a state of moodiness, of depression she was unable to fathom. Then, miraculously, as Christmas approached, he appeared to be his old self, boyish, gentle, helpful, having cast aside whatever demons that were pursuing him. Willingly, he took part, and carried the stacks of perfectly starched and ironed linens for the maids, chopped firewood for the greedy fireplaces, and took immense pride in joining his *femmka* in selecting and purchasing gifts not only for every member of their household but also for the children and the poorer families of St Moritz Dorf.

Recipes and Christmas decorations duly arrived from Vienna. Romola unpacked the *szalon-cukor* with utmost care. These were made of sugar, water, and some flavouring, such as vanilla or chocolate, moulded into square pieces and then wrapped in pale pink, blue, or just plain white, tissue paper. The centre of the candy was covered with foil and the result was a glorified Christmas cracker. Other decorations for the tree included golden balls, silver tinsel and white angel hair. In true Hungarian tradition, primarily gold, silver and white were chosen as the appropriate colours with which to greet the *Prince of Peace*. Romola instructed the cook how to make the *beigli,* essential to grace a Hungarian Christmas table. The *beigli* are delicious, very rich nut and poppyseed rolls, always sliced before serving and generously sprinkled with powdered sugar. These masterpieces were first served on Christmas Eve and after that, *ad nauseum* throughout the festive season.

Waslaw and Romola had procured a pine-tree, so large it touched the ceiling of the dining-room. On Christmas Eve, after lighting the candles, the servants were ceremoniously ushered in to receive their presents. Then Romola said the prayer and dinner was served to the family of three. It was very simple – fish, potatoes, a special brioche-like bread and lastly, the *beigli.*

They retired at the end of a 'perfect day'. Already the following morning Romola's happiness was marred by the intrusion of a trembling maid who announced that the Christmas tree had fallen down – an ill omen! Romola went down to study the havoc and was joined by Waslaw who assisted her in tying up the tree and salvaging the decorations, forlornly strewn on the floor.

When Kyra's Swiss nanny was compelled to leave the Nijinsky household to be with her mentally ill husband, she was replaced by another Swiss girl, who, according to Romola, had been brought up in England but had also lived in India. Romola claimed that she told them of her experience of fakirs and adherents to the philosophy of Yoga. Waslaw became so interested in the ideology that he began to study it. Apparently, it was she who introduced them to *séances,* much to Romola's amusement. Waslaw approached the subject seriously.

The young nanny must have been Marta, for in 1979, the News Editor of the *Daily Telegraph* received a letter from a Mrs Marta Grant in which she mentioned having lived with the Nijinskys in her early youth.

Igor Markevitch, Kyra's late husband, got in touch with Mrs Grant and her reply subsequently came into my possession. It makes interesting reading because it throws a rather different light on certain aspects of daily life in the Villa Guardamunt from those portrayed by Romola at some stage in 1918.

September 1979

'It was toward the end of the first War that I stayed with the Nijinskys in the Villa Guardamunt in St Moritz, Switzerland. I liked them from the first moment I met them. Mrs Nijinsky said some time afterwards that the same thing happened to them about me when we first met. They looked a very happy yet serious married couple.

When Mr Nijinsky was present we always spoke in French; with Mrs Nijinsky always English and when Kyra was present never anything but English as she was supposed to learn this language. With the servants I always spoke their native Swiss (not German). This put Mr Nijinsky rather apart as a person as he could only speak French (and of course Russian). Somehow, he was always a separate individual in more ways than one.

We led a very isolated life. No one ever came except Mrs Nijinsky's mother for a few days. There were no local callers either. I was their only link with the outside world. We did not even have a newspaper and as far as I know the postman seldom came... We sometimes called in at the Confisserie Hanselman in the village, famous for the good cakes, and sometimes at a small place where they served exceptionally nice creamy milk. This was about once a month only.

We used to go for walks on the slopes at the back of their house. You seldom met anyone there and those were the times when Mr Nijinsky used to kind of come out of his shell. He even laughed at times. He used to speak of his brother and his mother. It was evidently a sad life. He also spoke about his difficulties in dancing at present. He could not even practise anywhere, the house was too small, he needed space. One day they asked me to go to a certain hotel to see if he could perhaps use one of their halls. The second time I went I was to find out about insurance in case he had an accident. I knew before I went there, that they would of course not consider this and would probably expect rent. As good old Swiss, everything has to be paid for. So it all came to nothing. This was a great pity. Nijinsky looked like a caged animal at times. He was very concerned about his way of writing about dancing so that it could be read from paper, like music is written and interpreted. He wanted to discuss certain ideas that occupied him very much and there was no one but Romola and myself to talk to and he was ages ahead of all of us. How often I wished one had a tape recorder like today to perpetuate his sayings; someone might then have understood what he was trying to convey. What he needed was to get in contact with another sphere. The books by Dr. Rud. Steiner would probably have been of great help to him – someone who spoke his own language. I knew nothing of Steiner who was actually writing these now modern writings. But as with Steiner there were very few who understood.

It was typical of his dancing that he kind of stood still in mid air. Why should he not have had that connection with the Cosmos in this more substantial way? Like the coming generations will have a different level of consciousness, Nijinsky had it already at the beginning of this century.

I suppose I should have realised his loneliness. He said to me he did not want the Russians to know where he is, as they would enlist him and he said: *'Je ne peux pas tuer'*. Which of course you would know at once if you had known N. at the time. He was a creature of his own.

My thoughts often tried to visualise the tremendous difference if Diaghilev had not acted as he did when he (N.) got married to Romola. He was like a child who could not understand WHAT had happened to him, *when as a wedding present he was sent THE SACK*. He was very unhappy about the way Diaghilev used him...and he expected his marriage would release him from that connection. Mrs N. also spoke to me about this, just ONCE she mentioned it, but it puzzled them and probably made a lot of difference to all their thinking about human beings.

It might have helped N. if he had lived at a different place than amongst the gentle slopes of surrounding St Moritz. Somewhere in the wilds of the mountains with the perpetual snow, the descent of thousands of feet in front of him, where you could be above the clouds in the sunshine, while below you a wide blanket spread out and you knew it covered the valleys and the people and all their busy little lives. Or up north with the rough sea, the forces of nature. That would have helped him. But it was not to be and so it happened that the turning point came.

Romola was ill in bed in the storey above, quite away from where I was with N. and, as usual, the door probably shut. I mention this because it is quite inexplicable to me how Romola could possibly have known of anything that happened downstairs.

N. came into the dining-room where I was. I noticed nothing different about him. He then asked me if I had seen the key to a certain drawer. I said no, but would go and ask the servants, when he suddenly leaped at me and held me by the throat...and I could hear Romola yelling 'Vaslav, Vaslav...' and he at once let go of my throat and tore out of the room... I was terrified. I would not even go to my room to fetch anything and borrowed a hundred francs from the cook to get the next and last train out of St Moritz that night to get away as far as possible, which was Zürich where I had to stay the night at a hotel. I even looked in the cupboard and under the bed...if N. was not there. And I took the train from Samaden, not St Moritz as I thought he would follow me there. I had to go through a wood for about half an hour and I thought he would leap out from behind every tree. Months later I woke up suddenly thinking of this terrible happening... I saw or heard nothing from St Moritz. Months later when I was already in England I had letters from Mrs N. which I answered after a while; in fact it is only 6 months ago when I found an unanswered letter from 1940 and I tore it up.

Quite frequently now I suddenly remember the things N. used to say...One thing I must add, Romola was the most wonderful, kind, patient and loving wife any man could ever wish for. Till his breakdown when he was going to strangle me, if Romola had not called him off, and it is quite uncanny HOW she knew he was in danger of doing something VERY wrong.

Signed *Marta Madeleine Grant*
     6 Surrenden Road
     Brighton BN1 6PT'

In a postscript to the above letter Marta Grant wrote that she used to be an avid reader, particularly of philosophy. She added that she would love to know what happened to Kyra. 'I only know that Mrs N. asked me to take her to live with me in England, which was impossible. But would be so glad to know more of her life, how it took shape etc... I am sorry all is written so badly, talking would have been easier.' Marta Grant died a few years ago. Her son recalled how often she had spoken about her Swiss adventure and of how deeply attached she had become to the young family who outwardly seemed to have every ingredient for happiness whilst, instead, a tragic drama was being enacted behind the closed doors.

It was a few weeks into the new year that perceptibly a change came over Waslaw, a change that was to grow at an alarming pace. His bouts of meditation became prolonged. He withdrew to his room where he sat until dawn broke, working away on his mechanical inventions.

> '*I have invented a new fountain-pen and a bridge – a cable railway which can destroy all steamers. I know everyone will tell me that I am talking nonsense, but I can prove it to technical scientists who will understand me.... I know of a method for the destruction of coal mines. I do not like people who force the poor to dig the earth. I have invented a method for obtaining physical power without coal...I know that if coal is destroyed there will be no smoke to harm men's health....*
> '*I shall invent a fountain-pen without pressure. The pressure of a fountain-pen does not give beauty to writing...*'

He went on shopping sprees for paints, pastels and brushes. Soon thereafter he was to forsake the circular sketches and instead Romola would find his study cluttered with the most bizarre creations 'strange faces, eyes peering from every corner, red and black, like a blood-stained mortuary cover...Then other designs came; fanciful butterflies with faces which bore a resemblance to Vaslav's and big spiders with the face of Diaghileff...'. He worked with lightning speed and it was not long before even his bedroom and bathroom were covered with his grotesque drawings.

Waslaw applied himself to the winter sports with frenzy. He learned to ski and while Romola stood paralysed watching him zigzag down the slope, the ski-instructor turned to her and commented on what a practised skier he was. He possessed such perfect balance and held his body in position like a trained skier; certainly not the amateur they have been led to believe he was. It was useless for Romola to remonstrate. But she experienced raw terror the day he drove the sleigh with herself and Kyra as passengers and, contrary to his usual care, had whipped the horses to such a speed, they came within inches of colliding with an oncoming sleigh. When Romola admonished him, he turned to her 'with a hard and metallic look' she had never seen before. Episode after episode from this crucial period is recalled in her biography, testifying that something was drastically wrong. But what? Danger signals were alerting her when her otherwise so gentle Waslaw began to show signs of uncontrollable temper. One day he pushed her and Kyra down the stairs when he accused her of making such a noise, she disturbed his work.

Once more he adamantly refused to partake of a meal in which meat of any kind was served and on occasion created such a fuss in restaurants that Romola would have to take Kyra to another table to enjoy what she considered a healthy repast. In Romola's view the lack of meat weakened bodily strength. Had she not experienced that earlier when Waslaw had adopted Tolstoy's philosophy? He would push the plate away at dinner when served his favourite *shchi,* cabbage soup, if it contained a trace of meat.

'I know how animals are killed; how they weep. Besides, meat creates lust. I do not wish to feel lust. Physical strength comes from the mind, not from food...I do not like eating meat. I saw how a calf was killed and a pig. I saw it and felt their tears. They felt death...Since I have stopped eating meat I have noticed my digestion is better, my thoughts are better and I run instead of walking...'

One afternoon, Waslaw arrived home from yet another shopping expedition. Under his arm he clutched four black copy books, very simple ones, the kind children used as exercise books. It was after that he confined himself daily to the solitude of his room, locking himself in to be certain he would not be interrupted. He would not suffer Romola to see his writing. To these copy books he confided all his thoughts, his political views, his spiritual experiences, his sexual desires – LIFE, DEATH, FEELING. It was all jotted down in Russian, gushing out from his fountain pen until both it and he ran dry. To the ordinary reader, perhaps most of what he wrote would be incomprehensible, indigestible, passed off as the ramblings of a distorted mind but to me there are so many passages of beauty and lucidity that I have felt a compulsion to quote them in this book. Through them, I learned to know my father and a clearer picture emerges of those months before his mind clouded over forever. Too, one gets his view on his own early life and the people around him.

'I write in small handwriting because notebooks are expensive. I was in a shop in St Moritz which is called "The Road". I went

in at God's command...I asked for notebooks. There was one woman, thin, with black hair and pince-nez on her nose. The pince-nez had a golden chain. I realised that the woman had shares in that shop, for the simple reason that she mentioned one price and the (other) woman in the shop another...

'I want to write, to write and to wipe away my tears. I must not weep so loudly as to disturb my Romola in the other room. I must weep alone. This fountain pen tires my hand as I write, so I must invent a fountain pen without any pressure, a pen with which I shall be able to write the truth, the truth about God and Mankind...

'I write as I can. I do not pretend. I write the truth because I want everyone to know. I know everyone will say that Nijinsky has become mad because he writes things without seeing. I see everything. I know everything...

'...this book will be published in many thousands of copies. I want to sign "Nijinsky" for the sake of publicity, but my name is "God". I love Nijinsky not like Narcissus, but like God...Nijinsky is I...'.

Waslaw took to going for long walks by himself without letting Romola know. Or else she observed him running quickly on the road leading to Chanterella. She was gripped with icy fear that he was endangering his health in such a high altitude. When he did not arrive in time for dinner, she shook with terror at the thought he might have met with an accident. She began to find it more and more difficult to draw out of him what was the matter. She was unable to probe his mind, nor could she find where he hid his copy books. And would she have been able to glean anything from them had she found them – her knowledge of Russian was very scanty.

'One day I was in the mountains and got onto a road which led up the mountain. I went along it and stopped. I wanted to speak on the mountain because I felt a desire to do so...I wanted to jump from the mountain into the little town of St Moritz...I went further and saw a tree. The tree said to me that one could speak here because men did not understand feeling...I went up to a height of 2,000 metres. I stood for a long time...

'I went out for a walk once, toward evening...I stopped on a mountain which was not Sinai. I had gone far. I felt cold... I

185

gazed at a star which did not say to me "How are you?" It did not twinkle. I know that twinkling stars are life and those which do not twinkle, death... I was frightened and wanted to run, but could not because my knees were rooted to the snow. I started to weep. My weeping was not heard... I screamed at the top of my voice "Death"...suddenly felt an immense strength and started running...The snow was crunching underneath my foot. I loved the snow. My step was full of life. I looked at the sky and saw the stars which started twinkling at me. I became cheerful and did not feel cold any more... I walked quickly as I walked down the mountain. I went past the Hotel Ciantarella.'

He was filled with the firm belief that he was the World, the Earth. He began to communicate more and more with God, with Christ.

'I am man. I am Christ.'
'I am not an ordinary man. I am God. I love God and He now loves me...
I am a man in God.'

In the early part of 1919 Romola's ever faithful cousin Paul arrived unannounced in St Moritz and paid daily visits to the Nijinskys and for a few brief weeks made life bearable for Romola. To her it was an antidote to have him around. He was indefatigable in catering to her whims, running errands, returning from St Moritz with delicacies which were too expensive for the family to afford. At Romola's request he would accompany Waslaw on some of his walks. She made known to him her concern over Waslaw's health; needless to say, the whole picture was unveiled during his frequent visits to the Villa Guardamunt. Waslaw's manner had become unstable, unpredictable. At first, Paul put it down to the dancer's inherent sensitivity, regarding the fits of depression or frenzied gaiety as natural to a genius of Waslaw's calibre. But then he started to study him more closely; watched him sitting in front of the window for hours at end, scratching his thumb. He also learned that Waslaw was writing a diary until the early hours of the morning. Again, he tried to analyse his friend's behaviour; the effect of the many pressures Waslaw had to endure; the heartache he must be suffering worrying about his mother and sister; the distress over his brother's death; the almost unbearable frustration of not being able to perform on stage.

A minor happening, incongruous by normal standards, occurred on one of the customary, silent walks Paul and Waslaw took to St Moritz Dorf. There was a tiny tobacco shop wedged between a couple of smart boutiques and Waslaw had indicated he wished to enter the shop. To while away the time, Paul preoccupied himself looking around and had not paid attention to the discussion between Waslaw and the proprietor at the counter. The former had asked to see all the postcards on the rack. Some fifty-odd were strewn out on the counter. Waslaw appeared to be undecided which to select added to which he was not able to find any money in his pockets. An altercation ensued but as Paul hurried to his friend's side, Waslaw found some money, tossed it on the counter without counting it and commenced to stuff both his and Paul's pockets with the cards. Without uttering a word, he turned on his heels and left. They returned to the Villa in silence broken only once by Waslaw's gleeful chortle as he explained the postcards were for Kyra – how she would enjoy them. Paul related the episode to Romola and also expressed his growing belief that a doctor should be consulted before the strain from which Waslaw appeared to be suffering became too great.

And others were soon to voice the same opinion. Romola had to face the day when their own servants came to her to warn her that something was terribly amiss with the master of the house, that he was acting just like a man in their home village who had had to be sent to an asylum. They told her how he was walking around in St Moritz Dorf with a 'big golden cross over his necktie, and stopping everybody in the streets asking them if they have been to mass and sending them to church.' The same servants, who had so adored him, began to be frightened.

With growing clarity, Romola accepted she had to seek professional advice but how to do it without bluntly telling Waslaw she feared for his sanity? So she pretended Kyra was in need of a physician's attention. The latter made a close study of Waslaw, camouflaged by a social cup of afternoon tea to discuss Kyra's condition. The doctor later told Romola 'Mr Nijinsky needs a rest; he has a slight case of hysteria, probably due to overwork. I would advise you to go into a sanatorium with him, and in the meanwhile I will get a nurse, so that we can have him under observation.' The nurse was introduced to Waslaw as a masseur. They felt secure that it would allay any suspicions he might harbour especially as he had for some time stated he wished to have a masseur. The male nurse who arrived the following day had a remarkable effect on Waslaw; for a short interlude peals of laughter reverberated throughout the house as Kyra and Waslaw played games together.The nurse, a German, had been with the Münich State Asylum some twenty-odd years, a kindly, reliable fellow and a natural actor because no one suspected his real profession. It was at that time, in one of his joyous moods, Waslaw suggested that Tessa should come to visit them.

Tessa's arrival temporarily dispelled the gloom. Her nimble fingers gave new life to the piano and the house resounded with mellifluous Strauss waltzes. She prompted Waslaw to join her and the marvelled at his uncanny ability to hear a tune played once and then to render it faultlessly. Uninhibited flirt that she was, Tessa seemingly made no effort to hide that she was attracted to her brother-in-law. Waslaw's notebooks reveal he was a shrewd judge of human nature.

> 'I understand very well, because I noticed she flirted with me, lying down on the bed in her underclothes to excite me. She thinks she can do it by showing her knickers made of silk. She wears small knickers, and very thin vests to excite people. I understand her very well. I know her tricks. They are like those of a tiger who waits for her prey. I came to her room on purpose when she was naked. She was not ashamed in front of me. A well-brought up woman must feel ashamed in front of a man...'.

Waslaw saw Tessa not only as a coquette but also found her addiction to the stimulus of wine objectionable, a bad habit she had probably acquired from living with Erik. He wrote about it at some length in his *Diary*.

> 'I do not like Tessa because she drinks and enjoys herself, but I do like her because she feels art...She cannot force her husband not to drink and, in fact, drinks herself. She drinks Madeira, liqueurs, etc. etc... My wife gives her wine because she knows that she drinks in secret. She is a drunkard...'.

Then he goes on to say

'Besides this, Tessa feels music and dancing and understands everything I do... She does not love me...and therefore she is a beast, a Tiger. I wanted to nickname her Tiger Cub, but thought that was too beautiful a name. I will ask her to go away as soon as possible...'.

Immediately upon Tessa's arrival, Romola had confided that due to Waslaw's odd behaviour, she was near collapse. In an attempt to involve him in their daily life, she wheedled Waslaw into giving Tessa dancing lessons, and to go with them on shopping expeditions.

'The bell is ringing. It is Tessa who has gone off to enjoy herself after my dancing...She wants me to take her into my Company. I do not want to take her because she does not feel her work. She wants to join the Company for her own convenience...'
'Tessa feels me because I give her a lot of presents. She loves presents...I bought shoes for her today because she hadn't any herself...She felt that I loved her and burst into tears for I gave her to understand that I would give her a ring. She liked the ring...'.

Romola wrote: 'One morning he arrived with a load of sweaters, in every colour of the rainbow. "But why so many?" *"Femmka,* the shades are so beautiful. Why not?"'
It was inevitable that Romola and Waslaw should exchange harsh words during that stressful, dark period. She was still unable to grasp what was taking place nor could he himself fathom it. He suffered increasingly from severe bouts of headaches. His writing became more and more incoherent. His temper flared up more and more often. There is no doubt that he still loved his *Romushka* deeply but he had begun to distrust her after the all too frequent visits from Dr . . . who presumably was their house physician. He rebelled fiercely against eating any food which contained meat. A simple bagatelle could bring on a quarrel.

'...asked her not to eat a sausage in the evening because I know its effect. She says to me that "What is good for you is not good for me."'

189

Behind the door to his room he scribbled down his real fears.

'I can no longer trust my wife for I have felt that she wants to give these notes to Dr . . . for examination. I said that no one had the right to touch my notebooks...I have hidden them...He wants to examine my brain...He cannot examine my brain because he has not seen it. I am afraid that I will be taken to a lunatic asylum and that I shall lose all my work...'.

Dr . . . is referred to time and time again. Waslaw confided to his *Diary* that he hated him, then that he loved and trusted him. Pathetically, he addressed his qualms and disarranged state of mind to Romola in a rambling 'letter'. He was plagued by the thought she no longer understood him.

'To my dear and darling Romushka

I made you angry on purpose because I love you. I wish you happiness. You are afraid of me because I have changed. I have changed because God has willed it so... You have called Dr . . . You have trusted a stranger and not me... I cannot dance the way I used to because all these dances are death... You will understand me later because everyone will say that Nijinsky is God... You think I am ill. You think that, because Dr . . . told you I was ill... You do not want to live in Russia, I want to live in Russia... You do not know what you want, but I know what I want... I do not wish you harm. I love you, you...'

He was apparently acutely aware that the physician was so often invited to the house to study him; not for a moment did he appear to be fooled that his visits were purely social:

'We ate at the same time because my wife has invited him to our house. He was observing me because he wanted to understand whether or not I was mad. He is still convinced that there is "something wrong" with me...'

Romola has written that on one occasion when they had guests, among which were the Duc and Duquesa de Durcal, Waslaw had teasingly remarked that he had played the part of a lunatic for about six weeks much to the alarm of his family, the servants and the villagers; that the physician had not realised he was merely playing a part to amuse himself as he no longer had a theatre audience for whom to perform.

Sometimes he would bring up the subject of dancing again and declared he would return to Paris to the Châtelet; other times he said he would give up dancing forever and go back to Russia to work on a farm. It was on one such occasion that Romola completely lost control of herself, and tearing her wedding ring off her finger, threw it at him, screaming she would divorce him and marry a wealthier man.

> '*She loves me and is therefore worried about my health. I told her that if she did not like anything I did we could divorce and I would find her a good and rich husband... I am not afraid of her abandoning me because I will not marry again...I love her very much and shall therefore ask her forgiveness if God will it...*
>
> '*My wife wants money and therefore she must be given it. If they promise me money I shall sell these manuscripts...*'

Of his marriage to Romola he wrote:

> '*I married quite by chance. I married in South America...I was introduced to my wife on the ship "The Avon"... I must say that I married without thinking. I loved her and loved her. I did not think of the future. I spent the money which I had saved with great difficulty. I used to give her roses at 5 francs each. I bought these roses every day, from twenty to thirty each time. I loved giving her white roses. I realised my love was white not red... I felt a lasting, but not passionate love. I loved her terribly. I gave her all I could. She loved me. It seemed to me she was happy...*'

The pages of his black copy books became filled with his religious fantasies, coinciding with the period when he started walking the streets of St Moritz with a cross.

> '*People understood that I was mad. I was not mad. I wore the cross to make people pay attention to me...*
>
> '*I know that men do not understand the Church but go there out*

191

of habit, because they are afraid of God. God is not an icon. God is in the soul of man. I am God. I am the Spirit. I am all… I know that God wants to help everyone…
'God is fire in the head. I am alive as long as I have a fire in my head. My pulse is an earthquake…'

It must have been bitterly cold that winter in the Villa Guardamunt because Waslaw complained *'my fingers are becoming numb'*. He brooded over what was wrong with him, how to convey his feelings to the outside world.

'My sickness is that of the soul and not of the mind. I know what I need to become well again… I am a man and not God… I want to dance. I want to draw. I want to play the piano. I want to write poetry. I want to compose ballets. I want to love everyone. This is the aim of my life…I am the whole world. I am the earth… I do not want to have property. I do not want to be rich. I want to love, love… I want happiness for everyone. I shall be the happiest of men when I shall know that all people share things with each other. I shall be the happiest of men when I shall act and dance…without monetary or any other kind of reward. I want love for people…
God is within me. I am within Him. I want Him. I seek Him.'

Then came the day when to Romola's surprise Waslaw announced he would dance again – a performance to which all their friends and acquaintances would be invited. From what Romola wrote, he himself was solely in charge of the preparations. He contacted Hans Bon, owner of the fashionable Suvretta House Hotel, and selected a ballroom he deemed suitable for his purpose. He even made the arrangements for tea to be served. Bertha Gelbar, a Viennese pianist of some repute, was to accompany him. She and her husband, M. Asseo, were friends of the Schmedes. Waslaw was extremely secretive about the costumes to be worn. He chose the material, hundreds of yards of fabulous silks and velvets and enlisted the aid of Romola's Italian dressmaker, Negri. Not even Romola was permitted to see the creations nor was she told what dances were on the programme. From Waslaw's own account one gathers that she and her husband were quite poor. The latter was a violinist in the Palace Hotel at night.

'...I went to the dressmaker on foot. The dressmaker has done her work well. She had understood me...I gave her husband a pair of underpants and a sweater...She took the present with love. I like Negri, this is how she is called. She is a good woman. She lives very poorly...She has no warm clothes. I shall give her a warm jersey and a cap to wear...She has a boy of about six and a girl of about two. I want to give a present to the children because they are very poorly dressed...She knows I am an artist and therefore she understands me...'.

The recital was due to commence at five in the afternoon. Romola only once broke the deep silence that prevailed on the way to Suvretta to innocently ask a simple question: what was Bertha Gelbar going to play for him?

'"I will tell her at the time. Do not speak. *Silence!*" he thundered at me. "This is my marriage with God."'

It is not difficult to imagine the cold shivers that must have passed through Romola's slender body. It was with trepidation she put on a brave face and went inside to greet her guests, some two hundred in all, both invited and uninvited. Her worst fears were confirmed when Waslaw manifested himself without any of the beautiful costumes he had created, simply garbed in his training gear. He paid no heed to the audience. Striding over to the pianist he said: 'I will tell you what to play. I will show you how we live, how we suffer, how we artists create' and with that he sank down on a chair and stared at his audience for what must have seemed like an eternity yet in all probability lasted a mere half hour. The atmosphere was by then laden with violent undercurrents like moments before the outbreak of a thunderstorm. The people who had gathered to see the great Nijinsky dance just sat there, hypnotised, Madame Asseo softly played the first few bars of *Sylphides* and carried on with *Spectre* as a cue for him to start. When Waslaw still remained motionless, Romola, unable to bear the sinister silence any longer, went over to Waslaw and beseeched him to begin to dance *Sylphides*. Again, in Romola's version of the event, he shouted at her in front of everybody 'How dare you disturb me! I am not a machine. I will dance when I feel like it.'

There were those who gave a different account of the beginning of that ill-fated afternoon recital on the 19th of January 1919. I will quote here, however, Romola's words. Suddenly,

> '...Vaslav was dancing – gloriously and frighteningly. He took a few rolls of black and white velvet and made a big cross the length of the room. He stood at the head of it with open arms, a living cross himself.'

She went on to describe how terrifying the scene in front of them was. Waslaw had proceeded to proclaim that he would 'dance...the war, with its suffering, with its destruction, with its death.' To his petrified audience 'he seemed to fill the room with horror-stricken humanity.' He danced as he had never danced before. When he finished, and his audience had snapped out of the weird spell he had cast upon them, wild clapping commenced – the last applause he was ever to hear.

He summed the event up as follows:

> *'I was nervous because God wanted to arouse the public. The public came to be amused. It thought that I was dancing for amusement. I danced frightening things. They were afraid of me and therefore thought that I wanted to kill them. I did not want to kill anyone. I loved everyone but no one loved me...I was nervous and therefore transmitted this feeling to the public. The public did not like me because they wanted to go. Then I began to act gay things. The public cheered up...started laughing...I danced badly because I kept falling on the floor when I did not have to. The public did not care because I danced beautifully... I wanted to dance more, but God said to me "Enough".*
> *'I felt God throughout the evening. He loved me. I loved Him. We were married. In the carriage I told my wife that today was the day of my marriage to God.'*

A few days later, Tessa departed for Vienna.

> *'I did not go to see her off because God does not want me to leave my writing.'*

In Budapest, Emilia was fraught with painful uneasiness over what was happening in St Moritz. She had received fragmentary reports from Tessa and she realised that her son-in-law was on the verge of a total nervous breakdown or worse. But she, too, had grave problems to cope with on her own doorstep. In the aftermath of the Great War, she saw her secure existence threatened, her world crumbling before her eyes. She still lived in the Villa, cosseted by Oskar. She still had a maid and a cook but the other servants, like the chauffeur and the gardener, were long since gone. The country lacked food, frightening slogans appeared daily in the streets, there were rumblings of a new political and social upheaval, wounded soldiers, the 'basketmen', presented a totally unfathomable and alien picture.

Within the confines of the Villa, however, Emilia struggled to carry on as normal. According to Oskar, never did she give up the ritual of preparing breakfast herself. It was a household chore she took particular pride in. A round drop-leaf table would be set every evening by the maid in readiness for the following morning. Milk, sweet butter, jam and croissants would be sent up by the cook in the dumbwaiter as soon as she came back from the local bakery. To watch Emilia brew the tea was a theatrical performance in itself. She would fill a handsome porcelain teapot with water that had just come to a boil, roll the pot with a gentle movement and then pour the water out. Only after that did she place two to three teaspoons of her favourite blend of tea into the pot, immediately filling it up with piping hot water. This done, Emilia would cover the teapot with a gaily decorated flannel and with a flourish set it on the table. Mimi, a beautiful white Angora cat and her cherished pet, was always present. She would enjoy her breakfast of fresh milk while her mistress indulged in her tea.

Emilia was fifty-nine, her face and figure still youthful, although telltale lines had appeared to signal that the autumn of her life had come. Her name held magic to her public as strongly as ever and she could savour the sweetness of success after each performance but Oskar was to confide to me she was physically and mentally drained. Worry and concern for her loved ones had taken their toll.

One afternoon, Emilia's maid burst into the drawing-room sobbing her heart out. It transpired that her fiancé Joska had been shot and seriously wounded in a fracas in their village. She wished to return home at once. The episode might have been brushed to one side as a trivial private act of violence in a peasant community but Oskar was acutely aware of what it signified – he calmly tried to

195

explain what was going on throughout Hungary, that they were facing the birth of a revolution. It was on that apocalyptic afternoon that he told Emilia in a few terse sentences what had happened to three of their Jewish friends, a banker and two businessmen. They had been found shot dead in the basement of their homes. The air was rife with disturbing rumours that anyone – be he aristocrat or peasant – who did not agree with the reigning forces risked being killed. Oskar wished to protect his Emma and she in turn thought only of his safety; not only was he Jewish by origin but he held a high position in the Ministry. They decided it would be wise to leave the country for a time and thus made the necessary preparations to go to Vienna to stay with Tessa and Erik, and possibly from there continue to Switzerland.

Meanwhile, in Villa Guardamunt, Romola observed the grave deterioration in Waslaw's behaviour with growing apprehension. He devoted himself almost wholly to filling the pages of his *Diary,* writing at lightning speed. She managed once to catch a glimpse of the text. It was all in Russian but she could discern familiar names: Diaghilev, God, the politicians of their day – Wilson, Lloyd-George, Clemenceau – Dr . . ., and many others. There was hardly a subject he did not cover; God and love, sex, philosophy, criticism of the statesmen who ruled the world. He reassured himself that he was not afraid of the Press were they one day to read his work because *'the press has already said a lot of bad things about me...but print cannot transmit the same feeling as writing...'.*

It was only natural that he should dwell on the past, ponder over his relationship with Diaghilev.

'I made the acquaintance of Prince Paul Lvov who introduced me to a Polish Count. I have forgotten his Christian name and do not want to offend the whole family. This Count bought me a piano. Lvov introduced me to Diaghilev who invited me to come to the Hotel Europe.
I hated him for his voice which was too sure of itself, but I went in search of a fortune...I was poor, I earned 65 rubles a month – not enough to feed both my mother and myself.
I know terrible things because I learned them from Diaghilev. I was young and did silly things but I do not practise them any more. Prince Paul Lvov wrote me love poetry. I wanted to live with him always because I loved him...He forced me to be

unfaithful to him with Diaghilev because he thought Diaghilev would be useful to me... Paul Lvov wanted to continue his friendship with me but I realised that it was dishonest to be unfaithful.

Diaghilev is a wicked man and loves boys...when he used to tell me that love for women was a terrible thing, I used to believe him. Diaghilev's smiles are artificial. He does not want love for everyone. Diaghilev wants love for himself.'

Diaghilev thinks he is the God of Art...I want to challenge Diaghilev to a duel so that the whole world will see. I want to prove that all Diaghilev's art is sheer nonsense...I know all his tricks and habits. I know his weak sides and strong.

'...I have punished him by revealing his faults so that everybody knows them. I have punished myself for I have told everyone about myself.'

Although Waslaw worshipped his daughter Kyra, he was unable to obliterate from his conscious state his longing for a son. *'I want to make love to Romola, not out of lust but to produce a child.'* They had discussed the subject earlier. 'Vaslav one morning suddenly declared: *"Femmka,* do you know of anybody – a great physician – who is a genius like Lombroso?... I want to talk to someone who would understand me...I want to have a son now, and I want him to be perfectly healthy, not only physically but mentally."' Romola seized upon this as an opportunity to visit a leading psychiatrist in Zürich, Professor Eugen Bleuler.

Emilia and Oskar arrived from Vienna. Tessa had told them in graphic detail about the disastrous recital and peculiar goings-on in Villa Guardamunt. Emilia had become exceedingly agitated. She believed Romola to be in imminent danger.

Waslaw was in his room when he heard people talking and recognised his mother-in-law's voice and that of Oskar.

'I realised that they had come...I heard my wife's sobs...I heard the threats of my wife's mother...I wanted to comfort my wife but God would not let me...I heard what was being said about me.

My wife's mother has calmed down because she saw my love for my wife'.

197

It is undeniable that Waslaw and Emilia did not always see eye to eye. They were both temperamental artists, both possessive in their love of Romola. In her book, Romola painted a very dark picture of her mother, and quite naturally, Waslaw was influenced by his beloved *Romushka* and often referred to his in-laws in anything but flattering terms. He mentioned Emilia scathingly in parts of his *Diary* but he also conceded;

> *'I want to speak to my wife's mother Emma and her husband Oscar. They are good people. I love them, but they have their faults like everyone else...I want to order a frame for Oscar's photograph because I want to show him my love...I have given him several of my drawings because I see that he likes them.'*

Waslaw was sufficiently in possession of his faculties to understand that he was suffering from some kind of nervous disorder. He and Romola had read about Cesare Lombroso, the Italian criminologist, who had been a professor of psychiatry as well as director of a lunatic asylum: now they were both overjoyed to have found a present-day psychiatrist of similar fame. Waslaw was in doubt, however, that anything truly serious was wrong.

> *'My wife is urging me to go to Zürich to see a nerve specialist in order to have my nervous system examined. I have promised her 100,000 francs if she turns out to be right that my nerves are not in order. I shall not give her that money if she proves to be wrong.'*

Yet, irrationally, he later writes:

> *'I hope I shall be committed to a lunatic asylum. I shall rejoice at this event because I like to tyrannise everyone.'*

He also admits he feels alarmed that he might be forced to go away because he fears death of the mind.

> *'I shall be horrified of loneliness but I shall not weep because I know God loves me and therefore I am not lonely. I know that if God abandons me I shall die.'*

He grieved that little Kyra had been told he was ill and that he might have to go away forever, as witness the following:

'My wife came to me and told me that I should tell Kyra I would not be coming back. My wife felt tears welling up and said in some agitation she would not leave me... I said I would not remain in Zürich if she was not afraid of me, but if she was afraid of me I would prefer to be in a lunatic asylum...'.

Regarding the trip to Zürich Romola appears to contradict herself. She writes at first that 'In a few days' time my parents arrived and we all four left for Zürich', confirmed in Waslaw's own writing. *'Tomorrow I shall go to Zürich with Oscar, my wife and her mother.'* Yet in the following chapter Romola writes: 'The day when Professor Bleuler made his statement, the day when I decided to save him (Waslaw) from the fate to which he was condemned, my fanatic parents arrived in Zürich.' The two couples had journeyed by train and stayed at the Hôtel Baur en Ville. It simply does not sound plausible that Emilia and Oskar went back and forth from Zürich to St Moritz to return the next day.

Whatever the order of events – I can visualise how Romola must have been too beside herself with shock over what she heard to record it with absolute accuracy later – there are far too many gaps in her account. On the first visit to Professor Bleuler she had gone alone. She had a two-hour conversation with 'an old man with infinite understanding in his eyes.' He listened patiently to her story and when she came to the end, he lifted her spirits with hope when he said 'Genius, insanity, they are so near; normality and abnormality, there is almost no border between the two states. I should like to meet your husband; extremely interesting. If you spoke of any other man I might be worried, but the symptoms you describe in the case of an artist and a Russian do not in themselves prove any mental disturbance.'

To quote Romola, she was relieved and happy and could not wait to tell Waslaw about the Professor's optimistic standpoint. They were to see him together the following day. Meanwhile, they went out on a shopping tour that afternoon and Waslaw purposely stopped in front of a window of a store displaying babies' clothes and he smiled in anticipation of the future. What risk could there possibly be? Had he not been brought up in the Imperial School under strict and constant medical care? Sound and healthy except for typhoid fever? His present condition was doubtful due to strain and stress under duress and the break with Diaghilev.

It was about three o'clock in the afternoon that they set off to see Professor Bleuler. This time it was Waslaw who went into the consulting room alone. She recalled so clearly every minute of what transpired. How her husband strode into the Professor's room, his step once more buoyant, shoulders thrown back with boyish confidence.

To while away the time, Romola idly flicked through the illustrated magazines strewn out on the table in the waiting-room. Everything was going to be all right. She and her Watza would pick up the threads once more from whence they had been so rudely broken. The dark shadows would be dispersed.

The Professor's door opened slowly. She barely had a chance to give Waslaw a smile as he came out when she caught the sound of the Professor's voice.

'Madame Nijinsky, *bitte kommen Sie herein...* I wish to give you your prescription.'

At first, his words had not registered. Prescription! What prescription? All at once she felt a throbbing of her temples, icy fear gripping her heart. Something was terribly wrong.

The Professor gently ushered her on to a chair and then...

'No, no, I don't want to hear it!' She covered her ears with her hands, but the words penetrated like nails driven into steel with harsh metallic blows. They would echo and re-echo for all the years to come.

Professor Bleuler was trying to tell her she should divorce her husband. Be brave. Take Kyra, their daughter, away with her. Leave Waslaw, for all their sakes. He was incurably insane... 'I must seem to be brutal, but I have to be able to save you and your child – two lives. We physicians must try to save those whom we can; the others, unfortunately, we have to abandon to their cruel fate...'.

She had no recollection of how she got out of the room, her legs had threatened to give way under her. Through a blur of tears she saw the figure of her beloved husband standing there in his Russian fur coat, the Cossack cap rakishly at an angle though not enough to shade his eyes as he gazed at her with pleading childlike pathos.

He uttered just one phrase.

'*Femmka,* you bring me my death warrant.'

That was the moment when the God of Dance died.

'Death came unexpectedly...I have been told that I am mad. I
thought I was alive. They gave me no rest. I lived and was glad
but people said I was wicked...I feel very sad...
I know what death is. Death is life extinguished. People who
have lost their reason are an extinguished life. I, too, was with-
out reason but when I remained in St Moritz I understood – in
my room – the whole truth, because I felt a lot. I know it is diffi-
cult to feel by oneself, but only when man is alone can he under-
stand what feeling is...'.

Due to the intervention of Emilia and Oskar, in an impulsive gesture meant not to harm but governed by a blind belief they were
helping Waslaw seek treatment, whilst simultaneously protecting
their Romola, the latter states that Waslaw was taken by force from
the Hôtel Baur en Ville in Zürich and placed in the State Asylum
among numerous other patients. Romola was to claim it brought on
his first catatonic attack. I am ill acquainted with legalistic proceedings but find it hard to believe that Emilia could have had the
authority to take such action of her own accord, and so speedily.*
Likewise, I must plead ignorance to any profound knowledge of
mental illness. Like most laymen I do know that any condition, be it
psychological or physical, can be triggered off and worsened
through extreme shock.

Romola, deeply distressed, went straight back to Professor
Bleuler who immediately arranged for Waslaw's transfer to the
Bellevue Kuranstalt, Kreuzlingen. A Dr Binswanger was in charge.
There, as he entered the gates for the first time, Waslaw looked up
to the sky and said, *'Femmka, courage, ne désespéres pas, car il y a*
un Dieu.'

For six months Waslaw stayed at the Sanatorium in the hands of
competent, friendly doctors and staff. But despite skilled care he
did not improve, on the contrary, his condition worsened to such a
degree that he began to suffer from hallucinations and became quite
violent. When, finally, he refused nourishment in any form,
Romola decided on July 29 1919, to take the drastic step of bringing

* In fairness to Emilia, I must add that recently acquired official documents have
substantiated that she was not responsible for having committed Waslaw to the State
Asylum.

him back to Villa Guardamunt. Perhaps, she reasoned, what he required most of all was the sanctuary of his own home, to feel the daily routine of normal life pulsating around him. Consequently, two physicians and three nurses provided round-the-clock care.

All this required vast sums of money. Much of it must have stemmed from Oskar and Emilia. When they embarked on their trip to St Moritz, Oskar was allocated the sum of 10,000 korona to take with him. As former counsellor to the Office of the former Prime Minister, he was granted the money under the subterfuge that he would send the Ministry reports of his work.

From the Hungarian National Archives, Ministry of Foreign Affairs, Commerce Department, the following extract from a cable relates to this affair,

'Párdány, who was counsellor to the Office of the Prime Minister, is at present in Switzerland at the request of the previous government. His wife, Márkus Emilia, member of the National Theatre, is with him. The couple have run out of money. Their son-in-law became seriously ill in St Moritz, suffering from a nervous breakdown. Payment for medical treatment is also required. Therefore, Elek Bolgar (the Austrian Ambassador) has put forward a request that their salaries be sent or transferred to a Swiss bank, thus allocating the money in said manner. Párdány plans to hold an exhibition of paintings (in Zürich) in June at the request of Kernstock.'

Kun Béla, leader of the Bolshevik Uprising in Hungary, sent a cable in reply to Elek Bolgar on the 26th of April, 1919, to the effect that the necessary steps had been taken to ensure that the requested salaries were transferred and that 'at present, the exhibition of paintings in Zürich is irrelevant.'

There must have been an interim period when Emilia and Oti-Papa absented themselves from Villa Guardamunt. It was the alarming news that her 'mad' son-in-law was once more ensconced under the same roof as her daughter that brought Emilia swiftly back to St Moritz, together with Oskar. Daily, she beseeched Romola to come to her senses, heed the wise professor's warning – to divorce Waslaw. Pleading was to no avail. Emilia's exhortation about the security waiting for her Molly and little Kyra in the Villa in Budapest fell on deaf ears.

The older couple were filled with good intentions but the pressure from all sides was so intense that Romola was on the point of a nervous breakdown.

It was Emilia in after years who furnished me with her version of what transpired during that strange visit. On the surface, at least, life pursued its normal course. Waslaw would often join them for tea in the salon although he now seldom participated in any conversation. There were the black days when he refused to move from his bed; refused to eat. Neither Romola nor the nursing staff could rouse him from his lethargy. Either he feigned sleep or merely lay there, staring into space, a vacant look in his eyes. There were the violent days when he erupted into paroxysms of wrath. Was it then perhaps that he was fighting against himself, trying to break away from the world of fantasy into which he appeared to have subsided? Unexpectedly, a young professor called at the house, one of the many Romola already had been in touch with. After an hour-long discussion in private he had taken his leave and Romola, prodded by Emilia, recounted what the professor had suggested. His advice had been simple; to erase the two words 'incurably insane' from her mind and to do everything possible to recreate the early days of her marriage, to surround her husband with a tranquil normal home-life. He had put it to her bluntly – that she should arouse Waslaw's sexual urge once more.

Emilia recoiled in horror at the mere thought and a cruel exchange of words followed. It shows what turmoil Romola's own mental state was in. After all, it was Bleuler who had discovered and identified *schizophrenia*. Was any man better qualified to judge the patient's condition? And there were Dr Binswanger as well as two physicians in constant attendance. Emilia frantically tried to make her daughter face the truth. Suppose Waslaw tried to kill her? A docile, gentle man one moment, he was like a beast the next and strong as an ox. The more Emilia carried on, the more Romola rebelled, calling her mother pitiless. Did possibly the thought of Waslaw longing so desperately and pathetically for a son cause her to arrive at her decision? Helplessly, Emilia had stood there as Romola stormed out of the salon and headed straight for her Watza's room. Emilia never forgot that night in September 1919 in the Villa Guardamunt, St Moritz Dorf. Was Romola's behaviour an act of bravery or sheer dogged foolhardiness? Events in 1920 with repercussions lasting into the late forties were to suggest she abhor-

203

red accepting the responsibility for the consequences. Indeed, she was to ride roughshod over innocent lives and cause immeasurable heartache. But that comes later.

Emilia and Oskar departed, thwarted in their last-minute plea that Romola should change her mind and go back with them. It had been a grim farewell. Romola vehemently maintained that nothing would induce her to forsake Waslaw. Ironically, only a few weeks later the situation at the Villa reached a dreadful climax. In the Epilogue to her first book, Romola has admitted in a few terse phrases that 'the home atmosphere did not soothe him. On the contrary, the efforts to behave normally provoked periods of violence...I decided to take him back to the place where he felt happy – where he was well-treated and cared for at the beginning of his illness – to the Bellevue in Kreuzlingen.'

A far more frightening and realistic picture of that period was brought to my attention when I was half-way through my writing.

Kyra and I were approached by Dr Peter Ostwald, Medical Director at the University of California. He had written a book on Robert Schumann, *Schumann – Music and Madness*, and requested permission to do a similar piece of research on Waslaw Nijinsky. Permission was granted and Dr Ostwald most generously provided me with some interesting facts gathered during his visit to Switzerland. Naturally, his probings also led him to Villa Guardamunt.

In the medical records dated December 2-3, 1919, a male nurse described Waslaw's condition as 'intolerable', so much so he must have been kept away from the Villa from time to time under guard. 'The patient had been assaultive, trashed the room, destroyed the furniture, throwing his food on the floor and then eating it from the floor etc.' In fact, when Dr Bezzola and attendants (or policemen) came from Chur to try to evaluate the chaotic situation at the Villa, Romola locked herself in and refused to meet anybody. Dr Bezzola declared that Nijinsky's wife 'is without insight and that she may even create difficulties for us in which case the patient would have to be taken to the Cantonal Insane Asylum in Chur.' In the opinion of the doctor the patient was extremely dangerous.

According to Dr Ostwald, 'Professor Bleuler never made the statement that Waslaw was incurably insane,' and he added that investigations are currently under way on the entire question as to what really was the nature of Waslaw Nijinsky's mental disorder;

whether it was a form of schizophrenia or possibly a form of bi-polar-affective illness.

Detailed medical reports by doctors and nurses from that period give a very coherent picture of what actually took place during those years when he was a patient and clearly indicate he was given the best possible psychiatric care available at that time. In Dr Ostwald's opinion there should never have been any need for Romola to suffer a guilt complex with regard to Waslaw's lengthy stays in various sanatoria.

CHAPTER 7

BREAK-UP OF A FAMILY

'Weibilie, I have just come from the Villa
Guardamunt, where you got your start in this
world in September of 1919...I am sending
this to you as a souvenir.
You are "made in Switzerland" – good stock.
I kiss you...Meme.'

This brief comment appears on a postcard from my mother dated July 11th, 1963.

On June 14th, 1920, Romola gave birth to a second daughter. She was back in the *Wiener Sanatorium Dr Anton Loew* as on the previous occasion six years before. Dr Halban was her personal physician. Her mood must have vacillated from joy to sorrow. She had virtually risked her life in the hope of presenting Waslaw with a son. Now, she could only lie there and ruminate on what the future would hold with yet another mouth to feed; to reassemble the shambles of the present.

It was Emilia who was to record the family's descent upon Romola to view the new arrival, a tiny bundle all white and pink with a tuft of barely visible fluffy blonde hair. Oskar and Emilia led the procession. Tessa swept in with Erik in tow, carrying an enormous bouquet of wild flowers; and lastly, Waslaw had come attended by his male nurse. In Emilia's own words, Waslaw had eagerly held the *bébé* in his arms and cradled her gently.

My mother had to remain in hospital until the 7th of August. She suffered from post-natal discomfort and severe abdominal pains. I found part of the original bill covering the cost of her hospitalisation for this period. It came to the princely sum of Austrian Kr. 32,839.60. Small wonder she was later to face a financial crisis.

It was to Tessa that Romola unleashed her acute fear of leaving the security that surrounded her within the white-washed walls of her room. She harboured no illusions about what was waiting for her in the bleak world outside. Unless a miracle happened, she

206

would once more have to shoulder all the responsibilities for the family. The simplest solution would have been to give up the struggle and 'come home' as Emilia had begged her to do time and again. There was ample room in the Villa, even to house Waslaw and his nurse. Mentioning that period in Vienna, Romola claimed it was only when he showed signs of extreme agitation that she took him to the Steinhof Sanatorium. Her primary fear of bringing him back to Budapest was that his condition might be aggravated were memories to flood back of the cruel climate in the Villa during the War.

To lessen the vehement strain of indecision, she called on Oti-Papa for guidance. The animosity she had borne against him in her youth had burnt out to be replaced by a wholehearted trust in a man, sensible and calm, with a shrewd business head on his shoulders. He had arrived alone and immediately plunged into a discussion on how to disentangle and find an answer to the intricate problems at hand. Romola had not shrunk from baring her deep concern – where to find a roof over her head for six people, i.e. herself, the children, Waslaw and his attendant, and also a nanny. From what source would she expect to find the money? Her preference was to remain in Vienna, a city to which she had become attached, and more practically, where there was an abundance of skilled doctors and psychiatrists. Oskar agreed that Budapest was unsuitable but so was Vienna, in his view.

Irrationally, she had clung to a flimsy straw – waiting to hear Oskar reassure her that any arrangement would be temporary, that he would tell her that Waslaw would dance once more. Oskar, the pragmatist, felt he was duty-bound to quell this self-delusion. He had, however, broached the subject of my health with concern. Was the baby 'behaving normally?' And he could not refrain from chiding her about the additional burden she had inflicted upon herself.

It was with a heavy heart Oskar retreated to report to Emilia verbatim his abortive mission. His attempts to channel Romola's thoughts away from Vienna had failed. She had shrugged off the suggestion that there she was far removed from the artistic society of which she had been part and that it was essential she settle down where she still had influential friends and where she perhaps could establish a business. To him, Paris had seemed the most sensible choice.

On the 8th of August, Romola left the Loew Sanatorium with me in her arms. She headed straight for Tessa and Erik's apartment where Kyra was staying. My father was by then back at Steinhof. Tessa bubbled with happiness at having two young charges in her home. Childless herself, she derived great pleasure from children so long as they did not become a full-time preoccupation. Her life was at a low ebb just then because her relationship with Erik had grown increasingly strained. His addiction to drink was escalating at a rapid pace and consequently they were faced with dire financial problems. When alone to mull over it all, she was wretched and listless.

It must have been shortly after leaving hospital that Romola engaged a nanny to look after me. She was an Austrian girl from a small village; her name was Laura Dietrichstein. She had been recommended to Romola through some mutual friend in the aristocracy. Like so many young women of the day, Laura aspired to further her education and widen her horizons. She loved children, performed her duties in an exemplary manner, and soon established herself as an official member of the family.

On September 10th, 1920, I was duly christened Zsenia Anastazia Marie de la Consolation Madeleine. Romola swore it was Waslaw who insisted on calling me Tamara.

After his violent attack in St Moritz in December, 1919, which brought him back to the Bellevue Kuranstalt, Romola had again consulted Professor Bleuler and even Carl Jung in Zürich. Unable to get any satisfactory answers, it was then she took Waslaw with her to Vienna in the spring of 1920. In her notes from that period she mentioned that she sought the aid of both Julius Wagner-Jauregg and Sigmund Freud. Neither could offer any real help. The former had said 'that as long as a schizophrenic patient has periods of agitation, there is a hope for an improvement toward normality.' Freud had bluntly stated that psychoanalytical treatment was utterly useless in cases of schizophrenia.

In 1936, Alfred Adler, the famous psychiatrist, wrote an assessment of Waslaw Nijinsky's illness, claiming 'it sprang from a deep inferiority complex; that he developed grandiose expectations during his childhood;...constantly disappointed because life was not like his childhood dreams.' An Associated Press article, published on July 19th, 1981, stated that the psychiatrist's analysis went unpublished for years because Nijinsky's wife Romola was upset by its conclusion 'that Nijinsky suffered from an inferiority complex'. A variety of theoretical justifications have arisen as to what triggered off the unhinging of a brilliant brain; perhaps the truth will never be found.

There was no abatement in Romola's quest to find a cure for Waslaw. But, meanwhile, she also took stock of the unmistakable signs of a breakdown of her sister's marriage and looked upon it as an indication that she must hurry to find another home. And, one way or another, she must seek to eke out a living that would bring in the funds now so essential. She yielded to Emilia's plea to return to Budapest but on Kyra's behalf only. It would give her freer hands to organise matters. Laura was entrusted to look after me. Kyra was elated at the prospect of being pampered by her grandparents. Romola was a strict mother, who was never to shower us with any outward display of affection. By nature, she seemed incapable of showing unfeigning warmth and tenderness toward a child. Perhaps she was too drained at that stage; ever since she had first set eyes on Waslaw, her emotional depths had pivoted around him and him only. Not until later did a thaw occur when she was attracted to other women.

Relieved of some of her responsibilities, she set about the task of renewing old friendships, ransacking her mind to be certain no one of influence had been omitted. She sought the advice of solicitors, discussed the sordid problem of money, or rather the lack of it, with bankers. In line with Oti-Papa's sage advice, she set Paris as her goal.

Then, quite out of the blue, a chance conversation was later to alter the course of her destiny. She and Waslaw had been invited to lunch at the Sacher Hotel by an old acquaintance, a staunch supporter of my father. Waslaw had been in one of his calm, docile moods and throughout the meal, not a syllable had passed his lips. Romola and Mr X had carried on an animated conversation, the topics ranging from politics and the current economic situation to finally touch upon Waslaw's fantastic American tour. It was then that a few magic words, 'New York' perhaps, transformed their hitherto mute companion. Without faltering and in a clearly audible voice, Waslaw declared *'Moi, America, j'aime beaucoup America.'* At first his audience of two had been visibly shaken but later Romola was categorically to claim that those few words were to steer her upon the path she then interpreted to be the right one. She was thereafter haunted by Waslaw's declaration of love for America, although she dared not be so foolhardy as to abandon her Parisian move. Shrewdly, she analysed what strategy to pursue in order to procure the necessary official documents for entry to the United States; an arduous, time-consuming process. And would Waslaw even be allowed in? No longer the God of Dance but a prisoner in his own impenetrable world.

In June, 1921, Waslaw's sister Bronia arrived in Vienna, accompanied by her two children, Irina, aged seven, Leo (Louvrushka), aged two, and Eleonora Bereda. In Romola's version, 'I succeeded after many difficult attempts to get my mother-in-law and my sister-in-law out of Russia. My great hope that the meeting between Vaslav and his mother might re-establish his normalicy failed.' Bronia was to claim that, upon hearing of Waslaw's mental breakdown, she then and there took the decision to flee from Kiev with her family. At that stage she was already separated from her husband. Romola greeted them at the station and booked them in at the Bristol Hotel. It was their first meeting with Kyra, then seven, and myself, one year old. Mother and sister lost no time in going to see Waslaw at the Steinhof Sanatorium but Bronia substantiated that Waslaw showed no sign of recognition at seeing the two women who had once been closest to him. As mentioned earlier, it was only when Bronia had carried on a lengthy conversation about dance and ballet that he uttered one sentence in Russian, 'the *ballet* is never devised, the *ballet* must be created.' This event is reported in Bronia's memoirs. Irina had been permitted to accompany her elders and recalls how her uncle had reached out his hand and given her a gentle pat on the head.

Romola's whole being at this point must still have been one filled with hatred for Diaghilev, combined with a frantic fight for self-preservation. Irina tells a most extraordinary story of the chain of events which followed. The family had arrived impoverished in Vienna, as Eleonora had been unable to smuggle anything of value with her. It was to fall on Romola to pay for their lodgings and she also promised to provide for their subsistence until they got settled. Bronia approached her daily for a few *schillings* with which to buy the barest essentials in the way of food. One day, Bronia came to see Romola, overjoyed with the good news she had to impart regarding herself. Eagerly, she pressed the cable in Romola's hands.

Très enchanté vous rencontrer. Espère continuons ensemble.
Maître Diaghileff

Romola had flown into a rage – her uncontrollable 'paprika' temper – and had torn the offending piece of paper in half. From that moment onward, she withdrew her financial support. To keep the little family going until she could join the ballet company from which she had been parted some seven years, Bronia was forced to demean herself to dance in cabarets.

A massive exchange of correspondence started to build up between Romola, Emilia and Oti-Papa, a measure of Romola's dependence on them. A few letters have been selected at random and inserted where appropriate to convey in her own words her moods, her snatches of maternal caring, her persistent lack of funds, her euphemistic hopes and her depths of despair.

26th June 1921

Dear Mama,

Thank you so much for your kind letter. Bébé joins me in thanking you for the Tetra diapers and the basket which arrived yesterday. I sent a package for Kyra via Uncle Elli; some lingerie as well as a dress. Do you remember that dress? I do not know if I ever thanked you for the deerskin, the cake and the toys for the bébé. I did mean to but I have to split my thoughts in so many directions, it may have slipped my mind. I am extremely worried about Waslaw's drawings. They could not be found at the Embassy nor does anyone even want to discuss them. The Courier Department stated that two parcels addressed to the Consulate had both been numbered 42. Yet only one was found; the Tetra diapers. This same courier lost the jewellery belonging to Princess Lichtenstein.

His name is Umlauf. Some months ago Princess Lichtenstein's jewellery, worth millions, disappeared. It could not be found anywhere. Two months later, however, when the Prince demanded a police investigation, the jewels appeared in a closet in the Embassy. The courier and the staff said in their defense,

211

they had locked them in the closet and then forgotten about the matter. Rumour grew that the gems were stolen but when the police began a thorough search, whoever was responsible took fright and deposited them in the closet. Now the disappearance of Waslaw's drawings appears to be extremely sinister. I beg you, Mother, to go to the Ministry for External Affairs and demand a search be launched for their recovery. Perhaps you can ask Bánfy.* He is an artist himself and will understand that it would be an irreplaceable loss to us and the Arts if the parcel is lost. The Embassy categorically claims it has not been received by them. It must be in Pest. Will you look into the matter straight away?

'Did you know that poor Kárpáthy is seriously ill? Do write to him. I am happy that Kyra's presence gives you such joy. Hopefully, you do not spoil her too much. Things are not going well for us here. All I do is spend money. The bébé is darling. Day by day she grows prettier. Bronia danced for us; she was phenomenal. How is your leg? Take good care of yourself and try to rest.

I kiss you many times.
    Molly'

On November 3rd, 1921, Romola filled in Form No. 228 'Declaration of Alien about to depart for the United States' at the American Consulate in Vienna. She gave as the purpose of her visit to attend to business matters. Her references included Professor Richard Strauss, Vienna, and Mr Otto Kahn of New York City.

She received an affidavit from the Bankers Trust Company, 16 Wall Street, New York, dated December 6th that same year, certifying that Mrs Romola Nijinsky 'has had at all times on deposit with us securities and cash in excess of $12,000' and 'She has on deposit with us as of this date securities and cash aggregating $12,309.57.' Not an impressive fortune but still a tidy sum to own.

To ease her current imperative demands, my mother capitulated to Emilia's suggestion that I, too, should be sent to Budapest.

---

* Count Nicolas Bánfy was the Minister at the time. He was a great theatre-lover and later became an author and playwright of some repute.

perhaps deep in her heart Emilia hoped that if both children were in her custody, Romola would decide against the drastic notion of moving to the new continent.

Subsequently, I was told how I was tucked into a basket with infinite care and taken to the steamer in the company of faithful Laura. Although the boat trip from Vienna to Budapest took nearly seven hours longer than by train, Romola chose to send me by boat on the Danube which she considered a far more healthy and hygienic means of transport.

Kyra remembers vividly how lavishly our maternal grandmother poured out her overflowing warmth and affection on us. So in contrast to our aloof mother. It seems I was a quiet, good-natured baby who seldom cried. Hence, a physical malformation went unnoticed until one day Laura became alarmed when she realised I was not kicking both legs as babies normally do. One leg remained limp in spite of vigorous massage. Emilia's house physician was called in and, after a cursory examination, he recommended that Professor Ignacz Pétery,one of the leading paediatricians in Budapest, should be consulted. He diagnosed my condition as *Csipöficam,* a condition whereby the hipbone had become dislocated, resulting in one leg being shorter than the other. It could easily be remedied by surgery as I was so young.

Within a few weeks I was bundled off to Vienna. Further consultations with Professor Laurence resulted in the use of a new method not requiring an actual incision. It was carried out by the professor's son. I emerged from the ordeal, pronounced fit and well, except that I would probably not be able to partake in sports or dance when I grew up. For eight months I enjoyed Aunt Tessa's loving care.

The early part of 1922 must have seen Romola toiling and planning for the day she could take Waslaw back to the States. That would be her moment of triumph. Her goal came nearer to achievement when on February 17th, 1922, the American Consulate sent her a visa permitting her to enter the United States. Ironically, this valuable document, Visa Number 1233, could have gone astray as she carelessly kept people uninformed of her whereabouts. It was addressed to her care of the Bankers Trust Company in Paris.

Romola was quite undaunted in whatever she undertook. One must remember she was Hungarian by birth, yet in compliance with the prevailing law at the time she had automatically become a citizen of her husband's country – Russia. To add to the confusion,

Waslaw became 'stateless' after the Bolshevik take-over. Curiously enough, the Russian Consulate General in Paris granted her a visa for America on the 27th of January, 1922.

It has not been possible for me to pin Romola down to any fixed address prior to our move to Paris some time in 1922 or early 1923. Samuel Untermeyer, of Guggenheim, Untermeyer & Marshall in New York, who handled her affairs there, wrote a letter to Romola dated March 1st, 1922; his tone was exasperated to say the least. She had evidently asked him to communicate with her in Paris yet she neglected to supply him with an address. In desperation he addressed the letter care of Suvretta House, St Moritz. Untermeyer was keen to know if she had received permission from the State Department for her entry. He warned her that the prospects of employment in the States were slim. 'It is very good of you to say you should have taken my advice but I greatly fear that unpleasant advice is one of those unwelcome things that it is difficult, if not impossible, for you to take.' He carried on with the sage warning 'You do not say whether you are coming alone or whether you intend to bring the children. Would it not be better and safer for you from a financial standpoint to come alone and look about on the chance of getting something to do rather than to take the risk and incur the expense of having the children with you?'

Romola did heed his advice and went to New York on her own, where she stayed at the Biltmore Hotel. On the 3rd of July she had a letter from Doctor Henry Cotton of the New Jersey State Hospital to the effect that he in turn had been notified by the Commissioner-General of Immigration, Mr W Husband, declaring that Waslaw Nijinsky could be admitted to the United States for a temporary period of six months under medical bond of $1,000 on the condition that he would be confined to and treated in the New Jersey State Hospital, Trenton, New Jersey.

Dr Cotton made an appointment for Romola to visit him at his office the following Wednesday. What transpired at that meeting Romola kept to herself but the outcome was that she returned to Europe. Who knows, perhaps she could not rid herself of the feeling that a 'home environment' would still be the best cure. Or had she been able to visit the hospital and found it too much of a 'prison'? Maybe the naked truth at that stage was that she felt incapable of taking on the heavy responsibility and the cost it would entail.

Ultimately, in the early part of 1923, Romola succeeded in finalising arrangements for the move to Paris. She rented a flat in the Avenue de la Bourdonnais and bravely set about to create– once more – a healthy, normal family ambience. By now the household had swollen to include a cook and a maid, and most important of all, Waslaw's male nurse.

She nourished the implicit belief that Paris, the city of his greatest triumphs, would awaken at least the dimmest spark of recollection in her Watza. People have told me in later years how hard she tried, taking him to the theatre, the ballet, to the haunts he had frequented in happier days, long strolls through the Bois de Boulogne, motor tours of the environs. All to no avail. It was shortly after their arrival that in desperation she sought every means she could think of to save Waslaw from the void to which he had been condemned.

To quote her: 'Naturally we consulted all the eminent French psychiatrists also. But orthodox medicine was helpless to cure. Therefore I began to turn to unorthodox treatments; natural healers, Christian Science healers, and Dr Coue of Nancy, and in the summer of 1923 we went to Lourdes...We spent several days there. I went with Vaslav to the Grotto. I washed his forehead in the spring and prayed. I hoped and hoped, but he was not cured...Maybe my faith was not deep enough.'

In Budapest there is still a dossier marked in Oti-Papa's handwriting 'Romola's Affairs'. It is crammed with bills, bank statements, miscellaneous business correspondence; some sixty-odd letters reflecting Romola's life in those days. On some occasions, when her heart-breaking struggle to fend off economic ruin pulled her down to the depths of despair, she would send off two to three letters the same day, penning them separately to Emilia and Oskar.

Her existence teetered on the brink of total collapse. In early December her ramblings in a letter to Oti show she did not know which way to turn. She mentioned the hope of a conference with a publisher. She toyed with the idea of starting a taxi cab business. A Mr Black was apparently involved but she admitted to being frightened regarding the viability of such a venture. 'An auto costs approximately Fr. 25,000. If I only buy four or five, they will merely bring in four to five hundred francs a day. At least two hundred or more francs go to repairs, etc. If I earn no more than Fr. 8,000 – 9,000 monthly, how will I make ends meet?'

Romola suggested to a friend, Magda, that they should become partners in a business venture which sounded very speculative indeed. She had been approached by a man called Aranyi to deposit Fr. 150,000 or 200,000 in a bank toward a business fund. He would act as their 'advisor'. The proposition was that the two women take over a medication from a French chemist to cure toothache. A 'bitter tonic', a laxative, would be included in the deal and other items would be incorporated later. Aranyi would not ask for any money on the latter, and the chemist and the producer of the medication would only receive a percentage of the profit.

Sensibly, Romola did ask for Oti's opinion and put it to him to write to Aranyi. *'I am all mixed up...If I were to set up a business you should be here. Concerning Aranyi, if I risk the money, surely I should earn the larger portion. And what about Magda, my partner? Nothing is moving forward and I am worn out from nerves and the worry about money. Please help...'.*

Romola's pecuniary lamentations accelerated in volume. Exactly one week after sending the aforementioned letter she wrote to Oti, acknowledging the receipt of one from him together with $2,400. She admitted to facing the future with dread. It seems that already by November 20th her dollar fund at the bank was depleted and she had a deficit amounting to $400. Consequently, a cheque bounced. *'I just found out that here this is regarded as a felony and because of the delay in clearing cheques, one can land in the "csaló"* (a Hungarian nickname for prison). *Mme X told me that the police were making enquiries about my source of income.'*

She still pursued the idea of a taxi-cab enterprise even though half-heartedly, as she realised the overhead expenses would be too high. She referred to a film proposition for which she had made a screen test but with which she had been extremely unhappy. Her performance had been under par and the make-up had made her too pale. *'It is more inexperience than maladroitness that shows up in my acting. Another reason why it is not an acceptable offer is that they do not wish to pay me outright; I might perhaps receive a small dividend.'*

An historic meeting took place between Sergei Pavlovitch, Anton Dolin, the rising young English ballet dancer, and my father in February 1924.

Dolin described the event so poignantly in his recollections that I asked the publishers, Routledge & Kegan Paul for their kind permission to quote it.

Nijinsky has always been to me a legendary inspiration. I never saw him dance, but any work of merit in my career with the Russian Ballet was inspired first by the man I had never known and then by the haunting memory of someone I had seen more in a vision than as a living person. During my first season in Monte Carlo, I asked Diaghilev to arrange for me to see him and he promised that he would.

Before I realised the desire of my life – a meeting with this genius of the dance – I remember an incident that stands out as a sheer contrast. One afternoon I went with some friends to a Chanel dress parade. I have been bored many times but somehow never quite so bored as on this occasion. My one wish in life was to meet someone who, I thought had worn clothes far finer and more magnificent than any mannequin of Chanel's could ever hope to display.

About two days later I saw Diaghilev, who told me he had telephoned Madame Nijinska and had arranged that we were to go to tea that afternoon. How the day dragged on. The taxi drive seemed interminable. Eventually we arrived at our destination. Facing us was a block of grey granite flats: I do not remember the address: my French at that time was very imperfect and I failed to observe it. All I remember is going up in a lift three or four flights and knocking at a door which was opened by a short Russian manservant abut 30 years of age. The large door was swung open. We entered the hall, our hats were taken and we were shown into the drawing-room. There, sitting in front of us, like a convalescent invalid, was the greatest of all dancers – my inspiration – the man on whom I had built all my ideas, the man whose achievements had always spurred me on in life.

His wife greeted us. I was presented to her. hardly a word was spoken, but somehow in this man's face there was something more expressive than a volume of words. There were the same eyes I had seen in pictures, the same beautiful mouth, the upper lip clean-shaven and dark, hardly any hair on the head at all, white hands that were never still.

This was Nijinsky!

All around the room were portraits. I distinctly remember Sargent's famous painting of the great dancer. There were various photographs, flowers in the window, lace curtains – it was almost suburban...and then, above a desk, a doctor's chart recording the varying temperatures of the invalid.

Diaghilev tried to make him speak. He wouldn't say one word. He just sat and laughed. I asked him something and he answered 'Je ne sais pas.' Four words that expressed the whole tragedy – he didn't know.

Altogether we were there for sixty minutes. It seemed like sixty days. It was and ever will remain the happiest and most tragic moment of my life.

I found Madame Nijinska, who spoke a little French, most charming. Their little daughter came in, a pretty child, a really lovely child.

I often wonder what Diaghilev's feelings were: whatever they were he succeeded in hiding them. During tea Nijinsky would not eat or drink. He seemed powerless to do anything. He looked as healthy as any of us, yet somehow his brain refused to work. He sat in his chair trying to understand. I believe he did understand a great deal but I think his brain was tired.

At last we rose to go. Diaghilev embraced him. By this time I was feeling the strain of the meeting and could hardly hold out my hand to say goodbye. I put my arms on his shoulders. Perhaps it was my fancy but he seemed to resent it. After a moment, however, he lifted up his hand and, placing it on my shoulder, kissed me on the cheek three times as all Russians do on leaving. He came to the door with us, said goodbye in Russian and then, when Diaghilev asked if we should come again, nodded his head in a wistful way as much as to say: 'I am very, very tired.'

I wish I could say I remember that occasion but I must truthfully admit I do not. What I do dimly recall is a motley parade of faces – the former colleagues who paid their homage; friends of Romola and Waslaw's from all over Europe. The ever inquisitive journalists could not be kept at a distance. How could all these have impressed a four-year old? It was the less significant details of daily life in that apartment in Paris which registered in my memory – the 'nice' feeling of the high-ceilinged rooms, the windows which in reality were French doors. They opened wide to reveal waist-high iron balustrades.

I had a white bed with bars set against a wall. I can still vividly recall how one afternoon I awoke screaming; huge monsters and deformed figures danced in front of me and closed in on me in a threatening manner. Kyra rushed in, cradled me in her arms to calm me down, and reassured me it was only a dream. Apparently, the rays of the sun gleaming through the window and mixing with the shadows had created my nightmare. Somehow, Kyra got me out of bed and manoeuvred me into the kitchen. There she placed me on a chair while she walked over to the cupboard to prepare a big slice of bread spread with lashings of butter and apricot jam. Like a little mother, she stood there patiently, watching me gorge myself on my afternoon snack. Every once in a while she would wipe my face with a blue-white checkered towel. Strange, how unimportant little details of daily routine can stick in one's mind like teasels. But then, Kyra replaced my mother most of those years in Paris. She was six years older than I; she realised far more what was happening around us. And it was she who gave me the love and affection that Meme never had time to give.

When Romola was at home, she would usually emerge from her room around nine or ten o'clock to have her second cup of tea and then go straight to Waslaw's room. She would stay with him for nearly an hour. What transpired behind those closed doors, I could not fathom at the time. Only when I was older did I learn that every day she meticulously went in to find out how he had slept, how he seemed, what his temperature was, what his requirements and wishes were. Day after day, she watched over him, conversed with him to ascertain what direction his mind was taking toward the world outside; or was he perhaps slipping deeper into his own mystical world. If she saw he was in an amicable mood, she would cajole him into joining her for lunch somewhere or visiting friends. Days would go by when everything went smoothly. The two of them would leave the apartment together, as if they were just an ordinary happy couple. But there were other days, and they were unpredictable, when Tatakaboy would come out of his room, all dressed up, only to stop at the front door, like an automobile suddenly braking, turn around and march back to his room, not to reappear that day.

Life became fairly much a matter of routine for the various members of the family in the Avenue de la Bourdonnais but although it was the only time that the four of us ever lived together, there was a total lack of sharing of activities or conversation. The reasons, of course, were obvious. Romola, when not caring for Waslaw, was off in pursuit of her objectives, Waslaw was locked in his chambers, Kyra was at school. In addition, she regularly attended dance classes at the Opera and even participated in some ballets. She already showed a strong inclination to go in her father's footsteps. My days flowed by in the company of my toys, most of which had been sent to me by Emilia. My greatest treat was to be taken to the Bois de Boulogne. Certain days, and how precious they were to me, Tatakaboy would join us. We must have presented a strange little group – my nanny, an Englishwoman who had replaced my beloved Laura, walking in front of Tatakaboy, holding my hand in a firm grip; Tatakaboy, with his hands behind his back, a stooped figure, frequently kicking some stones on the path with the tip of his shoe, sometimes pausing to draw weird patterns with his foot. His male nurse was usually only a short distance behind him, furtively smoking a cigarette. Kyra, when she joined us, was the soul of the party, bubbling over with enthusiasm, rushing back and forth from her father, to Nanny or myself, then skipping ahead of us laughing at her own antics. Often, she would clasp my hand and tease me into racing off with her as fast as my chubby legs could carry me.

I was not as blessed as Kyra, who had had the advantage of being with Father before he became so ill, but registered in my memory are the brief moments I spent with him – how always a warm, compassionate, loving smile would brighten up his face. As I grew older I used to impart that impression upon my classmates and I can still feel the hurt, when talking about my father, someone blurted out, 'But, of course, insane people have an imbecile smile...' How I wanted to rub the arrogant smirk off that person's face.

Among the few treasured snapshots in my possession is one of me standing in front of the Eiffel Tower together with Kyra. It must have been taken in wintertime as I was wearing a fur coat, hat, and *gamasni,* an extraordinary piece of wearing apparel, resembling a stocking but made of thick textile with buttons along the side, to be worn on top of the regular white stockings; in actual fact, a female version of spats. Both Kyra and I were dressed in the latest fashion like little princesses. Small wonder that Romola floated on a constant sea of financial trouble.

How I worshipped Tatakaboy, my father. On those rare occasions he was in the drawing-room, seated in a comfortable armchair beside the fireplace, I would climb up on his lap and thrill over the protective way he would place his left arm around me. It was as though an unspoken conspiracy developed between us. We did not need words to communicate with each other. We were so different, his two daughters, the embodiment of his own split personality: Kyra, the explosive, colourful artist already as a child and I, shy, withdrawn, peace-seeking. I felt totally at ease in Tatakaboy's presence. Romola made me feel awkward and self-conscious. It was a relief when she was not present.

Looking back, there was one episode that made me feel miserable and gave me great discomfort. It happened at one of those intimate dinners my mother was so fond of giving to a close, select circle of friends; people fascinated by art in all its forms, intellectuals, compassionate to the genius Nijinsky and the tragedy that now enshrouded him. She would choose her list of guests with the utmost care to ensure that Father would have an enjoyable evening. Certainly, she must still have been filled with that ever constant hope that these encounters would be beneficial to him and perhaps even pull him out of his hallucinations and nightmarish world.

The table was set, as usual, with her finest Limoge china and lead crystal glasses. Romola was an extraordinary hostess, skilled at making her guests feel at ease and at organising the work of her tiny staff. Although she herself was not gifted in the art of cooking – I cannot recall ever having seen her preparing a meal – she had that knack of supervising the creation of a perfect feast. She loved rich Hungarian dishes, in addition to which caviar, *pâté de foie gras* and other delicacies were her favourites. As a special concession I was sometimes allowed into the dining-room when my mother entertained. In those days, well brought-up children normally had their repasts separately with either their nanny or governess. This particular evening Romola gazed at me proudly when I entered, dressed in an expensive 'Callot Sisters' dress, white socks and black patent leather shoes. Mindful of my manners, I hesitated at the door,

220

clutching Nanny's hand. Romola called me to her side and with an unusual display of affection hugged me and then introduced me to the guests.

'*Alors, tu veux un canard?*' My mother's tempting invitation was music to my ears. This ritual was one which gave me intense pleasure and my eyes raptly followed every movement she made, from reaching for the silver sugar tongues, daintily picking up one lump, dipping it into a cup of coffee and then carefully placing it on a spoon which subsequently found its way to my mouth. What delight. What bliss. In the process of swallowing this delicious 'sweet', I happened to glance at one of the guests, going through the same motions as Romola. Thrilled at the possibility of receiving yet another *canard,* I looked beseechingly at my mother.

'*Mais bien sûr, tu peux avoir un autre canard. Dis bien gentillement merçi à Madame.*' The guest temptingly held out the spoon with the *canard.* Alas, overcome by greed, I made a hasty, clumsy movement in reaching out for the spoon with its precious cargo and the sticky *canard* slid off, somersaulting over and over again down the elegant silk dress of Madame X, to finally come to rest on the rug. I froze, mortified, engulfed with shame over the disaster. Madame X brushed the incident aside with a few polite phrases. Romola apologised on my behalf but I could tell from the tone of her voice she was furious with me. I dared not look at her but I pursed my lips, withholding the hot tears burning my eyelids. To be perfectly honest, the tears were probably more due to the loss of the tantalising delicacy than to the shame I had caused my mother. I was summarily dismissed from the room but just as I had reached the threshold, I heard my name being called. As I looked in his direction, I saw Tatakaboy standing by his chair and holding a huge, dripping *canard* between his fingers. To this day, I can still taste the warm, sweet coffee in my mouth and recall wistfully Tatakaboy's gentle, understanding face...

How true it was when Father wrote in his little black book: '*I am a man in a house. I do not like a crowd. I like family life. I love all children. I am a child. I like playing with children. I am a father.*'

A pleasant disruption to the humdrum everyday life – at least for us children – was the sudden advent of Aunt Tessa. Ostensibly, she had been corresponding with Romola over a period of many months. Her request to join our family in Paris had caused Romola grave concern. She was deeply attached to her sister, her bewitching

221

personality and good-hearted disposition, but was also fully aware of her Bohemian nature. And how would she, Romola, cope, feeding yet another mouth in the ever-expanding household?

Against her better judgment, Romola ultimately consented to her coming. Perhaps selfishly she thought Tessa could be useful around the house, help with the day-to-day shopping, keep an eye on us when Romola was away. More importantly, she felt it would be good for Waslaw to have the companionship of someone who shared his interests in the arts.

And so the day came when Aunt Tessica joined us. Erik was by then incurably alcoholic and she sought a divorce. Erik Schmedes was to die of *delirium tremens* in Vienna on March 21st, 1931, barely sixty-three years old.

Tessa's worldly possessions consisted of a few pieces of jewellery and a modest sum of money. Romola started scheming to introduce her sister to eligible men about town in the hope that Tessa would find a rich husband. Only in her early forties, she was still a most attractive, beautiful and highly talented woman. It did not take long for Tessa to become drawn into the social whirl of Paris thanks to her wit and vivacity but sadly, a wealthy suitor eluded her.

Poor darling Tessa – it would not be an exaggeration to say that in all probability she nearly drove Romola mad. She tried so hard and wanted nothing more than to be of help. She was more than willing to do the shopping but the money she was given slipped through her fingers like fine sand and she spent it all on the frivolities of life, leaving little or nothing for essentials like bread and milk. When in the mood, she would give the maid a hand at cleaning but it was a gesture made at random and never very thoroughly at that.

By mid-July, the Nijinsky household, by then comprised of *nine* persons, seemed doomed to crumble. What Romola jotted down was unparalleled in all she had hitherto written to Oti and Emilia; a note to Oti was scrawled in black pencil and further down the page she poured out her grievances to Emilia in a dark purple pencil. Evidently she had planned to send Kyra and me back to the Villa but she had no money to pay for a cable to explain she was unable to buy tickets for us.

'I have moved heaven and earth these last three months to avoid a catastrophe but have failed. To find work for a foreigner like myself, especially without any qualifications, is impossible. I

tried to place Waslaw with Bronia for two or three months and the children with you, but both Bronia and Diaghilev have left Paris. I am sharing my last piece of bread with Tessa, who has been staying here since April. I fear she has turned the heads of the servants. I will have to send them away anyhow as I have no money. I am unable to pay this month's rent. Please try to convince the Wiener Bank Verein to wait until December. If they decide to sue me, all they can do is to auction my lingerie since I am without funds or other valuables. I do not see a way out.'

To Emilia, she confided more personal matters. *'Please do not be angry with me for not having written since April but I did not wish to complain and make you sad.'* Romola mentioned that someone by the name of Alexander had behaved very badly and mistreated Waslaw; that she had had to send the man away. Possibly he was a nurse temporarily in charge while Wolmersdorf, the regular nurse, was in Vienna. He, poor man returned, having been jilted by his bride-to-be, and worse, who had stolen all his possessions. Romola complained bitterly about the English governess, to whom she then owed two months' salary. The woman was not working hard enough and was untidy.

'Tamara has suffered from an intestinal infection the past four weeks. She picked it up when I sent her away on a visit because of Kyra's illness. She is now on a diet. Kyra contracted diphtheria a month and a half ago and still looks unwell. She is very thin. Two months ago I fell on my back from a horse and my spine was injured. It is extremely painful and I cannot afford any treatment. My stomach, too, hurts. The doctor would like to send me to Vichy.'

Romola goes on at length about the two servants, Mariska and Emma. They took time off without permission and refused to fetch up coal and wood from the cellar with the result that meals had to be cooked on the gas range which was very expensive. Under the circumstances, Romola had decided not to renew their permits but instead to send them back to Budapest as soon as she had a few spare francs. Nor was she paying them a salary.

She told Emilia how hurt Tessa was that she did not write to her but she, Romola, felt unable to comment on what had happened in

Budapest since she had not been there. She confided that Paris had been an unfortunate choice for Tessa to make, professionally untrained as she was. How sad in retrospect to feel that her one great talent was overlooked by everybody. She was a brilliant pianist and with her background and famous name, Tessa could readily have found scores of wealthy children to whom to give piano lessons.

Some light broke through the clouds of gloom with the unanticipated arrival of Paul Bohus on the scene. His unspoken devotion to Romola had never wavered nor had his genuine, very deep affection for Waslaw. It was to be he who shouldered the burdens that Tessa was unable to; he hastened to come whenever Romola beckoned him; ran errands, never returning empty-handed; choice fruits for Waslaw, bouquets of flowers and bon-bons for Romola and masses of toys for Kyra and myself. He was an excellent stand-in at any dinner or other social event and was liked by the servants for his generous tips. He was also a talented cook which delighted Romola because he not only prepared delicious Hungarian meals but provided all the ingredients himself. I do not remember for how long he stayed in Paris during that phase of our lives. He was an intrepid traveller and was involved in art and antiques all over Europe. But it was he who was to refresh my memory many years later concerning an amusing incident which took place in the Bois de Boulogne.

One day, our little retinue was headed for the customary walk in the Bois. Paul had arrived early in the morning to assist Romola in serving breakfast for Waslaw, drawing his bath and in general being at hand the whole day, while the male nurse was absent. Before noon a carriage was called for and we departed – Paul, Tatakaboy, Mademoiselle and I. For whatever reason, Kyra did not join us. We had enjoyed the pleasure of a brisk walk along the winding paths when Paul suggested we sit down on a bench and relax. He had brought with him a bag full of *brioches* and *croissants* which he ceremoniously opened and with a flourish offered Tatakaboy first choice. He eagerly selected two and commenced to eat with his usual hearty appetite. Furtively, I watched the proceedings out of the corner of my eye to see if I would be offered some as well. One of Mother's golden rules was that we children should not eat anything between breakfast and lunch but I adored pastries and sweets, a weakness I seemed to share with my father. Paul diplomatically

224

invited Mademoiselle to taste one of the *brioches*. With an elegant gesture he handed it to her but deposited the bag with its remaining contents on my knees. In my excitement to peep into the bag, my teddy bear dropped to the ground. It was a gift from Paul and was nearly the same size as myself. Seconds later, I jumped up and hid behind the bench, while my childish screams rent the air. I was hastily joined in my refuge by Mademoiselle. Paul sat glued to the bench. The object of our terror was an enormous, very much alive leopard. A beaded collar adorned his sinewy neck. With utmost nonchalance he picked up my teddy bear between his teeth and stalked off with it across the path where he squatted on the grass, still holding his treasure, once mine, now his. We all watched paralysed as Tatakaboy, who had remained oblivious to all the commotion, calmly stood up and walked over to the beast. He bent down and offered the leopard a *croissant*. Smelling the bait in front of him, the leopard dropped the toy. Luckily, by then its owner arrived quite out of breath, shaking the chain and apologising profusely for the misbehaviour of her precious 'pet'. Paul had regained his composure sufficiently to express his indignation in no uncertain terms. No matter that upon closer scrutiny he observed it was merely a young cub, he rebuked its owner for her callousness in letting her wild pet loose in the park. Tatakaboy paid not attention to the heated argument but instead stepped behind the bench where I was still rooted, placed one arm of the teddy bear firmly in my hand and took hold of the other himself as he slowly propelled me to continue our walk.

A few letters in August reveal that Romola was still using Oskar and Emilia as her 'wailing wall'. But she was giving serious thought to the imminent future and how to rid herself of her burdensome debts. *'I have now learned one should never make debts and once I have money I will sit on it like Aunt Irma!* (Emilia's sister). She was contemplating relinquishing the lease on the apartment by the 1st of October at the latest to find a smaller place in Neuilly, just large enough for her and Waslaw, Wolmersdorf, the one maid Emma, and naturally the children.

Romola resisted the idea of bringing Tessa along. She said it was intolerable even to live in the same city as her sister. She found her too highly-strung and with irritable mannerisms. Besides, she was anxious about Tessa's obvious inability to earn money, refusing several offers put to her. Romola implied Tessa was constantly daydreaming about America, an indulgence in fantasy that would get her nowhere.

Another worry had surfaced, to which I a toddler of four, was oblivious. It concerned Kyra.

'I received the answer from Bleuler. I have to send him more information and consult a doctor here, recommended by Doctor Bleuler. According to Bleuler it is not a question of mental illness but an abnormality of character which is the cause of the problem. At any rate Kyra has to be closely watched during the coming month. She is sluggish and a habitual liar but she is not a bad child. I will let you know in my next letter how I imagine her treatment should be. According to Bleuler, if the same symptoms crop up, she ought to be raised away from the family.'

My mother still harboured visions of sending us both off to Emilia and in the above letter she suddenly showed spurts of genuine caring for us. She admonished our grandmother how to handle us; to keep us in the fresh air as much as possible; to watch what I was eating, taking into account my intestinal infection; to use butter – meals cooked with lard could be 'harmful unless used sparingly.' At the most Kyra could have meat once a day; she should preferably have lots of vegetables and compot. Tea and coffee were forbidden. Both of us should have a daily bath. It was necessary that I wear orthopaedic shoes and that my leg should not be subjected to too much strain. An important issue was languages. She wanted Oskar to converse with us in German and a family friend, in French. For six to eight weeks Kyra should learn English and French, nothing else.. It was an enormous responsibility to thrust upon the shoulders of a couple getting on in years and it never came to pass that both of us were sent back.

Every so often in her correspondence the name Blumenthal cropped up. Ostensibly, he was connected with the film and theatre community, but not based in Paris. She kept nagging Oskar to convince the man that she would like to have a go at acting. She considered herself quite capable of playing on stage in English.

Waslaw had 1,000 francs in his Russian bank and after exhaustive enquiries she was able to release the money, which ensured ten days' livelihood. She was also successful in selling their car which had been standing unused in the garage and with that lump sum was in a position to pay off some nervous creditors; a month's rent, food and medicine. Somehow or other, she always managed to scrape through at the last moment, despite many doors closing in her face, like an American friend who had solemnly promised to lend her money during one of her many crises and then failed her.

At some point in early 1925 she reached the end of her tether. She had fought poverty long enough and been unable to mingle with society. There were priorities to consider; her cherished Waslaw had to be ensured medical attention regularly as clockwork; her daughters, to receive a proper education.

She mustered the moral courage to break up the family home. Once more, Emilia dipped into her purse and cleared the backlog of rent and wages for the servants. She generously paid the fee to place Kyra in a boarding-school in Switzerland. I was despatched to Budapest. Romola persevered in hunting for smaller and less expensive living accommodation in Paris and had to rely on Tessa to be in charge of the depleted family while she herself embarked on the search for a money-spinning career.

Perhaps it was at that juncture that Romola Nijinsky's lonely, soul-searching odyssey began.

CHAPTER 8

ROMOLA AND FREDERICA

However much I ferret through my mind for more recollections of those brief years in Paris, it is to no avail; they are too misty. But I can vividly reconstruct my arrival in Budapest. I still clearly visualise my grandmother Emilia and Oti-Papa, two pillars of stability and comfort, standing there on the platform. *Nyugati Pályaudvar* (The Western Railway Station) was in those days rather foul-smelling and stifling and it was with relief one emerged into the open after hugs and kisses of welcome had subsided. My eyes lit up in wonderment at the four-door semi-convertible Chrysler parked by the pavement. An enormous spare tyre was attached to the side and a polished horn was securely in place next to the driver, who was not protected from the elements.

In this splendid vehicle we crossed the Margit Hid (Margaret Bridge) and sped through the old part of Buda to reach *Hüvösvölgy* (the Cool Valley), a suburb of Budapest. As the automobile turned into a broad avenue, Oti-Papa slowed down purposely to allow me to absorb the atmosphere of new surroundings. On either side there were magnificent villas, solid buildings erected for the bourgoisie, all enclosed by well-kept gardens, protected from outsiders by wrought-iron fences or high brick walls. Vast, majestic chestnut trees lined both sides of the avenue like sentinels, their intertwining branches forming a canopy over the road. I was to experience all the changes of the seasons through those wonderful trees; in springtime, when the pink and white flowers, shaped like miniature Christmas trees, gave delight to the beholder; in the autumn deriving almost sensuous pleasure even as a small child from scuffing my feet through the mellowed, golden leaves which had formed a thick blanket on the pavement, listening to the faint rustling sounds as I walked. In the winter I enjoyed picking and caressing the smooth, polished, brown chestnuts. Although not good to eat as they were a wild variety, I loved to use them to make necklaces and other decorations.

With a fanfare of screeching brakes Oti-Papa stopped in front of the entrance to the Villa. Eagerly, I jumped out and just stood transfixed, my head swirling as I took in what was to be my home for many years. The huge balcony overhead, decorated with five small stone lions, made the deepest impression upon me then. My grandmother gently took me by the hand and escorted me to my living quarters, luxury to a little girl, as they comprised a bedroom and a combined living-room and study. Mother had used the bedroom for a brief period when she was a young girl before she left Budapest. Two doors outside the bedroom boasted a singular feature. They were covered with tiny square mirrors which gave fragmentary, grotesque impressions to the beholder. The rectangular-shaped living-room, ingeniously designed, had yet another pair of doors, one leading out to the terrace with the ferocious lions, the other to the corridor above the atrium.

I celebrated my sixth birthday that first summer in the Villa. Every facet of my young life had undergone a change; a new home; a foreign country, whose language I had as yet not mastered; loving, almost overprotective care bestowed upon me by two doting grandparents. To add to it all, for a short time I was treated like a 'celebrity', with journalists flocking to write their stories about the arrival of the Great Márkus's younger granddaughter, and to take pictures. It was important that I learn to speak Hungarian and in the beginning I had to be tutored at home. My ensuing grades were completed in a private elementary school.

Emilia, although already in her mid-sixties, was still called upon to give numerous performances. I became steeped in the classics. I thrilled to watch her from the wings of the stage, and a play that particularly etched itself in my memory was Schiller's *Maria Stuart*. I was fascinated by the scene in which the queens, Elizabeth I, and Maria Stuart, had a clash of wills. The atmosphere on the stage would be laden with drama more electrifying than perhaps required because the two women facing each other were the real-life queens of the Hungarian theatre – and rivals. Emilia Márkus and Mari Jászai. I cannot refrain from reflecting how could it be that the western world knew so little about this charismatic actress – my grandmother – who played to perfection so many title roles. She was a true professional.

The move from Paris to Budapest not only changed my environment but my whole lifestyle. From the strict, disciplined routine enforced upon me by Romola, I was tossed into a carefree, sometimes rather chaotic ambiance. Unashamedly, I must admit that

Emilia pampered and spoiled me. On days when school was closed I was allowed to sleep in the mornings as long as I wished. If I showed the slightest sign of any indisposition, I would be kept indoors. Eating became an occasion. The three of us – my grandmother, Oti-Papa and myself – always had dinner together, so different from the days in the Paris apartment. And long before my teens, I was asked to assist Emilia when she entertained; I supervised the table setting and saw to it that the hors d'oeuvres were served on the appropriate silver trays. Jealousy was Emilia's Achilles heel. We had a cook, Eszter, a comely, buxom woman in her early thirties, whose only claim to beauty was her rather nice, black eyes. Yet Emilia was convinced that Oskar was ogling the cook's shapely figure through the window as she was bending down to pick vegetables in the kitchen garden. Poor Oti-Papa, he was most likely admiring the sunset over the hills while grappling with more earthy matters such as finance. Nonetheless, I was given the role of 'mediator' between kitchen and dining-room.

Sometimes I was taken to the cinema, thus by courtesey of Hollywood's Al Jolson, Charlie Chaplin, among others, yet another form of entertainment unfolded itself to me. After such an evening Emilia would regale me with stories about Tatakaboy: how she had learned from Romola of his keen interest in the film industry and how he had enjoyed meeting the stars when in California. I think back on those formative childhood years as my happiest. My horizons were widened, new impressions changed me. I never tired of listening to my grandmother as she told me about my natural grandfather, Károly, the brilliant head of the Fine Arts Museum. I became saturated with the humanities and the glorious past of Hungary. Emilia's rich voice comes back to me as I write this and I can see her in front of me, my emotional, exuberant, colourful grandmother who, to her last breath, played out her part, whether on stage or off. Oti-Papa, on the other hand, was the soothing, down-to earth element of my life. It was he who saw to it that I met young people of my own age.

Our immediate neighbour was a very successful playwright who lived together with his mother and a niece in a spacious villa architecturally built to resemble an English country house. It was rumoured that he courted a lesser-known actress, Theresa Csallig. One of her daughters had married a baron and their son, István, was the playwright's godson. Almost always during his visits, István would come over and join me in some game or other. Another of my close playmates was Zdenko Kostka, the grandson of Irma Márkus, Emilia's older sister who had married Count Kostka.

In my teens I acquired a close friend, a girl named Alexandra, who lived on an ostentatious country estate in Hátvan, a town some sixty kilometres from Budapest. Her father was the head of a vast sugar refinery, a family concern. Alex's parents were immensely wealthy, snobbish and unbearably formal. After a long, tedious weekend at the manor, it was with a sigh of relief I entered the Villa to inhale its easy-going Bohemian atmosphere. It was after that visit, upon hearing my 'verdict' on the Hátvany grownups, Emilia told me the story of Romola's 'lost weekend' years previously. With a mischievous twinkle in her eyes, my grandmother exclaimed: 'Just think of it, Weibi (her pet name for me), you could very well have been Alex's cousin.' Seeing my baffled expression, she hurriedly went on to say that my friend's father was in fact a brother to Bandi Hátvany who had been spurned by Romola.

It was inevitable that I should become drawn to the theatre and all that evolved around it. I was nine when I made my modest debut on stage in a Hungarian play, *Csongor és Tünde*. My name was even given mention in the extensive review covering the event. 'Little Tamara Nijinsky was a delightful butterfly'. And later, when I studied at high school, our new headmaster, Mr Jékely, also a well-known poet whose works were published under the pseudonym Lajós Aprily, selected me to recite a poem in Assembly for the celebration of our forthcoming national holiday. Although I initially suffered the all too common malaise known as stage fright, I must have conducted myself well, because I continued my role as orator on commemorative occasions until I graduated.

Otherwise, my early years passed very much like those of other girls in the same social stratum. One of my favourite sports was swimming and in the summer I would be taken to the Hotel Gellért, which had one of the first pools in the country with artificial waves. Tennis was another pastime in which I excelled but my one and only attempt at horseback riding ended in failure. The creature took an apparent dislike to me and I was unceremoniously thrown off. Wintertime, my friends and I would go skating on the lake in Varosliget, the park where years previously Romola had strolled with Bandi.

More and more, I drifted apart from my mother or rather, she from me. A wide gulf separated us both physically and mentally. Her self-indulgent nature did not permit me more than a rare postcard now and then. Only those and the letters she wrote to Emilia and Oti-Papa kindled a resurgence of memory about her person. Tatakaboy had been 'far away' for years.

In 1927, Romola was in Culver City, California. It appears that she had participated in some 'Miracle Plays'; that she was also trying her hand as a scriptwriter in Hollywood. Her missives to Emilia were as plaintive as ever. Life was still fraught with problems. Tessa had written to her from Paris that the furniture was in danger of being repossessed and that she, Tessa, daily faced the more and more gruelling task of eking out an existence for Waslaw and herself on the meagre money provided by Romola.

Romola wrote to Emilia, imploring her to spend Christmas in Paris. She complained that Emilia did not reply to Tessa's letters, and rather pointedly said that she lavished much more time to correspond with Kyra.

She was disappointed that Reinhardt (Max?) was not in California but in New York where he was enjoying a great success.

'This week I was together with Dr Jacobi, the director of the trade bank... With regard to my being homesick, it is not Europe but Waslaw I long for... I am very disheartened that I am unable to care for him as I should, give him the clothes so imperative for him, take him out in the fresh air. I am very upset and concerned about it... Yes, I would love to return to Europe with lots of money, to straighten out my affairs there and rest a little, take radium baths, but who knows how and when matters will be settled. The future is truly unpredictable, especially if I am not able to earn more money...'

She reproached Emilia for not addressing the envelopes correctly. 'The mailman will be angry if you do not write California, since there are several places in the United States with a similar name. Also please write USA.'

Toward the end of the summer in 1928, the Villa became a bee-hive of activity. We were expecting Kyra. Ever since the break-up of our home in Paris she had been in one of the most expensive and exclusive Swiss boarding-schools. It transpired that she could not stand the mountains, something she had often complained about in letters to Emilia who paid for her tuition and board. She loathed the environs so much she had even run away once. A tedious and lengthy correspondence on the matter ensued between Emilia and Romola. Emilia had pointed out it was unwarrantable that Kyra should be deprived of an equally good schooling in Hungary; that we two sisters should no longer be separated and that Kyra would savour a much needed home and family life.

And so Romola capitulated – but only to a temporary stay. With Kyra's arrival the entire household became joyful, the atmosphere overflowed with renewed life and vigour. Emilia and Oti-Papa vied with each other to suggest the evening entertainment – concerts, the opera, theatre. Yet again, friends poured in to meet a grand-daughter of Emilia Márkus. Kyra's spellbinding features had already begun to blossom; she was almost a carbon copy of Tata-kaboy, with the same oblique dark eyes and olive-coloured skin.

Alas, our happy reunion – togetherness – did not last for long. Romola refused to relinquish her plans for her older daughter. But oddly enough, it was through another woman that Kyra's new life was to present itself – in the form of Natalie Rodgers, a young American, whose husband was a hotelier in New York. She had no children of her own and begged Romola to let her become Kyra's mentor. She wished to contribute to Kyra's education and study of ballet in the United States. Kyra expressed no regrets over so sudden an upheaval but instead looked forward to the opportunities that beckoned. Romola travelled to New York from Hollywood to greet her and proudly introduced her to old friends there – the Steinhardts, the Vanderbilts, Fritz Kreisler, Ignace Paderewski and many others. Certainly, she was initiated into the highest cultural circles that existed in New York in those days.

On the 2nd of September, 1928, Romola wrote from Hollywood expressing her deep regrets that I could not have joined Kyra, but she promised my time would come. Not for one moment did I suffer any qualms at having been 'left behind'. I was perfectly content to remain stagnant in Budapest with my grandmother. I felt no desperate wanderlust nor have I since. Upon reflection, I wonder if it would not have been more beneficial to Kyra, in those formative teenage years, to have enjoyed a stable home life, surrounded by relations who gave freely of their love, rather than be thrown from one alien family to another, change environment every few months. But then, that was her destiny.

Romola was staying at the Savoy Hotel in London when she wrote the following to Emilia, dated the 8th October, 1929. She was there to negotiate the possible publication of her memoirs as well as the printing of a portfolio of Waslaw's drawings.

'*Dearest Mama,*

I received your letters of September and the beginning of this month and wish to thank you so much for them. I am always so happy to hear from you. And thank you for the play 'Boszorkany' ('The Witch', written by Sardou). It was not possible to get hold of it here and we needed it badly. In Paris, yes, but only with the greatest difficulty and that is why I turned to you. I hope I did not cause you too much trouble. Thank God, I have had good news about Kyra...she is making progress both with her dancing lessons and her other studies. General Donovan, Hoover's righthand man, sent me a cable informing me that the State Department have renewed Kyra's permit so that she will be able to stay on and continue her studies. So, thank God, for the time being everything seems to be all right with Kyra. The Untermeyers are very kind to her and she is often invited to Greystone, their country estate. I can hardly wait to see you and Tamara. We have not seen each other for so long. I cannot even imagine how Tamara looks but everybody tells me such lovely things about her and for that I am very happy. I do hope she is in good health...

Thank you for writing to the Consul and for taking care of my belongings. Maybe hopefully by Spring I will find my way out of my difficulties and make a payment, if my possessions have not been auctioned off by then. Please try to find out what has happened to the furniture and other items left behind in the flat, in particular the Sargent picture. I would also like to know what has happened to the old photograph albums. I desperately need them for the memoirs I am writing. I already have an English and an American publisher for the book which means I shall really have to start working hard at it. This past summer,*

---

* The Sargent drawing was of Waslaw Nijinsky in *Le Pavillon d'Armide*. It had hung in our flat in Paris and we all loved it.

due to Kyra's illness, I had no peace of mind to write, nor of course, because of the state of affairs in Paris.

Please ask Tessa what she has done with the pawn tickets for my gold purse and Waslaw's rings. Also what about my jewellery? I really would like to know if she has sold them or pawned them?...

I managed to get two fur coats from storage in Paris and it appears that I shall be able to get Waslaw's wintercoat as well. I am very happy about that.

It is quite certain that we will come to Budapest although we do not know the exact date as yet. It all depends on whether Lya will be making a film or whether she will perform on the stage here in London. She has not made up her mind yet because we are waiting for the third act of the play which the author has just finished... She is very gifted. She has great dramatic strength, is a very colourful performer, and her voice is deep and warm. It reminds me of your voice. It would be a pity not to make use of all that talent.

London, as always, is beautiful, the English people are charming. It is a very sympathetic nation. Please write as soon as possible and when we know we are coming, I will let you know.

Million kisses to you from Romola
Give some of the kisses to Weibi and Oti'

Many months were to pass without further news about Kyra. But Emilia was to learn from reliable sources how Natalie faded out of the picture as Kyra's mentor. For a short while she had faithfully kept her promise to Romola and done everything in her power to help her. Then a hidden side to her nature manifested itself. Natalie began to drink. And she became involved with another woman friend, who had a pretty blonde daughter; a girl who was neither gifted nor talented in any way. Natalie's new companion cunningly turned her interest away from Kyra toward her own offspring. Consumed with jealousy, she wanted the financial benefits bestowed upon Kyra to be transferred to her own daughter. And she succeeded. Kyra was abandoned.

A few years later, the trio came to Budapest, where Natalie rented a house in a smart suburb. Apparently, she regularly had to consult a famous Hungarian psychiatrist. I remember being introduced to her one day at the *Gellért Szálló.* I could hardly believe my eyes. Could that fat, sloppy woman, with the cigarette dangling from her mouth, be the same charming, beautiful Natalie I had seen pictures of ...? A rather bizarre characteristic of hers was that she usually carried around with her two very much alive monkeys. Everyone who approached her was terrified that they would bite. I would keep a safe distance, fearing I would contract tuberculosis from the little beasts.

Romola's determination to find a cure for Waslaw became more and more an obsession with her. She was single-minded to achieve this goal. Somehow, some way, she had to find the necessary finance to place him in the best institution, to seek advice from the most knowledgeable doctors. She was never once to falter. Eleven years had passed since Professor Bleuler had given his verdict. She must have realised that Nijinsky the dancer would never again resurface but she refused to accept that his name might fade into oblivion. Consequently, she started afresh to renew old contacts to revive interest in him. She embarked on a succession of trips between the States and Europe, ultimately earning her the title 'The Flying Dutchman'.

She met a number of Hungarians in America who were already on the stepladder to fame in the field of films: George Cukor, Alexander Korda, Mihaly Kertesz (Michael Curtis), and it was at that stage she reopened her friendship with Lya de Putti. Lya was born in Hungary in 1897. Her father was a Hungarian officer and landowner of a vast estate, her mother, the Countess Hoyos. Lya had married very young. Whether her husband subsequently died or she was divorced, I do not know.

It was said Romola and Lya had often been together in Berlin, when Lya was acting in films at the UFA Studios between 1918 and 1926. Like so many of her contemporaries in the world of stage and screen, she migrated to the States, to Hollywood that beckoned with promises of fame and fortune. Romola was deeply impressed by Lya's personality and beauty. She declared that Lya was singularly gifted. Quite likely, too, in her own shrewd way she calculated that remaining close to Lya would prove to be a stepping stone toward achieving her own goal; to organise a foundation for the support of Waslaw's stay in a sanatorium. For a time she acted as Lya's secretary and companion.

Romola still leaned on Oskar as her Nestor and when he learned about her involvement with Lya, he gave her fair warning not to rely too much on that friendship. She was soon to grasp the wisdom of his words. Sometime in 1930, Lya had promised Romola to pay for Waslaw's stay in the Bellevue Sanatorium in Kreuzlingen, a promise clearly defined in a registered letter sent by Romola from New York to Doctor Anton Bockli on the 4th of November,1931. *'Den Frau Lya de Putti hat sich verpflichtet mir gegenüber die Schuld von Sanatorium Bellevue (in Mai 1930) bis den Tag also ess war damals 8,717.36 zu übernehmen und ess zubezahlen...'* In the same letter she pleaded with the doctor to have patience a while longer and that she, Romola, would find the necessary money to pay the debt; that she was working on setting up some sort of foundation, which would then support Waslaw in the sanatorium until his death. As it happened, Lya did not keep her promise and Romola was compelled to resort to legal means to clear up the matter with Lya's attorney.

It was to Oti that same year that she poured out her heart in a jumbled mixture of despondency, aggravation and wounded pride.

'December 11th, 1931 New York
c/o Richter, 400 Park Avenue

My kind Oti...

I received your letter dated November 5th for which I thank you and also for your good advice, for which I am always grateful, no matter the circumstances. You were and are so right that I could not rely on my friendship with L. (Lya). And it was not my intention to do so. Although L. did everything possible to keep me under her control, in spite of her wretchedness this summer, I told her truthfully that even if she were to rectify her indebtedness to me immediately, I would in future stand on my own two feet and only if she behaved herself and I had any time to spare, might I possibly be of assistance to her. In spite of the fact that she then and there tried to inveigle me to go to Hawaii and California with her, I refused to do so although she kept waiting for me to change my mind. I wasted no time in renewing Waslaw's and my acquaintances and this has kept me preoccupied.

To date, I have achieved the following concrete results. From February 1st through the 15th next year, Waslaw's drawings *will be exhibited in the Legget Gallery of the new Waldorf Astoria Hotel. (This will be one of the first exhibitions in New York of his work). Claudel Vernissagon, Mrs Vanderbilt and I will host the occasion. Possibly, I might sell a few, but in any case I will offer a subscription so that the drawings can be published in 10-15 bound editions. During this period I will be giving lectures on 'The Art of Dance' and my talks will simultaneously be interpreted in dance by Waslaw's friend, Gavrilof, who will be in full costume. In this way we hope to be hired on a full time basis by some artistic academy or university. From this, Waslaw's dream – the Bayreuth of Dance – may develop. Vanderbilt and Cotten have vested interest in this idea and they are playing into my hands... Meanwhile, Elisabeth Marbury is trying to bring together twenty individuals willing to undertake to pay for Waslaw's sanatorium for life, and to cover past expenses... Morris Gest offered a contract of $200 weekly to have a performance at the Metropolitan (Opera). However, he suffered a concussion and went into hospital, so nothing will come of this for the time being.*

I do not wish to go into details but Lya refused to accept that she had lost both Blumenthal and me; she cannot torture us any longer. In her anger she swallowed a bone, which, wrecked internally as she was by alcohol, caused a terrible gas poisoning (this is an unusually strong bacteria many soldiers caught in the war) and in the aftermath of surgery she caught pneumonia and died. Who nursed her, who called for Walter to come to her deathbed? Who gave the servants support, the very ones who had plotted against me all summer? Who called the best doctors, who called the priest, who nursed her day and night... the kind, stupid Romola. And now, I have had to take care of everything together with Walter; the funeral and all the details... She did not leave anything except for a couple of thousand dollars in debt, which Walter is paying although he is under no obligation to do so.

He too has had to soothe the personal maid, the servants, to rehabilitate them, assist with the funeral, everything... And who is attempting to find a small income for Countess Hoyos? I am! Whether I will succeed or not, I do not know. Up until now Walter has behaved like a big brother to me. According to him, two people ruined their health, two people suffered hell at the hands of Lya: he and I and – that is the truth...

May God save everyone from such a sadist... Walter wants me to go away for a holiday – to his friends in Palm Beach who have a beautiful home there, since I am drained, exhausted, you can imagine... Enclosed I am sending Uncle Elie's letter. If he imagines for a moment the money he sent was too much, send word to him that he should try to make ends meet on that little in America... Others must have $500 in order to enter into this country.

I have been asked to write an article about how it feels to travel around without money; if it is published, I will send you the royalties as an advance... Now, I wish to discuss two serious business matters, which are important. According to Untermeyer, I am under no obligation to B... He has no right to use the material and information concerning the Russian Ballet and Waslaw that I gave him. On Capri I handed to him a manuscript written by me earlier in California about 'how I met Waslaw' and now I would like this back, immediately. Please ask for it back in my name – diplomatically – so that there will be no problem with Natalie on this account. You know best how to handle this. Secondly, please find out from Tessa what she has done with my luggage and the Sargent picture. I will buy it back if she has sold it. Tessa should not force me to have to settle this with the French and the Danish consulates, because it could mean her expulsion from France or something worse. But I must know at once what has happened to my things; the luggage is essential because it contains material concerning Waslaw...She should be happy that I don't cause a great ado on account of the mysterious disappearance of my jewellery. Please make her understand this, otherwise I shall be compelled to take the drastic action to deal with the matter through my lawyer and the Consulate. She neither responds to my forbearing letters nor to my requests. ...I regret that I have to burden you with this...But what can I do? I hope this will not add to your worries. Here, too, economically, the situation is indescribable... I implore you both to write. Within days I will write to Mama. All good wishes for a happy holiday and for the New Year. I wish the three of you good health and lots of money for the coming year.

With love from the heart and kisses to you all.

Romola'

Although Romola suffered many setbacks and much heartache through false friendships, she did have one true friend in a Dutch woman, Frederique or Frederica as she was called. They had first met each other somewhere in Europe before Romola commenced her endless commuting between countries and continents. Their relationship blossomed anew through correspondence at a time when Romola was going through harassment from all quarters. Then a wonderful thing happened – Frederique Dezentje decided to join Romola in the States. A tall, blonde young woman, outwardly very calm with a winning smile, projecting a soothing effect on those around her, she had a healthy, positive influence on Romola. It was she who encouraged Romola to tackle the writing of the Memoirs; who prodded her to stop smoking, and warned her against the misguided motivations of others. Her own health was frail, she suffered from tuberculosis and had spent months in a sanatorium, but her love for Romola was so strong it did not prevent her from a drastic upheaval of her own roots to go to an alien country, where she was to find herself in an uncertain financial situation. She had torn herself away from a cossetted life with a Frenchman. The 'new' world was completely different from anything she had previously experienced. In all fairness, Romola had warned her that she would not find either comfort or luxury in her new surroundings yet she never capitulated to doubts but came to be at Romola's side.

Romola kept her promise to write to Emilia.

'30th December 1931

Dear Mama,

Happy New Year to the three of you....I have little time to write, just my news in brief. Thank you for your letter of the 20th November. I have so much to do, "Azt se tudom fiu vagyok e vagy lány,"* which I do not always know anyway. People are tearing me apart with their invitations. I am busy day and night attending to matters regarding Kyra, myself and Waslaw...Even though I have a secretary, she too is laden with

---

* 'I don't even know if I am a boy or a girl' – literal translation of an old Hungarian proverb expressing a state of confusion in one's mind or life.

*work... In addition to which I have now become a writer –
already one book and one essay have been sold. Don't you dare
tell Natalie now, because they, i.e. her entourage, are capable
of leaving me in the lurch. B..., Natalie's friend, would explode
with envy. That little sneak laughed at me on Capri and tried to
discourage me. Here, C.N. nearly fainted with awe over my
scribbling... It goes so fast I am now writing two books at the
same time. Next week, I will go for three weeks down to Palm
Beach together with friends of Walter's just to absorb a little
sunshine.*

*I can thank Frederica for all these positive happenings; she is
the one who has not let me sink into despair, who beseeches me
to rid myself of bad influences. If I do become somebody, it will
be because of her. Kyra has not written for a long time. But I
wrote to her, advising her to go to Paris to study under Lifar,
which I feel is an important step. Please induce Tamara to lose
weight. It is terrible to hear how fat she is – she must have a
problem with her glands. And that is bad for her heart. Please,
do it...I have met several doctors, lawyers, who were all in love
with you and, allegedly, when they confessed this to you, you
answered them all with "Why didn't you tell me before?" Well,
what more shall I discover about you?*

*Following the teaching of Christ, I did everything to ease
Lya's last days. I protected her and her interests, even though
her behaviour toward me was shameful. Only two days before
the accident she said to me: "Romus, if you stay with me and
you promise not to care any more about Waslaw and that Dutch
whore (Frederica) we could live for three years like little kings,
and then commit suicide together, alternatively, you can go and
starve to death in the street with your husband. You will be
either with me or nobody." I replied, "I will always be your
friend but for the past thirteen years I have struggled for
Waslaw, who, to me, is a saint, and now in our fourteenth year I
will not forsake him for anybody."*

*Well, that is your lot, Romola de Pulszky Nijinsky. Noblesse
oblige...Oti should not worry himself sick over taxes, things
will get better. Here, nobody has any cash, merely worthless
stocks and shares. Even Otto Kahn is moaning. "I" will give
him 5... Please tell Natalie to send Kyra to a doctor who will
give her some vitamins.*

Waslaw has not been well, he has had two heart attacks. This
worries me terribly, although they tell me not to worry. Please
do send some Gerbeau chocolates to Lydia, the head nurse. I
beg you to do me that favour. You would make her very happy.
I did send her some lingeries for Christmas. Watza is to stay on
in Kreuzlingen and the debts will be paid... I am watching my
own health. I am very nervous. It seems I suffer from nicotine
poisoning. But I am not going to smoke any more, as I have
given my word to Frederica that I will behave... Now I will aim
at establishing the Bayreuth of Dance and win the Nobel Prize
in Literature; with God's help...this is my humble ambition for
the time being...

Romola'

1932 found Romola still in the States. She had become increasingly upset by Tessa, who, it appears, had disposed of both Romola
and Waslaw's belongings in order to survive. In fact, she had gone
to such extremes that for years Romola wrote in the French papers
publicly accusing Tessa of living off money that rightfully was
Waslaw's.

In a letter to Emilia of February 14th, 1932, Romola once more
gave vent to her grievances.

...How she (Tessa) lives, what she does, is none of my business
and therefore I do not have the moral right to criticise her.
Every human being has the right, even more important, the
duty toward himself to arrange his life as bearably as possible.
Especially if one has to support oneself and, in addition, in a
foreign land. I feel that you, my dear Mama, cannot understand
that, because ever since your childhood you have enjoyed
success, security, means to live. You have had someone who
belonged to you and who loved you. To live alone and to fight
alone for survival is not possible. You see, even Lya, who had a
handsome income and was courted by men, could not face life,
when she realised she had lost Walter and me. To my last breath
I will always do what is my clear duty toward Waslaw.'

Her consuming interest at this crossroad of her life was the
writing of her memoirs about Waslaw. Feverishly, she set
about contacting everyone she could think of who in one way

or another had been connected with him. One of many positive replies came from Anatole Bourman who had set up a Ballet Studio in Springfield, Massachusetts. Earlier in January he answered:

'Dear Madame Nijinsky,

...I think that your idea of writing a book of "Memoirs of Nijinsky" is a very splendid one. Your husband is my very best friend and I remember his whole career very distinctly, but I have just recently conceived the same idea.

If your object is to explain his entire life; his birth, his family, his success, and all the events which made him one of the most interesting dancers of all time, then I will be only too pleased to co-operate with you. As he and I grew up together, I can remember many humorous as well as great achievements which dotted his past.

...I am sure that a book of his life would be far more interesting than Karsavina's book of her life, because of his far greater success as a dancer. Not only dancers would want to read it, but everyone would be interested.

I wish you every success possible in your new venture and remain,

Most respectfully yours
Anatole Bourman'

Romola must have sent copies of her synopsis of the story about Nijinsky to a number of publishers in the States and England. At least three expressed sufficiently deep interest in the subject to reply by return that they would eagerly await to read the finished book: Dutton's, Alfred Knopf and William Heinemann.

Eleonora Bereda, Waslaw's mother, died of diabetes in Paris in 1932 at the age of seventy-five. She spent her last years in a wheelchair, having had one leg amputated. I have been unable to find any reference as to Romola's reaction. It must be assumed that she never conveyed this sad news to Waslaw, and even if she had, it would not have penetrated his obscured mind.

The intensity of the relationship that existed between Romola and Frederica is surely revealed in a letter Romola wrote to Emilia in early 1932.

'...I have heard from someone that you do not speak well of Frederique. It really hurts me. Why are you so against her? Especially as she admires and respects you. What wrong has she done to you; the only faithful friend I have who stays by my side for better of for worse, even endangering her own well-being. Who gave up a man with 70 million French francs for my sake. If I achieve anything, it will only be thanks to her. If I would not have her friendship, I would have followed Lya's advice (commit suicide).

Thirteen years of tragedy is too much even for an animal. Nobody can ask of me that I should live alone. I could not do so anyhow because of my health problems and I have to be capable to work. I was told by my doctor I have a serious heart condition. I should have a calm, tranquil life, without undue excitement...'.

Looking back on Romola's life so many years later, reading through letters that my grandmother so carefully kept, I cannot help but reflect on what constituted her inner nature. She yearned for love and affection and as soon as she found someone for whom she cared, Tatakaboy, Lya, Frederica and scores of others, she lavished upon them whatever she could give – nursed them if they were ill, shared their worries – yet sadly she was incapable of the same devout attention to her own flesh and blood, Kyra and myself.

There was a long interim in correspondence between Romola and Budapest. Then, after a silence that lasted many weeks, the extremely sad communiqué reached Emilia that Frederica was dead. Romola was devastated. She raged against Fate that once more had robbed her of a beloved. To her, history was repeating itself – had she not 'lost' her Watza in 1919 when his mind had shut her out. Now she suffered yet another blow – the physical death of her dearest companion. She poured out her heart in a disjointed, agonising letter to her mother, who had sent her condolences immediately she heard the news.

'Camp of the Two Ranges
North Dorset, Vermont
3rd October 1932

My dear Mama,

I received your letter. I realise how hard it is for you to write

244

because of your eyes, yet still you wrote to me for which I am eternally grateful. It was very thoughful of you to remember Frederique and I am also grateful that Oti expressed his sadness about the terrible tragedy that has befallen me.

As I already told you in my brief communiqué, I am trying to scrape together enough money to take Frederique back to Holland. That was her wish. I gave her my sacred promise I would do it. She came over to America despite the fact she did not like this cold, heartless place. She accepted it all gracefully, even the enormous problems in my life, the lack of necessities. She was always ready with a consoling, encouraging word to keep me going. She tried everything to help me so that I would be in a position to secure an existence for Watza and that we ourselves could have a little home together. Without her I would have given up long ago...

A few moments before her death, her last gesture was to share some champagne with me, so that I should be able to bear her passing. The doctor gave her a glass of it to ease her own suffering which she endured with such patience. When Frederique breathed her last, I felt as though I, too, stopped existing. I have no more willpower...no desire to go on living.

I am not referring to the love which is inherent in us toward our mother or our children but to the love we feel toward those we have chosen of our own free will. For me, only Waslaw and Frederique counted. They both had goodness in their souls and noble hearts. I am unable to live alone...

When Waslaw became lost to me, do you remember how I rebelled, the tantrums I threw? I did one mad, crazy thing after the other in order to forget the emptiness – the void – which was left in my life without him. My friendship with Lya was nothing more than a dose of narcotics to make me forget... Now I do not want to repeat the same mistake. I do not want to become an alcoholic or a drug addict. Just as I could never remarry, I could never again share my friendship and life with anybody... Fate can have only one thing in store for me – that I may be reunited with Frederique as soon as possible...

My permit to stay here has expired. As it already has been renewed twice, I shall have to leave the country for a while before filling in a new application. At present it is impossible to earn money here. Those who have any, hide it, those who do *not just sit and stare into space. Everybody is complaining yet they seem unable to comprehend that nothing is solved by itself. The future looks bleak, without any hope of betterment, people are drowning in their own agricultural and industrial surplus which they cannot sell. There are no jobs, especially for foreigners...Everybody is cutting down and the prospects are no better for women... Now I will turn my back for good on the New World. I have been staying here for a few weeks on the estate of a friend of mine but shall be going back to town tomorrow. I am determined to do everything possible for Watza and get my papers in order to enable me to travel.*

I have to find the amount needed for Frederique's and my grave since her mother is penniless. I want to look after her little son as well...to see for myself how her husband's family is raising her child.

I would like to see Kyra and Tamara...but to go back to the places where I have been with Frederique is impossible – I could not bear it.

I worry terribly about Watza's fate, he could live for yet another twenty-five to thirty years. I cannot hand over to Kyra the burden of taking care of her father, that would be asking too much. If I have nothing else to leave her, certainly I cannot let her inherit a responsibility of this magnitude. I cannot count on Bronia. I wrote to Madame Polignac in Paris and to Lord Rothermere in London that they should take some action to benefit Waslaw. I believe that if we could only get together 10,000 dollars, it would be possible to keep him at Kreuzlingen for the duration of his life.

Here in this country there is not one good friend, at least no one who would seriously consider helping me. There are just a few who were good to Watza. I can only pray they will stay that way. I fear that before I am able to go to The Hague I shall have to face some very traumatic days. But I shall not have fear because I no longer desire anything for myself. I learned long ago that time does not heal nor allow us to forget those we so sincerely have loved. At least I am incapable of that. If I have not written often enough, please try to forgive me. I have not wanted to moan about how hard my life is...If I have not cabled you on your birthdays, please forgive me for that too. Despite my negligence I only wish the best. I am still unable to fathom the ghastly thing that has happened. It all went so quickly. Frederique was ill for two weeks. I feel that the lung specialist she first consulted, who is the head of a very exclusive hospital, did not give her the right treatment earlier. America, and the fact that she came to be with me, killed her. Her last few days she was in the care of the doctor who saved Kyra's life but by then every treatment known to medical science was in vain, as were all my prayers. For seven days she was in an oxygen tent, close to death. I begged God to save her life. The first doctor who treated her died only a few days after Frederique, allegedly of a heart condition... If there is a life after death, why does she not come back to me, even for the briefest moment? Since she knew so well I cannot live without her. If I ever had to leave her alone, say for half an hour, we would 'phone each other and she would say: "Schazi. Liebling, kommst schon zurück, ich lang-weile mich so furchtbar ohne Dich..." When anybody sug-gested something for her to do, she would merely reply: "I have found that I cannot live elsewhere, my heart and my soul will forever belong to Romola..." Yet now she has left me so suddenly, how is that possible...?

Do you honestly believe in an after life? And a reunion? I will remember you and the children in my prayers but you, too, must pray for me that my miserable life might end and that we shall be together, Frederique and I, as soon as possible...

Forgive me for this letter, I cannot write any other way... I am like a dog who has lost his master...

I kiss and hug all three of you. From the heart
Romola'

Romola was to dedicate her first book *Nijinsky* to her darling Frederica.

'To the memory of Frederica Dezentje, without whose affec-tion and friendship this book could not have been written."

Gradually, the shock and sharp pain at losing Frederica subsided into a dull ache and her resilient willpower enabled her to survive. But she needed answers to so many questions and being possessed of an inquisitive nature, she turned to spiritualism. Emilia received the following in which Romola defined her ultimate objectives.

Dear Mama,

*Mr Shaw informed me that you had written to me enquiring
as to my whereabouts and my well-being. You must forgive me
for not having sent news of myself and most of all for having let
the holidays slip by without any sign of life from me. You must
be aware, however, that I always wish you well, even if I do not
write it down on paper. That I am completely breaking all contacts with the outside world is only to ensure that if the inevitable
happens, it will be easier for everyone concerned. I am incredibly busy with the three things that I have made my goal – to
secure Waslaw's future, to finish the book within a couple of
weeks. It will truly be first class. In addition to that, all my time
is taken up with tests carried out by the John Hopkin's Psychiatric Department in conjunction with the clinic here attached to
the Psychic Research Society.* **

*They are carrying on scientific research and experimentation
on a regular basis with the world's finest mediums to determine
whether after death everything terminates or whether individua-
lity and personality live on in another form. Truly remarkable
things have happened to me during the past three months based
on the postulations which these scientists are now researching;
that the undeniable phenomena that occur in my room and in
my presence are due to some unexplained force in my subconscious memory which they are as yet unable to identify, or,
is indeed all this caused by the spirit of Frederique? In any case,
these eminent scientists, English and American doctors and
psychiatrists, claim that I am an extremely rare and strong
medium and decidedly valuable for the furthering of scientific
research. Since I, too, am infinitely keen to know whether there
is a Great Beyond and a reunion, you can well understand that I
am making myself available to these experiments... Perhaps,
after all, I will be of some use to mankind...*

* My mother kept notes of two of these sittings:
March 6, 1933, 2 o'clock at the Psychic Research Society in New York with a Mrs
Larsen from St Louis; a sitting with Mrs Ruth Vaughn, July 12th, 1933 at the London
Spiritualist Alliance.

248

During these experiments I am not only in contact with Frederique, who is constantly by my side, but in a number of instances I have had the opportunity to talk with Papa (Charlie-Papa), Teréza Pulszky, Grandmother Márkus, Jozsi Bacsi (Uncle Joseph). All this is recorded by a stenographer and into a microphone in the presence of the scientists in their clinical laboratory. I cannot explain it fully in a letter, it would take too long and be too complicated. Don't think that I have gone mad. I have never been more sane than at this moment...

At the end of March I will leave for Holland and will notify you before my departure. I would like to have Kyra's address, I need it urgently, please send it immediately...

I hope all three of you are well and have had a good holiday... Naturally, I did not take part in any celebrations but tried instead to forget it was the Holiday season. At the moment Kyra's portrait is displayed here at an exhibition. I hope that she is well and that she is doing something. It would be about time... And Tamara, is she healthy and diligent? How is your eye? What is Oskar doing? Is he still racking his brains over taxes? Here, too, it is a strange world, everything has changed a great deal since last winter. Mrs Laszlo (Leslie) Széchényi has been infinitely kind toward me and Waslaw, doing so much on his behalf. Right now I am in the process of organising an International Committee for "The Nijinsky Memorial Fund."

Lord Rothermere, Lady Cunard, Lady Morrell, Lady Duff, the Aga Khan, the Duke of Westminster are the English members; the French: the Princess of Monaco, Comtesse de Neuilly, Marquise de Polignac, Comte de Beaumont, Rolph de Maré, Princess Murat; the Americans: Mrs Vanderbilt, Mrs Széchényi, her older sister Mrs Whitney, Anne Morgan, Mrs Rockefeller Jr; on the artistic committee: Ignace Paderewski, Chaliapin, etc...

These are the ones who are acting to gather together the funds for Waslaw's care, and I have stipulated that after his death, the money should go to the education of a few talented dancers. You should have seen how they took to this idea. I hope that shortly it will gain great success...

I have received an invitation to visit Russia during the summer and I would need to go back to Europe, to Paris and to Cannes. But by then I may be with my Frederique, I can hardly wait. Truly it is only for Waslaw's sake that I am carrying this yoke...

Otherwise, what is the news in your part of the world? What is Tessa doing? Papa (Charlie) is always asking about her. He sends you many kisses and says that he is well and that I should write to you and let you know. Is it true that Papa spoke Dutch? He is constantly telling me 'yes' and says that he is together with Frederique, whom he has learned to like very much... Jozsi Bacsi really did sing the "csak egy kis leanyt," it came across so clearly that the technicians who handled the microphones during the séance almost fainted. Now, I am able to laugh but at first I was genuinely frightened...

All good wishes. Write to me care of Mr Shaw, as I am wandering from hotel to hotel. I find no peace anywhere without Frederique. You must believe me... I kiss all three of you. Romola'

I was barely thirteen when that last letter arrived to bring the first rumblings of disharmony to our hitherto peaceful way of life in the Villa. My grandmother was distraught with anxiety. Rising blood pressure made her increasingly irritable. Perhaps with her inclination to dramatise everything, she suddenly imagined that Romola might, indeed, do something foolhardy. Subtly, the milieu was overshadowed by sadness, the surroundings rife with an impending crisis. I grew to dread the daily delivery of post, especially when I could distinguish Romola's typewritten capitals on the envelopes or Tessa's bold handwriting. It went so far that sometimes I would secret any letters that aroused my suspicion, hoping by this act to erase any further interruptions to our normal routine. Only when my guilty conscience grew too unbearable, did I retrieve them and hand them over with some lame excuse or another.

With hindsight I realise that my grandparents must have had many other problems to cope with as well. Blistering winds of economic chaos in the aftermath of the Wall Street crash found their way even to Hungary. To support their great Emilia Márkus, the Ministry for Culture had granted her a franchise to a fairly large complex which included shops and an ice-skating rink in the summer season conveniently turned into a tennis court, in addition to a building that was at one time the National Theatre. The property was situated on the corner of Rákoczy Road and Museum

Körüt. Although rents flowed in, the income did not always justify the enormous stress and strain it imposed on Oskar. He had by now retired from the Ministry on a small pension to be at Emilia's beck and call whenever she needed him. The daunting task of finding the necessary funds for the upkeep of the Villa – heating alone absorbed tons of coal annually – rested on his shoulders. Both he and Emilia had generously scooped out of the Horn of Plenty to help Romola whenever she was in dire straits, to pay for Kyra's schooling, to keep me. Now the tide had turned. Money merely trickled in.

Typically, instead of showing appreciation for past favours, Romola dealt the elderly couple a further cruel blow when she accused them of having used her and Tessa's inheritance from Charlie-Papa's estate to build the Villa, a blatant distortion of the actual facts. With the exception of a few paintings, books, some furniture Emilia had found it impossible to part with, everything had been acquired through Oskar's skilful financial manipulation.

Tessa's letters descended with uncomfortable frequency. She issued veiled threats that she would face imprisonment because of her inability to pay the ever-mounting debts in Paris. Yet, throughout the whole of this distressing period, she received 200 pengö monthly, a tidy sum considering that in those days a postman had 40 pengö and a civil servant 80 pengö per month.

From the age of ten I kept a diary and, like most young girls, diligently confided my thoughts to it. Then the entries petered out to one or two sentences and the diary was replaced by a small calendar. But on June 10th, 1933, I had scribbled with great excitement that Meme was planning to come to Budapest. I was torn between the desire to see her again and fear that her appearance would give rise to quarrels and misunderstandings. My grandmother was by then in her seventies and although outwardly she did not show signs of ageing, her health was frail.

For whatever reason, Romola did not come but another event was to take place that made her 'presence' felt to a harmful degree.

Meanwhile, however, my father's state of health was a continuous topic of conversation and bulletins regarding his progress or otherwise were eagerly anticipated. On August 1st, 1933, Romola had a letter from Dr Binswanger at the Bellevue Sanatorium, Kreuzlingen '...that the month of July has passed without any change in your husband's condition. Although I had not seen him for several months, he recognised me and greeted me most amiably

251

and with a smile. He has occasionally suffered slight irritations of short duration. As usual he spends most of his day in the garden. His physical condition is, as always, good...'.

Then the dreadful day came to pass that was to plunge us into misery for weeks. Oversensitive and a worrier by habit – I worried to the point that if there was nothing to worry about, I would worry about exactly that – I had become almost paranoid about my grandmother's wellbeing, so close had I grown to her. From the moment I stepped over the threshold, home from school, a sixth sense conveyed to me that something was horribly wrong. My instant thought was for Emilia and I bounded up the stairs to my grandparents' bedroom. In a daze, I took in the picture of Emilia lying prostrate on the bed, mumbling incoherently. Oti-Papa, his face ashen-grey and drawn, sat slumped beside her. Suddenly aware of my presence, he got up and brusquely ordered me to leave the room. Stunned by his harsh command, to which I had never ever been subjected before, I obeyed but not before my eyes had caught sight of an airmail envelope and a thick, clothbound book on the bedside table.

For weeks Emilia lived on tranquillisers and the doctor came more and more frequently. Both she and Oskar obdurately refused to discuss either the contents of the offensive letter or the book that had sparked off the drama. Slowly and inevitably my grandmother recovered, my well of tears dried, and a daily semblance of normality resumed. But my instinctive desire was to know the why and wherefore of it all. Furtively I searched in every conceivable nook and cranny for 'the culprit' – the book – but it had vanished. An old retainer to the family finally took pity on me and told me that my mother's book, *Nijinsky* had been published in London and that in it, Romola had written some flagrant untruths about her mother. She did not elaborate any further and the matter was brushed to one side.

The biography was highly acclaimed by the British press. The reviewers vied with each other to heap superlatives on it. 'A picture of engrossing interest, remarkable for its devotion and devastating candour...', 'the life of Vaslav Nijinsky is not merely a record of a great dancer's artistic triumphs; it is one of the strangest stories ever written...', 'Mme Nijinsky has created a work of art...', 'In this enchanting volume there are romance, adventure, pathos and tragedy, enough for half a dozen novels...' 'She has given us a fascinating sociological document...she has provided material of far-reaching speculation in the region of psycho-pathology, and she has written a deeply moving story of a dramatic human relationship'. In the United States and other countries where *Nijinsky* was published in 1934, the praise was as lavish. It became a best-seller and the royalties gave Romola much needed financial relief for Waslaw's upkeep. I believe she had several collaborators in writing the manuscript, foremost of whom was Lincoln Kirstein.

Una Lady Troubridge wrote to Romola that the book was '...a great tribute and memorial to one of the greatest artists in his art of all time. It has brought back memories of my personal meetings with him, of an entire world that is gone forever, and confirmed me in my determination never to see another ballet till I can see Nijinsky dance in Heaven!'. Una Troubridge had sculpted 'Nijinsky-Faune' from life (his head only) and the original in marble is said to be in the Museo della Scala in Milan.

When the storm subsided Romola became reconciled with Emilia and correspondence between mother and daughter resumed its usual pattern.

On November 16th, disquieting news arrived from Romola, while she was staying at Mayfair Court in London, to the effect that Kyra, who was studying ballet in the city, had been taken seriously ill.

> '...The specialist was able to ascertain from blood tests that her parathyroid gland was not functioning properly...the basic cause of her difficult nature, her poor physical health, and if the ensuing tests support this theory, then accidentally, we may have found the key to Waslaw's illness...Kyra can be cured in a few months with proper treatment...and maybe even Waslaw's condition can be improved...would not that be a miracle...?'

Unfortunately, I only have hazy recollections of information about Romola's movements during the following couple of years. Nor have I been able to find further reference to the cure mentioned in the above letter. She flitted from continent to continent, city to city, on a ceaseless round of lecturing engagements and cultural events to keep her name in the fore, to which a number of programmes, yellowed with age, bear witness. She was in London on Sunday, the 6th of November, 1934, invited as guest of honour at the Mayfair Hotel on the occasion when Miss Vera Brittain spoke on the subject *Why I wrote "The Testament of Youth"*. In 1935 she gave lectures from Minneapolis as far down south as Fort Worth, Texas. A press cutting from the latter event is curiously headed, *'Mrs Nijinsky prefers farm to fame, potato to plaudits'!* In the interview she is quoted as saying that she would like best of all to have a farm home and a garden where she might grow vegetables. The article goes on to say that 'she is travelling alone and it is "the first and last time" she intends to do so. She finds being secretary and maid to "Mrs Nijinsky" is quite a job.' The article continues, 'Kyra, older daughter of the Nijinskys and idol of her father before his confinement to a hospital in Switzerland, is dancing now in London: The younger daughter, Tamara, is in school in Budapest. Tamara, her mother says, is a mathematical genius, "the only one in the family who knows how to count." Mrs Nijinsky...hopes Tamara will scorn careers of all kinds, marry and settle down to a quiet life. If she (Romola) can't have the quiet home she wants, she would like for one of her daughters to have it. ...Mrs Nijinsky last saw her husband six weeks ago. He recognised members of his family, she said, will listen to no talk of the dance and sometimes sits silent for hours. He hasn't seen Kyra for seven years, nor will he look at her pictures. He pushes them away along with everything else connected with the field of art from which his illness has severed him.'

With unflagging spirit Romola pursued her plans to get together as many patrons as possible for her 'Foundation' project although she faced numerous refusals upon her approach to the rich and famous. In May 1935, for instance, she had a polite no from the Duchess of Kent. In a handwritten letter from the Lady-in-Waiting it was regretted that Her Royal Highness owing to heavy engagements was unable to undertake anything further. In September, Rolf de Maré wrote to her from Paris that he would be delighted to discuss with her the subject of a Nijinsky museum. Others pleaded for her support to further their own cause. When she was staying at the Hotel Ambassador in New York in October she had a communication from Edward Warburg to the effect that '...it is most important that at this time, when we are all working towards a greater interest in the ballet...I hope that our tours may coincide in some places so that you might be able to see the work Mr Balanchine has done with the American Ballet...It would be more helpful than I can say if, during the course of your lectures, it would

254

be possible for you to mention Mr Balanchine and the work of our group. Every kind word helps in building up what we hope will be eventually, a great American institution...'.

On the 2nd of July that same year, Romola sent a terse letter to Emilia requesting the latter to intervene on her behalf at the Ministry for the Interior to arrange for her Hungarian passport to include a visit to the USSR. She explained in her letter that she had been assigned by the Hearst Newspapers and others to write articles about the arts in various countries; that she had to go to Scandinavia and from there to the Leningrad Art Festival. She wished to combine the work on the articles with a thorough preparation for her forthcoming lecture tours on the contemporary Russian Ballet and Theatre.

> *'...Laval will give me a letter of introduction to Stalin, so I presume that everything will be in order, but without Hungarian clearance, I am unable to travel. Please arrange this for me immediately. Many kisses to all of you and Tamara.'*

I cannot find anything to substantiate that the tour did take place at that stage in Romola's life. Lengthy newspaper articles quite firmly established her presence then in the United States. The headlines splashed across the *New York World Telegram* on Thursday, January 2nd, 1936, reveal the tidal wave of emotion in the Nijinsky family triggered off by her book. They revolted openly to what Romola had written, in contrast to Emilia who discreetly was to take matters in her own hands when the Hungarian rights were sold.

NIJINSKY'S WIFE IS SORRY SENSATIONAL REVE-
LATIONS TURNED DAUGHTER AGAINST HER:
'Family Feud Rages Over Her Biography of Her Insane Husband'.

'Mme Romola Nijinsky is a gracious lady, slender as when she too tripped for Diaghilev. Magyar born, she's as live as a bottle of Tokay and there is no hint in her Danube eyes of the feud that is raging about her.
...Even her daughter Kyra has now turned against her. And there may be suits and countersuits – ...her biography *Nijinsky* – a stark narrative of her insane husband whose brain is now a Petrouchka whirl in a Swiss sanatorium. His sister and daughter are incensed at her characterization of the famous dancer.

The controversial book is to be filmed...and this has touched off a whole...of family temperaments. "I told the truth about my husband and his relations with Diaghileff," she said, "and now my daughter too has been won over by the

enemy. Poor child, she is too young to know she is being misled.
…Let them sue. I shall simply say, very well, you take over Nijinsky's
support, pay for his hospitalization. My sister-in-law says that I have written…brothers are insane. She does not like to be reminded."
…Madame Nijinsky sees her husband when in Europe as often as physicians
permit. He recognizes her and is grateful for the visits, but the specialists will
not allow her to remain over night…'

Douglas Gilbert, the staff writer, described her as a slender,
pleasant woman, clad in a black pyjama ensemble. She was interviewed curled upon a couch in her hotel room, exuding
complacency and understanding and quite unruffled by the storm
she had created. She herself was contemplating taking legal action
against Arnold Haskell on the grounds that his biography of Diaghilev implied 'a defence of the impresario to the detriment of
Nijinsky. Romola had hastily added that she did not seek money,
merely public retraction.

And on February 2nd, *The Hartford Daily Courant* wrote FOR
THE SAKE OF THAT MENTALLY DEAD GENIUS, HER
HUSBAND, AND FOR THE DANCE, MADAME NIJINSKY
WRITES AND LECTURES. 'Wife of famous dancer tells *Courant*
reporter intimate family fact. In New York, Romola Nijinsky
admits constant dread that fate will curtail her contributions to
support of insane mate – proud of daughter who won't speak to her.'

'Romance, adventure, gaiety and tragedy – all these had written their traces in
the deep blue eyes of Romola Nijinsky…facing me in her suite at the Ambassador in New York…
A gracious hostess with the sparkle of quick wit and charm of old-world
courtesy…Of medium height, dark-haired and trim, she was an arresting
figure in her tailored black gown, which was ornamented only by three metallic buttons.
"I live in daily terror…I think – what if I should close my eyes tomorrow –
what would happen. The income from my work is not great, but it has paid for
hospitalization and if it should stop – what of Nijinsky."
…"But what of Kyra?"…Madame Nijinsky indicated the mantelpiece with a
sweep of her hand. "That," she said, singling a card out from the array. "is
from Kyra. It is because I sent her a check at Christmas. You know, we are not
on speaking terms."
"She is a very talented person, my daughter Kyra. She can draw well, writes
beautiful poetry and is a born actress. She has great promise as an actress, but
she has chosen to continue with her dancing lessons." Was there a shade of
regret in her voice?'

She carried on to elaborate on a book of dance she was working
on and discussed the role she played in founding a new School of the
American Ballet. The book, she explained, 'begins with the dawn of

creation, and traces the history of the dance up through the time when the Russian Ballet was at its height in the 1900's.'

When the time came for an edition of *Nijinsky* to be distributed in Hungarian, Emilia was in a quandary. She adored her Molly in spite of the insensitive, cruel blow the latter had dealt her, and was intensely proud of her, yet she refused to suffer the humiliation of people reading the slanderous, false allegations made against her and the people of Hungary by Romola. After private consultations on the highest level, involving an audience with Governor Horthy, the decision was reached that the translator omit every one of the offensive, malicious passages. The foreword to the Hungarian edition was written by one of the country's most prominent authors.

It was the revised version that was to fall into my hands through a chain of events emanating from the necessity of Oti-Papa entering hospital for an operation. Emilia decided to remain in the clinic to be close by his side and I was despatched to Emma Hegedüs, Romola's former chaperone. Miss Hegedüs was the old retainer who had told me about Romola's biography in the first place, and it was she who now assumed the responsibility of lending me the book on the promise I would not tell my grandmother.

I recall so distinctly how I plunged into the pages, absorbing every word that brought to light a fabulous world, hitherto unknown to me. It was the first time that Waslaw Nijinsky, the world-famous ballet dancer, was unveiled to me, this almost unearthly being so different from Tatakaboy, my father. I became indifferent to food, read on until the early hours of the morning, working myself into a state of giddy intoxication at the thought I possessed such a remarkable parent. My poor grandmother believed I was suffering from the first pangs of 'puppy love'. I dared not confide in her but my conscience compelled me to tell Oti-Papa, who expressed relief when he learned I was reading the Hungarian edition. But I pressed him to unveil the mystery of the original book. He made me solemnly vow never to raise the subject with Emilia and then proceeded to relate the contents of the chapter Romola had written about her and Waslaw's stay in the Villa during World War I, the innuendoes, the renunciation of all the older couple had done for them, the acrid and false accusations against Emilia, indeed, against her countrymen. The gross injustice had nearly killed Emilia. At first, she had wanted to have the book banned but then accepted a compromise.

Governed by Emilia, my future as an actress seemed to be

crystallising. But she saw to it that I developed in other directions as well. I took piano lessons and also ballet lessons. Although my leg was now fit, I felt totally uninspired to take up ballet dancing as a career. For a brief spell I became a pupil to Maestro Troyanoff, who later left Budapest to further his career in New York. When I was barely sixteen my grandmother concerted all her efforts on getting an audition for me at the National Theatre. I genuinely wanted to make the stage my career, I won't pretend otherwise nor that, thanks to Emilia's influence, the opportunity was practically handed to me on a silver platter. She hoped, nay, she was certain that I possessed the same qualities as she had had at that age. The strict rules would be waived; no need to study first for three years at the Academy of Dramatic Arts; no need to face a highly critical panel to pronounce judgment on me 'to be or not to be'. And what happened? I lost my nerve. Or rather, instinct told me the time was not yet ripe. I would not live up to her expectations. Emilia was sorely disappointed, Oti-Papa greatly relieved. Instead, I was enrolled at the French College and looked ahead to an intensive four-year programme, shortened by a year as I spoke French fluently.

When Kyra came to Budapest in 1936, fresh from a performance at the Mittlerer Concert Hall in Vienna, a Hungarian journalist wrote at the time:

'She who wants to dance around the world; Kyra Nijinsky... This name could easily be found in a Pushkin poem or a Lermontov novel. Its bearer is like a Pushkin poem herself, blazing eyes, secretive, cultured, and still she sustains in herself the romanticism of distant worlds.'

'Yesterday, I watched Kyra practise. I believe it is impossible to reach higher in elevation than she – it was miraculous.' Emilia's voice choked with pride as she turned to the journalist. He himself was unable to take his eyes off the vibrant young woman in front of him.

The barrage of questions continued and the journalist wanted to know if she planned to go on a North American tour after her London engagement. She replied that had been her original plan but that now she had separated from the Russian Ballet. She had been asked to tell about our father on English radio as well, about how he had trained her; confided to her the secrets of the art of dance, like perfection lay in the strength of the toe, the perfect 'point'; that the secret of being light as a feather lay in one's breathing...when he had practised his jumps in the meadow in St Moritz Dorf, the flowers barely bowed their heads under his magic step...Her face was animated, a fascinating, tense face. I could hardly believe she was my sister. I could have sat there for hours, listening to her.

The interviewer finally channelled his questions onto more personal grounds – about love? Marriage? 'Never! To dance, to dance, to embrace the entire world, to dance around the world, that is my plan.'

On several occasions during those few days I accompanied Kyra to the Royal Opera where twenty-four years earlier our father had captivated his audience. She had been invited to teach, direct and dance her own choreography. I seem to recall that one of the ballets was based on Liszt's *Mephisto Valse*. At her first rehearsal there was a hushed silence when she walked out on the stage and introduced herself. I was amused to eavesdrop on the exchange of conversation between the young dancers, puzzled as to how she was able to make such fantastic leaps, '...a woman, and she isn't exactly petite, either. Look at her strong calves and legs!'

Some snapshots of a glorious weekend on the shores of the Danube bring back nostalgic memories of that transient interlude when Kyra was with us. Her warmth and charm made both Emilia and Oti-Papa forget their aches and pains and their many problems. And I had a wonderful companion until long distance telephone calls took up more and more of Kyra's time between rehearsals. It became amply clear that someone very close to Kyra's heart was at the other end of the line. Once in a while, Oti-Papa would shake his head anxiously while he muttered that telephone calls between Paris and Budapest were not the cheapest means of communication, but 'who could convince Cupid that...'

Even with Kyra's words to the young journalist still ringing in my ears, I found myself addressing the following invitation:

Emilia Márkus P. has the pleasure to announce that her granddaughter Kyra Nijinsky and Igor Markevitch will unite in holy wedlock on the 24th April 1936 at 12.30 in the Coronation Church, Budapest.

The sudden preparations for Kyra's wedding turned our lives upside down. It became widely publicised overnight...a big event...a wedding out of the ordinary. The elder daughter of the great Nijinsky to be joined in matrimony with a promising Russian composer, whose career was said to have been launched by Diaghilev. I later found out he had been Sergei Pavlovitch's last protégé.... The cynics might have shrugged their shoulders and exclaimed: 'Like mother like daughter'.

Romola cabled that she would attend the ceremony. We had not seen each other since her brief visit two years previously. I wish I could recall details of our encounter but I draw a blank. She must have been her usual poised, arrogant self. Used to being the centre of attention, she was temporarily upstaged by Kyra. Whatever thoughts she harboured about her new son-in-law, she kept to herself. His connection with Sergei Pavlovitch must have aroused long faded memories. The mother-daughter relationship between Romola and myself had even at the best of times been precariously unhealthy. Unwittingly, perhaps I did not know how to handle the situation after having read her biography. To me, a susceptible young girl, it had had all the overtones of a beautiful fairy story...a tale of romantic love. But once the initial euphoria had died down, I perceived the glaring omissions, the darker sides. 'He smiles only when he sees Kyra.' That short sentence in the Epilogue had begun to act like a poison in my mind. Not with a single word was I, Tamara, mentioned. Always awkward and ill at ease with her, I was too cowardly to face her and to ask her outright: *Why?* And she departed almost immediately after the wedding.

The Coronation Church was built in Gothic style during the early centuries and was commonly known as Mátyás Church (Matthias), named after Hungary's most influential and cultured Renaissance king. The wedding took place with great pomp and circumstance. The bride wore a striking and unusual wedding outfit, a gown made of thick, ivory taffeta, fragrant ivory-coloured gardenias in her hair, and a red velvet cape flung over her shoulders. Emilia excelled as usual in her role as hostess. The wedding luncheon was held in the vast dining-room of the Villa. The caterers came from the finest hotel in Budapest, whose cuisine was world-renowned. Igor had invited a friend from abroad to be his best man and Kyra's witness was none other than Tamara Karsavina, once Waslaw's favourite partner, now married to an English diplomat who was assigned as Ambassador to Hungary.

Igor had to depart the following day due to previous concert commitments and Kyra was left to face the opening night of her ballet without her husband. Not long afterwards she left for Switzerland where the couple settled down temporarily. The pure air there was beneficial to her health. Snippets of information to reach us revealed that they appeared to be very happy. Igor had had a most successful concert in Paris and Kyra had resolved to stop dancing for a year or two in order to enjoy marital bliss despite newspaper gossip that she was to make her American début in 1937 in a series of concert programmes with which she would tour the country. It was hinted her partner was to be Grant Mouradoff.

1936 was an eventful year in other respects as well. It was then Romola heard through the Poetzl Clinic that a young Austrian doctor, Manfred Sakel, had discovered an insulin shock treatment which yielded positive results in curing schizophrenia. Whatever else she was involved in, she never ceased her relentless search for new treatment that might bring back her Watza. Already in 1927, she had been in touch with Professor Poetzl who had told her to approach them again when certain experiments had been successfully tested. Romola hurriedly departed from the States for Kreuzlingen, where she consulted Dr Sakel together with three eminent Swiss physicians. The path ahead was to be a hard struggle. It was to take two years to wring the consent out of Waslaw's guardian and the medical staff at the sanatorium to commence treatment. Old friends of Waslaw's were wholly opposed to it, claiming it would be too cruel to awaken him from his dreams at this late stage, particularly as there was no hope he would be able to dance again. But, Romola persevered. In August, 1938 the experiment started.

In 1936, too, Romola's literary agent succeeded in finding a publisher for Waslaw's *Diary*; Jonathan Cape, London. The three copy books, in which he had exposed his soul in laborious scribbling during those fateful months in Villa Guardamunt, were translated from Russian into English. Some 30,000 words were expurgated from the original version by Romola because his writing also revealed the tortuous, maniacal fantasies that infested his brilliant mind when he lost all control over it. She had no wish that the outside world should be given access to the 'long erotic passages, poems, including one on defecation, explicit sexual references and obsessive repetition'. The latter quote is derived from an article in the *Daily Telegraph* of July 25th, 1979 when, after Romola's death, the original copy books were sold at Sotheby's for £45,000. Anton

Dolin, together with John Gilpin, placed a bid on behalf of all those dancers who feared Waslaw Nijinsky's memory would be besmirched. They failed in outbidding an Oxford book dealer, who was acting on behalf of a customer who wished to remain anonymous.

Experts had authenticated that the copybooks on view were in Waslaw's handwriting. The first two were written in ink in his familiar bold handwriting which deteriorated noticeably later, became cramped in style and almost illegible; perhaps by then he no longer possessed a pen but wrote with a very blunt pencil.

The royalties from the revised *Diary*, and the sale of foreign rights that followed, provided Romola yet again with much-needed funds to carry on.

Whatever is contained in the original copy books, it is certain there is nothing that can ever tarnish the name of my father, Waslaw Nijinsky. He has played his intrinsic part in ballet history which will survive until the last curtain call comes down on that form of art.

A letter written on the 14th of July, 1936 to Emilia reflects Romola's mood at the time. The contents are similar to so many other letters written during those years. She was then back in London.

'I have to scout around a great deal with regard to the movie (the film mentioned in newspaper articles). *Korda is unable to pay, hence he has decided to postpone the film until 1937. I cannot wait that long. Ah well, I have enough problems to cope with. I am writing day and night to provide for the everyday needs. There is so much I have to squeeze out of my brain, that soon it will become totally dull and vacant. My only consolation is that Dostoievski and Balzac had to struggle likewise and that it is only the mediocre writers who earn the money. Unfortunately, I have had to reprimand Tessa severely and since then she has not written to me. Wishing you the best from my heart, I embrace all of you...Romola.'*

Back in Budapest, I plodded on with my studies with the goal in sight to receive my diploma in the French language and then to enrol in the *Magyar Királyi Szinmüvészeti Föiskola* (The Academy of Dramatic Arts).

Slowly but surely, I was absorbed into the adult community, and I was thrilled when the first invitation arrived to attend the Hubay Concert, the highlight of the social season for the 'older generation'. Jenö de Hubay, known also as Eugen Huber, famous violinist and composer, and his wife, a countess by birth, would hold four to five chamber music recitals at their home during the winter season – early on a Sunday afternoon. The guest list would have been carefully selected from aristocrats, artists and diplomats. They rotated their guests to ensure that everyone they wished to invite would be able to come at least twice during the winter. Their small, elegant, two-storied palace faced the Danube on the right bank of the river. The guests were inevitably greeted by the Countess at the top of the staircase which led to a large salon. From there they were ushered into the rectangular-shaped concert hall. Heavy, gilded baroque chairs awaited the guests. After the concert, they had tea and sandwiches in two adjoining drawing-rooms. The 'distinguished patron' of the concert would have indicated in advance who should be granted the honour of having tea with him. This honour usually befell Emilia or, on those occasions when the Archduchess Augusta (Emperor Franz Josef's younger sister) was the patron, Oti-Papa would have this honour bestowed upon him as he was one of her favourites.

The social life was further enhanced by the frequent visits of the Prince of Wales who later became Edward VIII and subsequently abdicated to marry Mrs Simpson. He revelled in the hospitality of Budapest and boosted the liquor industry by favouring the Hungarian Barack Pálinka (apricot brandy).

It was at about this time a young man entered my life; Michael, whom I rechristened my Cyrano. We met at a tea-party. It was on his shoulders I was to cry out my pain and seek comfort in tragic hours. He was to prove his love and devotion throughout the years, being the most sincere and faithful friend I have ever had. Michael studied philosophy but was drawn to the theatre and attended practically every performance Emilia Márkus acted in. He remained a bachelor and to this very day we are still in touch.

In January, 1937, a cable arrived from Romola announcing the birth of Kyra and Igor's first, and as it turned out, only child, a blond boy who was christened Vaslav. The happy tidings gave us the impetus to visit the young family in Switzerland during the summer holiday. It also provided a golden opportunity to visit Tatakaboy. The plans for the journey were made weeks ahead.

At long last, the big day arrived. The shopping and packing were completed, the servants had been given last minute orders to rotate their own holidays so that the house would never be unattended. The trip had to be made as comfortable as possible – after all, Emilia was approaching eighty and Oti-Papa was recovering from a recent operation in addition to suffering from a weak heart and diabetes. We spent one night at the Hotel Vier Jahreszeiten in Munich, and then continued at a slow pace to Corsier-sur-Vevey, where Kyra lived. The reunion was a happy one for all of us. My little nephew was showered with the usual gasps of admiration all babies patiently have to endure and I could not get over my astonishment at seeing my artistic sister who previously had never been exposed to domestic life, so skilfully portraying the rôle of the perfect mother.

After a few relaxing and exhilarating days there, we prepared for the next stage of our journey. Our destination was Kreuzlingen, and the sanatorium. Emilia had felt that the family reunion would not be complete without Tessa and therefore, with a generous gesture so typical of her, she had dipped into her purse and sent a ticket to Paris. Not having seen me since I was four, Aunt Tessa did not at first recognise me when she arrived. We were booked at a conveniently located hotel. By pre-arrangement we were all to meet Romola that evening at the sanatorium where we would dine together. Not until the following morning were we to be taken to meet Waslaw. My heart beat faster as we drove through the large well-kept park. I was overcome by mixed emotions. My hands felt clammy and I was unable to control my trembling. When last I had seen Tatakaboy, I had been a mere child, who looked upon him as a solid, comforting father figure. Now I was grown up and through my mother's book I had been introduced to a superhuman being, transcendent to all others in the realm of ballet. What was my reaction to be on this first encounter after so many years?

Dinner was a convivial affair. Throughout most of the meal I was engaged in a merry conversation with my aunt Tessica, making up for lost time. I found her very endearing and girlish, quite different from the picture I had built up in my mind when her letters used to arrive and cause such consternation. One of the patients, a Spanish count, had been invited to join our table. By eavesdropping, I gathered he had suffered a dreadful shock when four of his brothers had been killed. Coffee was served in a spacious salon and shortly afterwards we retired to our hotel, having received implicit instructions from Romola when and where to meet her the next day.

The following morning, our little group headed for another building in the park. Romola asked us to wait outside. She disappeared through a narrow doorway and after a short interval reappeared with Tatakaboy at her side. He was wearing a grey suit and moved toward us with a measured stride. He looked us over like a general who reviews his troops. Involuntarily, I gasped. Could this rather insignificant, slightly balding individual be the Great Nijinsky, The God of Dance, my famous father? My heart felt leaden and I was overwhelmed with sadness. If only I could have crawled away to some hidden corner and given vent to a flood of tears.

Romola spoke to him, almost imploringly: 'Watza, look, my mother, Oti, Tessa and Tamara have come to visit you.' He turned his head slowly in my direction and furrowed his brow. I had the definite feeling that he was searching hard to place me. I was afraid to utter a sound, afraid to break the spell, should a flicker of recognition begin to stir.

'Watza, Watzuska,' Romola prodded him gently, placing her arm under his. He regarded her somewhat sombrely, then glanced at me, smiling shyly. I stood there immobile, the lump in my throat more painful than ever. Would it not have been the most natural thing in the world to rush up to him, to hug him and smother him with kisses? Surely, he needed to receive expressions of warmth and love. But how could I have risked taking such an unprecedented step in front of my mother. Suddenly, I felt so awkward. The silence was almost unbearable. Could nobody speak...react with some measure of spontaneity to this mute genius standing there before us...our closest kin... Dear sensible, levelheaded Oti-Papa relieved the tension by offering to give Waslaw a drive in the car, an offer that was gratefully accepted. Beaming all over his face, Tatakaboy clambered into the car together with his male nurse and off the four of them went. Incidentally, for the rest of our stay, the car ride became one of the regular daily features and each time they returned, Oti-Papa would ask Waslaw, 'Waslaw, c'était joli?' And he would nod his head vigorously in assent. How I yearned to go with them on those excursions but I never screwed up the courage to ask my mother. It was she who made all the decisions.

Then it happened one day, just before lunch, that my patience was rewarded when Romola linked an arm with Tatakaboy's and urged me to do likewise. We strolled down one of the parkland paths like any normal family. Tatakaboy's steps were light and springy, in perfect rhythm, and I had a problem to keep pace with him. Once or twice I stumbled and he gently squeezed my arm to give me support.

Little by little, I got to know another side to Romola when I observed how she handled Waslaw. It was almost uncanny, the transformation she underwent whenever she was with him. A radiant smile would lighten up her features and she would converse with him in a soft, compassionate voice in French. She was every inch the gentle, devoted and understanding wife. She would take hold of his hand like that of a child, teasingly pulling him up to join her in a walk, kissing his cheek when she had to part from him. And then, the incredible metamorphosis – the moment he was out of sight, the poised, cold, elusive Romola was back. In my opinion, she had one vested interest, to protect him from the outside world, from any more hurt. She was his shield, the Chinese Wall between the Waslaw of her youth and all those who had been the cause of their tragedy – directly or indirectly. In fact, she never allowed any of us to be alone with him, not even in the presence of the male nurse.

Our departure was drawing closer and the prevailing mood become strained and subdued. Even the insouciant Aunt Tessa was smitten. That last afternoon, Tatakaboy was lounging in a lawn chair under a spreading oak tree. Romola and I were seated near to him in white wicker armchairs, with the nurse in attendance a short distance from us. My parents appeared to be sunk in quiet contemplation. I, however, felt restive and wished I could have a few precious moments alone with my father. The seconds were feverishly ticking away and I knew that our departure was imminent. Would I ever see him again? And then, miraculously, the gods in their kindness came to my rescue. An attendant came running, bringing Romola a note on a round silver tray. A long distance call – urgent! Before departing, she magnanimously gave me permission to stay. A most extraordinary gesture on her part.

My misery vanished as if by magic. I smiled timidly at my father. He smiled back and instantly I recognised *my Tatakaboy* from childhood. Impulsively, I raised myself in the chair, ready to dash over to him and embrace him. But my mother's warning that it was essential to remain calm in his presence and never make sudden gestures that might provoke him restrained me. With utmost caution I stood up and made my way to some wild daisies I had noticed in the long grass. From the corner of my eye I could see that he followed every move I made. Almost on tiptoe I stepped forward and offered him my humble bouquet of flowers. He reached out his hand and in my nervousness I clumsily dropped the flowers into the palm of the outstretched hand. Without uttering a sound, he gazed at the daisies, lifted them upward to the sky...like an offering, then sank back in his chair, shut his eyes and pressed the flowers to his heart... I floated on a cloud as I rushed to join the others. I had experienced an instant of sublime happiness and was bursting to share it with the rest of the family.

My exuberance was quickly cooled, however, when I came down to dinner. A frosty, forbidding atmosphere reigned at the table and with the exception of the usual polite phrases common around a dinner table, lips were tightly sealed. Toward the end of the meal, Meme rasped in a harsh voice, 'Look, Mother,' but got no further, observing Emilia's face white with anger. My grandmother clearly indicated that whatever had transpired before my arrival, it was not to be discussed in front of me.

It was Tessa who broke the embarrassing silence by offering to escort me to the cinema. Instead, we ended up in a *konditerei,* where over a cup of hot chocolate, Tessa said that the time had come to bring the matter of the heated dispute out to the light. I sat there, bewildered and painfully aware that I would not like what I was about to hear. Romola had demanded that Emilia relinquish me to her. My aunt's tone was slightly edged with malice as she went on to explain that Romola was a snob. She considered my present environment unsuitable and wished to groom me for a more dazzling future, most likely with the ulterior motive of finding me a rich suitor.

Emilia had reacted violently at what she considered was a slur against her. She accused Romola of abandoning Kyra to the four winds whereas I had a secure home in Budapest, a sound education, and a future with the National Theatre.

Poor Tessa carried on in a tedious monologue on how badly *she* had been treated by Emilia, how she had always been rebuffed in her love and attentiveness toward Emilia and how the latter now got her just desserts for having favoured Romola. I barely bestowed my attention on her. There was one question to which I wanted a reply. Why had Romola despatched me to Budapest in the first place? Rather evasively, Tessa answered it had had to do with financial matters. Possibly, other factors had played a part as well. She cautioned me to forget the whole matter, that it most probably was another of Romola's whims. Of one thing I was certain. I would never leave my grandmother. I belonged to her. It was she I loved, her warmth and protection I needed. Romola did not pursue her claim on me. Emilia never referred to the painful occurrence.

I feel I have described the end of the Kreuzlingen intermezzo rather inadequately, but it was all a confused muddle at the time. And it left me feeling drained that my natural mother harboured such a strong ambivalence toward me. She drifted out of our lives after that only to reappear during World War II.

In 1937, the Nijinsky Foundation was formed, thanks to the efforts of Tamara Karsavina, Anton Dolin and other devoted friends. Most certainly, Romola would have collaborated with them. A Nijinsky Matinée was held at His Majesty's Theatre in London on Friday, the 28th of May at 3pm. The Chairman was Lady Juliet Duff and the Deputy-Chairman, Lady Diana Cooper.

The statement of objects of the Foundation read as follows:

Vaslav Nijinsky, to whose inspiration and marvellous power the modern ballet owes so much of its success, has suffered for many years from mental trouble; and though extremely sensitive and susceptible to his surroundings, is quite unable to look after himself or earn any money. He is at present living in a Swiss nursing home, in a kind of mental twilight, with very little hope of recovery. All his savings have long ago been exhausted, and though his wife, by her devoted efforts, has hitherto succeeded in supporting him, it is impossible for her to continue to provide for him without considerable help.

The object of the Nijinsky Matinée is to assist in raising a sufficient fund to provide for the proper care of Vaslav Nijinsky during his life, and subject to this, to give assistance to any other artists of the ballet who by reasons of sickness or similar misfortune may be in need of help.

All money collected will be paid into a trust fund, and administered by the committee of the Nijinsky Foundation, of which Madame Karsavina is Chairman and Sir Edgar Bonham-Carter, K.C.M.G., and Sir John Sykes, K.C.B., are the Trustees.

The artists are generously giving their services, and the necessary expenses of printing, etc., have already been contributed by Nijinsky's friends so that all money raised by the sale of tickets will go directly to Nijinsky's benefit.

The list of patrons and donors added up to some two hundred names and included much of the British nobility and aristocracy. The performers ranked among the most famous of our era. After the overture, three psalms were sung by the Russian Choir; Alicia Markova and Frederick Ashton danced *Foyer de Danse*, choreographed by Ashton for Marie Rambert; Mary Honor and Harold Turner, the *Casse Noisette pas de deux;* Markova and Serge Lifar, *The Blue Bird pas de deux* from *The Sleeping Beauty*. A poem, written especially for the occasion by Christopher Hassall, was spoken by John Gielgud.

> *'I sing the Ballet, and I sing the man,*
> *The Phantom and the Faun, who first began,*
> *Creator and interpreter, to weld*
> *Into one art, whereat he so excelled,*
> *Traditions mixed and stray, so that a new*
> *Pre-eminently graceful science grew.*
> *A child of earth, yet one that seemed to be*
> *The true and only wingèd Mercury...*
> *At once defying Gravity and Time.*
> *His mind now, like his urgent body then,*
> *Has flown beyond our ordinary ken,*
> *Leaving the great foundation that he laid*
> *In others' charge, dependent on your aid.'*

> From Christopher Hassall's
> *Poem in Aid of the*
> *Nijinsky Foundation.*

The overture after the interval was appropriately Schumann's *Carnaval;* Lifar danced *L'Après-midi d'un Faune;* Lydia Sokolova her own choreographic work *Tarentella*. Margot Fonteyn and Robert Helpmann danced a *pas de deux* from the *Ballet Pomona* choreographed by Ashton; Markova and Anton Dolin a *pas de deux* from *Aurora's Wedding*. It is impossible to list everybody who contributed to make that afternoon memorable but the voice of Giovanni Martinelli who sang arias from *Turandot* and *Pagliacci* must surely not be omitted. Tamara Karsavina ended the programme with a speech about Waslaw Nijinsky.

CHAPTER 9

ROMOLA DISOWNS HER DAUGHTER

I attended classes at the Royal Academy of Dramatic Arts with mixed emotions. I found it hard to endure the sarcasm and almost sadistic humiliation heaped upon me by one of the professors. It seemed he held it against me that I was related to a celebrated actress. It was then I met Miklós Szakáts, a fellow student. He was the one person who adopted a protective attitude toward me, who showed compassion and who bolstered my shattered image.

Miklós was immensely charming, with blonde, handsome features and a velvety, reassuring voice. His manners were impeccable. I learned something of his background; that his ancestors had belonged to the aristocracy in Transylvania, how they had owned not only a castle but vast acres of land which they lost during the First World War. He was one of three brothers. His older brother had entered the priesthood, the other the Army. His own driving ambition was to become an actor.

For two whole years our friendship consisted of him accompanying me to the tramcar or dropping in to the chapel which was part of Rokus, a very old hospital located a few yards from the Academy. Our short walks grew longer and longer, until one day he uttered the words 'I love you'. But he made no attempt to kiss me. I flew into ecstacy. Beautiful red roses arrived for my birthday and other occasions. It was impossible for me to hide my feelings and it was not long before my colleagues found out and made rather crude jokes about the 'saintly lovers'.

Emilia must have noticed the floral tributes but tactfully refrained from asking who the donor was. Brimming with youthful exuberance I itched to introduce him to her, certain that she would approve of him wholeheartedly; his circumstances unimpeachable, his career in the same sphere. So I invited him home to a birthday party I was giving. To my horror and disbelief, Emilia received him graciously enough but a slight frost lingered in the air and when later I revealed my depth of feeling for Miklós, my otherwise so supportive grandmother left me in no doubt but that my erstwhile suitor was *persona non grata*. I was shattered and my joy evaporated. I had to resort to subterfuges to keep my trysts with the man I loved.

Miklós graduated from the Academy with the highest honours, indeed, he was so talented he was invited to become a fully fledged member of the National Theatre of Kolozsvár. Normally, gifted graduates first had to have a year at the National Theatre on a scholarship. Naïvely, I, too, applied for a transfer. But Emilia's influence was still far-reaching. My endeavour failed and for nine unbearable months I was separated from Miklós, carrying on instead in Budapest where, as a senior Academy student, I was given small parts at the National Theatre.

Emilia saw to it that my social programme became more and more crammed, in other words a cunning strategy to keep me so occupied that I hopefully would forget Miklós. Dear Oti-Papa did his utmost to maintain a dextrous balance between Emilia and myself with regard to the man of my choice. I was too fainthearted to have it out with my grandmother, and Oti's only comment was that theatre and marriage were not a compatible combination. What did puzzle me was that no matter to whom else I turned, relatives, friends or colleagues, they all broadly hinted that Miklós was not the right match for me. If Emilia was behind any rumours, she could not have attempted a more undiplomatic solution to the problem.

Wrapped up in my own private miseries, I had paid scant attention to the sound of war drums beating a more and more frenzied alarm as Germany began its ominous march through Europe. Inevitably, in Hungary, too, young men of military age were being drafted. The uniform became a common sight. Hitler's *Blitzkrieg* was accelerating.... As the days were torn off the almanac, Oti-Papa suddenly aged. It was no longer possible to tell that he was eleven years younger than Emilia. His eyes were sad, his face extremely pallid and his hands shook perceptibly. It was as though demons from an outer source had taken a strong grip on him. I noticed that the light in my grandparents' bedroom was on far into the small hours of the morning.

In Paris, Aunt Tessa's financial plight was ruinous. She again feared imprisonment because of mounting debts. As it was well-nigh impossible to send her money, Emilia felt prompted to write to her to come home. So she did. Tessa, fifty-seven, a little on the plump side, still smiling in spite of everything, arrived with her adorable Dzinn, a wire-haired fox-terrier, under her arm. It did not take her long to fit into our lifestyle.

271

Letters arrived sporadically from Romola. She wrote sanguinely and at great length how much better Waslaw was, practically cured, that they went to the theatre like in the old days, and that they now and again visited their grandson Vaslav. The only disturbing news was that Kyra's marriage was headed for failure. The two temperamental artists were unable to live together in harmony.

We knew that Waslaw had undergone a gruelling succession of insulin shock treatments in 1938. Dr Sakel had personally given the treatment in Kreuzlingen. According to medical opinion, the shock in itself triggered off an epileptic fit, which in turn could cure schizophrenia. Romola said afterwards, 'I suffered indescribable anguish. I wondered whether I could endure the torment. But seemingly, he stood the treatment well, and when he recovered consciousness he would answer quite clearly and logically questions put before him.' She found great comfort when Professor Bleuler came to visit and gave her the ray of hope. According to her, he had said, '...now I believe you will be rewarded. He will once more become himself.' As the world knows, his prophecy never came about. Friends and former colleagues of Waslaw were pessimistic from the start. The patient was fifty years old, his physique not too good, taking into consideration that he was overweight and had already suffered two heart attacks. Still, the letters from Romola at this juncture ended on a triumphant note. 'Vaslav is beginning to behave quite normally...' She refused to accept defeat, whatever her reason: inextinguishable love, guilt or compassion.

When Dr Sakel departed for the United States,it was arranged that the treatment should continue at the State Asylum in Münsingen, Canton Berne. It was said that Waslaw received a record number of 270 shocks.

In his book, *Nijinsky,* Richard Buckle has written that Serge Lifar came to visit Waslaw and Romola in June 1939 and that he had found 'Vaslav fitter, more supple and more sociable'. Lifar was to write a vivid description of the occasion, implying that Waslaw had regained the use of speech. '...When we entered his room, Nijinsky was talking to himself...in a language all his own, quite unintelligible to others – a mixture of the most unexpected combinations of Russian, French and Italian words...'

Buckle also mentions another Gala performance from which the Nijinsky Foundation benefited by 35,000 francs. I have found no reference to this Gala among Romola's papers. Again, famous artists from all over the world had participated: Dolin, Lifar, Vera Menchinova, Ram Gopal, among others.

Upon the advice of her son-in-law, Igor Markevitch, Romola decided to rehabilitate Waslaw in a more intimate atmosphere, a move which was endorsed by the doctor. Temporarily, she found a haven, a hotel in Adelboden, a small mountain resort in the Bernese Alps. It seemed that my parents had settled down to a relatively problem-free, normal routine. Then, one disruption after the other manifested itself. Waslaw's regular attendant was mobilised. Romola almost ferociously clung to the belief that all she required now was a companion for Waslaw to relieve her from the bondage of care whenever she had to leave the premises. A rapid succession of nurses came and departed. Waslaw frightened them away with his odd behaviour. Romola categorically denied at that point he was dangerous, simply 'mischievous', wanting to 'be alone with me and to be once more the boss in his own home.'

Against blunt warnings from Dr Müller in Münsingen, with whom she was in constant communication, Romola took on the heavy responsibility of caring for Waslaw entirely on her own. But a couple of near-catastrophic incidents brought her rudely back to reality. On one occasion during a walking tour Waslaw gave her a powerful thrust with his arms so that she toppled down a slope. Minutes before, they had been walking on the edge of a precipice and then the outcome would have been fatal. On another occasion he started to throw the furniture at her. She still persevered, however, and made plans for them to go to the United States. Hadn't he years previously exclaimed he wished to return to 'America'?

Christmas arrived and with the holiday, Kyra with her little boy, Funtyiki, as he was affectionately called.

Rumours began to seep into the world press that Waslaw Nijinsky was so improved that his comeback to the stage was imminent. Romola even claimed that an impresario had sent an offer for Waslaw to appear in New York but she prudently declined. the time was not yet right.

She fought a valiant battle to gain entry to the States. Dr Sakel was still there and Romola wanted him to look after Waslaw once more. Oddly enough, she acquired permission from the State Department in Washington but when it came to the crux, the Consul in Berne refused to recognise Waslaw's Nansen passport. My father was stateless. No amount of pleading altered the Consul's refusal and Romola lost the battle. The Swiss authorities were harassing her to reveal financial security if she and Waslaw were to stay on there. Her purse was empty. The frontiers were closing around them, they were hemmed in on all sides.

Acting on the counsel of old and trusted friends, Romola decided to write to Emilia to ask for sanctuary there. Hungary was, after all, her own country, and still neutral. Sadly, none of the household in the Villa were too enthusiastic about the forthcoming visit. Images of the past – the lengthy traumatic interlude during World War I – once more stirred from the murky corners. Emilia's age, her high blood pressure and nervous condition, coupled with the fact that she and Romola had had violent disagreements, provided no inducement to an amicable reunion. Oti-Papa, with his diabetes and heart condition, was not fit either to cope with the strain of the impending events. Too, the grave political situation was taking its toll on his psyche – he was, after all, of Jewish origin. And, once more, another weighty factor reared its ugly head – the financial one – because gone was the flow of plenty from yesteryears and all that remained was a franchise as the main source of income together with Grandmother and Oti-Papa's pensions. Certainly not sufficient for a swelling household. We were four in number excluding the maid and the cook.

Emilia owned a small but quaint two-storey house tucked among the old palaces in a district called Vár. Narrow, curving cobblestone streets led to that historic quarter situated on a hill on the right bank of the Danube. At first, when it was known that Romola and Waslaw were definitely coming, Emilia offered them the use of this house, quite large enough to accommodate them. Tessa and I would be willing to take turns to help them. But it appears that most plans are made to be rejected, as in this case. For reasons best known to herself, Romola refused and thus the 'tower' on the top floor was once more refurbished.

Page after page in my diary bears witness to the trials and tribulations after their arrival, July 1940. Thus, with the exception of Kyra, the family was together once more, in body if not in spirit. I had steeled myself to the shock of seeing Tatakaboy again since that magical moment three years earlier in Kreuzlingen. Yet to all outward appearances he had changed little. Balder, perhaps, which aged him somewhat, but otherwise he seemed to be physically fit.

No matter how hard I tried, I found it impossible to believe that he was 'practically cured'. To me his gaze was just as it had been in the past; seeing without being present. His step was still sprightly and his behaviour was extremely calm and docile, more that of an obedient, repressed child, particularly in the presence of Romola. He obeyed her, but it was a loving obedience as though he was saying 'It is so good that someone takes care of me. I have no worries...'

The news of Romola's homecoming with her husband spread like wildfire and the telephone at Hidegkuti ur 51/a rang incessantly. The press arrived equipped with cameras and clamoured for interviews. One journalist wrote:

'Waslaw Nijinsky has come to rest. His wonderful, artistic career, unequalled in the history of dance, which began in the Russian Ballet, continued throughout every great city of the world, and which culminated in the *Spectre de la Rose* and in *L'Après – midi d'un Faune*, was cut short because of a serious, nervous breakdown. It seems it is a law of nature that during our lifetime we have to pay for being a genius.... And for many years now Nijinsky has been paying his penance. Perhaps the room in the Swiss sanatorium or the silent pine trees can tell the real story because the artist either cannot or will not recall his meteoric past. He does not utter a single word to anybody. If he is asked something, he does not appear to hear, if he is told something, he does not appear to be interested. With his deep eyes, he just stares, locked within himself.... Maybe he is searching...for the artist, the ideas, the rhythm, the dance? Will he ever find it?'

The interviewer was talking to Emilia and Romola on the balcony. When questioned, Romola willingly answered but was unable to hide her sadness when she admitted even she could only get her husband to speak a word or two. She said his best friends were the valley and the trees, he could watch them for hours. 'And here in Budapest?' Patiently, Romola went on to explain he had already chosen two silent friends, Sio and Ficko, her mother's dogs. It was only their companionship he sought on his daily stroll in the garden.

The article finished, 'Suddenly, the door opens. Waslaw Nijinsky comes across the terrace, down to the garden. He does not notice anybody, no sound passes his lips, just walks to and fro like a child whose first steps augur it will be able to walk the difficult journey through life.'

Once the novelty of the new occupants in the Villa had died down, the days slipped back into well-worn grooves. My parents withdrew to their old habitation in the Tower. Thankfully, they partook most of their meals there. I was so inhibited by the stories I had been fuelled with of their previous stay, I dared not approach that part of the house of my own volition.

Waslaw did not always feel inclined to get up, but whenever he did so, Romola would shave him, select his clothes with utmost care and then the two would go out, disappear, arm in arm, down the wide lane of chestnut trees for their habitual walks. In the stillness of the afternoon they would usually come down and sit in the Gobelin Salon. It made an idyllic picture; Emilia engrossed in her favourite game of solitaire, Oti-Papa and Romola absorbed in the newspapers and Tatakaboy reclining in one of the comfortable, deep armchairs. On the whole he was very still, except for the rather irritating habit of once in a while picking his thumb until a tiny trickle of blood appeared. He never engaged in a conversation, but sometimes he would mumble a few incoherent words under his breath.

How uncanny it all was somehow – the stage was set for yet another act in a drama that had had its opening night many years previously, when Tatakaboy had lived in the Villa with Romola and their first-born daughter. Now, he was once more under its roof, this time with his younger daughter. Instinctively, I sensed that he remembered the Villa. Was it helpful to him to look back upon the past or would it prove to be far too painful?

For a short space in time peace reigned, then the storm broke loose. Almost immediately upon their arrival Romola had admonished us not to make sudden movements or any loud noise in Waslaw's presence. In other words, do nothing that could possibly provoke fear in him.

Emilia was not adept at walking on eggshells in her own house. Her nature was outgoing and explosive with a penchant for melodrama. In a sense, Romola laid down the rules and Emilia found this a bitter pill to swallow. She obdurately refused to ignore Waslaw. One day, for example, she strode into the salon, casually carrying a basket laden with fruit. In her strong, theatrical voice, she cried out, 'Look, my children, what fine fruit. Do have some,' and, stepping over to Waslaw, swung the basket in front of him. At this 'cue' he jumped up, flapping his arms ecstatically, and accidentally knocked the basket out of the bewildered Emilia's arms. A scene erupted, with Emilia rebuking Waslaw in no uncertain terms for what he had done. I hurriedly went down on my knees to retrieve what I could of the pears and apples rolling about helter-skelter.

Romola heaved a barely audible sigh and in a tone tinged with reproach reminded Emilia of her warning. She grasped Waslaw's arm and in a firm voice said, 'Come, Watza, let us go upstairs and take a nap.' Sheepishly, like a child caught doing something wrong, he climbed the steps to the Tower, an expression of extreme sadness registered on his face.

The tension in the Villa mounted with every passing incident. Tatakaboy's volatile moods were wholly unpredictable; he could change within minutes from a soft, gentle personality to an antagonistic and violent being. His strength was then such that he once broke Emilia's favourite Renaissance rocker, snapping it into pieces like flimsy kindlewood. At other times he would pick up sundry large items and with jerky movements throw them off the upper terrace.

The culmination to a strained relationship between my mother and myself, which had been building up for some time, came to a head toward the end of an otherwise uneventful day. It was the twilight hour, and we were as usual gathered in the salon. The lights had as yet not been turned on. As usual, Emilia was absorbed in her card game and Waslaw was slumped in an armchair, listening with rapt attention to a broadcast of classical music. Suddenly, he got up and with light steps moved in her direction. So engrossed was she, she was unaware of him until he leaned over the table, resting his palms on top of it. She looked up and involuntarily emitted a faint scream upon which he bent closer, giggling impishly. Emilia froze to her chair as he with one sweeping gesture flung the cards on the floor, still chuckling and with a complacent look on his face. Emilia could take no more. Her long-suffering forbearance snapped and she asked Oskar to accompany her to her room.

It had all happened so quickly that neither Romola nor I had had a chance to react. Tatakaboy had by now retaken his former position in a chair. But I expressed deep concern over my grandmother, being all too familiar with her high blood pressure and the effects of any undue excitement. Just as I stood poised in the doorway, prepared to join her and Oti-Papa, Romola stopped me. I was totally unprepared for the onslaught that followed.

In an acrid tone she accused me of rushing off to my 'dear one', and of forgetting or wishing to ignore the fact that my place was with my parents. When the torrent stopped I stammered that poor Emilia needed her cold compresses; that I merely wanted to help her as I had always done, and that I had no desire to hurt anyone, least of all show nonchalance toward my parents. Through my tears I could see Tatakaboy. He gazed quizzically at us, sensing from Romola's strident voice that something was amiss. It was all too dreadful. My mother shrugged her shoulders and through clenched teeth ordered me to go; she would not prevent me performing my duties.

Sleep did not come easily that night as I fretfully tossed in my bed, churning the episode over and over in my mind. I could not fathom what was alienating my mother from me. How could I stop caring for my grandmother, who after all had replaced Romola as my mother when I was a small child? Romola had never lavished any maternal love upon me, not even in her irregular sketchily written correspondence devoid of any soft, emotional undertones of caring about me. And now, it seemed, she was trying to push me further away. What horrible wrong had I unwittingly done her?

The ensuing weeks passed without any major eruptions. I tried to organise my days so that I would not have to face Romola alone. She, in turn, went about her business as if nothing had happened. My composure returned as I persuaded myself that the issue was now buried and forgotten.

More practical matters pertaining to the household cropped up demanding urgent attention. Eszter, the cook, advanced in years, had trouble with her legs and complained it was too much for her to prepare meals for so many people with dissimilar tastes. One after the other, the locally hired maids left, finding various lame excuses for their departure. The naked truth was they were terrified of 'the gentleman in the Tower'. Certainly, I had no fear of Tatakaboy even though his behavioural norm since coming to live with us had proved conclusively that he was far from 'practically cured', as we had been led to believe. In all fairness, I must admit there was a positive side; he had become more approachable living within a family. On rare occasions, I would take him by the hand and lead him out into the garden to sit in the white wicker chair. I would sink down on the lawn beside him. We never communicated verbally with each other. I simply relished being in his presence because there he always radiated serenity and love. Romola never failed to be in the proximity. Engaged in her writing, she would glance up now and then with a vigilant eye.

By now, I was the proud possessor of a driver's licence. I loved driving and Romola happily accepted my invitations to take her and Tatakaboy up to the hills that surround Budapest. Oddly enough, I was never nervous to have my father seated just behind me even though I was acutely aware that the slightest disturbance from the outside world might bring on one of his attacks.

The day arrived when Romola had to give in and employ a male nurse for Waslaw. It was the same nurse, incidentally, who was to make a statement in October 1940 in connection with Waslaw's violent outbursts; how he had hit a child and how, when Romola intervened, he had tried to inflict grievous bodily harm on her. The stifling climate in the Villa was unhealthy for all of us. The fear of traumatic scenes recurring at a least expected moment took its toll on Emilia. Her blood pressure rose precariously high. To appease her Molly, she continued, however, to make sacrifices. Her few friends, who were still alive and who normally gave her much pleasure by their visits, stayed away. The meagre household budget was stretched to the limit to provide for the additional three mouths to feed. Romola herself must have felt the shackles that bound her to Waslaw's side night and day well nigh intolerable, although to her credit it must be said that never did a word of complaint pass her lips. She paid frequent visits to the American Consulate in the vain hope of arranging visas to the United States before it was too late.

It is still distressing to recall the black day that my mother summoned me to the Tower; she had something of the utmost importance to impart to me and insisted I come up without first paying my respects to my grandmother. Her steely, blue-grey eyes glittered angrily.

'Listen, my dear daughter, after all you *are* my daughter. It is about time you think of your own parents.' She did not even ask me to sit down but grimly let me stand there like a culprit on trial before a judge. The gist of what she had to say was that she had not returned to Budapest out of longing for the Villa, nor the company in it. She found the pervading mood decidedly bad for my father, who, ill though he was, sensed the animosity with which he was treated. I Tamara, Emilia and Oskar were constantly whispering behind his back... throughout this chastening monologue, she lit one cigarette after the other, flicking each match to the floor with her thin, nervous fingers.

Conscious of a noise downstairs, I turned my head slightly and she pounced on that innocent gesture, accusing me of not wishing to listen; that she might as well talk to a blank wall; I was solely concerned about Emilia's nerves, but that she, too, had nerves, that she might suffer a heart attack at any moment. She grasped my hand and forced it to her breast to feel the beating of her heart. She rounded off her tirade by coming to the point. I was to ask Oskar for 500 pengö which she required without delay. I felt physically ill, lost for words, then stammered I knew such a sum was not available. After debating to myself whether to ignore Romola's request or to tell Oti-Papa, my instant reaction was the latter course of action. What a preposterous idea. Between them, Emilia and Oskar had less than 1000 pengö a month in pension. How could they possibly spare 500 pengö? Inescapably, a bitter feud ensued, when I capitulated and referred the delicate issue to my grandparents.

As funds shrivelled, Emilia was faced with the cruel prospect of putting up some of the Pulszky antiques and furniture to auction. Oskar convinced her it was her only option if she were to help Romola. It was with a heavy heart she agreed to part with cherished possessions from the past. The worst was yet to come. A short time after the announcement that Emilia Márkus was to auction belongings dating back to her marriage to Charles de Pulszky, an official document arrived stating that she and Oskar were being sued by her two daughters, Romola and Tessa. They claimed the legal right to everything left by their father. After Charles' death the Pulszky Estate had been placed in trust for his two daughters; Romola had received her share while not yet of age, when she embarked in pursuit of her 'God of Dance'; Tessa had squandered hers many years ago. And yet Romola had had the audacity to accuse Oskar of having used part of their inheritance to build the Villa in 1912. Tessa, who had kept a discreet profile in the shadows after Waslaw's appearance in our midst, capriciously shifted her loyalty from mother to sister to suit her own needs. Unquestionably, she loved Emilia dearly but she had lived too long on the borderline to poverty to have many scruples left. To be fair, however, she did withdraw her claim. On another matter, I have no recollection of her actively giving a hand toward Waslaw's well-being during those trying days. Perhaps that, too, stemmed from her unpleasant years in Paris when Romola left her in charge of Waslaw. She was noticeably absent whenever a storm broke out within the confines of the Villa's walls. I never pried as to where and how she spent her idle hours.

To aggravate the already noxious aura of the 'happy family' the subject of my adoption cropped up. When I had received a scholarship to the National Theatre, I would only be eligible for membership if I were a Hungarian citizen. Acting upon advice, Emilia took the only course open to safeguard my future. She legally adopted me. As her daughter, I automatically became a Hungarian citizen and I was entitled to use the name Tamara Nijinsky Márkus. Absurdly enough, it also made me my mother's 'sister'. To say she was not amused was an understatement. Once more, I was summoned to her room, once more she lashed out savagely against me.

'Tamara, I do not want you to use the name Nijinsky any more. I do not wish to discuss the matter further.' I recoiled, my cheeks burning as though she had struck me with a whip. She turned her back on me and I rushed out to the refuge of my own bedroom. Was it wounded pride or jealousy that prompted this terrible onslaught on me? I could not bear to involve my grandmother in yet another stormy quarrel, and therefore kept this latest outburst from her. I felt wretched and sick at heart. What did Romola have against me? Tessa's cryptic answers to some of my questions that evening at the *konditorei* sprang to mind and it brought home to me yet again that I had been ignored in my mother's biography. I needed to have no fear that the subject would be dropped and forgotten. It resurged months later to darken my life for years onward.

The circumstances in Hungary overshadowed all personal conflicts. There were several factions, each vying for supremacy. The official Government was under compulsion to fight against Germany's enemies, a fact seized on by a group which blindly promoted Germany's cause, ever ready to sell our country to the Germans. Then there were those who were totally indoctrinated by Soviet ideology, working underground. A small handful of Hungarians remained who had one goal, one dream and one wish: a neutral, independent Hungary.

Emilia came face to face with the political tidal wave engulfing the country the day she received an official visitor who tried to press her to lease the Villa to a high-ranking German military official for an indefinite period of time. As a bait, she was offered a most rewarding pecuniary settlement. Under duress, she promised to give the proposal her consideration. Within her, she was torn apart. For thirty years the Villa had been her home. Where could she go at her advanced years? Besides, she was a patriot to the core. On the other hand, Oskar, the realist, could see their current problems solved with the stroke of a pen. He had frantically been searching for a scheme whereby to procure money for us all, even toying with a plan to convert the Villa into flats. But it was futile to reason with Emilia. Sadly, though, she eventually had to capitulate.

To my infinite relief, Miklós returned to Budapest where he was now under contract to the second largest theatre. Through influential connections he managed to be posted in the city to complete his military service. My only escape from the tedium of daily chores happened when I was engaged to play minor roles at the National Theatre. Although I was often mentioned in the theatrical reviews, I do not believe Romola ever came to see me perform. If she did, she never let on.

Then a ghastly thing happened. I had accepted an invitation to spend a brief holiday in the country with a close friend. The first few days on the estate were harmonious and relaxed, until one morning her younger brother breathlessly rushed toward me, clutching a newspaper. Glaring, black headlines screamed at me on the front page. 'WHAT IS THE TRUTH BEHIND THE BATTLE BETWEEN EMILIA MARKUS AND THE NIJINSKY FAMILY?' Waves of nausea swept through my body as the contents of the article slowly registered. It comprised of an interview Oskar had reluctantly agreed to give. He felt duty-bound to clear the air of the malevolent gossip that had leaked out of the Villa following an incident that had taken place there. Cowardly, I thanked God I had missed it. He explained the facts briefly: why and how Romola and Waslaw had come to Budapest; that contrary to what Romola had said, Waslaw was not wholly cured. He dealt with the rumours of violent action against Emilia by Waslaw; the real reason for the auction, their plans for conversion of the Villa into flats, and went on to discuss Emilia's health. He then carried on about the controversy surrounding my position as Emilia's adopted daughter. In a final defiant gesture, he had taken the journalist up to the

Tower and shown him the broken windows, the blood on the couch, and the chaos in the bathroom where the large wooden stove, normally used for heating, had been thrown into the bathtub. He finished the interview with the terse report that Romola on the night of Waslaw's frenzied outburst had been forced to call a nearby doctor for help as even the male nurse had refused to enter Waslaw's room. An ambulance had been ordered and Waslaw Nijinsky was now in the State Asylum (ironically only a few minutes' distance from the Villa).

Life in the Villa was destined never to be the same again. Conditions deteriorated rapidly. The auction had been a failure and most of the items had been returned. Emilia was forced to cede to life's harsh realities, and work on the conversion commenced with builders, architects and their assistants treading us underfoot. Doctors took turns visiting Emilia and Oskar. Soon, two bureau drawers were required to house all the tranquillizers and medicines prescribed. Days would go by without a glimpse of Romola. She was preoccupied seeking to discover a way to leave the country, a possibility which faded with every passing hour.

Then came Romola's rebuttal to Oti-Papa's interview to prove conclusively that 'a coin has two sides'. We should have been able to foresee this would happen. She described in glowing terms how successful the insulin treatments had been and produced a certificate signed by the head of a Swiss State institution to the effect that Waslaw no longer required to be institutionalized and that he could travel freely; that her stepfather's statement that Waslaw could prove dangerous was a blatant lie; that he had never at any time meant to cause Emilia grievous bodily harm. She had simply startled him one day when she had entered his room unannounced and, nervous as he was, he had grabbed an object, as it happened a tin of bicarbonate of soda, and thrown it on the floor, not *at* her. Romola's only reason for removing her husband to the State Asylum was that she wished to free him from the hostile environment that prevailed in the Villa. Her stepfather had refused to give her the 450 pengö needed to place Waslaw in a private institution, consequently she had no alternative but to seek State aid. Now, however, the problem had been solved, and her husband was in a private sanatorium. On one point only did she make a concession – it had been a disastrous mistake to bring him back to a place that held so many sad memories for him. She concluded: 'I did not wish my daughter

(Tamara) to become an actress. I am the daughter and the wife of an artist myself. I know the great price they have to pay for success. ...It would hurt any mother to find out, purely by accident, that her daughter had been adopted.... It is my duty to defend Waslaw Nijinsky's interests over and above the interests of my children and myself.' (Quoted from the newspaper *Független Magyarország,* 13th July).

Emilia was unsuccessful in her attempts to wrest me from Miklós. I was madly in love and would happily have accepted a proposition in lieu of a proposal. But in February 1944, I was invited to dinner at his parents' home, upon which occasion he solemnly proposed and slipped an engagement ring on my finger.

A few days later, Miklós called on my grandparents to ask for my hand in marriage. As he described it to me afterwards, Oti-Papa had entered the salon alone excusing Emilia's absence with '...a sudden attack of migraine...'. Clearing his throat, he honestly but bluntly expressed his and her views on the matter. 'We are against this marriage, but Tamara is of age, there is nothing we can do...'

Because of the refurbishment of the Villa, we had to abandon it temporarily. Emilia, Oskar and I stayed in the Hotel Gellért on the right bank of the Danube (the Buda side). The hotel reputed for its hot springs was an elegant establishment, much frequented by the wealthy who took the cure there. Romola and Tessa moved to a boarding-house not far from the sanatorium where Tatakaboy was staying.

When we returned home we found the Villa transformed. Emilia's bedroom and my two rooms had been turned into one flat and her former study on the same floor was now a smaller flat with a diminutive kitchen and bathroom. The once splendid dining-room was Emilia and Oskar's bedroom; the old pantry, their bathroom. I was to inhabit the Gobelin Salon. In other respects the ground floor remained unchanged. Because of lack of coal, the central heating had been cut off and woodstoves installed in the bedrooms. There was no longer the luxury to which the occupants of the Villa had been accustomed but we coped and were still surrounded by a measure of comfort.

On Sunday morning, 19th of March, 1944, I was getting ready to go to the theatre for a matinée. I looked for Oti-Papa to say good-bye, and found him in the Atrium by the vast arched glass entrance that was never in use. He had pulled the muslin curtain to one side and was staring out on the road. His shoulders were hunched and he looked so desperately tired. Sharp commands and the loud clatter of boots on the cobblestones filtered through to break the serene silence in the Atrium. In rows of four the soldiers marched in their smart uniforms, an endless procession of more, more and then more.... The Germans were marching into Budapest. Oti-Papa bowed his head and cried unashamedly. It was the first time I had ever seen tears roll down his cheeks. 'This is the end,' he murmured.

News of horrifying, alarming happenings in Poland, Austria and Germany reached us concerning the Jewish population there. At home, those who had influential friends and enough money began to make preparations for their exodus from Hungary. Shortly, orders were issued that everybody had to declare if they had any relatives of Jewish origin. For a while, this applied only to those who were one hundred percent Jewish. However, the day was to come when everyone who might have had the remotest connection with Jews had to prove by way of an official document going back to their forebears that they were Aryans. At first, those Jews who were married to Christians were exempted from wearing the David Star on their clothes but then they, too, like all other Jews, had to conform to the rule if they wanted to step outside their homes. It was from that day onward that Oskar refused to leave the Villa even to go into the garden. Rumours reached us that many Jews had even been forced to leave their homes and enter a ghetto. My heart bled for Oti-Papa and for those many friends of mine I no longer could reach. Eszter, our old cook, was still in our service but the remainder of the staff, who had not already fled the Villa when 'the madman' occupied the Tower, departed, claiming they could not work in a household that was not purely Christian.

I shrink with shame at having to confess how up to that point I had shut myself out of the world around me. I had a fiancé, my mother's tyrannical, omnipotent presence was gone from the Villa. I had pressed my grandmother to tell me outright why she had opposed my forthcoming marriage. I adored her and could not carry on with such a barrier between us. Calmly, in her resonant voice, she said she selfishly did not wish to lose me. 'I want you beside me until the end of time...' Weighing every word carefully, she went on to explain her assessment of Miklós, good-looking, cultured, one of the most promising young actors of our day, yet instinctively, she found something amiss in his character. She feared I would be hurt. Had I but heeded her warning!

One day, I declared my intention to introduce Miklós to my father. No matter that Waslaw would in all likelihood not comprehend the purpose of our visit, but I was filled with a desperate need to do so. As we climbed up the steep lane, we paused now and then to inhale the intoxicating scent from the acacia trees. What strange twists and turns the path of life takes. I was on my way to the same sanatorium where my grandfather Károly Pulszky had stayed before he departed on his ill-fated trip to London. Miklós and I had been apprehensive as to whether any restrictions would bar me from seeing Tatakaboy and I prayed fervently that Romola would not be there. To our good fortune, we were received and ushered into a fairly large room, comfortably furnished. On the threshold, I held Miklós's hand in a tight grip while balancing a tray of sweet pastry in the other. A male nurse greeted us and announced our presence after which he discreetly left the room. I observed, however, that he left the door slightly ajar as a precautionary measure.

My father turned slowly toward us from where he was standing by the window and for a few split seconds we remained motionless. Then Miklós bowed slightly. Tatakaboy scrutinised us carefully, and with a quick movement walked over to Miklós and tapped him gently on the shoulder. I became so elated over what I construed to be a display of approval that I impulsively grasped my father's hand and kissed it. Alas, my sudden gesticulation alarmed him. He jerked his hand from me and uttered something in a high-pitched, agitated voice. Like a flash, the nurse was back in the room to see if anything was wrong. Miklós signalled reassuringly that he could leave. In slow motion, my fiancé offered Waslaw some pastry, all the while speaking reassuringly in French. His subdued dulcet tone must have calmed my father because he approached us once more. His eyes lit up in anticipation as he saw the delicacies. I could tell he coveted them. Like a child he devoured all three pieces with unbelievable speed and then glanced dolefully down at the empty tray. Miklós gingerly wiped telltale remnants of whipped cream off his face with a paper napkin and promised that the next time we came, we would bring more sweets. Tatakaboy reacted by tossing his head back and pursing his lips in a peculiar manner. Evidently, he enjoyed being pampered. Tears splashed down my cheeks as I mumbled a farewell and we took our leave.

Somehow, the news must have reached my mother that I had been to see Tatakaboy and that I had brought my fiancé with me. A message arrived at the theatre that she urgently wished to see me. We met in a well-patronised tearoom on Vörösmarthy Tér. As I squeezed my way between guests and waitresses, I noticed she had company, Paul Bohus, whom I had not seen for years. I found out that when he had heard that Romola was in Budapest he had contacted her and offered her his assistance, as he had so many times in the past.

When I reached their table he jumped up and gallantly kissed my hand. I squirmed uncomfortably, listening to him lavish praise about my appearance. I now found his mannerism intolerable, far too contrived, and frankly, he was an enigma to me. Romola asked him to leave us alone, promised to get in touch with him later and dismissed him with an impatient wave of her well-manicured hand. Like a well-trained pet he departed.

We sat there facing each other. I felt clumsy, all hands and feet. She asked me what I wished to order and then continued in her slightly arrogant tone to point out the bizarreness of a situation where she had to meet her own daughter in a tearoom. She had heard of my engagement. Caustically, she went on to say she hoped I was not merely trying to escape the unfortunate predicament of being torn between two opposing factions. She rebuked me once more for what she deemed was my unpardonable behaviour toward her, my father and Aunt Tessa. She then plunged into yet another stern sermon about how wrong it was that I had been adopted by Emilia. I tried unsuccessfully to interrupt her flow of speech. The nerves of my stomach had started to churn and I did not wish to hear any more. But there was no escape. She continued how she wished I had not taken up acting as my profession. When I demurred, pointing out that her own mother had been one of Hungary's finest actresses and that Tatakaboy, too, in a sense had been an actor, she told me sharply to stop talking and to listen to what she further had to say. That I was under no circumstances to use the name Nijinsky in my acting career. I must only use the name Márkus.

I excused myself a few moments and when I returned to the table, it seemed to me that her expression was warmer, more relaxed. She actually acknowledged how pleasant it had been that I had gone to visit my father but went on to say it was a pity it could not be repeated. I listened dutifully as she talked about the imminent

287

possibility of Waslaw and her leaving the country. She wrung a promise from me that under no circumstances would I relay our conversation to 'the couple' in the Villa. I heaved an inward sigh of relief that she would soon be out of sight, hopefully out of my mind. Still, I could not refrain from feeling compassion for her, my poor, proud mother, who continued with supreme sacrifice to protect the man to whom she had dedicated her life. Taking me into her confidence was perhaps her way of 'forgiving' me and of saying goodbye. It showed her duality of character, a woman with a heart but who had forced herself to bury emotional feelings a long, long time ago.

At the end of August, 1944, on a Tuesday morning, I started to dress for my wedding day. Miklós and I were to be married at the 'Chapel of the Palace', not far away from the Coronation Church where Kyra had stood bride eight years previously. Just as I was ready, the piercing sound of an air raid siren broke the stillness. Resignedly, I took off my lovely white wedding gown and veil, laid them carefully on the large, semi-circular divan under the tapestry, tuned in the radio and waited patiently until the All Clear signal came. A second air raid actually sounded en route to the church and we all had to abandon our cars and flee for cover under the arched door of an old house. The bombing now was much heavier and I felt uneasy qualms about our safety until I found myself standing at the altar with Miklós at my side. I was blissfully, blindly happy, determined to live with him for all eternity. 'Remember, dearly beloved, your life can be compared to a rose, but the rose has many thorns...' That is all I can recall from the ceremony. The circumstances of a war raging around us curtailed Emilia from holding a grand wedding reception. Ours was an intimate occasion, the guest list limited to close family – Emilia, Oskar, Tessa, Miklós's parents, his brother and sister-in-law – and a smattering of friends. From Romola there was not a word. That she could not attend was understandable but a message would have meant so much. After a late lunch we took our departure to spend our honeymoon in the most luxurious hotel in Budapest, situated on the left bank of the Danube. Miklós had been unable to obtain permission to leave the city boundaries as he was on call to his military unit.

What followed was to me an unparalleled nightmare. A telephone call disrupted our idyllic existence, at noon on the following Thursday to be precise. His face drained of colour, Miklós said flatly that he had to report to his headquarters. I became filled with a terrible feeling of doom. He refused to elaborate and attempted to get me to leave him to make his own way back. To his discomfort, I stubbornly declined. Mutely, we journeyed back to the main gate of the grim-looking army building. There, an officer, who apparently had been waiting for Miklós, seized him by the arm and barked 'You are under arrest.' In a hoarse whisper, Miklós ordered me to hurry to the Villa and to wait there for further word from him.

Temporarily numbed, I obeyed without a sound coming from my lips. It was pitch-black when I pressed the bell to the front door, a bewildered, bedraggled bride of forty-eight hours. My grandparents behaved splendidly, promising me all the support they were capable of giving. Rigidly, I kept vigil by the telephone. I nearly fainted when Miklós did telephone. His message was that he would perhaps face the firing-squad within twenty-four hours. I must not lose faith, however, but listen carefully to what he had to say; I should contact a Father Tamás at dawn. He was familiar with the dire situation and together with his compatriots would do everything in his power to help.

For a cruelly long week I lived in a vacuum, not knowing whether I was a bride or a widow. Then, one bleak morning, Father Tamás arrived to say that the execution had been stayed and that Miklós was to be put on trial that very day. I was driven to the Court and we parked outside its forbidding exterior. I sat from nine o'clock in the morning until six in the evening, my eyes glued to a bay window on the corner. Behind that window, I was told, my husband's fate was being decided. The clock had just struck six when I caught a glimpse of him being led out by some soldiers and one civilian. I leapt from the car, impulsively wanting to rush over and embrace him. But something held me back. His once elegant suit hung creased and soiled on his gaunt frame. His face was unshaven and his head bowed down. He must have sensed my presence because he stopped, hesitated for a moment and turned his head in my direction. A soldier prodded him on and our eyes never met. I was kept in suspense regarding the verdict until late that evening when Father Tamás rang to tell me that Miklós had been sentenced to several years' imprisonment. He had been taken to the military prison on the Buda side. I learned that Father Tamás had been Miklós's confessor and spiritual guide for a number of years. Fragments of that oppressive period were relayed to me; it had been Father Tamás who had schemed that Miklós should pretend to be insane, for example, and therefore abetted him to escape the death penalty. But the salient facts behind the drama were obscured until long after Miklós had permanently vanished out of my life.

It turned out he had been engaged in underground activities against the Communists and possibly also the Nazis. Allegedly, a Jesuit Order was also involved and it was through them he was spared from execution. His position as an actor, often touring the provinces, his skill at portraying different characters, diplomatic in manner, and well-spoken, made him a useful adherent to the underground movement. Throughout our engagement and married life, I never once suspected that he participated in so dangerous a task. He never lost his nerve nor his patriotic fervour and he resumed his activities during the 1956 Uprising, was eventually caught, sent to prison and almost died from maltreatment. He was released after seven months. Although it is all past history by now, his involvement was of such an international nature, it is safer buried with him. He and his second family came over to the United States some years ago and settled in South Dakota where his wife established a ballet studio. Moody, disillusioned, he did not fit into the American way of life. He was a continental through and through. And he seemed forever to be furtively looking over his shoulder, fearful that some shadows from the past were tracking him down. He returned to Europe to die.

But let us turn back to when the husband I then so dearly loved was in prison. I divided the hours of the day between him and the theatre. All my ingenuity was applied to finding new sources of food to take to him. My 'ally', a sergeant whom I had bribed with several packets of cigarettes, taught me the rule whereby a prisoner 'needs a clean shirt every day'. When he was on duty I could smuggle in food camouflaged under a shirt that was not crushed together. At the theatre, feelings were running high because changes had to be made in the repertoire just to please our uninvited 'German visitors'. There were days when we had to study new parts to replace the actors who for political reasons were forbidden to perform or who, because of their Jewish ancestry, had been deported.

Shall I ever forget the 19th of October when Miklós Horthy, the Regent of Hungary, went on the air to grant pardon to all political prisoners. This was one of his last official acts. The American Army later sent him to Germany as a prisoner-of-war. There, for a couple of months, his fate hung in the balance – had he been with or against the Germans? As it turned out, he was not sentenced as a war criminal but instead exiled to Portugal with his family. He died there.

Having for days on end lived through every variety of torment, I could scarcely believe it when Miklós rang to say he was free, free! I hastily packed a bag and picked him up outside his gaol. Our honeymoon resumed where it had been so rudely broken off. We locked ourselves in, the world outside. The following Monday, Miklós had to report to his regiment in the eastern region of Hungary and a few weeks later I joined him in the small village where he was stationed. Winter had descended upon us with a vengeance. It was bitterly cold but I was blissfully happy. I was expecting our first child.

Early in December, I received an urgent message to hasten back to Budapest as Emilia was in hospital. The only means of transport was a freight train, a trying journey in freezing temperature and I was grateful for the protection of a heavy hunting coat lent to me by Oti-Papa. A tragic story was unfolded by my Aunt Ilona. Emilia had given refuge to some Jewish friends. Unbeknown to her, the granddaughter of the handyman was an active member of the Nazi Party and had reported her. Soldiers of the puppet régime had broken into the Villa, shot down one of the Jewish friends and dragged Oti-Papa out to a jeep. Emilia, then in her eighties, had rushed out and climbed up beside her husband, refusing to abandon him. After a night of agony, they had been released thanks to the brave intervention of Tessa, who had stormed into the Office of the Ministry for Cultural Affairs and delivered a dramatic speech about the disgraceful behaviour to which Hungary's greatest actress had been subjected. Emilia, however, succumbed to the shock and strain of the ordeal and was rushed to hospital. Oskar went into hiding together with several prominent authors and artists who shared his predicament – victims of anti-semitism.

Through some ingenious scheme, the details of which I can no longer recollect, we managed to bring Emilia and Oskar to the Hotel Géllert in time for Christmas. Relieved over their safe reunion, we decided to celebrate our first Christmas Eve together in style, all worries thrown to the winds. I donned a cocktail dress of soft brown Chantilly lace, my handsome Miklós, a tuxedo. We paid a call on his parents, continued to my grandparents at the hotel and planned to be home before dark for our intimate Christmas together. Our rounds completed, we hastened to await our tram but none arrived. A sergeant ran toward us, shouting brusquely that the Russians were approaching the inner city and that we would be advised not to attempt to go home. Our Yuletide spirits quelled, we had no choice but to retrace our steps to the Géllert. New Year's Eve found us still there – I in my cocktail dress, Miklós in his tuxedo.

1945 did not give birth to any joyful tidings. Already early in January intimidating news spread that an intense search was going on for soldiers absent without leave, and when found, they would face the firing squad. The German Army accelerated their vicious manhunt and while we were still at the hotel they set up firing squads in front of it and men who were not in uniform were selected indiscriminately, irrespective of age, lined up and shot. Miraculously, Miklós narrowly escaped sharing that fate twice in less than a week. When we first learned that the Russians were advancing, we naïvely believed they would come as our liberators. All too soon the cruel truth was to penetrate our minds.

How is it possible to recount the full horror of the ensuing months? We realised our safety would be jeopardized if we remained at our present premises. On January 6th, Epiphany Day, we bid a tearful farewell to my grandparents. After a hazardous trek, with gunfire too close for comfort, and thwarted in our first attempt to find shelter, we reached the National Theatre, which was to become our living quarters for several months. The basement boasted an immense boiler-room with luxuriously hot water dripping from its pipes. Fuelling presented no problem as the theatre was well-stocked with coal. Nature supplied fresh water in the form of flurries of white snow. How did we cope? How did we survive? Sadly, not everyone did.

Miklós's father had been ordered to dig graves and it was while engaged in this grim task that he suffered a severe gallbladder attack. He was refused admittance at the hospital, the chief surgeon's excuse being that every square inch from wall to wall was filled with wounded, dying and dead soldiers. The Nazi commanders had explicitly forbidden him to operate on civilians. Before daybreak, my father-in-law died in the theatre at the age of fifty-nine. Half a mile down the road the Hungarian Army was engaged in house-to-house combat against the Russians. Burial in the cemetery was out of the question. It was imperative to bury him swiftly to avoid risk to our own health. In the early light of day, Miklós, together with a handful of volunteers, cautiously crept out of the building with their burden, their goal to reach the small green park across from the main entrance, near the statue of the Hungarian troubadour, Tinody Lantos Sebestyén. Together with my grief-stricken mother-in-law I kept watch, the sound of shooting coming nearer and nearer. There was no time to dig a fresh grave and so they were compelled to place the body on top of another corpse. Later, in April, an official decree declared that all persons who had been buried during the Siege of Budapest had to be exhumed and properly buried. My presence was required. It was the first time in my life, and hopefully the last, that I had to witness a body being exhumed.

By now, our haven had become a conglomerate of resistance fighters, political refugees, soldiers who had deserted rather than fight side by side with the enemy. Food was so scarce it grew into an illusion. Then came the moment we had all dreaded. Russian troops entered the theatre. We stood with bated breath and listened to their footsteps overhead, the harsh tramp of their boots on the marble floor. They were to ferret us out and call upon the men, young, old, no matter, to work for them – to perform the most menial and laborious tasks. Anyone who showed the slightest opposition would receive a nudge from a 'davaj-guitar' (Russian sub-machine-gun). Many of the men who were marched away to work units never returned; those who did showed physical evidence of their involuntary assignments. We women had other reasons for not wanting to be sent out alone with the soldiers. How I grew to detest the sight of that red star on their uniforms.

With military efficiency Soviet soldiers built pontoons over the Danube while German soldiers on the retreat were equally methodically blowing up all our bridges. The sporadic fighting on both sides of the river continued for quite some time after the Germans had gone into hiding in the dark caves of the Géllert Mountain.

In spite of everything Spring arrived. Tiny buds appeared on trees and shrubs. The welcome, caressing warmth of the sun enticed us to leave our 'dungeon'. What we saw spread out before us was devastating: torn-up streets, unclaimed, headless corpses stretched grotesquely out on the dirty, melting snow in the company of decaying dead horses. There was no water to be had, no gas, no electricity, no manner of transportation or communication.

Bombed-out houses stood silently like empty shells, deserted by the people who had once lived and loved there. Only the sound of a stray bullet disrupted the ghostly silence. But we were alive...

By April 4th, 1945, the country was liberated from the German invaders, nearly four months after a truce had been signed by the Hungarian provisional government. As far as we were concerned, it was a signal that war was over and we began to rebuild and reconstruct our lives. A group of actors surfaced and with *élan* we helped them clean up the theatre. Strong, willing hands and nimble fingers miraculously transformed it back to a semblance of its former glory. Performances were to begin at two o'clock in the afternoon to allow everybody to be indoors by curfew at six.

Throughout the ordeal I had fretted with worry about Emilia and Oti-Papa. We had lost all communication with them since that terrifying night we had fled from the hotel. Hilda, a gifted young actress from the National Theatre, came to my rescue. A dynamic woman, it was she who organised meals and set up a proper soup-kitchen. A member of the new ruling party, she performed miracles and it was she who brought my grandparents back to me. I was wrenched from that fleeting moment of immeasurable joy upon learning her mission had been successful, when I saw their haggard faces, their gaunt, almost emaciated bodies. There was no doubt but that Oskar was seriously ill. We managed to get a bed for him at the Rokus Hospital, a couch for Emilia in a dressing-room at the theatre. Poor, dear Oti-Papa, his broken eyes pleaded with me to take him back once more to the Villa, to the sunshine and the huge chestnut trees. How could I tell him that I did not even know if their home was still there and not just a heap of rubble? The expression in his eyes continued to haunt me and I discussed the matter with Hilda. Once more, she proved to be the benevolent samaritan and manipulated his transfer to a hospital run by nuns, conveniently located on the hillside only a few miles from the Villa. Emilia, frail though she was, insisted on going with him. And thus the contact was yet again broken but not for long.

In the middle of May, a pathetic, scrawled, pencilled note arrived from my grandmother. Three words. *'Oti-Papa died. Come'.* Grief-stricken, I made arrangements to see her. Miklós was unable to accompany me. I was seven months pregnant and the only means of reaching the hospital was some thirty kilometres by foot. My baby weighed heavily inside me and I felt uncomfortable and clumsy stumbling over debris in my path. On the verge of despair, I was given a lift by a brewer's drayman on his low cart. We had not gone far, however, when the combined odour of Pálinka, a strong liquor which he was imbibing from a flask, and the sweat steaming from his body, so nauseated me, I asked to be let down. To reach the hospital I had to pass the Villa, and to my amazement I noticed that the front door was ajar. I could not refrain from entering. Dust and cobwebs were everywhere, the *objets d'art* and most of the furniture missing, but otherwise the Atrium seemed undisturbed. Surprisingly, even the huge mirrors facing each other were intact, as it had been used as a stable for army horses. Hesitantly, on tiptoe, I approached the Gobelin salon. Blinded by the rays of the afternoon sun, I could only just discern a silhouette seated by the window. The silhouette became clearer, more focused. 'Waibi, my dear Waibi.' How weak my grandmother sounded from the depths of the huge armchair. I cradled in my arms what was left of the Blonde Miracle, a shrunken skeleton covered by a black dress many sizes too big. An inner force had compelled her to return to the home where she had spent so many happy years with her beloved Oskar. I stayed with her over-night, then had to leave her to weep, perhaps it would ease the heartbreak and the pain. More practical matters required my atten-tion. Compassionate, understanding neighbours promised to keep an eye on her while I visited the hospital.

I struggled up the hill where I was warmly greeted by the nuns. They consoled me by saying that Oti-Papa had died peacefully, his kind, gentle heart had simply given up. The responsibility I now had to shoulder was to see he got a decent burial. Where to obtain a coffin? Proper trading had long ago come to a grinding halt and was still chaotic. Acting upon the advice of the nuns, I found a labourer willing to make one, provided he could scrape together sufficient wood. I faced yet another big problem. Would Emilia have the strength to attend the funeral? The ludicrousness of our situation struck me – there were no funeral parlours, no horse-drawn carriages, no pallbearers, no organist to play a requiem.

Emilia Márkus still possessed the stamina that had served her so well those many decades on the stage. Nothing could deter her from following her Oti to his last resting place. Our former handyman took pity on us when he learned of our predicament and arrived in the morning with a cart, having collected the coffin en route. Emi-lia, in sombre black from head to foot, was hoisted up and I clambered up next to her. The little procession must have made a comically macabre sight to the beholder; our 'chauffeur' pulling the heavy load with the two chief mourners resting their backs against the coffin, their feet dangling unceremoniously in the air. With every jolt I feared for the baby I was carrying. It was peaceful at the cemetery. Oti-Papa's favourite trees, the chestnuts, had burst into bloom. They made up the floral tribute. The birds sang as we stood around the grave, Emilia, myself, the priest and the handyman.

The following day, I moved Emilia back to the dressing-room in the theatre. There I would be able to keep an eye on her. A concession to normality began creeping into our lives once more. Slowly, streets and buildings were cleared of rubble and the stench of decay. Human nature being what it is, everyone started to plan for tomorrow, to look ahead into the future.

Summer arrived, bringing with it a sultry heat. On a particularly sweltering afternoon Aunt Tessica reappeared unexpectedly. She, too, was marked by the ravages of war. Deprived of her customary makeup, her features looked pallid and drawn, her hair, tied in a knot, betrayed the lack of proper dye for months. A brown silk dress, frayed and grubby, hung loosely on her thin frame. Little Dzinn was tucked under her arm.

Our elation at seeing her was shortlived. In a torrential flow of words, barely pausing for breath, she launched into an incredible account of what had happened to her. She had, of course, been stunned by the news of Oskar's death, which had been relayed to her together with Emilia's present whereabouts. But she was in dire trouble. She had been given the responsibility to care for the villa of a Jewish couple when they were compelled to flee the country. Her story was garbled, and to this day I could not say for certain whether they had managed to escape the ultimate horror of death in a concentration camp and turned up without warning, or whether some relatives came. No matter. It was claimed that valuable jewellery was missing that had been stacked away under a staircase. An accusing finger had been pointed at Tessa and the police were searching for her.

For a few wild moments I had cherished hopes that Tessa would stay with us and thus lighten my burden in caring for Emilia. In consultation with Miklós, however, we voted unanimously that it would be highly unpropitious for her to stay. The sooner we got her out of the country, the better. She still had her Danish passport – the magic wand to freedom, her one precious legacy from Erik. And thus, like a whirlwind sweeping into our lives, so, too, she left. Emilia, knowing she would never see her tempestuous Tessica again, unclasped a long golden chain, her thin veined hands shaking. It was one of the last remaining mementoes from former days and she wanted her daughter to have it. We scraped together a parcel of food for Tessa's journey and with that we wended our way to the railway station. What a droll sight our trio must have been. Like circus clowns. Miklós, in his tuxedo trousers now much the worse for wear, a frazzled light-blue shirt open at the neck, Tessa, teetering on her high heels in her shabby finery, hugging Dzinn, I, in my faded cotton dress now far too tight, my stomach bulging.

The temperature was still soaring, not a whisper of wind to cool us when we reached the station at dusk. It was smokier, smellier and dirtier than ever. Soldiers were milling around, raucously calling out to each other, heavy rucksacks on their backs. Peasant women, brightly-coloured babushkas tied under their chins, and laden with unwieldy bundles, added to the general chaos. Above the din, Miklós could hear that a train was just about to pull out, destination Roumania. We elbowed our way through the throng and Miklós unceremoniously lifted Tessa onto a carriage platform. She was still desperately clutching her Dzinn but as the whistle blew, he tore the dog from her arms and dropped him into mine. 'Please take good care of Dzinn' were her last, parting words. Ironically, we were to learn that in the general confusion we had put Tessa on a train going in the opposite direction to Denmark. She did eventually reach her haven safely but I was never to see her again.

Fed up with all the excitement fermenting around her, our baby announced her impending arrival in no uncertain terms the following evening. We had no means of transport to the clinic. Every step seemed a mile and I had to pause now and then to rest until the sharp labour pains subsided. A Russian jeep was rumbling past and Miklós waved it to a halt. Language barriers were broken when the soldiers observed my condition, and within minutes I was delivered to the entrance to the clinic.

I felt sadhearted that I could not share my happiness with Romola and Tatakaboy over the birth of their grandchild, Miklós's and my daughter Kinga-Maria, blonde, blue-eyed, unquestioningly delightful to behold. Fortune smiled upon us and we found suitable accommodation not far from the Villa. We succeeded in getting

Emilia to join us but it proved futile. She wanted to be home, no matter the current squalor of the Villa. Her homesickness vanquished us in the end, and after a brief spell in hospital suffering from a bout of pneumonia, she stayed at a small hotel on the Pest side. Meanwhile, with the aid of my friend Michael, we put part of the Villa into a habitable state; the dining-room, her bedroom and the Gobelin salon. The wife of our former handyman was entrusted to look in on her daily, and I was within calling distance.

There had been no news about Romola and Waslaw. Then, it must have been around Christmas time, an enquiry reached Emilia through the Red Cross in Vienna. Romola had sought their help to find out what had happened to her. There was no mention of my name in the enquiry. Thus, in 1946, correspondence resumed between Romola and her mother.

It was in subsequent letters and newspaper clippings which filtered through that we could piece together what had transpired after they left Budapest. An article in the Overseas Service edition of *Life*, dated September 10th, 1945, yielded a terse but nonetheless expressive account of their tribulations before reaching Vienna. The interviewer described Romola as Waslaw's 'alert, birdlike wife and biographer'. He went on to give his impression of Nijinsky himself.

'At 55, decay has not yet touched him physically as it has mentally. Before the war he grew fat, but rationing and wartime hunger, as well as increased exercise, have taken care of that. Now he is amazingly strong and supple for a man of his age. Only his face betrays the ruin within, a face of Mongoloid cast seamed by the fears and suffering of his disease but still capable of relaxing into the warm, humorous face of a happy Slav. Sometimes the face shows terror or cunning or anger, sometimes merely the blank vacuity of a loon. At dinner it is likely to be sullen. Nijinsky, locked in his private world, cannot understand why the table is not loaded with his favourite foods. Often he accuses Romola, his faithful protector, of plotting to starve him. He grows suspicious and sometimes violent. Nor can he understand anything else about wartime dislocations. Like a very young child, he is unable to understand the irrationality of war which, ironically enough, is understandable to a rational adult'.

298

The article was accompanied by pictures; an excellent one of Romola and Waslaw together in front of the Victory Monument overlooking Vienna, shows them as a smiling, happy, middle-aged couple.

In 1952 Victor Gollancz in London published a new work by Romola entitled *The Last Years of Nijinsky*. In it she wrote a portrayal of their gruesome ordeals during World War II. She included in it her version of the brief interlude in the Villa which I found to be a distortion of the actual happenings. However, I must confess I have no other source of information than her own to either prove or disprove the rest of the story leading up to the safehold in Vienna. I am therefore taking the liberty to summarise it here to fill the gap of the intervening years.

Whatever her shortcomings, this second volume clearly indicates that she suffered the most harrowing and excruciating deprivations to pull Waslaw through safely. I could not fathom, however, why this same woman continued to write false accusations against her mother with such a vitriolic pen, to dispose of Kyra, her first-born in a few dispassionate sentences, and still to ignore any mention of me, her second daughter.

Although he had not reacted adversely to the piercingly shrill air raid sirens, the sight of German soldiers and tanks on the roads and streets of Budapest had agitated Waslaw more and more. A friend, Pali Strauss, had found them a refuge in a convalescent home in Buda.

Upon the advice of a Jewish friend who was seeking to return to Hollywood via Russia, Romola had applied for transit visas to the States. She was encouraged to hope that Moscow would grant permission because the Russian officials she contacted assured her that the great name of Nijinsky was not forgotten. But only a few months later, the shocking news came that Germany had declared war on Russia and her plans were yet again thwarted. Fearful of waiting any longer in the capital, she took Waslaw to a tiny summer resort near Lake Balaton. Apparently, they had found it a peaceful haven and settled down to a tolerable existence, even a male nurse to attend to Waslaw. The bliss did not last for long. One day, they were accosted by a couple of grim-looking officials who had heard rumours that they were Russian spies. A distraught Romola had hastily gathered together their few meagre possessions and retreated back to Budapest. There she succeeded in finding shared accommodation on the top of Svabhégy. Her lack of funds worsened by the hour. The bitter struggle to provide for Waslaw, and to buy fuel to keep him warm, seemed endless. She had prepared a Hungarian edition of his *Diary,* which had been published. Casting aside pride, she demeaned herself to go around to all wealthy and influential people she could think of, imploring them to buy copies. She wrote that she felt like a door-to-door salesman, but her plight roused sympathy with many and in years to come she was to reap financial reward for this selfless devotion to her husband through contacts made during this stressful period.

She virtually haunted the Swedish Embassy which represented Russian interests, and also the Red Cross, in vain attempts to get Waslaw out of the country, back to neutral Switzerland. She became gripped with panic when she heard that the Germans were intensifying their efforts to track down the mentally ill who were being herded onto cattle trains in the company of the persecuted Jews and sent to the concentration camps to face extermination.

Paul Bohus was instrumental in finding shelter for Romola and Waslaw in a small inn in the forest near Sopron, once a favourite ski resort on the shores of Lake Neusiedler near the Austrian border. Once more, she attempted to normalise their life as much as possible. They would go for long walks in the deep, pine woods and explore the little medieval town. A gypsy girl assisted in the household chores and, from her, Waslaw learned some gypsy dances. It is interesting to note that throughout her narrative of this time, Romola always referred to Waslaw as a perfectly normal person, taking an active part in discussions and what went on around him. Enigmatically, she still clung to the idea that he would once more resume a brilliant career, if not as a dancer, then as adviser to international ballet dancers and choreographers.

Paul, himself a refugee, spent as much time as he could with them and supplied them with bulletins of the progress of the war, which daily grew more alarming, and in August of 1944 they learned the Russians had penetrated Roumania and that Hungary was next. She realised their position was precarious and they were forced to move from one place to another. Devoid of funds, Romola had to risk a journey to Budapest to raise cash by selling her few remaining family gold heirlooms. During that time Waslaw again had to spend days in a hospital, in a special ward for mentally sick. She wrote that that visit to Budapest was her last. She also mentioned that it was then she bade farewell to Emilia and Tessa, something I had no knowledge of at the time.

In March 1945, the Russians bombed the area, bombs falling thick and fast. Romola and Waslaw sought cover in the dense forest. The night sky overhead was brilliantly illuminated by Russian signal flares, 'Stalin's Candles', tracing fierce patterns in the atmosphere that made the villagers huddle together in terror. Not so Waslaw, who like a child enchanted by fireworks, had stood exposed throughout the raid, ecstatically watching the phenomenal bursts of light.

The danger was now so imminent that, together with Paul and several thousand others, they sought protection in caves beneath the Carmelite Convent. For days they had to stay in the overcrowded caves under the most appalling conditions. Paul had contracted measles and lain in a high fever. Romola had to shoulder the responsibility to seek food for them, to boil all the water for drinking as there was a threat of typhoid. She had to fend off people hostile to the idea that a man who was rumoured to be insane was among them. Waslaw was growing increasingly weaker from the lack of proper nutrition.

Easter arrived, and they crawled out of their dark, dank holes underground and returned to the house they had temporarily been living in. Everywhere, there was the movement of Russian troops and within a short time the entire town and the surrounding forests were occupied. Overnight, Sopron had been transformed into a Russian town. One morning, Romola was brusquely ordered to accompany two military policemen to the Russian Commanding Officer. He interrogated her at length and was astounded to hear that her husband was Nijinsky, the great dancer. The name was still revered in Russia and she was treated with deep respect. A friendly Russian officer, one Stephan Danilovitch, was attached to their household and Romola claimed she could discern a gradual change in her husband. He listened with undivided attention to his mother tongue, mingled with the soldiers who came to him with presents. His eyes lit up again and he came to life in a way he had not done for years. Romola related how one evening he had sprung up and begun to dance with some of the soldiers, and inspired by their clapping and the accompaniment of the balalaikas, executed breathtaking leaps. A grey-haired, balding, rather stout figure, yet still graceful, still in control of his movements. It was then that remorse had flooded over her. Had she been sufficiently far-seeing she should never have permitted Waslaw to be locked up in solitary confinement in the early stages of his illness; he should have been allowed to return home, home to his beloved Russia. Perhaps then he would never have fallen into a catatonic stupor. Perhaps...if... How could she blame herself? Every hindrance reared its ugly head when war was declared. Yet I feel certain she carried this doubt with her until she died.

Waina Kontechales – the war is over. Late on May 5th, Romola was relayed that wonderful news by Danilovitch. She was posed with a dilemma. Where to go? Budapest was a ruined city. She was offered passage to Russia but what guarantee did she have that promises so readily made then would be kept. And she would be totally isolated from her own world. Vienna seemed to be the only sensible solution. The first step on the road to freedom. It had been declared an international zone – divided up among the Russians, Americans, British and French. She learned that Kyra was in Italy, in Florence, and that Waslaw's sister Bronia was in the United States. Together with Paul she went to Vienna by train to reconnoitre the situation. To her dismay, she found the once beautiful city ruthlessly scarred by the war; Soviet flags and portraits of the Communist leaders were prominent everywhere. Paul succeeded in inducing the manager of the famous Sacher Hotel to provide them with accommodation. To divert attention from the authorities, the hotel had been made to look uninhabitable but the magic name of Nijinsky opened the doors. Borrowing a motorcar from the Austrian Red Cross they returned to Hungary to collect Waslaw. That trip was to test their nerves yet again as on the return journey to Vienna, they were taken prisoners by the Russians and were released only after a terrifying night during which they were uncertain of their fate. It appeared that it was the motorcar the soldiers had coveted. Romola professed that Waslaw had at no time shown any sign of fear of the Russian soldiers. He had calmly sat throughout the ordeal and the following morning dressed and taken his breakfast as though nothing untoward had occurred.

It was with a sigh of relief that Romola reached their sanctuary. The manager had performed a miracle in their absence and a luxurious suite of rooms was in readiness for them. The shortage of food was the only problem. A guardian angel entered their lives, a Mrs Margaret Power, a widowed Englishwoman, a balletomane, who had been asked by friends in London to find the Nijinskys. She arrived, not only with a parcel of provisions, for which they were deeply thankful, but she also brought the glad tidings that a small sum of money awaited them from the Nijinsky Fund. She was at the time posted to the Allied Commission in Austria. She was to become a valuable friend and later contacted Anton Dolin to raise more money for the couple in the United States. Contrary to what Romola averred, she, too, found Waslaw a very silent man. She grew exceedingly fond of him and his gentle nature on the many occasions they met in Vienna but despite the fact that she tried to converse with him, either in French or in English, he always remained quiet, never engaged in conversation.

Summer came and once more the theatres flung open their doors and there were performances at the Opera. Tirelessly, Romola continued to involve Waslaw in cultural events, concerts, the Opera, an exhibition of paintings at the Hofburg in the Imperial Gardens, to Sunday Mass in one of Vienna's splendid churches. The Bolshoi Ballet, Oistrach, the great violinist, and Oborin, the famous pianist, made guest appearances in the Capital.

For a brief period, the Russian Army took over the Sacher Hotel, so that history repeated itself in that Romola and Waslaw were again surrounded by his fellow countrymen who eagerly tried to persuade him to come back 'home'.

But then the military deck of cards was reshuffled and the British Army requisitioned the hotel. Stiff, new rules were applied, and everybody was told to leave. Romola pleaded with the British Commander, and was reluctantly granted a temporary reprieve under the condition she and Waslaw did not receive any civilian callers, thus to some extent cutting them off from the outside world. Through the auspices of the International Red Cross, Romola was provided with food parcels for Waslaw. The tinned food, however, did not agree with him and with growing alarm Romola watched him wasting away. She succeeded in attracting the attention of a Colonel Gordon Smith who held a high post at the British Headquarters. A keen balletomane, he wielded his influence and Romola was supplied with one hot meal a day for Waslaw from the Army kitchen.

A notable event in their cultural life was an invitation to a performance of the Leningrad Ballet at the Ronacher Theatre; their host, the Russian Commandatura. It was planned as a surprise for

Waslaw. The settings and costumes were breathtaking and the dancers gave an outstanding performance, perhaps inspired by the fact that one of their greatest artists was sitting there in the audience in front of them. Kapoustina, Boris Borisoff, Chabukiani and Sergeiev were among the illustrious names on the stage but it was Galina Sergeievna Ulanova, who brought rapture to Waslaw's face. In her notes, Romola described Galina as looking fresh as a rosebud on a June dawn. She also claimed Waslaw watched the dance with relish and when the evening ended with Fokine's *Les Sylphides,* he clasped his hands and accompanied each step with a perceptible movement of his body.

The following day, he and Romola visited Ulanova at her hotel. Artists and army officers crowded around Waslaw in the entrance hall and with tears in their eyes handed him an armful of red roses. Their tribute to the *Spectre de la Rose.* Romola and Waslaw spent several hours with Ulanova, reminiscing over the past. Ulanova's parents had been former classmates of Waslaw's at the Academy and she had known him since childhood. She also talked about the latest achievements of the Soviet ballet, the advancement in modern technology, the aid of motion pictures to record and copyright choreography.

Romola fought an ongoing battle with the authorities to obtain exit visas and permits to go to other countries. Pressure was brought to bear on her and Waslaw to vacate their suite. She feared, too, that the continuous intrusion of military life was having a depressing effect on Waslaw. She had made the acquaintance of an American, Colonel Yarborough, who did everything in his power to ease their situation. He was the Provost Marshal and arranged for Romola to travel around the countryside to select a place suitable for Waslaw in the custody of the American authorities. At first, she went to Salzburg and then toured the surrounding districts in the American Zone to find a fitting dwelling. Thus she came across what she termed a fairy-tale castle from the 11th century, complete with a drawbridge, dungeons and towers, innumerable passageways and even a torture chamber: Castle Mittersill, high up in the mountains near Gross Glockner, between Kitzbühel and Zell-am-See.

It must have been in July 1946 that Waslaw was comfortably installed on the ground floor of the residence Romola called the 'Castle of the Knights'. The suites boasted up-to-date facilities, electricity, central heating, private bathrooms. His windows overlooked the majestic Alps and the Valley of the Salzach. He had free access to the lovely garden and the inner courtyard. Food and other commodities were no longer any problem. They poured in from all directions and according to Romola she found willing servants, only too glad to work in exchange for the precious items in abundance at the castle. Nevertheless, bills were to shower over her, the monthly rent alone being 1,000 schillings, excluding utilities, nurse and servants.

Immediately following Emilia's receipt of Romola's first communication in March 1946, she commenced a correspondence with her Molly. She kept the contents from me and it was not until I read through a bundle of her letters after my mother's death that I found some rancorous allegations against me. Without flinching, I looked my conscience full in the face. Did they contain any substance of truth? Were they not rather the rambling and piteous outpourings of an old woman wishing to ingratiate herself with her daughter after so long a breach between them. I racked my brain to understand what prompted her to write as she did.

Emilia's reproaches hurt more than a dagger plunged through my heart and caused me great unhappiness. She blamed me for making her return against her will to the dirty shambles of the Villa.

'If you could see how ugly it is now. It was on Oti's orders they set to work on it with a hammer because he and Tamara wanted more income. They would not listen to me. I did not count, only Tamara's opinion...then, when she got married, she left us...You were right about Oti but also about Tamara, who is completely under the spell of her Svengali. She is only looking after her own interests... and so did poor Oti I am disillusioned with her. It is too late now...'

She conceded, however, that she would have to take me with her if she were to make a trip to Austria to visit Romola. Kyra's well-being preyed on her mind and she felt frustrated over her silence. *'A lock of Kyra's hair is in my prayerbook as well as a calling-card which reads "Miss Kyra Nijinsky, 38 West 58th Street, New York"'*

Emilia carried on in numerous letters about her worldly possessions:

305

'I have to discuss with you the matter of my will for the benefit of poor Kyra and poor Tessa, too...When I mentioned that to Tamara, she replied: "If it will not interfere with my child's interests." Incidentally, the child (Kinga) *is very good natured, lovely and intelligent. I have not seen her for two months. I do not wish to bother them. All I ask is that Tamara should be happy and not quarrel with me.'*

'...The writing-desk is yours, the two Buddhas, and also the pearl earrings. I have the peculiar feeling that they are waiting for my death inorder to obtain certain small things, that neither of my granddaughters really cares for me...the only one who cares, is the little doll who has inherited the brain of the Pulszkys, all my charm and impishness, and whom they keep strictly away from me (again referring to Kinga).'

To Romola, Emilia also confided her own financial problems.

'If I go abroad to see you, how will I get my pension, my money? It is a serious matter. Another important issue is that I have to sell some valuables. I would not want to leave money to Tamara's husband. If Tamara is not lying, they are already "eating" the 300 square foot property...sold the fortress (the house I had received as a dowry). *Tamara now has a wonderful coat and dresses...Tamara's family do not give me a penny... All I hear is "We cannot let our child starve." Always the same refrain...'*

There were other letters in a similar vein. She sounded pathetically joyful that Romola replied and showered her with the love she so desperately needed in 'her devastating loneliness'.

'Perhaps we made many mistakes but we always meant well. We just did not see into the future. Poor Oti suffered so much, do not carry any anger in your heart against him. On his deathbed he said repeatedly we should have handled many things differently. Although I am dead-tired from my recent illness, I want to gather all my strength so that I can "fly" to you, but first I have to arrange certain matters here. I do not want to sell the house but have to sell whatever else I can to raise money.

Oti left Tamara, our adopted daughter, the house in the Fortress and 300 square feet of the ground here. Concerning Tamara's marriage, she would have eloped rather than lose her chosen man. Oti tried to talk her out of it, he was immensely worried for her future happiness. Love triumphed and to avoid any scandal, Oti accepted the situation like a gentleman but from then on he complained often about his heart. Maybe, if you would have been here with us, maybe... A mother's eye sees more wisely what is for the best, but we adored Tamara, we did not see clearly; let us face it, we were not so young... How fortunate that the family like her. When Mrs ... offered to take Tamara to her, so that she could raise her, maybe that is where I made the mistake in not accepting... Now I turn to you in deep sorrow and ask you to forgive me for the way in which we decided upon your younger daughter's fate...we made her a Hungarian citizen, we let her choose a profession which you never wished her to have. I have paid for it bitterly.'

In September, a letter arrived from Romola, congratulating her mother on her birthday, the 10th, which coincidentally was Romola's wedding anniversary. It was not written from Mittersill but from the home of Colonel Yarborough, where she was staying as a guest. She planned to go to Paris on the 20th October and to take Waslaw with her. She asked Emilia to make preparations for a visit to Mittersill. A certain number of formalities would first have to be dealt with. She advised Emilia to contact Major Tamas, director of the National Theatre in Budapest, who would help her with obtaining a visa and passport. Toth Miklós of the Ministry for Foreign Affairs in Vienna would give assistance once she reached there. Romola had heard from Tessa that all was well with her. She hinted at a journey to the States with Waslaw. *'I am a little bit concerned about such a long trip with him and for the fight for a new existence, but what else can I do. One has to work although I am so weary. All I would really like to do is rest.'*

Paul and his mother Gisella were in Mittersill at the time and he must have corresponded with Emilia concerning Romola's perpetually strained finances.

'I see from Paul's letter that you are in great financial trouble. Instead of lamenting my problems and my loneliness, I beg you

to stop smoking... If you are too tired, ask Paul to read my letters to you. May Heaven bless you, my dear Romicza, do not forget your old mother who will love you to Eternity. I kiss you and Vatza. With love...'.

Romola had made no overtures for me to accompany Emilia but when the time finally came for their reunion, Emilia was afraid to undertake such a strenuous trip on her own in her frail condition. And, who knows, perhaps she saw it as the ultimate goal to a reconciliation between me and my mother. For years, it had preyed on her mind that we were alienated from each other, of that I was aware. How could anybody guess what qualms I suffered, not certain of where my loyalties lay. I could not allow my grandmother to venture away on her own, yet at home I had my little daughter Kinga to consider. The relationship between Miklós and myself had slowly begun to degenerate – the honeymoon was long since over – 'Like as the waves make towards the pebbled shore, so do our minutes hasten to their end...'* How well one of my favourite sonnets by Shakespeare reflected my mood. Sensitive to the core, I was aware an invisible wall was building up between us. I loathed uprooting myself from my habitual environment. I subjected myself to self-interrogation, coming to the conclusion that uppermost on my list of subterfuges for not going was my fear of meeting Romola again. But in the end, duty to my grandmother won.

In early January 1947, Emilia and I were on a train bound for Vienna. There, Paul met us at the *Bahnhof* where we were to change trains. His incessant flow of chatter and flattery was unnerving. It was a lovely drive from the station to the castle – the landscape was clothed in a coat of glistening white snow. The Schloss Mittersill could not have had a more dramatic setting, and with its turrets and ramparts it presented a breathtaking sight of beauty, romance and the magical atmosphere of a long bygone age. In short – it was enchanting.

Upon our arrival, we were ushered into a pleasant-looking salon. My parents were seated in front of a roaring fire, playing cards. Romola rose from her chair and with outstretched arms walked swiftly over to Emilia, hugging and kissing her. She barely afforded a glance in my direction but after the effusive greetings subsided,

* *Sonnet LX,* William Shakespeare

she regained her normal, cool composure and acknowledged my presence by giving me a quick peck on one cheek. 'Isten hozott, Tamara' (Welcome, Tamara), was all she said in a tone implying that I was far from welcome.

Throughout it all, Tatakaboy had remained seated. He was dapperly dressed in a dark-striped suit with a finely dotted tie. He was a shade thinner, looked more relaxed than on the previous two occasions, but still observed me with a searching look; not a flicker of recognition was sparked off in his eyes. With a resigned shrug, he leaned his head back in the armchair. Hesitantly, I took a step forward but came to a halt at the sound of my mother's voice crisply commandeering us to freshen up for dinner. When I came downstairs again, I noticed my grandmother and mother were engaged in profound conversation with Paul. Feeling unwanted, I strolled out to the conservatory. My father was there with his nurse by his side. It was so poignant, that third encounter with him since childhood. And it was hard to accept the unvarnished truth that he did not know of my existence. We could not even communicate. I had no part in that mysterious dreamworld in which he had locked himself even before I was born.

Gingerly, I approached the nurse and asked if I could take my father for a stroll through the garden. He nodded agreement and tenderly I took Tatakaboy's hand in mine. Only the crunching of snow under our feet broke the quietness that enveloped us. He pulled me to the side of the path where the snow was neatly piled several feet high. It gave him childlike enjoyment to poke his feet one at a time into the soft white verge. The spell was rudely broken by the clanging of a bell and the nurse came running to fetch Monsieur Nijinsky in to dinner. The time had come to bid goodnight. I raised myself on tip-toe and kissed Tatakaboy on the cheek. He giggled ever so softly and embraced me before meekly following his keeper. I stood immobile until they had vanished indoors. It was the last time I was to see my father.

Conversation at dinner flowed innocuously at first. Romola told of her forthcoming plans to pursue a writer's career if only she had the stamina, and how Laura, my nurse from when I was a baby, had promised to relieve Romola off and on with the household chores. Kyra was to have come from Florence and Romola had gone by car to meet her at the Brenner Pass. She never turned up and Romola was completely in the dark as to what had happened. Neutral, harmless topics dispensed with, Romola trespassed onto the dangerous subject of money. She launched into a belligerent attack against Oti-Papa, claiming he had never helped support Emilia's two daughters and that he had lived off his wife. Like clouds gathering before a storm, the atmosphere became laden with recriminations. What was so diabolically wrong with the chemistry between the women of my family that we could never meet without blood pressures rising and sparks flying in ugly verbal exchanges?

The events of the next day were much worse and painful to relate. Paul asked me to accompany him to the village where he had some errands to attend to. I seized upon the opportunity as it would leave Emilia alone with her Molly to seek a truce between them. During the course of an otherwise impersonal conversation Paul cast forth the suggestion that Miklós and I should leave Hungary and its unhealthy 'climate' stirred up by the new régime. I agreed in principle but pointed out the futility for a gifted actor like Miklós to establish a career elsewhere. Besides, he would never be granted official permission to leave the country. The time ticked by as we wrangled over the pros and cons. Consequently, we arrived back too late for lunch. Romola pounced on me like a tigress, demanding to know the cause of the delay. I loathed the thought of yet another acrimonious confrontation and was determined to stand my own ground. With a boldness unusual for me, I simply reiterated Paul's proposal that I and my family leave Hungary. I turned round to gain Paul's support but he had conveniently slunk away. She behaved like a woman racked with jealousy and screamed at me to go to my room. Her angry posturing, still treating me like a child, was the last straw. Something snapped in my brain and I heard myself shouting at the top of my voice that I would not go to my room but out of the castle and home where I belonged, away from her hysterical tantrums and apparent hatred of me. Before she could muster an adequate retort, I had turned on my heels and sped up the stairs. The next time I spoke to my mother was thirteen years later in Canada.

I pleaded with my grandmother that she should stay but of her own accord Emilia decided to go back with me and consequently we departed the next day. Whether or not Emilia bade goodbye to Romola, I do not know. Once back home, life slipped into its usual routine.

Undeterred by the conflict that had arisen between us, Romola continued to write to Emilia, beseeching her to come back. She must have felt wretchedly forlorn. Paul was away on business trips most of the time. She put forth the suggestion she should write Emilia's memoirs. She had been to Paris on several occasions in the vain hope that there she could once more establish roots for herself and Waslaw. The American plans appeared to have been shelved. She turned her attention to England. Quite naturally, in a sense, because after all, Charlie-Papa had been born in Highgate. In June 1947, she was in London, lunching with Tamara Karsavina at the Hungarian Club in Manchester Square.

In a letter to Emilia from Mittersill, dated October 18th, 1947, she confided that she was desperately worried about Kyra who was all alone, ill and starving. Romola felt overwhelming distress at not being able to help her make ends meet. She confessed that she was exhausted after her own struggles during twenty-seven years. She had had enough.

'I do not have one true friend now who is on my side, Waslaw is a saint and an angel and Tessa has been with me most of my life. Poor little Kyra, whose life has always been so difficult, I feel so sorry for her. I am afraid to pick up the wanderer's stick once more and travel to the unknown with a seriously ill person.'

Then, a heartening communiqué arrived that she had been successful in obtaining a British passport for herself, and through the auspices of Duff Cooper, the British Ambassador in Paris, permission for Waslaw to accompany her and to live in England.

The news that her daughter would soon be leaving the Continent made Emilia determined to have a last reunion with her. Summoning up her strength she departed once more for Mittersill, this time in the company of her nephew.

Emilia wrote to her Romicza on November 10th, soon after the former's departure from Mittersill.

'I know I am a difficult and suspicious woman and that I do not always judge things clearly. If you think about it, you will understand that at my age my exhausted heart requires quietude and peace and much loving care. I have been very quarrelsome and also very much afraid. When you were angry I did not know where to hide. Surrounded by all your frightful worries and strife you are unable to control your nerves and you are not

always capable of feeling the suffering of others. You invited me with love yet my presence did not bring you joy and happiness... (They) deprived me of my last piece of bread. But should I lament? Duse, chasing a piece of bread in America, died there. Emma Grammatice is starving there. I was faithful to the National Theatre for seventy-five years, from the age of fourteen, not like my colleagues. Poor Charlie-Papa thought so highly of my talent that he wanted to send me to Paris – the entire aristocracy wanted to – yet I stayed. The wheel of fortune turns and turns. If you do not seize it, that is the end. And so it is with poor Kyra. Can't you send her some money? Could she not write to Natalie who loved her so? She would certainly help. It is terrible that Kyra is starving... My dear Romola, the tone of your letter is very sad. I do comprehend everything. You should never have been alone. What is the use to beg you to take care of your health, in the midst of so much conflict, so much grief, it is to no avail. I can only pray for you and Vaca, that the Good God will protect you from tremendous sorrow. From this distance I can feel your immeasurable pain. I suffer that you have to suffer in this way. Remember me sometimes. Feel that there is someone who truly loves you, waiting for you to come home. This is your mother whom fate has treated badly.'

Once more, Emilia survived a bout of pneumonia. Whatever I was to read later of her views on resuming residence in the Villa, it was she who insisted on going back yet again when she was fully recovered. Recurrently, she implored me to write to Romola, to apologise (for what?), but I adamantly refused. I could not even bring myself to ask her how she had found Romola and Waslaw.

Henceforth, it was only on those rare occasions when Emilia imparted snippets of news to me from England that I had an inkling of what happened after my parents left Mittersill.

They had travelled to England in November 1947, in the company of Paul, stopping over in Zürich for consultation with Dr. Rohr, who confirmed the Austrian village doctor's diagnosis that Waslaw suffered from high blood pressure. He prescribed a strict diet and medication. The first few days they had stayed at a hotel in London but Romola was eager to get Waslaw to the serene seclusion of the English countryside where he would have more freedom to take long walks amidst the nature he so loved.

19. Romola Nijinsky, Paris, 1926. Dedicated with love to her mother and Oti (Oskar Párdány). Photo by Cr R Manuel Frères

20. Romola and Waslaw Nijinsky in Kreuzlingen, 1934. Photo by Helen Fisher

21. Wedding of Kyra Nijinsky
to Igor Markevitch in
Budapest, April 24th, 1936
Background: Portrait of
Emilia Márkus as *La Dame
aux Camélias*

22. Kyra Markevitch with
Tamara Karsavina, one of
the wedding guests

23. Waslaw Nijinsky
    (Tatakaboy) in the garden
    of the Villa, Budapest,
    during World War II

24. Waslaw Nijinsky at Great
    Fosters, Egham, Surrey in
    1947

25. Waslaw and Romola
    Nijinsky at the Alexandra
    Palace. Standing behind
    them Norman Collins and
    Imlay Newbiggin-Watts,
    April 4th, 1950

26. Teruko Akashi, The
Takarazuka Theatre, Japan
Two pictures of Romola
Nijinsky and Teruko
Akashi, 1959 or 1960

27. Romola Nijinsky,
November, 1964. Courtesy
of Psychic News, London

Alexander Korda, who as an old acquaintance of Romola's, suggested that they move to a large country hotel in Egham. It was a delightful Tudor house and the suite comprised of four rooms.

Letters to Emilia arrived at that time with more frequency. Romola enthused over Waslaw's increased participation in everyday life.

'He watches me with interest when I type a letter or play solitaire. I decided I would take him to London to a few ballets and concerts. You should have seen how enthusiastically he applauded the performance of a young Mexican, Luisillo, who appeared with a Flamenco troupe.'

She dragged Waslaw to the theatres and to the cinema. It was revealed that his favourite actress was Paulette Goddard. In March, a gallery in Brook Street held an exhibition of Waslaw's drawings and Romola sent an invitation to Queen Mary to come. Whether she did or not, I cannot say.

On one of my regular visits to Emilia, she proudly waved a newspaper cutting in her hand. It was taken from *News Chronicle* of Friday, March 12th, 1948, and headed *Applause for the Man in the Box*. Waslaw and Romola had gone to the Saville Theatre the night before to watch Ram Gopal and his Indian dancers. 'They (Romola and Waslaw) stayed to the end of the performance, and when he rose to go there was a sound Nijinsky had not heard for many years – an audience applauding him.' The article was accompanied by a picture of Waslaw seated in the box. He had a crew haircut and wore what looked like a thick overcoat. He appeared to be old and weary; I barely recognised him.

In the spring of 1948, having found that the hotel environment was not suitable, Romola set about house-hunting and leased a charming place in Virginia Water in the proximity of Windsor Great Park.

To judge by her letters Romola was full of plans. She was working on a book to which she had already sold the film rights. She mentioned interviews in which she stated that she and Waslaw had decided to settle down in England for good and that together they would in due course establish an international theatre of ballet; a kind of University of the Dance. The newspaper cutting accompanying that letter read: 'My husband would devote himself to advising the artists and doing choreography.' How well I recall how Emilia shook her head in disbelief, as she carried on reading. I asked her why and she replied in her quiet way: 'I simply cannot understand the situation. I am bewildered. As much as I wish all the best for my Molly, I find it hard to accept the fact that Waslaw is well enough to be an artistic adviser. Surely you can draw to mind his strange behaviour when he stayed with us during the war. And then, Mittersill?' Sadly, yes, I remembered it only too well.

Romola continued to make every effort to put up a brave front not only to Emilia but to many in the entourage that flocked around Waslaw. But sometimes his true condition leaked through in the press. A tiny notice in the *Daily Express* of the 8th of April told how the greatest ballet dancer of them all had sat in the front stalls of the St Pancras Town Hall 'waiting to go on stage as patron of *Le Petit Ballet Imperial*' but that he had been unable to face it and Romola had been forced to take him backstage to rest and then to a seat in the 12th row. 'There, unsmiling, he accepted the bouquet he should have received before the once-familiar footlight.'

She warned Emilia against me and my family, i.e. my husband, in a letter dated July 23rd, 1948.

'Forget about Tamara's family, and, first and foremost, forget her. They only tear you apart. It is they who should help you, not you them. I haven't known your love since Tessa and Pár-dány appeared on the scene. You were lost to me...'

In a letter of December 16th that same year she informed Emilia that Kyra's former husband Igor had remarried. Vaslav, her grandson, was studying somewhere in England but nobody had troubled to give her his address, so she was unable to contact him. Tessa was useless and impossible. Romola had written to Kyra, asking her to spend Christmas with her, so that neither would have to spend the holiday alone, but she had not had a reply.

Romola's letter dated May 29th, 1949, was plaintive:

'Since the beginning of March I am alone with Vaslav. I cannot be a writer, a breadwinner, nurse, all rolled in one – I, with my sick leg. There are too many burdens heaped upon me...it is intolerable. I am not superhuman. Maybe we will leave here and go to the States or to South America, if only I still have

314

enough strength. It is terrible that neither Bronia nor Kyra help
support Vaslav. Unfortunately, the fact that Paul brought his
mother over has caused us all a great deal of trouble...Pray for
us, and write.'

Her game leg was due to a fall outside the house in Virginia
Water. She had torn a ligament and was laid up for many weeks and
subsequently could only move about with the aid of a cane.

Romola never mentioned an ambitious venture on a large scale,
the purpose of which was to bring sorely needed funds to the
Nijinsky Foundation. In a sense it became a non-success and I
imagine that is why she ignored it in her later book.

A letter from the Aga Khan in June 1949, reveals that Romola
had tried to contact him at the Ritz on a number of occasions. 'I
leave tomorrow for France, but letters are always forwarded. If
there is any way in which I can help you, please write to me.' As
later correspondence showed, she must already then have wanted
to sound him out about her idea. 'I am so very glad to hear that a
Committee of "The Nijinsky Foundation" is being formed. Of
course I am happy that my name should appear with the names of
Lady Mountbatten, Lady Astor and others....'

On the 15th September, Leon Hepner wrote to Romola, confirming that in November, he would organise 'a big "Nijinsky Gala" at
the Empress Hall, Earls Court, all profits from which, after deduc-
tion of Entertainment Tax and 10% Managerial Expenses, will be
handed over to you for the benefit of your husband... All profits
from the sale of programmes of the first Gala will also be handed
over to you....' An ensuing letter from Hepner stated, 'We have
received a telegram from Toumanova, asking us to contact her, as
from Wednesday, in Paris... I am also hoping to get Babilee and
have already spoken to Kochno offering to help us with the artistic
direction for the Gala...'

On the 27th October, the Aga Khan wrote a long letter to
Romola in which he expressed deep pessimism about the forthcoming event. He feared that 'there will be little, if any cash over
once the very heavy expenses are paid.' He went on to enumerate
his reasons; a vast number of tickets at high prices would have to be
sold; that the event was ill-timed – the end of November was not the
season when rich tourists frequented London; other ballets might
prove a counter-attraction; and he summed it up by saying he

believed 'the only proper place where one Gala Performance ought to be given is Covent Garden, the home of Ballet and the scene of your husband's great triumphs.' At the end of the letter he re-affirmed his fears that the proposed Ballet at the Empress Hall would not produce sufficient money after all expenses had been paid. He was to be proved right.

According to a report in the *Daily Herald*:

'Six thousand people watched entranced last night while world famous stars danced at the Empress Hall. Two seats were vacant. They should have been filled by the man in whose honour and for whose help the show had been organised, Vaslav Nijinsky, and his wife.'

Only a few short hours before the curtain was to rise, Romola had telephoned to say the excitement and emotion would be too hard a strain on her husband. Mrs Audrey Wordsworth, one of the organisers, said: 'Our disappointment and that of the artists gathered to pay him tribute must have been as great as that of Nijinsky.' For all the stars – Toumanova, Chauvire, Babilee, Tall-chief, Massine and Skouratoff – the show had meant personal sacri-fice in one form or another. Toumanova, for example, missed four performances in Paris, and she would not need again new costumes costing £55 each. It was hoped that a cheque for £1,000 would be handed over to the Fund.

In a letter of the 27th October, 1949, Romola confessed to Emilia she was very run down, her own health impaired; she was still extremely anaemic and lacking in calcium. She had begun to worry about Waslaw's physical condition, and when one day he was seized by a sudden and violent attack of hiccups, she had grown alarmed and telephoned to Professor Rohr in Zürich for advice.

Going through Emilia's papers many years later I was unable to find any further correspondence from Romola to her after the end of October.

As Miklós's career soared and he became more and more successful in the theatre, so mine dwindled to nothing. I was offered a position as announcer, and later as actress and director to the Youth Programme on Radio Broadcasting, an opportunity I eagerly grasped even though I found it somewhat daunting. And remarkable, considering I did not belong to any political party and

316

was assumed to be unsympathetic to the government on account of my family background. Once and once only, did I drop my mask of neutrality when reading the news. Halfway through the text handed to me, I unwittingly jumped up and exclaimed: 'But this is....' A steely look from my supervisor stopped me from carrying on: '...outrageous, a lie.' Biting my tongue, I calmly continued: 'Yesterday, at the trial of Mindszenty (no mention that he was a Cardinal), he confessed to treason in conspiring to overthrow our new government.' Reading that bulletin was probably the best performance of my life. My voice gave no indication that I felt like a traitor to my firm beliefs nor that tears lurked behind my eyelids. The security system at the broadcasting station was tight to the extreme. Intimidatingly militant guards stopped every visitor at the main gate and asked for identity cards. How stifling it was to breathe in a moral climate that kept one repressed and in constant fear.

Then, a cryptic telephone call came from an attorney in Budapest, urgently demanding my presence in his office. A matter of grave importance had arisen involving my mother. I pleaded with Miklós to come with me and as we entered the attorney's office I could feel the pulse in my temple throbbing. Mischief was brewing, that was my automatic reaction, but I was wholly unprepared for what was to come.

Without preamble, the attorney went straight to the crucial point. His client, Romola Nijinsky, had empowered him to persuade me to renounce the name of Nijinsky and to sign a document to that effect.

Flashback after flashback pierced my numbed brain: Romola in the Villa years previously accusing me of 'hostility' toward my parents; taunting me about Emilia's adoption of me; my Hungarian citizenship which made me an 'enemy' of my father; her accusation that I was a pawn in Oti's hands, abetting him to incite Emilia against her. Her strident, shrill voice resounded in my ears like a bad dream from the past and I recalled how she had wished that I give up acting. Why? She had muttered some lame excuse that no one but Waslaw should bear the name Nijinsky on stage.

I roused myself from my stupor and studied the document in front of me; a piece of paper I had no intention of signing. Why should I? Legally, I had the right to bear my name. I had a birth certificate to prove it. In a hollow voice, I enquired what the consequences would be if I refused. The attorney shrugged his shoulders and in a resigned voice declared that he had no option but to bring legal action against me. I stared at him in disbelief. Why would my own mother do such a thing? On what grounds? How would it benefit her? He cleared his throat: '…the question of inheritance…and to protect the moral rights of a mentally sick person.' The words did not quite register. By then, my thinking was blurred. But feebly I pressed on. What would be the outcome of a lawsuit? There was a deathly pause and then came the dénouement: 'In order to have sole access to any inheritance, your mother will declare you illegitimate.' I burst into hysterical laughter, tears streaming down my cheeks. I strode over to the window, looked down at the Danube, on whose shores stood the Academy of Science, the majestic building in which my mother had been born. Watching the steady flow of the river, unperturbed by the antics of mortals, had a soothing effect on me and I regained my composure. I turned to my mother's 'messenger boy' and stated my case briefly. His innuendoes could be interpreted to mean that my mother might have had an affair with another man. That was none of my business. Whether or not I ever inherited was the least of my worries. Whatever my mother wished to do was up to her, although I deplored that she had to stoop so low to secure her own financial gain. Having said which, I repeated that I would under no circumstances relinquish my birthright.

Leaving the musty chamber, I fumbled down the wide, marble staircase, followed by Miklós. He was already formulating an excuse to absent himself, when my defences crumbled and I began to sob uncontrollably. My mother had turned her back on me, Miklós was in the process of doing the same. Our relationship had been building up to a climax for a long while but I still loved him profoundly. I beseeched him to spare me a few moments. Chiding me for creating a scene in public, he led me to a small, smoke-filled espresso bar around the corner, one of the many that had sprung up after the war, unofficial rendezvous for the intellectuals.

What Miklós revealed to me during the ensuing half-hour sapped me of what little strength I had left. He wasted no time. I heard my husband confess that shortly after our engagement he had been in touch with Oskar, unbeknown to either Emilia or myself. He had wished to probe into certain unsubstantiated rumours regarding my parents and me. Oti-Papa had told him frankly about that evening in the late autumn of 1919 when Romola declared her intention to

318

go to Waslaw's room to make love to him; to prove to the world that she could cure him and give him the son he so desperately desired.

But then he pressed on how a young doctor, who attended Romola and Waslaw in St Moritz, had fallen passionately in love with her. Gossip would have it that he had been flattered that the wife of such a famous personality as Waslaw Nijinsky favoured him. Besides, Romola was only in her late twenties, beautiful and elegant, capable of turning any man's head. With the worsening of her husband's unbalanced state of mind, she sought sympathy and a shoulder to lean against. Not an inhuman frailty. But there was one drawback. The doctor was a happily married family man.

Then came the fateful night she forced herself upon her husband. Soon after that she discovered she was pregnant and the full cognisance of what she had done must have dawned on her. Waslaw had been declared incurably schizophrenic. Suppose she gave birth to a child who would inherit his madness? Miklós hastened to add that much of this was conjecture. She had panicked, so the story went, and had gone to her friend the doctor, demanding he should perform an abortion or else she would announce to the world that he was the father. He had blankly refused on ethical grounds and apparently Romola in revenge had carried out her threat and gone to the Medical Authorities. The doctor had been temporarily suspended from his practice pending an investigation. The ensuing smear campaign involving the doctor and his family was rumoured to have driven him to suicide, but Miklós had been unable to find concrete proof of this and was sceptical that it was true. The case had been held behind closed doors. Miklós had pursued his investigations even further and had been in touch with high-ranking officials in court whom he knew through certain connections, but had been unable to glean further information.

Miklós brought the matter to an abrupt end by getting up to take his leave. I just sat there, torpid. It was as if I had been struck by lightning. I dreaded the thought of being alone and entreated Miklós to allow me to accompany him to the theatre. But he callously pointed out that I had my duty to perform as a mother. A peck on my cheek and he was out of sight. When had he started to drift away from me? Was it all my fault? Had I neglected him? He yearned for the glamorous side of life and admittedly, after Kinga's birth, I had perhaps devoted too much time to her. In a despairing mood, I wandered home, weary to the very marrow of my bones. Romola's monstrous and cruel action toward me, the sensational scandal surrounding her past, were too much to cope with. My brain cells refused to coordinate to find the answers. But Miklós's fickle behaviour eclipsed the horror of my mother's.

In the end, Romola never did pursue a lawsuit against me and we were years later reconciled as mother and daughter. The episode in the attorney's office was to ferment in my mind for years. Nor was I able to screw up sufficient courage to raise the issue with my mother when I eventually did meet her again. However, it must have constantly preyed on her mind because she had sworn to Irina that I was Waslaw's daughter – that the evening she had forced entry into his room he had been in one of his rare, calm moods. This was substantiated in a furiously scathing letter which Romola addressed to Irina, accusing her of having taken the *Faune* notations from the Opera Museum in Paris for her own use, a fact which Ira strongly denied. In that same letter, Romola pursued several other matters. She lashed out at Ira that she and Kyra were spreading the false rumour that I was not Waslaw Nijinsky's daughter. Ira had become deeply upset and declared that it was a gross misinterpretation of the truth, that actually it was my sister and she alone who had taken upon herself to make such an allegation. What impelled her to do so, I cannot say.

It was in early December 1949, I was to learn the truth about my husband's late nights, his frequent absences from home. 'Well-meaning' friends told me that Miklós had lost his heart to a promising and gifted ballerina. She was described as very young, beautiful, willowy, dark-haired.

In September 1949, Emilia celebrated her eighty-ninth birthday. Frail, yes, physically shaky, but mentally in full possession of her faculties. Her face was remarkably free from wrinkles and her voice could still charm her listeners. She had resumed her visits to the theatre and was still an avid reader. Her favourite literature was stacked high on her bedside table as in previous years. She adored her great granddaughter, Kinga, who could twist her around her chubby little fingers.

Then one day Emilia fell. At first it appeared to be a trivial accident which she brushed to one side. Nonetheless, from then on she declined rapidly. On the 13th December, I was visiting her when our family doctor took me to one side. He gave me the tragic news bluntly; she was not only suffering from jaundice but also incurable cancer. He wondered if I would wish her to have a blood transfusion as she was very weak. After consultation, it was decided to spare her that distress and pain as it would be to no avail. '...like pouring water into a barrel riddled with holes,' the doctor sighed. He was a trusted friend as well as our family doctor, spanning many years, and I could tell something else was weighing on his mind. I asked him point-blank what it was. He hesitated a moment, then said that I had to contact my mother and tell her of Emilia's condition.

At first, I fulminated over this demand from him, of all people, to whom I had confided the ill-fated trip to Mittersill and its consequences. When I reminded him, he merely shook his head and reiterated that I would have to do it for my grandmother's sake. It was not the time to pursue a personal vendetta. Selflessly, I had to cast all else aside and concentrate on my dying grandmother. A cable was despatched to Romola.

On December 20th, Emilia's condition deteriorated and a Franciscan monk was sent for to administer the last rites. Miklós, his mother, and little Kinga were also present. Emilia lay with her eyes closed. The priest took his departure together with my mother-in-law and Kinga. Miklós and I sat silently by her side. Suddenly, she opened her eyes, and with her last remaining strength groped for our hands and clasped them together. In a barely audible whisper she said: 'My children, be at peace.' After that, she slipped into a coma. Providentially, she knew nothing of the disharmony between Miklós and myself and she was spared the knowledge that her warning against him had been right.

My vigil at Emilia's side began. A strange phenomenon was to take place. The doctor arranged for a nurse to come to administer morphine if necessary and to relieve me now and again. When she arrived we went to the bedroom. We stood transfixed on the threshold, staring in the direction of the bed. Slowly, Emilia was lifting her right arm at the elbow, then dropping it to her side. Uninterruptedly, this inexplicable procedure continued day and night. The doctor was nonplussed, unable to give it a medical explanation. Sister, a dependable, warmhearted woman, exclaimed that it was as though Emilia was trying to reach out to someone.

Christmas Eve was approaching. I had done nothing to prepare for the 'joyous and glorious' feast traditionally celebrated that day in Hungary, but I was confident that Miklós's mother would see to it that my little girl was not deprived. My place was with Emilia to her last breath. Sitting there in the semi-darkness of the room, looking down at her, it dawned on me how very much I owed her, foremost, one of the most precious gifts of all – genuine love, especially in those adolescent years.

Two jarring events occurred. One day, the doorbell rang and outside stood a formidable woman who, without introducing herself, wondered if the premises were available. Like vultures at the sight of prey, people were ruthless in their pursuit of a roof over their heads, the war having destroyed so many habitable dwellings. A second caller was the postman with Emilia's pension. The money was sorely needed but I had to tell him that Emilia could not sign for it. 'Is she still alive?' he queried. I barely had time to nod assent before he tiptoed into the bedroom. Grasping Emilia's right hand, he placed a pen between her fingers and guided them to mark an 'x' above her printed name. He then pressed her thumb on it, a symbol that he had carried out his official duty. Methodically, he counted out the money and bade a solicitous farewell.

Hour after hour I sat there, patiently waiting, hoping against all hope that she might wake up. By now I had despaired of hearing from Romola although I had written, clumsily apologising for my behaviour at Mittersill, and going into detail about Emilia's illness. In doing so I felt I was atoning for any wrongdoing against Emilia and perhaps it would penetrate through to her that I had at last obeyed her wishes. Just before midnight a terse cable did arrive. It was from Romola in London to the effect she regretted being unable to come, that she wished Emilia well and us all a happy Christmas. I showed the slip of paper to the sympathetic nurse. She told me to lay it on the pillow next to Emilia and to whisper in her ear that her Molly sent her a message of endearment, how much she loved her and how deeply sorry she was that she could not spend Christmas with her and me. I stared at her vacantly. My grandmother was in a coma, beyond my reach. The nurse stubbornly prodded me forward. I bent down and whispered.... I straightened up to behold a miracle had taken place. Emilia's thin, veined arm was resting peacefully on the silk blanket. That was all she had been waiting for, to hear from her Molly. She died in the early hours of the morning. She lay there all of Christmas Eve in her bedroom of the Villa until the undertakers arrived around six o'clock in the evening with the coffin. Only my friend Michael was with me then. He placed a red rose over her heart, I, her rosary. However much

Death is expected to take a loved one away, it is almost unbearable to face that moment when it does come. When they carried her away, the dam burst. Michael had to sort me out, turn the key in the lock, escort me home to have Christmas with Kinga and Miklós, the last the three of us were to have together.

The funeral was barely over when I fell ill and had to be hospitalised. I had become pregnant in what I believed was a rapturous moment of reconciliation with Miklós, but the strain of the past weeks had taken its toll and I had a miscarriage. It was faithful Michael who visited me in hospital, who saw to it that the remaining bits of Emilia's furniture were temporarily stored. He brought the news about the tenants who had taken over the Villa – a woman's organisation. Their occupancy was beyond my control. He had salvaged in safekeeping for me the few valuables, Emilia's correspondence, comprising mostly letters from Romola, as well as family photographs and documents.

I heard nothing further from Romola after Emilia's death nor, sadly, did any letters arrive from either Kyra or Aunt Tessa. But by then I was past caring.

* * *

1950 – Spring scented the air with the fragrance of acacias and lilac blossoms. Tables and chairs sprang up like mushrooms outside the sidewalk cafés. People had shed their long overcoats, heavy shawls, galoshes and thick boots. The capital had awakened from a long winter's slumber and the battle scars were fading.

Miklós had walked out of our home in late January, having made it amply clear that our marriage was an utter failure. He promised to take care of the usual, sordid formalities involving a divorce. Ours was not to be an amicable separation. We were to wage a bitter tug-of-war over the custody of Kinga, Miklós ruthlessly demanding that she should live with him, his new love, and his mother. I had no work. When I reported back to the studio after being discharged from hospital, I found that my identity card had been checked against a list of 'undesirables' and I was summarily dismissed.

One afternoon in April, I was waiting for Michael at a quaint old coffee shop I used to frequent. He arrived late and with profuse apologies handed me a dark red rose. We sat there, basking in the sun, carrying on a low-key conversation about nothing in particular, avoiding any topic that might have bearing on my recent experiences. A shadow obscured the rays of the sun, and I looked up to find Miklós standing in front of me. An electric shock passed through my body. I still loved him blindly and would have done anything to have him back. He looked as debonair as ever, impeccable in a pin-striped suit, ivory cufflinks in the white silk sleeves of his shirt, the elegant tie, my last gift to him. I studied him closer and noticed he was without his usual composure. He cleared his throat, uncertain what to say. Then it came. He had been to our flat to collect something and found a cable which he had opened by mistake. He apologised for being the bearer of such bad news. He handed me the cable. I read it out loud.

> 'Vaslav died Holy Saturday, April 8
> Romola'

Michael kissed my hand and begged me to accept his deepest sympathy. Miklós stood there silently. What could he say? I thanked him for taking the trouble to track me down, and then walked away without a backward glance at the two men standing there.

Returning to the flat I picked up Kinga, and with her little hand in mine walked to the Villa. Kinga pushed the wrought iron gate wide open. It greeted us with a rusty, creaking sound. The premises had as yet not been taken into use. My child rushed up the steps between the two stone lions. She begged me to let her go inside. Maybe we would find Dédi* still there waiting for us.

I sank down on the grass, leaning my head on my arms, too shocked to find relief in tears. I saw Tatakaboy sitting in the white wicker chair, complacently picking his thumb with his forefinger, a gentle smile on his face.

'*Tamarushka*, courage...'

---

* *Dédi*, the nickname for *Dédnagymama*, Great Grandmother.

CHAPTER 10

TURMOIL IN BUDAPEST

Late Spring 1950 found me in despair, still shocked by the events which had wrenched so many loved ones from me; my grandmother, my husband, my unborn child, and then my father, virtually all within the past six months. It was hard enough even to bear the loss of the Villa, forever stripped of its vibrant personality and the echoes of joyful childhood, today confiscated by the grim, new régime; the harrowing divorce proceedings; and the abrupt dismissal from work.

Although some years had elapsed since the end of the war I trembled at the sound of a loud noise; the fear of a bomb attack still haunted me. And the enemies from across the borders had been replaced by enemies within every community – that 'fellow neighbour' whose ideological views were so alien to one's own.

Another grave problem was the acute shortage of housing with which the government had to wrestle. Budapest had not been as fortunate as Paris, which had been declared 'an open city'. Scores of buildings had been destroyed, not only by bombs dropping from the sky, but by the incessant street fighting. Hundreds upon hundreds of refugees now crowded the city, the surviving Jews who had ruthlessly been evicted from their homes and were now wanted back, the farmers who had lost their land and, rather than work in the communes, sought labour in the factories. Hungary had been defeated, bled dry, in two world wars, and faced financial ruin. From once having been a rich agricultural country, she was now slowly being transformed into an industrial state. Pressure had been brought to bear by party members needing decent flats to live in. The statute was plain-spoken, no mincing of words: one had to apply through the City Hall for a place to 'live'. The appropriate forms had to be filled in complete with legal stamps and signatures. If one was a high-ranking party member, a blue-collar worker, had a 'flawless' background, i.e. unblemished by any connection with the aristocracy, if one swore allegiance to the dictatorship, if one had one child, then, and only then, would one be eligible for ONE room.

In that respect I was favoured although not for long. When Miklós moved out of my life, I stayed on in the flat we had acquired years previously and shared with his mother. My mother-in-law occupied one room. I remained in the room I had formerly shared with my husband. Kinga had her own little room and the fourth we used as a salon. We were an odd trio. Miklós's mother was a tight-lipped, domineering woman. But her presence had its advantages. Cleanliness was an obsession with her, consequently she kept an immaculate house for us, and she performed magical tricks producing savoury meals with the meagre food we could procure either on the open or the black market.

Miklós visited his mother and daughter on a regular basis. Sometimes, he brought Kinga's future stepmother along. Officially, we were not yet divorced. I refused to discuss the matter. Drowning in my own self-pity and vanity, I shrugged off the episode as a passing affair. When Miklós so dispassionately walked out on me, I lost my happiness; no longer was I fulfilled as a woman, no more dreams, no love, no sharing. Romola, too, had lost her husband. But if a loved one is taken away by death, it is absolute. The cord is severed. Had it been more gruelling for her than for me? Physically, Waslaw was gone forever but my Miklós was vibrantly alive. For many months I was to be haunted by hope that he would ring the doorbell, look at me with the tenderness he had once bestowed on me, and beg my forgiveness.

Every once in a while I spent a relaxing evening together with my friend Michael who lived with his mother Zelma and a brother. Michael was later to become assistant director of Budapest's Theatre Museum, where official records of the Arts were kept. Their home radiated warmth and friendliness, and over a cup of tea we would while away the hours talking about sundry things, the risky todays, the uncertain tomorrows, and our yesterdays, a mixed bag of joy and sorrow. Never once did Michael reprove me for any foolish, false steps I had taken in the past. It was he who snapped me out of my current saturnine temperament and spineless approach to life by means of a simple pastime. It was on the occasion that we drew up a list of the women in the Nijinsky and the Pulszky families, outlining their tragic fates. Last on the list was my name. I was suddenly jolted into the realisation yet another name could be added, Kinga's. That was the moment my eyes were opened and I threw aside my self-indulgence and pretence. For her sake I would try to break the jinx. I owed it to her. It was essential that I find employment. I was to learn that was easier said than done in the harsh 1950's. Bureaucracy and restrictions challenged me at every turn.

The ink had hardly dried on the signatures of the divorce papers before Miklós married the dark-haired ballerina with whom he had had an affair. Weekends, he continued to come over to pick up Kinga and it was on one such occasion he suggested I should apply for an audition on a new government scheme for actresses who were unemployed. The acting profession was still held in high esteem and the reigning party in Hungary wished to establish the same standards for them as their counterparts enjoyed in the Soviet Union, better living quarters, higher salaries, etcetera. To my delight, I passed with flying colours but when I learned that I would have to join a repertory company and go on the road to play in the smallest villages throughout the country, spreading culture impregnated with the new ideologies, I flatly declined. Not only were the political motivations behind the scheme abhorrent to me but I shuddered at the thought of being away from Kinga any length of time.

A second choice was offered to me by the forbidding woman in the Ministry for Culture's drab office. She was a repellent-looking creature, garbed in a threadbare, grey skirt and yellowish blouse, her hair tightly pulled back in a chignon, her teeth nicotine-stained. A position with the State Puppet Theatre! The idea revolted me at first. I knew absolutely nothing about this 'children's world'. Hesitantly, in a quavering voice, I ventured to ask if there were any other vacancies. The dragon demolished any illusions I might harbour on that score by hinting at what could be in store for a fussy person like myself. I drew to mind the terrible reports of what happened to people who did not comply with the wishes of the State and quickly accepted.

With apprehension I entered a new world the following morning as a member of the Hungarian State Puppet Theatre. It was to take me nearly two years to learn not only how to manipulate the puppets but also to understand what a wonderful form of art it really is. Before the war, only an amateur group of puppeteers existed in Budapest but now, under new masters, a professional Puppet Theatre for children and adults had been built up. To my astonishment, I learned that puppetry was an ancient art; that Napoleon had ordered puppeteers to entertain his troops during his

327

Egyptian campaign; that Goethe had observed some satirical puppet shows in the market place when he was a little boy and it was from this image he got the idea for *Faust*. The more I gleaned knowledge of this art form, the more I enjoyed and appreciated it. The rehearsals were endless. We had to stand, holding the puppets high above our heads. Our theatre was not a marionette theatre, where the puppets are manipulated from above with the aid of strings. We used small hand puppets and the so-called *Wayang puppets* (also known as rod puppets). The Wayang puppets originated in Asia and were adapted to the modern puppet stage by the great Russian puppeteer Obrakov.

I was self-sustained now, earning money, which provided mental fortitude. I had at last proved, not only to myself but to Miklós, I could stand on my own two feet. Since the fateful day the cable arrived announcing my father's death, I had lost contact with my family. Rumours reached me that Romola was in the States and that Aunt Tessa had settled down in Switzerland after her lengthy sojourn in Denmark where friends of Erik Schmedes had been successful in arranging a small pension for her. Kyra and I had lost track of each other during the war; I assumed she was still in Italy.

The pressure on the individual was hard. Stalin was still alive. We were separated from outside communication by an Iron Curtain. Even a whisper that one had association with the West could mean imprisonment or worse. It was only at infrequent intervals we were able to tune in to 'Radio Free Europe' behind closed doors and shutters. In spite of the element of danger, those news bulletins were exchanged in hushed tones, often at secret rendezvous.

The black market was a flourishing business and one day I stumbled upon an address where a woman was selling her belongings, mostly clothing. I went in the hope of finding something useful with which to replenish my wardrobe. I purchased a sweater and a couple of blouses. Once home, I could not wait to try on my treasures. When I eagerly pulled the blouse over my head, I felt a hard object in the left cuff. Upon closer scrutiny I found that something heavy had been sewn into the cuff. Ripping up the seam, I uncovered two shiny 'Napoleons'. It was a crime to possess foreign currency. I dared not return the blouse; besides, sound logic told me I had paid for it. But where to hide the two golden pieces I clutched in the palm of my hand? I jumped with apprehension when the doorbell rang. I suspected the police had come to claim the coins, and I stood frozen to the spot. The piercing ringing of the bell ceased, to be replaced by loud banging, and it was only then I detected Kinga's voice above the din, begging to be let in. How can I possibly convey to those who have been fortunate enough never to have lived in the shadow of a dictatorship how one reacted even to the most insignificant events. Persecution reared its sinister head everywhere.

The problem of how to dispose of the Napoleons nagged me for weeks. By a stroke of luck, I learned that a colleague's boyfriend commuted to and from Vienna at regular intervals on errands cloaked with mystery. I decided to take her into my confidence and seek her advice. She assured me that her friend could take the coins with him on one of his 'business' trips. She queried what I wanted to have in return. A gold chain? A Swiss watch? I quickly decided upon the latter and then pushed the whole affair out of my mind, having found a secure place to secrete the coins.

Months later, the telephone rang and it was my colleague who wondered if we could arrange to meet on the Margit Bridge. Would I wear the blouse she had so admired as she wished to sew one similar. At first I was puzzled. Then I understood. Of course, THE blouse, with the Napoleons. I retrieved the coins from their hiding place. It was dusk by the time I reached the bridge. Not many people were about. My friend came toward me with a big smile, and grasped my hand in greeting. I slipped her the coins, which she quickly substituted for a gold watch. Once the merchandise had changed hands she vanished. A trivial adventure, perhaps, in the light of what went on in that Cold War but all the same, it had me hovering on the threshold of suspense and danger. Today, some thirty years later, that watch is still my faithful companion.

It was a trying time in which to bring up children. Distrust and suspicion hung in the air and one had to teach them twisted morals, to become secretive, and under no condition to repeat outside the home what they heard from their parents. Kinga went to a nearby grade school. She was fast growing up into a quiet, industrious girl. At her school, the pupils had to study Russian as their second language; daily, they were indoctrinated with the newfangled 'liberated ideals'. One particularly wintry afternoon stands out from all the rest. It had already turned dark and Kinga had not arrived from school. Fearing something had happened, I rushed to the bus stop. After an interminable wait Kinga arrived. I alternately cried and scolded her as I hugged her to my breast. When I reproached her for having given me such a fright, she said she was sorry but that she had been to church. She made me faithfully promise not to tell a living soul what had transpired, not even her father. Fearing that the walls had ears, she lowered her voice and divulged the wherefore of her belated return. She had two very good friends in her class. The three trusted each other implicitly and had come to a grave decision – to take an oath in front of the painting of St Filomena that as long as they lived, they were determined to fight against Communism. My girl was eight years old.

It must have been a year or thereabouts after Miklós and I parted that I first met László (Laci) Weninger at a rehearsal. He was an extremely versatile man; orchestra leader, musical director, composer. The stage was devoid of heating and I can still see him now, how he sat in front of the piano, wearing a heavy overcoat, a cigarette between his lips. His face was so lined and with an expression of deep melancholy. An enigmatic and complex figure. Sarcastic and cynical in his behaviour to the other artists, he treated me with infinite understanding; his professional awareness diagnosed first-class stage fright. Quietly, reassuringly, he started to sing, clearly enunciating each word of the song that had stuck in my throat. All the while, his fingers ran smoothly over the keyboard. Like magic, I mastered the song.

Now and then I would encounter him either in the theatre or in one of the popular gathering places in the city. Casual greetings were exchanged, nothing more. Desperately seeking extra income, I heard of a State Theatrical Group who performed in the fashionable provinces and who required a stand-in for an actress who had suddenly taken ill. As luck would have it, I was given the opportunity to replace her and I also managed to place Kinga in safe hands. By sheer coincidence, Laci was on the same tour.

The following weeks it was he who brought some rays of sunshine into my recently bleak and barren life. He became my constant companion, and with his dry humour he dispelled the clouds of gloom that had encapsulated me for so long. It was during one of our strolls along the shores of Lake Balaton, his own past came to light in an exchange of confidences. His mother had born ten children, two of whom died in the influenza epidemic during the First World War. He confessed that he had despised his father because of the latter's abuse of his mother. Heartbroken at witnessing her suffering, he had gone so far as to threaten his father's life when he was an adolescent. An ill-judged wartime marriage ended in the divorce court, and together with his son Peter, who was about Kinga's age, he now lived with his mother and a younger sister, who went to college. It was on the tip of my tongue to ask about his ex-wife but at the last moment I decided against it. I did not wish to become too involved in his life. I had come to regard him purely as a good friend and therefore, when Laci made known his feelings for me at the end of the tour, I rejected him. Miklós still remained the shadow between me and other men. I fenced off definite advances, resisted intimate relationships.

In Budapest once more, I threw myself with renewed energy into my work in the Puppet Theatre. Doggedly, I learned all the tricks of the trade, foremost that one had to practise every single day for hours in order to attain perfection. There were no performances on Mondays, otherwise the theatre's doors were open six days a week, including matinées for children and students from schools in the provinces. On Sundays, we had as many as three performances. For the children we played much-loved fairy tales such as *Cinderella* and *Little Red Riding Hood* as well as animated stories with a 'moral' attached to them. The evenings were devoted to variety shows; humorous or political one-act sketches. Although in theory every syllable was censored, some anti-government references did slip through the net, much appreciated by audiences.

The director of the State Puppet Theatre was a former stage hand from the National Theatre, who well remembered me. He was a quiet, intelligent man. Under his management the performances were sold out weeks in advance. The secret of his success lay in his uncanny ability to acquire leading playwrights, musicians, actors and stage designers. I could not help but deeply admire his brilliant 'juggling' to retain a cultural and intellectual staff, and this in a decade in Hungary's history when the régime tried to efface all but the blue-collar workers.

That turbulent period contains so many bitter remembrances of things past. I was oppressed by the humiliation many of my friends had to endure. Shorn of the dignity of being treated like human beings, there were thousands among the gentry and the opposition who were deprived of their occupations, lost fringe benefits, pensions, everything. They were reduced to selling their few worldly goods on the black market to stay alive. When the housing shortage became precariously acute, the government solved the situation by singling out this class of society to be sent to distant villages hundreds of miles away from the capital with sometimes merely twenty-four hours' notice.

One such tragic case came to my attention when I decided to look up a friend of mine, the wife of a colonel, who had three darling daughters. We had lost touch with each other shortly after the end of the war. As I neared the building where they lived, I saw to my relief it had not been damaged by bombs, shoddier perhaps, but that was all. I glanced through the names on the letterboxes but theirs was missing. Hesitantly, I rang the bell marked *concierge*. I was rebuffed in no uncertain terms by the coarse female who answered. In short, she hoped my friends had gone to Hell and that I should follow them.

It was not until many weeks later that I was able to track them down. Their fate resembled that of countless others; involuntary resettlement. After a hazardous journey, they had reached a tiny village where a sympathetic farmer offered them the use of an old barn. There, the family of five had made their new 'home'. Their beds were hay, their staple diet milk, bread from the farm, and root vegetables. No running water, no electricity, no heating of any kind. My heart ached for them but what could I do?

Late one Sunday evening after a performance, Kinga excitedly rushed into my dressing-room, hugging a beautiful doll. Clothed in silk and lace, it bore all the hallmarks of Vienna or Paris, not an item one could purchase in Budapest in those days. I was naturally curious as to who had given it to her. She had spent her usual weekend visiting her father and it was when she was taken to dinner with him at a restaurant, a foreign man, a guest of Miklós's, handed it to her. She bubbled with pride as she recounted the incident. Miklós was punctilious about delivering our daughter back safely to me and I rushed out to the stage door. I found him still lingering about, waiting, as it happened, for me to come out. He had something of importance to convey to me. For a split second my heart skipped a beat. Was he perhaps going to ask for a reunion; his marriage had failed? But I was brought down to earth by his next remark. His foreign friend, the donor of the doll, knew Romola and had met her in the States. I tried to arouse a flicker of interest. What news did he bring?

'Not much,' he retorted, 'but apparently she has had a new book published about your father entitled *The last Years of Nijinsky*, which has appeared both in the States and in England.' What did it contain? Was there any mention of either Miklós or myself in it? He could not say. And to my surprise I found I was wholly indifferent. I did not have her address and, besides, what did I have to tell her? That she was right – my marriage had been a gross mistake? Rub salt in my wounds? The instinct of self-preservation warned me not to contact her under any circumstances. So far, I had managed to survive despite not being a member of the Party. I did not wish to draw attention to myself by communicating with someone in the Western World. Let sleeping dogs lie.

The following week, a more sinister occurrence arose which was to make me feel like a hunted creature. A subpoena was thrust in my hands on the very day I was due for the dress rehearsal of a new play. I was summoned to appear in court regarding the custody of Kinga, a matter I innocently believed to have been dispensed with legally, and that the law was on my side. Alas, a tedious and ignoble battle was to commence. Miklós held the trump card because the flat in which I lived officially belonged to him. Unscrupulously, he had worked it out that he could oust me and move in with his new wife. However preposterous the idea, he had a perfect right to put me on the street, thus providing him with an excellent weapon to gain complete custody of our child. A homeless mother stood no chance and I had nothing to barter with, nothing to offer in exchange for another flat. Reluctantly, I abandoned my usual reserve and sought Laci's counsel. Acting upon his advice, I filed a petition with the housing authorities for one room in the flat to be registered in my name. I hired two husky men to move my paltry possessions into the one small room on a day that my mother-in-law was out. She returned before the deed was completed, and rushed to the telephone to call her son. The speed with which he arrived only surpassed his rage. The horrifying brawl that erupted made me hysterical, and I fled out of the flat, coatless and wearing only thin slippers in the freezing cold. My one clear thought was to seek Laci's help but there was nobody at home. A colleague of mine found me aimlessly wandering about, distraught and shivering.

It was to be this loyal friend who sorted me out. She pointed out the incongruity of attempting to live under the same roof as Miklós's mother; saw to it that Kinga was collected after school, contacted solicitors, opened her home to Kinga and myself until we were settled elsewhere. She wheedled me out of my apathy and was instrumental in finding a vacancy on the second floor of an old baroque building, whose once noble interior had been chopped up into flats. It must have galled and infuriated Miklós that I managed to get authorisation to use in exchange the room that we had fought over. A baser side to my nature filled me with malicious glee at the thought of my fastidious mother-in-law having to accept her new tenant, a scruffy, dirty fellow. I had to swallow the bitter pill, however, of moving into his dim, seedy room, so long, roller skates could admirably have been used to commute from one end to the other. The marble bathroom had rusty taps and the water froze from time to time. We shared a communal toilet with two other individuals on the same floor. No matter, I was now the master of the 'house'.

When the day came that Laci proposed to me I turned him down. I told him I was touched and flattered but was unable to accept his devotion; I was still incapable of burying my craving for my ex-husband. My blunt honesty did not deter him. At least once a month thereafter he asked me to marry him.

What a sinister decade we lived in. One day, Kinga came home from school, her face ashen-grey. A sad tale unfolded itself. The head teacher had entered the classroom and solemnly announced that their great leader Stalin had died. The entire school, children and staff, were ordered to assemble in the auditorium where the record *Fel, fel Ti rabjai a földnek* was played. (To arms, to arms, you proletariat of the earth). For two solid hours they had been forced to stand rigidly at attention, listening to speeches dedicated to the memory of the fiendish dictator.

The court hearing for Kinga's custody dragged on for months. Miklós was determined to establish that he was better suited to bring her up. Laci was a consolation during that gruelling period when I felt I was being crucified. There was no abatement in his faithful support, without which I would have gone under. Throughout those excruciating weeks when I lived in dread that I might lose my daughter, he dauntlessly repeated over and over, 'Please, I beg you, marry me. As your husband I will have the legal right to fight for your child. She will be provided with both a home and a family.'

Then, miraculously, it was all over. I had won! Gained the security of knowing that Kinga could not be wrenched away from me. But the psychological strain proved to be too much and I suffered a complete nervous breakdown, and had to be placed under doctor's care.

It was in 1953, after Stalin's death, that a slight chink could be observed in the Iron Curtain. I actually received an *uncensored* letter from Romola. How she had traced me was a mystery unless it was through the stranger who had given Kinga the doll. The old postman handed it to me gingerly as though it might be a bomb ready to explode. Out of concern for me he had not pushed it through the letterbox below, knowing that the concierge was an old busybody, all too eager to report anything untoward. She belonged to 'the other side', those who spied on their fellow human beings and were only too happy to pass on titbits to the AVO (the Hungarian Secret Police).

Unbelievable as it may seem today, I was overcome by such a state of nerves from holding a letter with a foreign stamp in my hand, I locked myself in the toilet to read it. A single, naked lamp bulb dangling from the ceiling provided a dim light. Laboriously, I tried to concentrate on the text. As I scanned through it my feelings towards my mother melted. Her tone was friendly; she apologised for not having written for so long and indicated that she had been extremely worried about me as she had had no news. She was optimistic about her work, a television production she was currently engaged in; how she was travelling back and forth between New York, Hollywood and San Francisco, where she had a darling little apartment furnished in her own inimitable style – 'like a Baroque house in Budapest's Vár district'. She wrote that 'they' – no names mentioned – wanted to make a film about Nijinsky in Hollywood, and that the French and Russian film companies planned a co-production in Paris and Moscow. Kyra had gone through a terrible ordeal in Italy during the war and Romola was taking the necessary steps to get her over to the States. Aunt Tessa was well, but why had I not contacted her? I was rather amused at this naïve rebuke. Not only had it been impossible for any letters to reach the West unless smuggled out but I had not the slightest notion of Tessa's address. Romola went on to query about various relatives and friends. She was particularly concerned as to who was taking care of Emilia's grave.

'Is there a monument raised? How she loved life. What a pity she could not have lived another ten years.' She rounded off her letter with a phrase so typical of her; a slice of her own philosophy. *'How is Kinga? Do not sacrifice your life for her. Do everything you can for her, but remember that you have responsibilities toward yourself. Please write to me at length, my dearest Tamara, I wish you health and happiness.'*

It was not until I retired the same evening that I surreptitiously took the letter out to re-read and found a flimsy piece of paper I had previously overlooked. It was written in English and addressed to the British Ambassador. It concerned a pair of earrings that Romola had inherited from Emilia – the famous pearl earrings which according to family history had been handed down generation after generation from Krisztina Pulszky.

When Emilia was dying, she left the earrings in my charge, extracting from me the promise that one day they would go to my mother. Unwilling to shoulder the responsibility for them on my own, I took them to one of our relatives who agreed to keep them as 'ours' because we were not allowed to harbour jewellery or currency belonging to foreigners. Romola had acquired British citizenship while Waslaw was alive and they were living in England. As her father, Károly, had been an English subject, the matter had been arranged smoothly without undue protocol. Under these circumstances it would have been out of the question to let it be known the jewellery was Romola's property. Any involvement with the British Ambassador might land me in prison or in a labour camp, but how could I convey to her how things stood in Hungary?

In a fit of exasperation I unburdened my problem to Laci. As always, he listened patiently to my tirade and then came up with a solution. Among his numerous acquaintances was a foreign musician married to a Hungarian ballerina who now enjoyed dual nationality and was in the enviable position of being able to travel in and out of the country. I got in touch with her and explained my ticklish dilemma. She memorised Romola's address and promised to contact her on her next trip abroad and to do her utmost to clarify the extreme predicament in which I found myself. Some months later, my go-between and I met again and I was handed a letter she had received from Romola. I recognised my mother's characteristic handwriting. The letter was addressed to Madame X, care of the *Magyar Királyi Opera Haz* (The Royal Opera). Romola thanked her most profusely for her intervention, but stated peremptorily – in perfect Hungarian – that Tamara should do what she had been instructed to previously – return the earrings without delay. I was stunned!

Gradually, more letters filtered in which thankfully had escaped the censor's eagle eye because she kept on harassing me about other bits of jewellery. What had happened to a diamond and topaz brooch? Who had it? She would willingly buy it back. She had contacted Michael in the matter but had had no reply. Now she threatened to write to the Head of State if I did not let her know by return as to the jewels' whereabouts. Her attitude was maddening. She had no comprehension whatsoever about the gruesome realities of life behind the Iron Curtain; that she jeopardised my safety. I tore my hair in sheer frustration when she suggested I should take her 'case' to the Russian Embassy. I would not go within miles of it, given the treasures of Midas. To my intense relief, this sensitive subject petered out. Possibly, someone alerted her to the danger of pursuing it.

I remember she once asked if there was anything in particular I would like her to send me, some nice lingerie for instance? I promptly replied that a CARE parcel would be very helpful. These CARE parcels were organised by charitable organisations. The method was quite simple. If Romola paid in a certain amount in the States, then I would be entitled to go to a designated place in Budapest to collect some flour, margarine, bread, beans or other sustenance necessary for one's daily meals. I never did receive one, instead my mother wrote that she could arrange 'that kind of a package for half the price in California...' Quite so. One day, a small parcel arrived. Trembling with anticipation of what it contained, Kinga assisted me in opening it. When the wrapping unfolded, a round tray of dried fruits lay on the table.

In one of her sporadic missives she congratulated me on my victory in obtaining full custody of Kinga. *'At last, the family quarrelling is over. It is also reassuring to hear you have found a good and faithful friend in Laci. It is not right nor proper for a woman to wander through life without a supporter or protector.'*

Piecemeal, a clearer picture of her life after Tatakaboy's death started to emerge. She had embarked on her new start in life in New York but California had beckoned as her base, partially due to the seductive climate but also to the proximity of Hollywood and the film world there. She had established *'The Nijinsky Productions Incorporated'* under which she optimistically planned to conduct most of her business. One of her projects was to make films about ballet, which she named *Ballet Miniature*.

Romola expounded in such glowing terms about her multifarious activities, I visualised her living in the lap of luxury, going on tours, lecturing at universities and womens' clubs, writing. There she was in her element, and somehow, she must have wielded an almost hypnotic power over most people she met. Yet to the many admirers and the hangers-on to the charismatic name of Nijinsky, she remained extremely secretive about her private life and even about her own family members. To illustrate the point, some years after her death I met an official of a well-known organisation, who had known Mother purely on a business level for a considerable number of years. After I had introduced myself, I wondered if he could possibly share some of his memories of Romola with me. To my utter surprise he replied, 'I never even knew she had children. Neither you nor your sister were ever mentioned to me.'

Romola succeeded in her efforts to get Kyra over to the States. She arranged for her to teach ballet to children of wealthy New Yorkers at the Ballet Art Academy there. It lasted only for a brief spell. After a controversy, possibly blamed on her teaching methods, her restless spirit drove her to San Francisco. In her heart, Romola always nourished the hope her beautiful and talented daughter would re-marry. Kyra had been divorced from Igor some ten years. It was he who had been granted custody of their son Vaslav. But Kyra, with her strong Catholic ideology, could not dream of breaking with her faith; in the eyes of God she was still married to Igor.

Reading about my mother's grandiose plans, her flair for carrying on a lifestyle on par with millionaires, yet often without a sou to her name, her superficial concern about us in Hungary, I could see she hadn't a clue as to the crystalline truth. I would sit there hunched up in the chill of the draughty 'corridor' and think about it. How could I dare to tell her of the misfortune and sense of doom that hung over us? The menacing machinery of politics that controlled us? The fear of going hungry on days when there might not be enough food? Of once prosperous people having to stand in line at the baker's from midnight onward in rain, in snow, in freezing temperature, only to find that when it came to your turn in the queue at around 8 am, there were no coupons left for bread that day?

My mother was a very astute woman. Surely, she must have read what was going on; journalists of the Western World must have written something, yet she resolutely turned a blind eye. Instead, she wrote of a lecture tour in which she had participated in Canada and described the gorgeous, impressive Red Wood Forest she viewed from the window of her room at a resort she had gone to afterwards to relax.

'It is beautiful, like Switzerland. Kyra stayed behind in San Francisco. She has to practise. She has ambitions to resume dancing and to go on tours. Unfortunately, she is not young enough for that any more. I would like to buy a small estate in Oregon, where there are mountains and hills and huge pine forests, similar to Austria. We should have a pleasant home, furnished in European style. Une bonne retraite for the family, a haven for the wanderer. I would like to bring Tessa out here next year. She is living under such strained financial circumstances in Switzerland. Then I hope you will come to visit me and we will all be together...'

On April Fool's Day, 1954, I married my second husband, Laci. It was ten years since I had stood as a bride dressed in a traditional long, white, wedding gown. In church. Now I was garbed in a strict navy blue corduroy ensemble. Laci and I exchanged vows as man and wife in front of the Justice of the Peace. As irony of fate would have it, it was Michael, who performed the ceremony; a temporary assignment he had undertaken when he was discharged from his military post after the war. My matron-of-honour was the blonde young woman with whom I had exchanged my Napoleons for a Swiss watch. Under the portraits of Lenin and Stalin, Michael proclaimed 'God bless you both.' And that was that.

We settled down to married life in a home-like, two-room flat on the hillside close to the Franciscan Church. Thanks to Laci's connections, we managed to acquire a room for Kinga to have on her own in the same building.

Laci's son Peter stayed with his grandmother, who had raised him as her son from when he was a baby. She would be overwhelmingly distressed if she were to be separated from him. In all honesty, I must confess that I heaved a sigh of relief when this arrangement was put forward to me. To shoulder the responsibility of bringing up a boy who was virtually a stranger to me, was more than I could cope with just then.

Slowly but surely, I started to regain momentum, to courageously face each day as it came, learned to enjoy life more fully, prompted by Laci, his optimism, his indulgence and gentleness toward me. I was no longer unnerved at the thought of Miklós. For the first time ever, I had a strong shoulder to lean against. We led a good life in spite of the unsettling political pressure poisoning our country. We lived in one of the better suburbs of Budapest and 'Junior' entered our lives, raising our social status even higher. Yes, an automobile, almost unheard of in those days except for high-ranking Party members. Countless forms had to be filled in and many weeks were to pass before Laci triumphantly announced we had the right to purchase a car. How we deliberated over this treasure, our 'Rolls Royce', its colour, the model, size and so on. I bored Laci with my description of the splendid Chrysler Oti-Papa had owned when I was a little girl. And then the big day arrived when we were to select our automobile. We were ushered into a rather ramshackle building on the outskirts of the city. After our forms had been thoroughly investigated, we were invited to go outside to choose the vehicle that caught our fancy. My immediate impression was that we were surrounded by a load of scrap metal. Undeterred, Laci suddenly called out that he had found *it,* a small two-door convertible, sans motor, radiator or batteries. It did possess four wheels and a steering wheel. The saga of the grey Adler commenced. Petition after petition had to be signed for each item, gathered from an assortment of different models. But Laci's determination won and almost a year later to the day, he proudly escorted me to a shiny car parked outside our lodgings.

Upon learning of our union, an affectionate letter arrived from Romola. Reading it, a sense of genuine happiness flowed through my veins. At long last I had done something of which my mother approved!

> *'Dear Laci, I read with great joy that Tamara had found in you a true friend, who stood by her when she so badly needed it. Now that you are married, please continue to take good care of her. Be patient with her. She is a dear, honest, warmhearted person who richly deserves a calm life, free from worries after all the tragedy she has experienced. If at any time you or she need my help, please do not hesitate to let me know. I greet you with love as a new member of our family.'*

Laci's mother died suddenly after a bout of influenza. The strain on her heart proved too much. She was only seventy-four. My husband was devastated with grief, and it was to take him years to accept the loss. I was presented with a delicate problem, to shoulder the responsibility to care for a step-son. Kinga and Peter had each been brought up as an 'only child'. Kinga was in the enviable position she also had a father whom she visited regularly and who spoiled her. Peter's mother, on the other hand, showed very little interest in her son.

News kept cropping up ever so often from Romola and what she was doing. She carried on at great length about her Nijinsky film, which was to become an ongoing topic for the next twenty years; I named it 'The Saga of the Nijinsky Film'.

She mellowed more and more, and let some of her former reserve down. She actually expressed happiness that we had spent a good summer and, thank God, that both Laci and I sounded pleased with life; this in the opening paragraph of a letter dated September 7th 1955. She herself was suffering from a terrible depression brought on by a lawsuit she had been compelled to take against a *multi-millionaire theatrical man who wants to rob me. But he will lose.* Taxes were another cause of her low spirits. She was saddled with enormously high taxes and felt at her age she should be in a position to rest and not have to work constantly. Kyra had upset her. She had moved out of Romola's place in May.

'During the summer she taught in a dance school, work which I found her. Now, she could have had a position in Hollywood as a dance instructor with a six months' guarantee of $800 per month but she refused to accept it. She said that neither I nor Bronia, who lives in Hollywood, should give her advice. She could marry well but refuses to consider it. She is also in the company of black men... I do not approve of her lifestyle. Your grandmother would turn in her grave if she knew about it.

Thank heaven, my health is fine and I am planning a vacation. Maybe I will go to Mexico. They have their hot springs and the country on the whole is so fascinating. Next year, I will try to come over to Europe to see you. Tomorrow, I will mail you a parcel with the black doll and the football (items Kinga and Peter had asked for as Christmas presents but they never arrived). *I am glad that the children are well and diligent in their studies and that you are happy with the car. I have not bought one as I am far too nervous to drive and, besides, there are too many accidents here. It is far safer to go by 'plane. An invitation arrived to attend the opening of the Opera House in Vienna but the trip is too expensive. Am working on three books and maybe one of them will be a financial success in which case I will tour the world. I cannot help it but I am a gypsy at heart, too restless to remain in one place. California is lovely but boring. I guess I am too much a European and I do miss you. Tessa is having problems with her eyes. I try to do everything I can for her now that she is old and alone. All her life she has needed someone to lean against...the opera season is just starting. Every Autumn the Metropolitan comes here and this year Tibaldi, the famous Italian singer is due to perform...I have attended several sessions at the United Nations. Most interesting...'*

Later on, she mentioned her decision to travel to Mexico to find a cure for her arthritis in one hand. Her tone was more discriminate. *'I am afraid I will find it a wild and dirty country, similar to ours* (meaning Hungary). *The people there are like our peasants...they are half-Indian half Spanish...'.* She went on to say that she would continue to Guatemala, depending on what the Internal Revenue had to say with regard to her finances. I suspect she was having further problems with her tax situation. Her chitchat about her travels and her financial state were beginning to become monotonous. We were facing more frightening prospects on our doorstep and across our borders. Covertly, we listened to what was being broadcast on 'Radio Free Europe'. We learned there had been an uprising in Poland against its oppressive government. An insignificant paragraph in our own newspapers dismissed it as a local incident in Poland but the radio bulletins spread like wildfire. If our Polish brothers, who had been so close to us throughout history, could achieve a measure of freedom, why couldn't we?

During the summer of 1956 Laci came home one day in a fever of excitement. He had heard rumours of an underground movement intent on overthrowing the Communist oppression. It was alleged that a group of university students had banded together and formed a so-called 'Literary Club'. They had set up small printing presses in the basements of their homes and were spreading out anti-government leaflets. A hazardous, yet heroic step to take.

What was later to be referred to as 'The Agony of Hungary' started on the 23rd of October, 1956. Step by step, the events that preceded this and their culmination have been recorded in contemporary reference books in unemotional, factual terms. How, as the opposition to Mátyás Rákosi grew, even within the Communist Party, he was dismissed from his post as First Secretary in the middle of July and replaced by Gerö. But the intellectuals were seething with resentment and wanted the return of Imre Nagy as Premier. There was talk of unrest and disenchantment not only among the students and their supporters but among factory workers as well. They wished to be unshackled; regain freedom of speech and the press, free elections, freedom for political prisoners; demanded the removal of the hated Soviet troops from the country.

I fear that I closed my eyes, covered my ears, to the increased rumblings of unrest that had been accelerating. As responsible head of the family, Laci decided the children should stay away from school and that we should remain within the safe confine of our home pending news of further developments. To me, it still had not registered that any danger could be afoot and hence I set off in 'Junior' for the evening's performance at the Puppet Theatre, only to find it had been cancelled. Crowds jostled each other on the street. Scores of army trucks, packed with men shouting 'Freedom! Freedom!' left little room for other vehicles on the roads. Some of them were zealously waving the Hungarian flag with a prominent hole in the middle. Our national flag with its horizontal lines of red, white and green, had in the past borne the Imperial crown in its centre but when the Communists came to power, the traditional emblem had been replaced with the hammer and sickle to demonstrate their unity with the USSR. The 'hole' was in itself a strong symbol of the feelings of those brave souls on the trucks. I retreated home as fast as 'Junior' could muster. Laci embraced me upon my return and said 'Never again'.

What followed, happened quickly, spontaneously, and unabetted by outside forces. As thousands of Soviet troops poured into the city, grim fighting spread and was to take its dreadful toll. The freedom fighters exploded in a blind fury for revenge. They systematically wiped out as many of their tormentors as they could find – the State Security Police, the Russian soldiers, the gaolers of the prisons in which thousands of political prisoners had suffered for years. We learned that evening that a group of valiant patriots had marched in silent demonstation to the statue of General Josef Bem, the Polish hero who had fought on the side of the Hungarians in the Revolution of 1848. At the foot of the statue they had placed a wreath in red, white and green, prayed for their dead comrades, then commenced singing patriotic songs which had been censored for years. The swelling masses had thereafter crossed the Margit Bridge, continued to Városliget, where they had come to a halt in front of another statue, that of Stalin. As if by a given signal they had stormed the statue. Using a welding torch to separate it from its base, they had strapped round 'his' neck a heavy rope and pulled it all the way to Budapest's widest boulevard amidst the screaming and chanting of the throngs of humanity comprised of university students, professors, housewives, mothers with babes in their arms, blue-collar workers, peasants, young and old.

Although the Voice of America for many months had implied that aid would be forthcoming if the necessity arose, the half-hearted promises were never implemented. The disastrous failure of the Suez invasion was possibly the major contributory factor. Hungary had to go it alone. Despite that, our rebels did not give up and they wreaked a terrible vengeance on their tormentors. The fighting went on for a week and by the 29th of October, the Russians began to retreat. Weary of the battle, the soldiers left the corpses of their dead behind them. The church bells peeled out the joyful sound of victory. Imre Nagy was reinstated as Premier. The cells of political prisoners were flung open and one of the first to emerge was Cardinal Mindszenty after eight years' imprisonment. The loathsome red stars and flags vanished overnight, torn to shreds. The euphoria lasted barely one week. Liberty! Breathing fresh, uncontaminated air as free Hungarians once more. Nobody went to work. Food became plentiful because the warehouses, where bountiful supplies of victuals had been stored for party members, were opened to the general public. The sumptuous villa, once owned by Rákosi, was broken into. It was found to possess every sign of the most opulent capitalism: two pianos, white telephones in every room, a home movie, the bar filled with the finest vintage French and Spanish wines. The two bathrooms were said to be enormous and housed all kinds of exercise contraptions. Exquisite carpets covered the floors. An enlightening insight into how one of our 'comrades' had lived.

For hours at an end we sat glued to the radio, eager to absorb every fresh item of news. But Laci, so unlike his usual carefree self, still refused to allow us to leave the premises. He would sternly ask me to make out my shopping list, depart, only to return with more provisions than we normally required. He took a pessimistic view of the outcome. I, normally the pessimist, was fused with a feeling that victory was in the air. Had not one of the high-ranking Hungarian Red Army officials joined the freedom fighters together with his entire platoon? Did we not now have Imre Nagy, a caring Premier who was on our side? Were we not at long last in control of the radio, the militia...'Radio Free Europe' was congratulating us and encouraging us to hold on; repeating assurances that support was on the way. I can still visualise Laci as he stood in front of me, when I eagerly turned toward him after one such broadcast. His face was drained of colour, and I studied him with alarm, assuming he had been taken physically ill. He assured me that he was all right but that he instinctively felt something appalling was about to break out. 'Mark my words, it will culminate in disaster.' How prophetic that short sentence proved to be.

Alas, the bubble burst. Already, after the 30th October, ugly rumours spread – a warning signal of what was to come. Russian reinforcements were pouring over the frontiers and by dawn of the 4th of November, before we had the chance of offering prayers of thanksgiving for our liberation, we had lost the independence we had fought for. What transpired on and after that fateful date is also part of the pages of modern history. Innocent pawns in the cruel game of power and dictatorship, we had once more to fight for survival. On that particular morning, Laci and I awoke to the sound of cannon fire. Bewildered, we switched on the radio, only to be met by a stony silence. On that day, too, the proudly waving flags vanished as if by sorcery. The streets were emptied of people; the inhabitants of Budapest appeared to have been swallowed into the bowels of the earth. The Russian foe had returned backed by massive columns of tanks, artillery and infantry. A gruesome and ruthless war was declared against the Hungarian people. All major road crossings into the city were guarded by Soviet tanks. Contingents of Red Army soldiers marched through the deserted streets two abreast. Free Hungary was to bleed to death, her people slaughtered, houses burned to the ground. Those who did not die in the street fighting were subsequently caught, tortured and executed, even young boys, mere children. The last feeble cry for help could be heard on radio on the 7th of November. The cry went unheeded. The bitter truth was that the Russians, contrary to gullible belief, had never actually left. The revolution had caught them unaware but before pouncing yet again on their prey, they had waited to see how the rest of the world would react. The free world turned a deaf ear. Had there been some strong reactions from the Western nations, backed by the United Nations, I believe the story would have been different.

As it was, my country put up a courageous but futile fight. To a large extent, it was a 'teenagers' battle. The ingenuity of our young freedom fighters was unbelievable. In the early hours of the morning, fourteen-fifteen-year-olds would slip out of their homes and pour petrol on the roads which they would light in front of oncoming Russian tanks. When then a Russian soldier jumped out to inspect the fire, a sniper would shoot him. Similarly, they improvised makeshift replicas of army land mines simply comprised of china plates stolen from household cupboards and strategically laid out in the path of the tanks. Again, when a soldier risked the safety of his steel enclosure to study the objects more closely, he was shot. Childish pranks came to serve a deadly serious purpose. On the steep hill leading to the fortress of the Royal Palace liquid soap was spilled out by the gallon, hampering military vehicles proceeding along that route. The adult population struggled to organise a temporary government to unite the people; radio broadcasts were resumed in dingy, anonymous basements. But the carnage of defeat was visibly evident everywhere on the streets, in front of Parliament...piles of dead bodies, men, women and children. It was all over. An eerie silence enveloped the land, only to be broken by the hushed whispers of those still alive.

Two major events resulted from our tragic, unsuccessful dream; one, feared but anticipated: retaliation; the other, an act which took the authorities completely by surprise: the massive exodus of Hungarian people across the borders to the West. At first, it was mainly the Freedom fighters and others who knew with certainty they would either face the death penalty or slave-labour camps if caught. But within a few days they were joined by thousands of others who no longer could bear the thought of life behind the Iron Curtain. Like lemmings they fled, spilling over the borders by riskful means, seeking freedom. Some of them already had close kin in the West. Only the most treasured belongings that could be crammed into a suitcase went with them together with scant items of clothing. All conceivable transportation was used; any vehicle on four wheels, city buses, trains. No one asked for tickets. The authorities observed what was taking place with growing consternation and decided to seal off as many frontiers as possible. Escape routes to Czechoslovakia and Roumania became impassable. Yugoslavia showed greater latitude but even there, refugees were detained and subjected to rigorous and searching cross-examination. Austria was the only haven; close by and neutral. Stories abounded of the many ingenious methods adopted to flee the country. Weekend after weekend an athletic acquaintance of ours checked in at a romantic little hotel on the shore of a lake across which was Austria. He would daily go for a swim, return to the hotel, and repeat the exercise following weekends. In the end nobody paid attention to him, brushing him off as either an eccentric or somebody training for a competition, until one day he continued across the lake, 'forgetting' to return.

Although neither Laci nor I had actively participated in the uprising, we feared the worst and for days virtually imprisoned ourselves at home, too shattered by the horrific nightmare to venture out. But after two weeks Laci was unable to stand the strain of uncertainty any longer and decided to take the risk of going to the theatre. I pleaded with him not to go but he was adamant. When he finally returned, I rushed over to greet him, tears choking my greeting. In my eagerness to embrace him, I nearly crushed the priceless bag of eggs he had managed to procure. He told us that the few people on the streets spoke in subdued tones; our colleagues at the theatre were cautiously discussing the rehearsal of their next play, making small talk about the weather. Utterly non-committal. Suspicion of the unseen enemy had taken its grip on them. Only one woman approached Laci and asked about me and the children.

And, unbelievably, though disillusioned and stripped of pride, life once more slipped into a set pattern. Daily, the radio blared forth stern commands to return to work, to send the children back to school. The show must go on.... And we obeyed; we learned to be mute, to walk about with a poker face. I carried on my work at the Puppet Theatre, but concentration did not come easily.

Imre Nagy disappeared, presumably seized by the Russians, and was executed after a secret trial in 1958. Cardinal Mindszenty was given political asylum in the American Embassy in Budapest, where he was to spend sixteen years. János Kádár replaced Erno Gerö as First Secretary of the Party on October 25th, 1956. At first, he was heard to proclaim 'the freedom of the people and the independence of the country'. Then, inexplicably, in November, when the

Russian troops renewed their grip on the country, he announced the formation of a 'Hungarian Revolutionary Workers' and Peasants' Government'.

Our harrowing plight intensified. We lived one day at a time. At night, when sleep deserted me, I would lie and think about Romola. There was now no way I could communicate with her. Her last letter to reach me had once more come from Mexico City. I could recite it by heart – her fairytale life.

> *'Write to me diligently, to my address in San Francisco. I will be staying another two weeks here in Mexico City, where I have come alone for a cure and a good rest. It is so very peaceful here. Everybody remembers Tatakaboy, and they spoil me. Since I speak Spanish, I find it even more pleasant. Many people come to visit me. I am crisscrossing the country, which is gorgeous, with 5,500 meter high mountains towering above us. I have just returned from a small town, where I visited divine churches and the world's largest silver mine. I escaped from Acapulco, which is Mexico's Riviera, because of the presence of scorpions and immense lizards. I also stayed in Guernavaca, where the American millionaires enjoy life on their estates. If I wish to I can go out and pick delicious fruits of my choice, banana, papaya or mango. I plan to fly to Peru. It is only three hours away by plane, but I will be returning to Mexico to attend the Opera, the concerts and the bullfights. I hope to stay here until the middle of October and then in November we will go to Japan or Hawaii.'*

I pondered over who 'we' could be. Kyra, possibly? She finished her travelogue by saying that the latest lawsuit regarding the film rights had been postponed until February. She rambled on that before going to Japan she might go by train to Lake Louise, Canada's equivalent to St Moritz to stay for a few weeks. I could not help but admire her pluck, her stamina. Laci, on the other hand, sarcastically wondered with *what* was she dashing from continent to continent.

Even in the adverse situation in which we found ourselves, I never harboured envy of my mother's travels, nor longed to be abroad like my sister or my aunt. My somewhat passive nature found changes of environment disharmonious and hard to cope with. It therefore came as a shock when Laci on a late November evening quite prosaically posed the question, 'Would you want to leave the country?' Momentarily, I was flustered. 'Laci, you know that where you go, I will go too. But it is becoming more and more dangerous.'

Laci persisted and assured me there were ways and means of getting out without endangering either our lives or those of our children. Turmoil welled up in me. I was in conflict with myself. Whatever Laci said to the contrary, I knew that the borders were heavily guarded, that peril lurked everywhere. Even in the centre of Budapest it was impossible to travel freely without systematic interference by police and patrolling militia. Laci and I had secure positions, his entire family were still in the country. And Miklós, how would he react if he learned that Kinga would be taken away from him? He abhorred the idea that Laci was her stepfather.

On the other hand, mulling it over, I found it very appealing to look forward to breathing free air once more like a normal human being; no more hardships to grapple with. And had not Romola time and again written that we should come to the States. My battle over, I readily agreed to Laci's proposal. I was dismayed, however, when he said he would contact Miklós and let him know of our decision. dreaded the confrontation of two husbands, past and present. I envisaged the tug-of-war that would ensue for Kinga. Laci laid down the law. Kinga was, after all, Miklós's daughter. Besides, Laci intended to ask if Miklós and his wife would join us in the flight for freedom. He knew Miklós was bitterly opposed to the current régime.

The date for our departure was set for December 13th – St Lucia Day. On the evening of the 12th, Miklós cancelled his departure with the excuse he was a Hungarian actor of note, his work was here, and where else could he similarly establish himself. Laci's profession was international. As a musician he stood a chance anywhere. As for me, did I not have my mother in the States to fall back on. He wished us both all good luck with our venture and then rounded off by asking when would it be convenient for him to collect Kinga. It would be too dangerous to take her along. She could join me later, possibly through the Red Cross.

A scorching pain penetrated my midriff as though I had been dealt a physical blow. I was incapable of speech and Laci took control. Firmly clasping my hands, he turned to Miklós and calmly stated that we were going home to unpack. With that, he led me away. Such was his character that he did not for one moment think of deserting me and it was inconceivable that I should leave my daughter behind. He was well aware of Miklós's devious streak; that if I were to hand her over to his care, she might never be returned to me. A terrible sense of guilt flooded over me. For my sake, Laci was willing to sacrifice freedom for himself and his son.

Just before Christmas, a letter reached me from Romola through the auspices of the Red Cross. It contained a garbled message, obviously coded, to the effect that she was concerned about our well-being and that Laura, my old nurse, was expecting us for the Christmas holidays. Reading between the lines, I took it to mean she wanted us to get to Vienna, where help might be at hand. But we remained. Kinga spent that last holiday in Hungary with her father and grandmother; Laci, Peter and I stayed with Laci's married sister, who had children of her own.

It was not until mid-January 1957 that Laci repeated his question. 'Do you want to leave the country?' Without hesitation this time I nodded my head in assent.

'Fine, the four of us will go together. I will soon let you know what has to be done but until then, not a word to anybody, not even the children.'

For days, I walked about in a trance. How would our plan escape Miklós's attention? And unverified reports were rife that fewer and fewer people stood a chance of reaching safety, especially on their own. But Laci had been reassured that there were members of the Hungarian Army and the border patrol who would conduct refugees into Austria at an enormous price. Laci had found an individual, simply called Joe, who was willing to take our car in payment. But the obstacles were far more treacherous this time; icy winter had transformed the landscape into a forbidding picture of snow with drifts piled many metres high in places, and relentless, cold winds. Two persons only were taken into our confidence; my uncle, to whom I gave the beautiful pastel portrait of Emilia for safe keeping, and Laci's sister. At the very last minute I tossed some clothes into a suitcase under the cloak of darkness, so as to avoid raising the suspicion of our next door neighbours. A couple of letters were scribbled, donating our sparse furniture to various relations.

We decided that the best day to leave would be a Monday as that was our day off. On Sunday evening, I went to pick up Kinga, who had been spending the usual weekend at her grandmother's. An extraordinary little incident followed which I took as a good omen. Over the years, Kinga had been given many toys but her favourite was a Teddy bear that Dédi had given her. It had become her mascot that spent the winter months at the home of Miklós's mother to await her visits. When my ex-mother-in-law opened the door, she held Kinga's coat in her hand. I exchanged the usual pleasantries with her, determined to act as normally as possible. Buttoning my girl's coat, I happened to glance into the living-room and saw the Teddy propped up in an armchair. I felt a twinge for Kinga's sake, realising I could not possibly suggest that she take her loyal companion with her. After goodbyes were said, and the door was locked behind us, to my astonishment, Kinga knocked on the door. When it opened, she dashed into the living-room and picked up the Teddy. Humming a little tune, she cradled it in her arms as she skipped down the stairs. Intuition? To this day, that same Teddy has a place of honour in Kinga's home.

The first light of dawn of our own decampment broke. Stealthily, we brought our luggage down to 'Junior' and stuffed it all in. I had told Kinga we were off on a day's outing to Lake Balaton. Barely twenty miles past the city limits, we were stopped by a patrol. Our hearts sank. Now, we had to put on the best act of our lives. We were asked to produce our identification cards and declare where we were headed and why. I wanted to blurt out we headed for FREEDOM, away from tyranny; to be able to sleep peacefully at night with both eyes shut; to send our children to church without being threatened; to avoid ideology classes at seven am.... Instead, I smiled feebly while Laci launched into an explanation of how he had been commissioned by the Ministry for Culture and Education to buy a piano for the theatre to replace one that had been destroyed. To our intense relief, the soldier accepted Laci's word, and even bade us God speed on our journey. An ironic twist that a representative of a godless government should wish us that.

After several hours' travelling we reached Lake Balaton where our anonymous friend 'Joe' was waiting. He and Laci went through the drill and it was found I had packed far too much. I was given exactly fifteen minutes to repack, keeping only the barest essentials. My task completed, we were driven off in a Russian car, Joe seated next to the chauffeur. Our tension accelerated now that we had left behind the security of our own vehicle. We were sped along narrow, extremely slippery back roads. Night fell swiftly but fortunately the light from the moon gave some comfort. Suddenly, the car slowed down and Joe admonished us to keep silent, no matter what happened. From nowhere, two Russian soldiers approached us. We could not discern what Joe said to them but I noticed that he handed them a parcel. Later, I was told it was a bottle of Vodka. Bribery is international.

We continued our arduous trek, each sunk in deep thought and the same question uppermost in our minds. Would we be lucky? Later, we stopped at a village inn to partake of a spartan meal. Joe was the only one who showed a healthy appetite. Gulping down a final glass of wine, he curtly asked us to wait and without a word stepped into the blackness outside. Panic gripped me as I felt certain he had deserted us but Laci calmed me down and promised that Joe knew what he was doing. Barely had he completed the sentence when Joe re-appeared and bundled us into the car. We travelled on the freeway, parallel to the Austrian border. After a couple of miles, we came to a halt and the headlights were switched off. We were told to abandon the car and follow Joe. The only sound was the crunching of the hard snow underfoot. We ploughed on. Sometimes the drifts were so high, I feared I would disappear into their depths never to surface again. My steps grew heavier and heavier as though I were treading in cement. The silhouettes of Laci and Peter faded into the distance. My heart pounded as Kinga and I tried to keep pace with them. I opened my mouth to beseech them to wait but then remembered in time and nearly bit my tongue off. After what seemed an interminable age, Joe stopped in front of a low barbed wire fence. He said that was as far as he could go; that we were to carry on a few more yards, then turn right and we would be in Austria. After a hasty embrace and wishing us good luck he vanished. We were now in 'No man's land'. From a distance we could hear shouts and the barking of dogs. Every once in a while, the sky was lit up by searchlights. I slumped down, unable to take another step. Every cell in my body was screaming from pure exhaustion. Suddenly, the surrounding fields were illuminated by a 'Stalin Candle'; a flare used by the patrols sent off in search of refugees. We pushed on another few yards and then, like a mirage, a house appeared in front of us, welcoming lights gleaming in the window. Laci told us to wait behind some shrubbery while he made enquiries. If he found that we were still in Hungary, we were to retreat as quickly as possible in a westerly direction.

From our position we were not able to see the person who opened the door but I recognised my mother tongue, spoken with an impeccable accent, *'Isten Hozta önöket.* Good evening. Welcome. Come in. Make yourselves at home.' Laci was confounded and demanded to know whether we were in Hungary or Austria. The man assured him that we were safe. He loved Hungary and the Hungarian people. He guided us to the kitchen where a gratifying cup of tea was poured out to help us thaw. Our host's friendly hospitality to the strangers who intruded upon him so unexpectedly will never be forgotten.

Much refreshed, we were picked up an hour later by a relief worker in a Volkswagen and taken to another small village where they were prepared to accept and eventually relocate Hungarians who sought refuge in the West. The highway that we found ourselves on ran parallel to the one we had left some hours earlier on the Hungarian side. The moon smiled brightly at us. Frosty little clouds of our breath filled the air as we inhaled FREEDOM at long last.

CHAPTER 11

REQUIEM FOR THE GOD OF DANCE

'I am not afraid of anything except spiritual death...
We are an infinite part of God in the Universe,
and when we create something beautiful we perfect Him...'

From *The Diary* by Waslaw Nijinsky

At some stage after Waslaw's passing Romola set down the following:

'On April the 8th, Holy Saturday, 1950, Nijinsky departed this earth. 1950 was the Roman Catholic Holy Year. April 8th is also Buddha's birthday. It might seem only a strange coincidence that this pure soul had to leave us on this very day. Nijinsky, the god of dance, the genius of choreographic art, was in life a very humble and kind person... Thirty-one years have passed since the spring of 1919. Thirty-one years of martyrdom for Nijinsky and unspeakable suffering for me. The young, violent and rebellious Vaslav gave place to a peaceful sage, who accepted his fate. We could not penetrate into Vaslav's inner life, we had only glimpses of it...he seldom spoke. He smiled and thus seemed to be expressing his thanks for all the care he received. He was docile and affectionate. His physicians, attendants, friends and family all had the impression that it was not we who had given him care, devotion and affection, but that he in his silent, tender manner had given us a spiritual uplift, a great lesson in faith. To those theologians, who have studied his diary and his life, Vaslav Nijinsky, who disappeared like a meteor from the world in 1919, today emerges a Saint, like St Jean de la Croix.'

About my father's last illness and the details of his death in a London clinic I was kept in total ignorance except for the terse cable thrust in my hands that sad, sunny day in Budapest. It was not until many years later that I could piece together the full account: from the numerous newspaper cuttings preserved by Romola announcing that the world's greatest dancer had lost his battle against declining health; and from the sequel she wrote to *Nijinsky*. In my mother's book, *The Last Years of Nijinsky*, the final lines read:

'...Watza sighed just once. The sun beamed through the window. The nurse stood helpless, while the attendant laid Watza back. His eyes and mouth closed. Thoughts and feelings were racing through my mind, but the enduring thought was: "You were privileged among so many millions of women to share his life, to serve him. God gave him to you. He has taken him back."'

When I was in England some years ago to discuss the editing of my own book, I was introduced to a Mrs Sheila Bate, who had been present that momentous afternoon at the Alexandra Palace when the Paris Opera Ballet were rehearsing for the BBC Television Service. Her then husband, Philip Bate, was involved in the production. Romola and Waslaw had been especially invited. Serge Lifar had also been there. As it turned out, it was to be Waslaw's last public appearance. Although Romola did not say so, it is quite possible that everyone had hoped for a reaction from Waslaw when he watched the performance. She commented enthusiastically on how lively Waslaw became and how he had keenly observed everything that was going on. Contrarywise, Mrs Bate recalled how he had sat throughout the afternoon, hunched in his chair, his face expressionless.

The next day, his physical condition gave cause for alarm, and the Hungarian doctor who was hastily summoned had blood tests taken. When the results were known, he immediately gave the order to transfer Waslaw to a London clinic. Romola panicked and tried to contact Professor Rohr to get him to fly over from Switzerland. He was unattainable. The end was to come swiftly. Waslaw lapsed into a coma. His kidneys had failed. He rallied from the coma for a few split seconds, cried out *Mamasha* and shortly afterwards slipped into his final sleep. Could it have been the young boy calling for his beloved mother Eleonora? Paul was with Romola at the bedside. Rays of sunlight flooded the room and Romola is quoted as saying that she all at once felt Waslaw's presence, that he was in communication with her, asking her not to give way to grief and despair because he now belonged to God, who had lent him to her. A sense of deep calm had momentarily filled her being. And in future years she was to seek solace on her visits to mediums, hoping for messages from him to her.

But once the temporary anaesthesia wore off, she crumpled up, sank to depths of misery and desolation. For three decades she had tried to find a cure somehow, somewhere, for her Watza. Nothing had intimidated her. Time and time again, she had swallowed her fierce pride to go with her 'begging-bowl' to keep him in the best of health. And she had obdurately ruled out the prospect that he would never return to the scene of his former triumphs. Blindly, she tossed aside the inevitable – that he would never waken from his mental death. Now, the magnificent obsession she so relentlessly had pursued had vanished forever.

He died penniless, the *Spectre de la Rose,* who at the height of his career earned more than a thousand pounds a week, a fortune in the early 1900's.

Sorting out the mass of papers relevant to the actual funeral, I came across a few typewritten pages from which I gained a clear and poignant picture of my father's funeral. The words of Cyril Beaumont yielded an infinitely detailed and moving account of the Requiem Mass at St James's Church, Spanish Place, London W!, followed by the burial in a nameless grave in the Marylebone Cemetery in the Finchley Road on Friday, the 14th of April.

According to Beaumont, the body of Nijinsky had lain in state for two days at a private chapel in Baker Street. The coffin was simple, of unpolished oak, a brass crucifix its only adornment, and a brass plate engraved: VASLAV NIJINSKY DIED APRIL 8, 1950. Aged 59. R.I.P. It seems that the curiosity of the press had been aroused by the blue and gold cloth with which the coffin then was draped. Could possibly the colours be associated with those of the old Imperial School of Ballet? As it turned out, the cloth had simply been supplied by the undertakers.

Eight pallbearers had been chosen: Cyril Beaumont, Richard Buckle, Anton Dolin, Serge Lifar, Michael Somes, George Raymond, Frederick Ashton and George Balanchine. At the last moment, Balanchine had sent his regrets that he was unable to come. Consequently, it was agreed that only six pallbearers be present, George Raymond graciously dropping out. As the church filled up, Beaumont recognised many familiar faces, among them that of Lydia Sokolova. Beaumont was quite evidently touched by a couple of minor episodes. A very old woman arrived and handed Somes a wreath of primroses she had picked that very morning. Humbly, she had requested that her floral tribute be placed among the other wreaths. And F. Zenon had come to pay his homage. Barely able to walk and supporting himself on a stick, he had asked for assistance to be led to the coffin where he had knelt in prayer. Zenon had for many years been associated in business with Diaghilev.

The hearse arrived at approximately five minutes past eleven with the coffin, now draped in rich, black velvet embroidered in gold with a large cross and with a gold leaf design in each corner. The trestles on which the coffin rested were similarly covered as was the underlying carpet. Beaumont described the scene thus: 'On either side of the coffin stood a line of three tall brass candlesticks, each holding a lighted coral pink candle. In the distance could be seen the pleasant grey stone of the lofty walls with their deeply inset arched windows, and the altar of white and gold with its soft candlelight reflected in the gleaming brass candlesticks. Above the altar, the stained glass windows, like a jewelled mosaic of ruby and sapphire, alternately glowed and flamed as the sun outside shone through them or was dimmed by a passing cloud.' Beaumont contributed this account of Waslaw's funeral to *The Ballet Annual* and in a letter from A. & C. Black Ltd, dated 30th November, 1950, Romola was granted permission to use the material on Nijinsky that Beaumont had written so long as its source was duly acknowledged. She was at the time on the verge of leaving for a lecture tour in America.

When the mourners were all seated, Serge Lifar left his place and walked to the head of the coffin and laid a wreath of primroses. A Father Casey conducted the service in Latin and in English. The coffin was sprinkled with Holy water, after which an incense burner was gently swung over it, creating wisps of aromatic smoke that drifted slowly through the church. Thus, the service came to an end and the six pallbearers took their places: Lifar and Dolin at the foot, Ashton and Buckle at the centre, and Somes and Beaumont at the head. Beaumont complained about how heavy the coffin was and how the weight of it had taxed his strength.

Romola had expressly asked him to attend the burial and he had taken his place next to the driver, with Romola, Karsavina, Lifar and Dolin in the back. In the car behind them were Margaret

Power, Marie Rambert, Frances James and Rupert Doone. Beaumont had observed how packed with spectators the steps of the church were when they left, and also the crowds who lined the pavement.

The open grave awaited them upon their arrival. Many more floral tributes covered the ground. The service was brief. The priest sprinkled the coffin with a phial of holy water which was handed in turn to Romola, Karsavina, Lifar and Dolin. Lifar scattered a little earth on the coffin and Beaumont did likewise. Romola had tossed roses onto the coffin and bowed her head in silent prayer. What torment and anguish must have engulfed her at that moment. Most certainly, too, a sense of abject defeat as the paramount aim to her existence was covered with earth.

In his last sentence, describing the funeral, Beaumont wrote: 'Nijinsky the man had passed from our midst, but Nijinsky the dancer will live forever in the history of the Dance.' As he had turned to leave the graveyard, he had caught a glimpse of yet another great figure in Dance, Ram Gopal, who had come to pay his tribute.

A handwritten letter, dated the same day as the funeral, is substantial proof that Romola, torn to shreds though she was in her grief, had already made up her mind that Waslaw's final resting-place should be in Paris, the city which had hurtled him to fame and where he had been so happy. The burial in London was a *force majeur*. She was drained of financial resources. Consequently, she sat down in her room at the Welbeck Hotel and on their letter-heading penned the following legal document.

'I, the undersigned, Madame Romola Nijinsky, give full permission to Monsieur Serge Lifar to transfer to Paris the body of my husband, Vaslav Nijinsky, deceased and buried here in London. I authorise him in my name to take the necessary steps for the transfer as soon as the organisation of the ceremonies will have been arranged in Paris. My wish is that after my death my body will repose next to my husband.

London, 14th April 1950

(s)   Romola Nijinsky'

Pathetically, however, her wish was not to be granted when the time came. Frailty of mortal pride was to decide otherwise.

There is little doubt that psychologically Romola was plagued by self-interrogation with regard to Waslaw's physical health. She had reached a watershed emotionally. Much-thumbed letters from the 1950's reveal how, after his death, she contacted a number of eminent doctors, probing to find out if she had done all in her might during his last illness.

She wrote, for instance, to a famous urologist in Budapest, who had been a close friend to Emilia. The Hungarian specialist responded that he had carefully studied the medical report she had sent him and he assured her that everything possible had been done to cure her husband of the uremia from which he suffered. From Switzerland, Professor Karl Rohr gave a similar verdict and stressed that Nijinsky's rapid decline had been aggravated by extremely high blood pressure.

With regard to his final breakdown, however, she absolved herself from blame, i.e. overwork and marriage were merely the hypotheses of the outside world. In her second book, *The Last Years of Nijinsky,* she listed the 'certain phases of Nijinsky's life-…upsetting enough to encourage any predisposition to mental illness…', namely, his childhood dominated by his love for his mother, the far too strict training in the Imperial School of Dancing at St Petersburg, his association with Diaghilev, and lastly, the fact that his dancing career was stopped, much against his will, through World War I. Was she here merely trying to clear her own conscience by so publicly dismissing her role in the whole affair?

For months after the funeral she lived in a mental vacuum. She sought comfort in visits to mediums, went on a pilgrimage to Paris to St Germain l'Auxerrois, the church to which she had gone years previously to pray to God that she might gain the friendship of the great Nijinsky. Between May and November of 1950 she flitted like a nomad between countries – France, Switzerland, Italy, unable to settle down, chasing after her own particular blue bird. It was to be the commencement of her ceaseless travels.

Communication between us had of course been broken off for years and was only resumed in those short spurts in the early 1950's. Even then, there had been something muted about her intimate private life which she closed tightly around her like an impenetrable shell; Kyra had as yet not joined her, contact with Tessa, sporadic, and Emilia, her *Anyuci,** forever lost to her, as the supportive tower against whom to lean and to come to for aid and reassurance. However deep the altercations had been between mother and daughter, Romola never questioned but that she had been Emilia's darling. Hence, however withdrawn she was by nature, she must have brooded over the absence, either permanent or temporary, of the mainstays in her life. I suspect that Paul remained faithfully by her side much of the time as witnessed by a number of letters from persons I am unable to identify, who asked about his health and whereabouts. Letters from Jean Cocteau, Tamara Karsavina, Ida Rubinstein and Charles Cochran, among others, reveal that she once more took up old contacts, but then with a specific purpose in mind. She asked them to write articles or eulogies about Nijinsky.

Her health was worsening and as a concession to her doctor, she went from Paris to Zürich for a complete rest. Was it possibly there in the solitude of her hotel room that she jotted down the random notes about what a medium had told her shortly before Waslaw's death. I have been able to decipher the odd phrase: *'You are finishing with the past...Surrounded by an aura of depression...'* She had scribbled her own contemplative comment that she had found the medium's choice of words odd, because she had been in a fairly optimistic mood then. Waslaw had seemed happy, content to be in England. At the same time, she was in the process of arranging for the two of them to go to the States. It had just not seemed right that she should be in a depressed state of mind. But according to the medium *'she was to rise from a most difficult time and fight the fates to live on and find happiness once more'*.

With every passing year Romola's engrossment in obtaining an option for film rights based on her book, *Nijinsky*, grew more and more into such an intriguing web of claims and counterclaims of yeas and nays, it is hard to disentangle. In Spring 1950, she had made contact with a fellow Hungarian, Alexander Paal of Alexander Films in Hollywood, offering him exclusive rights to negotiate a deal for a period of six months only. Paal got in touch with Vanguard Films but Selznick was away and had left the message he would only be interested in the Nijinsky project if there already was a story or outline. Later correspondence was to clarify what he must have had in mind – the last years of Nijinsky's life had

---

* Term of endearment for Mother.

as yet not been put down on paper. On April 30th, 1951, Paal confirmed this in a letter to her in New York: 'As I told you before many times, I am unable to do anything until I receive from you the second book...which I am most anxiously waiting for...then maybe I could arrange that some of the major studios would assign you to write the proposed treatment of this film...'

The first person with whom she had signed a contract back in the 1940's had failed to honour the stipulated time limit. Consequently, the rights reverted back to her. She had then approached Alexander Korda, who could claim friendship with both the Márkus and the Nijinsky families. It was he who later was to assist her in her endeavour to gain her entrance permit to the United States. Due to lack of available funds, however, he had had to decline making the film, and agreed that the rights revert back to Romola if his firm, 'London Films', were advised that she had another backer; a formality on paper to allow London Films to turn the project down politely and legally. It was after that she contacted Paal.

Like with everything else pertaining to Waslaw Nijinsky, she refused to accept that funds were not readily forthcoming for what she deemed a paramount, world-shaking subject. Perhaps, despite her vexation and frustration over all the negative replies at the time, the whole operation was beneficial to her. To some extent it must have acted as therapy to her in her bereaved state. And in June 1950 she received a glimmer of hope in the form of yet another letter from Paal that a wealthy director had expressed interest and that Gene Kelly as well wished to become involved in it.

She worked tenaciously on acquiring a visa to enter the United States, and in October 1950, her efforts were rewarded, abetted by Korda. At that time, too, she became the recipient of more good news in the form of a contract covering a lecture tour in the States. Stepping off the ship in New York, she must have been struck by the winds of optimism and prosperity charging round the majestic skyscrapers untouched by the ravages of a great war. She had left behind her a Europe still scarred and bleeding; most countries there were in dire financial straits. The Americans were on top of the world, and Romola was swept along with the tide. For a while, she settled in New York where she speedily adjusted herself and took up old ties.

It was in New York City that she set up the Nijinsky Productions Incorporated – on East 82nd Street, to be exact – because I found a letter from a Mr A. E. Davidson, Private Secretary to the British Ambassador in Washington, addressed to her office there. In a desperate bid to acquire some form of work, she had written to the Prime Minister asking for employment with the British Information Services. Mr Davidson's reply was polite but non-committal, merely an acknowledgement on behalf of the Prime Minister, and stating that her request had been forwarded to the British Information Services. Of the final outcome I haven't got a clue.

She put much effort into her brainchild *Ballet Miniature* and discussed this project at great length in correspondence with Robert Tenger in Paris. He was a lawyer who had been a close friend of Waslaw's, and still remained an adviser and friend to Romola. She always referred to him as *Maître* T.

Apparently, some of the ballets had been performed by the Paris Opera. Alas, like on many similar occasions, the lack of funds terminated the deal with the Opera. Undaunted, and still brimming over with optimism, she confided to *Maître* T her hopes to sell the ballets to American television. Several companies, such as the Radio Broadcasting of America and Columbia Broadcasting, had shown some interest but the most likely one to come forth with the appropriate finance would be one of the greatest of them all, the American Foundation. 'They spend millions to educate the public about art and culture through the media of radio and television.' *Maître* T had responded keenly to her postulation about working with artists and choreographers from different countries, and consequently she was all the more eager to add available dancers, costumes, orchestra etcetera from the Paris Opera Ballet to her stable.

She expounded further, 'I will come personally from the Foundation to discuss if they should wish to work with us on a percentage basis or rather be paid for each individual ballet. We would shoot the film on location: *Spectre de la Rose. Petroushka.* Naturally, we would film some of Lifar's ballets as well and those of other choreographers. For your information, but pray, do not repeat this to Lifar or the press, we will proceed along the same lines together with the Vienna Opera and the Copenhagen Opera.' She concluded this letter by emphasising that in every respect it was a serious endeavour, based purely on a non-profit basis by the Foundation since the ultimate goal was to raise the cultural standards of the American people. 'As soon as my book, *The Last Years of Nijinsky*, is published here, I plan to come over to Paris. With the same mail, I am writing to Lifar, so that meanwhile the two of you can get together regarding the *Ballet Miniature*. I embrace you with all my heart.'

She must have intended to incorporate with this ambitious project a series of special Dance Poems for television. In her notes, she gave Waslaw the credit for this idea, claiming he had invented a new technique to photograph dancing especially for television. The Dance Poems were to represent a new form of art, integrating all interpretive art forms with dancing, singing, acting, pantomime. The subject would be carefully chosen from the most beautiful fairy tales and legends of world literature, to woo the great masses, adults as well as children. Romola would supervise the production of the programmes and would also be the narrator. Only the best-known artists would be asked to participate. Her list of potential sources was grandiose, to say the least: the Paris Opera Ballet and Orchestra, the Vienna State Opera Ballet and Philharmonic Orchestra, the Japanese Court Dancers, the Kabukis, the Siamese Court Dancers, the State Opera Ballets of Iran and Turkey, the Bolshoi Ballet and the world-famous Moiseyew Ballet. Igor Moiseyew and M. Lavrovsky were to stage the Russian fairy tales, Wieland Wagner, director of the Bayreuth Festival, the German fairy tales, Jean Cocteau, the French stories; and so forth. All an indulgence in wish-fulfilment. She *wanted* Waslaw to have masterminded such a glorious scheme.

A letter from Robert Tenger throws a rather amusing if somewhat disconcerting light on her extravagant habits during one of her Parisian visits. He wrote to her:

'...I have to confess to you that there are two people who are deeply offended. One, is the M... fashion establishment who were paid French fr. 17,690. They find it a bit much when you state rather impertinently that the remainder of the debt of fr. 10,000 is for a dress made out of material provided by you...If you have not collected the dress, it is your own fault, and the dressmaking fee must be paid. Why don't you? And then we have Madame T... who screams that you owe her, not 37,000 fr. but 137,000. Agreed, you have paid 37,000 but you still do owe her 100,000. She has threatened to come over to New York. Well, that is all I have to say for today. You must understand how my friendship with you forces me to make sacrifices on your behalf all the time, or rather, whenever I can do so, and that some of them relate to matters which are not always amusing to an attorney of the court. Please write to me. Believe me, I am your affectionate and devoted T...'.

Among the pile of scribbled notes which she had put to one side for use in a future book she was planning, was one she simply entitled 'The Ruins'. A rather extraordinary little vignette. I cannot date it, but quite possibly it belongs to that period in the early '50's. It is related to a visit to a medium, and it would seem logical she sought advice from such a source not long after she took a trip to San Francisco. According to Romola, the medium told her about a house that she, Romola, must buy, and even gave her the address. My mother snappishly replied she could barely afford to rent an apartment, hence to buy a house was out of the question. The medium persisted and Romola, purely out of curiosity, decided to have a look at it. Upon arriving at the location given to her by the medium, she stared in disbelief at what were the ruins of an old house. No war had reduced it to its squalid state, merely the neglect and decay of untenanted years. Fired by indignation at having been 'hoaxed', she returned to the medium to complain. Her tirade of reproach was ignored. The medium insisted that Romola must buy that particular house. Because of her deep-rooted faith in spiritualism, Romola, quite against her own sound reasoning, went off and borrowed money to purchase the property. Months went by until one day an official-looking letter arrived from the City Hall. The text was brief and to the point...plans were being drawn up to widen the road, create a park in that specific area etc. etc...A fairly large sum of dollars was offered for the ruin and the ground upon which it stood.

Most likely, it was this unexpected dividend that enabled Romola to rent a flat in one of the steep streets of San Francisco. With her vision of a great film never leaving her subconscious, she had mulled over the advantages of living close to Hollywood, the magic world of films. She rejected Los Angeles and chose instead to plant her roots in the city that to her was more continental, the climate kinder, despite the fog. Romola possessed inexhaustible energy to whatever she applied herself, and within a very short time created an Oriental atmosphere with Chinese furniture and knick-knacks in addition to a shrine to the memory of Waslaw; every nook and cranny had photographs of him. The flat was to become her *pied-à-terre* for many years onward.

I unearthed a most interesting letter from Oskar Kokoschka. Romola had written to him, asking for a photograph of the charcoal drawing he had made of Nijinsky in Vienna in 1912 on the occasion of the first performance of the Imperial Ballet in Europe. He claimed it was by far the best portrait of Nijinsky as other artists missed his extraordinary beauty, and 'satisfied themselves with a mere decorative design which could apply to any dancer.' He went on to say 'I knew them all and was always upset about their lack of insight in view of such a meteor-like genius who never had his equal.'

Kokoschka was introduced to Diaghilev by Adolf Loos, a great architect-pioneer who was Kokoschka's mentor. The day after the performance at the Opera-house in Wien, Kokoschka made sketches of Nijinsky for an entire week while the latter was undergoing his daily routine training. I was fascinated to read his vivid impression of my father:

'I never forgot how many battements he could do while spinning into the air and flying like a feather with no weight straight through the window high up in the wings. ...when I was invited to lunch by Diaghileff, I dropped my serviette on purpose in order to feel his (Nijinsky's) muscles because I could not understand the power which allowed such a child of slight build, who only had eyes as large as a gazelle, to be capable of a physical feat which all the much stronger dancers in his group never could equal. At this moment, while touching his thigh, I was alarmed as if I had come into contact with a creature of the ancient Greek myth – a centaur. When we left the table, I asked Diaghileff for the favour to let me try to lift this miraculous creature. He, being a giant as you know, smiled, and threw Nijinsky into my outstretched arms. But suddenly he made himself heavier and heavier and would have thrown me off my balance, if I would not have put him down quickly. He was the most wonderful dancer I ever have seen in my life and I knew them all.'

He finished his letter by saying he had contacted a certain art dealer in Zürich and asked her to obtain a good photograph from the present owner, a Mr Böhler in Luzern. It has formerly belonged to the Imperial graphic collection Albertina in Vienna, but Mr Böhler had acquired it during the 'first revolution'. A later letter suggests that Romola wished to have the drawing for her book together with an explanatory text from Kokoschka because the artist wanted to know if and when the drawing was going to be published.

A programme issued by Musical Artists, New York, advertised a forthcoming series of lectures by Romola during the season 1952-53:

'Romola Nijinsky offers for the first time in the United States a completely new series of highly dramatic and vivid demonstration lectures relating the highlights in the life of her husband. She will show, in actual concert form, the relevance of ballet to the lives of men and women of today.'

The lectures were to be held in association with Paul Szilard, internationally known dancer and choreographer, whose artistry, in Romola's opinion, was in the true tradition of Waslaw Nijinsky. 'He is not only a dancer, but also a creator. His creative power is extraordinary.' Quote from *The London Times*.

She had previously toured all over the United States, lecturing on the art of dancing. To quote *The Town Hall,* Tulsa, Oklahoma, 'Madame Nijinsky was everything one could wish for...the audience was captivated by her unusual, personal charm and the graciousness of her manner. Every seat in the Hall was taken...' In the same vein, she was praised by other Town Halls, by the Institute of Arts and Sciences, New York, and the Women's Club of Wisconsin.

In 1952, *The Last Years of Nijinsky,* the sequel to Romola's first book, was published in the United States by Simon & Schuster, and by Victor Gollancz in England. In Hollywood, Louella Parsons, in her gossip column on September 24th, spread the rather incongruous rumour that Yul Brynner had agreed to accept the role of Nijinsky in a forthcoming film and that 'Romola says she feels that Brynner is the one man she wants to portray her famous husband.' According to the columnist, Romola was in London negotiating film rights with Sam Spiegel.

Overriding all her undertakings, however, was her dauntless spirit of resolution to keep the vow she had made on the day of Waslaw's funeral, to have him transferred to Paris where he belonged. Ever since, she had kept in close touch with Serge Lifar in the matter. He was then chief dancer and choreographer at the Paris Opera. How could she have prophesied that it would actually take three arduous years before their mission was completed?

Raising the necessary funds conducive to arranging the practical aspects for re-interment, was a formidable venture in itself, but they had not foreseen the miles of red tape they would have to wade through: official permission for exhumation; resealing of the coffin in a suitable wooden casket for transportation to France; purchase of a permanent grave in Montmartre's Cemetery; endless forms and documents to fill in for the second burial. The services of both British and French funeral parlours had to be found. Romola was inundated with a sea of correspondence from her attorney and Lifar, not to forget countless others involved. Under the aegis of bureaucracy, they encountered obstacle after obstacle yet they persisted.

When, finally, the *niaiserie* pertaining to legal matters had been dealt with, the human, more personal side had to be tackled: pallbearers to be found; appropriate music and hymns chosen for the solemn, religious service in the *l'Eglise de la rue Daru* (The Russian Church). At the very last minute, Romola had pointed out that Waslaw had been Roman Catholic, not Russian Orthodox, as his mother had brought him back to Poland to be baptised in her faith. It seems, however, that Bronia had intervened, insisting that he be buried with Russian Orthodox rites. The long list of invitations had to be written.

Madame Romola NIJINSKY
Monsieur Serge LIFAR
L'Institut Choreographique
Les Anciens Camarades du Ballet Russe
ont l'honneur de prier............

....

de bien vouloir assister à l'inhumation de
Vaslav NIJINSKY qui aura lieu au cimetière
de Montmartre (Nord) le Mardi 16 Juin 1953
à ll heures

.........sign.

La cérémonie religieuse sera célébrée
le même jour à 9 h. 30 à l'Eglise Russe de la
rue Daru

The almost unbearable irony was to be that Romola could not accept her own invitation! Despite the fact that she had chosen the United States as her base for acquiring funds, she had no thought of relinquishing her British citizenship. Thus, she sorely needed a working permit. True to character, she did not waste time by filing an application through the usual channels, but instead wrote to a Francis Bolton on the Committee on Foreign Affairs in the House of Representatives. On January 13th, 1953, he replied to her letter of the previous December, and enclosed several copies of the new bills he had introduced on her behalf.

The Bill for the Relief of Mrs Romola Nijinsky was referred to the Committee of the Judiciary before the House of Representatives on January 3rd, 1953, to the effect that 'for the purpose of the immigration and naturalization laws, Mrs Romola Nijinsky shall be held and considered to have been lawfully admitted to the United States for permanent residence as of the date of the enactment of this Act upon payment of the required visa fee and head tax. Upon the granting of permanent residence to such alien as provided for in this Act, the Secretary of State shall instruct the proper quota-control officer to deduct one number from the appropriate quota for the first year that such quota is available.'

Not even Romola's bulldogged tenacity could sway the American legislature to move the wheels faster. In fact, it was to take until the spring of the following year for the 83rd Congress, Second Session, under Eisenhower's presidency, to grant Hungarian-born Romola Nijinsky, a British citizen, permanent residence in the United States of America through the 'Special Bill'.

In June 1953, Romola's attorney strongly advised her against leaving the country so long as her papers were not cleared. It must have been a soul-searching, agonising decision to take – not to be at her Watza's side to his journey's end. Her common sense and logical mind won, and she steeled herself to refrain from making the trip. Instead, she contacted two loyal friends who, she knew, would represent her and fill her in with all the details: Nadia Nicolaevna Legat, second wife and widow of Waslaw's teacher Nicolas Legat; she was head of a ballet school in Tunbridge Wells; and the other person was Margaret Power, who promised to go to Paris on Romola's behalf.

And so, on June 4th, 1953, the gates of St Marylebone Cemetery were kept locked, while the body of Waslaw Nijinsky was exhumed and placed in the Marylebone Chapel.

Robert Tenger, who made the identification, later wrote to Romola: 'When Waslaw's body was exhumed…prior to his reburial in Paris, I made certain that everything should remain the way you had arranged it when he was first buried in London: the silk bonnet and the silk arm bracelets (from his costume in *Spectre de la Rose*)…' It was then taken by Garstin's, funeral directors, to their private chapel and placed in a lead-lined coffin which was sealed. The new coffin was of light, unpolished oak and the inscription, the same as before.

Margaret Power had promised Romola that she would accompany Waslaw to Paris and wanted Romola to advise Lifar of her arrival. But she must have had a last minute change of plans according to Nadia Legat, and did not turn up until the funeral.

Nadine Nicolaevna Legat wrote to Romola on the 17th of June:

'You will be pleased to know that not only I, but about 20 of my girls were with Vaslav all of yesterday morning until his train took him away from us. Before his departure from the chapel we wanted to decorate the crate…with loads of flowers. The day after the exhumation, I saw his new coffin. Although the cover could be taken off, I could not actually see him because the top was sealed. He was lying very peacefully in the same chapel on Friday, and I stayed a little while with him. I made enquiries whether there had been other visitors but was told no, nor was anyone expected. I am sending you a little cutting from the newspapers where you can see me at the end of the line and the girls putting flowers for the second time at the station. They went and bought flowers themselves. The first lot were brought from the garden at school, white, red and purple rhododendrons, the latter were roses, carnations and all sorts of beautiful things. I saw with my own eyes how the crate was put into the motor hearse. I followed in a taxi with a few of the girls. At the station we saw him placed into the special goods van, and with all the flowers it really looked quite nice. I was expecting some others to come. I alerted Beaumont and Ram Gopal as you requested. Beaumont never showed up but Ram Gopal came 15 minutes before the train left. Mrs Power was nowhere to be seen. Still, darling, you must be satisfied that Vaslav was not alone. I have been with him from the moment of his exhumation, and all morning from 9 a.m. until 12.30 we have not

left him. And so he has left England accompanied with love, from myself and girls of all nationalities, English, French, Brazilian, Indian, Russian, German and Swiss. I hope that when he arrives in Paris our flowers will still be on the crate so that the French people can see that, although you were not in England, he left this country with the love of his friends and little admirers, and covered with flowers. I hope to hear from you soon. With all my love.

Nadia'

Was it possible, that while she had held vigil at the coffin, Madame Legat recalled the occasion in 1948, when my father stood godfather to six-month old Paula, daughter of dancers John Gregory and his wife Barbara Vernon? The christening was held at the studio of the Legat School in Tunbridge Wells. It was a rather unusual ceremony in that, although the parents were English, they wished their child to be christened in the Orthodox faith as a tribute to their many Russian ballet friends. Archbishop Sava of the Russian Orthodox Church performed the ceremony. There is a newspaper cutting showing Waslaw together with the Archbishop and the godmother Vera Volkova, who was holding the baby.

On another visit to Tunbridge Wells, he attended a performance by Nadia Legat's pupils and Tamara Mikhailova at St Pancras' Town Hall. Afterwards, Waslaw was ceremoniously presented with a gold laurel wreath trimmed with the colours of Imperial Russia. The article in the *Tunbridge Wells Advertiser,* recording the event, also stated that 'Nijinsky is much improved in health and hopes in the near future to work as a choreographer in co-operation with Madame Nicolaevna Legat....' I can almost hear my mother giving the interview. Pertinaciously, she clung to the belief that the miraculous would happen because, in statement after statement to the press and to the world at large, she spoke of Nijinsky's steady progress toward normality.

Upon his return home from the final farewell to Waslaw at Victoria Station, platform No. 12, Ram Gopal wrote a long letter to Romola, a sensitive, touching, revelation of his feelings that sombre day, 'cold, grey, sad, and mournful, bleak-like mid-winter':

'...Remember always that in my heart and purest thoughts, there is ever a place of prayer and love for both You and

370

Vaslav. YOU did more for him than any one living person. Nobody could have withstood such trials, such sadness, with so much bravery and heroism. Remember, Romola, that in the eyes of God, nothing goes unchanged or forgotten. While little "worms" squirm and make noises, only little "worms" wriggling in the mud hear them and take notice. But Vaslav and you are of the Heights, the heavens... We (Nadia Legat) spoke of you, and standing at the side of the platform was the wagon, and in it a large wooden crate with many flowers on it and inside, the body of Vaslav. It made me so very, very sad, I felt suddenly thousands of years old; inside, the shell of a soul now gone into God and perhaps, who knows, future incarnations in this world or other worlds of forms. What great beauty and joy he gave on the altar of God, and what great suffering and tragedy for being able to give it. ..And so did Vaslav dance, his dance of life, and love and death, the cycle of God, creation, preservation and destruction. But his image will only grow greater as the years and centuries pass. ...What an ache and pain is now in my heart, since this morning. I never saw him dance, but yet I can say that I "felt" his Eternal spirit of God, perhaps more than most who saw the visible "form" of his dances. Vaslav danced in 1910 or 1911, here in London. Then all was glory, arriving in a blaze of glory, and now here was the big, grey, cold wooden wagon, holding a casket of wood, like that of Jesus of Nazareth's cross. I put yellow roses on the wooden casket: yellow is the Buddhist colour of renunciation as his life was. ...I prayed with all my heart that Vaslav, His little child (God's) rests in great gardens of infinite peace, with beautiful eternal flowers and with wonderful music where Vaslav can dance and dance and create...Then the lights of the railway signals which were red...suddenly turned green, and a whistle of death blew from the guard of the train, green like emeralds, green like the sea, green like nature. The doors of the wagon were shut, jammed and bolted. And with a creaking of steel the carriage was moving away, just fading past into the steam at the far end of the platform, passed the green lights, bending, and finally in the steam lost in the mists, and suddenly the green lights got red again, two of them, like the eyes of some dragon, and then my eyes were getting misty from my soul...from the sadness of heart...I think of his divine dancing and match this with YOUR loyalty and faithfulness to him in life and death, and to me the picture as I see it, is a masterpiece of God's work.

None of the so-called self-styled critics were there. No dancers from any leading companies either. How poor must be their souls to be so wrapped up in themselves. I am sad today, Romola. My heart is heavy...that nobody can come to pay homage to the greatest dancer on his farewell to this great city...

I have in my sitting-room a statuette in porcelain of Taglioni, and Pavlova, please give me something of Vaslav's one day, Romola, to keep as a holy relic... When will I see you, Romola? I do miss you, but my prayers and thoughts are often with you, always will be. I shall close this letter written as in a trance, so excuse the ramblings, and expressions and thoughts, but you will, I know, understand their substance.

God bless you then, and my love, yours ever.

Ram'

He mentioned *en passant* his own plans for the future, such as going to the Holland Festival. He had recently completed two films, one, a non-dancing part, together with Claudette Colbert called *Outpost Malaya* and the other, *Elephant Walk* with Vivien Leigh. In the latter, he had been responsible for the choreography and had played the leading dance role. Like Waslaw so many, many years before him had enthused over the 'new-fangled' art of movieland, so Ram Gopal expressed the optimistic view that films enabled the acting profession to reach a far wider world public.

On June 13th, the *S/S Worthing* departed on its regular Newhaven-Dieppe run with its precious cargo on board.

On the morning of the funeral, the pews in the Russian Church soon filled. There was a profusion of floral tributes. The Parisians were eager to express their welcome to the man who had given them so much of his genius years back. According to one of those present, Manuela Messe, everybody of note in Paris was there. The solemn occasion was only marred by the absence of Waslaw's *femmka*. The great Matilda Kchessinskaya, poor health notwithstanding, arrived accompanied by Grand Duke André and his son. She laid down a bouquet of white lilies, a farewell gesture to a former colleague. Messe noticed that the last signature on the list at the entrance was that of Cléo de Mérode. The name brought back a surge of memories of '*La belle epoque*', and of one particular ineffaceable moment in her early youth when she had had the privilege of attending a dress rehearsal (in the guise of an editor's assistant) of Diaghilev's *Ballets Russes* with its star performer Waslaw Nijinsky. Ida Rubinstein, Cléo de Mérode and numerous other famous women had been there, sparkling with beauty and jewellery. It had been difficult to decide which of the spectacles had excited the public more, that on the stage or in the theatre.

Margaret Power, describing the impressive service, wrote that the wreaths had been very beautiful and enormous, the largest consisting of deep-red roses and oak leaves with a ribbon on which was printed '*A mon Vatza de sa femmka!*

Her letter continued...

'Bronia was there with her husband (I think) and Maître Tenger...I was amazed to see Bronia looking so old and worn. Surely, she is younger than Vaslav? Her hair is quite white and she really looked very ill and pale. ...I think "everybody" was there, all the ballet people – Kchessinska, Préobrajenska, and many of the old emigré Russians, and also many of the young dancers from the Opéra and the Ballet School... The Archbishop spoke in Russian, of course, but someone told me that he spoke very tenderly of you and of the splendid example of your love and devotion... My thoughts were with you at the time because I felt that the real Vaslav was with you and not here in Paris... Then we went to the Cemetery and I think you would have liked the priest who took the service at the grave. He had a very saintly face and he wore a white habit...and he spoke of the beauty of Vaslav's life, of the talent given to him by God and of the wonderful beauty and pleasure he was able to give to the people who saw him. He said that the joy which Vaslav gave to us was still with us, held in precious memory in our hearts... They also spoke of the genius and of the great artist which I did not know, but I remember the simple, affectionate childlike man whom I loved. I think perhaps Bronia was remembering him as a little boy when the children met us at the cemetery. There were a number of small boys and girls from the Opéra Ballet School who led the procession from the gate to the

grave...I think you are right – Paris appreciates her artists much more than London and I think it is therefore better that the body of Vaslav should rest there and be honoured in memory....'

The coffin was taken from the church to the Montmartre Cemetery; the pallbearers were young dancers from the Opéra. Crowds watched the procession along the streets, and the children mentioned in her letter – *les petits Rats de l'Opéra* – were in the cortège to the cemetery.

At 11 a.m. Waslaw Nijinsky arrived at his final resting-place. Serge Lifar sprinkled holy water on the flower-strewn coffin before it was lowered. Addresses were given by Lifar in the name of ballet, Maître Tenger for the family, Monsieur Darcaute for the National Artists Union, and Maurice Lehman on behalf of the Opéra, in addition to a representative of the French Government. The Reverend Father Carré, Dominican Chaplain of the artists of Paris, bade a touching farewell on their behalf.

'He has rejoined the God of his Art, the Creator of all things, the Source of all beauty, the great Artist, who has given the power to certain beings – to this genius – to express by dance rhythm, harmony, the joyful or painful sentiments of Mankind and the anguished or calm passions of Mankind.'

The dancer, who had become a legend in his own lifetime, had at last been given a niche among other famous artists, no more to be forgotten in an unmarked grave. His close 'neighbour' is Auguste Vestris, acclaimed as the world's greatest ballet dancer long before young Waslaw rose to fame. It was Diaghilev who, when he saw Waslaw dance, said there had been no one like him since Vestris, and hence, what could be more appropriate than the two geniuses of dance resting so close to each other.

He is not forgotten. A few summers ago, a friend of mine, who was spending three days in Paris, visited his grave and found that two fresh, long-stemmed red roses had been placed on the unpretentious slab of stone shortly before her arrival.

Seemingly, the last curtain had gone down for Waslaw Nijinsky, but Romola was determined it should not be so. Whatever bitterness she may have felt over her great loss, whatever frustration and pain she harboured over the sacrifices she had made, which in the end were to no avail, she hugged her feelings close to herself. After a bout of depression and introspection brought on by the reburial, she carried on unswervingly to ensure that her Waslaw's name would never die. Kyra and I had no part in that side of her life. She never wrote a word to me about my father's death as well she might have done. Nor did she seem to care about how Kyra felt at the loss of her father and his subsequent re-interment.

Having written two books about her life with Waslaw Nijinsky, she proceeded to plan a third book to which she gave the working title *Anthology of the Eulogies*. The history of what gave her the impetus to this idea was quite simple. After Waslaw's death, tributes and appraisals of his career emerged in a flood of writing, both in prose and poetry. In the process of gathering this material together, Romola also dug out extracts from works already published in Waslaw's lifetime, gems of portrayals by Auguste Rodin, Alexandre Benois, Prince Peter Lieven, to name but a few.

Her new book never saw the light of day, a fate which was to befall scores of other projects in later years. She would make preliminary notes and then push them to one side, diverted from the task in pursuit of something else further afield. She became more and more restless, unable to settle down to regular hours of work, too distracted by all the schemes buzzing inside her head to perpetuate the name Nijinsky, to give it eternal life. Yet her notes reveal how much she wanted the world to read what his contemporaries had to say about Nijinsky.

Out of respect for her wishes and out of love for my father, whom I knew so fleetingly, I include a handful of the eulogies. It is with a feeling of profound pride I do this. My father comes vibrantly to life once more and I can clearly visualise the youth with whom Romola fell in love, to such an extent that she discarded everything else in her life to be at his side. One woman's almost blind obsession, oblivious to its fatal consequences.

The *New York Herald Tribune* devoted several columns to the dancer hailed 'as Greatest Dancer' and noted that 'immediately after his graduation, Kchessinskaya, then Russia's favourite ballerina, invited him to be her summer partner. He was only eighteen, and during his entire career, he never danced except with a première ballerina.' She recollected that until the graduation performance (at the Imperial Theatrical Academy in St Petersburg) in 1908, she had never seen him dance or even heard of him. 'I was at once struck by his outstanding ability especially by his incredible lightness in "flying" jumps. Without any hesitation I chose this unknown young man as my partner for the summer season at Krasnoye Selo, in spite of the fact that he was only beginning his artistic career. At that time I played the leading role on the Imperial stage and I wanted, by this act, to help an obviously talented youth in his first steps. And I was not mistaken in Nijinsky. From that time on began his brilliant career.... After London, I danced with Nijinsky in Vienna, in Budapest and in Monte Carlo. We danced together for the last time in Monte Carlo. There can be no doubt whatsoever that ballet suffered a great loss when Nijinsky left the stage so prematurely...'

Lydia Sokolova, recalled how nervous and concerned she was at her first rehearsal for *L'Après-midi d'un Faune* in 1913, when Nijinsky told her to 'step and move between the beats of the music', and how he taught her to dance the part of the young girl in *Le Spectre de la Rose* at the Metropolitan Opera House in New York. She wrote: '...I experienced a sense of thankfulness that he is free at long last, but at the funeral today my heart ached for Madame Karsavina, whose beauty and fame were linked with him in a perfect harmony of dancing, which has never been surpassed...'

Elisabeth, Duchess de Gramont, lauded him as the most extraordinary dancer who ever existed. With his leaps, he reached incredible heights. No one who had not seen him fly and disappear through a bay window in *Spectre de la Rose* could say he knew Nijinsky. 'The blazing trail which he left behind on the stage will never be extinguished.' She made the same remark as Alexandre Benois and others; how, in everyday life, he was a short young man, pale and insignificant, but that he applied his skill and tricks with makeup to transform his silhouette, his neck, shoulders and calves, underneath which were the famous muscles of steel. She finished by quoting Renaldo Hahn, the great connoisseur: 'When one has seen Nijinsky dance, nothing else matters.'

Marie Rambert (Mrs Ashley Dukes), whose affection and admiration for Waslaw Nijinsky so many years ago had been far deeper than that of one colleague for another, concentrated on 'the purely physical aspects of those infinitely poetical movements of his. No one held more firmly to the ground in order to obtain that fabulous spring. He had an exceptionally long Achilles tendon and was one of the very few people who could do a full *plié* (that is until the thighs become horizontal) in the fifth position... in every grand *jeté* whether it was straight forward or *en tournant* he did the *battement* with the second leg without dropping the first, and for a moment held that position in the air...it was his consciousness at that moment of the position he held, and the supreme happiness of being suspended in the air that communicated a corresponding delight in the audience... Nijinsky came nearer the stars and made you forget the earth altogether. His pirouettes were brilliant...the incredible lightness and swiftness of his head movements...His feet were extraordinarily supple. I remember him showing me how to hold the foot *sur le cou-de-pied*... "Clasp it as though with the hand", and indeed his foot had the intelligence and sensitiveness of a hand- ...Nothing and nobody will ever make me forget his soaring into the air in *Spectre,* his sparkling brilliance in *Le Pavillon d'Armide,* his irresistible mischief in *Carnaval* and all his other roles, but above all his Albrecht in *Giselle.* I meant to write only a few words, but I could think and talk of Nijinsky all day long, so I will not embark now on talking about his choreography. His achievement as a dancer alone makes him immortal.'

Cyril Beaumont contributed a glowing endorsement of Father's comparatively brief career, ending as follows: 'I shall never cease to venerate Nijinsky, whose equal I have never seen. In those far-off days just before the first World War he dominated the ballet scene like the god of the Dance that he was. How sad it is that I cannot show our dancers and ballet-goers of today how Nijinsky danced in the days of his glory. Some have doubted the legend of his greatness. It is true. I ask you to take my word for it.'

Throughout the appraisals of Waslaw, there is one consistent theme – the transfiguration of the ugly duckling to that of a beauti-ful, graceful swan. Of course, a person of renown, like Jean Coc-teau, put it far more succinctly.

'It is hard for me to speak of Nijinsky. He was a drama and an enigma, just as Beauty is. That "little young man" to whom a Taxi-girl from Tabarin said, while bringing him back to our table: "You're awfully nice, but you can't dance", that young man whose muscles bulged under his clothes and whose long neck, jutting out of his collar, held a small ape-like head with sparse hair, that unat-tractive and rough-looking young man – for he lived with his dream – that young man would come out of his dressing-room and into the stage-lights with such beauty, such powerful grace, that the least sensitive of beings, the most aggressive critics, were pervaded by a sort of bliss. In him all was Dance; stillness as well as springing; and his gestures; and his look; and the way he would turn his head from left to right and from right to left; and even the final bow, which in itself was a spectacle and of which the public never tired, calling him back and acclaiming him until his aides and his servant Wassili could shower, rub and pamper him behind the scenes, as if he were a boxer at the end of a contest. Undoubtedly, there never was anyone who could compare with Nijinsky, and there never will be. I have seen him in all his parts. I have seen him challenge the law of balance, fly straight out of the window of the *Shadow of the Rose;* I have seen him die under the snow of *Petrouchka* and bring tears to our eyes with one gesture; I have seen him killed by a sword at the end of *Schéhérazade,* beating the ground like a fish beats the deck of a boat. I saw him bow again and again and once more, with a sort of delightful military salute, in a storm of applause and before a raving audience that would not sit down. I saw the public demand another performance of *Spectre de la Rose,* not realising the exhausting effort it meant for him, because he dispelled it, showing only the utmost ease, as if he was saying: "It is very easy, you can all do it." Nijinsky is now dead. Why tell our dreams when no one will believe us?'

Nadia Nicolaevna Legat wrote at great length about her husband's former pupil. I only wish that space would permit me to include it in its entirety.

'Nijinsky came to this earth with a super-earthly capacity, with a soul so great that the body was an inadequate medium for the manifestation of the powers of his soul and spirit. ...The most remarkable and amazing fact about Nijinsky as an artist and dancer was that he had that rare quality of being so natural...The first person to notice this, and to point it out to me, was Nicolas Legat, who was his teacher from his earliest days. It was well known that Nijinsky as a pupil somehow appeared to be completely transformed when in Nicolas Legat's class, where he appeared exalted, vibrant, free and so ecstatic that his enchanted teacher would lay aside his violin and forget that there were other boys in the class except Vaslav. There, in that plain, dingy dancing classroom, stood another Plato and Aristotle – master and pupil – both great, both free, and both above the average man...His powerful, effortless dancing often caused the teacher's eye to be focused on this boy, who seemed to him to be the incarnation of "harmonious movement". This earth was not his true home: all material things took a second place in his life. I, myself, was fascinated by Vaslav the dancer, because I always felt that he belonged to a plane above ours, and that he could link himself with us only through his powerful medium – the dance. The rest of his inner self he knew we should not understand – therefore he lived in his own world. I, who was always searching for the "unknown", felt that Vaslav was perhaps the one who could, if he wished through his super-artistic and super-physical dancing, show us the way to reach that "ideal". He was supreme in many other directions. At the present time I have been entrusted with the task of translating and editing his book on dance notation. His ideas were ingenious, because they were not only simple, but complete, easy to learn, and logically conceived. The work is still unfinished, but I hope it will soon be published for the benefit of future dancers, and as a proof of Nijinsky's many-sidedness. He possessed the capacity of thinking symbolically, as I have seen from his drawings, which were full of mystic meaning...They are so much above the world in which we live that some people will pass by and not notice them – others will proclaim them as merely the works of a madman, the reason for this being that they do not understand. To me there were, and always will be in my memory, two Nijinskys – Nijinsky "the dancer", whom the world enjoyed watching, loved and even idolised, and Nijinsky the "superman" – barred from us through his detachment from the material world which he had outgrown, and to which he did not wish to belong, but in which he was inevitably involved and, being involved there, he showed "greatness" both in feeling and family life. He frequently visited my school, and shortly before he died, came there and watched the classes. He especially enjoyed the children's classes and very much admired and encouraged them. To me Vaslav was never mad. It was the world that was blind (if not mad) because it could not see, understand, or reach his height...'

Carlos Salzedo, the French harpist, who became a close friend of the Nijinskys during their stay in New York, touched upon another faet of Waslaw's 'many-sidedness' – his inordinate love of music. 'Nijinsky was music personified. I was vividly made aware of this when I introduced him to two composers with whose music he was not thoroughly familiar: Brahms and Scriabin. He was standing at the piano, in his well-known posture – on one foot – his eyes fixed on an imaginary horizon. As I was playing, the music seemed to filter through his relaxed motionless body, as in a trance. It was an unforgettable experience... During the summer of 1916, in Bar Harbor, we had made definite plans for a touring company which would have included four or five dancers and an orchestral ensemble composed of four harps, a few string, wind and percussive instruments, for which he had asked me to orchestrate our repertory and lead our prospective orchestral ensemble. Our repertory included several of Scriabin's immortal last piano preludes, most of them unknown at that time – and even today. Regretfully, this interesting and artistic project of ours never materialised.'

'What remains of Nijinsky for the eye to behold? Many photographs, some paintings, a few drawings.' Jean-Louis Vaudoyer, French poet and a member of the *Académie Française,* pursued the idea that either or all of these media betrayed the picture formed in the memories of those fortunate enough to have seen Nijinsky dance and that if these memorabilia are shown today to those who are too young to have attended *ces spectacles* they will only inspire incredulity or deception. It was Vaudoyer who had the original idea for *Le Spectre de la Rose,* inspired by Théophile Gautier's romantic poem. How could he hazard a conjecture at the time that it was to become Nijinsky's most famous role. Fokine was the choreographer. Bakst created a stage design of ethereal beauty, quite possibly the most enchanting picture ever to frame a ballet. The costume he designed was actually fitted on Waslaw himself. Romola described it in detail. 'He sketched it on the shirt Nijinsky was wearing. Bakst had painted samples of silk pongee, in rose, rose lavender, dark reds and various pinks, and these were given to Maria Stepanova to have bolts of the material dyed. Bakst cut the forms of the rose-petals himself. Some had to be tight, others loose, and he instructed her just how to sew them on so that the costume was created anew each time Nijinsky danced. It consisted of a close-fitting, fine silk, elastic jersey, into which Nijinsky was sewn, covering his entire body, except part of his breast and arms, where bracelets of silk rose-petals bound his biceps. This jersey was stitched with rose-leaves, which Bakst would colour as they were needed. Some were ragged, as from a dying flower; others were stiff and firm; while still others curled even from his thighs.' Marinelli, the London impresario, had attended the première and had gasped in disbelief at the sight of Waslaw's single bound across the entire stage. Afterwards, he had asked Vassili to show him Nijinsky's shoes. He suspected that the soles were made of rubber. Waslaw had become irritated over all the attention focused on his leaps and is reputed to have said *'Je ne suis pas un sauteur. Je suis un artiste.'* Vaudoyer, who had also been at the première, had called the ballet perfection, that it was a triumph, more Gautier than the actual poem.

In his eulogy, Vaudoyer said: '...Away from the theatre, back to daily life like everybody else, Nijinsky was nothing more than a silent boy, secretive, not timid but lacklustre, absentminded. Somehow, he faded, became invisible, neutral. He was very much like the butterfly who only in flight displays the brilliant colours of her wings...' It was the same incredible transformation that so many others had been struck by. '...Nijinsky appeared to be a ghost of himself, an illusion, a capricious projection of the mind...', and then sharply everything changed under the influence of the dance, '...a marvellous, miraculous phoenix burst truimphantly forth out of the chrysalis.'

On the 16th of June, 1953, André de Badet wrote in the same vein in the opening paragraph of his *éloge* to Nijinsky. 'It is impossible for those who have not seen him dance to form an opinion of what Waslaw Nijinsky was like. It would be illusory on their part, like making a blind man see the birth of a bird and the marvellous progress of its flight.' Badet dwelt on his meeting with Waslaw and Romola in South America, how the couple would spend their leisure hours in the seclusion of the tropical garden surrounding the vast house in which Badet and his mother lived on the outskirts of Montevideo. Waslaw had confided to him how he felt persecuted by the other members of the troupe, how three times his life had been endangered at the Téâtre Colon in Buenos Aires. Badet retold the story of how Waslaw, a profound pacifist, has contacted him regarding the soirée to aid the French and British Red Cross in Montevideo. 'Never had he been more aerial, more prodigious, more touching than that evening on the stage of the old, magnificent Théâtre Solis, accompanied at the piano by Domingo Dente, with a few of the more romantic passages from Chopin. Waslaw had composed some new dances for the occasion.'

Badet claimed that he had received numerous letters from Waslaw when the latter first settled down in the Villa Guardamunt in St Moritz Dorf, and that these letters, like others written to Badet in Argentina and Brazil, were proof of Waslaw's command of

French, contrary to what certain people pretended. He had shown the letters to Romola, who, taken by surprise, exclaimed: 'But he writes French far better than I.' In closing, Badet recounted how Waslaw had let him into the details of his shipboard romance; how charming he had found Romola, seated in a deck chair next to him, and the incongruity at that initial stage of being unable to communicate with her other than through expressive mime; the trauma of misunderstanding and embarrassment during the honeymoon, both anxious to prove their love yet unable to talk to each other, question each other, confide to each other. All the while evoking the memory of the adventure, Nijinsky's slightly Asiatic face, small in comparison to the vigorous column of his neck – a neck as powerful as a Donatello – had lit up in a smile that gleamed maliciously in his eyes, then, flashing his teeth as he laughed, his fabulous, flexible features took on the expression of the Faun, of Daphnis, of Petrouchka, of Narcisse, of the favourite slave in *Schéhérazade,* 'of all the personalities of dream and legend that blended into one with the memory my heart retains of him.'

Jacques Rouche, ex-Director of the Paris Opera, commented on how Sergei Diaghilev, with his new ballets, suddenly transformed the traditional trend and how he introduced an unprecedented revelation, Nijinsky, a consummate artist, a liberated dancer. 'In *Le Spectre de la Rose,* to enter the stage through the window was not to conform to the fairy-like romanticism of the libretto. He created the illusion of a spirit. He did not revolve around and around the young sleeping girl as a man nor as a dancer but like a veritable reflection of her dream. The departure into the night did not have the pace of a normal leap but of a bound into space...'

Valentine Hugo, President of the Society of French Scenic Artists in 1950, summarised Waslaw Nijinsky's career in an eight-page testimonial, ending as follows:

'I hope one day that I can produce his dancing life in such a manner that it will not be lost to the dancers to come. This would be my last gesture of admiration and homage to that charming young man, petit, thickset but of perfect proportions, who presented himself to the world rather like a sportive character, ill at ease in his civilian clothes, a homage to that brilliant dancer who on the stage miraculously turned into a romantic creature soaring above mortals, a mysterious young faun, a bounding Negro, a dream, graceful and light, an adolescent, supple and silent, a sunburst gushing like a fountain, a puppet so moving he brought tears to the beholder; finally, a prodigy with a mortal body, one of those ephemeral beings whom destiny takes back and plunges once more into nothingness as if he inadvertently was forgotten on earth by God.'

Maurice Rostand, son of Edmond Rostand, the French dramatist and poet, and famous in his own right as a playwright (he created a sensation in 1928 with the production of Napoleon IV), recollected how, during a couple of seasons prior to the first of two horrible wars – before 1914 – when everything was colourful, the climate right, a breath of poetry filled the air. Nijinsky, the god of the day, would come to Larue's to partake of supper with Marcel Proust and himself (Rostand). The god, having descended from his altar, and devoid of make-up, was transformed into a dreamy, Russian lad. Rostand mused how the years rolled by...the dance was interrupted...'but the memory we had of the unique dancer was unforgettable... Even during those hours when he perhaps forgot himself, we were able to reach him. There were always great bonds joining us together... And after many years, a new impression of him was brought to life, which I set down in a few lines of verse... In March 1948, the newspapers announced that Nijinsky, after many years of illness, had gone to watch a young man dance, and I wrote the following, joining the present with the past:

Après tout ce temps de folie,
Ce temps de délire insensé,
Nijinsky, la face pâlie,
Regarde un jeune homme danser!

On voit, dans l'ardente atmosphère
Où le mème dieu les conduit,
L'immense danseur de naguère,
Le jeune danseur d'aujourd 'hui!

Mais, poursuivant l'envol sublime
De ce passé qu' il reconquit,
Nijinsky, dans son rève intime,
Regarde danser Nijinsky.

Maurice Rostand'

CHAPTER 12

THE LURE OF JAPAN

On March 6th, 1957, Romola wrote to a Mr A G Heltberg, the American Consul in Salzburg, supplying him with details regarding Laci and myself, presumably requested by him in a letter to her dated February 26th. She ended her letter: 'I do hope that the family Weninger will soon be called for medical and other necessary processing and that it will be possible for you to grant them permission to enter the United States.'

A subsequent letter to a Mr Rieger, dated April 9th, from the American Embassy in Vienna, reads as follows: 'Mr and Mrs Weninger (she is the daughter of the famous dancer Nijinsky) were in to see me recommended by a dear friend. Mr Lehman tells me there is a good chance that in about a week things will be clearer and that she still might be able to leave for the U.S. Since she is in Camp Roeder, may I recommend her to your kind heart...?'

Thus, Romola earnestly tried to help us, but the ultimate road to freedom was not going to be as smooth as we had been led to believe.

After the initial, genial welcome to Austria on January 29th, 1957, we had been taken by bus to a school where we were temporarily housed and where we savoured our first real breakfast for ages. Later, Building 209, Camp Roeder, Siezenheim, near Salzburg, was to be our domicile for the unforeseeable future together with thousands of other souls escaping the tyranny of their homeland.

To be the daughter of Romola Nijinsky had its advantages, and we were given free rein to visit Vienna. In compliance with my mother's earlier message, I contacted my old nurse Laura, and she in turn put me in touch with Dagmar, Erik Schmedes's daughter. She lived in Dürer Gasse, and I cherish the warmth of her hospitality and help. She also advanced us funds that we sorely lacked, which were later settled by Romola.

How marvellous it was day after day to stroll through the street of that lovely city. We stayed far too long, intoxicated by its beauty and by the freedom we breathed. But after a few days, alarming news reached me that Miklós was preparing to come to take Kinga back with him to Budapest. With my inherent honesty, possibly naïvety, I had felt duty bound to let him know of his daughter's whereabouts; that she was safe and sound. I was stunned to learn that, according to the Hungarian legal system, he was in his full rights to accuse me of kidnapping despite the fact that I had the custody of Kinga. I was in no position to seek protection from the Austrian authorities. They were powerless to intervene; we were Hungarian citizens and theirs was a neutral country. Rather than risk a volatile situation, we swiftly left Vienna and sought the anonymity of the Camp.

That night, we sat up unable to sleep. Laci made the suggestion that I call Romola. It had been all of eleven years since last I spoke to her. Bitter memories stirred in me; I could still hear her acid voice reverberating in my ears from that last conversation. Laci assured me that her attitude had changed but my courage failed me, and so he telephoned. She exploded with fury; it was three o'clock in the morning, and she had just fallen asleep after returning on a night flight from New York. Laci broke off her outpouring to explain the troublesome set of circumstances in which we found ourselves. Admonishing him that a telephone call was far too expensive, that she had already sent the necessary papers on to Vienna, and that he should give further details in another letter, she hung up.

Her ensuing letters presented a changeableness that could only be compared with April showers. She was commiserative about our plight, promised to send us money, and was extremely apologetic that the sum would not be large but she was just then engaged in a lawsuit. She offered to move Heaven and Hell to get us out of Europe. Already, she had spoken to the Head of the Bureau of Immigration in Washington, personally visited their local office in San Francisco, and she expanded further on the matter by stating she was going to write to President Eisenhower. She showed deep concern about Kinga's safety and suggested that I place her under the protection of the United States through its Consul in Salzburg. She went even further, advising me to send Kinga alone to the States.

Time crawls along at a snail-like pace when one is waiting for news of any kind. To employ our long hours usefully, we threw ourselves into various activities in the Camp. Our knowledge of languages came to good use. Laci worked with the Red Cross and I acted as an interpreter in the office. We joined the privileged minority who enjoyed special favours. Before that, we were part of the 'herd', men, women, families, some eighty odd, crammed together in a barrack whose sole furnishings comprised of bunkbeds. I found it disquieting that 'events', often of a most intimate nature, during the night, should be heard by our children. It was therefore with intense relief we departed with our meagre belongings to our own quarters, a room no larger than a monastic cell but there were mattresses on the floor, and we had total privacy.

April arrived, the glorious month pregnant with the promise of summer to come. By now, both Laci and I had grown restless and hungered for something to happen at last, as already thousands upon thousands of our fellow compatriots had left the Camp and been flown to 'the promised land', USA. No influential mother had helped them, but a Church organisation. Finally, unable to bear Laci's mounting misery any more – *'I did not leave Budapest to sit and rot some measly miles from the Hungarian border'* – nor my own growing anguish, I paid a visit to the American Consulate in Salzburg. There I received the shock of my life.

The Consul, flicking through my documents, sounded what seemed to me a death-knell. We had crossed the border into Austria in January 1957, and the Bill allowing refugee Hungarians to enter the United States had expired on December 31st, 1956. We would have to wait for a new bill to be passed. I mustered sufficient courage to ask for how long.

'Dear Mrs Weninger, only the good Lord knows when. It may take six months, six years.' He shrugged his shoulders. 'Who can tell?'

Grimly, Laci absorbed the calamitous news. He clammed up like an oyster and for two days I suffered his silence. On the third day, he departed without a hint as to where he was going. Some hours later, he returned and without preamble handed me a couple of forms, stating brusquely that we would have to have our identification photographs taken. I had two choices – South Africa or Australia. A wave of giddiness swept over me. At first, I refused to take him seriously. As far as I was concerned, either choice would be like stepping off the globe.

Laci put his cards on the table. There was a strong possibility that he would be offered a directorship at a music conservatoire in either of the two places. Australia tantalisingly promised him a villa and a car as well, anything he asked for. I wrote to Romola seeking her advice. She replied promptly that she was sad fortune had turned against us but she would still try her utmost to get us over to San Francisco. She strongly advised against going to South Africa, forecasting bloody events between the whites and the blacks. As for Australia, she hesitated to recommend going there. *'It is still a very barren place. I have heard the English are extremely prudish, full of prejudices, and art simply does not exist there. The few artists who go there for concert tours, mention them in the most unflattering terms. Besides, it is a socialist country. Everybody has to do everything himself...'*

Laci relentlessly pressed me to state my preference. I could not. Throughout the interminable black nights I lay awake, racking my brain how to find a solution that would bring me and mine to the States. And then, the miracle happened, purely by chance. One day, as I was leaving the Cathedral in Salzburg, I noticed a breathtakingly beautiful poster in a travel agency window opposite. One word stood out in bold lettering: CANADA. Of course, why had I not thought of that before?

The following morning, I took a bus to Vienna and went to the Canadian Embassy. There, I had the good fortune to meet a compatriot, a Hungarian countess. I poured out my despair at the prospect of emigrating to a strange continent, and how I longed one day to be reunited with my mother. Canada was after all a 'close neighbour'. She immediately took me under her wing, and pulling strings, which were to remain her secret, managed to simplify the procedure for acquiring the right papers. On the 25th day of April, 1957, we boarded an old, four-engine converted World War II plane bound for Canada. The flight lasted a gruelling twenty-two hours with a stop-over in Iceland.

When our plane finally touched ground at Montreal Airport, I could not thank God enough. At last I was in the New World, on the same continent as my mother. Perhaps the granite wall of the dark past that so long had separated us would now crumble and we would be reunited without acrimony on either side.

Together with the others, we were bundled into coaches and taken to the outskirts of the city to a former army barrack, which had been converted into a refugee reception centre. There, we had our own room, three square meals a day, and were assured that we could remain as long as we liked until we had found suitable work.

With $10 between us, Laci and I set forth the very next day to seek our fortune in Montreal.

It was not going to be a primrose path to prosperity. I took a temporary job as a waitress in a very exclusive private club. But for Laci the situation was different. Laci could not embark on his professional career until he had lived in Canada for at least six months. Only then would he be able to join the Musicians' Union and as a member be allowed to apply for suitable work. He went through an extremely frustrating time. His world had centred around organ music, concerts, the theatre, but finally, to support his family, he was reduced to playing as a part-time pianist in Montreal's top-star hotel, where he sat at the ivory keyboards, playing background music barely discernible over the din of the guests' table talk and the clatter of cutlery in the dining-room. Definitely not his dream come true but we were at last living in freedom, and he was providing for his family.

Thanks to the charitable organisation in charge of rehabilitation of refugees, we moved from our tiny efficiency flat to a larger one in September that year. It boasted two bedrooms and was located in the heart of Montreal. The children were sent to English schools. Soon, we acquired a car and reminiscences of jaunts in 'Junior' flooded over us on our excursions into the countryside. I now felt we were settled and yearned for a visit from my mother, although I was apprehensive as to what my reaction would be. One moment, I envisaged myself greeting her affectionately, the next, the memory of the last encounter overshadowed my assumptions, and I went limp with uneasiness. However, I wrote to her, asking her to come to see us.

Her reply arrived a few days later. She apologised for having forgotten my birthday, but she wrote she had been very ill in the summer. She urged me to force the children to learn English and French, and praised me for having spoken French so fluently as a little girl. She hoped it would now come back to me.

'...almost died; it was a miracle that I survived. I caught a microbe which infected the brain and ended up in the kidneys. It was the beginning stage of uraemia and it was only due to my strong heart I survived the massive dose of antibotics. I cannot come to visit you now, but I hope to do so soon. I cannot tell you how happy I am that you are out of that Hell. I never

wanted to let you go to Hungary. I am sorry to this day that I did send you to your grandmother, but my financial situation during those years gave me no option. Please do write to Tessa. She is very hurt that you appear to have forgotten her. Remember, she did take good care of you when you stayed with her eight months in Vienna when you had the operation on your leg. I would also like to know how Kyra is faring. I have not been on speaking terms with her since June, when she wanted to bring a priest to see me. Write to her, but please do not tell her that I asked you to do so. She should come to me and apologise for her behaviour but still I am concerned about her welfare. She is all alone, and without any protection; it must be very difficult for her. I am fully aware that she can earn very little teaching dancing.'

Typically Romola, she did not heed the fact that all communication had been broken off between me and Tessa and Kyra for years, a situation of which I had already made her aware.

The long-anticipated day did arrive. 'D-Day', the family called it with mock humour. Before that, I suffered every conceivable emotion. Laci, Kinga and Peter accepted with tolerance the frenzy with which I tackled the house-cleaning of our flat, not one inch was spared my scrubbing and dusting. Hungarian dishes popped in and out of the oven. About half an hour before she was due, Laci took the children downstairs, and waited for her outside. Then I heard footsteps on the landing, and the door open.

At first, I could only stare at her. 'So this woman is my mother.' She had gained weight, was a little on the stout side. First-moment impressions darted signals to my brain; I was appalled to notice how the years had ruined her wealth of shiny, auburn hair. It now hung in thin, harshly red strands around her face. Far too much dyeing, I concluded. Melancholically, I recalled Emilia's thick, golden tresses which even when mixed with silver threads were beautiful. Romola wore a simple, long-sleeved, maroon dress. Her expensive jewels attracted the eye: a magnificent brooch adorned her cleavage, a thick gold bracelet graced her wrist. On her fingers I noticed a grey pearl ring and one with an enormous sapphire. She, in turn, gave me a searching look. Without preamble, she extolled the virtues of Laci, although she had only just met him. Romola could not abide my first husband and she was keen I should not forget it.

It was not easy to bridge the gap of past years. I felt ill at ease and clumsy in her presence and the conversation was stilted. Like most men, Laci was bowled over by her magnetic, bewitching personality, and chided me for not responding to her with more candour. He claimed my judgement was unfair, and that she did love me but was unable to show it.

Our long drawn-out evening talks shed some light on her travels, her books and the eccentric, complex lawsuits. I do not imagine it will ever be possible to assess how many lawsuits she was involved in during her lifetime. After her death, I was to find bulky files dealing with one case after the other. One letter, for example, dated January 25, 1956, was from the Private Secretary to HM The Queen of the Netherlands, replying to a letter from Romola. The last sentence reads '...You must understand that the Queen cannot enter into a lawsuit...' To which one it referred I have no idea. I merely learned that my mother had had no qualms whatsoever about going to the highest levels when she felt she had been wronged.

During the course of one conversation, Romola confided she had approached Ivan Mestrovic, the famous Yugoslav sculptor, who, among his other works, had made numerous religious reliefs and figures. She had written to him in January 1956, when he was at the University of Notre Dame, to ask him if he would make a base relief for Tatakaboy's crypt. In his response, he had mentioned how well he remembered her husband, going back to their first meeting in Rome when Diaghilev had brought Waslaw to his studio, and how thereafter he had seen his performances and admired his extraordinary talent. He had been most interested in her request although he was extremely busy with other work, but he required some more pertinent information; photographs of Nijinsky, a photograph or drawing of the crypt, its exact size, and so forth. He would then quote Romola the price for the relief in Carrara marble.

Romola evidently let the matter rest until a year later. I have a letter of the 1st of May, 1957, from Mestrovic in which he quoted the cost. '...You are asking me for the approximate cost of this monument – stone, carving and my fee.... Despite that Vaslav Nijinsky was a genius in his field he has certainly not left a fortune. Therefore, I would be disposed to make a relief for his tomb for less than half of my usual price. It means $3,000.... To procure a fine piece of marble, cutting the relief in it would cost the same amount... Transportation of the finished stone to Paris has to be at your expense. I am not able to tell you exactly how much packing, insurance and transportation would cost, but roughly it will amount to $1,000... It seems to me it has to be a very simple shape, rectangular on the top, to avoid banality...' Of course, the whole idea came to naught. Evidently she was befuddled regarding the ownership of the grave. It belonged to Serge Lifar.

She made an indelible impression on Laci through her 'names-dropping', casually scattering illustrious names like so much multi-coloured confetti while she chatted away – Jean Cocteau, the Aga Khan, Serge Lifar, Tamara Karsavina....She made it sound as though they were part of her intimate circle of friends. The dull mediocracy of our flat became transformed. Romola monopolised Laci's attention in telling of her recent contact with Dr Carl Jung on the subject of dreams in colour. She waxed enthusiastic on a topic which revealed a hitherto unknown side of her early youth.

As a child she used to have very vivid dreams, many of them telepathic or prophetic. So sensitive was she then that Emilia had taken her to Professor Ranschburg, one of the foremost neurologists in Hungary. He had diagnosed her as a highly-strung, imaginative child and ordained bromides. She was forbidden to read before going to bed at night, and was restricted to far fewer theatre visits. Her dreams persisted all the same and they were invariably in colour. She became so fascinated that she began an intensive study of the subject, going so far as to bombard friends and acquaintances in order to gather statistics on how people dream. The result showed that most people's dreams were in black and white but that on occasion some would also dream in colour. She pursued her probing for an explanation, interviewing psychiatrists and physicians.

She delved into the pages of Aldous Huxley's book, *Heaven and Hell*, pondered over his observations and conclusions as well as those of Dr Calvin Hall, and pronounced dissatisfaction with their verdict. In a letter from Aldous Huxley, he recalled what a miracle it had been to see Nijinsky dance in *L'Après Midi d'un Faune* but it seems he had not wished to enter into a debate with Romola on her pet 'hobbyhorse'. Dr Jung, on the other hand, wrote her a long letter in the latter part of May 1956. Jung suggested that if there is contact between the conscious and the subconscious mind ('the approach of the conscious to the unconscious exists or vice versa'), then there will be colour in dreams ('a special accent') as well as other 'impressive qualities' in waking behaviour. If, on the other hand, there is no such contact, 'no expressed necessity that the conscious should make contact with (the) unconscious', i.e. the subconscious mind, the dreams remain rather without colour. Romola had known Jung since back in 1919 when she had first sought his advice on Waslaw's mental behaviour and had never lost touch with him.

Bit by bit we elicited from her some of the highlights of her public life, thus filling in a few gaps. Romola had donated to the London Museum a fur-lined coat and fur bonnet, worn by my father on his departure from Russia in 1911. She had been extremely touched by a phrase in a letter from Helen Hayes, inviting her to come to a luncheon. 'Whenever I remember that I have had the privilege of seeing Nijinsky dance *Spectre de la Rose,* I don't regret my growing mountain of years.' Romola collected praises about Waslaw like precious pearls to add to a necklace.

Margaret Power had continued to be a bastion of strength. Romola turned to her to sort out a number of problems that she herself was unable to solve from distant San Francisco. At times, she taxed Margaret Power's patience to the point of rebellion by the latter. She went so far as to demand that Margaret should negotiate a few delicate issues with the Soviets. Romola insisted on presenting Ulanova with a very special photograph of Waslaw when the prima ballerina was dancing at Covent Garden and also to discuss with Asaf Messerer the donation of Waslaw's System of Notation to the Soviet Union. Margaret Power had reacted irascibly in a letter of November 18th, 1956: *'I know perfectly well that dancers have nothing to do with their government's policy but I simply felt that I did not want to speak to Russians, knowing what their soldiers were doing in Hungary.'* One of the interpreters for the company had said: 'Why does Madame Nijinsky want to give them anything at all. They are quite unworthy of the generosity and they certainly will not value such souvenirs.' Ulanova was given the photograph, however, after the final performance and the star had graciously accepted the gift with deepest thanks. *'...that she would always remember the meeting in Vienna because it was a moment of the greatest importance in her life.'*

As far as the System of Notation was concerned, Messerer told Margaret Power that they now had a far better system in the Soviet Union, but, if Romola wished to give them the manuscript after the book was published, they would gladly have it in the Museum of the Bolshoi Theatre in memory of Waslaw. *'But I shall be ashamed of you if you do give it to them...When I feel less bitter maybe I will be able to write in more detail.'*

Among Romola's notes was one that she entitled *'Le Système de Notation Choreographique de Vaslav Nijinsky'*. It reads as follows:

'Vaslav Nijinsky invented a system of dance notation during the years he studied at the Imperial School of Dance in St Petersburg. Nijinsky had carried on research to enable him to develop a precise notation of the steps and movements in a ballet as well as the choreography.

1) To be able to note down the choreography of ballets, dance steps or any human movement with the same exactitude as musical notes,

2) To note down the entire choreography of a ballet and thereafter to obtain the copyright. According to international law, all works – literary, musical or choreographic – are protected by the law (copyright of the author). Consequently, another choreographer is forbidden to create another version because this will then be seen to violate the right of the author. This is a judicial point of immense importance.

3) The system thus preserves the ballet in its original arrangement for future generations.

4) It allows each artiste to receive his role written down, which he then can study so that upon arrival at rehearsal he knows his part, facilitating the work of the choreographer, the ballet master and of the ballet dancer himself. Nijinsky's system is based on the laws governing anatomy and geometry. He uses a circle (360°) of which only 80° are feasible for the human body. Two circles cover the vertical and the horizontal. Within these circles all dance movements are to be found. Nijinsky always said that he considered his system the most important work that he had created.

Nijinsky's system is the most accurate, legible and simple of all the systems existing today.

My husband, whose pupil I was, taught me this system.'

Romola was unfaltering in her belief that she would amass a small fortune through renewed sales of her book about Waslaw; it was being reprinted in Great Britain and was due to be published in Russian, Japanese, Polish and German. She revealed that she was pressing hard to see the fulfilment of her highest goal, the film about Nijinsky, based on her book. Among others, she had contacted Tamara Karsavina, imploring her to shoulder the role of technical adviser. The latter had politely refused, claiming she was no longer equal to the strain of such a responsibility, and besides, she was very much behind schedule *vis-à-vis* a contract with her publishers.

Romola showed us cuttings from a Mexican newspaper and the Mexican edition of the *American New York Journal* covering interviews with her in late 1956. The latter consisted of an article by a Marjorie Farmsworth entitled *'A Story of Tragic Love'* and described how the meeting with Romola had taken place in an 'enchantingly gay patio with the bright plumage of tropical birds, *marache* music and the soft swish of palms as the wind blew through their branches... After a short while Madame Nijinsky came into the garden and it became more enchanting, more alive, for this woman who has known tremendous tragedy is an enormously alive person...'

The content of the actual interview was no different from hundreds of others supplied by Romola, dwelling basically on the romantic meeting with Waslaw and the proposal on board ship; the tragedy of his insanity. One single sentence, however, presented a notable exception. According to the interviewer, she said: 'We were married for 38 years but we spoke together only four of those years; we learned each other's language but by that time my husband's mind was such that he never spoke again.'

It was a contradiction to previous statements that Waslaw had to some extent regained his power of speech, something that never ceased to puzzle me because on no occasion that I met my father did I hear him utter a word. Perhaps during those agonising years prior to his physical death, she played a desperate game of pretence to boost her own morale. But I discreetly kept my thoughts to myself.

Laci was eager to pick her brains and unfolded his idea to build a puppet stage for me so that I could carry on with the career that had been so rudely cut off in Budapest. He had a far more commonsensical approach to life than I and was a shrewd man, who read me like an open book; on no page could he find reference to a predilection on my part for the drudgery of housewifely chores.

Surprisingly, Romola was utterly ignorant about puppetry. To her, puppets were synonymous with dolls or toys. But with her usual fervour to learn something new, she prodded me to tell her all about it. Zealously, I launched into a detailed narration on the intricacies of a puppeteer's work; how the puppet customarily was made of wood or papier-mâché; how it achieved character and a full range of emotional depths simply through skilful manipulations of one's arm. I went on to explain how I hoped to translate into English and French some of the most famous Hungarian puppet stories for children. We would form our own little theatrical company; Laci would provide the musical accompaniment on the piano, Peter would be the stage hand and Kinga a puppeteer. I confessed that my most ambitious aspiration was to acquire Wayang puppets with which to recreate *Spectre de la Rose* for an adult audience. These puppets, approximately 25-28 inches in height, have two rods attached to the hands and can give the illusion of dancers. The technique originated in Asia, but had been modernised by Obrakov, the world-famous Russian puppeteer.

Romola listened engrossed, and after I concluded, she said that she would try to get me and my puppets on the Ed Sullivan Show; that he was a good friend of hers and a powerful and influential personality on American television. She implied that if he did take me on, my career in the States would be made. Like so many indulgences in wishfulfilment, this one faded away with Romola when her stay came to an end.

Our lives subsided to an even tenor after Romola's departure. Weekends, Laci spent scanning through real estate advertisements in the hope of realising his lifelong ambition to have a house of his own. His dogged determination bore fruit, and in 1958 we bought a brand-new, spacious house in a modern development in the suburbs, an hour's drive from the centre of the city. Advantages counterbalanced disadvantages, then the latter began tipping the scales in the wrong direction; the burdensome bank loan, the remoteness from urban life such as cinemas and theatres, the hostile attitude toward 'outsiders' in this predominantly homogeneous French section. Other thorns in our lives manifested themselves. It began to dawn on me how hard it was for Kinga to accept her stepfather – shades of Romola and Oti-Papa – and likewise Peter shied at the idea of me as a replacement for his mother. Adversity had bound us together, security was tearing us apart.

The most ironic twist was to come when Laci found himself

unable to tolerate the bitterly cold winters in Canada. The biting winds and persistent snowfall were too much for his mental and physical well-being. Increasingly, too, he pined for his paramount passion, an organ on which to play.

A triumph for me was the arrival of some puppets from Hungary and the 'Tamara Nijinsky Puppet Theatre' became a reality. Kinga and I were the voices behind each character. Laci accompanied on the piano, and Peter managed the props and stage setting. Our small troupe performed in English and French. Slowly, our fame spread and we were called on to give performances at summer camps, Sunday schools and children's birthday parties.

My own humble contribution toward keeping Tatakaboy's candle of fame burning arrived one day in the form of two Wayang puppets. Months previously, I had sent photographs of Waslaw and Tamara Karsavina to a friend of mine in Budapest. Aided by these, she had sculpted an exact likeness of their faces and dressed the puppets in authentic copies of the costumes, even colourwise. The blood circulated faster in my veins as I envisaged the challenge of recreating *Spectre de la Rose*. My gratitude to my friend was boundless. With these puppets I could advance from children's audiences to adult performances as well.

Over and over again, I cajoled Laci to play von Weber's piano piece, *Invitation to the Dance*. Daily, I studied my treasures while trying to figure out the steps and movements. Unfortunately, I was handicapped in that I had never seen the ballet performed, hence the choreography was a total mystery to me. Laci had the brilliant idea that I should contact Romola and ask her. A terse reply arrived on a postcard. *'Read the biography. I have already written it down once.'*

I read and reread the book but the movements eluded me. My frustration had reached its peak when rescue arrived in the shape of Romola herself. We had come home at 1.30 am after one of our rare concert evenings. It was Siberian winter weather, we were frozen to the marrow, longing to crawl to a warm bed. A note was pinned to my pillow. 'Romola called from a hotel – in Montreal. Call her back whatever time you get home.'

Romola was on her way to Europe on one of her regular trips, but the plane had developed engine trouble and been diverted to Montreal. The passengers were accommodated at a hotel in the centre of the city. Under no circumstances would she come out to us; instead, she gave the order for us to come over to her immediately. To me, it was like a royal command. Laci muttered under his breath. Nevertheless, he accompanied me.

We found Romola sitting in bed, dressed in glamorous silky, lilac-coloured pyjamas, surrounded by Agatha Christie thrillers, the inevitable cigarette dangling from her lips. She was in one of her most ebullient moods, and when I begged her to demonstrate the steps I so frantically required, she complied without demur.

It was almost dawn – an unforgettable moment – when my sixty-nine-year old mother leapt out of bed and gracefully executed the two roles, explaining, as she danced, the technique, the arm positions, the young girl's encounter with the Spirit of the Rose. The only musical accompaniment was Laci softly whistling the waltz. Feverishly, I scribbled down her instructions on two frayed paper napkins I found on a tray.

She retold again how the ballet had been one of my father's greatest triumphs; the first performance had been at Le Théâtre de Monte Carlo in April 1911; how the success had been repeated wherever Waslaw and Karsavina performed.

In late 1957, early 1958, Romola was engaged in correspondence, peppered with her most irritable tone, regarding a death mask of Waslaw by a certain Michel de Bry. Before the burial in London, the latter had entered the funeral parlour under false pretences. According to Romola, he violated the sanctity of the coffin, and it was only through the intervention of Madame Valentine Hugo that she did not take legal action against de Bry. She desperately wished to retrieve the mask and to donate it to the *Musée du Théâtre de l'Opéra de Paris*.

Madame Françoise Reiss, who had written *Nijinsky ou la Grace,* inadvertently stirred the whole matter up again when she wrote to Romola asking if she could help her acquire the mask for an exhibition planned on Nijinsky.

Romola's reply expressed her anger and distress over de Bry's action; that she regrettably would be unable to attend the exhibition, but that, when she returned to Paris in the spring, she would pursue the issue regarding the death mask, should Monsieur de Bry meanwhile not have presented it to the Museum. '...*de ma part, je suis scandalisée par sa conduite...*'. She apologised to Françoise Reiss for having bored her with the proceedings, and hoped that the two of them could meet in May.

In April 1958, I had a long letter from my mother recapitulating in her usual breathless manner her bustling, indefatigable modus vivendi. The 'Nijinsky Productions', making films on ballet for television, for instance, sounded like a full-time occupation.

'...I am the head of the entire production – director, artistic adviser, and main stockholder. As we have 13 films to make at the same time, writing the stories, choosing the actors, choreographers, scenery designers, and selection of music, you can well imagine what this all means – to do the work of a director, writer, producer; I am also responsible to those who give money. They call it a 'package', and I have to watch that profit is made on it.'

In the next paragraph she revealed that she was in the process of writing yet another book. She went on to say she had been appointed as professor of the Arts and History of Dance at the University, a post demanding that she give innumerable lectures. In addition, the City of San Francisco had asked her to establish a 'Museum of Dance' and to become its curator.

I prize this particular letter because in it, for the very first time, she paid me a genuine compliment.

'I am pleased, my Tamara, that you are so gentle and accommodating – an ideal daughter – for a mother. The many praises I heard about you from everyone – they were right. It seems that in Budapest you were under your grandmother's thumb – because there you were not so kind to me.'

She went on to warn me not to let Kinga go from my side, that were she to be raised by somebody else, she would become a stranger to me.

'Learn from my example. I should never have let Kyra and you go away from my side. But living in the same house with a mentally sick person, I could not keep children there. My own life being so uncertain, I was not sure if I could procure you a comfortable and good life; the one I thought you would get from your grandmother. The result was that you were alienated from me, and I can imagine how much untruth they said about me. I tried to forget and to forgive...'

Romola's insatiable wanderlust got her in touch with Tenzing Norgay. Judging from letters, she knew Raymond Lambert well, and contacted him in the matter. She requested him to write on her behalf to the famous Sherpa that he could anticipate her arrival during 1959. Lambert himself was departing for Mexico in January to show Mexican mountaineers some films he had made at the time of his expeditions.

Tenzing Norgay replied to her on April 25th in a very cordial letter. 'I am all the more happy to learn that Raymond Lambert also happens to be a great friend of yours as well as Mr Mallory. This coming autumn I shall accompany my daughters on the Cho-Oya Expedition although it is an all woman expedition and its leader is Mrs Claude Kogan from France. If you have a definite plan to visit Thyanboch this autumn, I can arrange for you to have four reliable Sherpas in advance.' He went on to say that his wife would be happy to receive Romola if she arrived late in Darjeeling. He had just learned that Raymond Lambert had been accorded permission to climb Mount Everest in 1961. Meanwhile, during 1960, an Indian Expedition was planned to Everest but he had not as yet decided if he would participate.

It must have been in the latter part of 1958 that Romola visited Japan for the first time. There, she was to experience an emotional upheaval second only to the one many years previously when as a young girl she attended the Opera in Budapest and beheld her Harlequin, who from that very instant took possession of her heart and soul and became her lifelong obsession.

Since her teens, Romola had been fascinated by the Land of the Rising Sun, and when she studied in Paris, she often visited the Oriental Museum, lingering in front of the priceless treasures of the Far East, overwhelmed by the lustrous silks, the exquisite kakemonos, the intricately carved lacquer and jade objects. In her last notes, which sadly never were published, she claimed that she had had the privilege to meet and make close friends with Fujita, the famous contemporary Japanese artist, who lived and worked in Paris. It was he who taught her to appreciate the classic Japanese masters in painting and who initiated her into the realm of Japanese poetry, specifically the poems by Lady Akashi. When Romola and Waslaw had been Paul Claudel's guests in Rio de Janeiro, the latter had spoken with great enthusiasm and admiration for Japanese dramatic artists and their theatre. He had familiarised her then with the

Nō and Kabuki dramas, and the dramas of Chikamatsu Manzae-mon, Japan's 'Shakespeare'.

It is evident from the material Romola left behind that she was planning to devote an entire chapter to Japan in a forthcoming book. She had drafted pages on the subject; her keen observations and impressions not only of the artistic side, on which she dwelt almost to the point of sheer adulation, but she recorded conversations with Hideyo Noguchi, the world-famous bacteriologist. She had made his acquaintance back in the 1920's, when she was in the States in the vain attempt to get a permit for Waslaw. Noguchi was with the Rockefeller Institute for Medical Research in New York. She had discussed with him at great length the subject of schizophrenia. In her distraught frame of mind in those days, going from clinic to clinic in search of the truth about Waslaw's madness, she pleaded with everyone she met in the field of medical science to give her advice, or supply her with the magic formula that would cure him. According to her, Noguchi held forth his own theory about the malady's origin, suggesting that it had been caused by a virus; that schizophrenia was a physical disease and only the symptoms were mental.

'My husband loved Oriental art and studied it a great deal... It was our wish to visit this country (Japan) but we never had time to do so as it took weeks to get there...He intended to compose a Japanese ballet based on Japanese music. He showed me the dances and it was only in later years when I visited Japan I saw what a marvellous creativity he had...He knew the Japanese art instinctively... Seeing the Kabuki theatre and the great actor and dancer Tokizo, I realised how inspired and authentic Nijinsky's composition of the Japanese ballet was.... Decades passed and still I had not had the opportunity to realise my long cherished dream to visit Japan. Then, suddenly, unexpectedly, out of the blue, my fancy became reality.'

She had returned to San Francisco from Europe after an enjoyable albeit hectic social whirl. Among other events, she had been to a performance by the Bolshoi Ballet in Munich, and had also attended the Bayreuth Festival. The idyllic summer holiday was rudely shattered by an unheralded summons to come back to the

States to deal with an urgent business matter. Once the problem had been settled, she felt destiny had cheated her out of a glorious autumn.

'I was supposed to spend it in a castle near Pau, given to my friends' ancestors by Henri IV...partake in some shooting on the estate of some other friends in the Loire countryside. Having instead some spare time, I had the sudden inspiration to go to Japan. I booked my ticket for Tokyo at once.'

She expatiated with a glowing account of the trip en route and elaborated in detail on the thrill she experienced when the young Japanese steward, a mere boy of nineteen, timidly approached her and asked if she was related to the famous dancer. When she nodded assent, he proceeded to amaze her with his profound knowledge of ballet. Her respect for Japanese education was strengthened even further when he told her he had acquired it in school.

Romola wrote a five-page essay on The Takarazuka Theatre, whose headquarters are in the spa town of the same name, picturesquely nestled in the hills which run from Kyoto to Kōbe.

In 1914, the Takarazuka's founder, Ichizo Kobayashi, a man of great vision, realised that the formal classical Japanese drama drew little response from the younger generations and the Western visitors. He boldly set about blending the traditional plays and operas with Western musicals. The performances open wide a window to the complexities of Japanese life and culture. Romola wrote:

'Millions of theatre-loving people visit this art centre which takes the place of the Salzburg, Bayreuth and Edinburgh festivals in Europe... The Takarazuka Hot Spring House has three theatres, many restaurants, a children's playground, botanical garden, zoo and a sports stadium... The village is studded with Japanese inns and restaurants, and is easily accessible by plane or train. The productions are lavish and well staged. The costumes and scenery, superb. Excellent directors and scenic designers are employed. The stage is a revolving one, and the actors can approach it from three sides. The entertainment includes the classic Kabuki plays, as well as modern light opera in Western style. Their shows sometimes border on what we in the West would call variety shows but done with great taste and in a lavish, colourful way. The company and the school are almost run like a convent, and the girls are not allowed to marry nor are they allowed to be seen with or associated with men. Their whole lives revolve around the theatre, and they usually work some sixteen hours a day. Although they have no holidays they seem to be satisfied with their lot and very happy. Twice to three times a year they perform in Tokyo. About one hundred girls are members of the company, which is divided into four groups: the "Star" group, the "Flower" group, the "Snow" group and the fourth group, which rehearses for the new show. They are a sheer enchantment to watch and everybody who goes to Japan should visit this unique theatre.

The greatest and most beautiful star of the company is the young Teruko Akashi, who portrays the male parts. She is very gifted, an excellent dramatic actress of great depth and strength, who is equally good in comic parts. She has a deep, velvety mezzo soprano voice which she uses with fantastic skill. She is an excellent dancer. Her interpretations of Japanese Kabuki roles are as wonderful as her enchanting acting in the part of a young European boy... The whole of Japan worships her and all the women and young girls who come to the theatre are bewitched by her as she creates the illusion of an irresistible young man...'

Who was instrumental in introducing Romola to the young actress? She was utterly uncommunicative about her innermost, personal relationships with other people. Paul was always at her side, I never questioned his presence; he had become a permanent fixture, so to speak. An essential part of her, forever at her beck and call. It was with a sense of shock that I read of her devotion to a young actress, an affection of a magnitude that she had never bestowed upon her two daughters. Malicious rumours have been rife as to how she and Teruko actually met, but I have no proof as to their authenticity nor do I wish to pursue the matter.

I try to visualise the first time that Romola set eyes on Teruko. Did perchance history repeat itself when Romola saw a slender figure on the stage, a bewitching personality with warm, slanted

Oriental eyes? Did she relive that moment decades ago when a Harlequin pranced upon the stage of the Opera in Budapest?

She sent me a letter from the Imperial Hotel dated the 1st of October, 1959. There was not a hint in this letter of what had transpired. She began by admonishing me for behaving like Kyra who never heeded her advice. For some time, I had felt a physical discomfort and she urged me to go to the University Clinic for a thorough checkup. She carried on in her rambling fashion about how Princess Chichibu, a sister-in-law of the Emperor, had given her a royal welcome and invited her to the première of the Moiseyew Ballet; how flowers and gifts had been bestowed upon her; how she could barely cope with the flow of invitations, not only from the Japanese but also from the Europeans and the Americans.

Never allowing business opportunities to elude her, she was simultaneously engaged in discussions about the publication of her book in Japanese, and various film projects.

> 'After a wonderful week, I flew to Takarazuka which is about 500 miles from Tokyo... A combination of Bayreuth, Salzburg, Vichy and Wiesbaden. It has a theatre which can seat 3,000 people. It is packed every day. ...It is close to Kōbe, Japan's largest seaport, and only 30 minutes from Osaka, the greatest industrial city. It is half an hour from Kyoto, the Florence of Japan. Narat is to be compared with Siena. All of the villages and cities are ancient, filled with objects of art in their temples. You can imagine how I enjoy my stay here... The entire village is helping me learn Japanese although I do take private lessons as well...'

A fairly concentrated travelogue, not a whisper about the intoxicated frame of mind in which she must have found herself then. A letter she wrote to Teruko from San Francisco some months later illustrates clearly the almost unbelievable attachment she had developed for the much younger woman. My mother often kept copies, and indeed, drafts of her correspondence, even of the most intimate nature, altered in her handwriting.

> 'The sun is always shining in California, but this morning when your letter and your lovely gift of records arrived, it was shining even brighter. I thank you gratefully; you do not know how much it means to me that you wrote.

You must forgive me for having intruded upon your life so unexpectedly; it had to be. When I meet you again, I will explain everything. I am a stranger to you, Teruko, but you are not a stranger to me; the first moment I saw you in Takarazuka, I felt I had known you forever. I am very thankful to you that you are so understanding. It gives me great joy to hear you sing on the records, I feel you are near to me. Also it made me infinitely happy to talk to you on the 'phone. If you don't mind, I will call you every month; the next time the 3rd of May. In this way, we can keep contact with each other.

I was anxious to know if you were coming over with the company, as I have to go to Europe for two months in June. But had you come to America, I would have stayed here at home to receive you. If you cannot come now during the summer, I will arrange for you to come as my guest whenever you have the time, and also I will take you to Europe. I want to show you Italy, France, Switzerland and the other interesting countries. I will arrange for you to appear on the stage, television or films, whatever you wish... I want you to be happy and a great success not only in your glorious native country, but all over the world. I know that I can help you in this as I have powerful and influential friends everywhere...I realise you are very busy and unable to write often. I myself am tremendously occupied with my artistic work and social obligations, otherwise I would have returned long ago to Takarazuka. If you do not come here this summer, then I will be in Tokyo in September and will see you there. I will be staying at the Imperial Hotel. I am so glad you are learning English; it will be of great use to you...I am studying Japanese to be able to talk to you without interpreters. As I speak six languages, I hope I will learn Japanese quickly too... My home is yours. If you honour me with your friendship, I will tell you all when we meet.

A dear friend of mine, a Mr Hans Popper, is flying to Tokyo next Saturday... I have asked him to take with him a ring for you, please accept it. Not knowing the exact size of your finger, it was impossible to fit it here, but I am sure it can be fixed for you. I hope it will please you...I want you to know that in me you have a loyal devoted friend, who would do anything for you.

Dear Teruko, take care of yourself, do not work too hard...'

404

Was it with the eagerness of a young girl longing to hear her beloved's voice that Romola telephoned faithfully on the third of May, because she wrote a letter the same day from Mexico where she was then staying:

'I want to thank you for so kindly answering my telephone call. It was a joy to talk to you. I can still hear your lovely voice and laughter ringing in my ears while I tried to speak to you in Japanese... Until I return to Japan next September I must be patient; then I will be able to converse with you...I fear that both my teacher and Simako feel that I am too bold and too European when I tell you that you are lovely, charming, that I miss you and long to see you...In the beginning of June I will telephone you again, otherwise I would feel you are only a beautiful dream and not reality.'

Her almost instantaneous infatuation for the young actress was perhaps the only light relief she was to experience in the 1950's. Without exaggeration, problems poured over her like hot volcanic lava. She had become increasingly concerned about Tessa's health. My aunt suffered from arteriosclerosis, which had reached the stage where she was incapable of recognising anybody, and was unable to look after herself. Romola's financial situation was so strained, she found it impossible to offer sufficient assistance. Poor Tessica had to be placed in the Psychiatric Clinic at Gest, bundled together there with some forty-odd other inmates. Gone was the feckless, radiant beauty, the giddy, happy-go-lucky flirt of yesteryears, all that remained was an empty shell.

That period in Romola's life was cursed by a series of bitter disappointments, and whenever she came to visit us, she brought with her an aura of tension from frayed nerves and the acrimony she felt toward a number of people. She had become involved in yet another lawsuit and it was one that she lost in 1959. At the height of Waslaw's fame, John Singer Sargent had made a charcoal drawing of him as Armida's Favourite Slave in *Le Pavillon d'Armide*. According to Romola, it had been commissioned and paid for in 1912 by the Marchioness of Ripon. Again, in Romola's version, Lady Ripon had stipulated in her will that Waslaw should inherit it, but although she died in 1917, it was not until 1923 that the portrait was received by Romola and Waslaw, possibly owing to all the red tape in the aftermath of the war. It hung at first above the fireplace in our flat in Avenue de la Bourdonnais. Later, when our little family had been separated, and prior to Romola's departure to the States, the household moved to 10 rue Conseiller Collignon. While Romola pursued her quest to seek asylum for Waslaw in America combined with working in Hollywood to make as much money as possible, Tessa was left in charge in Paris. At some stage up to 1929 the flat was allegedly broken into and many valuables were stolen, including the Sargent portrait. The news came as a severe blow to Romola, particularly the loss of the drawing. She swore that if it were ever recovered, she would donate it to the Louvre.

It was purely by a freak coincidence that Paul discovered the portrait in 1958 in the elegant Bohemian Club in San Francisco, where an exhibition of Sargent portraits was held. The club claimed it had been bequeathed to them by the late Senator Phelan, who had lived in Paris and been a staunch supporter of ballet. Romola carried on at great length about it and evidently she had been to a séance because she said: 'I know that Tatakaboy organised all this. Is it not strange that of all places, the drawing reappeared in San Francisco. I believe more and more that there is a heavenly Providence, where after our death we continue to live...'

She started proceedings against The Bohemian Club but lost. She was extremely bitter about the outcome, and claimed it was unjust. Never prone to give up a fight, however, she sought advice from a Paris solicitor as late as 1965, but she must inevitably have been hampered by the fact that she did not have enough facts to back her case – no exact date of when the theft actually occurred, no witnesses to verify when last the drawing had been seen in the flat, and so on. Her efforts to regain possession of the famous portrait were doomed to failure, and I only wish I could carry on the battle for her. Incidentally, in Richard Buckle's book, it is said that Lady Juliet Duff presented the drawing to Romola.

One battle she did win was when her solicitors received a letter from Igor Stravinsky dated August 22nd, 1959, to the effect that he would delete a paragraph from his autobiography to which she had taken grave exception. In the letter, he also agreed to eliminate reference to a Nijinsky letter that purportedly revealed the discontinuity of Waslaw's thoughts. The offending lines in Stravinsky's typescript were damning to the Nijinsky name, asserting that everybody knew that Waslaw would lapse into insanity, that his brother had been insane, an uncle blind, a cousin deaf, and in a final virulent attack, Stravinsky claimed that Diaghilev had said that the Nijinsky family was syphilitic. What could have prompted Stravinsky to make such a grotesque allegation without a shred of tangible proof remains inexplicable to me. To this very day, medical science is debating the issue as to what caused my father's mental illness. That a mere layman should pronounce such a harsh judgment, albeit to some extent through hearsay, was more than Romola could tolerate. It was humiliating and degrading to the memory of the man she worshipped. With red-hot obstinacy she pursued the matter until she had forced Stravinsky to retract his statement.

Throughout 1959 Romola continued with unflagging spirits to seek film or stage adapters interested in her book. A massive dossier of correspondence bears witness to her struggle. An actor for whom she had great esteem was John Gielgud, and she wrote to him for advice. She received an extremely courteous reply in which he cautioned her of the many pitfalls she would undoubtedly encounter in her endeavour. I read with interest the PS at the end of his letter in which he suggested some names he considered suited to play the two main characters: Yul Brynner as Waslaw, Charles Laughton or Orson Welles to portray Diaghilev.

Two staunch friends of Romola's, Campbell and Greta McGregor, took steps that year to give her financial support. McGregor was a diplomat. From what I have gathered, they lived globally, but did have a permanent residence in Switzerland, Villa Greta in Chambésy, Geneva. In late August, McGregor and Romola entered into an agreement by which the former should guarantee to shoulder all the fees and expenses she would be encumbered with in her attempt to terminate, modify, or cancel the film rights she had given to Vidor and subsequently to his heirs. In return, she was to hand over to McGregor all rights, titles, interest and estate pertaining to her two publications, *Nijinsky* and *The Last Years of Nijinsky*. By 1959, Romola had already obtained $7,500 under this contract. It appears that the contract was updated to January 17, 1962 by which time McGregor had advanced a total of $11,089.32. Curiously enough, this contract was not signed by my mother.

In August, Greta and Campbell placed the whole matter of the film rights in the hands of a Californian lawyer, Angelo Scampini, at which point McGregor sent a handwritten letter to Romola – with a copy to Scampini – intended to enlighten the lawyer regarding the background to the Nijinsky film saga.

Briefly, the letter declared that Romola had been toying with the idea of producing the film in Russia in close co-operation with the Bolshoi Ballet already while Charles Vidor was still alive. Together with the McGregors, my mother had undertaken a trip to Munich when the Ballet Company were there on tour. They had been extremely impressed by Romola's vision of a Russian-made film and she reported back to Vidor what had transpired.

McGregor went on to say that he, too, felt that the Bolshoi were the only suitable ballet group to be involved in the film. He was also of the opinion that the Russian Minister for Culture would be only too glad to give full support.

In ensuing letters, McGregor suggested that Romola should go to Hollywood to talk to Mrs Charles Vidor about a Russian-made film and that she should strike a bargain with her for a fair percentage of the gross sales and a down payment on completion of the picture by the Russians, say $50,000 to $100,000; impregnate in her mind that she would be offered the picture at no cost to her. In Hollywood, it would cost in the region of $3 million. If she demurred about the terms, then Romola should tell her to go to Billy Wilder and make a 'one run' film. Having evidently given much thought to the structure of the picture by now, McGregor warned Romola against making a 'ballet only' film. He quoted *Red Shoes* as an example, with no story to tell. Billy Wilder himself had said that 'the Nijinsky story is the saddest in all theatrical history'. The big money in the film industry came from films with stories that gripped the hearts of the general public and had long runs as revivals year after year. Romola's film should have strong dramatic appeal, just like the book it was based on; 'the vicissitudes of the tent show circus travelling through the villages of that era in Russia. After the death of Vaslav's father, the struggles of the widow bringing up little Vaslav in their flat in St Petersburg...his meeting with the Czar and appointment as student in the Imperial Ballet School... then the school's graduation class doing their dances before the Russian Court in the very palace where it had taken place...Diaghilev should be played up as the strange, fascinating, sinister character he was...'. These were merely some of the suggestions from McGregor. He stressed that Romola should consult the Russians as they had the true artistic touch. He expressed the sentiment that the Russians would immediately turn thumbs down on the project if they were approached by anyone other than Romola. It would be 'just another commercial deal'. If, on the other hand, she went to them for the sake of Art and Culture, and to perpetuate the name of their most famous dancer, they would not refuse. McGregor was certain he could put pressure on them to finance the cost of production. He enjoyed a very cordial relationship with Russia. Gromyko had often stayed at Villa Greta, and on the strength of this alliance, he was sure of success. In several of his letters, he re-iterated his willingness to go to Moscow with Romola to the Minister for Culture. In his dealings with the Russians, they had always kept their word to him and he had been deeply impressed by their friendly attitude.

In mid-1960, McGregor learned that Romola intended to go to Hollywood to see Mrs Vidor, and he stood by his promise to reimburse her for all expenses in connection with the trip. Romola wrote a month later telling him of the outcome of her visit. Delighted with the favourable results, he wrote: 'You could not have expected better results if you had dictated your own wishes to Mrs Vidor.' His wife Greta added: 'We hope you are happy now. Mother Becker and the Spirit Friends always wanted you to see Mrs Vidor and work on the project, not go to Europe for nothing. Now you have a goal...'.

Romola's film plans must have leaked to the media because on October 24th, 1960, Marie Rambert wrote to her:

'We get in touch about every twenty-five years it seems, though the last time I saw you must have been eight or ten years ago. I saw in the paper that you are going to do a film of Vaslav. I think it such a marvellous idea to do it in Russia as there you are more likely to find at least an approximate type for him, and also the production would have a great deal more authentic style than would be likely in the West. ...I wanted to congratulate you on this brilliant idea, but at the same time I was wondering whether you might find it useful to see a little film of "L'Après Midi d'un Faune", which I had made by an amateur friend in 1930. It was only a short while after Diaghilev's death, and Weizikowski had been doing it during the last seasons so that at that time he remembered it perfectly and produced it with the real style. As nothing seems to exist of Vaslav's choreography, perhaps it might be helpful just to have a look at that

film when you are passing through London. My best wishes in this great undertaking...'

Throughout those years, Romola kept us in the dark regarding the McGregors' funding. Instead, she attributed her cash flow to her 'business partner'.

'I learned in life not to keep worrying about how the telephone bill will be paid, but try to avoid getting into debts. I have charge accounts because sometimes they are unavoidable. Believe me, the Little Infant Jesus of Prague always pays my bills. This has been going on for nigh on fifty years. He has never let me down. I highly recommend him to you.'

Although this rather naïve philosophy might be labelled self-deception, taking into account her countless debts and cliff-hanging financial crises, yet was there not perhaps a measure of truth in what she wrote, because she always managed to float to the surface in grand style. And I am certain she helped keep many airlines in business with her incessant travel to and from nearly every capital of the world.

She must have been elated at the thought she might soon reach the end of her rainbow – the triumph she had striven for – to have her beloved Watza immortalised on the screen. It would be an added tribute to him, too, the young man who decades earlier had been so impressed by the newfangled entertainment industry on his first ever visit to the United States, and who then envisaged the greatness of the movies in the future.

But along with all her involvement in the world of film-making and her many other projects, she apparently yielded to a deeper and deeper attraction for Teruko Akashi, which the few drafts of letters clearly signify. At the top of some letters, she had scribbled in her own handwriting the day they were sent off. 'Terry', as she nick-named the young actress, wrote a few cool, taciturn letters in reply, excusing their brevity by the fact 'it is only to be regretted that I cannot write to you because of my ignorance of your language, with my desire. I'll study your tongue. I look forward eagerly to your visit to Japan. I wish you a healthy life.'

Romola, on the other hand, poured her heart out in flowery prose, unable to disguise her ardour.

'Soubarashii Terry, I was so deeply touched (to hear your voice) that I could not talk to you, I could only cry...I am ashamed that I behave like a young girl who has lost her head. I tell myself continuously what a fool I am but I just cannot help it. The present situation is beyond endurance for me but I would be a very poor and bad friend if I would think only about myself and what would give me happiness. I have to think of you... Terry, I have the feeling you are worried about your future? Am I right?'

Romola went on with a prolonged discourse about Terry's career, what would happen after a few years' stardom, a detailed analysis of the pros and cons of working for the Takarazuka Theatre; probing into every aspect of the young woman's life. *'Tell me frankly everything'.*

Romola reminded Terry how she had once told her that if circumstances ever permitted, she would be willing to go abroad, willing to give up her career with the Takarazuka Theatre. But Romola did warn her to think this over very carefully.

'You do not know the world, you have never been outside of Japan, you cannot know now if you would like life in America and Europe... That was the reason why last winter I was so anxious to spend some time with you in Tokyo and in Europe...to see your reaction to the different way of living to which you are used...I wanted you to have this experience before giving up Takarazuka...Unfortunately, Umeda San made the realisation of this project impossible, and I am convinced that in the future he will also refuse any leave of absence for you...

I want to help you, Terry, unselfishly...The other side of the problem is my problem. You are young and beautiful; you are just beginning life; I am finishing it...If I could do what I wish, I would fly over to Japan immediately and say to you, "Terry, close your house (or leave it in care of your maid), resign the Takarazuka Theatre and come with me abroad. I will take care of you." It would give me the greatest happiness...

You could have a Japanese maid with you who speaks English and with this, the language barrier will be eliminated...If you get bored and want to, I can always arrange for

411

you to go on American TV or films in London; Paris, on the stage...they would adore you...but you might only get restless for your career...now you are in the limelight before your public; you might miss it...

Another reason why I cannot ask you to come with me is because you do not have the same feelings towards me as I have for you...

You, only you, must decide about your life and future. I await patiently for your decision; you can take weeks, even a few months to decide. You have to think it over. Only, please, do not discuss the matter with any member of the Takarazuka Theatre – they would only intrigue... I am so unhappy, Terry, without you.'

Only thirteen days later, Romola wrote:

'If God ever grants me the happiness to see you again, I will just lie down on the sofa in your drawing-room and cry...You ask me how I am. I am feeling better but am losing weight steadily. My doctor scolded me, saying that unless I am happy, he will not take the responsibility for my health and life. He finds that since I came back from Japan my health has deteriorated and I have not the resistance I used to have. He explained to me that continuous mental worry and unhappiness causes physical illness. He told me that he could relieve my pain by giving drugs and sleeping pills – but what I need as a cure is happiness – and this only you can give...

The little insignificant souvenirs I am sending you are only to show you that you are constantly in my thoughts. I would love to spoil you, to give you beautiful things but (because of the Customs) I can merely send you these when a trustworthy friend goes over to Japan. A mutual friend of Colonel N van Meter's, Mr L..., is flying over to Tokyo the 29th of April. He will bring you a golden bracelet and will mail it to you from Tokyo. I hope you will like it.

I wrote to Kikouchi San, the jeweller at the Takarazuka Hotel. ...He mentioned to me that you had looked at the pearl necklaces and you liked them. I told him to go and see you, to take some pearls to you. Please choose the size, the colour, you like. I told Kikouchi San to make up a lovely necklace for you as a present from me. Terry, I would like to bring down the stars from Heaven for you...In the article which appeared recently the reporter mentioned "adoption" of you by me. The idea is not bad at all.'

Romola continued, explaining that she did not believe the law would permit adoption because of the age difference. She went on to say, however, she had taken legal steps to ensure that Terry would have lifelong security; that her (Romola's) bankers and lawyers were working on it.

'As soon as all formalities will be completed, Kyo Minoura, the husband of Yoko San, will go and see you and explain all to you. You will have to sign certain documents...'

Whether this liberal gesture by Romola ever came to pass, I do not know. Certainly, I never came across evidence of it. Taking into account my mother's chronically 'unhealthy' bank accounts, I cannot understand what motivated her to give such a promise, when she was perpetually short of funds. How blind is love! Her behaviour was excitably beyond self-control, perhaps not only induced by her feelings for the young actress but also for Japanese culture itself. In a letter of February 5th, 1960, Princess Chichibu thanked Romola graciously for the three Sterling Silver rose plants my mother had sent her. The Princess wrote *'The roses have reached here in perfect condition and have at once been planted in my garden. I now look forward with great pleasure to seeing their lovely rare flowers...'*

The letter of the 25th April, 1960, laid bare the nature of Romola's feelings for Terry in no uncertain terms.

'I do not wish to repeat myself all the time; by now you know well how I feel towards you... The reporter of that article must either be very naïve or very shrewd by making up the "Mother-daughter" story... I suppose he invented this for the sake of the public. Very wise. Of course, all forms of love contain a certain amount of maternal instinct. But my affection for you, as you know, is very different. You are a grown-up woman, Terry, you understand me. My love is the love of a sister for a sister, a love of a friend for a friend, a companion for a companion, a

413

mate for a mate. I love you passionately with my whole being, with every particle of my body and soul. YOU are part of me, therefore to be separated from you is torture.

At night, when I cannot sleep, I see you before me as Roberto, standing on the bridge, and later, in the second act, I see you drinking and laughing. You created so perfectly the illusion of a carefree, gay, flirting Italian boy, that you became one, and with this image you have captivated me. I can never forget you as Saemon in "Ashikari"...when standing at the door (in the second act) you talk to her (Mayumi) and won't let her in in spite of loving her...There and then, you revealed a part of your soul to me, and your capacity to love. Moiseyew, the great Russian director and choreographer, who attended the performance with me, said "Romola, you are right, Miss Akashi has a great talent." Terry, I know so much about artists, about artistic creations. An artist is only able to portray what is a part of him, what he is in reality. You are ROBERTO, SAEMON, VITTORIO, and all the other characters you act...and when you are those, then, Terry, you are irresistible. You are my Akachan-No, but you are also the devil, who bewitched me. Therefore we have to take the consequences. It is now I, who say, "Terry, give me happiness."

You asked me in your last letter what I am doing? I have to write two books which I must deliver to my publishers before December 1960. I have to supervise and produce 13 ballet films for television for the United Nations, which will be broadcast all over the world. I have to supervise and partly direct the NIJINSKY film (the life story of my husband and me) which will be made jointly by the RUSSIAN GOVERNMENT and HOLLYWOOD... To be able to carry out this very heavy programme, I need perfect health and strength...It depends on you if I shall have it...I hate Umeda San, and I am desperately jealous of Kiko-San, don't make too much love to her...it kills me.'

One long letter, partly typed out and then altered with her familiar scribbling all over the pages, is undated. In it, Romola apologises profusely for the invasion (apparently of Terry's dressing-room after a performance) by her friends, Colonel van Meter and Yoko Minoura San. She had asked Yoko San to see Terry alone. Colonel van Meter was merely to have telephoned. However, he had not only attended a performance but afterwards he had introduced himself to the actress. Evidently he had written to Romola that he had fallen in love with her.

> *'I understand him... he is a very good, old friend of mine, trustworthy. Please do not think that I am broadcasting my affection for you all over. I hold this sacred. Only my friends know me so well that they know that I never took such a deep interest in anybody, and they see that since November 1958 I am a completely changed woman. I hope you understand and forgive. I am a discreet person.'*

Romola goes on to ask Terry to send her best gramophone recordings to some friends.

My mother had an almost paranoic fear of illnesses of any kind. She believed in 'preventive' medicine and went at least twice a year to have a complete check-up. There is hardly a letter to me in which the issue of health is omitted. And she kept admonishing Terry to fulfil her wish and go to the University Clinic in Osaka, where all the necessary facilities would be available. Romola pleaded with her not to stave off the visit; she herself had been saved from death some two years previously by going for a check-up, when she was suffering from a kidney ailment.

> *'...Even if you think this is unnecessary nonsense, do it, please. I will be greatly relieved to know from the doctor's report that you are well. Please let me know how much the examination will cost. I will send you a cheque at once for it, payable to the Osaka Bank. My bank there is the Tokyo Bank.'*

In May, Romola wrote to say she had received a long letter from Yoko San, giving an account of a talk the latter had had with Terry about her friendship with Romola. Terry had confided she would be happy to be a friend but that she wished to know Romola better, as her intrusion into her life had come suddenly and unexpectedly. Indeed, Terry had confided she had become frightened of Romola the previous autumn upon learning the latter had come to Japan solely to see her.

> *'You see, my dear Terry, my instinct last Autumn was correct when I felt that you had changed and were avoiding me... You*

*were afraid of me, but why? I would never harm you, and I
always respect your wishes. Because I am a foreigner? I am of
another race than you are, but although I am a European,
although my skin is white, my eyes are blue, I have the same
feelings, the same joys and sufferings as any Japanese woman
might have. I have written this last year many long letters to
you, so that you should understand me better through them.*

*Yoko San told me that you did not wish our friendship to be
kept a secret, that you want to have the blessing of your fellow
artists... I would be delighted if this could be done, but I am
afraid that they will be jealous of our friendship.'*

Again and again she weaves into her letters the same theme:

*'My dream was to be happy with you, to make your life
carefree. I hoped I could teach you about art, life...to introduce
you to the world-famous artists, to international society, to
make of you (if you so wish) a world-famous star...to spoil and
cherish you. This was my dream...'*

One tiny fragment of that dream manifestly came true. Press cuttings dated the 24th November, 1960, bore the headline 'Takarazuka Actress Leaving for Paris'. Briefly, the article announced the
impending departure from Tokyo for Paris of the actress Teruko
Akashi of the Takarazuka Opera Troupe. She was expected to stay
one month as the guest of Mrs Romola Nijinsky, widow of Vaslav
Nijinsky. Teruko, whose real name was Takako Murakami, had
been given one month's leave of absence from the troupe so that she
could accept the invitation. I have been unable to find any trace of
correspondence relating to Teruko after the Parisian encounter if,
indeed, it actually took place. This intermezzo in Romola's life
appeared to have evaporated into thin air. There is only one line to
Paul in late 1975 mentioning her name: *'I am very sorry for Terry. It
is terrible.'* Perhaps Romola had heard that she was gravely ill. Who
knows? Subsequently, I have learned that the beautiful and gifted
actress retired from the Takarazuka Theatre in 1963 as the troupe's
superstar; that she married and gave birth to a daughter. She died
on December 31st, 1975, only fifty-seven years old.

It was with a melancholy sigh, I put the last of those letters to one
side. As more and more shadows from my mother's past unfolded

themselves to me, I wondered how many revelations were yet to come.

Romola's letters to me were of a distinctly different calibre and dwelt mostly on family matters. Her mood fluctuated from being an encouraging parent with sage advice on how to bring up our children to an angered, hurt, frustrated woman in the throes of legal harassment, money shortage, bickering with relatives, incessant globe-trotting. The postbox was often flooded with communiqués, not only to me but to Laci, Kinga and Peter as well.

She had become immensely fond of her granddaughter. '*...I am very happy with her. She is a bright, intelligent girl, well-behaved...*'. She was eager to impress Kinga with her own skills and never failed to remind her of the numerous languages she, Romola, had mastered: her native Hungarian, French, German, English, Russian, Japanese and Spanish, adding a smattering of Italian, Greek and Latin for good measure.

Overnight, or so it seemed to me, Kinga and Peter graduated from grade school and were enrolled in a Catholic High School. I still kept myself busy planning, organising and rehearsing the puppet plays. By now, we were qualified to call ourselves semi-professionals and my engagement sheet was filled up. The harmony was not destined to last for long. We were yet again to find ourselves on the threshold of another phase in our lives. Laci's services at the hotel where he had been playing were terminated. A new manager, a new broom! He entered into a critical phase. Ever since he had arrived in Canada, Laci had fought hard and valiantly to reconcile himself to his debasing work. But the crippling chill of the winters had penetrated too deep for any thaw to snap him out of his melancholia. Frankly, we were all dreading another season of sub-zero weather, of having to shovel snow from the garage entrance and repeating the same process to park.

In the autumn of 1960, Laci reached breaking-point and prevailed upon me to contact distant relatives as well as Hungarian friends living in the States. I could not bring myself to write to Romola about this issue. However much closer our relationship had grown, I was still dogged by discomforting memories of past confrontations when seeking her aid.

To my surprise, Romola learned of our plans from Ilus, a cousin who had escaped from Hungary with her family before us. September 11th, 1960, she wrote: '*Ilus told me about your plans. It would*

417

make me very happy because I miss you.' She went on to say that Ilus would be forwarding the necessary information and added that she herself would do everything in her power to help us. *'If I was successful to "bepanamazni" Kyra into this country, then I can bring you in too. Just trust me. I will figure something out. All I ask is a little patience until March, which is when I go to Washington.'*

It was a most conciliatory letter. Not only did she go out of her way to promise to help us but she praised both Kinga and myself in glowing terms. I had a 'heart of gold' and was 'so encouraging' to her in her fits of depression. Alas, it was now Kyra's turn to suffer from her erratic evaluation of her kith and kin; Kyra, her first-born and favourite.

Kyra had been to visit our mother who was aghast at her voluminous size. Romola blamed it entirely on Kyra eating far too much ice cream and chocolate cake, possibly due to frustration. My sister had been extremely upset over certain allegations Igor had written.

'She is completely in the hands of the Church, which to a certain extent is a good thing. She is a strange mixture of intelligence, talent and stupidity. She does not know how to live well. Here, I could have married her off to someone fantastic. She is still very beautiful and could have had a life free from worries, have an honest, rich husband. Instead, she plays the role of a Catholic martyr – "sitting on a cloud". I could explode.'

Querulously, she ranted on about how she had given my sister some money out of Tatakaboy's estate; had promised to send her back to Rome if she so desired; offered to find her a position as an official hostess at the airport at a salary of $500; set up a dance school for her, ending her 'diatribe' with *'I do not have time to quarrel with her.'*

Romola had telephoned the clinic in Genf to enquire about Tessica. They reported that physically my aunt was better but mentally she needed all the care and supervision she could get. My mother had intended to fly over to see me to discuss family affairs but had instead been forced to go to Hollywood regarding the rights to *the* film. *'Vidor's widow is willing to return (the rights) to me for as "little" as $1,000,000 – therefore I must now rush off to London and Moscow to raise the money because an English consortium and the Russian Government want to buy the rights. I will get back the rights*

from Mrs Vidor and go half and half with whoever does the film. On
September 20th I am flying to London, Paris, Genf, then back to
Paris, on to Moscow and Leningrad, Tiflis, New Delhi etc., etc. Per-
haps to Tokyo – we shall see.'

On the whole, it was a gossipy letter about this and that. Dagmar
Schmedes had written to Romola from Tokyo, and confessed she
was quite frightened because she did not understand one syllable of
Japanese. She was there on a three-year contract with the Imperial
Music Academy, which Romola had negotiated for her. Romola
promised that the next time she went to Japan she would send me
books and pictures relating to *Bunraku,* the Japanese Puppet
Theatre, which she claimed was the greatest in its genre in the
world. She even hinted that she might take me with her the following year so that I could learn the art, and become the first to produce
it in the States. She reiterated an earlier promise to give me all possible assistance in promoting my Puppet Theatre: *'We can do a lot, if*
you are beside me.'

Although she could foresee a rosy future for me in the States, her
prognostications concerning Laci's chances were pessimistic and
cheerless. She would do her best to sound out what opportunities
there might be for a man of his talent, *'although here there are as*
many musicians as there are stars in the sky.' She never frequented
night-clubs but Ilus had suggested trying various orchestras and
hotels. She ended her letter by saying that she was going to have a
Mass said for Emilia's birthday.

It was in late 1960, that Romola made one of her most memorable
trips, her first visit to the Soviet Union. It was natural that she
should wish to see the country her Waslaw had spoken of so
wistfully and tenderly, his beloved Russia. She had a dual purpose
for going, to take his place on that journey home he had dreamed
of, and to further the plans for a Russian-made film of the book.

When she applied for a visa, her friends said she was mad and
painted gloomy pictures of what might befall her. Contemptuously,
she shrugged off their warnings, and it was with a feeling of elation
and triumph she boarded the Aeroflot Jet at Le Bourget Airport in
Paris, passport in hand. Random notes about the flight revealed the
thrill she experienced, cosmopolitan traveller though she was.
Never did she give the impression of being bored or blasé. She had
devoted the flying time to a guessing game as to what nationalities
and occupations her fellow passengers might hold. In lyrical terms

419

she described every moment; the morning was sunny, the plane flew swiftly and smoothly like a swallow, the light repast that was served was excellent. The young woman seated next to her worked for one of the embassies in Moscow but was of Russian descent. She was a balletomane, had studied dancing in Paris, and was very knowledgeable on the subject of the Russian ballet. At around eleven a.m. visibility had become poor and the captain announced that because of the prevailing weather conditions in Moscow, the plane was heading for Leningrad. Most of the passengers expressed their displeasure over the change in destination, not so my mother, who wrote 'I told my little companion, Mademoiselle S., that I knew the real reason why we were landing at Leningrad..."It is my husband's wish that I should first step on Russian soil in his own city, St Petersburg, ..."'

To her it had been an unforgettable sight when the grey, misty clouds dispersed, revealing below the winding Neva River, the myriad of tiny canals, the impressive pink-and-grey coloured palaces. Emotionally, she experienced a togetherness with Waslaw, a reunion.

At the airport she was met by a tall young woman who introduced herself as Natasha. She was to be her watchdog, chaperone and interpreter for the duration of her stay in the country. They immediately proceeded to Moscow. Her hotel room was vast, with high ceilings, decorated in Baroque style. The parquet floor was covered with rich-looking rugs.

The very next day, she had a meeting with the Minister for Culture, which had been arranged beforehand. The purpose was to discuss the matter of the film, which they agreed would be a co-production with English speaking actors and, naturally, dancers from the Bolshoi-Kirov Ballets. The filming would be made on original locations, and Romola was escorted to the different ballet schools to find a dancer to take the part of Waslaw. When the interview was coming to a close, Romola turned on her most beguiling charm, and asked the Minister for one favour. She made it clear that the request she was about to utter was not for herself but on behalf of her late husband. Gallantly, he assured Romola that her wish was his command. However, when she blurted out that she wished to have an audience with Nikita Khrushchev, his poise deserted him, and he looked staggered. Covering his consternation at such an outlandish idea, he politely enquired how long she planned to stay in

Moscow. Two to three weeks was her reply. The Minister made no further comments.

She recorded that she enjoyed the ensuing days immensely. People everywhere treated her most cordially. She attended various concerts and theatre performances, and also visited ballet schools throughout the country. She praised the schools, they were marvellous in her opinion, run exactly like in the days of the Tsar although now subsidised by the State. Children who were accepted stayed from eight to ten years and were rigorously trained. Unlike American dancers, they did not have to work at other jobs; they were wholly absorbed in the art of dance for art's sake. She had been very moved by an incident that occurred in a school in Leningrad. Invited to stay for lunch, she was led into the vast canteen. At each table, a number of pupils sat together with a teacher. But at her table she sat alone with one of the teachers. At first, she had taken umbrage, feeling she was being isolated from the children. Then someone told her that she had been given the place which had been Waslaw Nijinsky's for the nine years he attended the school. Their display of sentimentality won her heart. She felt particularly rewarded because it showed that Waslaw's creative genius was still alive in people's memories, and that the students knew what he had contributed to the world of ballet.

The time passed all too quickly. Convinced by then that her wish would not come true, she made reservations to fly back to the States. On the morning before her departure, the unexpected happened. An invitation arrived by special messenger to the effect that Tovarich Khrushchev would be honoured to see Madame Nijinsky at noon the following day. Imbued with a feeling of triumph at having achieved her objective, she had lain awake half the night planning her attire. So important were clothes to her, she never failed to mention what she wore on specific occasions. For this exceptional occasion, she donned a burgundy dress with her favourite two strings of pearls around her neck, and wrapped her sable stole casually over her shoulders.

This historic meeting lasted one hour. Her host was most courteous and the conversation, with the aid of the interpreter, centred around ballet and Waslaw Nijinsky. According to Romola, Khrushchev was extremely well-informed on the subject. As she was leaving, Romola's stole slipped off her shoulders, and Khrushchev politely picked it up. He remarked on its fine quality and wondered

421

if Romola was aware that it was Russian. Assuring him that she was, she asked him if he knew the story of how Fanny Elsler had received a full-length sable coat as a gift from Czar Nicholas after one of her performances. Retorting that he had not heard the story, he bowed and bade Romola adieu.

Later that day, Romola boarded her plane, settled down comfortably in her seat, mulling over the events of the past few weeks, how superbly it had all come off.... Her reveries were rudely interrupted by a harsh voice on the intercom requesting all passengers to disembark. They were unceremoniously hustled into the airport waiting-room. No explanation was forthcoming. Romola nervously lit a cigarette. She examined her own conscience and began to have qualms about her movements – had she unwittingly said or done something tactless that might cause her to be detained? Her fears appeared to be justified when, after a nerve-racking hour's wait, the door was flung open and a Red Army officer marched in, and demanded to know if a Madame Nijinsky was there. Outwardly unruffled, she felt a throbbing in her temples as she made her presence known. Then, to her unconcealed astonishment, the young man stepped forward and placed a long, white box on her lap, saluted her smartly, turned on his heels, and vanished. Her fellow passengers surged forward and clamoured for her to open the box. Thus roused out of her stupor, she obeyed. Inside lay a full-length sable coat.

Whether or not this extraordinary story ever reached the Western press, I do not know. As I have mentioned earlier, my mother had aspirations for a number of books, including one about herself and the incredible things that had befallen her. She was never loathe to boast that her life was a charmed one, that the world was her oyster. I can only believe that much of what she related was true; the most unusual adventures seemed to befall her.

How insipid and prosaic my own daily life was in comparison. In Canada, we were trudging on, steeling ourselves to face yet another cruelly cold season. Taking into account Romola's letter and discouraging replies from others, repeating that it would prove virtually impossible for Laci to acquire a work permit, our efforts had been negative. But then, Laci had a greeting card from an Aunt Rosa, who lived in Twin Cities, St Paul, Minnesota. She was an elderly Hungarian woman who had been a close friend of his family. She had been given our address and expressed disappointment that we were not living in the States. Perhaps it was the Little Infant Jesus of Prague who prodded me to sit down and reply at once, spelling out our current situation. To my astonishment, her answer was not long in forthcoming. When I opened it, a Church Bulletin fell out. Penned to it was a note that the organist and choir master of St. Mary's Church in Phoenix, Arizona, had been murdered, and consequently, the position was now vacant. Aunt Rosa advised Laci to write and apply.

None of us had a clue as to the whereabouts of Phoenix. Hastily, we dug out the Atlas. I sat down that evening and wrote an application on Laci's behalf. February descended upon us with a vengeance, bringing with it a snowstorm that virtually paralysed our lives. Schools had to close, transport was brought to a halt, we were cut off from Montreal. Electricity and heating failed. Our spirits had been dampened by a stony silence from Phoenix, when on a particularly gale-swept Saturday the telephone rang and a voice at the other end introduced himself as Father Victor from St. Mary's Church. Was Laci still interested in the vacancy as organist? If so, he was cordially invited to fly down to Arizona for an interview. A round trip ticket would be in the post.

And so, in late March 1961, Laci set forth in search of his Utopia. It had been a gruelling trip to the airport; another blizzard had all but blocked the major roads. My husband bundled himself up in a heavy winter coat, scarf, boots, furlined gloves, hat – all the trimmings to protect himself against a Siberian freeze. He arrived in Phoenix, Arizona, where the temperature stood at 90 degrees, and men were walking about in their shirt sleeves. What did it matter to him the sideward glances and the odd snigger. He had come to Paradise. A room had been reserved for him at the Adam's Hotel! He was escorted from there to the Rectory where Father Victor welcomed him. The interview went smoothly. He was offered a contract to become choir master and organist of the church in addition to taking on the position of choral director and band leader of St Mary's High School. The church and the school were owned and run by the Franciscan Order. Today, incidentally, St Mary's Church is a Minor Basilica and it was there that the Holy Father, Pope John Paul II, addressed the people of Phoenix on his trip throughout the United States.

Laci returned home overjoyed by his good fortune. By then, I had read all about Arizonia, its deserts, its rattlesnakes, and other choice bits of useless information. However, I had by now reached the stage that all I wanted to do was to go where Laci went – and where he would be happy.

Our path was still paved with stumbling blocks. For instance, we discovered that the quota was indefinitely closed to Hungarian nationals. Romola was unable to provide assistance, although she had assured us earlier she would be in a position to 'pull strings'. Then a lifeline was thrown our way from unexpected quarters. I was advised I could come in under the Austrian quota as I was born in Vienna. Father Victor gave his support by making use of the Special Preference Bill. As Laci's employer, he could prove that no one else had come forward to claim the position despite widespread advertising.

Feverishly, we began our preparations for the big move which was to take place at the end of term. We put our house up for sale, made all the necessary overtures to depart, when gallbladder complications forced me into hospital to face surgery. So, instead of June, we started our journey by car on August 5th, 1961. The bulk of our belongings had been shipped on ahead. We loaded the little Austin Healey with our more personal possessions and, of course, Betyár, our dog, and set forth on our adventurous jaunt into the unknown.

The last communication I had from Romola before we left Montreal came from Bayreuth where she was staying as a guest of the Wagners for the *Festspiele*. She rejoiced that my operation had been a success but warned me against undue exertion during the next few months. *'The travelling and change of climate will be tiring enough. I am sorry that I am not in the United States right now to give you a helping hand... The performances here are truly phenomenal; Wieland Wagner, Richard's grandson, is a genius. Mrs Siegfried Wagner, charming.'* She complained that she felt stressed and weary. Therefore, she was going on to Marienbad for a three weeks' cure after which she would return to Zürich. As almost always, her letter contained news flashes about family members. 'Little' Vaslav, Kyra's son, had got married, no mention as to whom or where; Kyra maintained a deathly silence, and poor darling Aunt Tessica had broken her ankle. *'For a whole week I was in Engadine – Pontresina, St Moritz – heavenly air, gorgeous. Some day I will take you there. Please write me your new address. Much love and kisses to you all and thank Laci for taking such good care of you.'*

On August 12th, we reached the picturesque Salt River Canyon in Arizona, some 120 miles from Phoenix. Our hearts beat faster as we took in the view – high red cliffs on one side and deep green valleys on the other. We were getting closer and closer to our destination.

The thermometer registered 112 degrees Fahrenheit the following day when we entered the city of Phoenix from the east side. The culmination of the long drive found me utterly exhausted, and I gasped for air as the hot wind stung my face and the dust penetrated my lungs. On the verge of collapse, I gazed around me, not believing my eyes; the overall impression was one of flatness with some cacti breaking the monotony. Nowhere were the luscious green forests to be seen, the purple mountains, the azure-blue lakes. 'Dear God,' I muttered under my breath, 'why have I been brought here, to a dusty old cowtown.' Today, that insignificant, arid 'outpost' is a vast teaming metropolis, a concrete jungle of important industries, of culture. The main street is some forty miles long. This is my home, I love it, and it is the only place where I want to live.

CHAPTER 13

ROMOLA'S TURBULENT YEARS

We lost touch with Romola during much of the time that we were busy resettling in our new environment. Communication fell asunder. She was jetting around the world in pursuit of her own destiny, changing addresses so swiftly it was impossible to keep up with her. Did she ever pause for breath? The first contact I had with her after we left Canada was a scrawled note with which she had enclosed a copy of an insurance policy naming me as her beneficiary in the event that she met with an accident. It was penned on an anonymous bit of paper, possibly in mid-air during a flight. She said over again how fatigued she was, and pressed me to consider an offer to become her secretary once she returned to San Francisco. Barely had I a chance to digest the contents of this communiqué, when another arrived postmarked Zürich. There was no doubt but that Switzerland was the sanctum to which she retreated after her venturesome journeys, perhaps to relive those ephemeral hours of happiness as a young wife together with Waslaw before darkness descended. Repeatedly, she urged me to accompany her to the Engadine Valley. It was heavenly there, she assured me. She had visited Czechoslovakia, and expressed dismay over what she had seen. *'Thank God, you are out from behind the Iron Curtain. I have had a glimpse of what your life must have been.'* She was concerned about my health and implored Kinga to write, should I not be capable of doing so.

For the first couple of weeks, Laci, I, and the youngsters had lived in a motel, the blood in our veins thawing back to normal, gently adjusting to the subtropical climate. From the bustling, throbbing big city we had left, we now found ourselves in a relaxed, informal, *petit-bourgeois* Western town. The transition did not go all that effortlessly, but we enjoyed a breathing spell. Imbued with optimism, we applied ourselves to another way of life in the sprawling vastness of the sun-drenched valley protected by the mountains. It is uncanny the way valleys became the setting for my major roles in life. My conception took place in the Valley of the Engadine, my youthful years were spent in Hüvösvölgy – the Cool Valley

– in Budapest, and now another phase was beginning in the Valley of the Sun.

Cautiously biding our time to become property owners once more, we rented a three-bedroom house within walking distance of St Mary's Church and the High School. Both Kinga and Peter were enrolled at the school as sophomores. Laci relished his task as church organist and choir master. He was also busily occupied teaching music and leading the school orchestra.

Instead of circumnavigating the globe like my mother, I was engrossed in discovering the charm of the desert in my proximity. My imagination was stirred by the peculiar, tall Saguaro cacti with their waxy white blossoms; to me they seemed like dancing ballerinas. The Saguaro is the State flower of Arizona. The Palo Verde trees' thin branches projected intricate shadows over the pale sand. With each season, the desert offers the most gorgeous panorama of brightly-hued flowers and plants with exotic names that are exciting to pronounce. The wealth of wild flowers spread out like an intricately woven Persian carpet. I learned to admire the beauty of the red rock cliffs that surround our valley. Perhaps it was the sharp contrast, the thrill of fresh experiences in Nature itself, that prevented me from ever feeling homesick for the Hungarian countryside.

If I suffered any initial pangs of loneliness, these were soon dispelled when I made the acquaintance of a warm-hearted fellow Hungarian. She and her family were instrumental in drawing us into the small Hungarian colony. Slowly, but surely, we also gained a few dear American friends.

I had as yet not set up a puppet theatre, and could not avoid turning over in my mind my mother's tempting offer to act as her secretary. In a moment of abandonment I had visions of a carefree, financial existence, a cosmopolitan atmosphere, mingling with society, seeping in culture… However, it had one great disadvantage. San Francisco was not 'next door' but hundreds of miles away, and I simply had to stay with my family, they were my 'obsession'. I would not be able to function without them. And, even now, revaluating the situation, I harbour no regrets in spite of the vicissitudes that were already then lurking in the shadows. The undercurrent of disharmony between Laci and Kinga was bubbling to the surface with ever growing frequency. If only it would have manifested itself in loud shouting matches, I would have 'heard' it. As it was, I feigned ignorance, buried my head in the sand.

In early 1962, Romola entreated me time and again to fly out to her, apologising that I would have to come alone due to lack of space in her flat. She promised to pay for the fare. I kept hedging with one excuse after the other. The plain truth probably was that I still felt too immature to face her alone. My indecision was swept away by a telephone call from my cousin Cicó, who lived on the West Coast. She admonished me for not having accepted the invitation. Romola was ailing and feeling very depressed and hurt over my nonchalant behaviour. Filled with remorse and pity, I took a deep breath and decided to go.

Romola and Paul greeted me affectionately at the airport. I must admit I was consumed with curiosity over how they lived. Both had been brought up accustomed to luxury. The taxi stopped in front of a two-storey, granite-coloured building at the top of the hill on Pierce Street.

I was first ushered into my room, actually a separate suite comprising a bedroom and bathroom. After refreshing myself, I entered the spacious living-room, hallmarked with Romola's taste; opulently elegant, heavy furniture in dark wood, Chinese antiques, original drawings on the walls, photographs of Waslaw everywhere, the most outstanding one, the *Spectre de la Rose.*

Romola had evidently decided to make the occasion a small family reunion. My cousin Cicó and her husband Steven were already there, and shortly afterwards Kyra breezed in. It was an emotional moment for me, we had to bridge a gap of twenty-five years. Romola's criticism of her weight could not be faulted. Gone was the graceful figure of yesteryears, but to me her sparkling dark eyes and face were as beautiful as ever. The room suddenly became pulsatingly alive with her bubbly laughter and lovely voice just like all those years ago in Budapest. The conversation, which up to that point had been strained and stilted, mellowed and the atmosphere brightened. I relaxed and felt 'at home'.

Kyra didn't choose to be as frank about her past as one conceivably might have expected between sisters, but perhaps that was not surprising considering the atrocious conditions she had been subjected to during the war and its aftermath. Her marriage had failed and I was later to learn that her son Vaslav had been taken from her by Igor in 1948, the reason shrouded in mystery. Not until 1974 did Kyra publicly shed more light on her life. In December that year, *Dance Magazine* published a special Nijinsky issue. Pamela Gaye, who also interviewed me at the time, headed her article about my sister, *Portrait of Kyra Nijinsky*. The war had trapped Kyra in Italy and, according to her story, she had been captured by the Nazis, accused of being a spy. Only at the last moment was she saved from execution. When the Allies took over, she was appointed as director and principal dancer at the Opera in Florence. She left the Opera and for a short period worked for a high-fashion boutique. Irina, who had met her at the time, recalled how she was literally transformed from 'rags to riches', one day shabbily dressed, the following looking like a glamorous model. She was in Rome when our father died, but was too hard up to afford a ticket to London. The article dealt at length with her career as a dancer, and also revealed her talents as a painter and poet. Like our father, she keeps a diary.

During my stay, Romola went out of her way to shower attention on me. She and Paul took me on excursions in and around San Francisco. We lunched at Sausaulito's and dined at a few of the marvellous restaurants overlooking the Bay. I drew in the salty and refreshing, soft blowing wind from the Ocean, delighting in its caresses, so different from the torrid heat of the desert.

Paul was with us everywhere. At their home, he waited on Romola hand and foot. In fact, it was he who concocted all the delicious repasts we enjoyed when dining at the flat. I had ceased to ponder over their relationship. Romola never revealed her feelings for him; he was too much of a gentleman of the old school to talk to me of their private life. I accepted him now as part of her 'inventory'. It no longer bothered me, nor did I resent him as I had done when I was younger. No wounds from the past were reopened as far as his presence was concerned. Indeed, when I studied him furtively as he hovered around his 'Queen', my heart swelled with gratitude. He had been her faithful retainer those many years, bestowing dedicated attention on both Romola and Waslaw until the latter's death, and thereafter carrying on at her side.

I found I derived pleasure from the social whirl as Romola insisted on introducing me to her friends like the McGregors, Helene Romanoff, and others. I balked at first, though, when she wanted me to accompany her to a *séance*. 'Mama' Becker was a medium to whom both Romola and Greta McGregor had turned many times. Romola did everything in her power to influence me; to assure me that if I were to accompany her, the spirits of Tatakaboy and Emilia would disclose themselves to me. She went on to say how she had been in contact with both, even with Charlie-Papa. My own religious beliefs made me recoil at the suggestion, but she was so persistent, I finally surrendered, and tagged along. Sad to say, Emilia never answered the question I put to her at the *séance*.

My visit came to an end, and although I felt no pangs of regret at leaving, at the same time I felt uplifted, purged from my previous misapprehension, at peace with myself for having taken the plunge. I had come to appreciate I had a mother who actually cared for me, and it gave life a new meaning.

Only one minor incident struck a jarring note. Romola lost one of her precious pearl earrings, and in spite of a frantic search, it was not to be found. Its disappearance dampened our spirits, largely due to Romola's irrational reaction. Material possessions meant much to my mother. The matter preyed on her mind to such a degree that when the time came for me to return home, she totally forgot she had promised to reimburse me for my air fare. Not until some days later when she wrote to me, did she mention her lapse. She apologised, promising to send the money in her next letter, and in the same sentence she blithely announced the earring had been retrieved – it had been nestling under a lamp stand. Her idiosyncratic financial problems prompted her to write later: *'I will mail you the air fare soon. I have to pay $1,000 toward a lawsuit, which is why I have not as yet been able to send the money. But do not fret. Whatever is delayed will be done in time.'* To the best of my recollection, it was delayed forever.

> *'We miss you very much. I am sorry you arrived only to fly away so soon. We loved you before, now we love you all the more. Now, too, that you are familiar with the road to us, I hope you will come often to your second home. Everybody became very fond of you. You came, you saw, you conquered.'*

For the umpteenth time she repeated her promise to take me along with her to Japan, where I would be able to study Bunraku in its own setting. We would then proceed to Hawaii and on to Mexico. She was quite outspoken about it.

> *'Being an egoist, I do not like to travel alone and since I am not one hundred percent well, it is really not wise to wander about solo. Paul cannot always accompany me in view of his business engagements.'*

In subsequent correspondence, Romola referred with tedious regularity to her lawsuit, which I read between the lines to be what she herself had baptised her 'Hollywood Nightmare'. Paul had mentioned it briefly to me. As I understood the context, Romola had gone to Los Angeles to pursue the case against Charles Vidor's widow, who refused to part with the film rights. To complicate matters, Romola's previous attorney had sold her out to her opponent. The new attorney was of Russian origin; his son was suffering from the same illness that had befallen Waslaw. The British and the Russians had agreed to a co-production *'if this damn lawsuit against the Vidor estate wasn't holding it up.'*

In a desperate bid to find cash, Romola turned her attention to what she could possibly salvage from Hungary. She asked me to write to 'Misi' in Budapest to look for two pictures she was eager to lay her hands on, together with six or seven Lodz drawings. Purportedly, they had been hidden in the wall on the ground floor of Emilia's Villa when Aunt Tessica stayed there. In her jittery frame of mind, she even declared she would personally travel to Budapest to collect them if they were found. She was also eager to regain an old Renaissance watch left to Kyra by Emilia.

> *'In the names of Kyra and Tessa I will try to wring out of the Hungarian Government the equivalent of the value of the Villa in money.'* (In her will Emilia had left the Villa mutually to Romola, Tessa and Kyra). *'Since Kyra is an American citizen and Tessa a Danish citizen, this would be possible. As a British national I cannot ask for anything because the British Government has already had 40 million from the Hungarian Government to reimburse British citizens for the loss of factories, bonds, etc but not for the value of houses...'*

Romola had not heard from Kyra since the dinner party despite the fact she had sent her a ticket to a ballet performance. She complained Kyra made her feel nervous and added *'Thank God, you were born, you are truly a Marie de la Consolation...'*. How fickle Mother was. One had only to stroke her the wrong way, as Kyra inadvisably had, to be in her bad graces.

She had developed a proprietary air toward Kinga and chided me for not having taught her to cook. She proposed I send Kinga to San Francisco so that Paul could teach her some culinary skills. *'It is essential that she learn to cook, although we will try to marry her off to a millionaire from Texas. Then she will have a legion of servants. We must at last have one Capitalist in the family.'*

On a small scale, I resumed my puppet performances. My mother spared no effort in her campaign to introduce me to important contacts; time and again she came back to the Ed Sullivan show. How successful were the puppet performances?

'Pali (Paul) is seriously making the rounds on your behalf and there is already the possibility of an agent and also a sponsor. Next week, I too, will have a talk with them. Allegedly, they are looking for live shows, a stable company; they would finance everything. The question is whether you could show them a pilot performance here or in Phoenix. Please let me know. I will probably go to Europe before April 20th and would like to discuss the matter beforehand with them. Perhaps you should show them the 'Spectre'. They are quite willing to bring puppets from Moscow. ...They financed one puppet theatre here but it was not good enough for them. ...Naturally, it would be much better if Paul and I were present, because he is excellent in business matters; he demands high amounts and gets them...'

Romola had also tried to persuade me to believe that the very word 'Nijinsky' would be an 'open sesame' to the corridors of power. What she could not fathom was that I possessed very little of her extroverted, almost flamboyant personality. Where I crept into my shell, she flagrantly utilised Tatakaboy's fame to gain her ends. It became a ceaseless bone of contention between us. I demurred for several reasons, which to me seemed logical enough. I could not see myself breaking the strings that tied me to my family to embark on a career that would take me to the far corners of the earth in the company of my mother. But just as strongly, I felt that her whole demeanour indicated that she, and she alone, had the right to be the torchbearer of the Nijinsky name. Lastly, was it not Romola who, some twenty years earlier, had attempted to stop me from using my rightful maiden name?

She must have seethed with frustration and discontent when, on March 17th, 1962, she wrote the following letter to me, in which she pursued her attacks on western ballet companies.

'R.P. was here with his wife and mentioned you met them during the performance of the Denham Ballet. Concerning Denham, just entre-nous, he became the head of a ballet troupe twenty-five years ago and took over the name "Monte Carlo Ballets Russes". The MONTE CARLO BALLETS RUSSES was DIAGHILEV's private company from 1916 until his death in 1929. After that (Colonel) de Basil, a former Russian policeman, took it over and then Denham from him. Since everybody seems to be abusing the choreographic rights, the scenery and the props, like mushrooms after rain, one very bad ballet company after the other pops up. Like Massine's Ballet, Denham, de Basil... they bear no relation to the real Russian Ballet... They did not look down on the audience in Phoenix, my child, they simply do not know how to dance. Every ballet company on this side of the Iron Curtain is AMATEUR, including the New York City Ballet and the terrible SADLER WELLS COMPANY which is now called the ROYAL BALLET. Do not bother to know them, it is only the Bolshoi Ballet, the Ballet from Leningrad and the Moiseyev which one can have anything to do with...the others are full of wind and cheating...'

Every so often, news cropped up that Romola had prospective parties interested in turning her biography into a play or film. In May, 1962, for instance, she received a letter from Edward Padula in New York staking his claim to bring her great story to life in the theatre, and possibly one day, in the films. 'In fact, I have a passion to do so. To recreate the great era through a retelling of your husband's life, in terms of drama, dance, music and decor.' He was the producer of a successful musical, *Bye, Bye Birdie* and also of *All American,* starring Ray Bolgar. He was anxious to meet Romola either in New York or San Francisco to talk about the matter.

For years, Romola was in correspondence with Winifred Wagner. My mother's nomad life took her to far-flung corners of both hemispheres, but I imagine if an accurate record had been kept of the places she revisited time after time, Bayreuth would have topped the list. Hence, her disappointment in 1962, when she approached Madame Wagner with a request for a seat in the Wagner family box for the first performance of the season. It was politely refused by Winifred Wagner as she shared the box with her son Wieland, and he had already committed himself to others. A polite note from the Aga Khan expressed regrets at not seeing Romola at the Festival and hoped the opportunity would arise the following year.

As a romantic young girl, Romola had liked to imagine a bond existed between her and Cosima Wagner, the illegitimate daughter of Franz Liszt and Countess Marie d'Argoult. In her eyes, Liszt had played an important role in the lives of three women in her own family. Her maternal grandmother Teréz had been in love with him; her Aunt Janka had been his favourite student; and her Aunt Polyxena had taken care of his household in his old age when he was still Director of Music in Budapest.

Romola penned a comprehensive essay on her visits to Bayreuth; her commentaries on the various performances she witnessed.

'Cosima Wagner (art director of the Festivals when Romola first attended them) left an enormous impression on me and her example influenced my subconscious, so much so that later I dedicated my life to the Arts. Indirectly, I can thank Cosima that I became Nijinsky's wife...My friendship with Winifred Wagner goes back many years, and in all my artistic endeavours I enlist her advice. Winifred is the Twentieth Century's most outstanding woman and without a doubt, the saviour of Bayreuth. Without her, there would not have been a Bayreuth Festival after 1938...It was most difficult for Winifred. She had to fight for Bayreuth's existence all alone. Cosima, who shouldered the management of the Festival after her husband's death in 1883, remained the driving force behind it even after her son took over in 1908. She died in 1930. She had always had the moral support of Hans Bülow, Richter, Mahler, and legions of Wagner worshippers. All of us, who love music, owe eternal gratitude to Winifred.' She carried on with an in-depth criticism of the Ring in the new French version under the directorship of Patrice Chereaut brought in by Wolfgang Wagner. 'I think Patrice Chereaut's idea was to take the Ring's characters and turn them into modern figures to fit into today's technological world...To some extent he was successful in making the characters more human and the tetralogical stories more understandable. The new version has many interesting points but at the same time it contains a lot of absurdity...many parts have become unacceptable...'

As a token of her high esteem and affection for Madame Wagner, Romola would send her gifts, mainly in the form of delectable confectionery. And the courteous, old-world thank-you notes that arrived in return were carefully kept throughout the years.

'Gestern kam als liebe Überraschung von Ihnen eine wunderschöne Packung californischer kandierten Früchte hier an, und ich darf Ihnen für die grosse Freude, die mir Ihre Gabe und Ihr gutiges Gedenken, bereitete, meinen allerherzlichsten Dank sagen.'

Some time after my mother's death, I wrote to Winifred Wagner and had a very kind, warm letter in reply. I would like to quote the passages about Romola because they portray so eloquently the tireless energy and determination of a woman whose body already then was racked by a painful illness.

'As often as your dear Mother visited the Bayreuth Festival she called on me and even presented me her book on your Father. As far as I remember, it was in the winter of 1975 or 1976 that she stayed at Bayreuth for at least 6 weeks. She planned to stage a Parsifal Ballet during the summer of the following year in the wonderful old Markgraf-Theater of Bayreuth and asked me to be as helpful as I could. I managed to get her in touch with the right minister in Munich regarding renting the theatre and to recommend to her experts on stage design, lighting etc etc with which she began planning her ballet. During those six weeks she was often my guest and we talked for hours and hours about the realisation of her plans. After she left Bayreuth I suppose she fell ill, for I never heard from her again, and my letters addressed to Baur au lac in Zürich were returned to me with the notice: Empfänger abgereist. Your Mother was most active and full of ideas even at her high age and I am very grateful and proud that she considered me as her true friend...'

In late February 1980, I again wrote to Winifred Wagner. It was when the idea to write a book about my mother was slowly germinating, and I wondered if she would kindly supply me with any personal anecdotes she might have, reminiscences of their time together. This was not to be. A reply did come, but not the one I had anticipated. Instead came a poignant, handwritten note from her daughter to the effect that Winifred Wagner had indeed received and opened my letter but that she was too ill to respond. *'In grosser Traurigheit, Ihre Verena Lafferentz-Wagner.'* And merely a few days later, the obituary arrived. Winifred Wagner had died on March 5, 1980.

During the latter part of 1962, cards would flutter onto our hall carpet like variegated butterflies; the stamps from unusual places, the envy of philatelists. It was impossible to keep track of Romola. Her restless spirit could never remain in one place for long. She constantly seemed in pursuit of something intangible, a shadow she was never able to catch up with. Kinga and I devised a game for our amusement, the 'postcard' game. We would spread out the cards in front of us that we both had received during the year. The collection was formidable. A travel brochure could not have been more rewarding to skim through. One must bear in mind she was by then past her seventieth birthday.

On the surface, my own life presented a picture of smalltown suburban life but it was imperceptibly heading towards an upheaval. Laci had reached a stalemate in his work and changed it to become music teacher at the Bourgade Catholic High School. Father John Hillmann, or Father Jack, as we got to know him, was the principal of the school. A strong bond of friendship developed between us all. Romola and Father Jack struck up a congenial rapport on their very first meeting. They would sit for hours in animated conversation on a diversity of subjects.

It was Father Jack who sponsored us when we decided to take the major step of seeking to become United States citizens, and on one unforgettable morning, Laci, I, and the children took the oath and pledged allegiance to our new country. A foreign accent still betrays me, however, and when asked my origin, I reply with pride: 'I am a cocktail. My father was Russian, my mother Hungarian; I was born in Austria; French was my first language, but now I am an American.'

In September, I heard from Romola, who was then staying at the Hotel Normandie in London. She was very concerned about Kinga's health. Kinga had been feeling unwell for some time, and

Romola was anxious that she should seek consultation at a university clinic and under no circumstances rely solely on her family doctor. Romola had been to Professor Spühler who had cured her completely from a kidney problem, and Paul, too, had been to him for a medical checkup. After attending to numerous business matters, she was flying back to Zürich for a few days and then from there direct to Nepal. Evidently, she was going to realise her visit to Tenzing Norgay. It was a peculiar eccentricity of my mother's, that she kept me à jour in most instances of where she was going but I never heard in detail of how or with whom her time had been spent. From Nepal she was going to Tokyo. *'Yesterday, I talked to Emilia, Charlie-Papa and Tatakaboy through an excellent medium. They love you and care for you. Their message is to stop worrying for they will help you...At the end of my long voyage I will come to you and collapse on your doorstep.'*

Romola received a letter from Dr Franz Strauss. It was dated November 24th, 1962 and referred to plans to make a film of the ballet *Tyl Eulenspiegel.* Dr Strauss wrote:

'I would be grateful for a copy of the contract from 1915. The film rights are in any case completely free, even as far as the publisher is concerned, and I will gladly give you permission to make *Eulenspiegel* into a film in the hopes it will not take too modern a form. We could still have a discussion regarding additional terms because the publisher would possibly wish to institute a modest claim for the film rights. As it stands legally, the film rights are wholly mine and the publisher is bound to me. Should you have any correspondence between your husband and my father, I would be extremely grateful for photocopies.'

In the same letter, Dr Strauss told of an incident, related to him by his father, that transpired in Vienna during the First World War. Richard Strauss had been invited to an early lunch at the German Embassy. In the course of his conversation with Councillor von Bethmann-Hollweg, a nephew of the Chancellor of the Reich, Strauss had brought up the subject of Nijinsky and had demanded that the great artist should be released from internment on the grounds that a dancer had to keep in training, and that it was impossible for him to go on living under circumstances wholly unworthy of

437

him. Showing marked irritation over Strauss's request, the Councillor had responded: 'What do you mean, Dr Strauss, Nijinsky is a Russian and is not entitled to any other treatment than the rest of the war internees.' Strauss had become livid with rage and replied harshly: 'Herr von Bethmann, Nijinsky is among dancers what Frederick the Great was among kings.' Whereupon he had turned on his heels and left the other man standing there speechless.

I was saddened to learn of the death of Aunt Tessica even though her passing was not wholly unexpected. She had progressively gone into a decline in the clinic in Switzerland, where she had been kept for several years. Like Waslaw, although for different reasons, she had long since withdrawn into a world of her own, and had not recognised the few visitors, who wished to pay their respects to her. A severe bout of pneumonia ended her life on the 19th of March, 1963. I was glad, in a selfish way, that I had not seen her during those final years. Now I was left with unimpaired memories of her. Even though her ethereal beauty had faded by the time I last encountered her, I could still recall her vivacious manner, the characteristic lilt to her voice, her combined air of naughtiness and innocence. What cruel destiny was it that seemed to decide the Pulszky women should die so tragically forsaken? According to Romola, Tessa had had an admirer, allegedly a lover, from the time she lived in Denmark after the War. His name was André Barben, and his nationality was Danish, although he was a Swiss resident. Apparently, he would call on Tessa on a regular basis for the first years she was in the clinic. He had an idiosyncratic habit of holding his pocket watch in his hand, and at a given time he would suddenly rise and depart without preamble.

It was infrequently that Romola found time to descend on us and 'collapse', upsetting our fairly prosaic lifestyle completely. Whenever she announced her arrival, I would agonise over what menus to prepare that suited her taste. One of her peculiarities was a fear of animals, dogs in particular, and by now we had two pets. It was almost farcical how I still felt intimidated and overwrought at the prospect of having my own mother in my home. She was too European, too steeped in her *beau monde,* to mix comfortably with our casual American way of life. I recall with a shudder the rare occasions when she accompanied us to barbecues, Western style. She invariably sulked, pecking at the food on her plate and haughtily refused to be drawn into the conversation. She would smile graciously enough when spoken to, but I could tell by the icy inflexions of her voice that she was 'not amused'.

Her capricious nature often as not landed me in mortifying situations; bagatelles that were to fade without trace but at the time made one's cheeks burn. They left a sting for a while because I tried so hard to please her. Determined that one visit should run smoothly, at least as far as catering was concerned, I took the precaution to write to her in advance to ask what her favourite dishes were. Back came the reply that she was on a very strict diet, could only consume fish and steamed vegetables. Again the pattern repeated itself; friends of ours insisted we bring her along to a real 'cookout' with chunky steaks on the menu. I confided Romola's diet to our hostess, and we agreed I should bring a piece of fish along to be prepared specially for Romola. Dear, whimsical Romola barely touched the food on her plate but like a deprived child kept her eyes glued to the juicy steaks to the embarrassment of the other guests. As it happened, my friend later confessed that she actually had an extra steak in the refrigerator but felt it would have humiliated me, after all my effort, to bring it out.

I do recall one occasion when Romola showed signs of lively interest in an outing. There is an Indian Mission some twenty miles from Phoenix and during one of her stays, they had a festival. I was apprehensive about taking her there, bearing in mind the rather primitive, dusty surroundings, but to my delight she thoroughly enjoyed herself and displayed a surprisingly profound knowledge of Indian culture.

Thanks to a more frivolous side to her nature, her penchant for the most exclusive beauty preparations to enhance her well-groomed appearance, my mother was instrumental in introducing me to a totally different kind of culture in our vicinity. When she and Waslaw were staying in New York those many years ago, she became acquainted with Elizabeth Arden at a function. Impressed both by the woman herself, and later by the range of cosmetics, she faithfully carried on using Arden products for forty years. When a particularly favourite lipstick was discontinued, Romola wrote a personal letter to Elizabeth Arden, who instantly replied that she would ask her sister, Madame de Maublanc, at the Paris Salon, to have some Cyclamen Day and Night shades specifically made up for her. Romola would then be contacted at her address in Paris as soon as the items were ready for collection. 'With all my best wishes and I do hope you will enjoy the lipsticks as much as I enjoy giving them to you. Very sincerely, (s) Elizabeth Arden.'

Some months prior to receiving this generous gift, Romola had come over on one of her occasional sojourns. She asked me to accompany her to 'Main Chance'. She had heard it was a very successful health and beauty clinic run by Elizabeth Arden, and she was filled with curiosity. Gently rebuking me for my unfamiliarity with the subject, we set forth on a tour of exploration 'somewhere in the nearby mountains'. We came upon it, an imposing white edifice nestled like a Shangri-la on the side of our famous Camelback Mountain. The well-manicured green grass, suggestive of a velvety carpet, surrounded the building. Palms and orange trees dotted the lawns. Brilliantly red bougainvillea spilt over the wall to a smaller guesthouse.

Its history was a vision of the future by this perspicacious woman.

Years before Phoenix became a famous resort, Elizabeth Arden realised the enormous potential in a climate that heals arthritis and related illnesses, and promptly bought that particular piece of land for 'peanuts'. She was scoffed at for investing her money in 'red rock' but proved all her cynics wrong. She was amply rewarded for her shrewd foresight when the clinic grew and attracted women clients among the wealthy hierarchy, not merely in the United States but all over the European Continent. They arrived in droves to iron out their wrinkles and become 'younger'.

During our brief visit, when we were taken around the establishment, I learned that the charming guesthouse was reserved for Mamie Eisenhower. Although the clinic was officially out of bounds to men, the strict rule was waived for the former President. He would sometimes accompany his wife, and a golf course had even been installed for him.

Seemingly resigned to the 'plain plump fact', to quote Robert Browning, that she could not mould Kyra or myself to suit her, Romola wholeheartedly turned her attention to Kinga and Peter. The time was fast drawing near when their future would have to be considered. Kinga wanted to pursue her musical interests. Peter, on the other hand, was irresolute. He was fond of music but showed little inclination to follow in his father's footsteps. And Laci cherished the ambition that his only son should become a doctor.

It was Romola's earnest desire that Peter should continue his studies in Germany. Like an echo, the well-worn phrase crept into her letters. *'I promise to help with my special connections. He might even get work with Radio 'Free Europe' in München.'* True to her word, when his graduation day finally arrived, she had found a reputable college for him in Germany. Sadly, too many obstacles worked against the grand scheme, of which money was the decisive factor. In the end, Peter enrolled in the Arizona State University at the same time as Kinga.

Romola set her heart on Kinga engrossing herself in serious linguistic pastimes; learn French and German fluently. Again, her plans soared to the skies. Kinga should also devote herself to becoming an organist. Romola knew of the ideal place – Regensburg, 'the heart of organ music'. So possessive had Romola become, once she discovered she had a 'family', she invariably tried to dominate our lives, even down to trivia. Kinga had beautiful long, flowing hair. Observing her brought back memories of Emilia; of the countless hours I had lovingly brushed her golden tresses when I was a girl. On one of her rare visits, Romola asked if she could borrow Kinga for the afternoon. I readily acquiesced, thinking in a bemused way that they were off on a shopping spree. When they returned a few hours later, I uttered a gasp of dismay. Gone was Kinga's lovely mane of hair. In front of me stood a young girl with an almost boyish bob.

'Voilà,' Romola's voice rose to a triumphant pitch. 'That is the way a young girl should look. It is not unhygienic like long hair and does not give a sloppy appearance.'

January 1964 found Romola once more in Tokyo. Paul had been with her part of the time. She gave no hint as to the purpose of her stay. She seldom did. She was always very thoughtful about providing me with material for my Puppet Theatre. A new book on puppetry had been sent from Japan.

'Next Sunday, the 19th, I plan to fly home by way of the Pole and across Alaska; it is only an 8½ hour trip – it is nothing. I will endeavour to be at your place on the evening of February 18th. On the 17th I have to appear in a Los Angeles Court for a hearing...do pray for its success. I am already looking forward to seeing you again...last but not least give my love to Dr Frank. His face reminds me of Alec Guinness...Kisses, Meme.'

Dr Frank is Frank Allinson, an English doctor with a Hungarian wife, living in Phoenix.

That year was a photocopy of all the other years; her time was spent on the global carousel – Zürich, Pontresina, Engadine, Munich, Bad Gastein.

> *'From there I have to go to Greece for one month. I have been invited to attend the wedding of King Constantine...I will be extremely busy now with the plans for the film because my producer comes on Sunday to Zürich. It is possible I have to go to Moscow in the Fall. I may have to spend a couple of months in Paris as two books must be finished, and I can only find the necessary historical data in the archives there. I have also been invited to Nepal and to Jaipur to stay with the Maharaja, who is tempting me to come by offering me sapphires and rubies like last year. On that occasion he said he only enjoyed his seven palaces if I was there to tell him stories. Ah, well, at this moment I do not know how I shall be able to tear myself in so many directions. We will see.'*

It piqued me that she kept dropping these broad hints about her intoxicating life-style, her escapades at that age. It was maddening to be in limbo, so to speak, never to hear the end of each fabulous adventure.

1964 was also the year that Romola 'celebrated' the tenth anniversary of her film-lawsuit-saga. By then, she was considering three other offers, of which two were in Europe. *'It is necessary that my heirs should derive money and enjoyment from something I have written,'* she told me. Rudolf Nureyev's name cropped up from time to time to play the role of Waslaw but allegedly he had demanded half a million dollars for his performance. *'I said to the producers, in that case I want a million dollars,'* was her sarcastic comment in another letter.

In November, Romola made the headlines in the Spiritualist newspaper, *Psychic News,* published in London. 'WORLD'S MOST FAMOUS BALLET DANCER COMES BACK TO HIS WIDOW.' It referred to an interview which Romola gave during her stay in the English capital. She was reported as saying:

> 'I am quite convinced life goes on. We *do* survive. This life is like a page in a book. You may have forgotten the earlier

pages, and not know what is on the next, but the spark of life within us is a point of God. I have experienced it so many times in my life. It sustained me during the 32 years of my husband's illness. We passed through so many hardships. Without it we could not possibly have come through.'

One of the aims of her visit was to meet the famous clairvoyant, Tom Corbett. She had read his book, *Stately Ghosts of England,* and been favourably impressed by what he had written. Romola claimed that the subsequent sitting with Corbett had exceeded her expectations. 'He is a wonderful medium. Fantastic.' From what she told Anne Dooley, her sympathetic interviewer, he had gone into detail about past, present, and future negotiations with Russia concerning the Nijinsky film. All he said confirmed what Kotome Fujita, the gifted Japanese medium, had earlier told her. Corbett had given her a communication from her husband. 'Vaslav told me exactly how his life story should be treated in the film!' She relived that black hour when she stood by his bedside and saw him slip away from her. But now, miraculously, in the depths of her grief, she suddenly had become aware of his presence and she felt he was trying to say 'You should not be like this. Now I belong to God. He lent me to you...'

It was a longish interview, and Romola went on to relate a number of similar incidents, and of messages she had had from other mediums, including Florence Becker, the well-known American medium to whom I had been introduced in San Francisco. She claimed Waslaw himself had said, when they were living in St Moritz Dorf: '...Of course, life goes on in another form. Birth and death are very similar. Both are part of a circle which goes on...We are an infinite part of God in the Universe, and when we create something beautiful, we reflect him...'

The article ended on a rather amusing note. Romola related how she had taken the Austrian, Rudi Schneider, to meet the Irish Hester Dowden, both proclaimed two of the twentieth century's most outstanding mediums. The meeting had taken place at Hester's London home. Rudi was introduced under the Hungarian pseudonym for 'Tailor'. When Hester's control, Johannes, came through he asked Rudi bluntly, 'Why do you come here posing as a tailor?'

Romola was uninhibitedly lavish in bestowing gifts on the famous – she even used to send exquisite roses to the Aga Khan, and I too was to be a recipient of her whimsical generosity. I recall how one day I found a small box, casually wrapped in brown paper, wedged by the postman between the screen door and the entrance. Except for the tell-tale San Francisco date stamp, it was wholly anonymous. A strikingly handsome ring fell out once I rescued it from its rather scruffy cocoon. It was a flat, silvery band with a green stone inset. At first, I thought it was just an inexpensive bibelot. I studied it rather disenchantedly and, admittedly, with ingratitude, as I was not prone to wearing ostentatious costume jewellery. I must confess I was overcome by a sharp twinge of remorse, when I learned that Mother's birthday gift was a platinum ring enhanced by an emerald.

For us in Phoenix, the mid-sixties were characterized by problems, crucial in more than one respect. Perhaps the inevitable process of life itself was a contributory factor. How I stumbled through them I do not know. The puppet theatre was teetering on the verge of collapse, although it did survive another few years. Lack of capital led to insufficient advertising and encumbered us with nasty debts. It forced Laci into a corner. He had to look around for extra work, and in a fit of desperation took on night-work in a smoke-infested German restaurant in the evenings, playing a far too heavy accordian. It was wickedly strenuous, enough to break any man, and he was a sensitive, highly-strung musician. The wall between him and Kinga was solid. Both were stubborn, both were proud, both kept silent about their feelings. Like a tyre bursting from too much pressure, Laci exploded one night. For everyone's peace of mind, it was deemed best that Kinga stayed with another family for half a year.

Ever since my remarriage, Kinga had resented the intrusion of a stepfather. Possibly, Miklós was partly to blame. At my insistence, she carried on a correspondence with her father, and when the letters arrived, seeds of jealousy germinated and left Laci embittered. Kinga became more and more withdrawn, and the gulf between the two widened. Peter went through his own crisis. In the end, everybody was wretched, although we played our parts to the outside world, staging a mock performance of the happy family.

With the puppet shows diminishing, I developed a feeling of inadequacy. Here, again, Father Jack came to the rescue and bolstered my flagging spirits. He suggested that I should teach French and German at the high school. These languages were to be added to the curriculum. Only two requirements were necessary – that I show my diplomas and enrol for a refresher course at the University. It was with a sense of achievement and satisfaction that I took up teaching.

As was their wont, Romola and Paul spent weeks in Bad Gastein, where they took the cure. My mother confessed to feeling utterly drained after her latest trip to Russia, and that she was in need of a complete rest; this, in 1965.

'...I was exhausted from my Russian trip, where in nineteen days I attended no less than twenty-one performances. I was even asked to assist at a couple of rehearsals. I attended a performance by the Hungarian Ballet Company, who were on tour in Moscow. Their ballet instructor was the famous ex-prima ballerina Lepischinskaya, who spoke Hungarian fluently. She took me backstage to meet the whole company in the artists' lounge. The furnishings had not been altered since the days of Emperor Alexander; wonderful brocade wall coverings and beautiful chandeliers. Among the artists were Harangozó and Zsedény but I did not have the faintest idea who the others were. It is quite possible that Kinga's father's second wife was among them. After all, it is a small world. They danced extremely well to the music of Bartók sand Kodály but not the more classical ballets. I was taken to the various museums and shown all the precious treasures within their walls. It is impossible to describe how much they spoiled me. I received so many gifts that I did not know how to carry them back to Zürich; some seven kilos of caviar, several bottles of vodka. I don't know if I told you that I met a darling engineer, engaged on some Sputnik project or other; six foot tall, blond, blue-eyed. We met on a bench under a lilac tree in the park by the Kremlin. He is a widower, and he told me that he earns 1200 rubles a month, owns an automobile, a villa in the country and a four-room apartment in the plushest district in Moscow. He claimed he has two months' paid holiday and travels to the Crimea, Caucasus, etc. We were engaged in a long talk, and at the end of it, he said: "You are the widow of our beloved dance genius; you like Russia and our art, why don't you stay here and become my wife..."

I am glad that the youngsters are doing extra work and that they are making themselves useful. It is also good that they have moved from home. They will thus become independent, and

you will finally have peace so that you can live a little bit just for
yourself. Höchste Zeit. It will do Kinga good not to be tied so
close to her mother. Thank you for the addresses in Budapest
and Yugoslavia. I am not quite certain that I will go because I
dare not tire myself too much, as in the autumn I have business
in London, Paris, Copenhagen and Brussels. We would like to
stay here, (Pontresina) weather permitting, until August 20th.
Then we are going to Italy for ten days, to Venice. Our for-
warding address until the 15th November is the St Gotthard
Hotel, Zürich. Everything depends on the matter of the film. It
is possible that I may have to stay in Europe the entire winter but
otherwise we may return home via Australia and Japan. Take
good care of yourself. Do not eat anything with fat but try to
lose some weight. It will prove much more difficult later on...'

What perplexed me time and again was where did all the money
come from for Romola's grandiose lifestyle. It was astonishing, to
say the least, considering the *longueur* of the unresolved film case;
the marginal gain from some lawsuits balanced by the loss of others;
the apartment on Pierce Street; the gifts strewn lavishly about as
tokens of affection; the travels to spas, cures, festivals. I sometimes
tried to calculate the cost of just one year, and the inside of my head
would buzz like a hornet's nest. I had a partial answer to my query
long after her death. Both Romola and Paul had incurred masses of
debts but funds had trickled in from the sale of memorabilia and
valuable items in their possession.

Additional enlightenment on their various sources of income
came from Irina. Both of them had dabbled in real estate. As confided to Irina by Romola, Paul owned three apartment houses in
Vienna and before World War II had also acquired property on the
outskirts of an Italian city. The latter property was confiscated during the War and was used afterwards to build a city hall. Paul
succeeded in obtaining a rental income for that use of the property
by taking legal action. Not being allowed to take this money out of
the country, Paul and Romola lived several months every year in
Italy. The same money was used to buy Paul's baronetcy. In 1976,
when Romola stayed alone at the Lotti Hotel in Paris, she told Irina
that Paul was in *Marseille* to settle a dispute involving several docks
in the harbour, which were owned by him.

They evidently dealt in the buying and selling of gold on the

Market because on one specific occasion Romola advised Irina to buy, assuring her it would give a marginal profit. Once, in Amsterdam, Romola took Irina along on a trip to a diamond cutter. Irina recalls how they had to pass through two to three doors equipped with special security locks. Romola had produced a large yellow diamond that she wanted to have cut into smaller stones. She was cautioned that such an operation would be impossible as the diamond had a flaw in it. She had merely shrugged her shoulders and said she knew of several places where it could be done: Yugoslavia, among others. Paul's many business ventures included the purchase and resale of high-quality jewellery. Many of these transactions were of a very speculative nature and did not always come to a head. Taking into consideration their lifestyle, and Romola's incessant campaigns to keep Waslaw Nijinsky's name to the fore, it is no wonder that their well of plenty in due course dried up.

Although I grudgingly had had to accept the devotion of Paul to my mother, I had never felt 'comfortable' in his presence, stretching back to my very first encounter with him. His distant past was under a veil of secrecy, and it was only recently, when Irina ruminated over her impressions of him, that further light was shed as to his character. Their paths had crossed frequently from the late forties onward in Italy, France, Holland, and Bad Gastein in particular, where Irina often stayed with Romola and him. On their shopping expeditions down the steep hill from where they lived, Paul would plunge into lengthy discourses, dramatising his previous life. The inexplicable part of it was that his stories varied from time to time, proof that they were like as not fabricated. She had been baffled by his use of vulgar American idioms, which belied his cultured background. Her innocuous query as to where he had learned it was glibly explained. He boasted that he had owned vineyards in California, and that he had had two black employees from whom he had picked up the slang expressions. She found it hard to reconcile this baser side of his nature with his dapper, almost effeminite, appearance. Like Romola, he took great pride in being well-groomed; always wore the finest pure silk shirts embellished by expensive cufflinks. The other tales he spun were likewise inconsistent. He announced on one occasion that he was an American citizen, and that he therefore dared not return to the States because he owed so much in taxes, probably from the sale of the vineyards. Yet he did travel back and forth with Romola. He was deft in the art of taking care of the estates of elderly rich people, and Irina vividly recalls how in Rome in 1970, he 'played up' to a wealthy eighty-year old American woman, whose family had owned one of the most valuable sites on the waterfront in San Francisco. It was rumoured that after Romola's death he moved to the States to look after an old wealthy gentleman, presumably in the role of secretary and personal caretaker. In October 1987, Paul Bohus died of pneumonia in Tuscon, Arizona.

When Romola was in London in September 1964, she had been asked by the BBC to edit a programme on the reading of *The Diary of Vaslav Nijinsky*. The reader was the well-known actor Paul Scofield. On April 13th the following year, Marie Rambert wrote:

> '*My dear Romola,* I have heard this last Sunday the excerpts of Vaslav's Diary read by Paul Scofield. It was an unforgettable experience. The reading which lasted nearly an hour and a half showed what a beautiful mind and soul Vaslav had, and what a wonderful translation you had made of this unique document. Scofield read it with the utmost sensitivity – no monotony, no affectation, on the contrary absolute simplicity, directness and delicate variety. I was spellbound and now am looking forward to the repeat on May 4th and am ringing all my friends to tell them about it... *Much love to you.*'
>
> *Mim*

Romola went to Sicily in the autumn of 1965, and she hated every moment of the two weeks she was there: '...*it is the worst place in the world, dirty, hot. On a piazza, a car ran me down. It was a miracle of God that when it hit me I fell to one side and thus avoided being killed. But I suffered a severe shock and as a result my bladder infection recurred for which I have to have treatment. And, can you imagine, the film project appeared to be 99% certain when at the last minute the producer cancelled it. It is only the little Infant Jesus of Prague and your prayers that can help me now.*' She had not gone to Venice as planned, and apologised that she had therefore been unable to acquire some marionettes she had promised me for a *Petrushka* performance I was hoping to set up. She advised me that the colours for the costume should be white for the top, the tie black, and the pants green, red and white. She sounded weary and bored; the sparkle was missing.

Months were to lapse before I heard from her again. I sent her a cable for her birthday, and she responded then with a long letter, of which half was a reproof to me for not taking better care of my health nor of Laci. She advocated certain tablets to calm my nerves and insisted that Laci's insomnia was a combination of too many cigarettes and black coffee. *'He should go to hospital for three to four days for a thorough check-up...Make him do it, otherwise you will be sorry. I mean well.'* How accurate that prediction was to be. How little I knew at the time.

She had been in Zürich since September and then gone to Paris, where she and Paul remained until mid-December. They had attended the performance of the Kirov Ballet together with the McGregors. *'It was heavenly.'* Then, in the beginning of January, the quartet had gone together to St Moritz and Pontresina. Paul and the McGregors returned to the United States, leaving Romola behind. Barely had they left when:

'...I picked up a darling young Italian flirt. I am unable to decide if he resembles a portrait by Raphael, Carpaccio or Michelangelo. He has the zart (gentle) *manners of a Romeo but he is also as aggressive as a Medici Borgia, a condottiere from the cinquecento. No sooner had Paul and the McGregors departed when he sent me one hundred red carnations and became my faithful and constant knight during the remainder of my stay. I asked him if he had gone out of his mind and if he specialised on 'antiquities' like myself.* (Romola was seventy-five when this incident occurred). *"No," he exploded, "Pretty, stupid young girls I can find by the dozen in Milano, Paris, London, but a Mona Romola can only be found among the ladies of the Renaissance." Et voilà, I am now engaged in une amitié amoureuse. We conquered the mountains together via the telpher* (funicular) *and crisscrossed the Engadine Valley in his Alfa Romeo; we danced through the night in the Palace Hotel in St Moritz. "What more do you want," I said to myself. "Chestnut trees do sometimes bloom for the second time in the Autumn of life, and it is an élmény* (magical moment) *that nobody can take from you." One needs a little romance...I have since been to Paris and London regarding the film but will have to go to Russia again as soon as possible. For the past three weeks I have been encumbered with crutches due to the plane*

449

having to make a crash landing at London Airport. As soon as I am back on my feet, I will return to Pontresina for a few days, and then I continue to Leningrad, Moscow, Caucasus, Tiflis. I probably will have to cancel plans to go to Siberia; it will be too much for my leg. Write to me once a month if only a postcard, c/o Hotel St Gotthard, Zürich. They will forward mail to me. Kisses to all of you from Meme.'

In her advancing years, Romola more and more assumed the role Emilia had played so well; incorrigible in seeking a flirtatious digression to escape the tedium of everyday patterns; a drop of elixir to make the pulse beat faster. Tessa had been the same. Perhaps it was inborn in the Pulszky women from generations back.

Together with Karsavina, Romola was the guest of honour at the première of the Kirov Ballet's guest performance at Covent Garden. She wrote to me about the gala occasion, how she had met many of the British and Russian artists, but that apart from enjoying the ballet as such, she had gone with a specific purpose in mind. Dressed in one of her most eye-catching garments from Japan, a black silk brocade dress with an intricately embroidered blue silk jacket, she felt well equipped to tackle the Russian Ambassador on a delicate matter that had been building up to a seething climax for years: Emilia's Villa in Budapest, which Romola legally could claim was hers. According to her story, the Ambassador had listened sympathetically to her and her proposal to turn the house into a home for retired actors as well as a recuperation centre for those who were ill. She had received a diplomatic response: 'I will do my very best.' That the Villa today is still in the hands of the Hungarian Government is proof that his best was not good enough.

Whenever she was in London, Romola never failed to pay a visit to the top floor of a building in Berkeley Square where her literary agent, Eric Glass, has his suite of offices. Both Eric and his wife Blanche had become real friends in whose company she could let down her hair and erupt 'like a paprika in a furious mood' (*Ma Paprikás hangulatban vagyok,* she often said about herself) with regard to her frustrations over the film rights and the lack of progress in getting the film off the ground. The whole subject had become her Achilles heel, and her paramount aim was to triumph in the end.

It is surprising that she was not more successful. She sowed so many seeds that fell on infertile soil yet she did have a number of people who supported her and fanned her hopes yet again. Serge Lifar gave encouragement in a letter in 1966. He wrote to tell her how pleased he had been to receive a telegram from Konstantin Sergeyev of the Kirov Ballet in Leningrad, thanking him for the three prizes from the *l'Université de La Danse* in Paris, attributed to Lifar's influence. He confided to her what joy it would be for him to work with that wonderful ensemble in setting up *Icare* with decor by Picasso, and then *Suite en Blanc,* 'the pure ballet which demonstrates our achievement in the domain of academic dance'. He ended the letter on the optimistic note 'Then, too, my joy to work with you, my dear Romola, on your *film,* on the grand epoc of the *Ballets Russes* and the immortal Nijinsky.'

Romola displayed inexhaustible energy in sustaining contacts with everybody she could think of as potential stepping-stones toward keeping the name NIJINSKY in the limelight. For years, she had been in touch with her friend Ervin of the Olympia Distributing Corporation in New York. In May 1966, she had a letter from him to the effect that he had had a meeting with Goddard Lieberson, president of Columbia Records and executive vice-president of CBS, sounding out the idea of doing a Nijinsky Memorial record album together with a picture book explaining each sequence and its history as it happened. Lieberson's wife, Vera Zorina, had gone to school with Kyra. It was suggested that Romola narrate the record, and that interviews with people who still remembered Waslaw should be included in the album. They should seek to find hitherto unpublished pictures of Waslaw, herself and outstanding personalities associated with Waslaw's life. Toward the end of his letter, Ervin wrote, 'I am quite excited about this new turn, and it could make tremendous historical impact on the whole project, and the integrity of the company and the man will assure the success of this album.'

He had also discussed the film, and Lieberson had come up with the idea of a possible Broadway show which could serve as a forerunner to the long-delayed film, a production on the life of Nijinsky. Lieberson had been extremely successful in backing other shows on behalf of Columbia, such as *My Fair Lady, Camelot* and *Bye, Bye Birdie.* The producer of the latter show, Edward Padula, had of course approached Romola four years earlier on the idea of a musical about Nijinsky.

My mother had been forced to accept, albeit ungraciously, that she was now a great-grandmother. Krya's son Vaslav and his wife, who lived in Switzerland, first presented Romola with a great-granddaughter, and then a great-grandson. Romola fumed over their selection of a name for their newly-born son. She wanted him to be baptised Varoslav after The Lawgiver, one of the four princes who developed the principality of Kiev. To her disgust, the child was given the name Manfred. 'Every gigolo in Germany is called that!' she commented sourly.

Very meagre titbits drifted in from Romola from the latter part of 1966 onwards into 1967. I had the occasional terse bulletin. She was visiting all the old haunts, Capril, Pompeii, Naples, Rome, Milan, Pisa, Perugia, Assisi, Ravenna, Siena, and, of course, the obligatory Zürich. She kept imploring me to come over to Europe, the change of air and scenery would do me good. I had written to her ventilating my own problems. Both Laci and I were suffering a recurrence of ill health. I had been feeling unwell for some time. My mother expressed deep concern over the situation and begged me to have a checkup in Switzerland. She also put forward the suggestion that I go to a specialist in San Francisco, a professor well-known to her. Her apartment would be at our disposal: '*I must know ahead of time when you plan to go, so that I can advise my landlady to provide you with a key. All our valuables are in storage as a safeguard against theft but essential items such as linen, silverware, are there and you will find plenty of champagne in the bar...*'

We never did take up her offer. I trusted our doctors in Phoenix implicitly and underwent successful surgery at Christmas time. Kyra presented another kind of problem. She could not pull herself together to eke out a living. Paul had been forced to pay six months' rent for her, and our mother naturally was perturbed: '*...I am very worried; what will happen to her in her old age?*'

At the end of January, Laci came home from work one evening, deathly pale. In a barely audible voice, he asked me to call our doctor; he had severe pains in the chest. I telephoned our doctor, described the symptoms and was told to rush Laci to hospital immediately. When the physician had completed his examination, he gave us Laci's doom without preamble. 'It would be advisable if you put your affairs in order. The next eight-ten days will be critical.' God spared us that time. Laci survived his first major heart attack but when he came out from hospital he said, quietly but firmly: 'Tamara, I want to go home and visit my family. Eleven years ago we left Hungary. We have not been back since.' He had it all worked out; Kinga was now an American citizen and it would be safe for her to return and to meet her father. Laci would purchase a car in Germany and drive down through Yugoslavia to Budapest, there to revisit the old haunts and to go to his father's grave. It was to be an all-embracing tour and I hastened to write to Romola about it. She responded with alacrity:

'I am so looking forward to seeing you in Europe this summer. I have written to Laci, giving him our schedule. It would be best if we could meet in Bad Gastein where we will be from July 15th until August 30th...It is a lovely place, 1,000 metres above sea level; with its radium baths it would do you both a world of good, and we could have a wonderful time together. Do try and come...Take care, both of you, do not eat or cook anything containing animal fat. ...I have discovered a delightful grand-niece in Vienna, Judith Baroness Sebessy. She is charming, granddaughter of my cousin Baroness Henriette Szirmay (née Pulszky). If you go to Vienna, you must meet her. Judith and Kinga must become friends. In London you will be able to see Tatakaboy's choreography for 'L'Après-midi d'un Faune' in the British Museum, and, in the Costume Department of the Victoria and Albert, his wintercoat and hat. There is a beautiful private collection of his pictures and costumes at the home of Mrs Charles Gordon (Nadia Nerina), the prima ballerina of the Royal Ballet in Covent Garden. Her address is... You must also get in touch with Mrs Margaret Power...Write to her before you leave Phoenix. She knows everything and everybody in London. She has been our devoted friend for the past thirty years... Tatakaboy's exhibition is at the Musée de l'Opéra in Paris. 1 Place Charles Garnier. Only part of the collection is on display – if you want to see the entire collection, you must ask Mademoiselle Morillon there to show it to you.'

In July 1968, *The Diary of Vaslav Nijinsky*, edited by Romola Nijinsky, was published in paperback by the University of California Press. The following is a quote from the review by Nat Honig in the *Independent Press-Telegram:* 'When he wrote this diary he was near a mental breakdown. In the diary Nijinsky poured out his ideas on art, love, religion (with which he had become obsessed) and life. Lucidity and mental disturbance jostle each other constantly; it is among the most tragic of documents...It is a diary that could have been written by Gogol's Madman – yet the rational world is never entirely absent from these pages.'

A month earlier, we had embarked on our great European venture, Laci and I filled with anticipation and yearning to see the old familiar landmarks, Kinga to be reunited with her father. Romola had warned us not to be too ambitious; just come to see her in Austria, and then relax instead of galloping around Europe in a car in the aftermath of one major surgery and a heart attack. But Laci was inflexible, and it was not until much later, too late, we learned the wisdom of her words.

We arrived at Munich where we picked up a Volkswagen, and headed straight for Yugoslavia to be introduced to Laci's home town and meet some of his relatives. After a rather strained stay there, we proceeded on the road to Budapest to stay with Laci's sister.

One day, Kinga accompanied me to the Villa. It stood there still, forlorn, ravaged by its present unloving occupants, a depressing sight. The entire house had been partitioned into small, one-room flats with communal bath and kitchen. The outside of Emilia's 'palace' was in a terrible state of disrepair. We were shattered by what we witnessed. With a lump in her throat, Kinga spoke for us both, when she shrewdly observed: 'It is true when they say one should never go back.'

Then came the day I both dreaded and looked forward to, the reunion of Kinga with her father. I envisaged how I would present my lovely daughter after eleven long years, with my head held high, I the 'unfit' mother. The scenario was complete down to the last detail, how we would meet, exchange some flighty pleasantries after which I would nobly depart, leaving Kinga with Miklós, her stepmother, and her grandmother. Reality was quite different. We drove Kinga to the building where her father lived, kissed her goodbye in the lobby and watched her climb the stairs. The joyful greetings as the door opened for her reverberated down the corridors to where I stood. I learned yet another bitter lesson; people do not think nor react as I do, not even my own daughter, and also that Tamara cannot have everything in life 'her way'.

We stayed on for a time in Budapest, seeing more friends and relations, assembling together the missing pieces of bygone years. The graves were many that we visited. Kinga had by then departed by car on a tour of Austria, Germany and Belgium in the company of Miklós and Judy, her stepmother. Now, nearly two decades later, I find it extremely difficult to put down in words the emotional turbulence into which we were flung at the end of our stay. It should have been an occasion for rejoicing over meeting loved ones again after twelve years. Instead, we endured the wretchedness and envy of those who had not been as fortunate as we. We experienced the bitter hurt that those we had loved, nourished the dream of being together with once more, had changed with the political tide – perhaps their only salvation. One should not seek to revive the past; it shrinks, fades, sometimes even becomes grossly distorted.

With sadness in our hearts, Laci and I left Hungary and continued on to Czechoslovakia to stay with Laci's other sister who lived in a border town near Austria. Even there, the air was smitten by the political winds of the new era. It was piteous and frustrating to try to reason with the younger generation, to analyse the goals and actions of the mighty Soviet Union. Even Laci's young nephew accused him of distorting the facts and delivering imperialistic American propaganda. By an ironic twist of fate, the very next morning, there were reports of unrest in the vicinity of the township where we were; a flare-up that could have dangerous consequences. We both relived the inexorable terror of being hunted like animals in the wild, and bade a hasty farewell. We headed for the border as fast as we could, with the ghouls of yesterdays hot on our heels.

It was with sighs of relief we arrived at Romola's haven in Austria. I found my mother changed, more informal, more caring and gentler than I had ever known her. She had gained weight, her thin, white fingers slightly deformed indicated she was a victim of arthritis. The hair was more the colour of Hungarian paprika than ever before, but she was elegantly groomed as always, dressed in a sleeveless multicoloured shantung garment. Although she reprimanded Laci for smoking too much, she was rarely without a cigarette between her lips. Yet she could not resist lecturing us on how to live soundly. 'Health is the most important thing in life; no matter how much you need to earn money, you must settle down to a quieter life.' She turned to Laci and admonished him: 'Follow Eisenhower's example, who survived two heart attacks, and for ten years they have not recurred. Being a soldier, he knows how to discipline himself.' We had some long chats, she and I, when Laci was not present. She was in a reflective mood, as if she was trying to tell me how wrong it had been to 'deport' me at such an early age to Hungary and leave me in the care of two persons, who were already then elderly. I was overwhelmed by her manifestations of love and tenderness. I discovered that she, too, was a vulnerable human being underneath the arrogant, polished exterior.

Upon arrival, we had been briefed by Paul as to what subjects *not* to bring to the surface, and to talk about the film was taboo. She had suffered so many cruel defeats that it was not a suitable topic of conversation. She admitted she had to slow down on her travels, in fact she was reluctant to go far without Paul, and said she toyed with the idea of acquiring a small *pied-à-terre* in Switzerland. One evening over drinks Laci asked Romola if it was true that she had a house in Japan. He went on to explain why he had asked. Father Jack back in Phoenix was due to celebrate the twenty-fifth anniversary of his ordination, and his faithful flock and close friends were taking up a collection for him to visit Japan. Would it be at all feasible for him to stay at Romola's place in Kyoto? She regretted that she was unable to say yes because she had lent it to Princess Chichibu, Emperor Hirohito's sister-in-law. 'It is the retreat to which she can go when she wishes to be incognito. I hope, however, that you and Tamara will come there one day, and then perhaps bring Father Jack along, too.' Romola had countless times said how she wished she had a house of her own; the place in Kyoto had come as a total surprise to me when I first heard of it. I was filled with curiosity as to whether she actually possessed it or was it merely rented, but prudence restrained me from asking her, even face to face.

Irina confirmed that Romola did own a small house in Japan; with the exception of a modern kitchen and bathroom, it comprised the stern simplicity of a typical Japanese home. My cousin had been invited to go there on innumerable occasions but had never had the opportunity to accept the offer.

The day came when we had to take our leave. I tried to extract a date from her when she would come to see us in Phoenix but already she was busily engaged in making up her forthcoming travel plans; her buoyant spirit was back and she showed me her itinerary: Moscow, Crimea, Yalta, Leningrad, Helsinki, Munich. Incurable, insatiable bird of passage. As we said our farewells, she embraced me and promised: 'You will see. I will come!'

Our trip in search of *temps perdu* came to an end approximately two months after it began. Dispirited, Laci and I drove to Munich to deposit the car and flew to London, where we had arranged to meet Kinga. Briefly, on the night prior to Kinga's arrival, I had not had a wink of sleep. Poor Laci's health alarmed me. I implored him to let me call a doctor but he remonstrated and was in such a choleric mood, I did not dare to disobey him. I was seated by the bedside checking his pulse, when Kinga walked in. She, Miklós and Judy had taken the ferry from Ostende to Dover and driven up to London. Some warped feeling of injustice must have been gnawing away in Laci's guts. Livid with rage, he accused Kinga of not having had the decency to visit his relatives but, instead, of being with her father the entire time albeit Laci had paid her fare. He rounded off by reprimanding her for her unacceptable conduct toward me.

Throughout it all, Kinga had stood like a statue. Then, in total contrast to her normal retiring self, she unleashed a torrent in self-defence and turned to me. 'And you, Mother, on whose side are you?' In my hysterical frame of mind, I made my usual fatal mistake; I could not, would not, choose between them. Calmly, she picked up her suitcase and declared that she would stay in London. She and her father had already discussed the possibility of her moving in with friends of his there. I stormed after her, pleaded with her to return to Phoenix to finish her senior year at the University. After getting her degree, she would be free to go wherever she wished. Kinga agreed on the condition that she would be permitted to seek other lodgings immediately upon our return.

Three strangers flew back to the United States. I was crushed. By not having the courage to speak out, I felt that I had lost my only child, whom I had once fought like a tigress to keep.

457

CHAPTER 14

THE LAST YEARS OF ROMOLA

The European tour had swept us all into a whirlpool with some appalling consequences. The stony silence between stepfather and stepdaughter remained unbroken. True to her word, Kinga moved out. She went to live with Ruth and Ernie, the couple with whom she had stayed in 1965 in the aftermath of the first crisis. They were sanguine, sympathetic people, who were in a position to provide her with unbiased support at a time she sorely needed it.

To appease me and to soothe my frayed nerves after Kinga's departure, Laci contacted an estate agent. The house to which we had moved when we first arrived in Phoenix had hospitably provided us with a roof over our heads, but it was rapidly showing signs of the shoddiness that comes to structures which do not mature into relics with preservation orders slapped upon them. It was in January 1969, after numerous unsuccessful viewings, that our agent's car came to a halt in front of a fair-sized lawn, shaded by an immense carob tree. Its branches were weighed down heavily by the ripe pods nicknamed St John's Bread, filled with sweet, juicy pulp. Any lingering doubts as to whether or not we should take the property were swept away when I beheld the crystal-blue swimming pool at the rear. I could hardly breathe for sheer happiness. It was to take some time, however, before we moved in, hospitalisation yet again a deterrent to a smooth transition from one place to another.

The once so fragile relationship between my mother and myself was by now on a more substantial footing. I was able to unburden some of my deepest worries to her, the paramount one being the intransigent antagonism that my daughter harboured for Laci and vice versa, the two human beings I loved equally much, but with a different kind of love. Romola touched upon the subject at great length in an understanding letter:

> *'You are fenced in by a most difficult situation between Laci and Kinga. You are too patient, too honest, constantly sacrificing yourself...I can clearly see into your innermost soul. Too well aware of the sacrifices you made to bring Kinga out of*

Hungary to raise her in a better world. Your grandmother and Oti-Papa were to blame for much of your heartache. They were possessive, wanted to keep you for themselves. They brought you up as a true-blooded Hungarian, which you were not, this against my approval. When you completed your schooling I wanted to take you abroad... I was totally against you enrolling in the Dramatic Academy. Please do not get angry with me, but you made the greatest faux pas by marrying Miklós. He was not the right man for you. It was a pity he became Kinga's father... I fear that Kinga has turned against you, which is another reason why I thought that your trip to Hungary was insane...'

She meant well with her words of wisdom, but the past was irreversible, and I had the todays and tomorrows to grapple with.

She wrote to Kinga on October 17th, 1968, from Pontresina. It was a warm and compassionate response to a letter that Kinga had sent her on the 4th of that month.

'My dear Kinga, I am much relieved that Mr and Mrs Pieri are so kind and good to you and extend such hospitality. At least I know that you are in a pleasant and trustworthy environment. Thank them in my name, too...I was very interested in what you wrote. I regret that I did not know sooner that once before you had lived apart from Tamara and Leslie and that there was not a harmonious relationship between you and Laci bácsi (Uncle Leslie). *You were very wise to go back to Phoenix to finish your studies there. Otherwise you would have lost your many years of work and would not have a diploma, which is very important for your future. Now you have time until next Summer to think over what to do. Listen to my advice then before you make any decision. We must meet and discuss in person what is most beneficial for your future.*

I know Europe through and through, including each country's advantages and disadvantages...It is very beautiful, especially if one comes with an American passport and a stuffed wallet. It is altogether different if one wants to settle down and make a living. In European countries a work permit is required. Salaries, particularly for women, are very low. If you wish to come to study for a year or two and that is financially feasible, London or Paris would meet that need. But wherever you want to settle, you must first try out the climate, the people etcetera of the country of your choice. Everything looks better from afar. In my opinion, marriage is the best solution, if one finds a good partner. But even that is not easy. The American student marriages are absolutely awful. One should marry a man who makes a good living, comes from a good family, is cultured and trustworthy and who will provide his wife with security. To marry simply to work until the end of your days and in the meantime be both cook and Jack-of-all-trades is not worth it...Love passes, the worries remain.

Your cousin, your Aunt Kyra's son, who holds quite a high position in Geneva with the International Red Cross, wants to move to America with his wife and children and to leave his fabulous job. His only desire is to get away from petty European circumstances. You, on the other hand, want to live in Europe. I must admit I find it hard to figure all this out. What is there about Europe that you like so much?

Concerning your Édesanya (mother), I am very worried about her. You are the apple of her eye. She has only lived for you and endured every sacrifice in the past to provide you with a secure upbringing. If you were to live on another continent it would be a tremendous blow to her. This you must also consider. It hurts me deeply that after a serious surgery and with a weak constitution, she still must work. I am not even happy over the fact that she has to cook and clean house, since she was not brought up to do these tasks. But even when she was a young girl she refused to listen to my advice. I asked her to wait until the end of the War and then to come abroad with me, not to marry...now you see how it has ended... If you see your mother, tell her I would like to write to her privately. Where could I write to her so that only she will read the letter? ...Take care of yourself and write from time to time. Many kisses with much love. Meme.'

Any ambitions Kinga had evinced about wishing to settle abroad vanished the day she met John Gaspers. A quirk of fate brought them together. Their paths might never have crossed, had she not moved to her 'adopted' home. John had come down from Chicago to work for the Pieri's son-in-law. A few months after they had been introduced, John formally proposed to Kinga, and I was only too happy to give them my blessing, seeing in him the embodiment of all that a mother could wish for her daughter. He exuded masculine assurance along with good looks and a gentle manner. After their engagement, John purchased a house some ten minutes' drive from where we lived. For practical purposes, the young couple decided to wait a year before getting married. While John lodged with his parents, Kinga moved into their future home.

It was in 1969 that Romola once more announced she was coming to visit us. I arranged for a reporter from a local TV station to meet her at the airport. At first, she showed a trace of irritation over the fuss made about her when the cameras began to roll, and the interviewers barked their questions, but she soon regained her composure. I heaved a sigh of relief when she expressed delight over our house but she had barely made herself comfortable when I faced yet another inquisition about the heirlooms left by Emilia. It was an ongoing, hurtful topic of conversation that always cropped up. Romola remained inflexible regarding this abstruse issue yet I *had not* been present at the Villa when Oti-Papa was arrested nor during the ensuing chaos. It was only after her death I came to understand more fully the dreadful financial position she must have faced continuously, and how frantically she sought to find the means to unsnarl herself from a twisted web of debts. The chief purpose of Romola's visit was to become acquainted with her granddaughter's future husband. She had to swallow the 'bitter pill' that he was not the Texas millionaire she had envisaged for Kinga, but John's manliness and tact won her over. Kinga arranged a small reception in their newly acquired home, and Romola was quite impressed by what the young couple had achieved. What perhaps more than anything won her admiration and respect was the fact that they had not come to her to ask for a loan. The three-bedroom house was romantically set in a citrus grove. It was still very sparsely furnished. The wedding date had by then been set for June 6th. 1970. Years later, Romola was to remember Kinga and John in her will when she left them some of her beautiful furniture. Secretly, she must have been distressed over the meagre furnishings of Kinga's living quarters but never showed it. Only a brief comment in her 'thank-you' letter afterwards betrayed her actual feelings in the matter. She had consulted people in San Francisco experienced in the antique business, and had been told that Spanish furniture could be found very cheaply. *'I will look around myself and let you know what can be had'.*

As I recall it, my mother had expressly asked we do as little entertaining as possible. Her age was beginning to catch up with her. She had suffered a slight accident in late autumn which left her less agile. And from mid-August onward she was engrossed in aiding Richard Buckle with material and comments covering his massive tome on my father which was to be published by Weidenfeld & Nicolson in 1971. The book, simply entitled *Nijinsky*, is, to the best of my knowledge, the most comprehensive book ever written about Waslaw's artistic career.

Although frailer in body, her mental stamina was as strong as ever and she boasted of how she was now seriously tackling the writing of her two books; one, on the great ballet dancers from antiquity up to 1900. She added rather ruefully that she had been committed to Simon & Schuster on that particular project for some thirty-odd years during which time they had held the option. Flagrantly, she even admitted that they were pressing her very hard to produce the goods. She cloaked herself in self-deception, claiming she could earn as much as $100,000 on it. The other book, about which she had dropped broad hints in the past, was to dwell on Tatakaboy, and she had already decided on its tentative title, *The Private Life of Nijinsky*. She vowed that an English publishing house had requested it and were prepared to offer her an advance of £10,000. It would contain hitherto unpublished, intimate glimpses into his life. All I have been able to find is a brief summary which, condensed, reads as follows:

'The story of Vaslav Nijinsky has been discussed more than that of any dancer in history. I have written two Nijinsky biographies, the contents of which are accurate as they are based on events I have lived through with him. The Nijinsky book by Madame Françoise Reiss (Paris) is objective and also truthful. Many of the other books on Nijinsky were written from hearsay – by people who for one reason or another were not well-wishers, such as the late Mr Serge Grigorieff and Anatole Bourman...they have unwittingly or maliciously distorted Nijinsky's image. Therefore, in this new book of mine, I wish to portray Nijinsky's life in true focus. I want the new generation who have never seen him to know him as he really was...describe not only the events of his childhood, youth and adult life, his family background, his development as an interpretive and creative artist; his attitude towards life, art and politics and sex; his relations towards his friends and his enemies; his opinion about the First and Second World Wars; the Russia of the Tsars and the Soviet Union; his acquiescence to the various attempts to cure him – Prof. E. Bleuler, Prof. Krepelin, Prof. Wagner-Jauregg, Prof. A Carell, Sigmund Freud, Prof. Alfred Adler, Dr. Coué, The Christian Science Practitioners, Faith Healers and Charlatans, his pilgrimage to Lourdes.

This book will be the inside story of Nijinsky's life and of a loving and devoted couple; their attitude towards each other, towards fame, success, wealth and tragedy; their struggle against a powerful international perverted group who, resenting Nijinsky's marriage, persecuted him. In this book will emerge Nijinsky's martyrdom during the 32 years of his illness. As all people, Nijinsky had two lives – a public and a private one. I will describe, for the first time, how, after he became ill, he withdrew from the world and his art, how he really felt in his dream world. I will further describe what it means to live with a genius and a schizophrenic...'

I found the draft of a handwritten letter to Lincoln Kirstein, then Director of the New York City Ballet. It was Kirstein who had assisted her in 1930 to write her book, *Nijinsky,* which was published in 1933 by Victor Gollancz in London through the auspices of Arnold Haskell. It was the latter who originated the idea for Romola to write a book about her husband. She had lost contact with Kirstein for many years when he re-appeared indirectly, having forwarded a letter addressed to Madame Nijinsky care of the *Saturday Review* magazine. In her reply she reminded him of an episode that had taken place in an Italian restaurant in New York in 1931; how they all had sat around a table sipping *zabaione* when Romola submitted the suggestion that Kirstein should ask his ex-roommates from Harvard to help finance a project for a ballet school. '*...I want to refresh your memory...I advised you to take twelve white American, twelve negro and twelve Indian children of eight years of age, have them trained in the method of the Imperial Dancing School of St Petersburg for nine years, then you would have the nucleus of a real American ballet...*'

She had gone on to advise Kirstein to engage one or two eminent teachers from the Imperial School:

463

'Do you remember? I took you to St Petersburg to teach you all you know about the Imperial School and how we then tried to get as teachers Nicolas Legat, Tamara Karsavina, Bronislava Nijinska. They all refused... In 1933, my dear friend Lifar had a fight at the Savoy Hotel with Edward Jones, the sponsor of the ballet; the company was disbanded. Serge Lifar packed his suitcases and returned to Paris where he was ballet master.

Balanchine was left behind, ill, broke and lonely. My friend, Lya de Putty, and I took care of him. Then and there I had the brilliant idea to sell him to you as a ballet teacher. I wired you immediately, recommending George, saying that he is the biggest, the best, the most eminent teacher who ever lived-...Well, the thing clicked much to my joy, therefore George owes me his forty-one years' bread and butter, having become the ballet tsar in the United States...'

She carried on, expounding on her sentiments regarding Balanchine; that she held no grudge against him in spite of his refusal in Paris after World War II to give a benefit for the Nijinsky Foundation. Nor did she harbour any hard feelings because he had produced *L'Après-Midi d'un Faune* although he was fully aware that a valid contract existed with the Society of Authors in Paris, signed by Claude Debussy and Waslaw Nijinsky as co-authors, whereby Debussy granted all choreographic rights to Waslaw – dividing the royalties equally between them.

'...The French Courts in Marseille gave a judgment recently to Massine in his favour, stating his contract for the ballet 'Tricorne', signed as co-author with de Falla in 1920, is valid and nobody has the right to choreograph a different version of the ballet without Massine's permission which he can refuse... exactly similar to the Debussy 'Faune' contract...

The Jerome Robbins version of 'Faune' is an infringement of Nijinsky's copyright, so much the more as according to international law all literary, music or ballet works, if written down, are copyrighted. I presume you probably ignore the fact that Vaslav has written down by his own hand with his system of notation the choreographic score of 'Faune' which in 1950 I donated to the British Museum...a copy of which is at the Bolshoi Theatre Museum...'

This letter to Kirstein finished on a somewhat dissonant note. She wrote that it was harder to forgive and forget the fact that neither Balanchine nor he came to Waslaw's funeral, lamely excusing themselves that they had rehearsals to attend to. The last line reads: *'I just told myself that Mozart fared worse than Vaslav because Wolfgang Amadeus was taken to his mass grave in Vienna unaccompanied.'*

She went back to San Francisco, recharged with some of her old zest, eagerly looking forward to a new decade which would also mark her eightieth birthday. Paul and she had decided that they would move to Europe indefinitely, and Paul had already been busy making the necessary preparations while she was with us. Leaving only the skeleton supply of household goods and furniture in the apartment, they locked the door, destined never to return together.

Romola entered yet another phase of a nomadic existence. I received a letter from her dated March 31st, 1970, enclosing a photograph of Pope Paul VI. Easter had come early that year and she had spent it in Rome. She was filled with admiration for the Holy Father and spoke of his miraculous powers.

'Holy Week was storylike...a phenomenal pageant, all pomp. On Holy Thursday, after the evening Mass in St Peter's, they displayed part of the sword used by a Roman soldier to pierce Christ, also part of the crucifix, and Veronica's scarf with which she wiped the perspiration from Christ. On Easter Sunday I received the Holy Communion. It was unforgettable. Here, God truly comes close to man. After Mass, the Pope spoke beautifully about peace. There were millions of people in front of the Basilica... We had good seats close to the Pope, and hence we were able to see everything very well. First we had a guided tour of St Peter's but then a cardinal, who is a friend of Pali's, showed us parts not open to the general public. On Sunday, I am travelling to Florence to see Bronia for a couple of days. She is currently there together with her daughter Irotschka to supervise one of her ballets for the local opera, for the Maggio Musicale. Afterwards, we are going on to Zürich to stay at the St Gotthard Hotel. I have to be in London on the 16th and at the end of April in Paris. God willing, on May 10th we will go to Vienna for three weeks...'

When in London she usually stayed at her favourite hotel, the Cavendish. Her main objective on that trip was to read through Richard Buckle's manuscript, and to make comments and suggest alterations where appropriate. It was a daunting task but one which she tirelessly devoted herself to. Anything to do with ballet, and Waslaw in particular, was like elixir to her. But she was quoted as saying in an interview at the hotel: 'I have so much to do and not enough time.' The staff adored her because she was forever joking and laughing with them. She admitted to dyeing her hair red and only ordered tomato juice to drink, 'because I am on a diet since this morning.' In spite of her hectic programme she managed to squeeze in a performance of the Polish Mime Ballet at Sadlers Wells, which she said was magnificent.

The highlight of her stay was undoubtedly watching on television Waslaw's equine namesake, Nijinsky, the 2,000 Guineas winner, in the racing season's first classic. She thrilled to see the headline 'Nijinsky leaps into turf role'. She could not refrain from placing a bet, and when she won a modest sum, she cried out 'Waslaw has paid me.'

Once more, rumours and counter-rumours had surfaced as regards Rudolf Nureyev portraying Nijinsky. In *The Times Diary,* August 14th, 1969, it had been stated that Romola was displeased with the idea; that when she had been to Moscow three years earlier it had been decided that several of the Kirov Ballet Company's dancers should play Nijinsky's part: for instance, Soloviev in *Carnaval,* Vassiliev in *L'Après midi d'un Faune* and that the veteran Sergeyev should portray Nijinsky in his latter years. Romola stressed how much she admired Nureyev but that he was not in any way like her husband.

The following day, *The Diary* reported that Edward Bond of *Saved* and *Early Morning* was to write the script of the biography.

On March 10th, 1970, the *San Francisco Chronicle* revealed that Tony Richardson would direct the film version of Nijinsky's life with Nureyev playing the part. The only question then raised was as to who would take on the role of Diaghilev. Harry Saltzman reappeared on the scene and declared that he would produce the film, yet again with Nureyev in the lead role. He was quoted as saying that he was totally indifferent to the 'jinx which had befogged Madame Nijinsky's previous efforts.' On April 24th, he declared in the same paper that Edward Albee, the Pulitzer Prize-winning playwright, was going to write the screenplay.

466

Romola wrote to me that she wished to 'push' Auntie Bronia to be the leading choreographer of the forthcoming film. She also repeated her earlier wish that she herself be played by the Baroness Judith Sebessy. She described Judith as a very beautiful twenty-three year old, who commanded perfect English. Judith was the granddaughter of Harriet Pulszky.

The inglorious end to this film saga was not to come until two years after Romola's death and I can only be humbly grateful that both my parents were spared the sufferance of having to see this gross misinterpretation of facts. It stretched beyond the realm of credulity, and some of the finest names in the world of art were wasted, to name but a few; George de la Peña (Waslaw Nijinsky), Alan Bates (Sergei Diaghilev), Leslie Brown (Romola de Pulszky), Jeremy Irons (Mikhail Fokine), Anton Dolin (Maestro Cecchetti), Carla Fracci (Tamara Karsavina).

Gilbert Adair in the *Monthly Film Bulletin* spared no punches. The film *Nijinsky*, based on *Nijinsky* by Romola Nijinsky and *The Diary of Vaslav Nijinsky* edited by Romola Nijinsky, was made by Hera Products for Paramount. The executive producer was Harry Saltzman, the director, Herbert Ross. The reviewer gives a lengthy, in-depth analysis of the contents, too detailed to repeat here, but I cannot refrain from selecting a few passages toward the end.

'Hugh Wheeler's screenplay admirably conjures the suffocating world of high-powered ballet, the camping in hotels and staterooms, the petty and more significant jealousies and, in particular, the unorthodox sexual mores. Almost from the opening shot, in fact, homosexuality is treated as the (second) most natural thing in the world...and the film firmly resists the temptation to portray Romola as anything but a spoiled young woman, who, in lieu of possessing talent, determines to marry it. (Leslie Brown's groupie-like Romola de Pulszky, suggesting neither the formidable young heiress who wrested Nijinsky from his lover, nor, potentially, the devoted wife who nursed him through thirty years of mental illness). Onstage... Ross hardly puts a foot right: the ballet sequences themselves are uniformly disastrous. Not only does he disfigure pointlessly *Le Spectre* with slow-motion dissolves but he actually cuts in the middle of Nijinsky's legendary leap...and *Le Sacre du Printemps* is interrupted as much by Ross' clumsy reaction shots as by its scandalised audience. But these lapses pale into insignificance beside the moment when, as Nijinsky all but rapes Romola during the voyage to Buenos Aires, Stravinsky's revolutionary rhythms blast from the soundtrack; and, throughout, the film attempts to establish a spacious equation between the dancer's growing schizophrenia and the modernist violence of the music he dances to. It is unfortunate, too, that a film bearing his name should so complacently subscribe to the received idea of Nijinsky as an unstable and incompetent choreographer, when his innovations have clearly been the source of much contemporary ballet.'

Romola Nijinsky's epitaph could well have read 'The hope I dreamed of was a dream, was but a dream; and now I wake, exceeding comfortless, and worn, and old, for a dream's sake.' (Christina Rossetti: *Mirage*). It sums up her losing battle to illuminate Waslaw's fame to a younger generation via the media of film.

My mother was incorrigible on the subject of lost 'treasures' which she would not allow to lie dormant. When she planned to visit Hungary in 1970, she appended the following paragraph to a letter:

'With whom did you leave the bracelet left for me by your grandmother in both of her wills? It is a circlet of gold with the Lily of Bourbon set with a ruby cabochon. It was given to Mama by the Duke d'Aumale, who was the son of King Louis Philippe. I wish to collect it when I go to Budapest. With whom were the Pulszky paintings left? Grandmother's portrait...? Let me know. Where is the Renaissance watch that Mama left for Kyra?...'

This incessant niggling preyed on my nerves, but I tried to dismiss the whole insoluble issue from my mind, concentrating instead on Kinga's wedding, which had been set for June 6th. I was determined to plan ahead so as to make her big day perfect. Romola was steeped in business engagements in London, Paris and Vienna but reiterated how happily she would be waiting for the arrival of Kinga and John on their honeymoon. She congratulated me on switching my profession from teacher to that of librarian. *'This is less tiring than teaching. Ilus's husband just completed library studies, and he is now working as a librarian at Berkeley University...'*

Kinga and John embarked on their honeymoon. John had not been to Europe previously and Kinga was delighted at the thought of acting as his cicerone. They flew to Milan where they rented a car. After a grand tour of Austria and Germany, they headed for Switzerland to join Romola on the last leg of their journey. She had arranged for them to stay at her favourite hotel in Zürich before proceeding to Vulpera close to the Italian border. Romola and Paul greeted them with warmth and showered them with that genuine old-world hospitality Romola had inherited from Emilia, I will not linger in detail over their visit; suffice to say, a very contented young couple returned to Phoenix shortly afterwards.

In the aftermath of their stay with Romola, I received some

rather droll comments from her. She rebuked me for having so lavishly spent money on Kinga's wedding, and I should not have invited the entire Hungarian colony in Phoenix. In the same breath she told me how Tatakaboy always used to say one should stretch one's spending only as far as your blanket stretches, never incur debts, but forget half of the income and put it to one side for a rainy day. Yet she had the audacity to end her moral little tale thus: *'Well, dear Tatakaboy, I am not doing it.'*

In late August, Romola went to London once more, this time to see Aunt Bronia and Irina. Bronia was there to choreograph Waslaw's original version of *L'Après-midi d'un Faune* for the Kirov Ballet who were on tour in England. *'We will save Tatakaboy's most beautiful ballet for posterity because Kirov will add it to its repertoire and Lenfilm will film it...'* According to Robert Mead, who for years worked in close collaboration with Bronia, this performance was cancelled after a few rehearsals. From London, Romola planned to go to Biarritz for three weeks and then on to Paris because on October 4th, Nijinsky, the wonder horse of the century, would be running at Longchamps and she had been invited to lead him around the course after the race. She prayed he would win, as always.

Romola became more and more dependent upon Paul.

'Paul is very fond of Kinga and John; they understand each other well...he is a generous angel toward everybody and carries me in the palm of his hand. I give thanks to God that in my old age I am not alone, that I have someone who spoils me, defends me, is on my side through good and bad. This is God's reward to me because I stood by Tatakaboy for thirty-two years during his illness.'

It was only when they had to travel their separate ways because of business affairs or other commitments that they ever were apart. And even then, they kept close through their correspondence, proof of how much deeper Romola's feelings for Paul had grown with the years. She was profoundly grateful to him for his undying love and devotion, and rated highly his financial support. The tone of her letters became increasingly familiar, often addressing him as 'Daddy' and signing them *utálatos persona* or 'Mommy'. Some of the letters that I found among her papers were so intimate, so revealing in the very nature of the contents, they must, in all decency, remain sacred to the dead.

Bronislava's daughter, Irina, tells how assiduous Paul had been in acting as a stand-in companion and nurse to Waslaw whenever needed. Romola would have been at a loss coping without him at her side.

Just as with Waslaw, Paris was to remain her great love, going back to those first years when she had studied there and come home to show off her Napoleonic treasures to Tessa. During September, October, she had been busily working on her manuscript 'The Great Dancers', gathering material from the Opera Museum and Library. She never tired of going the rounds to all the cultural attractions. She sounded almost intoxicated when she described the various exhibitions she had seen; Janet (Jean) Clouet, a skilled miniature painter at the Court of King Francis I; Goya on show in the Orangerie of Tuileries Palace. Memories must have flooded back to her, too, of the many occasions that she and Waslaw strolled through galleries on whose walls hung the famous paintings of the centuries.

She wrote to me that she intended to pursue her quest for a house either in Zürich or Geneva. All of a sudden, she desperately longed for roots. Christmas she hoped to spend in Venice together with Bronia and Irina. And to partake in the celebration of Bronia's eightieth birthday.

On the whole, her communiqués in 1970 and throughout 1971 were mostly related to health matters, almost to the point of excessiveness. She had shared our intense alarm when it was discovered Kinga had to have exploratory surgery. Simultaneously, John found himself without a job. They went through a miserable and critical spell in their new life together. But as good fortune would have it, surgery revealed Kinga's condition to be benign and John obtained a better position.

Romola kept admonishing me to eat better, to rest as much as possible. She advocated fresh food, masses of vegetables and fruit and to abstain from tinned and frozen food. Sadly, after a long silence, I had a letter from her dated January 27th 1971, relating her own misfortune. She was happy that I was in good health, having followed her advice, but that she had been unable to reply sooner as she had been taken seriously ill in Vienna; a haemorrhage of the intestine which had become progressively worse and forced her to enter hospital in Rome. It was incomprehensible to her because her semi-annual checkup in October had shown her to be in good health. Now, the doctors had found her blood condition to be alarming, and she had been given cortisone tablets. She claimed she was being tortured, and on the whole sounded miserable. She had had to cancel her visit to Bronia over Christmas and was too exhausted to carry on with her book. She complained that Bronia was working herself to death, having had three strenuous engagements in Europe during 1970; young Vaslav was unwell and could only work part-time although he was saddled with responsibility for his own family; Lily Márkus had written that they were struggling along somehow to make ends meet. All communication between Kyra and herself had temporarily snapped. My sister had obviously tired of our mother's sermons, however well meant. Romola wailed: *'She is treating me like her enemy'*. Still she could not contain her anxiety. Had I heard from Kyra recently? Why did she insist on giving all those cocktail parties? Romola felt strongly that Kyra had ruined her own life and that she was past redemption. She beseeched me to keep in touch, if only with a postcard to give her the latest tidings. She sounded pathetically lonely.

By April, however, she had conquered her negative mood and once more she drew up a travel itinerary to include Nepal, China and Egypt the following year. She and Paul had spent Easter in Davos and their immediate plans after that were to go to Vienna, then to Tyrol until the middle of July when they would proceed to their usual haunt, Bad Gastein. She had resumed working on her two books. Behind her back, Paul had purchased a small house in Meran. His choice of location had upset her; she loathed the place as she was certain that the whole of Italy had been infiltrated by communism. But it was said the house was beautiful – Paul called it a castle – and it could constitute a base for her to unpack some of her many trunks scattered far and wide on the Continent.

It was heartrending to read of her ardent desire to settle down once and for all. Pierce Street had been the nearest to the home life she now strove for. The flat was to be dismantled once and for all. Paul was to go over in the autumn to finalise the arrangements, and to select the pieces of furniture to be shipped to Italy. She generously offered Kinga and myself the residue of the furniture. That she was in a dilemma was clear. The property in Meran had to be renovated and constant strikes made the prospects of moving in that year very bleak. She cried out for a home base of her own, having switched her preference to Paris. *'It would put to an end to being fed in restaurants and living in hotels, which is so boring.'* Switzerland was by now out of the question as property prices there had soared above her means. In a downcast moment she even wrote to John and asked him to find her a house either in Phoenix or Scottsdale. *'You know my taste. We require a large living-room, three bedrooms, two bathrooms. If there is a small study, even better. We need an ultra-modern kitchen. And a dining-room because I do not like to eat in the kitchen. I would prefer it if the garden was shaded by palms or other trees, and if it had a swimming-pool.'*

Barely had Romola regained her *sang-froid*, when she was plagued by arteriosclerosis in her right knee, or so it was said. Kinga received a letter from Paul in which he explained the pain made it impossible for her to walk. She had contacted doctors in Baden bei Zürich, who specialised in rheumatic ailments. A series of shortwave treatments only served to increase her agony. She then went to the Stadt Hospital in Zürich where she was given cortisone injections. Two-and-a-half months and 800 Swiss francs later – according to her – the doctor had had enough of her and recommended she return to Bad Gastein and the warm baths there. She described what transpired in a hilariously witty letter. There an entirely different diagnosis was given, and after an assortment of injections, she was ordered to 'walk, no matter how much it hurts, keep walking.' And walk she did, for weeks onward, only to wake up one morning to find her leg hanging from the bed like a limp rag. Paul became alarmed and demanded that an X-ray be taken. It showed that Romola had been walking about with a broken hip. When he learned of it, her regular doctor deserted her, vanished into thin air, according to Romola, and she took to her bed. On this particular occasion Paul and she had rented an apartment in Reitlweg, and Paul was rushing around like a demented soul, playing the part of shopper, cleaner, cook and nurse, while at this same time telephoning all the Swiss and German clinics for advice. In Romola's own words:

> ...they stated flatly I should not go to Ulm, or Freiburg, or München. Finally, one clinic said an immediate operation was necessary. Due to the weather, I could not be flown out by helicopter and a nine-hour trip by car was out of the question. I

decided upon the First Aid Clinic near Bad Gastein, where they performed thousands of operations a year on victims of skiing accidents. The operation was successful, thanks to the support of the Infant of Prague and Tatakaboy, although why I had to be so ill only to be saved, I do not know. Both the surgeon and Paul declared I behaved like a heroine...It was said, however, when I cam to from the anaesthetic, I threw the entire medical staff and the nurse from my room; they considered that a good sign. I had to stay in hospital for several weeks. The food was miserable but thanks to Paul, who brought me pâté de foie gras, Hungarian salami and French cognac, I did not starve...Seventeen days after surgery, the stitches were removed and the doctors were amazed how well I was progressing. I am certain this is due to my ballet training...'

Although her tone throughout this ordeal had been amazingly buoyant, she did have to face up to a new situation of being slightly handicapped and forced to use a cane. This did not impede her writing, though, nor distract her mind from *The Film*. She kept chasing Harry Saltzman about his plans:

'When do you intend to produce the Nijinsky film? I am anxious to know when you require my services. If a script is going to be written, please send the writer first to me as I am the only person who can give him the necessary information about my husband and myself. May I suggest you engage Lucchino Visconti as the director. He is a superb artist and nobody could handle my story better than he. As regards the casting, I beg you to take Paul Scofield as Diaghilev. he will be magnificent. The dance sequences should be performed by the Kirov Ballet from Leningrad and Nijinsky should be danced by the twenty-two years old Mikhail Baryshnikov, the greatest living dancer and actor...'

She had been given to understand that a member of Saltzman's staff had attempted to acquire some material for the film from the Opera Museum and the National Archives but insisted that this should not be done without her permission. She finished the letter with her assurance she would do everything to help make the film not only a big box office success but an artistic film that would win

Oscars and a prize at the Cannes International Festival. When the rights were sold to Saltzman, Romola had in actual fact been appointed artistic adviser but her services were never used.

Romola's maternal feelings stirred. When I wrote to her that I had been unable to locate Kyra during one of my infrequent visits to San Francisco, she bombarded me with questions about my sister. *'Don't you have her address? Isn't it in the 'phone book? What is she living on? How are things going for her? I want to know how she is but you must use complete discretion; she must not find out that I want to know. I would like to help her without her being aware that I am her saviour behind such an action.'* She carried on about having sent me a wild mink cape and that her next port of call would be Athens via Dalmatia.

Fragments of a letter written to her agent on November 25th, 1971, reveal that Romola was unable to produce the finished manuscript of her new Nijinsky book by the stipulated deadline. She excused it this time by voicing her opinion that Richard Buckle's book should have the limelight, at least until the following year. She intended her new book to be sensational, startling. She was to clarify her aim more precisely in a later letter:

'It is not, must not be a biography. It is written more in the manner of Malreaux's antimemoir. Half of the book is written in the first person. It is Vaslav himself who tells his story about his art, life, and his social and political opinions, recreated after his own notes on the various subjects, and his statements to friends, colleagues, physicians, nurses etc...The second part is my story which has never been told.'

It must have been galling to her literary agent and the publishers to swallow postponement after postponement of this much-heralded intimate insight into a 'legend'. Always for a different reason. At the end of 1972, Romola wrote: 'Now, my dearest Eric, don't jump to the ceiling and don't curse me...You know I almost died in January 1971...' And then she went on to expatiate on her various ailments amidst profuse apologies. 'I am a reliable person who has always kept my promises to my producers and publishers. I realise you have been a perfect angel in the matter and that our new pubishers...are very patient and understanding but I am in a mess now, and you simply have to bail me out of an awkward situation. I know the book was expected by the end of 1971 and then in December 1972. Well, my dearest Eric, I won't be ready. I cannot hand out a book which is not 100% good...Some of the illustrations are in San Francisco, others in Leningrad...My doctor does not allow me to overstrain myself...I will need time at least until Easter...Therefore, I leave it up to you and him (the publisher) to decide either to give me some time or to release me from the contract.'

The year 1972 offered a mixture of personal loss and of a certain measure of triumph. As regards the former, Aunt Bronia died of a heart attack in Los Angeles on February 22nd. Ironically, six weeks prior to Bronislava's death, Romola had finally succeeded in tracking down the ballet dancer Hideo Fukagawa through the courtesy of the Japanese Consulate General in Zürich. Apparently, he was on a two-year contract with the Stadt Theater in Stuttgart.

Unremittingly, she had refused to surrender the idea of a film being made of *L'Après-midi d'un Faune*, and her letter to Fukagawa clearly indicates that Bronia was in collusion with her.

'I have been searching for you all over Europe during the past weeks. We want to know if you would be interested to dance the Faun...The ballets (Nijinsky's) *Faun* and *Jeux* are going to be filmed in Germany early in June. Our aim is not only to show the ballets in their original form but also to preserve them for future generations. My sister-in-law, Bronislava Nijinska, is coming over in the Spring to rehearse and present *The Afternoon of a Faun* and *Jeux*...If you are interested to dance Faun, which I sincerely hope, please let me know at once...I will then put you in direct contact with the manager of the film company to make you an offer for the contract. My sister-in-law is anxious to have a dancer whose image is similar to my husband's and I feel you are the one...Naturally, we will do all we can to fill our schedule for the rehearsals with your other commitments. The actual shooting of the film must take place during June...'

Despite her aspirations and high plans Romola was cheated of fulfilment yet again, this time by Bronislava's death.

Romola had always expressed her admiration and respect for

Waslaw's sister. She proclaimed Bronia was one of the greatest and most prolific choreographers with some sixty-odd ballets to her credit. To my consternation, I was to learn that this feeling had not been reciprocated. Bronislava had confided to Robert Mead on the occasion that they were mounting *Les Noces* and Lifar's *La Giaconda* in Italy that she had distrusted Romola on a number of issues and could never rid herself of the feeling that Romola had been partly to blame for Waslaw's insanity. But she had exclaimed that 'blood was thicker than water', i.e. that she would never dream of letting any member of the family down. On one occasion she had even paid Romola's fare to Florence when the latter was temporarily out of funds. It was therefore distressing to learn that when the roles yet again were reversed prior to Bronia's death, Romola showed the same lack of compassion as those many years ago in 1921. According to Irina, her mother was going through a difficult phase financially during the period leading up to the filming of *The Faun* in Germany, and she had swallowed her pride and written to Romola, asking for an advance. Romola sent a curt reply by return that she was unable to comply with her request. Irina kept the letter from her mother, who died a few days later. Then a cable arrived from Romola. Opening it, Irina assumed it was a message of condolence. Instead it read 'Mail back Faune notations.'

Margaret Power died of cancer the same year. Whether their close friendship had weathered the storms, and she and Romola were still in communication up to Margaret Power's death, I am unable to say. She was a very down-to-earth, warm and giving woman, who had devotedly stood by Romola and Waslaw.

On the whole, however, it was a fairly rewarding year for Romola because during most of it she was to experience the euphoria of seeing the name Nijinsky in the headlines once more. She kept careful track of how many copies of Buckle's book were selling, and was likewise delighted that her own book had been published in paperback after forty years. She called upon me, not once but on numerous occasions, to purchase copies for future use. Another important event was the arrival of the highly controversial Belgian ballet, *Nijinsky, Clown of Dance,* choreographed and produced by Maurice Béjart and performed by his company throughout the capitals of Europe before it came to New York in late October. The damning critics she spurned. What did they matter? Others realised what a masterpiece Béjart had created. The inner voice of Nijinsky dominated the stage; his genius as a dancer through the portrayal of his most famous roles, and, of course, his religious belief, his closeness to God. Had he not written in his notebook: *'I appear as a clown to make myself better understood. I think that a clown is only perfect when he expresses love, otherwise he is no longer a clown of God...'* To Romola, it had been a supreme moment when she witnessed the performance at the 5,000 seat Palais des Sports in Paris.

The happiness she enjoyed was somewhat soured by a dispute over royalties. She had agreed to the use of certain phrases from Waslaw's *Diary* but did not mince her words that the contract covering 2% of the gross had not been honoured. She called Mr H, who had been responsible for drawing up the terms of the contract, impertinent. 'He does not seem to realise that I am a living person, my life story is not public domain. He had no right to put me on the stage unless I authorised him to do so... It does not interest me what their expenses are in connection with the production. H & L do not behave like business people but like gypsies.'

I did not have the good fortune to see the ballet but via the media I was able to follow its triumphant course on the stages of the world, not least its reception at Madison Square Garden's Felt Forum. Zealously, I scanned through all the critiques and studied every picture I came across. Romola's open-minded acceptance of Béjart's avant-garde interpretation of Waslaw's talent and soul was all the more astonishing taking into consideration that she was then in her eighties and could rightfully have been thought to be steeped in the traditions of the past.

So much stirred that year around the name Nijinsky. Lincoln Kirstein was the compiler of a superb picture book entitled *Nijinsky Dancing*, which presented my father's career through the use of many fascinating photographs.

Almost voraciously, Romola grasped every opportunity to partake in material written about her Waslaw. She became deeply involved in assisting the medical profession pursuing their search for the key to Nijinsky's mental breakdown. She took upon herself to correct the manuscript written by a certain Joseph Lyon, psychiatric professor at several West Coast universities. This book was to be published in 1973 under the title *The Case of Nijinsky*. Certainly, she must have felt that time was running out, and consequently she persisted in attempting too much.

For instance, in April she wrote how she was grappling with yet another lawsuit against Stravinsky. She now accused him of having stolen Tatakaboy's royalties from *Sacre du Printemps,* going as far back as 1913.

> *'This is a small fortune. The French courts ruled that the contract signed in 1913 entitled Tatakaboy to half of the royalties from Stravinsky and Debussy (The 'Jeux' Ballet), no matter if the works are performed in the guise of TV, radio, gramophone, concerts…because these two works of art are the result of collaboration… Hence correspondence with the attorneys, the Société des Auteurs and Société des Editeurs de Musique etc, not to forget my correspondence with Russia, such as the Ministry of Culture, the Sovkino Lenfilm Company, the Leningrad Ballet Company, the Leningrad Ballet School; museums, the University of Cambridge, the media of Paris and London: Paris Match, London Times, the Observer etc etc…'*

She went on to remind me that she had written to János Kádár regarding the Villa on Hidegkuti Street in Budapest. According to unverified reports, private property was slowly being returned to their owners but she still failed to get the Prime Minister to agree to her proposal to establish the Villa as a rest home for retired and convalescent Hungarian and Russian dancers.

> *'You must understand… I am unable to pursue private correspondence since I have only two hands and one Hungarian royal brain!'*

Despite her frenetic involvement in the revival of Waslaw's fame, Romola did not wholly abandon her interest in her family. She was grateful when I succeeded in my endeavour to locate Kyra and to win her confidence, so that she would not feel deserted or completely alone in the world. My sister had a small flat in the less fashionable quarters of San Francisco. Part of one room had been converted into a studio. She was earnestly involved in painting with emphasis on portraits. Profoundly religious in an explosively extrovert manner, her faith dominates not only her painting but also her poetry. When we were together, she unburdened her heart to me about wishing to go back to Europe. When this was brought to

Romola's attention, however, she saw to it that her eldest daughter's plans were thwarted, begging me to keep my own counsel in the matter, an unenviable situation for me because I felt a deep attachment for my sister. Our mother explicitly made it clear that she did not wish Kyra to come under any circumstances, as with her tornado-like temperament, she would make life unbearable. *'I need absolute quiet and simply could not stand it.'*

In all fairness, Romola required her share of solitude to cope with her innumerable commitments, added to which her nailed hip, as she called it, gave rise to much discomfort. She had to go to hospital every two weeks for treatment to build up her bone structure ruined by the cursed cortisone. She experienced another mishap on a visit to Hamburg; slipped while emerging from a bath and ended up once more in a hospital bed for some weeks. To make matters worse, Paul had stumbled on the street on one of his daily visits to her and broken his ankle.

One grave problem Romola had to resolve was her reinstatement as a permanent resident in the United States. When she departed in March 1970, her return permit was valid up to March 1972. Due to the hip operation and ensuing treatments, she had been unable to go back in time. In January 1972, she had requested the San Francisco Immigration Office to automatically renew her permit in view of her ill health. They had replied they were not in a position to grant her request. Indomitably, she sat down and typed a letter to President Nixon, introducing herself as the widow of the late Vaslav Nijinsky, the world-famous dancer. After the preliminary paragraph, she went on to say how in 1940 she had obtained permission from Congress for her husband to enter the United States thanks to the assistance of Eleanor Roosevelt and Laurence Steinhardt; how most unfortunately the visit had not transpired. 'After my husband's death in 1950 I decided to settle in California. With the help of the late President Dwight Eisenhower, I applied for a "Special Bill". My sponsors were Senator Lehmann of New York and the Hon. Frances P Bolton of Cleveland. The 83rd Congress granted my request and I was admitted to the U.S.A. as "permanent resident".' She went into detail about her current plight and the Immigration Office's refusal. 'In my great need, I am turning to you, dear Mr President, to help me to be reinstated as "permanent resident" to the U.S.A.'

In a letter to Father Jack in September 1972, she reported victoriously: 'Please vote for Nixon. He was most kind to me. I wrote to him asking him to reinstate me as a "permanent resident"...He fulfilled my request and wished me a speedy recovery. All this, two days before he left for Russia. I think it was very decent of him.'

In September, Romola was in Biarritz, staying at the Miramar Hotel, seeking fresh sea air and peace to work. Her schedule was again crammed with appointments in Paris and London. For Christmas she planned to go to Cape Town and in February 1973 she had been invited to stay with friends in Egypt. But she confided to Father Jack that her most important engagement was to return to Lourdes to thank the Virgin Mary for saving her from death on two occasions during the past years.

Romola's spells of silence grew longer and longer, and we in Phoenix faded into the background, not an incomprehensible factor, taking into consideration the well-nigh Herculean workload she was encumbered with. Her massive letter-writing on ballet alone sufficed for a normal working day with or without a secretary. For instance, there was an extensive exchange of letters between her and Vera Krasovskaya, who was working on a biography about Nijinsky which was published in Leningrad in 1974, and later in the United States in 1979. Romola was in close touch with Natalia R, who lived in the Soviet Union and who conscientiously ran errands for her in Moscow, kept her up-to-date with happenings in ballet circles and made certain that Waslaw's costumes from *Spectre de la Rose* were well preserved in addition to his Notes on Notation and other vital documents which she had donated to the Bolshoi Ballet Museum in Leningrad.

There must have been countless occasions when she found herself submerged in piles of unanswered mail, both personal and business. For example, among those Romola contacted when she had the idea to write her book on famous dancers of the past was Waslaw's half-sister, Thomas Nijinsky's daughter, Marina Nijinskaya Bolito, Marina had been delighted to hear that her father was to be included in the book and had gone into a detailed account of his incredible skill as both dancer and ballet master. She extolled his abilities, claiming no dancer before or since had been able to execute *sissonne ouverte* with *entrechat huit*. He would make twelve pirouettes and finish with an arabesque. His execution of the pirouettes was all the more unusual in that he would press his chin against his chest, thus maintaining his head immobile.

'I could write endlessly about my father as I loved him dearly and I can very clearly recall my childhood. Father was a truly good man and was much loved by ballet people. They never paid attention to his temperamental outbursts. Father could not tolerate lies. He would literally fly in the air if people started to relate stupid untruths.' She ended on a more bitter note 'I have no tears to spare for Bronislava as she offended me deeply. She should rest in peace.' Marina spoke only Russian and had had her letter translated into German. As late as December 26th, 1972, Romola had not acknowledged receipt of any letters because a *crie de coeur* was sent on that date from Natalia: 'I have telephoned your relative Marina Fominichna Bolito-Nijinskaya to give her your new address. Both she and her son are very much concerned that you have not answered their two letters, so please write to them soon. You can write in French or German or any language you choose – they can always get the letter translated.' Marina was by then a widow, her husband having died suddenly of a heart attack. She had confided in her letter to Romola that she had a small group of children to whom she taught choreography, a labour of love for the sake of the arts as it was wholly unpaid but it was also good for her physical and mental well-being.

With great expectations, Romola embarked upon collaboration with Robin Maugham, nephew of Somerset, to write a play about Waslaw. It was to be based not only on her two previous books but on new material from her forthcoming volume. Then, like a thunderbolt, came the news that Sir Terence Rattigan was commissioned by the BBC to write a play based on Richard Buckle's book *Nijinsky*. And that the television rights belonged to the BBC. Shattered to the core, she assailed first of all Sir Terence, demanding that he withdraw from the project. His reply was most conciliatory, explaining that he had no idea when accepting the BBC's suggestion of making a TV play out of Buckle's book, he was infringing copyright, and he gallantly 'capitulated', and offered to withdraw.

Momentarily, Romola's mind was set at rest. Sir Terence's play would have included not only Waslaw's career but his private life as well. And hers, too. She objected violently to any mention of her private life: *'I am very much alive.'* She had been given to understand that when she provided material for Buckle's book, she had never given clearance for use in any other medium. She felt strongly that if the BBC went ahead, it would mean annihilation of 'her' play: neither she nor Lord Maugham had found a producer as yet.

Pressure was brought to bear upon Sir Terence. BBC reminded him that he was under contract to them, and that Romola did not have a case. According to an interview in the *Daily Express*, Sir Terence was quoted as saying: 'I shall have to tread carefully and trust that she (Madame Nijinsky) cannot sue me.... In my script I intend to treat Madame Nijinsky very sympathetically.'

In *London Day by Day* (The *Daily Telegraph,* July 16th, 1973) it was announced that although Robin Maugham had recently suffered a heart attack in Bombay, he was to commence work on the Nijinsky play and that he would be moving to a hotel in Bad Gastein in early August to facilitate close co-operation with Madame Nijinsky. When questioned as to who was to play the leading role, he had replied he only knew it would have to be someone with a dancer's body. 'He has already decided on a completely empty stage with a backcloth on which film can be projected. He also intends to include a great deal of music.'

Romola had her own views regarding whom to get to assume Waslaw's role and tried to interest Oscar Werner, the German actor.

Surprisingly, only one play had ever previously been produced on Waslaw. A brief notice in *Variety,* dated July 11th, 1973, showed that Charles Bruce Milholland, who wrote the original *Twentieth Century,* had written a play about Niijinsky simply entitled *Fawn.* It was presented in Indianapolis, USA, in 1935.

Romola still pledged that her third and most sensational Nijinsky book would see the light of day. Bad Gastein was now her headquarters for prolonged periods of time. She kept meticulous tabs on the royalties that should come in from the *Nijinsky, Clown of Dance* seasons in Brussels, Paris, London, even down to the prevailing rates of exchange and in a series of eruptive letters both to 'the accused', and to those who she hoped would provide professional guidance, she ventilated her case that she was being swindled.

With naked sarcasm she referred to Saltzman. 'He has the very bad habit, utterly un-British, of not answering any of my letters. Anyhow, I hear through his Swiss jeweller, where he buys diamonds for his wife, that he had a stroke last year but that he is awaiting anxiously for me to go to the Great Beyond, because then he can produce the Nijinsky picture without any interference from me and make a real Hollywood nightmare.' Her prognostication was to prove right.

In April, she wrote to her close friends, Blanche and Eric Glass, begging them to come over to the Stollen in August when she would be back from various travels. She was going to Munich for a week to attend a performance of the Bolshoi Ballet and thereafter direct to Moscow where she would be present at the 2nd International Ballet Competition which was to start on June 2nd and last for twelve days.

The competitions in Moscow were to take place in the new, vast concert hall directly connected to the Hotel Rossia. Natalia had advised her to contact Intourist as soon as possible to book a reservation at the hotel but when the organisers heard of her impending visit, she was invited to be one of the judges on the panel.

A lesser mortal would have felt defeated by the countless lost battles, but Romola carried on, undeterred, in all likelihood sustained by her invincible belief that Waslaw was in constant touch with her through the various mediums she consulted. He was her guiding light. Even her strongest adversaries before and after Waslaw's death admitted to the transformation that came over her whenever Waslaw's name was mentioned; her faced smoothed, and she became youthful and tender; her harshness evaporated as if by magic. However much she may have idolised the dancer, there can be no doubt but that she genuinely loved Waslaw the man until the day she herself died.

One pilgrimage she found it heartbreaking to abstain from was the visit to Australia, where she had been scheduled to present a lecture at the Sydney Opera House on October 21st, 1973. Ill health forced her to cancel this much longed for trip to the land where her Charlie-Papa lay buried. For years, she had dreamed of going to his grave. The Australian Elizabethan Theatre Trust had sent circulars to their members:

'We are very pleased to announce that Trust members have been offered seats in the Opera House Theatre for a lecture by the fascinating Madame Romola Nijinsky – the widow of the world famous dancer, and authoress and ballet historian in her own right. Madame Nijinsky will reminisce on the Russian Ballet's first seasons in Paris and London, and Pavlova and Nijinsky. It will be a unique opportunity for ballet lovers and students of ballet history to have a visual interpretation of the legendary period when her husband, the great Nijinsky, took Paris and London by storm.

As the widow of Vaslav Nijinsky, she is practically the only living interpreter today of his world famous art, choreography – and of the dynamic personality of the man himself....

Madame Nijinsky is visiting Australia during the opening season of the Opera House. She will recount her impressions of Nijinsky and the Diaghilev Ballet in the OPERA THEATRE at 2.30 p.m. on Sunday 21st October. Tickets: $2.00.'

By a curious twist of fate, Romola had already learned where Károly Pulszky's grave was located, and had even been sent his wallet, intact with documents, such as his passport, photograph of Emilia and their two young daughters etcetera. Dr E F Kunz, a Hungarian-born social historian, who had arrived in Australia as a refugee in 1949, worked from 1951 in the Mitchell Library in Sydney. Browsing through its prominent collection of Australiana, he came across traces of a 19th century Hungarian refugee movement to the goldfields. He became so immersed in the subject that he was subsequently to write a book entitled *Blood and Gold: Hungarians in Australia.* This esteemed work led to him being invited to become a full-time Senior Research Fellow at Canberra University. In the course of further research on Hungarian refugees, the name Charles Pulszky cropped up. Pulszky's illustrious background, his infamous trial, his suicide in Brisbane, fired Kunz's imagination. He became fascinated with the subject and ferreted through the archives, where he found the coroner's report, and also learned of the existence of the wallet that had lain unclaimed all those years. Accompanied by a friend, he located my grandfather's grave. The nameplate lay some five yards away. Together, the two had refastened the cast-iron plate on the numbered but unmarked tomb and later Dr Kunz photographed it. He learned that the funeral had been paid for by the Consul for Austria-Hungary.

The wallet and its history had an almost mesmerising effect on Dr Kunz. Unable to erase the tragedy from his mind, he wrote an article about it in the *Magyar Élet* in Melbourne.

A friend of Romola's in Los Angeles happened to read the article and sent her a copy. Romola immediately contacted Dr Kunz, care of the editor, and told him how much it would mean to her to have the wallet as she had no mementos of her father. Thanks to his influence and his ability to prove that Romola Pulszky Nijinsky was the sole legal heir, he was able to get the wallet released and posted it by registered airmail to her. A cable came back 'THANK YOU THANK YOU GOD BLESS YOU.'

To my chagrin, I have no recollection of Romola ever telling Kyra or myself about this incredible incident. Even more frustrating is the fact that I have not been able to find any trace of the wallet.

In spite of the ongoing dispute with the BBC, and Romola's attorney's refusal to bring an injunction against them, letters between Romola and Robin Maugham indicate that they were still going ahead with their own project. Lord Maugham wrote to her at the end of April 1974 that he had not been idle but was working hard on revisions and improvements for the betterment of the play which otherwise had reached completion. He had had a meeting with Bill Freedman upon his return to London thanks to an introduction by Eric Glass. Freedman was the successful producer of a number of splendid productions such as *Hadrian VII, Staircase* and *Suddenly at Home*. Maugham was thrilled to be able to say that the producer was most enthusiastic about the Nijinsky project. Maugham could envisage that if he took it on, it would not only become a success in London but also on Broadway. Freedman had made certain suggestions which Maugham was eager to follow up.

'...your character (Romola's) would be more appealing to audiences if it were less on one note and they could see a little more of the gaiety and determination to win the man you loved so much – a truly romantic aspect with which they could sympathise and identify. And he feels that the tragedy of Vaslav's illness would have more impact if we would inject a little gentle humour into the earlier scenes up to the time of his illness.... My dear Romola, you know that I want only what is best for you and the play, and you know how dear to me is the memory of Vaslav, whom I feel I have come to know and love since working with you...'

There followed a big gap in the correspondence between Maugham and Romola. At his suggestion, opposed by Romola, Isobel Cogan was contacted. She asked for permission to send a copy of the play to John Neumeier to read. He had produced a Nijinsky Ballet Festival in Germany. The final act in yet another Nijinsky drama ended on Robin Maugham's optimistic note that the Chichester Festival might be interested to put on the play in 1977 but Romola, justly or unjustly, penned a virulent attack against him.

'What are we going to do about Robin's "miscarriage", the Nijinsky play? Something has to be done... I have shown the script to the director of the Berlin Dramatic Theatre, to the director of the Stadt Theater in Zürich, to the director of the Burgtheater. They collapsed, nearly fainted, and said it was unpresentable; they cannot believe Robin has written it. I really think it was William who wrote it as dear Robin was always dead drunk here...somehow this contract must be annulled...at once.'

Ailments continued to dog Romola. She had a polyp removed, and only some weeks later, she had to return to hospital to have the remaining tissues treated as a precautionary measure. A pathological check revealed no malignancy. She wrote to me about the latter incision, what a heroine the doctors said she was as she had it performed without anaesthetics.

At home, I suffered a number of personal setbacks which left me feeling trapped, and I could barely cope with the dull everydays of my life. Romola wrote to me:

'One has to trust in God, He solves all problems, so please do not worry too much. The Almighty takes care of the flowers and the birds and us humans as well. He knows best what He is doing... Only He knows, because more often than not, we do not understand what is good for us. So do not run in circles and be all up in arms.'

In the same letter, scribbled in a mixture of French and Hungarian, she mentioned that she was in Stockholm for a week, staying at the Sheraton, and making a television film for Swedish and Norwegian TV on her life with Tatakaboy. She had made the acquaintance of Ingmar Bergman, the world-famous Swedish film director, and was looking forward to working with him on a ballet film the following Spring. She was also negotiating with the theatre in Oslo to go there to reconstruct a televised version of *Jeux*.

'In addition, the Opera have hired me for the next season to stage two of Tatakaboy's ballets: 'Till Eulenspiegel' and 'Jeux', the latter with Debussy's music. For the Paris Opera I have been asked to stage the original version of 'L'Après-midi d'un

Faune'. In the autumn we are going to publish the Nijinsky System of Choreography based on his dance notations. Igor (Markevitch) is going to write the foreword to it. He claims that Tatakaboy was the master of music and that his invention is the new discovery of this century, stating that he created for dance what Arezzo did for music – the notes, the harmony, the counterpoint.'

Irina stayed with Romola for a week in Bad Gastein. They then flew to Zürich together and Irina went on to Stuttgart to see her mother's ballet *Les Noces* for which Stravinsky had composed the music.

'At my suggestion, Ira suddenly became a choreographic adviser. Now she is earning good money and she is forever invited over to Europe... She knows her art form because Bronia taught her to become a dance teacher and for years she directed Bronia's school in Hollywood... It was I who acquired Düsseldorf and Stuttgart for her, and today she is very much in demand. Ira is diligent.'

My cousin and her husband are happily settled in Pacific Palisades, California, and have two grown children, a son and a daughter.

Kyra was at long last brought back into the fold – the prodigal daughter? Romola announced she would be staying with her for a few weeks after which Kyra would be sent to a dear friend of Romola's, Schwester Simone at the Cloister in Freiburg im Breisgau. From our mother's account, Schwester Simone was a great painter and industrial artist, and the intention was that she teach Kyra to paint icons, in Romola's opinion an admirable way to earn a lot of money. She also tried to send Kyra off to Russia, presumably to continue learning the art of painting icons, but the offer was refused.

'I will send her to Geneva to her son and her darling grandchildren. After that, I want to take Kyra to Lourdes for a few days. I go there yearly to say thank you... Igor says "millions of people go to Lourdes to ask for something; you are the only strange 'bug' who goes to say thank you..." Monday, I go to Oslo,

487

*where Paul is supposed to meet me but you never know with
him, he is such a whimsical soul. Nonetheless, even if he does
not turn up, I shall fly to the North Cape and Lapland. Between
July 5th and the 13th I can be reached at the Hotel Plaza in
Copenhagen.'*

During the latter part of 1974, Romola got in touch with Leonide
Massine, whose home base was then on the Island of Galli although
he conducted classes all over the world – Paris, London, the States
etcetera. She wrote to him, asking him to assist her in reconstructing
some of Waslaw's compositions. He replied on a very positive note
and offered to meet her wherever it would suit her – Montana, London... she should name the place.

'Dear Leonide, I am overjoyed by the news that you want to
help...I thank you on behalf of Vaslav and myself. It will make
an important contribution toward choreographic art and to
future generations if we save those ballets...I feel that *Faune*
and *Sacre* should be done first. As I mentioned, I have the
choreographic scores of both ballets written down by Vaslav
in his *System of Notation* which I can read fluently...'

She set down her proposals which would require photocopies of
the piano score, the notes made by Bronislava, and any available
photographs. She put forward the suggestion that Massine, too,
should revive his oeuvres, such as *Le Tricorne, Les Femmes de Bon
Humeur* and *La Gaieté Parisienne*. 'We could make it a joint
Nijinsky-Massine season. The Salzburg Festival would certainly be
a possibility. We could invite a conductor, say, Carl Boehm or von
Karajan.'

Their first meeting took place in Montana and they were fully
aware of the enormity of the task undertaken but applied themselves to it with the verve and professionalism they both possessed.

Co-ordinating the grand scheme was to span a period of two
years. In fact, it was not until June 3rd, 1975, that Romola wrote as
follows to Massine on Isola de Galli:

'...Yesterday, I concluded the contract for the two of us
regarding *l'Après-midi d'un Faune*. Liebermann & Gail have
accepted the conditions imposed by you: 30,000 Frs cash for us

plus the trip Borken-Paris and return and 200 Frs per day for your room and food. It is the fee that the Opera normally pays foreign artists. At the same time, they have accepted to pay your assistant plus the fare London-Paris and return. The month of February has also been agreed upon for rehearsals. Mr Gail has assured me that you will have 40 to 50 rehearsals from the 29th of January through to the 1st of March. They wish to consult their legal counsellor to find out if one contract will suffice for us both or if two separate contracts are required, and whichever they decide upon will be sent to you for your signature. I shall send a cable to Misha to ask him if we can count on him to arrive by the 1st of August for rehearsals of *Till...* I depart on the 5th of June for Madrid, on the 15th to the Hotel Imperial in Vienna, and then, after the 20th, I will be in Bad Gastein.'

Letters to Paul reveal that Romola and Massine did work on the ballet in Paris but evidently they had exchanged rather hot-tempered verbal accusations when they interpreted every single gesture of the *Faun* differently. Massine was livid with fury when Romola cut in and remonstrated that his interpretation was too modern. She had even delivered a volcanic outburst against one of the *regisseurs* over which choreography to use. In a sharp rebuttal, she flatly refused to allow any other version than the original, and she waved in front of him photostat copies of Waslaw's Notation for *The Faun* together with photographs. To the amusement of the assembled staff and participants, she had mocked Massine by throwing at him: 'Your nymph walks around as if she had a tummy ache.' Undaunted by his disapproving countenance, she had carried on demonstrating the Faun's gestures when he reclines on the veil. Amidst the mirth of those present, she is reputed to have said: 'Do I have to teach you? The French people...? How you should...?'

Irina was at the Opera at the same time, working on *Les Noces*. Romola had the impudence to 'borrow' one of her ballerinas for the role of the Nymph. She also claimed that Irina gave her full support against Massine but Irina was to deny this, stating that she had far too much respect for him to intervene. Unashamedly, Romola admitted to the devilish idea of asking the Opera to pay Irina to teach the dancers the original choreography, which the latter had been taught by Bronia. In the knowledge that Massine would have to go to Pittsburgh for a month, she saw this as a golden opportunity to have matters her way.

L'Après-midi d'un Faune was ultimately performed in Paris in April 1976, actually in three different interpretations according to Robert Mead: Waslaw Nijinsky's, Maurice Béjart's and Jerome Robbins's. I believe the artistic director was Violette Verdi. The Opera insisted on making a film of the first ballet for their archives, but assured Romola that it would not infringe on her copyright.

On the 9th of April, Romola wrote that she had been to the première two days previously and that it had been a huge success.

'To the enormous surprise of us all, it was 'The Faune' such as it was performed in 1911. Neither my assistants nor I had been aware of this version and I am convinced that Tatakaboy directed it from Heaven. Miracles do happen, whether you believe them or not, dear Weibili.'

Yves St Laurent, who was then with Dior, had written to her to come and see their latest collection because he wished to design a gown for her to wear at the première. *'I felt like Cinderella...the beautiful green emerald ring with diamonds I wear all the time.'* Irina recollects how Romola regularly attended all the *haute couture* shows in Paris. The bills that arrived in the aftermath of choosing clothes must have been staggering. In a letter to Paul, she voiced her frustration over the fact that a red fox coat she had ordered from Reveillon in Paris was not ready as they were still waiting for ten red foxes to be delivered from Moscow.

Back in 1974, the BBC had contacted her in connection with their plan to make a documentary film to coincide with the twenty-fifth anniversary of Waslaw Nijinsky's death. According to Romola, their proposal was to base the film on interviews with people who had known my father, a narrative backed by photographs, a few select extracts from *The Diary* and, most important of all, dancers.

Romola was assured that the project would in no way conflict with any film version of Waslaw's life. She met the producer, Colin Nears, in Bern, Switzerland, to go through the details. She was delighted with the script that Mr Nears showed her, the music he had chosen and, on the whole, was enthusiastic about his expressed wish to pay homage to Nijinsky, the choreographer who had started the twentieth century school of modern ballet.

490

Her idea that Mikhail Baryshnikov was the only dancer who could shoulder the role of Nijinsky had been germinating for a long time. He was then with the National Ballet Company in Toronto. After a guest performance at the Metropolitan in New York together with Natalia Makarova, the *New York Times* had commented: 'At last we have seen really superb dancing, perhaps the best since Nijinsky was here in 1917.' She suggested to the BBC they should engage Baryshnikov, adding she was certain that she could negotiate reasonable terms. The BBC discreetly held their own counsel and went ahead with the production their way. In a letter to her agent, Romola burst out in an unprintable tirade against the BBC. What motivated her to grow more and more tactless as the years piled up? Was it that her pride would never allow her to yield graciously to a compromise; that she rejected anything that did not meet fully with her approval? Certainly, she fell out with the BBC. They took the decision to scrap a planned transmission of her Norwegian TV programme on Waslaw. One executive went so far as to say she jeopardised her own credibility in one brief sentence when they were discussing Diaghilev.

'You see, my dear, everybody got it wrong. I was the only woman Diaghilev liked.'

BBC's *Programme Correspondence* kindly supplied me with the confirmation that an *Omnibus* programme was televised on April 6th, 1975. 'Nijinsky was spoken (in vision) by John Hunt and danced by Nicholas Johnson. Kate Harrison danced Romola. Gideon Avrahami danced Diaghilev, and the choreography was by Jonathan Taylor.'

On the 19th of April, 1975, Romola sent me a card from Vienna where she was staying with her ex-son-in-law. She had just come from Munich, and together she and Igor were continuing to Budapest. She elaborated on the trip in a letter to Laci and me – that she was accompanying Igor on a concert tour. But was it not in fact a final adieu to the city where it had all started?

Her health was deteriorating rapidly, although she had had checkups at clinics in Stockholm, Zürich, Bern and Copenhagen. Tests had shown the polyp to be benign but one Swiss professor advised major surgery, asking for 150,000 Swiss Francs in advance. She even consulted a Cairo specialist by post.

From what I could gather, when she was in Sweden, a friend had introduced her to the wife of the Dean of the University of Upsala. She was a famous medium who carried out séances without charge. Romola attended one of these séances but her identity was not revealed. She received a message. 'I see a beautiful corps de ballet with only one male dancer in their midst. He is wearing white tights, a crêpe de chine blouse and a black velvet jacket. He leaps and flies in the air, exclaiming "Tell my wife not to undergo an operation."' To Romola, it was her Watza speaking, and she decided to live with her condition.

Whatever was burning inside of her she concealed it well when she arrived in seemingly high spirits in Budapest. My old friend Michael and Romola's cousin Miklós had arranged to meet her in the lobby of the Hotel Budapest where Igor was also staying. Michael had been nervous that he might not recognise her but the moment she stepped through the door, he saw 'Emilia' as he remembered her some thirty odd years earlier. Romola still spoke Hungarian fluently without a trace of an accent.

For a whole week, Michael was together with her practically every day. They would luncheon in the 'downtown' restaurants where, so he said, her every gesture betrayed she was used to being treated like a *grande dame*. She insisted on attending every one of Igor's concerts and was invited to a reception given by the French Ambassador in his honour. Michael recalled how she had a brooch taken out from the hotel safe for that occasion. It had been given to her by Indira Gandhi.

In his role as director of the Theatre Museum, Michael took her there to show her the tastefully displayed memorabilia that had belonged to her mother Emilia.

She expressed a desire to visit the Villa and Michael arranged it. She observed how tall the two pine trees in front of the house had grown. 'Time goes by, children and trees grow.' She had been saddened to see how it had been divided up into what amounted to no more than cubicles. It wrung her heart to find that the magnificent frescoes were gone. No resemblance remained of the stately Villa where she and Waslaw had found refuge on two occasions; where long before that she had spent a carefree youth.

To Michael's bewilderment, her grudge against Oti-Papa flared up once more and she irrationally placed the blame for what she now saw on him. She hadn't a clue as to what really had transpired after her departure. Inquisitively, she wanted to know what had happened to all the splendid furniture, and Michael had patiently listed the items left after Emilia's death and their present whereabouts. She suffered from a delusion that Charlie's brother, Agost Pulszky, had paid the government the money that Charlie had been accused of embezzling. Hence she was obstinate in her belief that the Piombo painting rightfully was hers; that if it was not returned to her, she would take her case to the International Court of Justice in the Hague.

There was rancour in her voice when she raised the subject of the little house in the 'Var' district. To whom had Tamara sold it? Wearily, Michael replied that it now belonged to an architect. She had never forgiven Emilia for leaving it to me.

Michael had recoiled inwardly as she carried on her vendetta against the dead. 'I told Tamara then, when she was on "the other side", not ours, that they had all better beware because "Uncle Pepi" (Stalin) would be in Budapest within six months. Mama had to leave her home, Oskar had to hide...the mills of God grind slowly. It was shameful how they behaved against Vaslav in both wars. But it is all over now and after death everyone receives his just reward or punishment...I do not think we will meet Oti-Papa in the other world.'

Romola could not even bring herself to pay her respects to her mother and step-father by visiting their graves. Michael offered to take her to the cemetery but she declined.

Her stay ended in a lighter vein during the last two evenings when they mused upon the arts. Michael had lent an appreciative ear to her comments on the various personalities with whom she had been in contact. In her opinion, Maurice Ravel had been the kindest, Jean Cocteau perhaps the wittiest. She shared with Michael her impressions of Kontantin Stanislavski, the Russian actor, as well as of Karsavina and Serge Lifar. About the latter, she claimed that he always threw away the flowers that she took to Waslaw's grave. Moissi and Raoul Aslant were brushed aside in an unflattering manner, whereas she heaped superlatives on Joseph Kainz. In her estimation, Gisella Werbezirk was the greatest comedienne and Max Pallenberg, the finest artist.

It was also during these tête-à-têtes that she told Michael the story of Picasso; how, when she and Waslaw lived in Paris, and she accompanied him to the theatre, Picasso on occasion had offered to look after little Kyra. In order to keep her from feeling bored, he would amuse her by making some drawings. Barely a year after Romola's visit, a brief notice in a newspaper caught Michael's attention. A few drawings made by Picasso during his youth in Paris had been sold at auction and Michael presumed that the drawings were the ones mentioned by Romola.

On her last day in Budapest, Michael had to escort her on a shopping tour. She bought goose liver pâté for Paul. Michael had been unable to refrain from a rather dry comment that it was hardly the most suitable gift to bring a man suffering from gallbladder complaints. But she did add a few bottles of Russian vodka and the sweet Hungarian Tokai wine, which had been the Duke of Windsor's favourite when he visited Budapest as the Prince of Wales.

Romola grew increasingly impatient over the lack of response to her lawsuit against Stravinsky and the ineptitude of the Ministry of Cultural Affairs in acting on her plea that Waslaw's choreographic works should be protected. When her demand that an 'inquest' should be held as to who had stolen the royalties dating back to 1913 went unheeeded, she brushed protocol to one side and sought an audience with President Valéry Giscard d'Estaing to discuss the matter. On May 30th, 1975, she wrote excitedly to Paul about the occasion which had left even her flustered. Paul must have been away on business at the time. She went into great detail about the event, even what she wore, a white, black and gold Tricot outfit; how she had to fill out a form at the entrance to the Palais de l'Élysée and, after clearance, how she had been accompanied by a valet in livery through a number of 'heavenly Louis XIV salons' to a suite on the first floor. After waiting barely five minutes, a door opened, camouflaged by the exquisite wallpaper, and the President came forward to escort her into his private study. She described him as a Grand Seigneur, intelligent, cultured and charming. His manner was without a trace of haughtiness, and he instantly made her feel at ease. He listened attentively and sympathetically to her outpourings on the burning issue of the 'stolen' royalties, which had earlier been brought to his attention in a series of letters.

With her she had the relevant documents including a joint petition signed by Leonide Massine, Serge Lifar and herself and, of course, a copy of *Le Système de Notation Choréographique de Waslaw Nijinsky*. What she was fighting for was that a bill be introduced to the Assemblée Nationale to protect the copyright of choreographic works in the same manner as books and music.

According to her, the President promised to take swift action and thanked her for bringing her case to him personally. Their dialogue continued for another three-quarters of an hour, and he bombarded her with questions about Waslaw and herself. Before bidding adieu, he made a promise to take his family to the première of *L'Après-midi d'un Faune*. He then went with her to the courtyard where one of the President's limousines was placed at her disposal to take her back to the Hôtel Lotti. It amused her to note the awestruck expressions on the faces of Lando, the old white-haired porter, and Monsieur Masson, the manager, when the limousine with the Presidential pennant waving on the bonnet came to a halt in front of the reception entrance.

During this phase of her life, Romola mentioned numerous people wholly unknown to me. 'Uncle Jacques' appeared frequently. He apparently had a chateau 'Gy' and Romola indicted to Paul that she would press Jacques to invite them for the Hunting Season. 'We will hunt there for something else, not for pheasant and deer.' She described this character Jacques as handsome and as youthful as ever. She went on to relate how 'Bobby' had been given some ground on the estate to enable him to build a smallish residence there. 'Bobby' was moving up in the world and had become the head of Musée Guillmet, the Oriental Museum, a position which entailed travel to Japan, China etcetera.

On June 4th, Paul received another letter containing mostly gossipy bits about their mutual friends and acquaintances. She mentioned that she had had lunch with André de Badet and had managed to persuade him to donate all the letters in his possession, written by Waslaw, to the Bibliothèque Nationale so that they would not be lost to posterity.

Together with Marcelle Morillon Romola attended an exhibition at the Bibliothèque Nationale to commemorate the centenary of Maurice Ravel's birth. She enthused over the phenomenal collection of paintings, the ballet and opera costumes, music scores, photogaphs etcetera, which included such familiar names as Picasso, Bakst and Benois. One photograph in particular had etched itself into her memory: Waslaw and Ravel playing *à quatre mains* on the piano. It had been taken by Stravinsky. They had been playing pieces from Chopin. Romola stood in front of it for a long time, then she remarked: 'Vaslav's hair is not well-trimmed. He looks so innocent, my *Dedushka*...'. She was deeply touched to find that a marble plaque listing the names of donors to this splendid building included the following: '1950 Mme la Comtesse Romola de Pulszky Lubocz Cserfalva – "Collection Nijinsky".'

It is interesting that some years later in 1984 the London galleries of Sotheby Parke Bernet held an auction of ballet memorabilia: ballet material from the collection of Serge Lifar consisting mostly of Diaghileviana and the *Ballets Russes*. The sale attracted collectors and dealers from all over the world, and the bids soared to the skies. According to an article in the American *Dance Magazine* of October 1984, Sotheby's took a gamble and held a week-long show of selected items at their elegantly 'minimalist' galleries in New York City, '...unprecedented sums changing hands even for items without claim to originality. Consider the unfinished *Portrait of Nijinsky,* a copy by the Studio of León Bakst which cost the Library of Congress $46,200. Or Alexandre Benois's portrait of Nijinsky as *Petrushka,* one of the many whipped up by the artist over the years...bought for $23,000...'. The writer of the article, Lynn Garafola commented 'I nearly cried in my champagne glass before the cast of Nijinsky's foot, squat, pathetic testimony to decades of idleness and pain, which rested in a display case next to Pavlova's leg...'.

At one stage, she advised Paul that he should go to a Monsieur de Frezzi with his papers. Frezzi would be able to free his French money investments, but first of all Paul must go to the States. She herself was jubilant because the vice-president of the Morgan Trust Guaranty Trust was letting her have Swedish Kronor *'at the drop of a hat – anything I want, and he personally escorts me out to the Place Vendôme.'*

On July 3rd, 1975, she wrote to Paul from the Hotel Danieli in Venice. Her opening sentence was one of reproof. *'You said goodbye to "this hateful person" in a very cold manner.'* She was penning her thirty-ninth letter since her arrival.

'The trip went smoothly. Rudi drove and behaved well although he chose a peculiar route. He turned at Villach, and after an hour-and-a-half we were up in the mountains. It was raining hard but later we found ourselves on an autostrada with

lovely vineyards on either side. It was past four o'clock when we arrived in Venice, and Rudi, not having been there for fifteen years, could not find the way to the terminal on the Piazza di Roma. Instead, we came to a dead end where the police told us to get out of the car as we could drive no further. There we were – stranded – without a porter, without a motor launch. I cursed Toni. Finally a kind 'gepäcksträger' arrived on the scene and grabbed all my things. Within minutes he had found a dilapidated rowboat. I handed over a cheque for Toni Maier amounting to Swiss fr. 300.00 to Rudi – whom I gave 100.00 Schilling and told him to go to... (Romola's expletives and very earthy language with which she strewed her letters are better left untranslated). *I was lifted into this terrible boat which danced on the waves and took twice the time it should take from the Lido to the Danieli. I thought my last hour had come. Safely ashore, there was still no sign of any porters. We found that this is due to a general strike.*

The cashier, the receptionist, everybody, greeted me with joyful shouts and they all asked "Dov' è il Barone?" They reserved a nice room for you next to mine. I have a lovely two-bedroom suite on the top floor where we stayed with Hattie. The room was filled with flowers from the manager... Yesterday, I had to carry the suitcases up myself, today, everything is all right. And yesterday, too, every eating-place except Harry's Bar was closed. I had lunch there. I began to enquire for Misa, Béjart and Neumeier. The latter had already left, Béjart was not in. I left a message "Nijinsky is calling you to the Danieli"... I spoke to all the English critics. Misa (Baryshnikov) *was heavenly. He danced in 'Le Spectre', 'Les Sylphides' and so on. The entire Piazza was in ecstacy. Venice is paradise. Every building has been cleaned up à la Malreux. I was so tired yesterday I thought this was the end, and I only wished to turn back but today the situation is completely different. I talked at great length to Leonide* (Massine) *and to Dunya* (Feuer) *who is due to arrive here on Sunday evening. On Monday we go together to Firenze where we will stay at the Hotel Excelsior because the Grand Hotel is closed. Misa went there today but I will wait for Dunya. Firenze does not have an airport, and I want to stay here and calm down a bit. Everybody spoils me so, and the food is good.*

'July 4th. Now I am chasing after Sergio Bostianelli. We want to go to the Frari to see the Ballet Exposition... The entire Ballet Festival is under the chairmanship of UNESCO, whose president, Señor José Romero Escuvia, I met at Dunya's place. Somehow it turned out well that Béjart did not show up. At midnight we hunted around to find a place to eat but as most restaurants were still shut because of the strike, Harry's Bar took pity on us and opened in secrecy and made us some sandwiches. 'Grässlich'. How can one live in a country like that? However, last night I had dinner at the restaurant next door where Hatti ate the 'gamberessi'. I was with the ballet critics of the 'Daily Telegraph' and the 'Corrieri della Serra' when to my great surprise who should walk in but Don Alvarado, Duque de.... Alba and Berwick...He had spoken to Señor José Escuvia on the telephone and arrived to see Misa as he is an ardent balletomane. At least I have an escort, and I do not have to pay which is fine because now a lunch or dinner costs 8,000 to 9,000 lire – at the Michelangelo 10,000 lire fly away in seconds. Today, we are going to Lido, not to swim. It is in fact forbidden as the water is so dirty in the sea, only the swimming pool can be used. Besides, I have just had my hair dyed...

Day after tomorrow I will go by boat to the Cipriani Restaurant. Afterwards, I will quench my appetite for art and study the Raphaels and Titians...take the communion in San Marco... Scrampi's, the beer restaurant on the corner of San Marco, does not exist any more. The other shops are still there. The public has changed catastrophically...hippies from all over the world are here...Americans in their shirt sleeves and without ties with six-eight brats...The millions donated by UNESCO four years ago for the restoration of Venice appear to have evaporated...only San Marco and some of the larger churches have been renovated. From the terrace, I am just now enjoying a wonderful view of San Giorgio Island, the sun is shining, and the temperature is about 28 degrees. The church bells are peeling. Now I have to telephone Menotti in Spoleto to ask how much he paid to Misa. The English critics say that Nureyev receives £1,000 for an evening and Misa £1,500. ...Take good care of yourself and do not stop loving that hateful person.'

498

Again and again, in her sporadic writings to us in Phoenix, Romola referred to the central problem of her poor health, the polyp, which she mentioned with increasing depression. She was by then weary and torn by indecision. *'I am not a guinea pig.'* She condemned the conditions in Bad Gastein.

> *'Here we are without doctors or hospitals or services of any kind. It has become impossible to live here. It is worse than in Russia as regards food. The people are rude, it is like a vast proletariat. Paul and I made a big mistake to leave the United States. We should have bought a little house in Phoenix, transferred our furniture and our effects there. You could have supervised the house, acted as my secretary. Now we are without a home, everything is scattered all over Europe, and our storage bill in San Francisco alone is $1,500 a year. It is idiotic...I am concerned, too, about Paul's health; he should undergo a gallbladder operation. If he becomes ill, both of us are lost.'*

Her letter had started off in an even more pessimistic vein, astonishingly enough on the subject of the world of ballet. She had returned from Italy, utterly exhausted and disenchanted, having attended the Ballet Biennale in Venice and continuing to Florence with Baryshnikov. The intrigues, the enormity of the difficulties and the pet jealousies caused her to collapse, choked with worries. In dire need of absolute rest, she vowed that she would cut off all her activities and her writings in connection with ballet and the stage. She had had enough. This was in November 1975.

> *'Take note of the following: there are three great powers in the world, The Catholic Church, the Masons and the Clan of the Homosexuals. The latter persecuted Tatakaboy and me ever since 1913. They continue to do so, because they are jealous of his glory.'*

On December 26th, Leonide Massine visited her at the Hôtel du Lac, Vevey, Switzerland, and presented her with a copy of *Nijinsky Dancing* with the compliments of Lincoln Kirstein. *'He writes in a fantastic manner about Vaslav, he calls him the God of Dance – it is I whom he slaps, me, but I do not care...'*

On February 8th, 1976, Romola made her way to the Montmartre Cemetery as she did whenever she was in Paris. She always brought with her cut flowers for Waslaw's grave but on this occasion she added a bouquet for Vestris. She remarked about this visit specifically because she had been concerned about Koska Kotyik, the cat who had taken up residence at the grave. He appeared to have vanished. The guard at the gate told her that it favoured the Moulin Rouge, Place Clichy in the cold weather. The cat had a special meaning to her, and therefore she slipped money to the guard, and made him promise to see that it should have milk whenever it appeared and tinned English catfood not French. She was very firm on that score.

At about the same time, my family had just surfaced from a tragic blow. Kinga had a miscarriage. Romola was sorry to hear the news but could not refrain from adding her own gloomy 'philosophical' viewpoint. *'Young couples yearn for children. Believe me, in our century, in our times, it is almost criminal to create a child. We are facing a nuclear war...'*

The doomful prognosticator was delighted, however, when she heard that Kinga had given birth to a healthy boy on October 6th, 1976. He was christened Mark Gerard. Possibly she was piqued because her advice had not been solicited for she quibbled over the choice of names. Why Gerard? *'Gustav or Gordon would have been better.'* But she melted completely upon receipt of a photograph introducing him to her. She claimed she had become lost for words in admiration of the baby. *'...beautiful, sunny, cheerful-looking, mischievous.'* Romola had it enlarged and framed. She nicknamed Mark 'his Lordship'.

Romola would not budge in her conviction that the only dancer who could portray Nijinsky on stage or on the screen was Mikhail Baryshnikov. Her letters abounded with glowing accolades concerning him. She jokingly referred to 'Misha' as her 'adopted' son and wrote: *'He is the first dancer in the last fifty years who resembles Vaslav in art, in technique, and in his flying leaps... I first saw him as a pupil in Leningrad when he was ten years old, and I care about him. I am forever saying that he is made of the same strudel dough as Vaslav.'* She made a heroic effort to secure him for a performance of *Till,* planned to be given in Stockholm in 1976, and the two met in Florence and in Munich to talk over the details. But the splendid scheme was virtually defeated already in its infancy when in June

1975 Baryshnikov's agent wrote that he was solidly booked for the forthcoming seasons; 'hopefully this beautiful idea will be accomplished at a later date.'

In despair she wrote to Leonide Massine. Presumably, they were working simultaneously on *Faune* and *Till*. She asked Massine to cancel the Swedish dancers and Dunya Feuer's trip to St Agatha as Baryshnikov would not be able to come due to his many commitments. During his short holiday he had to rehearse a new Hamlet ballet choreographed especially for him, and in October he would be dancing with Natalia Makarova at Covent Garden in *Swan Lake* and *Romeo and Juliet*. Romola had had to get in touch with Sven Gunnar Tillius to straighten out the reigning confusion about negotiated contracts. Still, at that point, she persevered. 'We two must establish the choreography...the trustees of the Nijinsky Estate insist that Misha shall dance at the première...'

Little wonder that her spirit was broken when she wrote to me in November. It was piteous and ironical that just as she was sure she had something tangible within reach, it slipped through her fingers. She became irritable and, unusual for her, eschewed company, so much so that she rebuked a friend, Felicia, who had been to see her and Paul in Bad Gastein. 'You and Paul are sociable people who love to talk. I cannot be bothered. For this reason I escaped to the *'Frühstück'* pension, but even there I was followed.'

She became more and more aware of her illness. Now the mediums were relaying messages from Waslaw that she *should* have surgery. 'Watza, make up your mind!' Her strong belief was that one lives on earth as long as God wants one to; at the time of birth it is already decided when we will die. In her darkest moments she confessed that she was not on speaking terms with her little Jesus of Prague, who had protected and helped her throughout her life. 'It seems that he does not bother with me now...I'd like to remain on this terrestial sphere for two more years because I have such interesting work left to do even though I find this crazy world loathsome.' Then her mood would change: 'I have made up with the Little Infant... and given him the benefit of the doubt that he will help me again.'

There was no way Romola could stand firm by her vow to give up either writing or the ballet. They were in her blood, as necessary to her as breathing. Preparations in Paris for *Faune* rekindled the spark within her and she kept going despite the excrutiating pain that was to rack her body more and more. To me, 'kind, good Weibili', her letters were crammed with the latest developments regarding her condition, the various medical opinions from specialists in well nigh every capital of Europe. They were interspersed with terse news of what she was currently working on. I gathered that she was frequently in Spain, invited there by the Duchess of Alba, with whose help she hoped to revive the Nijinsky Foundation. '...the Duchess had promised me to become president of the Spanish section...' A few postcards from Madrid dropped through the mailbox hinting that her private life was as glamorous as ever. She mentioned *en passant* that on one occasion she had met the famous heart specialist, Christian Barnard, at a dinner. Typically, she had shamelessly shown him the cardiogram taken at the clinic in Copenhagen. He had studied it and pronounced her 'prima'.

Romola never tired of collecting material on the subject of Waslaw, and she was evidently eager to impart such information to Paul. Hence, in a letter to him, scribbled from Munich at 2 a.m. on August 20th, appeared the following:

'Claudia found a divine book. Everything is in it, including 'Tyl' etc. Diaghilev presented Vaslav with a contract in 1909, signed by the poor boy as many as five times. For the entire season he received 2,500 francs and a second class ticket St Petersburg-Paris and return. Hotels etc. Vaslav had to pay. Such a pig was Sergei Pavlovitch.'

Perhaps it would be fitting here to introduce a chapter in Romola's life which was, and will probably forever be, cloaked in mystery. Her feeling for Waslaw was one of eternal love but simultaneously she had to satisfy her worldly longing for love and admiration. The older she grew, the more the flattery of younger and younger men appealed to her. It was like a tonic; she flaunted her luxurious lifestyle, and perhaps there were those crossing her path, who regarded her as a wealthy widow, an easy prey to flattery.

Dance Magazine (U.S.A.) of September 1976 reported the following in their 'White Night Notes' column by Arthur Todd.

'The most cherished memory of the trip is that of a long and leisurely luncheon in Leningrad's Hotel Astoria with handsome Konstantin Sergeyev and much beloved Natalia Dudinskaya. During the course of our conversation, Mme Dudinskaya mentioned that she had received word from 83-year old Romola Nijinsky announcing Romola's marriage to the 37-year old Spanish Duke of Alba this past May.'

Was there anyone gullible enough to believe so preposterous a rumour? Most certainly, we in Phoenix knew nothing about it, and only a sentence or two in letters conveyed the news that Romola had been the guest of the Duchess of Alba at the Palacio de Liria in Madrid. Had I given it second thoughts, I would have surmised that she had reopened old ties from the past when she and Waslaw had formed bonds of friendship with the Duc and Duquesa de Durcal and others in the Spanish aristocracy.

The only evidence I have of this 'fairy-tale' romance from 1975 up to the end of 1977 consists of a card to me from Segovia where Romola claimed: *'I am a guest of the Duchess of Alba. She takes me everywhere'*, and a flimsy packet of letters to Paul which must have been among her belongings at the Hôtel Lotti. She was taken to many of the historic places in Spain and extolled over them. Segovia was a phenomenal city where *'Isabella la Católica was crowned'*. They had continued to La Granja where long ago Farinelli had sung to Philip V in an effort to cure His Majesty of melancholy madness. The singer had stayed for twenty-five years, serving Ferdinand VI after Philip's death. The excursions included Escorial, an indescribably beautiful cluster of palace, convent, mausoleum and church. Romola wrote to Paul that her strength flagged at this point, and that she could barely drag herself into the Cathedral to pay homage to the graves of their Majesties Charles V and his son Philip II.

It was on June 4th, 1975, that Romola mentioned her impending flight to Madrid the following day. *'The Duchess of Alba wrote that someone will fetch me at the airport.'* It has been confirmed that Romola Nijinsky actually was a guest at the Palacio. But where does truth end and fiction commence?

In her first communiqué to Paul on June 11th, she painted a vibrant and glowing picture of the magnificence of the interior of the Palacio, the family members, the impressive guest lists.

One letter started off in a semi-humorous, semi-'delusions of grandeur' fashion.

'*Monseigneur*

I can say I made it. I am surrounded by dukes and the grand aristocracy of Spain – I, la Comtesse de Pulszky de Lubocz and Cserfalva, Princess de Matagascar... I am at a loss for words to describe the luxury, pomp and splendour here. Everyday we eat in a different dining-room, surrounded by frescoes, Gobelins, paintings by Goya, Velasquez, Murillo. You should see the marvellous banquet hall in marble, the vast library; the family's private apartments which the Duchess shares with her sons and one daughter are divine. The guest suites are fabulous, each comprising a bedroom, boudoir, salon and two bathrooms. I have a valet, maid and chauffeur at my disposal. The latter's name is Antonio. There are also two nurses at my beck and call in addition to a hairdresser and a masseuse, should I require them. Every evening the butler wishes to know my preferences for the following day's menu. I feel quite giddy by it all... Obviously, Doña Cayetana likes me because I am invited to her private salon for a chat every afternoon. It amused her when I related that I would not be sitting here beside her had her great-great-great-great grandfather succeeded in burning Charles de la Poule at the stake...'

It was on this first visit that she named some of the guests present at dinner. Dr and Mrs Barnard, the Marquis de Villaverde (General Franco's son-in-law)...She also confided to Paul that she had accepted an invitation to dinner from Doña Carmen Polo Franco. But an indisputable miscarriage of fact cropped up in that very first letter, the charade to be carried on until the end. Why? Romola told Paul that her handsome knight who accompanied her everywhere and who professed he loved her '*since that is the proper thing to do*', was Don Alvarado, one of the sons. None of the five sons is so called, and upon enquiry at the Spanish Institute I was told the name is a surname in Spain, not a christian name. In her next rambling letter, she gives all his names, some eight or ten, yet again self-deception appears to have crept in. There is no present Duke of Alba. The title is only passed on to the eldest son after the death of both parents. The Duchess of Alba is very much alive and has remarried. Her eldest son Carlos married not long ago. It is in this second letter that Romola hints to Paul that Alvarado wishes to marry her. She extolls his virtues, what a wonderful attentive companion he is, how he wines and dines her at the finest restaurants, sends her bouquets of yellow roses every morning, orchids for the evenings, and ends her letter telling of a visit to the Palacio Réal, the former royal palace.

On December 26th, Romola wrote an epistle to Paul scrawled on Hôtel du Lac (Vevey) stationery. Apparently, they had quarrelled over the telephone the day before because Romola starts off 'do not be so upset and mad and angry without reason. I had to hang up.' She went on to describe how she and de Soto (from what I can gather one of Alvarado's many names, ie de Sotomayor) had travelled by car through a wild, sparsely peopled forest across the French border. They must have made up a party because she mentioned two cars.

'...Everybody was armed with a revolver or a knife, as if we were going to war. I would not have been at all surprised if the border police had found a plastic bomb hidden somewhere in the car. But weapons are essential because here, too, there are hold-ups, kidnapping, bankrobberies daily, like on a conveyor belt. By eight o'clock in the evening we found ourselves moved back into the XVIII Century.... It is a beauteous place in the midst of the woods, no other houses than the former Auberge, its interior stuffed with original furnishings from the eighteenth century. In the barn stood a stage coach of the period, only the people of that era were missing. The house itself was very comfortable, well heated with fireplaces stacked with big logs. The outside world was covered with a blanket of snow. Only the cook, a Frenchman, and a housekeeper were staying there. We brought servants with us.... We were enveloped by complete calm, stillness. Some twenty-five miles from the Auberge is a lovely little village inhabited by French peasants. We went to their tiny church for the ten o'clock Mass but had to leave in time for the midnight Mass from St Peter's in Rome, which we watched on a colour TV screen.... On December 24th, we saw the Pope open the Sancta Porta, and then they showed Montini close it for the next twenty-five years. It will not be re-opened until the year 2000. Do you recall how we in 1950 went through that door...?

The Cathedral was a blaze of light, an unforgettable experience. There must have been at least half a million people on the

Piazza.... This was not created by Bramante, Michelangelo or Raphael. God had His hand in it, too, without a shadow of a doubt. This heavenly creation could not have been the work of mortals.... Montini had aged a great deal but he performed his task well. All the Cardinals wore purple robes. At least one thousand priests went outside to give communion to the crowds gathered there... During Mass the choir of the Sistine Chapel sang divinely. It was all so wonderful and moving that I started to cry. One forgot one was not there in body. We knelt during Mass, it would not have been possible to listen to the elevation and the papal blessing in any other manner. The Mass and the ceremonies lasted two-and-a-half hours. We did not return to the Auberge until 2.30 in the morning. We drank to your good health at the Christmas dinner, "Lanson Extra Dry". There was a diminutive gilded Christmas tree at the Auberge, rather more Biedermeier than Louis XVI. But I believe in those days they did not have Christmas trees. Glittering little ornaments hung from the tree's branches. One was particularly shiny, a wonderful Piaget bracelet watch studded with diamonds. I asked "What is that?" de Soto blushed and stammered that it was only something to remind me what time it was when I attended the theatre... This morning we returned to the twentieth century here in Vevey... I am sending you yesterday's luncheon menu. I have gained at least two kilos...'

Romola went on to discuss the seriousness of her condition. She was bleeding internally and required blood transfusions. Possibly she would have these in Salzburg, then she and Paul would decide in March where surgery was to take place: Salzburg, Vienna, Madrid. She missed Paul very much – God willing, next Christmas they would spend together. She worried about his health, his problems with diabetes and gallbladder complaints, and beseeched him to go to a sanatorium for a few weeks where he would be put on a strict diet. She vowed she would wean him away from medications and sleeping pills. She wrote:

'As I am unable to put up a great fight all the time and the three of you, Villaverde, de Soto (Alvarado) and yourself have entered into a conspiracy to extend my life, I capitulate. I have finally realised you want the best for me... Wherever I go every-

506

body asks what have I done to look twenty-five years younger?
Are you upset that somebody unselfishly cares for me, and wants
to make my life more pleasant? Now he is thinking of taking me
to Montini to arrange an audience with the Pope... I do not know
why? I told him that perhaps eventually I would go but that I do
not have time at the moment... Concerning lengthening my life, I
explained to him that the day of our death is already determined
at our birth and that if "you want to keep me alive for another
forty or so years, the simplest thing for me to do would be to go to
Hunza or the Caucasus where people easily reach 180 from
eating plenty of yoghurt etcetera.

Today I overslept breakfast because I am so nervous, concerned
about you. I had a curious dream, you scolded me, and still half
asleep I cried out "No, no, Paul." I woke to find Alvarado by my
bedside. He said, "It is only I, not Pablito. I will telephone him to
come." Please, Paul, be kind and understanding. Let there be
peace and love on earth and between us, as the Pope said
yesterday. Amen.'

In February 1976 Romola's letters to Paul to a large extent dwelt on
her progressively worsening state of health. He was absent from Paris
that month but must have advised her on what course to pursue.

'I am glad that you have decided what has to be done. I am
grateful to the priest of St Stephen's Kirche and to Thadeus. What
does Mrs Becker say? Dr Briggs? Operation or no operation?
Leonide is talking me out of one; he fears that if something
happens to me he will lose his money.'

She was extremely happy that de Soto was back. He was so calm
and determined – everyone listened to him: Martita dared not rush in
every five minutes day and night to check her pulse and blood
pressure. Romola had figured out that all she had to do was to play 'I
am dying' and *Su Altezza* (her pet name for Alvarado) would hasten
to her side. *'Querida mia,* I would not let you die...'

Nureyev was dancing at the Sports Palace. He had held a press
conference and among the questions raised was why was he not going
to dance the Faun. 'Because *la veuve Nijinsky* does not agree with
me,' he had replied.

Romola claimed that on his frequent visits to Paris, Alvarado stayed at his family's mansion in l'Avenue Martin. She confided to Paul that she had asked *Su Altezza* to accompany her to Versailles to meet la Duchesse Montmorency de Talleyrand Périgord concerning André de Badet. Again, according to Romola, Alvarado had said he would gladly help financially provided Romola kept her promise that Badet was kept ignorant of his involvement. The Duchess had assured them that everything would be done to assist André, and then went on to reminisce about her own life. According to Romola: *'the Duke had participated in the French Resistance and been shot by the Germans. Her son died in action during the war. Her daughter lives in Paris, but she prefers to stay in Versailles, because she loves to walk in the park. The Duchess is an educated, intelligent woman. She had great respect and admiration for Waslaw and said "There will never be anyone like him".'*

Judging from Romola's letters to Paul, she returned to Madrid in early March 1976. On the sixth she sent a postcard to Paul, who was then staying in Bad Gastein. The opening sentence must surely have come as a shock to him, left him utterly puzzled and bewildered, unless on some previous occasion she had personally discussed the delicate matter with him.

> *'This morning my future mother-in-law came to the hotel. Everybody fell down on their knees in reverence. She wished to be assured that I was being well taken care of. Tonight she will fetch me to stay at her palace for the week-end. There will be just a close family dinner...'*

Romola elaborated on her subsequent stay in a long letter a few days later. Alvarado devoted himself to her. Although now riddled with medication she enthused over one dinner in particular: caviar, goose liver in aspic, consommé, fresh asparagus, roast suckling pig. She told of a silly tiff she had had with *Su Altezza,* how she threatened to go back to Bad Gastein by the next plane but he had placated her and assured her his family had greeted her with open arms, that they loved her and wanted her to regain her health. She behaved now like a moody, spoiled child. *'Well, I do not want to hurt him. He is an angel from Heaven, and I am a stupid beast.'* Her letter ended sadly, however: *'I do not feel well, I am afraid I am bitter.'*

The following day, Romola had gone back to the hotel to enclose with a letter to Paul a medical report he had requested. She stated emphatically that under no circumstances should he let the contents be known to her family, naming Kinga and myself. She scribbled the letter there to ensure that Alvarado would not find out about it either.

'This boy is capable of shooting down Marta and Schmidt. He is so upset and concerned when surgery is mentioned, one practically cannot talk to him...I received fresh strawberries from Aranjuez for lunch... Jacobo, one of Alvarado's brothers, wants to meet me. There I can rest. Nobody will distract me. Last year he was away... You misunderstood Alvarado. He is filled with kindness and friendship towards me. He is not jealous. He says how fortunate you are to have spent thirty years with me. Tonight I said I would like to go to the movies just to change the subject of my illness. We decided to see Romy Schneider's new film. Tomorrow we are going to look at the Palace where Franco lived. I said I would show the spot in the garden where I slapped the Duke of Durcal's face because he kissed me.'

It was during this last stay that she said she had been introduced to Juan Carlo's sister, the Duquesa de Badajoz together with a friend, the Duquesa de Valencia de Don Juan. The former invited Romola to visit her in Avila, where she lived in a sixteenth century castle. Purportedly, she had imparted to Romola how delighted they all were that Alvarado had found a new lease of life. The amazing proposal was mentioned in Romola's last letter from Madrid. She had gone for a ride with Alvarado, seeping in the divine scenery, while at the same time imbibing in slightly more vodka than was good for her. A valet who was with them had poured out generous portions. Possibly they were on a picnic. At every village church Alvarado had pressed her to accept his hand in marriage. She had countered his proposals by saying she must discuss it with Pablito (Paul). Besides, she was and wanted to remain an English citizen. She claimed that after dinner that evening Alvarado had shown her a passport issued to the Duke of Berwick, stating proudly that he possessed dual nationality. She then went on to more prosaic, domestic issues with Paul and signed off: 'This is all for today.'

A letter written some time in 1977 reads as follows:

509

'Dear Pablito,

Today I am writing to you to clarify the situation in reference to Donna Romola's artistic plans, which are of great importance to the world and future generations. She feels it is her sacred duty to preserve Nijinsky's Ballets.
Of course, I agree with her, and am not as selfish as to hinder her in this task, on the contrary I will help her in every way to realise them.
Naturally, I would prefer to have her quietly at home in Almerida or Madrid but then she would feel as she says "like a bird caught in a golden cage". But above all I wish her to be happy. Her great sense of duty and love of Nijinsky are unique and admirable.
We both have the same aims to see that she should regain her health and be content, so I ask you to help me, to co-operate with me, towards this end. You know she misses you, is deeply attached to you, so I hope in the near future we will form a "happy family".
You should have seen her the evening of "Carmen". She was very beautiful, radiant, as happy as a child listening to Placido Domingo's Don José, but indeed he sang for her.
As you know, after our stay in Balmoral we are going to make a short tour of Scotland and rest for a while in my old ancestral castle with all the Spooks she wishes to meet.
So let's get together very soon
Until then, my dear Pablito
Au Revoir. Yours Ever,
Alvarado.'

On September 12th, 1977, a cable was despatched from Edinburgh to Baron Bohus, c/o Hotel Beau Rivage, (1200) Geneva.

'Taking Donna Romola to Royal Infirmary for tests and will phone you end of this week. Kind regards. Alvarado.'

Who was he, Alvarado, de Soto, *Su Altezza,* Duke of Alba and Berwick? An imposter? A figment of the imagination? The hallucination of an elderly woman facing death? The old ancestral castle,

510

Berwick, has been a ruin for many decades. The Scottish family history goes back to James Fitzjames, son of James II. In 1704, a descendant became Grandee of Spain, and I believe the title 'Duke of Berwick' became extinct after the early 1700's. Irina, who met Romola often during those last years, recollects distinctly Romola mentioning a dashing young Spaniard, although she never met him. Why should Romola deceive Paul? Surely not to arouse an older lover's jealousy because from all I have learned they were devoted companions, nothing else. Perhaps one day the mystery will be unravelled. Somewhere, there is somebody who holds the key to the solution.

Romola fretted constantly about Paul's and her belongings which she had authorised John to deal with. She hoped that Paul would be able to fly to San Francisco and Phoenix to reach a decision about the sale of china and porcelain. In addition to the furniture there were some thirty-odd packing cases containing valuable items.

At some stage after Bronia's death, Romola contacted Robert Mead while he was on a temporary assignment in Paris. At the time, his base was Germany. For years he had collaborated with Broni-slava, and now Romola asked him if he would be willing to mount *Les Noces* in Peking. The discussion also included *Faune*. Negotiations proceeded, contracts were drawn up, and even air tickets for the trip to China reserved when she withdrew, most likely due to her inability to cope with all the ideas that she was hatching.

To add to it all, Romola confessed to her London attorney that she was 'broke like the City of New York.' He would have to wait yet another year for gold to turn up.

She wrote to her agent and claimed: '...new book on Vaslav Nijinsky. Manuscript two chapters are sitting in my safe in the Hôtel Lotti, Paris, where I left it before leaving for Madrid in June. With God's help, I will be in Paris January 29th and will immediately despatch it to you...'

Without giving a second thought to finishing one task, she audaciously embarked on yet another literary undertaking that had been brewing in her mind; ie, of putting together a selection of short stories on prominent personalities she had either met or heard about in the wide circles in which she moved. A few of these sketches have already been incorporated in this book. Adolf Hitler and Henrik Ibsen were among the names on her list. She calculated that there was always a ready market for such gossipy titbits. They might just bring in the pot of 'gold' she sorely needed. With regard to one of the stories in particular, she tinkered with the thought of seeking legal aid. The topic concerned Diaghilev's seven lovers: Dmitri Filosofov, a cousin, Alexander Mavrine, a former secretary, Waslaw Nijinsky, Leonide Massine, Serge Lifar, Anton Dolin and her son-in-law Igor Markevitch, Diaghilev's last lover. The first three were dead and presented no problem but the remaining four were at the time very much alive and she feared that they 'would raise Hell' with her and her publishers.

Unquestionably, it could only have been through Emilia that she had material for one of the subjects she was contemplating writing about, namely, Henrik Ibsen. She had given it the tentative title 'Die Frau van Meer' and claimed it was about Ibsen's platonic love, who had inspired him to write *Hedda Gabler*.

The story about Hitler, on the other hand, was based on her own encounter with him. Adolf Hitler, the son of Alois Schicklgruber, a shoemaker, and Klara Poelzl, Alois's third wife, left the little border town of Braunau-am-Inn in his teens to seek his fortune in Vienna. His ambition was to become an artist but he failed his entrance examination at the Art Academy. Uncouth, surly, destitute, he was compelled to take a job as a building trader's labourer. Romola was staying with her sister and brother-in-law, probably at the time she 'fled' from home and broke off her engagement to Bandi. A young house-painter developed the habit of calling at the house to beg for tickets for Wagner operas. On one occasion when he called, Romola was alone in the apartment except for the cook. She noticed his extreme pallor and thought he was going to faint. Taking pity on him, she guided him to the kitchen, where he admitted he had not eaten a proper meal for days. Julie, the cook, served him some warm food and in the course of the ensuing conversation, Romola learned of his interest in art and in music, Wagner in particular. She became intrigued by his obvious intelligence, his political views and knowledge of various matters, and helped him to get a temporary redecorating job with the Schmedes. Whenever he arrived for work, Julie would see to it that he was well fed. He left Vienna for Munich in 1912, later to become the master of Germany '...a bloodthirsty guttersnipe, a monster of wickedness, insatiable in his lust for blood and plunder' as Winston Churchill described him.

Romola claimed that some thirty-odd years after having helped the starving labourer, her 'good Samaritan' act was rewarded. She wrote to the Führer, reminding him of the incident, and asked him for the release of seven Jews from Dachau (the names are not recorded) and Hitler complied with her request.

Two ambitious ballet scenarios consumed her last working year. She wished to mount a ballet which Waslaw had never completed. The title chosen was *Die Unvollendete* signifying it would be left where he had broken off. Scenery and costumes were to be designed by Alexandre Benois' son, who was then with La Scala in Milan. The music was to be based on some of the forty-eight preludes and fugues from Johann Sebastian Bach's *Well-tempered Clavichord*. Romola wrote to Laci asking for his advice on the orchestration. Igor Markevitch and F. Sauget, a well-known French composer, were also abetting her on the musical side.

Early in 1977, she telephoned her literary agent in London to say that she was pressed for time. 'Why the sudden hurry?' 'I want to finish what I have started before I ascend to Heaven. Watza is calling, but I have told him that he would have to wait until 1978.'

The second ballet was *Parsifal* which had been choreographed by Waslaw. She was in touch with Winifred Wagner and Eric Rappe, a musicologist from Bayreuth, in addition to Grigorovitch, the Bolshoi Ballet Master. Her aspiration was to have it performed in the little *Markgraf* theatre, accompanied by the Festival Orchestra on those evenings when the Bayreuth Festival House could not accommodate them. She wrote to Paul Scofield, for whom she harboured great admiration, asking for his assistance with regard to the *Parsifal* story, and on behalf of Winifred Wagner and herself invited him to join them in Bayreuth.

The actor wrote an encouraging and courteous reply, explaining that the only version he had was one taken from the original of Wolfram von Eschenbach, and queried if it was any different from that of Walter von der Vogelwide. He was due to leave for Scotland but hoped that in January (1978) Romola could spend a day in the country, and to please let him know of her arrival in London.

Weeks went by, and then picture postcards arrived with meagre messages as to her whereabouts and what she was doing. Temporarily, I was lulled into reassurance that her physical condition had not changed for the worse.

During the first week of September 1977, Romola was staying in London for a few days, after which she left for Edinburgh to attend the Festival, where a performance of *Carmen* was to be held with Placido Domingo, Teresa Berganza and Caballi. *'It will be divine. The voice of Domingo is more beautiful than that of Enrico Caruso – a superb artist.'* She stayed for three weeks in Scotland, described it as a 'heavenly country', the Scots as great. She was going to Loch Ness and was filled with curiosity as to whether or not she would see the monster, whom she referred to as the 'hippopotamus'.

While in Edinburgh she had also been to a concert of Beethoven's *Seventh Symphony in A Minor, Opus 92,* with Claudio Abado conducting the London Symphony Orchestra.

The last postcard was stamped Munich on the 11th October. *'I flew in yesterday to work at the Opera House. We are doing 'Till Eulenspiegel' and after that Tatakaboy's 'Les Papillons de Nuit.' I am very busy. Kisses to all of you. Meme.'*

After that, all communication between us was broken. Not until I went through her slim batch of letters to Paul, retrieved amidst all the boxes of correspondence, did I learn more about her Spanish interlude or how serious her health was when she wrote so lightly from Scotland.

Although Romola's contact with us had invariably been fairly constrained and lacking in intimacy, I nevertheless grew increasingly apprehensive as the months sped by without a word from her. The New Year 1978 began with Kinga's extremely serious operation. When the first sign of Spring arrived, so Kinga's health improved, and it was then I devoted my spare time to making long-distance calls. I began with the most feasible, Bad Gastein, only to receive a curt reply 'She left'. I tried six other places and as many hotels, to no avail. She had already departed. Nor was I more successful in tracing Paul. Neither had left any forwarding address. Despondently, I could only sit back and wait.

It must have been May when a letter of despair arrived from Paul, telling me how ill Romola was. They were again at the Hôtel Lotti, but now cramped in two very small rooms high up in the building. Already in Vienna, Paul had come to realise how hopeless it all was. She had terminal cancer. He knew that she wanted to end her days in Paris and to be buried next to Watza, so he resolutely set about bringing her back. She refused to be taken to hospital, terrified lest she be placed in a Psychiatric Ward.

He had been interrupted in his writing to me because Romola had rushed out of the room bleeding profusely. Most likely, the pains caused by a haemorrhage proved to be beyond endurance, and she sought to escape them. Paul had shrewdly hidden her acute condition from the management of the Lotti, aware of the fact that no hotel wishes to have dying guests under its roof. Tormented by the fear that they then would be forced to leave, the forlorn man had covertly washed the bedlinen in the bathroom in the middle of the night.

Paul nursed her to the best of his ability but a few days before the end a doctor had to be summoned to give some relief for her suffering. She died in Paul's arms on the 8th of June, 1978. So far as I know, he did not tell anybody about her death for twenty-four hours, just sat quietly by her side, not wanting to relinquish her, to let anybody take her from him.

Kyra's son Vaslav was informed and went to the hotel and together with Paul descended to the basement to search among her belongings for a suitable dress in which to bury her.

Nadia Gordon (Nerina) telephoned me from Paris to break the news. Paul was in too great a state of shock.

I believe that Maître Dumas took care of the funeral arrangements. Among the mourners were Paul, Vaslav Markevitch, Nadia Gordon, Maître Dumas and Madame Gilberte Courand. Romola was not buried next to Waslaw but instead in a perpetual grave she had acquired in 1976.

So ended this sensational and controversial chapter of ballet history.

EPILOGUE

Why did I not hasten to see Meme when I found out that her time was running out? I can think of many reasons for not doing so. Perhaps she would think that I had come at the last moment to ensure my share of any inheritance. Maybe the truth was simply that I had never been able to liberate myself from having been overshadowed and discarded by her those many years ago. Anyway, my passport had expired and I saw no reason to go to the funeral.

Shortly after her death I was faced with a serious problem. Romola's last lawsuit was heaped onto my shoulders when a Power of Attorney was handed to me to pursue the legal battle that had raged between my mother and Serge Lifar.

Briefly, Romola had wanted to ensure that she be buried next to

Waslaw in accordance with the letter she had written back in 1950. But in 1976 she learned to her dismay that Lifar intended the sepulchre to include himself and a woman who was close to him. He had had his own name inscribed on the marble slab to show to the world that he was the owner. Shattered by the thought of sharing the last resting place with anybody other than Waslaw, she had rushed off to Maître Dumas. Once she was the owner of a perpetual grave, she wrote to Lifar, requesting permission to have Waslaw transferred. He refused and an acrimonious dispute flared up.

When matters pertaining to the estate required my presence in Paris, I decided to delve further into the matter. To my consternation I was told that Lifar had no intention whatsoever of being buried in the Nijinsky sepulchre. In fact, today he lies in the St Genévieve Greek Orthodox Cemetery. He purchased this plot in 1979. My hands were tied. The Tribunal in Paris gave the verdict that my parents should rest in peace in their respective graves.

In due course, the executor of my mother's estate died, and I once more had to cross the ocean to finalise everything on behalf of Kyra and myself. Again I haunted the authorities, pleading with them to allow me to sell the new grave and re-unite Romola with Waslaw. The cost of the re-interment would be covered by the sale. To no avail. The French laws are rigid; perpetual graves cannot be sold or given away, but possibly if Lifar had agreed and I had found the money elsewhere, arrangements could have been made to move either Romola to Waslaw or Waslaw to Romola.

Dance and Dancers Magazine of London in its July 1978 issue made this comment:-

'Happily the spirit of Nijinsky lives on as an inspiration more important than which plot of land his bones happen to moulder in.'

The last obstacle is gone, for Lifar is now dead, and perhaps one day Romola will be joined with her God of Dance within a grave in Montmartre Cemetery marked

Romola and Waslaw

BIBLIOGRAPHY

Buckle, Richard, *Nijinsky*, Weidenfeld & Nicolson, 1971.

Dolin, Anton, *Friends and Memories*, Routledge & Kegan Paul, 1984.

Nijinska, Bronislava, *Early Memoirs*, Faber & Faber, 1982.

Nijinsky, Romola, *Nijinsky*, Victor Gollancz, 1933; *The Last Years of Nijinsky*, Victor Gollancz, 1952.

Nijinsky, Vaslav, *The Diary*, translated from the unexpurgated Russian text; *The Diary of Vaslav Nijinsky*, edited by Romola Nijinsky, Victor Gollancz, 1937

Shapcott, Thomas, *White Stag of Exile*, Allen Lane, 1984.

517

INDEX

The main characters in this biography are listed in the Index in respect of Birth and certain dates, the other references being too numerous to list.